WHERE THE
GODS LEFT OFF

Cover design: Sara Raztresen
Interior design: Sara Raztresen

All images from Canva and Shuttershock.

Paperback ISBN: 979-8-9864876-3-2
Digital ISBN: 979-8-9864876-2-5

Printed and bound in USA
First Printing September 2023

Published by Sara Raztresen under Sveta Lisica Imprint
Rhode Island, 2023

OTHER BOOKS BY SARA RAZTRESEN:

The Glass Witch
Discovering Christian Witchcraft (March 2024)

FIND SARA ON:

Tiktok: @srazzie97
Instagram: @sararaztresen
Twitter: @Srazzie97
YouTube: @srazzie97

www.sararaztresen.com

WHERE THE
GODS LEFT OFF

TABLE OF CONTENTS

Loki	1
Kresnik	12
Hades	19
Brigid	28
Cernunnos	34
Freyja	42
Hekate	52
Apollo	61
Persephone	70
Lucifer	80
Thoth & Anubis	91
Veles, Lada, & Zorya	104
Mary Mother of God	124
Archangel Michael	135
Archangel Raphael	143
Thor	153
St. Mary of Magdala	161
Jesus	170
The Morrígan	190
Archangel Gabriel	199
King Paimon	208
Isis	219
Judas Iscariot	228
Archangel Azrael	237
King Belial	243
Azazel	251
St. Dismas	265
Prince Stolas	273
Archangel Zadkiel	280
St. Nicholas	287
Morana	295
Frau Berchta	303
Archangel Uriel	311
St. Joseph	319
Archangel Metatron	325
Prince Vassago	333
Odin	341
St. Paul the Apostle	350
Baba Yaga	362
St. Cyprian of Antioch	370
Archangel Raziel	379
Leviathan	388
Princess Bari	395
Mokosh	404
Nehalenia	411
Amida Buddha	419
Quan Yin	427
Afterword	435
References	436
Special Thanks	437
Index	438

BEFORE WE START...

"I don't know, Sara; I find all this a little hard to believe," my dad said as we all clustered in the kitchen to talk. "You're telling me you're actually, like, *talking* to God or whoever? And getting answers and all that?"

It was a typical Sunday afternoon, later in the day, with my mom fussing with the dishes as she started working on dinner and my dad and I both taking a break from our work—mine being some writing and the laundry I'd just set to dry downstairs. It's true: I, like many other a mid-twenty-something year old, practice the age-old tradition of *living close enough to one's parents to use their laundry machines*, and the every-other-Sunday laundry schedule has become a dear and welcome ritual over the course of the three years I've lived on my own.

That ritual, naturally, includes catching my parents up on all the wacky projects and things going on in life, and that includes the work I do spiritually: the Christian witchcraft I do, how I'm building a platform to help others discover a spiritual practice of their own, and the education, exploration, and other professional development I'm doing to create safe, ethical, and empowering spaces for fellow believers to come together. Our conversations also bring us time and time again to some of the most controversial and unbelievable work I have the privilege of doing with and for my community, and that's actively seeking out the other faces and names of Divinity that have sewn this patchwork of people in the world together and created the kaleidoscope of cultures, traditions, art, stories, music, and faith that we have today.

I shrugged. "Yeah. I don't know how to explain it other than I've seen and heard things I didn't know about before."

My dad blinked at me, then shrugged. "Well, alright, I guess. But hey, did you hear about—?"

And so the conversation continued, with my mom, dad, and I all contributing stories from the past two weeks about things we'd seen, heard, done—people we'd talked to, plans we'd made, our thoughts on the latest headlines and news—and the afternoon sun melted away into evening twilight as mom's dinner went from stovetop to table. But as we talked, ate, and talked some more, I couldn't help but think to myself: *it is pretty unbelievable, isn't it?*

Unbelievable to think that the God we're all singing hymns to in churches, honoring on holidays, and using as a political sword and shield, might actually be an entity that watches us march around in His name. Unbelievable to the extreme to think that this faceless entity, this God known simply as God, might be someone we can talk to—*and receive an answer from.* But it's true, and I've known it's true for about twelve years now as a Christian witch. Ask God a question, learn how to listen, and more likely than not, you will find yourself in possession of an answer.

Answers you'd never think He'd give you. Answers that folks will tell you He *won't* give you, or, to my own shock, that He *can't* give you, as if there's anything that this God they tell us is so omnipotent and all powerful *can't* do. "No, that's not God talking to you," is the famous rebuttal to anything you learn from God directly: "no, we have the Bible. No, you're being led astray. No, those are *demons.*"

They, they, they of little faith.

It was by talking to God and developing the relationship I have all these years that made me realize something: God is nothing like mainstream Christianity has painted Him to be. *Nothing.* No, the mainstream Christian version of God—or the Evangelical Egregore, as I've come to call it, is nothing more than a shadow, a cardboard cut-out of Divinity, and it doesn't even begin to compare to the richness, the complexity, of God—or all the truths that got shattered and scattered across so many denominations fighting for the right to be called "true Christians." God is so many things, so many *incredible* and *unbelievable* things, that for a long time, I'd determined to never again listen to a human, or especially the manhandled, distorted, and abused *Bible*, tell me anything about God again.

Needless to say, things have changed since then. I study the Bible with fervor now, understanding the stories within to be not about fact so much as feeling, with how many creative myths and political tales are woven between the actual historical accounts of things that happened in this one area of the world thousands of years ago. I understand that this is a good tool to learn some things about the character of God and the nature of Christ's mission. But still, I default to asking God directly if I have questions about things that don't make sense. And likewise, after coming to understand these things, and the many ways in which the name of God has been used to destroy and maim and murder other people and their cultures,

I've also turned my eye on the gods of religions that flourished before Christianity. First for curiosity's sake—because if what mainstream Christianity said wasn't quite right about God, then maybe these gods had things to say that weren't tied to their stories, too—and second to light a torch that still feels too heavy for me to lift: one that brings the light of truth and knowledge back into places people of my religion tried to seal off and suffocate. One that reveals things that have long been hidden away, patiently waiting for the day where they could grow again unburdened by an evil empire masquerading as the righteous will of God.

So I started talking to these gods in order to know them more directly, and to remind myself—or maybe prove to myself—that they weren't just characters in a folktale or myths that were never true. I started talking to them to see what wisdom they had to share, and what they were like, and what they wanted from a world that was once again reminding itself who they were. I'll admit to quite the self-centeredness, too: I was curious as to what they would want or think of *me*, being of the religion that broke so many of their temples and desecrated so many of their holy sites. All I wanted was to experience them at first, to drink up their stories and feel their energy and know that everyone around me was right: that there *was* more than just One, even though I'd always known in my rational mind that it must've been so.

Over time, though, it became clear that what I was doing—interviewing pagan gods as if we were on a late night talk show, inviting Divinity in its many forms to come spare a word over a cup of tea or a bowl of fruit—wasn't just about me. Nor was it about the people who came to enjoy reading these interviews and seeing these videos I put out of my discussions with these spirits each week. Over the course of fifty interviews, each one slowly began to feel less like an exploration, and more like an apology. A reparation of some kind, even if all that came about was a sixty second video of tarot cards and a few pages of my explanation of their meanings.

Still, I think it's important. And I think, as you read on, you, too, will come to understand why it's important that I share these stories. Yes, I'm a Christian (even if a highly unorthodox one), and yes, I understand the role my religion played in the destruction of others. I understand so many people believe the gods of old are just stories, or minor spirits, or even demons and fallen angels, and I'm here to say with every possible ounce of authority and knowledge and experience I can:

Those people are wrong. They're wrong, and these gods are so, so good—as good as you'd want a god to be. They deserve the respect not only for the work they do now in the world, but for the work they've always done to keep our ancestors safe (as many of these pagan gods that *loyal* and *faithful* Christians now scorn are the reason any of their family lines survived and were able to learn about God in the first place). They're Divinity, through and through, and they have so very much to teach.

IN THIS B◉◉K, YOU'LL FIND...

Many things, honestly. But in here lies just a little bit of what Divinity in its many forms has to say, along with the way my own perceptions and culturally Christian shackles have broken as a result of repeatedly showing up, asking questions, and making the effort to connect. It's structured in exactly the way I experienced it, each spirit appearing in the order I spoke to them. However, if you're more interested in specific topics, or specific types of spirits (demons, angels, gods of certain regions, or Saints), please do make use of the index in the back of this book, where I've organized its chapters.

Please keep in mind that this book is *not* a how-to guide on contacting these entities. This is entirely my own experience, my trial and error, and my journey in discovering the spiritual landscape around me. I do not recommend you try to repeat these processes unless you're an experienced practitioner that is mentally and emotionally equipped to do so. (And even then, I don't recommend it, honestly.)

For each of these interviews, I used a specific tarot deck, which you'll find listed in the chapter. My experience of tarot has shown me the value of having more than one deck, as while the Hierophant may mean generally the same thing no matter what deck you use, each deck's art and descriptions will show you a different aspect of each card. Every entity I've spoken to had the opportunity to choose their deck beforehand, and I do believe that the reason for their choices is made clear in the language of each deck. As such, while I've tried to summarize the meanings as much as possible, I do still retain some of the unique qualities of each deck by paraphrasing their meanings.

The decks I used are:

The Golden Tarot by Kat Black
The Marigold Tarot by Amrit Brar*
The Angel Tarot by Doreen Virtue
The Weaver Tarot by Threads of Fate
The Universal Fantasy Tarot by Lo Scarabeo
The Guardian of the Night Tarot by MJ Cullinane

*Brar's deck is also used for reversed definitions of the Angel, Guardian of the Night, and Universal Fantasy Tarot, as these decks don't have specific reversed meanings.

As you flip through these pages, reading both my encounters with these entities and surrounding experiences, revelations, and other thoughts that came in between these weekly sit-downs, I hope you, too, can find something of value within the many lessons learned and the many themes and topics discussed, and I thank you for being one of the many who lets the voices of these deities and spirits come forward again, whether as a devotee of these entities yourself or as someone who's simply curious about what the Divine essence of societies old and young have to say today.

It's an honor to be able to show the results of a year of work to you all, and I sincerely hope you enjoy traversing not only the worlds of these many entities, but the long road I took to get from Interview One to Interview Fifty.

LOKI

Loki. What can be said about him that hasn't been said a thousand times? The Norse trickster god of chaos and mischief, he's one full of stories—some of which are more lighthearted and fun, like when he went to cheer up Skadi with an interesting (and painful) game of tug of war with a goat, and others of which are more tragic, like how Loki managed to arrange the death of Baldur (and keep him dead). Yet we need to be clear about this here: the idea of good and evil in many pre-Christian religions wasn't always so easily defined, and Loki is one of the cases where the question of him being good or evil doesn't really apply.

Loki simply is. And he's had his own fair share of heartaches at the hands of the Aesir, creating a family dynamic and general divine neighborhood that's far too complicated to paint with such broad strokes of the morality brush. Still, nowadays, you'll find mentions of him everywhere, with many a witch or magician, or just a Norse pagan with no magical cares or inclinations, honoring this god of mischief. However one might've worshipped him in times of yore, the common wisdom in today's online spaces is that Loki loves trinkets and bad whiskey, shiny things and snacks, cinnamon and snakes. (And we can't forget his love of sending spiders to people, whether they like spiders or not.)

This was the very first god I ever interviewed in my journey to understand more about the spiritual world I lived in, and I'll be honest with you: I was terrified. I'd never spoken to any of these gods I saw other witches and pagans invoke and worship, as one might expect from a Christian Witch. Hell, I was still at the point where I thought that meditation wasn't something I was capable of, because I still thought meditating meant sitting with your legs crossed and forcing your mind to go completely still and quiet for an entire hour (which this gremlin's nest of a brain will never be able to do). So when I looked up things associated with Loki to invite him with, and I checked and double checked and triple checked with God that I was, in fact, allowed to speak to another deity, and I set all my candles and cleansed my tarot decks, I wasn't sure how anything was going to go or what to expect.

My nerves were through the roof. My skills were pretty much solely limited to looking at tarot cards. My doubts were sky high. But still, with God watching like a Heavenly Dad at the Astral Park

Bench while I mucked about in the Divine Playground, I went and did the damn thing, and I am so glad I did.

So, without further ado, here's my interview with Loki—first of many.

I checked my table, checked my gifts: there were cinnamon sticks and apples, which I'd read were at least loosely associated with him, and likewise obsidian and garnet. Then there was a dragon statue (which was my attempt to have any snake, or least snake-adjacent, imagery), and a fox statue (because what animal is known as a trickster more than the fox?). All was in place. Perfectly spaced apart were two skull-shaped shot glasses, the only ones I own, and in them went a healthy shot of Fireball whiskey, per the repeated recommendations of his devotees.

As with every interview I would go on to do, I started the process by setting my space—or, as some might understand it, casting a circle—with the Lord's Prayer and some holy water. It wasn't so much that I was afraid of Loki; given I thought I'd felt him around once or twice already by that point, and that I'd seen how he acted with others who worshipped him, I had no worries there. Instead, I was more worried about a whole separate issue: the possibility of getting an egregore in the house.

Because what a waste of time it would've been, to have all this set up and take all this time to ask questions, only to find out that it'd been an astral copycat.

That's why I do the Lord's Prayer before encountering any entity: to invite God into my space first, and to ask Him to keep egregores and fakes and others unnecessary to the reading out. This was especially important for my first time speaking with another deity; the less distraction, the better. But once I was settled, and I'd burned some mugwort to try and boost what little psychic ability I thought I had, I held my pendulum up and thought hard about Loki, as if my brain were some kind of god-magnet. I called for him (out loud, in whispers under my breath, because at this time I had a real silly hang-up that I could only talk to God with the little voice in my head), and I asked him, "Are you there?"

The pendulum hovered above my palm. When it spun in a circle after a moment, in wide, strong arcs, I sat there relieved—only for the relief to dry right up when I felt a shower of prickles all up and down my arms, like someone was pinching and poking me. And there was a tapping in my ear, too! I didn't know where it was coming from at all, not until I caught a glimpse of my reflection in my phone screen and remembered that I was wearing snake-shaped earrings that day.

What a way to get my attention.

"I—alright, Loki, I'm glad you're here," I said, and I felt stupid, because who was I talking to? For anyone walking into the living room, it looked like I was talking to empty air. I hadn't felt this silly since trying out those four-stanza rhyming spells from Wiccan beginner guides as a teen. At least I had my own candles for this conversation, rather than the old ones I'd pillaged from my mom's long-unused collections and taken with me when I moved, but it didn't make it feel any easier to sit there and hold a rock on a chain over a bunch of cards. "Can you tell me which deck you want to use?"

It swung over each deck as I repeated the question, back and forth, back and forth—the sign for "no." Only after a few attempts did it finally start switching directions, making a wide circle over Amrit Brar's Marigold Tarot, marking his choice.

As I've said earlier, each deck has its own way of explaining the cards. I want to give each entity the easiest time possible when it comes to picking cards for questions, so I ask which one they want to use—which ones explain the cards in a way that'll most accurately get their message across.

"Okay, the Marigold Tarot it is," I muttered, and I cleansed them with smoke and asked God to let Loki borrow them for a bit before shuffling. "So, first things first... When I decided to start doing these conversations, everyone said I should choose you first. I know I felt you there, eager to talk even as I was just throwing the idea around. I'm curious: what interested you in being interviewed?"

I. WHAT HAS YOU INTERESTED IN BEING INTERVIEWED?

Truth, indecision, inadequacy, emotional detachment.

In love with the concept of love, tethered back to reality.

Separation, mistrust, low self esteem, disharmony.

Martyrdom, hardship, confusion, consequences. What can we learn from this?'

That was a lot of words. I stared at them for a long time, trying to turn them over like the many colorful squares of a Rubik's cube, as at this point, I couldn't just hear. I couldn't just see. And I know you may be wondering: *but Sara, hadn't you talked to God all these years with tarot? Shouldn't interpreting things directly from the card have been easy by this point?* Thing is, though, this wasn't God; this was someone else altogether, and looking at these cards made me feel like I was learning a new language.

"Um," I poked at the upside down Knight of Cups, "I don't get it; what do you mean?"

And then, from behind the dark of my eyelids as I searched for some kind of inspiration, I caught it: a flash of red, shoulder-length hair, gold rings glittering in his ears, eyes dark as night, leather armor black like shadows. Loki perched there in my mind's eye only for a moment. The image wouldn't stay, though. It was slippery, hard to hold onto. But still, he was there, and I got this idea as I looked at all of those cards together: it's for them. It's for the ones who need him.

"Oh," I whispered. "Are you saying that you're wanting to show up for the people that need you? You want to reach more people? And teach them to be more confident?"

My ears started ringing—a sure and clear yes.

"And you want to help? The world turned upside down, learning—you want to help in the chaos that is the world right now?"

Again, a ringing yes. I even brought my pendulum out to confirm, and it swung in a circle, which I know as a yes. Finally, I'd managed to piece together an answer that made sense. Let me tell you: when you're used to just doing a one-card-back-and-forth with your guides, and the answers are clear and simple each time, trying to stitch together such different cards and ideas into one lucid thought is a whole new level of challenge.

But challenge is good. Challenge is how you grow. And so, with one answer firmly tucked under my belt, I got back to shuffling and went onto the next question, all the while trying to hold onto that image behind my eyes of the man with red hair and black armor.

"Alright, alright, I see what you're saying," I said as I shuffled. "But then, you know, I'm pretty sure I've felt you around in my apartment before. I know some other Christian Witches work with you, but as far as I know, you and I have no history. If that was you that I felt, can you tell me what inspired you to come by, Loki?"

2. WHY DID YOU COME TO ME EARLIER THIS YEAR?

Transformation. Accepting changes and evolution, especially if hard won.

Indecision, unforeseen difficulties, unwillingness to change.

Unwillingness to see issues clearly, looming disaster, avoiding change.

Law, parental structure, ambition, power, leadership.

Wait a minute.

I blinked at these cards. Chewed my lip near raw over these cards, even. Why? Because they were nearly the exact same cards God Himself had been giving me for the better part of a month. Worse, the message here was clear, as if I'd been slapped with it. In my mind's eye, when I looked up at God, He stood there like He always did: arms crossed, eyes blazing, waiting for me to get the picture. This time, though, there was an unmistakable chuckle in the background coming from anyone other than God.

Bringing that red-haired man back into focus, I started, "Now, hold on a damn minute. Loki."

His teeth were so apparent in that massive grin he wore.

"Is there a reason you're telling me the same things God has been telling me?"

A black-gloved hand pointed up. *You know why,* he seemed to say. *But if you're that confused, then go ask the God you haven't been listening to.*

The tension of my clenched jaw shot from my teeth to my temple, and yet after a moment, I couldn't help but smile. Never in all my years of living would I have ever guessed that:

God would let me talk to other gods.

God would ask other gods to deliver one of His messages that I'd been ignoring.

The god to do so *would've* been the Norse god of chaos, of all beings.

You're too anxious. That was the message here that I was getting without actually hearing it. It'd be a long while before I really deciphered and translated the words the way I do now, but that didn't mean

I couldn't still get the picture. *You're too afraid of the unknown when you should just jump right in.*

My tarot journal was littered with the same message. Over and over and over again, God tried to tell me: *Lighten up. Trust me. Just go.* And yet.

"Okay, okay," I said as I cast one last glance upward to God, "fine. Fine, I hear you both. Let's move on, then. Loki, could you tell me what kinds of things you want to talk about? Surely you must've come to do more than just help God drive that nail into my head."

3. WHAT TOPICS WOULD YOU LIKE TO DISCUSS?

New beginnings, feelings, relationships, and projects.

Solitude and personal reflection, taking inventory of one's limits. Self care.

Steady, well deserved confidence. Complete comfort with one's identity.

Self satisfaction, good fortune, and contentment. Joy with what you have.

Of course. I could feel the answer in my gut, even without words, and the cards came quick, snapping into my hands.

In short, these cards said: *The things you're supposed to be focusing on.* That's apparently what Loki wanted to talk about, and it was getting easier to understand the way he wove the tarot meanings together. I just stopped myself from rolling my eyes as I got, once again, more of the cards I'd been seeing. First was the problem, second was the solution, and as my skin felt like it was lighting up with little pinches, and the air grew even thicker with a presence so very obviously not God's, I sighed. It seemed there was no escaping this message; if I wouldn't take it from God, I'd have to take it from the master of chaos himself. And that message was pretty clear to me:

You gotta take a step back, kid. Look at this mess you're making for yourself. You know what you gotta do to get to where you wanna go. How long will you ignore that?

Spoiler: I'd ignore this warning for another eight months or so before the floodgates burst and the fragile bit of stability I'd been clutching to got washed away. But that's a story for another time. Right then in that moment, I was sure that just rearranging my schedule for the fifth time that month, as if it were nothing more than a particularly challenging level of Tetris, would magically solve all my problems. So I committed to doing just that and got back to shuffling those cards, glancing at the clock every so often to see how long I'd been sitting on my living room floor. It was starting to hurt.

"Well, then, Loki, let's talk about your story. What do you want people to learn from it? Why?"

4. WHAT LESSONS DO YOU WANT PEOPLE TO LEARN FROM YOU?

Partnership, new romance or old romance enduring. Excited for new opportunities.

Greed, potentially shallow fulfillment, material concerns.

Calamity, struggle, misjudgment, a situation with potential disaster.

Success, discipline, enjoyment, focusing on what one finds good, seeing the big picture.

It was getting easier to see him. He leaned against something—a wall, maybe, or a wooden support beam—and he crossed his arms as he stared at me, eyes sparkling with something that seemed like a far away star.

This is one of those moments where we can fully digest a very important lesson: you need to know something about the spirits and deities you're contacting in order to put their answers in context. For me, after reading quite a few of the Norse myths starring Loki and understanding the way he'd been warped into a Norse version of the devil with the advent of Christianity, I understood in no uncertain terms what Loki was saying with the intensity of these card descriptions: his story was a wild ride.

Among it all is no one clear message, no consensus. As Loki stared at me and watched me piece it together, I got the sense that overall, this was just the story of someone who lived as true to themselves as they could and paid whatever price resulted from their actions. For better or worse, Loki was Loki, and there was no making him be anything else, not for all the punishment or misfortune or consequences that could've come his way. If his story proved nothing else, it proved that he wouldn't ever shy away from doing what he wanted or needed to do, no matter the cost.

I admire that. At the time, though, I hadn't really expected that answer—not with the way everyone talked about and described Loki.

"That's awfully noble in a way," I mused, "but now, Loki, what about all these modern representations of you? And the way people make you out to be online or in other public spaces? Because I'll be honest, this energy isn't exactly what I expected."

5. WHAT DO YOU THINK OF MODERN INTERPRETATIONS OF YOU?

Wastefulness, bad news, and preoccupation with projects over other priorities in life.

Calamity, struggle, misjudgment, a situation with potential disaster.

Loneliness, alienation, extreme caution, and isolation.

Too entangled in celebration, neglecting one's duties.

I tapped the pencil to my lip as I stared at the cards. There were images running through my head: Tom Hiddleston's Loki, the many comments I'd seen online, the whole genre of Goofy Loki Moments™ videos. Throughout them all, Loki stayed there in the background, shaking his head, and there was a feeling building in my chest, like a trapped sigh. It wasn't my sigh, though.

It's nice to be recognized. That was the first part of this odd feeling. But there's more than just silliness and fun and chaos here. Those parts, unsurprisingly, are the ones that tend to be ignored.

"I hear you." And I felt bad, too. Certainly, even if we started off a little silly, and even if Loki got a laugh out of my surprise earlier in the discussion, there was more to Loki than fun and silliness. There was an edge to him, hiding under each word like a little razor blade under the flap of an envelope. It took care not to get cut. "Then—okay, how about this for a question? People say you like to 'collect' followers. Why? Is that true? Is there a reason?

6. WHY DO YOU SEEM TO "COLLECT" NEW FOLLOWERS?

1. Loneliness, alienation, extreme caution, and isolation.

2. Indecision, unforeseen difficulties, and unwillingness to change.

3. Victory, superiority, confidence, pride.

4. Calamity, struggle, misjudgment, situation with potential disaster.

There was a pandemic! The words were coming in my voice, and yet they weren't my words. It was the strangest thing I'd ever experienced up to that point. These thoughts were just popping in all over the place: the Worldometer counter, the empty streets, the vague feeling of anxiety and dread that put me right back into March of 2020. *People give up too easy.*

Be brash in the face of difficulty.

Swagger through life.

Evolve through hardship.

These phrases pelted me like little raindrops—just large enough for me to take notice of them. Between these phrases and the occasional snatches of Loki's image I'd get every time I closed my eyes, it felt like there was something happening that I didn't understand: like I'd moved a muscle I'd never known how to move. I still couldn't move it well, but it was moving. I was seeing. I was hearing.

Which, as you might imagine, freaked me out just a little bit. No matter what way I cut it, I'd spent years of my life being told that no such entities like these other gods existed, that only God existed, that anything that I felt that said otherwise was just a demon. Even if I thought it was ridiculous to say that my God existed and none others did, I didn't pop into this world perfectly deconstructed and easygoing; I had ideas about other gods that I regret.

My upbringing was more on the mystical, European, laid back Catholic side, sure, and I had no real religious trauma to speak of, but I couldn't help but think at this time that these gods weren't quite gods, you know? My reasoning was that God was a word reserved for, well, God. Anything or anyone else could never deserve such a title, surely, because... *God.* So I solidified the idea in my head that these entities must've just been spirits or some great and powerful energy, but never a god.

(I know. You're fully within your rights to cringe and groan and roll your eyes. I am, too, thinking of myself just a short year ago—but that's why they call it character growth, right?)

Nonetheless, as I sat there just beginning to hear and see these things, I had this discomfort come up and sit on my head like a little imp. I couldn't shake it, I couldn't banish it, but I knew I couldn't bow to it, either, because the fascination and intrigue of talking to a god that wasn't mine—however I understood the concept of a god at the time—was thankfully stronger.

Imp or no imp, I kept going.

"Alright, I understand that perfectly well," I said, nodding along as if Loki were physically there, and I was just some reporter asking questions for a scoop, "but it does lead me to ask: what do you think of the state of the world now?"

7. WHAT DO YOU THINK OF THE STATE OF THE WORLD NOW?

1. Naïveté, disharmony, holding onto the past in an unhealthy way

2. Vulnerability, powerlessness, and a possibly inflated ego.

3. An unavoidable force. Righting wrongs, accepting consequences.

4. Victory, superiority, confidence, and pride.

It felt as if the air around me shrugged. Closing my eyes, I could see it clearly: Loki shrugging, eyes hooded as he then crossed his arms. It was a vivid image, but it didn't last very long before it shifted and smeared like oil paint across the darkness behind my eyelids.

I poked at the meanings of the cards for a bit, finding the threads that stitched them together into the quilt of Loki's meaning. It took some time before all these words and images and ideas—and the images of Loki himself, the snatches of thoughts that I wasn't sure actually came from me, if that makes any sense—came together to a conclusion: *the world's a mess.*

I mean, fair enough.

But it's a mess, in Loki's eyes, because of how people don't want to accept that the old ways of the world are no longer relevant. Out with the old and in with the new seems to be his way of thinking, and it's frustrating watching people try and hold onto power they're not due with social values that are no longer relevant. Still, that Justice card stuck out; that was Loki's main message. Change is unavoidable, as is justice; people will have it, and the world will change, no matter who likes it or not.

It's almost ominous, reading it like that.

"Still," I said, smiling, "I like it. Thank you, Loki. Now, I guess as we come towards the end of my list of questions here, I can't help but wonder: is there something you want me to do? Something that made you come here, something that made you want to go first?"

8. WHAT MADE YOU WANT TO BE INTERVIEWED FIRST?

Mistrust, neglect, fear, prioritizing others over oneself.   *Manifestation, seizing the moment, realizing goals, action.*   *Misfortune approaching, depression, unsuccessful ventures.*   *Healing, balance, and harmony. The inevitability of all things.*

I couldn't help but sigh, all while Loki gave me a big old grin. It was more of the same—more of what God had been telling me at that time, and what He would continue to tell me for months and months afterwards until I almost missed the last chance to take the advice.

You need a break, kid. I would say I didn't need to be told twice, but I apparently did. *You're in a place where things don't feel like they're working out. Just switch track. Find balance. Enjoy the moment. Trust the things you're manifesting are coming.*

It always sounds so frustratingly vague when gods say things like this. Still, I didn't know this deity well enough to groan and whine and pout like when God tells me this, so I wrote it down and kept moving, shuffling the deck again.

"Okay, okay. What about your devotees? Is there anything you want from them?"

9. DO YOU WANT ANYTHING FROM YOUR DEVOTEES?

Bad faith, burnout, and unfinished projects.

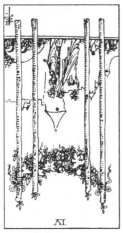

Social disputes, prioritizing others at the risk of one's personal development.

Assuming the worst, misunderstanding one's or another's needs.

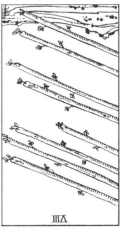

Quarrels, delays, slowing down to re-evaluate goals and circumstances.

Rally! That was the idea that popped into my head as I read the cards. Each one seemed to point to a separate thing Loki's followers were grappling with; that's what it felt like in my gut. *Gather your strength! Get through these things!*

Frustratingly vague, yes, but sweet, don't you think? I was tired by this point; it was late in the night. But as I rubbed my eyes, I couldn't help it: I felt a little better. The imp in my head, telling me all this was made up lies, faded a bit. There in those cards was a truth that didn't come from Loki's mouth, nor from God's, nor from anyone else's; it was just a realization.

They love us. These gods love their people.

"Well, Loki," I said with a sigh, "before I go, I want to know: how do you see yourself?"

10. HOW DO YOU SEE YOURSELF?

Loss, theft, uncompromising values, obsession with social accepted roles.

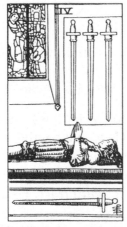

Solitude, re-evaluation, and rest. Self reflection and renewal.

Persistence and resilience in the face of adversity. Proudly rising to the occasion.

Navigating all kinds of relationships, including relationships with the self.

Whether you work with Loki or not, imagine him standing tall, arms over his chest. An edge to his brow, a toothy smile—like he'd won every war and every battle and still stood to tell about it. That was the energy coming off the cards, and that's what translated into words into my head as I wove all these cards together:

I'm still here after all I've been through. I never gave up. I never will—not until we break the bounds and binds of what's acceptable in the world and make something new.

It spoke to me, that last line, and by that, I mean it hit me in the head like the crack of a good hammer. But as I finished writing, thanked Loki for his time, and closed out that ritual space, I found that I, too, had something of a bandit's smile—a lightness in my chest I couldn't understand. There was also this feeling that the world around me had a layer on it, like a curtain I couldn't find the corner to. I felt the emptiness Loki left behind as I packed my cards up, and when I turned myself about in my mind's eye to find God, I found eyes brimming with the fiery golden light of the sun: warm, comforting, assuring.

I didn't realize it right then, but with that first interview under my belt, I'd just uncorked a bottle full of secrets I never even realized I wanted to know.

KRESNIK

If you want to know how I was feeling the next week, when it came time to pick this whole "Interview With the Gods" thing up again, I'll tell you: emboldened. I'd managed to successfully contact a whole separate god, and while the experience was tapping at my ideological and theological frameworks like an over-cautious Jenga player at the start of the game, I wasn't about to give up after the first one went so well—and how could I?

I still had other gods to talk to, like the gods of my ancestors. Of course, the very first among those was none other than Kresnik, who I'd recently learned about and wanted nothing more than to meet, because unlike other Slavic gods, this one was *specifically* Slovenian.

It also turns out that his name is something of a title rather than a name proper. The first part, *Kres,* means something like "Bonfire" or "Change of Seasons," and because *v skresiti* means "to resurrect," according to F.S Copeland in *Some Aspects of Slovene Folklore,* it could also be a title that means "Resurrector." (413), shedding more light on some of these folktales and the meanings behind them. Other possibilities are that this name has something to do with fire, given Kresnik is a god of summer, storms, and the sun, but it all points to a god with golden hair and hands, who sometimes appears as a deer with golden horns on his golden mountain.

This "Resurrector" is actually the Slavic god Svarožič, as Copeland explains, and this is the son of Svarog, a main creator deity of the Slavic pantheon. Svarožič means "little Svarog," and as is common of sun gods and their lore, he's considered to be born on the winter solstice, growing in strength each day until summertime, only to fall asleep and be reborn again for the next year. But as each Slavic tribe is different, so too are their stories about the gods, and for what I can piece together about Kresnik in a way that makes neat and tidy sense in my mind, Kresnik is intimately connected with Vesna (his wife, the spring goddess, or Snake Princess), Mara (or Morena, the dark winter goddess and mother of Vesna) and Veles (the god of the underworld, music, and mischief, known as the Snake King in Slovene myths surrounding these beings and a frequent antagonist of Kresnik and other gods considered similar or cognate to him, such as thunder god Perun).

I know. There are a lot of names. Trying to parse any of this kind of ancient pagan stuff is a mighty challenge; that I'll never deny.

Though over time, Kresnik went from god to folk hero—a mighty, magic-wielding king who still prefers tending to his cows over dealing with serious problems. His name has also become a title for other folk heros to wear, as it's said that children born with a caul on their head are destined to either become *kudlaki,* a type of evil spirit, or *krsniki,* or a sort of vampire hunter that learns his magic from the fairies. Both of these beings shape shift into animals at night and fight like hell in a big battle of good and evil. Kresnik's great celebration day, the summer solstice, has long since given way to the feast of St. John the Baptist, and his role as dragon slayer has likewise been absorbed by St. George, but still, Kresnik is out there, enjoying the sunshine of his mountain and tending to his cows with Vesna. Naturally, reading about Kresnik being this great protector of all Slovenes, I felt compelled to speak to him; I was far too curious not to approach one of the most beloved gods of my ancestors.

So without further ado, let me introduce to you Kresnik, the hero of Slovenia—and an entity that now, I do consider a wonderful friend, a loving ally, and a selfless defender of his people despite everything.

The table before me was littered with trinkets and tools that all had a touch of fire tucked some-where within. From tiger's eye to sunstone, carnelian to smoky quartz, bread with honey, chamomile tea, oranges—these were all things that had *something* to do with fire and the sun to me, at least in a more modern witchy sense. (Had I the wherewithal or the sense, I might've put some walnuts out, too, but I hadn't peered very hard into the more specific Slovenian aspects of magic at that time.)

One thing I *did* know was that chamomile was important to Slovenians, if only because it was something I associated with my mom and oma—and color me surprised when, months later, as I was reading Vlasta Mlakar's book, *Sacred Plants in Folk Medicine and Rituals: Ethnobotany of Slovenia,* I discovered that chamomile flowers and daisies were actually called *kresnice.* Sometimes Divinity re-ally does lead you forward like that, even when you don't know exactly what you're doing yet.

Nonetheless, I was excited for this interview, and a little nervous, too. God had given me His ap-proval, sure—but what would the god of my ancestors have to say to me? What would he be like? What would he think about *God,* or the fact that I was honoring God instead of him? I didn't know, and I wouldn't until I asked, so I said my Lord's prayer to set some protections against egregores, poured two cups of tea, and spoke.

"*Pozdrav,* Kresnik!" It felt like it'd be rude to not at least greet him in the Slovene language first. "Hello, and welcome! Please come sit with me; I'd love to talk to you if you're fine with it! I have some snacks here, some tea, and some questions for you."

Maybe it was because I'd just done some research on him a few days prior, with one picture sticking out so vividly in my mind, but suddenly, I saw a man behind my eyelids that looked about the same: one with long golden hair and a rough golden-brown beard, an embroidered headband around his head, with a tunic embroidered in red, and a twinkle to his honey-gold eyes. The patterns on both the shirt and headband were similar to Ukrainian *vyshyvanka* patterns. He was the picture of a pretty classically Slavic guy, blinking at me like he was surprised.

I couldn't help but smile. "Come, sit! Sit by me!"

Then I waved him over like I would an old friend, and funny god, he actually did take me up on it; for some reason the images were crisper this session, and I could see him walk over to me and sit beside me before my coffee table, shoulder to shoulder. He stared out at the things on the table like they were confusing, or like he hadn't expected them, but he didn't seem to mind, either.

With pendulum in hand, I took a breath and settled in. "Well, Kresnik, if you'd be so kind as to choose a deck to use, I've got a few of them for you here. Which one do you like best?"

Sunshine filled the living room, a light breeze wandering through the windows. It was just starting to warm up, what with it being early April, and it brightened the mood in the whole room as my pendulum sheepishly swung over each deck of cards. *No* to the darker decks, the Weaver Tarot and Marigold Tarot, Kresnik said—but the Golden Tarot!

Of course the god of golden hair and hands would pick the Golden Tarot.

"Alright, works for me," I said, all while Kresnik quietly watched me cleanse and shuffle the deck. "I guess we can just dive on in, then? I was hoping to know a little bit about your history as a god in Slovenia, so to start us off, how about this: what duties did you have in Slovenia before Christianity? What duties do you still have?"

Oh, came more of a feeling than a word, like a sigh.

I. WHAT DUTIES DID YOU AND DO YOU STILL HAVE IN SLOVENIA?

One person can make a difference. Seen and learned much, responsibility for putting this knowledge out. Live so others can follow the example.

Short term parting for reasons of circumstance, or ending a relationship altogether.

What a completely distinct set of cards. It felt like I was watching the birth and death of a hero, looking at the meanings and the imagery both. Knowing Kresnik's story—that he was god, then a king, then a folk hero, then nothing but a fairy tale, a whisper—it made sense. While I couldn't really hear him speak, I could see the hard curve of his frown, the bend of his head as if he had something heavy hanging around his neck and bending his back. Kresnik *was* in an important station once, I gathered: a station that had him being an example to the people, warm and just and powerful, a defender and a leader. But he's no longer in such a position due to Christianity; it was taken over, himself relieved of duty, from the looks of it. There's some of it coming back, per the Two of Cups Reversed: maybe it wasn't a permanently severed relationship after all, but just a hiatus. Still, it's not what it used to be.

"I understand," I said with a nod, and I could imagine myself easily leaning onto his shoulder, as if to try and give him any solace. We sat so close that it really did feel like I was sitting with a friend or family member I'd always known, though I wasn't brave enough to inspect that feeling just yet. "Well, I know two figures that took over bits of your role are St. John and St. George. Do you work alongside them at all?"

2. DO YOU WORK ALONGSIDE ST. JOHN AND ST. GEORGE?

What I would come to understand about Kresnik over the course of this interview was how *distinctly* Slovenian he was: his attitude was so nonchalant, his air so easy, even as he spoke about things that obviously dug a blade right into his chest. *It's not so bad,* he seemed to say with his energy, *though I miss the old days.*

Yet despite how he missed it, the cards were clear, as was the hard edge of determination that surrounded us: he may have stepped away, but he didn't abandon the Slovenian people. No, Kresnik just helped St. John and St. George be what his people needed them to be in his stead. There was a sense of *keep the children safe,* an urgency like a parent watching their children from afar, knowing they made the best decision no matter how hard it was. Kresnik's first, and only, priority was the people, and he wanted to see them happy, safe, and thriving, no matter who they worshipped.

Slow, plodding, reliable man. Sticks with project no matter what; responsible, reliable, keen to assist.

Innocence, love, and faithful acceptance. Remembrance of childhood joys. Yearning for simpler times.

I'll admit it: I teared up looking at these cards. My heart ached for him, this sweet and almost-forgotten god.

"Speaking of that fading role," I said as I blinked the first hints of tears away, "what was it like being depicted as a folk hero instead of a god? The krsnik?"

3. WHAT DO YOU THINK OF BEING DEPICTED AS THE KRSNIK?

 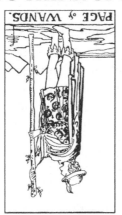

A man with great hidden sadness." Keeps emotions in; self destructive.

Bad news, unreliable youth.

It was hard. A snatch, a whisper, of words floated across my mind. All I could see was his face, downcast and crumpled as if he carried a deep pain in his heart. There was a feeling in my own chest of unease, uncertainty, as if I were walking across a rotten beam and wasn't sure where to put my foot, every step a risk of breaking the beam and plummeting down into the dark unknown. *Hard, hard, hard.*

As far as I can understand, Kresnik was dismayed to have his name chipped away at, his place as a god whittled down into a hero, and then to nothing at all. He loved his people and still does, but so many had forgotten him for so long. Still, he watches the people; his love isn't dependent on their worship or their memory.

I could've wept for him seeing his face, honestly. It still hurts to think about.

But there are people that know his name now, and that remember him as the god that he is, so it seems things are at least starting to turn around in that aspect. People are remembering him again, though I don't think he puts a lot of stock in the quality of their memory anymore. It isn't hard to understand why.

But after recording the answer, I decided it was best to just move on—to ask him something else, so maybe his face would stop looking so painful in my mind's eye.

"How about you, then?" The stock of the tarot cards was thick in my hands, the laminate making it hard to shuffle as elegantly as I wanted to. "Forget what the world thinks; how do you view yourself?"

4. HOW DO YOU VIEW YOURSELF?

 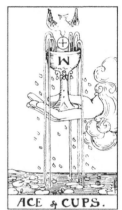

Beyond the card meanings, I had a sense of sunshine mixed with thunderstorms, lightning and fire viciously tearing up the countryside, just as much as warm sun rays kissed delicate green shoots and wildflowers. There was a shrug buried in the energy, a sheepish smile floating through the air, as if Kresnik were saying, *I get angry sometimes, sure, but I'm a good god! A good god.* One all benevolent and loving, even if that temper can become volatile and end in flashes of lightning, booms of thunder.

What I marveled at more than the images and feelings, though, was the fact that I was seeing and feeling things at all. It was happening more than it did with Loki. Don't get me wrong: the doubts were still there. The question of *is that really a sign, or am I just making stuff up?* was one

Fickle, flighty man with trouble controlling his anger.

Overflowing cup, love and joy. True contentment. Fertility and bountiful abundance. Spiritual fulfillment through unconditional love.

that would plague me for ages, but I had no choice but to keep going and hope I was picking up the right messages.

As I took the cards back and reshuffled them into my deck, I asked, "And how do you want others to see you?"

5. HOW DO YOU WANT OTHERS TO SEE YOU?

There were no cards for this, only Kresnik's warm smile. *The same.* That was the sense I got: he wanted people to see him as he saw himself. *See me the same.* It was too strong a feeling to deny, and too easily translated in my head, so I jotted it down. In the back of my mind, that plaguing question needled me—*how do I know he said that if I have no cards? How do I know I didn't just make that up? How do I know? How?*—but I decided to trust Kresnik's face and those few words I heard.

"Okay," I muttered, "fair. But how do you see Slovenians? What do you think about them now?"

6. WHAT DO YOU THINK OF MODERN SLOVENIANS?

1. Abandonment of materialism. Putting aside financial security for spiritual fulfilment. Cutting off from old, seeking new. Journeying.

2. Courage in the face of adversity. Taking a stand in adversity and overcoming obstacles. Bravery rewarded.

It was as if his feelings were my feelings. There was a swell of love and pride, warm and expansive in my chest, and when I closed my eyes, I saw Kresnik sitting next to me with such a big smile, like a proud father. Between the cards' meanings and Kresnik's very energy, I understood: he was proud of the Slovenians, and how they still valued the things they always did, like nature and peace and a modest, quiet life. He'd seen all they'd overcome in the past several centuries, and he was glad to see how they'd remained true to themselves despite others' many attempts to break them as a people. Their bravery paid off. They were their own sovereign people, finally, after so long. It'd taken a little over a thousand years, but they'd done it: they'd won their sovereignty, and their peace, back.

As a Slovenian myself, I couldn't help but feel a little puffed up by Kresnik's praise. He loves us! After all this time, he still cares! I don't think I'll ever get over that, but knowing that so early in this journey was so important. You must understand: while I knew logically that these gods were benevolent, and of course that they loved their people and their devotees, there's always that doubt, that fear, that burrows in the back of your mind due to the culture you grow up in. When you hear people say "they're not gods; they're demons" enough, even if you *know* it's nonsense, you can't help but be just a touch afraid. Here, though, there was no fear. I already knew claims of other gods being *demons* was nonsense logically, and this interview showed me that in the emotional and intuitive sense, too.

Now, after this revelation came an admittedly selfish set of questions. After all, I am a fantasy writer, and I had a book in the works (still do, actually) about exactly this kind of stuff—about a boy, the grandson of an unwitcher, who had to save the town from the evil counterpart of the krsnik, that awful kudlak. Given that I was speaking to Kresnik, the very origin of the idea of the krsnik, I wanted to know what he thought about the story I was writing, and how I might resolve the ending in a way that was true to the nature of the kudlak and made sense with the story.

So, yes: I asked a god how I might write a fantasy.

"Kresnik," I started, shuffling as I thought of how to word it, "can you tell me a little more about the kudlak? I'm writing a story with it and the krsnik in it, and I'd love to know your thoughts."

7. WHAT ARE YOUR INSIGHTS ON THE KUDLAK?

There was, once again, a sigh in the air, as if the topic was tiring. Kresnik pointed at the cards, and it was like trying to tune a radio as I made the connections, as I *listened*. There was something here that he was trying to say, and I thought it was obvious by the meanings of the cards themselves— how merciful Kresnik had been this whole time, to give me such easy cards to read—and finally, I found the right spot on that little spiritual radio.

It's the very nature of them that's the issue, Kresnik impressed upon me. *Their nature is what prevents them from getting what they want.*

I was confused, and baffled, at how these ideas seemed to just translate into English in my head. It may have been my very first time really experiencing, undeniably, what folks might call *claircognizance*. Because it certainly wasn't clair*audience*; I wasn't literally or spiritually *hearing* a voice. It was as if someone was planting ideas into my head like seeds, letting them sprout into their message.

Coveting others' success while wasting one's talents. Jealousy, envy.

Monetary success easily lost. Don't risk what you've gained.

So I asked a clarifying question: "What do you mean? How can the main character of my story stop them, if their own nature is in the way? How can I work that into the story?"

8. HOW DOES THE MAIN CHARACTER DEFEAT THE KUDLAK?

It's not about pure might, Kresnik insisted as he sat beside me, *but healing the wounds that got the Krsnik and Kudlak into their situation to begin with and finding ways to right the wrongs. Healing both party's souls, even if one is banished in the end.*

"Oh." It hit me like a sack of bricks, all those ideas I just translated into words for you. I understood, viscerally, through concepts and images and ideas that had to be finely teased into this comprehensible message, how it was the story needed to be resolved. It wouldn't do any of the characters any justice to resolve it any other way. "I understand now. Thank you. Thank you for that."

Irresponsibility with other people's money may lead to debt. Chance of fraud. Be wary.

In true victory, both sides are winners. Matriarchal power. Collaboration, compromise. Creativity. Bounty of good fortune.

And then I looked around at the table, at my cards, and knew it was time to pack it up. That was the last question I had for Kresnik, and I was thrilled that he'd bothered to answer me about something as frivolous as my own writing, but I didn't feel I had anything else to ask him—not in that moment. So I said as much, and I thanked him for his time, but before he left, I couldn't help but reach out for him one more time.

"Will you be around?" I was searching in my mind's eye for him. It felt strange to finally have someone like Kresnik in my space and just let him disappear again, though *strange* isn't quite the right word for it. Maybe, if you've encountered the gods of your own ancestors, you understand what I mean. "Can I continue to have you near, Kresnik? Can I speak to you again?"

I'd never seen a man, let alone a god, with such a warm smile. To this day, the image is seared in my head: of him and I, sitting shoulder to shoulder, heads tilted towards each other and touching, as if we were siblings or family. That image was enough of an answer for me, and I thanked him again and said goodbye for the time being, finally ready to close the space and continue with my day. I was satisfied with that, very much.

Since then, Kresnik has been a friend, coming around for conversation at times, and at other times, disappearing to do the work he needed to do. Anyone who's my friend knows that I'm terrible at staying in touch, so I've gone quite a while without speaking to him, but when I last visited my ancestral lands, I made sure to leave him flowers and say hello. He has his own tarot deck, now, too—one that all of the Slavic gods enjoy using when they come by to chat.

But all those developments were a long way off from where I was right there, cleaning up after my second interview with a god other than my own.

HADES

We all know Hades, right? Of course we do.

Now, this is undoubtedly the place where the wheels began falling off a little bit in this adventure—a whole two interviews in—but as the saying goes, hindsight is twenty-twenty. Before we dive into my insights looking back, however, let's talk about Hades himself.

In Greek polytheism (or *hellenismos*), Hades is the god of the underworld. One of the three major brothers (the other two being Zeus and Poseidon), it's said that Hades was given the underworld as his domain after casting lots with them to determine their kingdoms. Zeus received the heavens, Poseidon the seas.

As Hades is also known as Zeus Kthonios (Lord of the Underworld), Hades Agesilaos (the Inescapable), or Hades Agesander (the One who Carries Away All), his role in Greek society was pretty notable: he was the one who collected all the souls, and he was the one who made sure they didn't find their way back to earth. He was also a god of riches and wealth, as noted by his Greek title *Plutoun* (later romanized into the more recognizable form, Pluto), because it was thought all the gems and gold of the world were underground, deep in the earth, which was Hades' realm.

Hades took his job seriously and was a pretty grim figure, but he was known to be merciful at times, too. One of the most famous stories is that of Orpheus, a legendary musician that went down to Hades' realm to get his with Eurydice back. Hades and Persephone both said that if he could get himself and Eurydice out all the way back up the steps of his realm without looking back, then they could go.

Naturally, Orpheus took a quick peek at his wife just as they neared the top, and she died again.

But that's only a little sliver of the available myths and knowledge surrounding Hades. I think the most famous of all myths surrounding him must be the myth he shares with his wife in the Hymn of Demeter, one that shows him snatching Persephone from the field of wildflowers outside with the permission of her own father, Zeus. The ground cracks open, Persephone shrieks in terror as Hades comes out in his chariot and grabs her, and then Demeter wanders about, enlisting the help of some like Hekate to find the girl. When she discovers Hades took her daughter for a bride and that she was never consulted (as marriages in ancient Greece were arranged by the father), Demeter goes into a rage so cold and quiet that the world's vegetation dies and the humans on earth risk real starvation. She refuses to let the world come to life again until she's reunited with her daughter, defying even Zeus, and so they all convince Hades to let Perspehone come back home.

Before she goes, however, Hades convinces her to eat a few seeds of a pomegranate, and the number of seeds she eats determines how many months she has to spend down in his kingdom with him as his wife. In those months, the land goes barren and cold and dead again as Demeter grieves.

It's a heartwrenching tale of a mother's devotion, a commentary on the nature of marriage arrangements and the fate of young women, and a fascinating way to explain why a certain few months of the year are awful for growing food and trying to survive. And in modern times, it's been utterly bastardized, the moral of the story thrown away to paint Demeter as an annoying helicopter parent and Persephone as a total girl-boss with a big, spooky man—the ultimate Death and the Maiden trope.

I love Death and the Maiden; it's my favorite romance trope. So naturally, I wanted that idea of Hades and Persephone to be true. I wanted it to be true so badly that I was willing to *make* it true. Through my understanding and interpretations of the cards, I was fully prepared to hear what I wanted to hear, even though looking back, my original interpretations may not have been all that sound—and may have, in fact, been quite the misstep on my part to talk about.

Again, hindsight is twenty-twenty. But let's take a look now at the cards I pulled, what I originally wrote down, and what I think about those cards now.

This was part three of my haphazardly using Wiccan and New Age associations to try and put together some kind of table for an ancient god of a whole separate culture. I don't think I'll ever be anything other than exhausted thinking about it. But nonetheless, as I searched for information about Hades, I discovered that some decent things to put out would be exactly what I did: red wine and dark chocolate as food offerings, because I'd read that he likes those, pennies as a reference to the coins paid to Charon, and some purple dead nettle just for the name, though I don't recommend this looking back as they are a part of the mint family, and the story of Hades and Menthe the nymph is its own can of worms. Alongside that, I had onyx, garnet, and smoky quartz, as these were stones related to the underworld or death in some way and made sense to me.

Had I known anything about Hellenismos, I might've tried to turn the wine into a libation after. (I think I did toss it outside, but I had no idea what a libation—a poured out offering—was, so I didn't think to signify it as such.) I also would've washed my hands with living water, which is any water that comes from a running source like a river or a faucet, and I would've requested someone from this faith to invoke Hades on my behalf, as there are some specific ways of praying to and invoking these deities that show deep respect, but that I as a Christian Witch wouldn't feel comfortable doing. There's a lot of praise, a lot of use of epithets, and a lot of other devotional elements that go into prayers of other religions, and I would prefer to save those kinds of things for my own God— but many a wonderful person have helped me invoke their deities in a respectful way, as you'll see throughout this book.

Nonetheless, all I can say is that I called out to Hades as clearly and honestly as I could, even after I knocked over my own cup of wine and sent it everywhere. Was that an omen? Maybe, maybe not. But I pulled it together after cleaning up the mess and tried to search for any feel of Hades.

At this point, it was still hard to identify when a deity actually showed up. I had to rely heavily on my pendulum just to prove to myself that *something*, at least, was there. And there was! I trusted God to let Hades and only Hades through, and as far as what I've heard devotees of Hades describe, I had Hades show up—as an older man with a thick beard and longer dark hair, as well as some solid muscles on his frame and a straight-to-the-point expression

"Hades," I said, with a bit of relief riding off my voice, because I *was* worried that spilling the wine was a sign that he didn't want to be there, "thank you for joining me! Hello! Welcome! I'd like to ask you a few questions, if you don't mind!"

As the pendulum swung over the different tarot decks I had available, I got the sense that I'd be talking to a god of very few words. There was an ice to him—not a meanness at all, but just a coldness, a lack of *spark*, that lined up with what I understood a god of death to be at the time. The energy was certainly a far cry from the mischievous Loki, the sweet and warm Kresnik. It was a sobering feeling, one that would keep my spirits in check and my focus stable throughout the conversation. Once Hades chose Threads of Fate's Weaver Tarot, I hopped into the questions.

And... oh, man.

"So... the wine spilling is making me wonder if you're upset with me somehow?" Sheepishly, I shuffled the cards, not knowing the many mistakes I'd already made that night that had nothing to do with the wine. But as I shuffled, I got the sign to stop and pull some cards, so at least I got an answer to my very silly question.

1. DID 1 UPSET YOU BEFORE STARTING THIS INTERVIEW?

Stagnant. Stuck and unable to bring life forth. Focus on creating a foundation of self-love. Doubting yourself. Stay grounded.

Dissatisfied with current life. Relationships stale or disconnected. May be taking others for granted.

Unknown feelings. Embrace mystery. An unnerving time where working with the hidden parts of yourself is necessary. Rely on your intuition.

I was surprised at the clarity of the message in these cards. I was also surprised at how they had nothing to do with me or the table or anything else. It felt, to me, like it was distinctly about his current state—which, given that we were closer to May, meant that Persephone wasn't in his realm with him.

Funny story: I still have a habit of asking God what He thinks about each deity I'm about to talk to. Very rarely do I get any serious messages; God tends to just make harmless quips about their character or give me a shrug and a loving "don't be stupid." This time, however, I was actually intending to talk to both Hades *and* Persephone at the same time, and God told me quite clearly that *I should not do that during springtime.*

I didn't know why and didn't question it, either. But it's good I listened. Persephone was *not* there, and Hades was not happy about it.

"Okay. I hear you. And thank you again for speaking with me, Hades," I said as I shuffled. "I guess the first thing I'd like to know after that, then, is: do you and your wife Persephone keep in touch during these times, when she's come back to the surface? If so, how?"

2. DO YOU AND PERSEPHONE KEEP IN TOUCH DURING SPRING?

The biggest thing I took away from these cards was this: *they don't stay in touch.* Or at least, they shouldn't. I guess that was part of why God warned me not to try and get them in the same space. There was also a feeling of unease, a complete lack of joy, like a bitter winter cold. But Hades' face was like stone, stoic; even if that was the feeling in the air, there was still a sense of duty that kept it all tightly wrapped up. The second takeaway I had, even as Hades stood silent waiting for me to ask the next question, was that he didn't *like* to be alone, certainly didn't *want* to be, but he would be for the sake of the deal he'd made and the duties Persephone still had in the world of the living with her mother.

Dominion over all things mystical. As spiritual beings, we move between worlds. Spiritual realm serves us. Stillness, meditation, journeying.

Sacrifice. Accepting struggle in the immediate because of how it pays off. Temporary issues. The need to pause.

Arrival at who you authentically are and what you need. Spend time alone and prioritize your relationship with yourself.

With a nod, I said, "I see what you mean. Though, speaking of Persephone, I really can't help but ask: what *is* the real story of you and Persephone? Is it really like the original myth says?"

3. WHAT IS THE REAL STORY OF HADES AND PERSEPHONE?

Here's where, looking back, I could whack myself if I only had half the chance. My interpretation at the time was that Hades acknowledged he had *some* guilt, but that it wasn't *all* that bad, no—that there really *was* room for that Death and the Maiden love story I was so unnecessarily attached to at the expense of the real stories of Divinity! No, it was only because Demeter kicked up a fuss that Hades even felt bad at all; Persephone was just fine!

Again, how do I go back in time and whack myself? I would surely love to know.

Maybe it's because it's been a year, and my tarot skills are different from what they were, and I have a better grasp on

Life springing forth. Unseen to outside world, real to you. Urgency, insight. Seize the moment and check your doubts.

You were wronged or wronged another. Justice rooted in truth. Internal moral issues. Addressing wrongs, not turning a blind eye.

Secrets and illusions. Believing wrongly about yourself or others. Explore what needs to come to light to unburden yourself.

the story of Hades and Persephone in the first place, but as I said before: hindsight is twenty-twenty. Looking at these cards again, it's so obvious to me that I was reaching for that initial interpretation; I was wishing for it so hard that I didn't want to see the obvious truth.

Hades' and Persephone's story is as it's written in the Hymn of Demeter. Hades snatched Persephone up; he was enamored with her. The betrothal was a secret between Zeus and Hades, secret even to Demeter. What happened was by all legal standards allowed, but by moral standards, was highly questionable and left consequences—*as was the point the narrative was trying to address.*

Hades is aware of that. He still wants his wife near him, as I understand it, but he is aware of that. And it was my ego, and my selfish wishes, and my biases, that got in the way of really hearing him say as much, despite his answers being right there in my face.

Still, I plodded on. *See?* I thought to myself. *It's not all they made it seem! It's fine!* And as I shuffled the cards, I continued my questioning: "So how about all the retellings of your and Persephone's story? Like *Lore Olympus*?"

Pause here real quick for me; I need to tell you something.

And that is that *yes.* You are allowed to punch something inanimate. Or groan and roll your eyes. Or throw this book. It's okay. I know.

4. HOW DO YOU FEEL ABOUT MODERN RETELLINGS AND IMAGES?

Too much ambition blurs the lines of morality. One may stop at nothing to get what they want. A slippery slope. Sacrificing one's true self.

Tangible results and ideas, unbridled enthusiasm. Chase your dreams. Create a vision board and make plans.

Nurturing but formidable. Life experience. Supporting those around you. Stability and wealth, seeing things from a higher perspective.

Again, throughout this interview, one thing I felt was that Hades was a god of *very* few words. The answers I got came more as feelings, or as single words or snippets of a sentence. It wasn't a fluid, easy conversation, yet it wasn't difficult to understand, either—even when the cards became a little more abstract. The *just knowing* aspect of claircognizance is something I don't think I'll ever get used to (and it certainly isn't convenient, either, because how the hell does one explain to other people that they *just know* these off-the-rails things that they know?).

But here, I put these cards together and came away with a pretty clear picture: Hades is more than these cartoons and retellings. He has thousands and thousands of years of life and duty to draw from, a type of divine understanding humans can't fathom. While Hades thinks the retellings are interesting, and that it's nice that humans have such a passion in them about the gods in general, he also thinks they should be *dearly* careful about using the likeness of Divinity to air their personal desires and frustrations.

Especially if they start selling out and completely demeaning and twisting the name of Divinity for the sake of continuing to push and popularize said retellings.

"Okay," I murmured, "I think I understand what you're saying. It's a fair thing to say, all things considered. But to understand you a little better, could you tell me what your relationship to the other Greek gods is like?"

5. WHAT IS YOUR RELATIONSHIP TO OTHER GREEK GODS LIKE?

This one was tricky. I could feel Hades' eyes on me as I went between the three cards and their meanings, though he certainly wasn't about to make it easy on me by offering an explanation. This was a true tarot test—seeing how easily I could break apart the meanings of these cards and fit them back together like a LEGO kit gone horribly mis-assembled.

There was the wealth, yes—Hades Plutoun being all about wealth and riches—but there were also those aspects I associated with death, too. The stagnance, the darkness, the many ambitions and projects of human life left unfinished. And there was a frequent message *not* to focus on the material, but on the self. I took another sip of wine and tried as best as I could to fit these threads together.

New beginnings for all things material. Prosperity or way of aligning with the material realm. A new level, a total start.

Stagnance. Unable to bring life through. Don't focus on what you're not currently doing, but on grounding and self love.

Instability. Unexpected bumps in the road, projects falling to the wayside. Focus on building what you want. Focusing on more than the material realm.

And then I understood, all at once. A true "light bulb" moment. Hades was that which recycled the energy of the world, and he helped his fellow gods understand the power of distancing themselves from material things in order to focus on bringing their gifts into true radiance. This way, they might refocus, recommit, and be "reborn" in a way; the god of the dead helps these other gods understand what the value of the living is, and what things the living value that could become stumbling blocks for the gods.

I sat back and nodded. "Okay, I see! Interesting. Well, Hades, is there anything in particular you aim to teach your followers?"

6. IS THERE ANYTHING IN PARTICULAR YOU AIM TO TEACH?

As I shuffled, though, I got no signs that any card needed to be picked. No tingle in my ear, no feeling at my fingertips, nothing. Even after a few passes around, there was nothing.

"Um," the cards grated against each other as I shuffled them, "Hades, did you want to pull any cards for that?"

Still, no answer. At that point, I had to go ahead and call that a "no," and the only thing I could take away from that was that what Hades helped other gods understand, he also helped mankind understand. In fact, he's here to teach those lessons to anyone: the lessons of what it means to be alive, what it means to not put all one's faith in the material world, and what it means to find things more important and meaningful than the material things we think we love so much here on earth.

Nothing to be done about a god that didn't want to say any more than that, so I kept shuffling and nodded. "Alright, alright, I guess that's that, then. Let's move on: is there any relationship advice you might give to humans?"

7. ANY RELATIONSHIP ADVICE FOR HUMANS?

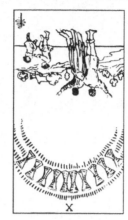

Broken bonds. Communication is difficult and out of balance. All parties have to want to mend something.

Arrival and completion, legacy. Financial success and relationship stability. Think long term and about the future generations. You're passing on patterns.

Potentially feeling dissatisfied. How are you showing up in your relationships when they start feeling stale? Don't take them for granted.

It's a silly question in hindsight. Not really his station, not really the point of his marriage, not really appropriate to ask. But I asked it because I was still new to this, overexcited and willfully misinformed, and thankfully, Hades seemed to be pretty patient about it. Maybe it's because so many people call on him for help whether they know about the proper customs of Hellenismos or not. Maybe it's because I wasn't picking up on any other signals that might've warned me off of the topic. Either way, he gave me cards this time.

There were at least two cards that had to do with something about communication and effort, with the only right side up card being about legacy. All the while, I could see Hades' bearded, near fatherly face, watching me as I scoured the booklet for clues about what this could mean.

There was certainly more warning in it than anything else. Looking back, I wonder if it's because of how his relationship with Persephone started—or if maybe he thought, with the modern people's view of the story, how he might've done things differently. Do gods reflect on their actions like that the way people do? Do they regret things and wish they could change things like that? I know there *are* stories of Greek gods showing regret, so it's possible.

But the practical takeaway here, I think, is that one has to be honest, up front, and invested in their relationship. They need to understand that their relationship, especially if they plan to have kids, is one that continues a legacy and a family name, and that the house they build is the foundation of their lives. Without proper communication, attention, and care, one's hard-earned foundation, and the safety and comfort it affords them, can crumble away to nothing.

With a nod, I shuffled the cards back into the deck and said, "That's sound, I'd say. Thank you for that. Next, what would you say are the best and worst parts of being god of the underworld?"

8. BEST AND WORST PARTS OF BEING GOD OF THE UNDERWORLD?

What an interesting collection of cards. The burden part jumped out at me, it being the most negative of them all, and I could easily imagine what a burden it would be to be the god of the underworld, the keeper of all this religion's dead. But it also seemed like, despite how stoic and quiet Hades had been the whole time, that there was a deep need for mastering emotional currents in it.

A land of raw, unchained souls. That's what the realm of Hades was. That's what Hades maintained each and every day since he'd taken up his station. The emotional currents of the underworld were high, and it took a lot for Hades to manage it; with Persephone around, it was easier to manage, but still difficult. The burden of being lord of the dead is heavy, but he bears it because there's no one else who can among the other Greek gods, no one who was chosen to do so.

The unknown, hidden feelings, the unconscious self. Embrace it. You can't rush the illumination of mystery. Unseen forces.

Carrying a large burden, brought on either by yourself or by others. You need to put it down. It's too heavy.

Anticipate others' needs and create containers for healing. Intuitive and healing arts. The use of one's intuition. No room for logic, only emotion.

"Wow." I will say, I'm not sure I expected an answer that vulnerable from Hades. "That's fascinating. I appreciate you sharing that; it's a good bit of context to see the work of a god of the dead through! Though I believe that was my last concrete question. Before we part ways for the night, though, I was wondering if you had any final thoughts or things you wanted to say?"

9. ANY LAST MESSAGES TO SHARE?

Nurturing new life. The intersection of love and creation. Deepen self love.

Highly energetic and gifted with ideas. Face discomfort of commitment.

Happy energy. Good things all around. Appreciate and celebrate your success.

I cocked my head and frowned at the cards—not because I disagreed with the message, but because I didn't expect it to come from a god of the dead. Yet there it was, loud and clear: *you're worth the effort to chase after what you want, but don't forget to slow down and enjoy where you are, too.* Like sucking venom from a snake bite, being able to stop and appreciate the moment will remove some of that fear of the future, no matter how the future turns. It was a message applicable to all people, and one I certainly appreciated, but one I wouldn't figure out how to incorporate into my life until much later.

"I got'cha. Alright, then! I guess that's a wrap! Thank you again, Hades, for joining me and answering my questions. I appreciate all the wisdom you've shared and can't wait to share it with others, too!"

And then I thought I'd leave it at that, but just before I closed my space, I caught an image: Hades, standing at the mouth of some kind of torch-lit cave, crossing his big arms and staring out at what looked like an icy city way in the distance. We were deep underground, and the only light besides the orange fire was this blueish, ghastly light radiating from the city. He looked out and smiled at it as if proud, and that was the last thing I saw before the images faded altogether, leaving me alone in my living room.

Looking back, I think that was a quick glimpse at Hades' realm—not so close that the privacy of its citizens would be encroached on, but just a glimpse of the city, and the way down to it leading from the cave. It was interesting, to say the least, and a vivid image that stuck with me for days afterwards, because it was the first time in this journey I'd gotten an image of *scenery* like that.

For all my ridiculousness in this interview, my childish overexcitement, I will say this: I did talk to someone I'm inclined to say is Hades, and I did crack the next layer of clairvoyant skill with that one image, as clear and vivid as if I'd seen it in a richly illustrated fairy tale book. Even if I hadn't gotten a single answer out of Hades, if I'd just had that image, I think I would've still called this experience a success—because progress is progress, no matter how small.

But even small steps of progress can lead to one becoming far too confident for their own good.

BRIGID

It was a fine Saturday: sunny and cheerful, with the air finally warming up a bit. Spring was here in full, and my stove was blazing away, taking a little bit of the sun's fire into my own house as I simmered a pot of milk, honey, and chamomile tea bags together. I was doing that, of course, to talk to Brigid, Celtic goddess of springtime, fertility, life, the sun, and the sacred hearth.

Brigid is such a fascinating figure. A goddess whose talents center around creation, she's known as a smith, a poet, a journeyer, a protector of the family and the flames that kept the hearth alive, and so much more. Whether she was a triple goddess like the Morrígan or simply a goddess with many names, faces, and skills is uncertain for historians, though she does seem split into separate aspects that concern themselves with the many things she governs. Nonetheless, with Brigid being the beloved of pre-Christian Celts, and the daughter of the Dagda, she is one goddess so revered and cherished that even after Ireland converted to Christianity, they refused to let her go altogether. As such, the goddess Brigid became Saint Brigid of Kildare—a woman of great miracles whose lore includes her even being the wet nurse of baby Jesus. (Somehow.)

This syncretic flare allowed Brigid the room and space to keep attending to her people, even as the pressure of Christian dogma pushed the other gods out and away. And while the Catholic church caught on eventually, declaring that St. Brigid was never a real person, it didn't mean a damn thing to the Catholic folks of Ireland, who protected their goddess from the cultural erosion of a new religion as much as she protected them from the many different ills of the world, including the life-sucking force of cold, brutal winters.

Many neopagans and Celtic polytheists understand her role in the festival of Imbolc, one that serves as a waypoint between first day of winter and the first day of spring. It's a time of cleansing, purification—of putting the old things of the previous year to rest for good and preparing the fields of our mind and soul for a new year, full of new love, new opportunities, and new lessons. Its cognate Christian holiday, Candlemas, contains similar themes, with Mother Mary as the central focus.

As a Christian myself, this was an aspect I wanted to explore: how *gods* become *Saints* in the crashing tide of conversion, whether gradual or forced. It's happened all around Europe, with Roman gods operating as Saints in Italian folk magic, or with Slavic gods still marking Christian graveyards with symbols so old that people don't quite remember what they mean anymore. But with three deity interviews under my belt—and a confidence that was rapidly growing despite my mind's eye only *just* beginning to crack open in the blinding rays of Divine light—I felt confident that I could get some insight on how this happened. Or, at least, how Brigid felt about it.

So the offerings went like this: a few fresh dandelions, as well as some common Imbolc items, blackberries and pumpkin seeds, because I heard she loved those. A bit of carnelian to represent fire and creativity. A little amethyst for wisdom and peace. A few piping hot cups of honey-chamomile milk and some honey-slathered bread, as milk is a big factor on Imbolc and chamomile and honey represent sunshine. And lastly, a couple lavender bergamot candles for the floral serenity factor. After learning a bit about Brigid, all of these things—and their associations with Imbolc, fire, fertility, wisdom, life, and creativity—felt appropriate to welcome her with.

Once I was settled, with rosemary smoke cleansing my space and mugwort smoke giving a boost to my psychic power, I went ahead and set the space with the Lord's prayer—a quick cast that makes sure, as I said before, that no pesky egregores or other silly things come to bother me. Then, when everything was lined up just so, I got to putting myself in the zone for some concentrated tarot, as I'd done three times already. Looking at my spread, I was reminded of Kresnik, as would make sense given them sharing associations of sunshine and life. It put me in good spirits (and that honey-chamomile milk was *delicious*), so I had a cheery note in my voice as I asked Brigid to come forward.

"Brigid!" At this point, I'd given up on speaking out loud. It just felt too silly for me. So I held the cup of milk tea in my hands and enjoyed its warmth as I shot thoughts out like arrows into the dark. "Hello! Wherever you are, please come join me, I have a few questions for you."

Between the treats I had out, the sunshine coming through the windows, and the sudden snap of something bright and cheerful that came popping into my space, I was quite content. But just to check, I confirmed she was there with my pendulum, and to my surprise, she chose the Universal Fantasy Tarot to speak through—a fun and whimsical deck that's always a treat to use.

"Alrighty then. Brigid, thank you again for stopping by. I guess the first thing I'd like to know is: given all the different things you have mastery over and are associated with, how do you see yourself?"

1. How do you see yourself?

1. Domestic bliss. Harmonious family life. Bountiful harvests, labors rewarded. Loyal and true friendship. Success.

2. Irresponsibility with other's money leads to debt. Fraud.

The first card was clear to me: they were things certainly associated with her as a goddess of life and fire and the family. And the energy I felt said as much: she was a goddess of the people, who kept them safe and kept life vibrant and joyful all throughout the land. But for all that sunshine, it felt like there was a frown lodged in there. I couldn't get a sense of her yet in the way I'd gotten a sense of the other gods—though I trusted the images would come eventually—yet still, she made her intentions known. That irresponsibility in the Nine of Coins Reversed? It wasn't about *money*. It was about *her*.

So what I got from this was that *she* has that very stable idea of herself, but the people she served seemed to have a way of mucking up her image; they were irresponsible with how they viewed her, and so they complicated something about her. There was a sigh in the air, a heaviness in the eyelids, as if the idea was enough to bring even a god to cigarette-smoking exhaustion.

I frowned as I shuffled the cards into the deck. "Irresponsible with your image? How?"

2. HOW ARE PEOPLE IRRESPONSIBLE WITH YOUR IMAGE?

Too much worry of the future distorts the present. Anxiety never a good guide.

Intense emotional turmoil. Loneliness and insecurity in relationships.

Too much! That's what screamed at me as I looked at these cards. *I was given too much!* And again, there was the sense of a frown buried in the very air itself—a set of deeply furrowed brows, a sigh waiting to be huffed out. Brown eyes twinkling as if full of embers. Red hair.

Snatches. I was getting snatches.

But it seemed to me that the main issue here wasn't people turning Brigid into St. Brigid, like I'd originally expected. Rather, it seemed pre-Christian folks ascribed *too many* areas of governance to her, mostly because they were afraid of so many different things in life and trusted her to fix all of it, even though there were other gods that could've helped, too. Brigid had specific duties, but people made her a goddess of a billion and two things because they wanted her, specifically, to come fix these issues.

"Well," my lips wrenched as I tried not to smile at the idea of a god being forced to work overtime, "how do you *want* people to view you, then?"

3. HOW DO YOU WANT PEOPLE TO SEE YOU?

The fire was bright in my mind's eye, but it was faraway, too: it was a little will-o'-the-wisp in a lantern, moving through a misty bog, with a woman carrying it easily over mossy tree roots and slippery stones. And that little lantern's orange light wasn't just an unliving flame; it was the very stuff of life, wild and proud and confident, dancing even through the concealing haze of the land. That was Brigid: a deity that burned away stagnance and insecurity, emboldening people to do what they needed to do to be their truest selves. She was telling me, through those cards and the wisps of divine flame, that she was a champion for those who needed help holding their head high.

"Wow," I breathed, "that's pretty intense. I love that." And I did! These sun gods, they had such incredible energy, and

A gilded cage is what we build with our own hands. Believe in yourself and stay faithful.

Withering of bounty through neglect and inaction. Weakness, indecision.

a way of making practitioners feel on top of the world. "Alright, well—how did you come to be connected to St. Brigid? And how do you feel about that?"

4. HOW DO YOU FEEL ABOUT YOUR CONNECTION TO ST. BRIGID?

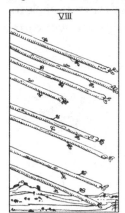

That which we have worked for will bear fruit if we have the patience to wait.

Irresponsibility with money leads to debt. Fraud.

Here, that flame dimmed a little. There was a red-haired woman with a small frown, with downcast eyes, and then an image of a church somewhere on a green hill. It seemed like an obvious answer, given the heaviness that hung off my shoulders in that moment, though the cards themselves spoke on it: patience. Waiting. Feeling like a fraud.

Brigid waited in the wings. She loved her people more than she loved her divine rights, though she knew one day she'd have both in her grasp again. That doesn't mean it was any less distasteful to have to be subjugated under the new religion the way she was, but Brigid did it for the sake of not being driven away from her people; she refused to let go, no matter what, and now it's paying off, as her name as goddess is coming back among the folks she waited so long for.

That's devotion.

As I digested that answer, I shuffled the cards with gusto. My heart brimmed with admiration for her then; I was in awe, and I was humbled to know how far Divinity will go for the sake of mankind (even though I'd already technically known it from my own faith—though at this point, I hadn't given the meaning of Christ's death and resurrection as much thought as I later would). But this brought a good segue into my next question.

"So how do you feel about working with Celtic Christians, then, given your feelings about becoming St. Brigid and the like?"

5. WHAT DO YOU THINK OF CELTIC CHRISTIANS?

I love it when the meanings of the cards weave a clear tapestry. Makes my job so much easier than trying to directly pull what they mean from abstractions and imagery and raw claircognizance. This was another one of those easy times, where as soon as I read the meanings of the Universal Fantasy Tarot's cards, I understood—and I saw why she chose them. This language was perfect at helping me figure it out right away.

While Brigid never forgot who she *really* was, and never truly let the Celtic people forget it, either, she absolutely made use of that foothold as St. Brigid to continue helping the people as they needed. Brigid is keen; she understands that this fluidity between goddess and Saint is what kept her, and by extension the old Celtic gods, anchored in their own lands, and that it's the lifeline that helped modern Irish

Fears of the past must not be forgotten, but kept like conquered enemies.

Understanding difficulties is the first step to overcoming them.

Christians and Irish pagan reconstructionists find their way back to her. As with many old gods who have retained some influence in the interesting sphere of Sainthood, it wasn't a welcome disguise, but it was one that undeniably worked when it came to keeping their people safe and their cultural practices at least somewhat retained.

"Okay, I got'cha," I said as I thumbed through the booklet. "But with all this said, let's turn it back to you. All these titles and areas of influence aside, I'd like to know: what's your *favorite* area to work in? Smithing, poetry? Something else?"

6. WHAT IS YOUR FAVORITE DOMAIN TO WORK IN?

Creation. Right away, as a creative myself, I recognized it: the feeling that the work is never *done*, the work is never *just right*. It's the work of creation, of art, of always being able to go back and keep improving something. The traveling, the journeying, it's necessary to make that art, but she prefers the moments she gets to make things with her own hands (poetry, smithing, or so on) than taking care of the many other things people have foisted into her sphere of influence. Those other things, they distract from the work she wants to do.

Labor with humility. Never thinking we achieved our goal. Best results.

Travel from an intolerable situation.

"Ah, I see." I put the cards back one by one, and when I blinked, I caught a glimpse of that red-haired woman again—Brigid—this time on top of a bear, with a face bright and strong, her eyes clear and focused. It seemed like a good place to end the interview, with her there at the very end, but before I could pack those cards away, I couldn't help but let one more question loose: "If you don't want to answer this, I understand, but Brigid... what do you think of God? After all this mess that happened with the church and the Sainthood and all that?"

7. WHAT DO YOU THINK ABOUT GOD?

1. Patience and perseverance are the key to solving many problems. Time to struggle; a wise man knows when to step up.

2. That which has been will be again. The eternal cycles of life dominate destiny.

Brigid's lips wrenched in thought.
Always there. Behind Brigid were two great and fiery eyes, burning hotter than the sun, and yet with an edge of cold to them—as if there was a barely-hidden, rueful half-smile hidden in the flame. The eyes of God. *He's always watching,* Brigid seemed to say; *He watches without being so overbearing.* And He wanted gods like Brigid to have their space to lead, to work, without interruption.

Cycles. It's all cycles. What was once destroyed will thrive again. There's wisdom in the hands-off approach, a discernment that mankind keeps trying to override. Through the cards and the imagery, through the ideas that vaguely translated into English in my head, it seemed Brigid was telling me something I'd always understood without saying:

God didn't intend for a lick of this mess we've made of the world and its many gods. Not a scrap of it. That was all us, *all* us, and finally, the Wheel is turning again, the things dead and buried reborn through new leaves and shoots, new faces and customs.

I smiled, then chewed on a blackberry I'd set aside for myself. There was something new and green in myself as I held onto this idea, something that had just poked its two baby leaves above the soil of my own spiritual awareness and understanding. It would be a while yet before that little something showed any true leaves, but it would stretch up for the light nonetheless over the course of this experiment, and it was up to me to continue tending to it all the while—that much, I knew right then.

"Thank you, Brigid," I whispered as I packed the cards back into their weathered box. "That's all the questions I have to ask you for now."

In my mind's eye, the woman with hair like the evening sun smiled, and the fire of her being, that little lamp in the misty bog, winked out, leaving me to stand alone in the light of the two burning, discerning eyes that would forever hang over me.

CERNUNNOS

So when it comes to Cernunnos, I actually didn't know that it was pronounced "ker-nuh-nos." I was thinking it was something like "tser-noo-nos." I blame my Slovenian inclination to make every letter *C* sound like a "ts," or the Cyrillic character ц for eastern Slavic languages. However, the only way I learned this was when a good few Celtic pagans reached out to correct me, which I'm thankful for.

All that aside, Cernunnos is an interesting deity—one of wild things, of fertility and forests, and more recently, one associated with death as much as life. He may have even had something to do with travel and communication, too. It seems to me that Cernunnos is more a *continental Celtic* name for this concept of a god: continental referring to Celts like the Gauls of modern day France. Perhaps an Isles equivalent of Cernunnos would be Herne of the Wild Hunt, or Welsh Arawn of the underworld and the wild things. His closest Germanic equivalent may be Wotan, who, in my view, seems to blend aspects of Odin and Cernunnos as archetypal figures.

However, as a horned god, Cernunnos gets lumped in a lot with Wiccan ideals of the Lord, or Green Man, or Horned God, which, given in Wiccan lore, dies every autumn and is reborn every spring, makes a lot of sense. One thing I will say, though, is that it's important to remember that Wicca is its own religion, and personally, I heavily disagree with how many folks act like the Lord and Lady are empty slots you can slap any deity into. Hekate is not a triple goddess the way Wicca understand a triple goddess, yet people pigeon hole her into this system. Cernunnos is not married to any of these goddesses, nor does his lore *always* follow this idea that people put on him through neopagan reconstructionism (it depends on which tradition you look at).

But I feel like I'm just speaking into the wind on this. People will do whatever fulfills them, regardless of what anyone else tells them. It's important they know that these gods had their own functions and cultures and significances before commercially viable witchcraft in the modern era, but if they choose to ignore it, you won't find me busting their door down with a battering ram and confiscating the Palo Santo they bought from one of those hack metaphysical shops (even if I'd really like to).

Anyway, I was fascinated with Cernunnos, and given I'd just started my Patreon, I wanted to start doing more with these interviews, something written. With this god of the wild things—so far removed from the order we normally associate with Divinity, as if to counterbalance their rule and law and civilization—I figured we had a great guest to start that adventure with. Here's how it went.

For this deity, I read somewhere that he was associated with deer—of course—but also rats. I had nothing related to a stag, but I did have a little statue of a rat with a Chinese coin, so I put that down, as well as some juniper, rosemary, pine cone, tiger's eye, and moss agate—all either things I read were associated with him, or things I felt represented his qualities of being of the forests and the beasts. An offering of strawberries and of blackberry and raspberry gin went with it, too, given gin is made with juniper, and berries are the epitome of wild fruits. With everything laid out, my prayers to God prayed and my space cleansed and fortified with mugwort and cinnamon, I was ready.

I was getting an image all the while of a deer skull. Maybe it's because I was still working on my debut novel, *The Glass Witch*, at the time, cleaning it up and beginning to think about self publishing, in which the motif of the deer skull is heavy. Maybe it's because I'd read about Cernunnos being associated with the stag. Either way, I saw it surrounded by mossy trees and slick stones as I invited Cernunnos into my space; whenever I closed my eyes, it hung there, suspended in the air.

"Cernunnos," I whispered into empty air, "welcome. Thank you for joining me; feel free to drink and share some fruit with me."

His glass tinkled throughout the interview—likely the ice, but it was loud and attention grabbing each time, much louder than my glass's ice popped. It was a solid sign, in my opinion and in my gut feeling, that he'd acknowledged me. He chose Amrit Brar's Marigold tarot to speak with, and he wanted *five* cards per answer.

So as I shuffled, I just decided to go ahead and ask my first question.

"To start, can you tell me your thoughts on the state of the world? Climate, modernity, anything."

"Oh. That's a big question to ask me on first pass."

It startled me a little, to hear—or, rather, *feel*—a whole sentence like that. I know I'd committed to really trying to hear these entities speak the way I spoke to them, to search for those threads of their voice and welcome them rather than wait for the cards to confirm them, but it was strange. And when I closed my eyes, even more startling was how that stag skull I'd been staring at moved. It tipped up, and a human hand came with it—and I realized the skull was actually a hat! It was a hat that could double as a mask, and underneath it was Cernunnos's face: a bearded man dressed in mossy, green-brown robes, a twinkle in his dark eyes and a smile hidden under his facial hair.

"I know," I said, cautious, marveling at this god I was seeing. "But I'm curious."

I. WHAT ARE YOUR THOUGHTS ON THE STATE OF THE WORLD?

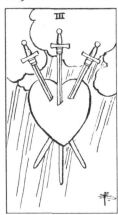    

Heartbreak, betrayal, division, rejection, hard truths, indecisiveness, pain.

Wishful thinking, imagination, concern with fantasy. Flighty nature of thought, third eye.

Healing, balance, harmony, cycles, natural order. Inevitability, manifesting future.

Misfortune approaching, depression, unsuccessful ventures.

Joy, moving forward, stagnation being the root cause of challenges.

Here was where I noticed something interesting. Yes, of course, I'd been talking to God and to these other deities through tarot cards the whole time, interpreting what these things all meant together myself, but as I looked them over, I let myself be vulnerable. I asked Cernunnos directly to weave these meanings together for me, to guide my pencil and make that graphite loop exactly the way he wanted against the page, to give me not just cards, but the *words* that connected them.

And he did.

"Well, if I can be entirely honest with you, I feel betrayed," he said as he solidified in my mind's eye, the Man of the Forest sitting there among the moss and dead leaves. "My people—they used to be focused on the things that mattered, that they could *see* and *touch* and that would actually keep them going. Nowadays, there's so much focus on these things, these abstract things—all the phones and noise and words and money, the *money*. Always the money, worse now than ever."

I dared to ask a follow up, a simple yes or no question, to see what else I would get: what feelings and images, and how they would translate into words. "And it's fair to say your people were also once concerned with nature, too?"

"Absolutely. That's why it feels like such a betrayal; they knew me. They knew the woods. I'm glad to see them start knowing them again, and knowing the concrete things in life again, but it'll get worse before it gets better, I can tell you that. It'll get a lot worse before it gets better. At least it *will* get better, though."

I blinked. This whole thing was so novel, so... strange. I felt like I'd crossed an ocean in one week, in one decision. How else can I describe it? To go from cards, scraps of words or ideas, little flickers of images, to this? Was it real or was I kidding myself? Was this just a product of seriously overactive imagination?

Or was it that I'd finally *allowed* these images, feelings, and abstract ideas to come and make themselves known without a shield of my own fear and doubt in front of me?

"Of course, yeah," I mumbled, unsure but unwilling to give up. "Now, can you tell me where you place yourself in the world? Where you work to make it better, if you do that?"

2. WHERE DO YOU PLACE YOURSELF IN THE WORLD?

Faith in ourselves and abilities of self expression. Optimism, navigation.

Cruelty, manipulation, ill intentions, injustice, and narrow worldviews.

New beginnings, spontaneity, change, innocence. Resting. Most important journeys are mental, not physical.

Wealth, prosperity, contentment. Spiritual and physical wealth. Protection, adaptation, a bright future.

Transforming force. Rest, rebirth, becoming stronger. Doing what needs to be done for our betterment.

Cernunnos watched me with a sharp, careful eye. "I'm a navigating force," he said. "People can use me to find the way to the truth, without the mists in the way. There's so much muck around the people right now, y'know? And in them, too. So much manipulation, all these ill intentions and injustice, and people with narrow worldviews getting in the way of real understanding.

"I always helped navigate that in the forest; that's where the *real* transformation happens. I'm here to get people moving forward, and I won't be nice about it if the people don't listen up."

"Understandable, definitely." I felt like I was at my job, interviewing a community partner for the next blog post I'd have to run by my boss. "With all that said, how do *you* see yourself?"

3. HOW DO YOU SEE YOURSELF?

Bad news, wastefulness, priorities in disarray.

Power, knowledge, success, reliability. Cooperative, abundant, keen.

Perceptiveness, sadness, honesty. Confronting painful truths.

Transforming. Accepting changes, new opportunities and obstacles.

Miscommunication, trauma, misunderstanding.

"Oh, me?" Cernunnos blinked as if the question surprised him. "Well, I can't say I was always the most present, I'll admit. There were things that came up—things that took my attention and time away for the people. You can guess."

Could I? "Was it the rise of Christianity? The move away from Celtic gods?"

"Yeah," he said, both through the cards and the way he wove them into words in my mind. "That took us all by storm a bit. It's worked out now, but I think it's worked out in an odd way. You see, I already said: I'm a navigator. I helped, and still help, people find the truth and recycle their energy, their mindsets, all that. And I'll always make the tough decisions that need to be made, if it's for the good of the people. But people kind of took this the wrong way, when I came telling them about *transformation.*"

"Oh, right. I can see that. Before we get to that, though, quick question: is how you see yourself, as a navigator and a facilitator for personal change and growth, how you want others to see you?"

4. HOW DO YOU WANT OTHERS TO SEE YOU?

I didn't get any sense that I should've been pulling cards here. At a time like this, it was the pendulum's turn to shine, and it did: I asked if he wanted to pull any cards and got a firm no, asked if he wanted to be seen how he saw himself and got a prominent yes. His voice came through as the crystal swung on its chain, a dry humor to his words.

"I wouldn't use such big words as that, but yes."

"Alright, fair." Here, I thought it was worth repeating, because my unease and doubt was starting to lay in my gut as if I'd swallowed a rock. "Again, Cernunnos, please do feel free to guide my words and interpretations as much as you like as I write them down. But to skip back to where we were: how do you find the modern interpretations of you, with the death and rebirth thing?"

5. WHAT DO YOU THINK OF MODERN INTERPRETATIONS OF YOU?

Transform-
ing force. Rest,
rebirth, becoming
stronger. Doing
what needs to be
done for our bet-
terment.

Denial, stale-
mate, indecision,
illusions.

Craft, dedication,
diligence, skill.
Adaptation neces-
sary to succeed.

Pessimism, dread,
resignation.

Directionlessness,
lost of ambition
and vision.

"It's too literal. Don't like it, not a bit. The change I want people to realize, that transformation, it's the internal type. It's not about literally up and dying, like the myths go now—but the *forest*, it's about the *forest*. You can absolutely take those parts of yourself you want to bury and bring it to the woods; the woods will take care of it there.

"The woods will recycle that energy. It'll take the bad you want to leave behind and transform it into the good to take home with you. *That's* the death and rebirth right there: purifying those rotten parts in the soil and growing new things from the waste."

Interesting. "So that sort of answers my next question, then: what constitutes 'death and rebirth'? And do you really die and come back?"

Again, there was no hint that I should've been pulling cards. But while I'd been advocating for Cernunnos to take my pen and simply *go*, to guide me in my efforts to translate his words correctly, I'll say this: I didn't expect the words to actually translate themselves into my head. From raw feeling and concept to the good old English language, the answer came all at once, forcing me to tease it apart into words that made sense.

I didn't need cards here. I just *heard*—or, more accurately, I *knew*. There wasn't any direct auditory experience like one would think of clairaudience; this was claircognizance through and through. And I'll be honest: it scared me for a thousand and two reasons. Just a couple of those reasons are the fact that it made my head feel overloaded, like pouring too much hot tea into a cup and splashing it all over oneself, burning and overwhelming and *intense*. Another was the fact that without the cards, I couldn't really put to rest the niggling doubt that I was just making all this up,

Because without cards, how could I have known? How could I have *possibly known* that this was real, that Cernunnos was really saying this, that I wasn't just having one hell of a fun time playing pretend in front of this table of trinkets? Without the cards, this physical thing, this *tangible* thing, this *indisputable* (sort of) thing, how could I know that it wasn't just *me* talking to *myself*?

I can't give you an answer. All I can say, though, is that by thinking like this, I'm no better than the average Christian that clings to the Bible's every printed letter because they're afraid to hear what God is *actually* saying in each moment—afraid to let go of the crutch of the physical and "provable."

But in that moment, I hadn't quite had that revelation. I wouldn't for many more months; I wouldn't until I wrote it here, alone in my living room on a Friday night, and watched Word's cursor blink. All I knew then was that I had to write this down, pencil to paper, in my little notebook.

6. DO YOU REALLY DIE AND REVIVE EVERY YEAR?

"Just like you said," came the words that spawned from this horned man in my mind's eye, "that answers it. It's not literal death. It's death of the bad things everyone gets stuck to them at some point or another, and changing them into something new.

"None of us ever come back the same when we go through this change, and it doesn't happen only once. You never wake up the same person even from day to day; the simple experience of being a *living* being means you're always dying somewhere and regrowing somewhere else. It's just how it is."

"And so, again, to clarify," because what if I was wrong, *what if I was wrong?* "your role in this world is to help with that?"

Cernunnos smiled at me, and I had no choice but to believe I didn't imagine it if I was to keep going without losing all my nerve and giving up the whole experience. "Yeah," he said. "To help go through this change and navigate the outcomes for the best results. Experience is what matters;

experience is what lets the hunter hunt and the doe learn to avoid the hunter. Always learning, growing, changing—that's what I help people do and get through."

I took a deep breath and gathered myself. *No time for doubt*, I told myself. *I'm here to be a reporter.* And a reporter I would act like. So I tapped my pencil to my notebook and said, "That's pretty intense, actually. In that vein, is there anything you want to tell your followers?"

I know, right? Who am I, as a Christian, to deliver a completely different god's messages to their followers? You may have asked yourself that a couple times now. But if God, the King of Kings, the Lord of Spirits, the Creator, the Whatever You Want to Call Him, could pull in *Loki* to deliver a message to *me* on *His* behalf, then I think it's plenty reasonable to say that something could happen in reverse, too—that maybe hearing a message from Cernunnos that these devotees had already received through a different filter would make it easier to listen.

Either way, he answered. So who am I to say anything at all, other than what he's told me to say?

7. WHAT DO YOU WANT YOUR FOLLOWERS TO KNOW?

False accusations, disharmony, general unfairness.	*Friendship, ties, bonds. Celebrations, good news and intentions.*	*Regaining inner strength and alliances.*	*Indecision, inadequacy, emotional detachment.*	*Unwillingness to see problems for what they are, looming disaster, avoiding change.*

See what I mean? That last card especially—that there's my point. But I just put my pencil to my paper and let Cernunnos do what he'd been doing all that time: braid those many card meanings into some solid idea, feeling, thought, that I would then translate into his voice, his mannerisms, and most importantly, his words.

"Ah, well, let's be clear, here," he said with a sigh and a scratch at his beard. "People *still* don't understand the old ways. All this time I spend on this, and they *still* don't get it, not all of them. Will they ever? Maybe. But they have to *decide* to get it—no more of this wishy-washy stuff, no more standing around and hoping problems just go away on their own without any work. It's easy to get beat down by the world, especially with all the muck in it, but my people, they need to hold onto the friends they know will help prop them up through this.

"They need to learn to be strong enough to acknowledge what's rotting on them and cut it off; they need to regain the strength to face these things head on. It's scary, sure, but it's worth it, and it's an adventure in itself, so people should embrace that and remember to be happy while they do the work!"

I smiled, even as my eyes burned while I re-read what I'd wrote. By this point, it was very late, and I'd essentially been working nonstop on a lot of things all day. I was very tired. I wanted to go to bed, but not before I finished these last couple questions. No, I couldn't give up, not until I'd satisfied every drop of my curiosity.

"So, as you're talking about the old ways," I started, "I was also curious: what do you think about modern lifestyles? Hustle culture and all that? Good, bad?"

My head felt like a walnut stuck in a nutcracker, with the pressure only increasing. And my eyes, how they burned, burned! Every blink was torture. But as I shuffled, I got no signs to pull cards; only a feeling to *go, go, go on, now!*

So I used the pendulum instead and asked my question again, asking if Cernunnos found hustle culture good. He said no. I asked if he found it bad. A resounding yes. And then came his voice like a hand on my shoulder, jostling me.

8. WHAT DO YOU THINK ABOUT HUSTLE CULTURE AND THE LESHY?

"Nah, no good—and you're a part of it right now!" His eyes were wide open, the whites clearly visible as I closed my own eyes and pressed my knuckles into them. "I see you nodding off," he said with a huff. "Go to sleep; don't push yourself so hard. What good is it, wearing yourself out?"

I rubbed my eyes a second longer and waved a hand. "Okay, okay. I hear you. But real quick, last question: what do you think of the Slavic Leshy? Please, I gotta know."

Again came that pouring-tea-too-fast feeling in my head. That, and the image of a great forest creature laboring through the woods, looking around between the trees—looking, itself, like a tree. A very Ent-like thing, surveying the forest.

"Ah, the Leshy," Cernunnos started, his voice a hammer to my tired brain. "A good friend, yeah. But they're more concerned with the guardianship part, keeping the physical forests safe. I live in those forests. I know the spirits of it; that's what I deal in. Leshy, on the other hand, keeps the bounds of those like me safe. They're good at what they're good at, if you know what I mean."

Did I know what he meant? Maybe. Maybe not. But I knew that was the last answer I was going to get from him, mostly because I felt that my mind would simply turn to liquid if I asked one more question. So I nodded and began packing up the cards.

"I guess I understand," I said. "Well, that about wraps up any questions I had, then. Do you want me to throw these things away that I have here, the strawberries and the drink, or would you rather I consume them?"

I know you're not supposed to eat things that are designated for deities that deal in death. Yet there was his voice, loud, insistent: "Don't waste them! I hate waste. Eat the strawberries, at least."

So, with a smile and a poorly stifled yawn, I said, "Fine, fine. But thank you for your time, and for coming to give me some insight. With that, I'm calling this a night."

FREYJA

I'll admit this: I knew very little about Norse gods before starting this series. You probably figured that, though. I knew very little about *all* gods, but Norse gods were, to me, an especially large mystery. I'd had Neil Gaiman's *Norse Mythology* on my shelf for years, but I hadn't ever had the maturity to read it. (And now, I still haven't had time to get around to it, so it sits there unread. But it is there.)

However, when it came time to look into Freyja, who was chosen in the Patreon poll for that week's interview, I found myself all but falling in love. What an interesting story she has; what an interesting goddess she is! It made me sad to know that she was essentially traded over to the Aesir as a peace offering in the lore of the gods, when there was that war between the Aesir and the Vanir, another cluster of Norse gods, but it's also fascinating to know that Odin showed her kindness as they were paired, and that she taught him the secret of the runes—magical tools and icons you've likely seen at one point or another. Turns out magic was considered women's domain in Norse culture, which is incredible: it wasn't something feared, but respected (and yet also looked down on as emasculating and shameful when men did it, as is predictable, but still disheartening).

Nonetheless, something I notice is that goddesses of beauty and love like Freyja tend to also have a warring aspect to them, too. Freyja is goddess of love, sex, and marriage, yes—and of course, of a specific old Norse magic of seiðr that let her see and influence the future and may have actually been used by men and women alike—but she's also a goddess of war and battle and wealth. She leads the Valkyrie, rides a chariot drawn by cats, and she has her own realm of the afterlife, Folkvangr, where the fallen soldiers who don't make the cut for Valhalla go and spend their afterlives in peace. All in all, Freyja is a major player in the Norse pantheon, both beautiful and brutal, compassionate and destructive. She may also be cognate with the goddess Frigg, according to some sources.

As I said, researching her had me enamored with her. She seemed incredible, and I couldn't wait to get to know more about her, so off I went to try—and it certainly was an experience. Take a look.

For Freyja, what else could I put as an offering besides mead? I had some of that on the table, as well as a chocolate covered apple, as I read apples were something she enjoyed as well. I picked some fresh lilac and buttercups for her, too, and set out some moonstone and rose quartz as a nod to her domains of love and magic. With candles lit and mugwort burned, as well as the Lord's Prayer said to set the bounds of my space and keep any fakes and egregores out per God's vigilant watch, I was ready to roll.

"Freyja, welcome." I was buzzing with excitement—or maybe anticipation, or anxiety. Maybe all three. "Please feel free to drink and share this apple with me, and thank you for joining me."

Freyja's energy was warm at my hands and feet, but still sharp, almost like Loki's was when we talked. I had an image of a woman with red hair coiled in beautiful, thick braids, and a dark cloak around her shoulders, layered with smooth fur and dark feathers, but her eyes seemed as if they were flaming, and she was a little more gaunt than I expected. This would switch, though, between the blues and blacks of raven feathers and the whites and pinks of a fine gown, brown fur cloak at her shoulders, a red belt around her waist.

There was duality, two modes of her nature, and it felt like looking at her with both eyes separately. You know how when an object blocks one eye but not the other, and your eyes can't quite reconcile both things, you see both the object and *through* the object at the same time? It felt something like that, and it made me nervous, because *why* was she doing that? Why not just show up one way?

I tried to let go of my creeping unease and find the base of our communication. To my surprise, Freyja chose the Universal Fantasy Tarot—one of my rarer, yet prettiest and most interesting decks. Before I could unnerve myself completely and start wondering if somehow I'd called the wrong astral number and invited something strange into my living room, I held my pendulum over the cards and asked, "How many cards do you want to use for readings? One, two, three, four, five?"

The pendulum kept swinging "no" for every number. I'd just done five cards per answer with Cernunnos, and that'd been pretty taxing on me, so I said as much.

"I'm sorry, Freyja, but to get through ten questions without sitting here for four hours, I think I can really only do five cards per question. Is that okay?"

After a moment, the pendulum swung in a circle—a yes, but a somewhat begrudging one. Either way, I was glad she understood, at least.

"Okay," I breathed. "Let's start off with something lighthearted: why cats to pull your chariot?"

1. WHY USE CATS TO PULL YOUR CHARIOT?

Greed, concern with material world. | *Quarrels, delays, reevaluating goals.* | *Disinterest, doubt, inability to see good.* | *A warrior who turns away from struggle has already lost.* | *Power isn't from materialism. but from the heart.*

"Oh, my cats," Freyja said, with a sharp curl to her lips and a lilt to her voice. "I was accused of being vain for wanting them, you know. The others—they said I was so focused on material things, that I should've taken a good, proper chariot animal. It made me doubt my choice in animal for a long time, because I didn't ever consider myself so obsessed with material things, but they insisted I was.

"So I put off choosing. But the more I thought about it, the more I was sure: I wanted cats. I wanted them, and I knew it wasn't just for material reasons, and if I denied myself that, then I couldn't call myself strong."

The quality of her voice was throwing me off, but I let it flow as I wrote, and I poked for some clarification. This time, though, I intended to pull a couple extra cards for that clarification—to see if these answers I was *knowing* in my bones were any reflection of reality. So as I shuffled, I murmured, "I see. But what about cats made you want them, outside of material reasons?"

Idols can help us look within our heart, but if we let them shine too much, they blind us.

Past regrets, ignoring the call to transform, disappointment, false accusations.

Freyja shrugged. "I admire them, plain and simple. They're powerful creatures. Sly and clever. And I refused to regret not choosing them for something someone told me I should've chosen."

"Fair. Well, with that said, I understand you are a goddess of both love and war. How do these fit together for you? What do they mean to you?"

2. HOW DO LOVE AND WAR FIT TOGETHER?

Overextending oneself or their resources and avoiding responsibility.

Bad faith, burnout, and unfinished projects.

Knowing how and when to risk it all is a quality of the far sighted.

It's only possible to seize opportunities by checking our most impassioned urges.

Wishing for the impossible, overabundance of options, indecision.

"Let me be clear: the urge to fight and the urge to fuck are not so separate at their core. What it boils down to is the urge itself, and the consequences of it. They're two sides of one coin. Tipping over into any of those urges without checking them leads to disaster, and that's what I warn against, among other duties. I should know this potential for destruction, too; I've good experience with it."

"What do you mean by that?" I puzzled over her answer for a second before I remembered a bit about the stories I'd read on her. "Oh, wait. The necklace, Brisingamen—there are two versions of that story. One where you choose to sleep with the dwarves to get the necklace, and one where you were bewitched into wanting it. Is that latter true, then? Was that a cautionary tale?"

"Yes. A *very* cautionary tale. Unchecked urges lead to quite the stupid decision."

There still felt like there was something off. Freyja had been speaking/channeling in a haughty, almost stereotypical lady's voice as I interpreted her meanings, and I felt that something wasn't right with that. At this point, I closed my eyes to try and get a sense of her again, especially to pull the next cards, and I got a face that was like the one I saw the first time, but covered in chips of ice, as if she were blighted.

Her eyes were icy blue and cold, and she leaned in with a wicked grin, very close to me. There were also two black eyes shining somewhere, but that very well may have just been my own mind or intrusive thoughts; I asked God to keep away any spirits trying to come through and invade the space (and to keep Loki on the sidelines if he was around, because at times I felt like he, or *something*, at least, was trying to pluck a card here and there).

But I was mostly focused on that odd image Freyja was giving me, and I asked her directly: "Are you trying to scare me right now?"

She pulled back and dropped the grin, smirking instead. Her eyes narrowed, too.

I wasn't sure what to do about this. Cautious, but still not wanting to be a coward, I said, "You seem to be a bit of a trickster yourself, if you don't mind me saying."

Freyja shrugged, still smirking. "Maybe. I like to play. But you aren't so easily rattled, are you?"

"Apparently not as much as I thought. But can you please show me who you are, truly? Not who you think I think you are? I get the sense I'm not getting the authentic Freyja."

This made her stare for a little bit, eyes orange again like embers reignited, and her smirk became more of a small smile. Then the gauntness of her face came back, and her frame was a little bony under the raven feather cloak, and she sat in a stone castle-like place. There was a cross-hatched window to stare out into a wintry forest, and a wooden stool and table to sit at. For the rest of the reading, she flipped between this wintry version and a more cherub-faced version, in a field of flowers and dressed in pink, with dark eyes and golden hair; it looked like a painting. I decided to move on, just accepting that these two sides of her weren't going to blend together into one cohesive image.

"So," I started, "with your associations to love and sex, I understand a large part of the reason your memory survived was because of the contempt you dredged up from the church. What was that like, riding that contempt to stay in the minds of your people?"

3. WHAT WAS IT LIKE TO BE HATED TO BE REMEMBERED?

   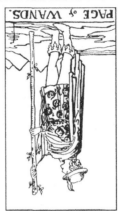 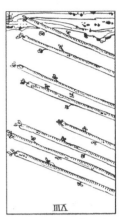

Knowledge requires sacrifice, but determination gets us where we need to go.	*Naïveté and recklessness.*	*Misplaced or lost faith, weakness, or feeling free thought is restricted.*	*Excess of excitement causing one to overlook key details when trying to maintain new projects.*	*Unrest and inability to move on.*

"I was in such grief, when my people turned away from me," Freyja said, with a scowl carved into her face. "I hated it. I wasn't sure what to do about it, either; I had no idea what I *could* do to stay there, in their minds. It wasn't until I understood how much they hated that one part of me that I knew what would keep me pinned to them, so I took on that role in full. I went unabashed with it.

"In hindsight, I regret this a little; people didn't know me fully anymore. They didn't see the real me anymore, the full me. They weren't allowed, by that church, to see any other side of me than the lustful woman in their stories; they didn't understand the full breadth of my station anymore, or maybe they just didn't want to. Even now, people get overexcited when they call on me; they call for help with love and marriage that they forget my other domains, and what I want to do."

I paused. "Like I hadn't understood, when I looked into you?"

A smile hovered in the air. "Yes," she said, "but you and others are seeing again. You're seeing all of it, not just some."

"That's good. I can't imagine what it was like, to deal with that. But what do you think of that church now—of God, and modern Scandinavian folk?"

4. WHAT DO YOU THINK OF TODAY'S CHRISTIAN SCANDINAVIANS?

   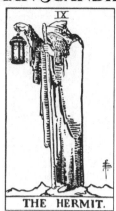 

Conflict with a person in power, a power struggle, or a need to confront one's relationship with power.	*Wishing for the impossible, too many options, indecision.*	*Falling in love with the idea of being in love. Jealousy, the need to be tethered back to reality.*	*Every answer must be sought in one's own soul. Avoiding others or refusing to confide can help.*	*Heartaches are often the symptom for internal desire for change in other aspects of life.*

Freyja let out a sharp *tsk*. She shook her head, folded her arms, and huffed, "I don't blame your God, if that's what you're asking. At the time, I didn't realize that a new era was coming; I was too desperate to keep my place among the people. I was afraid of fading. I would've liked to show my teeth to your God then, if it meant I'd be able to keep the life and world I'd known—but I see now that there were other ways I could've gone about this, and that this was an era that needed to come. For better or worse, it needed to come. And the Scandinavians today, as you call them—yes. Fine people. They're beginning to remember, too; they're beginning to remember the gods of their ancestors, and to find their way through a whole new era. It pleases me greatly to see it."

"Alright, I can see that. I'm glad the tide can turn again for you all, and that we're living in a world where people don't need to give up any gods they don't want to," I said, and I meant it wholeheartedly. Contrary to popular belief among my fellows in faith, God isn't a God that's supposed to be forced on people that don't want to follow Him. "But then, given all of these things we've talked about so far, I am curious: how do you see yourself now? In our time?

5. HOW DO YOU SEE YOURSELF?

A lapse in judgement, holes in one's intuition.	*Greed, shallow fulfillment, and concerns with the material world.*	*We're most vulnerable to attacks from within when others lose faith in us.*	*Closure, working for not necessarily positive resolution, hostility.*	*Tradition preserves good things about the past, but wisdom knows when to innovate.*

This was the part of the reading where she sat down at that table I described earlier, by the window. She looked out, her back turned to me, and there was such a bleak feeling to the scene.

The energy was that of a rainstorm that never quite became rain, instead just blowing cold mist around under a canvas of empty gray sky. Freyja stayed at that table and sighed.

"I was too attached to my station, and I marred my own name," she said. "I was so hurt, as my people began to forget me and turn away from me, that I lashed out at those insulting priests and their wicked words. It made me bitter; I dwelled in infamy without realizing it at first.

"Letting go was something I had to do, if I wanted to do anything different with myself. It was a bitter pill to swallow, and I did swallow it, but not without choking on it. I understand, still, that I had my own challenges with authority to face. God is God; I hold nothing against Him. It was I who poisoned myself, with my refusal to accept the new era He brought into my lands. There was nothing I could do, even if I hated to admit it. But now, the people are able to turn to me again, and I intend to show my full and true self to them, not the half-self I'd been constrained to."

My pencil pressed to paper, but it didn't move. "So you want to come back to the public eye?"

"Yes!" In my mind's eye, she whipped around, red hair flying about her face, a ferocity in her still burning eyes. "I'm here now. I'm not leaving, nor hiding myself, any part of me. Never again."

"Okay, okay, fair. And how do you want others to view your true, full self?"

6. HOW DO YOU WANT OTHERS TO VIEW YOU?

| *Defeat, loss of control, lack of direction.* | *Knowledge requires sacrifice, but determination can get results.* | *Too caught up in celebration, neglecting duties.* | *Fears shouldn't be forgotten, but kept like conquered enemies.* | *Naïveté and recklessness.* |

Here, I got that cherub image of her, in the sunny flower field. Round face, dark eyes, dressed in flowing fabrics. It was so stark compared to the other version of her.

That sweet cherub image said, "As an entity that represents mistakes, and learning from them. I'm more than my old station now; if people see me, let them see growth and change along with love and war, sex and death. I've grown. I've changed. Let them see it. Let them see that I'm determined now to be a true warden, both over Folkvangar and the people who look to me.

"You said I'm like a trickster; you may be right. But if I do my tricks, it's to test my people. It's to see their ability to make sense of situations and avoid folly, remove blindness. As I hadn't before."

"Wow. Alright." These gods, man. They're something else. I was thinking that to myself before I kept up my questioning. "In that regard, what do you want your followers to know?"

7. WHAT DO YOU WANT YOUR FOLLOWERS TO KNOW?

I didn't pull any cards. I just heard her, in that way I've been describing. I didn't dare question or alter a single thing I heard; I wouldn't have been able to if I wanted to, in fact, because the words repeated like the ringing of a cathedral bell, slamming into my head.

"I'm coming," she hissed, a fiery eye fixed on me. "I have tests. I will always have tests."

"Understood, okay." I blew out a long breath and paused to rub my eyes. They were starting to burn. "Now, another part of your story is that you are of the Vanir, and you went to the Aesir after a war. How is your relationship with the other Norse gods, given this history?"

8. HOW IS YOUR RELATIONSHIP WITH OTHER NORSE GODS?

Breaking bonds, freedom.

Length of journey shouldn't temp us to take shortcuts.

Unrest, an inability to move on.

Disloyalty, feeling pressured or lost.

Delusion regarding relationships.

"I have done a lot of work, I can say," Freyja said. "It was hard, and there was a lot that happened; I was antagonistic, I admit. Being traded over like a war spoil, it wasn't a good start, and marriage didn't make things that much better. But eventually, I learned I didn't need to be so harsh. They're a good bunch. We have fun."

"Like when Thor dressed as you to get his hammer back?"

She actually barked a laugh here. "Yes! Yes, like that. It's better now than it was, so much better. Eventually I had to pull my head out of the sand, put my shield down, and try. I couldn't get anywhere else if I didn't."

"Sounds fair to me," I said, encouraged by her mirth. "And regarding marriage, how did your relationship with Odin start? How did it develop?"

9. HOW DID YOUR RELATIONSHIP WITH ODIN DEVELOP?

Hostility, indecision, disharmony.

Wishing for the impossible, indecision.

Fears of the past should be kept like conquered enemies.

Too much celebration, neglecting responsibilities.

Preoccupation with perfect life, broken family, violence, discord.

That mirth quickly faded. Again, Freyja was back to the wintry window, cloaked in raven feathers—like she'd been sobered.

"I didn't really trust him at first," she admitted. "Nor did I know what to do about him, *if* there was anything to do. But there wasn't much other option for me, so I took the chance and married him. We had quite the time together at first; the celebration was near endless, to the point that we might've neglected our duties a bit."

"A proper honeymoon, then, as they say?"

A little fire came back in her eyes as she smiled at that table, but it didn't last long. She kept explaining the cards she had me pull, weaving the meanings into something I could understand, filtering it through images and feelings that I wouldn't know what to do with otherwise.

"Yes. But unfortunately, the mess with the dwarves and the necklace left a rift. That infidelity was no simple thing to brush off, it seems; we still respect each other, and we still rule together—he's a good man, Odin, such a good man—but what's been done cannot be undone. I have no particularly harsh feelings about it, and neither does he, but that rift will always be there. Still, there's love. Just not the same.

"But love itself is a fickle thing. It takes many forms, does many things. Sometimes love is like love, and sometimes love is like war. I'm still here to help the people navigate that, and find it in all its forms. It's something that needs help to be navigated, I think."

"Agreed," I said, and I caged a yawn. Last thing I wanted to do was make her think I found any of that uninteresting; I was just exhausted. So as I finished writing and started picking up the cards, I did what I do worst, which is say my goodbyes. "Well, I think that wraps up my questions for now. Thank you again for sharing your perspective with me, and goodnight."

Freyja smiled at me, but she didn't let me go without one last word. "Goodnight, then. But tell them. Tell them who I am and what I do and what I want."

Not the tallest order I'd ever received, but a tall one nonetheless. There was a weight to her request that I wasn't sure what to do with; it intimidated me. I mean, really, who was I to be doing any of what I was doing, anyway? But with the cards back in their box, I tipped my head to her.

"I'll do my best in that regard. Goodbye for now, Freyja."

HEKATE

Hekate, the ever-famous goddess—who hasn't heard of her, especially among witches? This Greek goddess of the underworld, the crossroads, of necromancy, sorcery, and the night itself, she's one that finds herself on many an altar of modern witches today.

I am not one of those witches. Even if I weren't a Christian, I wouldn't be one of those witches. Not because I have anything against Hekate, no—in fact, I hope you know that when she was chosen in the Patreon polls, I was over the moon excited—but because while Hekate is *a* goddess of witchcraft and magic, she is not the *only* one. It's something I wish people would remember rather than running after Hekate (and the misguided idea that she's somehow appropriate to suck into Wiccan triple goddess archetypes); their own ancestry has gods that can help them just as much as Hekate.

Gods like Norse Freyja and Odin, Slavic Veles and Zorya, Egyptian Thoth and *Heka*. (Hmm.)

But for those who do devote themselves to Hekate, I will say: it's a beautiful choice. She's an intriguing goddess, one of the only Titans allowed to stay free after Zeus and the other gods rose up against them, and the only that Zeus honored so richly, as she has her due share of influence in the heavens, the earth, and the underworld. She's shown herself to be a matron of tough love, yet is still sympathetic and kind, too, which we see with how she's come to have her two familiars, the black dog and the polecat. Hekate was also there to help Demeter in her search for Persephone, and after Persephone had to stay in the underworld, Hekate, a matron of the dead, took it upon herself to be Persephone's companion during those cold months in Hades' realm.

While it's common to see her in the mix with all kinds of different deities and entities, including with the infernal divine like Lucifer and others, it's important to remember that Hekate is a member of the Greek pantheon, and therefore still has certain customs necessary for approaching her—none of which I knew about. I can only be thankful that Hekate, being so widely known and venerated by so many different people, seemed to understand that I was just a simple fool playing with forces I still didn't understand (and, frankly, will never fully grasp).

So let's jump in.

The table around me was dressed with all the things I had available that I'd heard had anything to do with Hekate: lavender tea and grapes to snack on for this interview, which I'd heard she was fond of, moonstone and onyx as a nod to her associations with the moon and magic, and things traditionally associated with the underworld, like chive flowers and garlic, alongside pretty gifts like jasmine. For some reason—and I couldn't really tell you that reason, even after thinking about it—I also decided it was appropriate to set down some totems that represented her and myself. For Hekate, a frog, because magic and frogs just went together in my mind. For myself, a fox—the animal I most closely align myself with.

In recognition of how she's often depicted, with three heads facing one side of a crossroad, I had three candles lit, as well, and after setting my space with the Lord's prayer and burning mugwort to enhance what psychic skills I was finally beginning to flesh out, I settled down and opened myself up to meeting with the goddess of witchcraft herself.

"Hekate, welcome," I said as I closed my eyes. "Thank you for joining me; I've got some lavender tea and grapes here to share with you. Please let me get a sense of your energy, your full self."

Right away, before I was even finished calling her, I had this stark image of a woman with black hair, three faces, and burning golden eyes, dressed in black silks. She sat on a throne of black and gold, maroon curtains in the background. She looked stern, but not mean. However, she didn't stay here for long, as if that image alone wasn't enough.

A moment later, the scene shifted, and Hekate appeared in a large temple-like place, empty and dusty with moss growing on crumbling columns. Light streamed down through the holes in the ceiling. Beyond all that, though, I also saw her big dog, bigger than her, with sharp teeth and shiny black fur. Hekate turned back and smiled at me, almost laughing, as if her dog's thunder-like growl was something endearing. All I could see was all those shiny, bared teeth.

Then, once again, we were off to another point. This time, Hekate was standing with a staff over a barren planet, red like Mars, with rolling dune of sand that stretched on forever. She had wings here, black feathers that shifted sometimes into a cloak around her back and a hood over her face. The winds and red dust swept around her, though she stayed eerily silent.

Finally, though, she settled on simply standing, wrapped in black robes with gold edges, and wearing a gold spiked crown at her head. My pendulum swung over each of the decks of cards I'd laid out all the while, until it started spinning in a circle over Kat Black's Golden Tarot.

"Um," I blinked at her as she took me through these many places and barraged me with all these images I didn't understand, "well, okay, so to start off our questions, let's start light: a long time ago, I did a photoshoot representing you, and my dress kept slipping all over. Were you with me for that? Helping avoid a massive wardrobe malfunction?"

What a mess I'd made of that photoshoot. It was for a photographer friend doing a Greek goddess series, and I decided that if I were to be anything even remotely resembling Hekate, I had to go all out: a massive crown of willow sticks spray painted silver and lined with keys, a staff also full of chains and keys, and two homemade torches that were terrifying to fling around. Even holding them as far away from me as I could, they felt like they could melt my face off.

But the thing that made it such a mess was how the dress I'd chosen just *refused* to stay up on my shoulders, constantly slipping off and threatening a whole different kind of photoshoot. I remember though, against all my thoughts about other gods and my rigid theological framework at the time, I shot a quick little prayer to Hekate, hoping that somehow, God wouldn't notice:

Hekate, if you're there, and you don't want these photos to flop, please keep it from falling down!

And she must've heard me, because despite wrestling with it all morning trying to get it to stay on right, that dress did not fall down even once the entire time we were taking pictures.

I felt it was a silly question, but I was so curious that I had to ask about it, and sure enough, my pendulum swung in a circle.

"Yes," Hekate said, her voice soft.

I couldn't help it; I beamed. "Thank you. What did you think of that photoshoot, by the way?"

I. WHAT DID YOU THINK OF THE HEKATE PHOTOSHOOT?

Optimism and wanting to believe the best may confuse a big issue. Consider and prepare for all possible scenarios.

Travel, a speedy journey, ideas swiftly made reality. Messages, news, but hasty decisions may be regretted.

Beware of deception. Cowardice, fear of change. Disgrace and abuse of power.

She looked over her shoulder at me with a small smile. "It was cute," she said, in the way one's parents might when shown some stellar macaroni art. "You did well looking into my symbols. Though you could've done more to prepare yourself, so that you wouldn't have needed my help.

"Beyond that," her brow shot up, "if you didn't like how you looked then, you might've done something about it, rather than shift the blame to your circumstances. You had time and resources. You squandered both."

Ouch. One last thing that, in my eyes, made that photoshoot a mess was that I was not in the physical condition I would've liked to be; my muscles were soft and undeveloped, like pate. Given it was also my first time living on my own as a college student, with roommates all too happy to indulge my every silly food craving and snack idea, I'd achieved a certain puffiness to my cheeks and sunken-ness to my eyes that only late nights doing homework and eating spoonfuls of Nutella could make happen. It wasn't a great time for me, neither physically nor mentally, and I couldn't unsee it in those photos no matter how much I wanted to like at least the *effort* I'd put into the overall outfit.

I really didn't expect Hekate to smack me with that comment. Worse, all I could do was duck my head, because she was correct: I had the power to prevent that, or at least change it, but at the time, I was more interested in thinking that everything I didn't like about myself or my life was everyone else's fault but my own.

"That is entirely true," I said, wilting a little as I thought about it. "I do regret that. But!" Even then, I was determined not to get stuck in the quicksand of my feelings while I had this opportunity in front of me, the cards giving way to Hekate's messages, so I kept going. "I'm glad you enjoyed it nonetheless! Moving on, though, I read somewhere that you may have not originally been from Greece, but somewhere else. How did you come to the Greek pantheon?"

2. HOW DID YOU COME TO THE GREEK PANTHEON?

Hekate sat down in that gold-black throne and stared off at a spot on the floor. She started slowly, saying, "I followed a boy. He wanted my help and asked me to be his guide as he traveled elsewhere. But it seems what I had to teach your kind wasn't enough for him; he grew bored of me, impatient with my teachings, and he left me. Nonetheless, where that boy had no appreciation for my teachings, I found plenty in this land who respect them."

"A boy?" I stared at the Knight of Coins. "What did he want?"

Hekate shrugged. "Power. As most do. He wanted power to tame the sun, to be more than all the heavens, and I would not do that for him, or

Slow, plodding, reliable person who will stick with a project. Responsible and pragmatic. Honorable and keen to assist others.

Fear of boredom may result in rash decisions. Consider all consequences before taking action.

Transient regrets and disillusionment, but hope soon regained.

anyone. So he decided he had no use for me. I had no use for someone of such insolence, either."

"Oh, wow." I will admit: I don't think I'll ever get tired of getting millenia-old tea from divine beings. "That's intense," I said, because I couldn't think of what else there was *to* say. "I'm interested in that, but I'm also interested in your willingness to help others—like when you helped Demeter track down Persephone. Why get involved with them?"

3. WHY GET INVOLVED WITH THE PLIGHT OF OTHERS?

Interestingly, Hekate had another smile, cheery and reaching her eyes.

"First, let me say: Hades and Persephone are a beautiful couple," she insisted. "They compliment each other well, and they grow each other just as fine. One is no longer complete without the other, and no one would think to separate them now, not any more than they already are each year.

"However, understand: we though Hades had done something underhanded. Demeter was so distraught that it was easy to assume this. We tried to find her without knowing the situation, and that was a mistake."

Overflowing love, joy. Harmony. Fertility. Fulfillment via unconditional love.

Distrust and dishonesty. Suspicion may be justified. Unreliability, theft. Careful. Some are loyal.

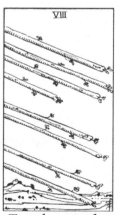

Travel, a speedy journey, ideas made reality. Messages, news. Hasty decisions may be regretted.

Now, I know. All of us who know the real story of Hades and Persephone may look at this response and feel something awfully close to discomfort about it. I did, too, reading it back. I wondered if I'd heard correctly, and where I'd gotten these ideas from. But the cards say what the cards say, and this is why I use them: I didn't pull these ideas out of thin air.

That doesn't mean what I interpreted from the energy Hekate gave me and the cards she pulled was flawless. Looking back, it's clear I missed some key hints she was telling me—filtering her answer through, once again, my own wishful thinking about Hades and Persephone as a couple. It's a shame to acknowledge, but my bias was blinding, and of course I couldn't see the deeper nuance to Hekate's answer then because of it. Maybe that's why she was smiling: because she knew I was a silly little thing who would hear only what I wanted to hear and not what was actually being said.

"I see," I pipped anyway, completely unaware of this blindness. "I can understand that happening. But moreover on this topic, beyond Hades & Persephone, why did you go against the Titans, being one yourself?"

4. WHY FIGHT AGAINST THE TITANS IF YOU'RE A TITAN?

Inaction, inertia, resistance to change. Hopeless attempt to fight the inevitable.

A woman of few morals, willing to use others for her own ends. Untrustworthy and fickle.

Pragmatism, collaboration, compromise. Victory obtained by working with others. Analyze the cause of problems.

Suddenly, we were out of the dark throne room. I started seeing flashes of her with her robes wrapped around her, somewhat hunched, eyes downcast. She sat on some stone ledge or wall on the red planet, a place that felt so dead and empty.

"I saw what was coming," Hekate muttered. "No one else did, apparently, but I knew my options were limited among Titans, and my future, too, so long as I stayed with them. The Titan ways created terror and chaos among people and Olympians alike. I, too, retain some of those ways, and I see how I earned fear from the hearts of men, but I like to think I use my gifts in ways conducive to man.

"But the Titans accused me of being a trick. A woman without morals, without loyalties, who would betray anyone for her own gain. They were wrong, of course. What I really was, was someone who knew the inevitability of their future and who knew how to change to avoid similar destruction. I secured a place for myself among the Olympians, so that I might continue to teach the skills and philosophies I came to teach without interference. To put it simply: they were brutes, and I was never so, and I refused to fall beside what I was not."

I had to sit with that answer for a minute. Between the imagery, and the severity of her words, it felt a lot like when someone finally gets old enough to be clued in on the many layers and intricacies of dark family history and drama that everyone whispered to each other about at family holidays—always *just* out of earshot of the children.

"Understandable," I said after a minute. Then I tapped my cards on the table and grasped for the next thing I wanted to ask, Eventually, I found the words. "Speaking of what you've come to teach, there is another faction of spirits who came to teach magic and such secret things to mankind: the Watchers. Given your talents and your wings, I have to ask: do you know them? Or have any relation to them?"

5. DO YOU HAVE ANY RELATION TO THE WATCHERS?

Her lips twitched as if she meant to laugh at me, but a laugh in a setting like this red planet would've been swallowed before it could even get past her lips. Still, Hekate answered my question.

"Of course I know them. The idea of these Watchers is not constrained to any one religion.

"But yes, I am like these Watchers you know of, and I had much the same function, but for a different group of people in a different time. I never overstepped my bounds, either. I came to teach magic and skills beyond man's understanding. However, man proved underhanded."

Laziness and desire for wealth without effort.

Great success accompanied by a little less contentment.

Travel for all the wrong reasons. You can run away from life, but not yourself. Detachment from reality, following unattainable dreams at the expense of what's good in life.

She kept a soft voice as she spoke, but her face was solemn over her shoulder, her back turned and beginning to hunch over.

"They saw magic as a shortcut to power and glory rather than the delicate and specific tool that it is," Hekate continued, "and they wasted their lives looking for more power, more, always turning over every stone to find something better than what they had, in order to become the most powerful of all. They could've spent that time cultivating themselves instead, growing their life with the tools I gave them, but they squandered their time; even for those who did grow powerful, it was never enough, and they were never satisfied. Like for that boy from Egypt."

"That's really fascinating." And I meant that. Slowly, but surely, a little network of Divinity was being mapped out in my mind, though I couldn't make heads or tails of it yet. "And you know," I said, tapping my pencil against my journal, "I also notice you appear a lot in witch circles—for obvious reasons, I can imagine—but I'm wondering: what has you so active now, in modern times? It seems you're more active than you were before."

6. WHAT HAS YOU SO ACTIVE AMONG WITCHES IN MODERN ERA?

*Don't take bless-
ings for granted.
A tendency to
yearn after that
which is forbid-
den or unattain-
able. You have
so much to be
thankful for.*

*Dwelling on past
sorrows may
prevent you from
moving on. Let
go of the past,
and confusion
and distress may
disappear.*

*A tendency to
enjoy the failure
of others and lack
of ability to work
together. A go-
getter not hesi-
tating to leave a
field strewn with
bodies.*

Hekate rested her chin in her hand as she stared out at that red planet. "Because people need me again," she said, as if it were the simplest thing in the world. "The old tools I taught are coming back, and I want to help people avoid the pitfalls that the magicians fell into before. Yet once again, people are using magic as a shortcut to power, and it's backfiring.

"This time, though, they're using it to refuse to acknowledge their past. Rather than do the difficult work to untangle the things they went through, and the people who hurt them, they're throwing a thin veneer of magic over their stunted selves to conceal those wounds, and it's doing nothing good. They're bringing pettiness to a respectable craft. I want to help people avoid such childishness and truly reach their full potential, and to not treat magic like some wonder weapon to bludgeon others with."

"Oh, goodness." I fought my lips as they tried to twist in a wry smile. "I think I know what you're talking about with regards to that. On that note, then, with using magic as a shortcut, why else would you say it's coming back into the modern age? Why is magic on the rise again now, and witchcraft?"

7. WHY IS WITCHCRAFT REVIVING IN FULL FORCE IN SOCIETY?

With this question, Hekate looked down, drew into herself, as if she were sad. "It's a tool, plainly," she said. "Tools have many uses. Some want to take advantage of others, and take that shortcut to power that I've mentioned. Others want it to look for and create stability in an otherwise wild world."

That was fair. "I figured," I said as I scribbled her answer down, and then I flipped through what questions were left. "Well, aside from all that, we're coming up towards the end here, so I wanted to know: how do you see yourself?"

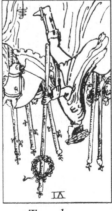

*Treachery,
intrigue, battles
which may be
lost.*

*A woman of few
morals, willing to
use others. Un-
trustworthy, fickle.*

*Love of one cre-
ates compassion
for others. Mate-
rial happiness
and security.*

8. HOW DO YOU SEE YOURSELF?

Bitterness and misfortunes clouding one's ability to see the good luck also dealt by fate.

Travel for the wrong reasons. You can run away from life, not yourself. Detachment from reality, chasing goals at expense of what's good in life.

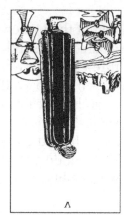

Regret and disillusionment, but hope will be regained.

Hekate stayed with her back turned for a while. Then she turned and looked at me; she said, with her head up high and her eyes glowing:

"I've made mistakes, and I regret them. But I have no choice other than to continue now, with the world being what it is. I built a good place for myself, so not all was lost, but I still carry that regret for past decisions. I don't wish for things to return to how they were—it's too late for that now—but I wish I'd known that no matter where I go, I would never find any more happiness or loyalty in any one place over another. All I discovered as I moved about was that fear is a constant, and people would always fear me."

"So someone who's made mistakes and carries burdens, then?"

"Yes."

"And how do you want to be seen?"

9. HOW DO YOU WANT TO BE SEEN?

Innocence and faithful acceptance. Remembrance of childhood joy. Wanting simpler times. Beware of nostalgia.

"As someone who loves. A dutiful force with a large past that I know I can't go back to. I don't really want to go back to that past, anyhow. I have children to look after; I can't sleep forever. I will continue loving them."

"That's really nice. As our last question, is there anything you want to tell your followers?"

10. ANY LAST MESSAGES?

No matter how much I shuffled or how much I tapped the cards to try and find one she wanted, there was nothing. I had to confirm with my pendulum that she didn't want to leave a message, just to be sure I was hearing her right, and then came her voice again, as those words I didn't quite hear, but simply *knew* in my soul.

"No. I don't need you to tell them; I'll tell them myself. Go. Goodnight, *fox*," she said with a wink and a teasing smile.

Then she turned away and walked off, all the images melting into nothing more than the darkness behind my eyelids. Still, I called after her, unable to just leave it like that without some kind of send off for her.

"Goodnight, then," I said as Hekate disappeared. "Thank you again for joining me, Hekate; I appreciate you speaking with me. Goodbye!"

Then I opened my eyes to a table much different than when it started: with one empty teacup, and one cold, with one branch of grapes stripped bare and the other still sitting there with the chive flowers and garlic. I poured the tea outside and threw the gifts out the door, not looking back for it as I locked the door in the face of the cool night. Even way back then, at the start of this journey, I knew better than to try eating something meant for gods of death and necromancy like Hekate, and I knew at least a *little* something, too, about crossroads etiquette.

As I went to bed that night, I remember feeling like I'd crossed something off my witchy bucket list: talking to Hekate, goddess of witchcraft. It left me giddy, almost, and I went to sleep with images of those burning golden eyes still shining in my thoughts.

APOLLO

For all of my excitement about Hekate, however, I was finally here: at the moment where the wheels completely fell off this operation. My patrons had chosen Apollo.

I didn't know what was about to happen as I set up a beautiful table for Apollo, even though God *had* told me earlier that day that I had to watch out—that there'd be someone who was sensitive and easy to offend. Though, in my mind, all that meant was that I had to be extra polite. How silly of me.

I only knew what I'd heard and read about this god, and how he seemed to be a favorite among so many people. Given that he'd taken on a bit of Helios's role as a god of the sun, I had nothing but high spirits, as sun gods had been pretty kind to me so far in this adventure.

But I'll remind you one more time: I knew *nothing* about Greek religion or proper custom when approaching these ancient gods. I only knew what I could find by researching on my own, and the thing about research is that you don't learn about topics you don't know you should ask about in the first place. So off I went, learning more about Apollo—and not from the right sources.

You see, while Apollo does now have some loose associations with the sun, he's mainly a god of prophecy, music, plagues, healing, poetry, and archery. He's depicted carrying a lyre, and he's got quite a few interesting—if tragic—stories about him and his many lovers. Son of Zeus and Leto, twin of Artemis, Apollo is certainly a beloved patron of many, and for good reason. Unfortunately for me, ignorant of proper decorum and with a serious talent for putting my foot in my mouth, I was on the other end of Apollo's might: the part that people don't want to find themselves on.

This is one of my roughest experiences in our little experiment here, and I make no excuses for the interview you're about to read, or any of the things that happen in it. It is what it is, it happened how it happened, I acted how I acted, and I said what I said. Had it *not* happened this way, mind you, I never would've learned why it *shouldn't* have happened this way, and I would've been worse off for it. A *lot* worse off.

So as we dive into this chapter, keep this in mind: you can't learn without being willing to run into trouble and get knocked on your ass as a result.

And boy, did I get *knocked* on my ass.

I'm not joking when I say this was one of my most beautiful table spreads to date, and that's another reason why it's heartbreaking to me that this interview went the way it did. You'll see what I mean in a moment. But to set up, I pulled out my old violin as the centerpiece, a nod to Apollo's lyre, and I dressed it with gold chains, gold sun icons, bay leaves (which are heavily associated with him thanks to the myth of him and his once-lover, the nymph Daphne), as well as cinnamon and orange, also both associated with the sun. Apples, too, because he enjoyed those, from what I'd read. I also had sunstone, carnelian, and tiger's eye there for their fiery qualities, and a raven, because I read about the white raven he used as a messenger. In hindsight, this is all very sun-focused for a god that isn't all that much connected to the sun, but it was what I had and what made sense at the time,.

All the while as I decorated, though, I felt as if I were being watched. And maybe judged a little. But eventually, after my usual routine of *holy water, Lord's Prayer, and mugwort,* I settled down with my several tarot decks and asked Apollo to come join me at the table.

"Apollo, welcome," I said. "Please join me, if you'd like. Are you here with me?"

The pendulum swung in a circle, which was a strong yes, and the ice in his drink—a bit of orange juice—clinked like a little bell.

"Great! Thank you for coming." And I couldn't help but ask, "Were you here this whole time? Watching me decorate?"

The pendulum swung in a circle again. I smiled; I knew I'd felt something while I worked.

"Ah, well, hi again!" I paused to set my pendulum over the decks of cards, in which Apollo stopped on the Universal Fantasy Tarot. "Good choice! Now, let's dive on in, if that's alright with you. Before we start, though, how many cards would you like for each answer? I personally prefer three because five can get kind of intense for me, but you can use however many you'd like."

With the pendulum swinging this way and that for each number, eventually swinging in a circle on three, I knew Apollo chose three cards. I also confirmed it was because I would've preferred three cards per question, which was nice of him.

I smiled as I shuffled the deck. "Alright, so to start: what do you love about music?"

I. WHAT DO YOU LOVE ABOUT MUSIC?

1. Understanding our difficulties is the first step to overcoming them.

2. Heartache is a symptom of an interior desire for change in other aspects in life.

3. Unexpected fortunes are best, but must be managed wisely.

Then came Apollo in my mind's eye: a blonde man with a band around his head, much like the man in the thumbnail of the lyre music I was playing in the background. He wore a white cloth on his hips, and his grin was toothy, his eyes bright.

"It's expressive," he said with a wave of his hand. "I love that I can use it to tell what happened to me over the ages. It sort of fell into my lap one day, the lyre—and I just kept playing it. Kept playing. I knew what it could do for the soul, so I held onto it."

The scratching of my pencil against paper fought with the music. "That makes sense." Once I set the pencil down, I closed my eyes and tried to hold that image of him in my mind—one that, oddly, kept shifting. He would sometimes have a face like a cartoon, and I didn't know why, but it felt like I was being mocked somehow. But soon the image was back to a beautiful man.

"Before we continue, could I get a feel for you?" I said. "It's hard to see you right now."

That's when I got the image of him in a field. There was a castle off in the distance, and I came into it from a shady part of a grove, like a forest exit. He was sitting in the flowers, sweating from the heat, smiling. I hesitated in the shade before pushing myself under the sunlight with him.

"Alright. Thank you." I strolled over to him, pen and journal in hand. "So to get to our next question: I'm assuming a lot of the things you mention happened to you had something to do with the lovers you've had throughout the ages. Why so many different ones?"

2. WHY SO MANY LOVERS IN ALL YOUR MYTHS?

Fear of change is inevitable, but it must be faced. Resistance is useless.

Withering away of bounty through neglect and inaction.

A woman with few morals, willing to use others. Untrustworthy, fickle.

In hindsight, this was a ridiculous question. Imagine asking someone why they've had so many partners? But I think what I meant to ask was more: if they kept causing such tragedy for him, these mortal lovers especially, why did he keep choosing them? This is why words matter. I know this as a writer, and yet I may as well have been chewing on my foot instead of a slice of apple before shuffling my cards.

He shrugged, a pout to his lip as if the question bored him. "They come and go, lovers—many were human, after all. It'd be a waste of my talent to hide myself away just because one left; there's always another. And **some**, of course, were no good, stealing my time and love! Those aren't worth my staying for, nor my celibacy."

Then his brow arched, and he stood up and towered over me, staring with sharp eyes. "Now, I have a question for *you*: why do you do this? These interviews?"

I'll admit, I was a little surprised. The gods didn't deally ask me questions up until this point. "Well, honestly, it's just fun," I said. "I know there are so many out there, and I'm curious; I want to learn more about them. I want to branch out and not feel constrained, or like anything is off limits to me; I want to explore the world and everything in it in full."

He cocked his head and pursed his lips, unimpressed. "Ah. So you want to walk into as many castles as you please without having to worship their kings."

I blinked at him. There was a heaviness in my gut, a sinking feeling, and a slight pressure building at my shoulders, as if gravity had gotten just a teeny tiny touch stronger. Whatever this meant, I knew, at the very least, that it wasn't good. Still, I answered him: "Yeah. I don't worship kings. I worship God."

He gave me quite the look: a smirk and a raised brow.

"Is that so? So all these things, these offerings you put out for me, that's not—?"

"This is to invite you as a guest. I am a host. I am not here to worship."

His smirk fell, and his face was washed with shadows. Apollo started to stand up straight like he was going to tell me something about that with more than words, and that pressure I'd just started to feel began building, as if it meant to crush me into the dirt. My stomach twisted; it was hard to breathe. And Apollo's face, the glow of his eyes, made me want to ditch the whole interview right there. But I wasn't about to quit, not unless *he* said he was done with me, so I did what anyone looking to get smote on the spot would do.

I pushed my own magic out, like a little bubble, and then both magically and physically shook that pressure off me. I lifted my arms, shook out my shoulders, and imagined that my little golden bubble was unbreakable, that Apollo himself was pushed back away from me. In my mind, and at that point in my journey, I was a child of God—just as divine and worthy of respect as anyone else. And this god, here, too, wasn't the One True God; he was a small one, a specified one, with no right to push me around given that *he* was born, created, just as I was.

"We are equals," I snapped. "I do not worship my equals."

I know, I know, I *know*. Go ahead and put the book down. Take a couple laps around your coffee table. Grab a drink. Then come back and remember where my mindset was during this part of my journey. As I said, until this point, I figured that gods weren't really *gods*, but just powerful spirits, because only God was worthy of worship as God (a view commonly known as monolatry). And like angels, God must've made these powerful spirits to help people who hadn't yet heard about Him; He must've assigned these beings to their own independent nations to keep them safe.

And if you were wondering, yes, there is *some* Biblical reasoning to this idea: Deuteronomy 4:9 and Psalm 82 both suggest the existence of other gods, and that God assigned them to nations other than Israel, even if they messed up their job a little bit and got a slice of humble pie at the Divine Assembly. Beyond that, per the narrative in Exodus concerning Moses's father in law, Jethro, it's made clear that Gentiles weren't expected to be monotheists that only worshipped God; they just had to acknowledge God's superiority when they came into Israelite lands. By extension, the Israelites were also mono*latrists* in this time, not mono*theists*.

It's worth also restating, again, that in the Roman empire, there was an idea of a *one high invisible God* among these more specified gods, such as the Olympians or the stars and planets or the *daimones*, that created all of these other divinities. I'll add onto this further from Wilken's work: to the Romans, worshipping the gods this one God created was to indirectly honor and worship that great invisible Divinity. And interestingly enough, the one high God was one that an actual *oracle of Apollo* stated the "holy Hebrews greatly honor," according to the research Wilken compiled of these many different arguments that early Christian critics were making against this new faith (152). It seemed that the God of the Israelites, to that oracle, at least, *was* this high invisible God above all the rest.

I still hold this henotheistic (edging towards monolatrist) view: that God is the Creator of all things, including these other divinities, much like the view the Romans had. Where I went wrong was denying these other gods had any divinity at all, denying their place in the hierarchy of spirits that keep this world in check, and denying that a God with a capital *G* and gods with a lowercase *g* could exist simultaneously. I thought these great spirits were important, and had their role, but were ultimately not so different from humans, who were also extremely divine and powerful in their own right. This was the arrogance I'd been approaching all of these gods with until this point, and I'm surprised it took this long to catch up to me.

Because boy oh boy, the look on Apollo's face after I snapped at him like that. If looks could kill, I'd have been obliterated to the point of no return But there was a tense moment, over my shoulder, I felt the stare of a Divine Being so strong and unbreakable that even Apollo paused. I knew it was God. I knew God was leering like a lion about to pounce, pushing out a force that made me want to just up and abandon that table altogether. Apollo was locked in a stare with God, right in front of me. And then, after what was likely the most tense moment of my life, Apollo settled back down. He went pretty quiet. I blew out the biggest breath and curled into a ball at the table; I ran my hands through my hair and gripped the roots, letting the pain of the slight pull anchor me a bit.

"Jesus Christ," I huffed. "Apollo, would you like to call it quits? I don't—if you don't want to be here, I'm certainly not going to keep—"

"No. Keep asking me your questions."

His voice sliced through my thoughts like a sharp wire. It was cold, low. But me, idiot, I thought to myself, *ha! That's right. I have* God *on my side. You can't touch me.*

Pour yourself another drink. Pour yourself two, and pour one of them out for my idiot self.

"Alright, fine. Anyway," I said, with the air of any front desk receptionist that had to deal with an annoying patron, "on that note, what do you think of God? And what do you think of the rise of paganism after so many centuries of Christian faith?"

3. WHAT DO YOU THINK ABOUT GOD AND CHRISTIANITY?

Rivalry, disharmony, and conflict, though of a transient nature.

We don't always recognize good luck, which sometimes arrives when we're unable to appreciate it.

Enjoying failure of others; the lack of ability to work together. A go-getter leaving bodies scattered on the battlefield.

Despite my cheeky question, Apollo smirked with a spiteful air. He said, "It's sweeter, watching paganism come back after how long it's been gone. I like watching the fallout, of everything crumbling back down. I don't hold anything against God personally, not really, but His people... they're monsters. Rude towards us old gods and our people, our ways. They liked watching everything burn. I'm happy to see everything finally rising from the ashes again."

If there was a pointed note in his voice, I missed it. I just kept going.

"I understand there's a statue of you *in* the Vatican. Thoughts?"

4. THOUGHTS ON STATUE IN THE VATICAN?

His smirk became a mean grin as he paced around the little field of grass and flowers we'd found ourselves back in. "I think I'm like a thorn in God's side," he purred.

I got the sense, as he grinned about that, that he was someone who liked to tease and poke. That he said he had no ill will, but that there was definitely some thin layer of resentment here, and that made him say things that God didn't appreciate.

How do I know God didn't appreciate it, you ask? Because it was at this point that I got a very clear image of God—or, rather, the Seraph that stands in for God as His representative. This Seraph is a specific one whose name I won't share: he appears to me as burning fire shaped as a

Knowledge enables us to see beyond the horizon and appreciate resources available to us, though we should use them wisely.

Unfair dealings; a cunning foe.

Our fear of the length of a journey shouldn't tempt us to seek shortcuts.

strong, sturdily built man, in blue jeans and a white shirt, with eyes colder and bluer than ice that still flicker like flame. He had his arms crossed and had this withering look that made Apollo's grin slip.

Then came Michael, big brown eagle wings out, red legionnaire armor glinting in the light of the other Seraph's flame. He sat beside me and looking at Apollo like a cat looks at a mouse. Apollo noticed and *tsked*. He went a little sour after that, no more smiles for a bit. To say the energy in there was heavy was an understatement. I was exhausted by that point, but I still scribbled in my notebook as Apollo looked away and spoke.

"I like to think I've left my mark. That statue lets me remind people of what they'd otherwise happily forget: that we were here. I journey to people who neither know nor love me, that they might keep the sunshine alive."

I shrugged. "Makes sense to me. But now, I notice things got a bit weird in here again. Are you sure you want to stay for the rest of the interview? Or would you like to go?"

Apollo blinked, his face stony. |I'll answer your questions; keep going."

"Okay. Alright," I said, and I just managed to cage a sigh. "How about... your relationship with other Greek gods? You know, with Hera and all that—?"

"I'm not answering that."

"Oh. Uh, well, okay." I was more than halfway to calling this thing quits myself. "How about your association with the sun? I understand Helios was in charge of that before it became associated with you; how did that happen?"

5. HOW DID YOU BECOME ASSOCIATED WITH THE SUN?

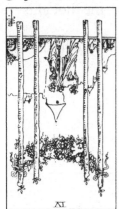

Still a card of success, good family relations, and labors being rewarded, but it's taking longer to come to fruition.

Intense emotional turmoil, loneliness and insecurity in a relationship.

Approach of victory announced by deceptive signs. Faith enables us to go on.

Apollo turned to me with such a somber look. It was as if the thought made him deeply sad once, but enough time had passed that the sadness was distilled into the one short sigh he huffed.

"He shined his light on me when I was at my lowest," Apollo said. "He gave me the light of the sun to guide me through the worst times of my life. I mastered walking into the light, and that's when I took over that symbol."

"Did those times have to do with your lovers?"

"Some, yes."

One thing I noticed, at least, among all these visions and the thoughts that came from outside me, and the very forces I felt around me, was that I was getting used to them. I was finding it easier and easier to just let an entity *speak*, without me there to second-guess; I was finding it easier to let the black behind my eyelids become whatever image these Divinities wanted to put there. I was able to actually hold a conversation, not just pull cards and hope. I didn't realize it then, but I was getting to a point where I was no longer just sitting in my living room; I was where the gods were. And I knew because when I opened my eyes for little things, it felt like my head was swimming, like I wasn't quite fully there, like I was seeing out my eyes as if they were aquarium glass rather than being fully present in the physical space that was my house.

It'd begun this way in Brigid's interview, piece by piece, image by image, and by this point, it was like watching a movie in full Technicolor with additional sensory details: seeing the god in question swivel about, the wind brushing through their hair, smelling the flowers and feeling their divine presence. I was determined to be in these spaces, to soak up everything and capture these experiences as this astral sunshine hit my face, and as the words in the tarot booklets seemed to weave together into what a god was trying to say without my having to think (too much) about it.

But right then, I wasn't able to appreciate this development. All I wanted to do was get this over with. At this point, though, I'd switched to different music on YouTube that had pictures of Greek temple ruins. Apollo looked through my eyes and grimaced at it.

"I hate seeing that. Our temples, all in ruins. Just abandoned."

"I can imagine. It's a shame; they were so detailed and beautiful."

He stayed silent, so I moved on.

"Well, okay, so I understand you're a god of both healing and harm, with your own arrows like Artemis. Any word on the duality of that? Healing and hurting?"

6. HOW DOES THE DUALITY OF YOUR EPITHETS WORK?

I got no indication that I should pull any cards, so I just sat by Apollo and listened as the thoughts came, the ideas translating from his raw meaning to my English tongue.

"No, no comment. Not much to say about it, really. If you can harm, you should be able to heal. What you can do, you should be able to undo. You're useless if you can't do that."

"That's not 'no comment,'" I said, lightly, in attempt to unsour this air around us.

But Apollo only shrugged. "I thought about it, is all."

"Okay, fair. We're getting towards the end here, so how do you see yourself?"

7. HOW DO YOU SEE YOURSELF?

He stayed somber here, then said, "I see myself as someone who resisted change for a long time before I saw how it could serve me. I found out how to change to cope with strange times, where everyone disappeared and our temples were empty and un-kept. I had to stay alive, so I did what I had to do. That's all."

"I see. A survivor; I understand. But how do you *want* to be seen by others, then?"

Inaction, inertia, resistance to change. A hopeless attempt to fight the inevitable.

Fate has a surprising way of revealing itself, sometimes linking distant thoughts and feelings.

Rules and traditions often preserve things that were good and useful, but true wisdom knows when to innovate.

8. HOW DO YOU WANT TO BE SEEN BY OTHERS?

Understanding our difficulties is the first step to overcoming them.

Disregard for risks, negligence, withdrawal from society, apathy, a lack of action.

Sentiments take us to great heights if we keep our feet on the ground.

The mood finally lightened a little bit. "As an artist," he said, with a small smile. "Art is everything. It's easy to get swallowed up by every terrible thing happening in this world, and all the ways we learn what's happening, but it's important to turn away and create something nice. Know your limits. I am someone who retreats to my space to create when things become too much, and that's what I want for my followers, too: to be able to step back and go to the places that make them happiest, so they can keep going when things are hard."

It sounded like this was an answer to both this question and the one I was going to ask next. I put the tarot deck down and looked at him. "So that's your message for your followers, too, then?"

9. LAST MESSAGES FOR THE PEOPLE?

He nodded. "Yes. To get out of the mess of this world and find someplace to create."

"Fair, fair. Alright, well," I sighed and clapped my hands, "that's all I have for us today. I appreciate you stopping by and chatting with me, Apollo, and I guess I'll see you around?"

He gave me a look then, not a mean one, but almost a sly one, as if he knew something I didn't. Then he slipped away, and I was pulled out of the field of flowers and back into the darkness of my own head. When I opened my eyes, I was a little disoriented, but there was a very clear feeling of *disconnect:* the silence was loud, buzzing, and the shapes and colors of my living room felt too concrete, too exact. I was no longer in a place where the world around me could shift and change.

So, exhausted as I was, I set about to cleaning all of my offerings up. Then I went to bed. As I nestled in for a good night's rest, I found myself feeling not too shabby about all that happened there; it was certainly interesting, a visceral experience I'd never had before, a new level of contact with Divinity. As exhausting and scary as it was at the time, I could only marvel at it as I went to bed then. And knowing God had come to protect me there, too? That he'd defended me from whatever Apollo was trying to press on me? It only made me more confident, and more firmly rooted in my position about Divinity that I still had at the time.

I distinctly remember thinking, as I closed my eyes and let myself fade into sleep, that I was starting to have everything figured out. That the proverbial rug underneath my feet was nailed down, and that it would never be ripped out from underneath me. That I could keep on as I'd been going, the whole world available for me to root through and explore however I liked.

Then the sun rose on a new day, and the knowledge and experiences I'd gathered from every day that ever came before it burned up in its light.

PERSEPHONE

The next day, I posted my video about speaking with Apollo. I wrote my interview on my Patreon. And then, over the course of that week, I got totaled like a car flipping and rolling on the highway after a direct collision. Each roll of the car along the proverbial pavement was a single day, breaking me apart more and more in front of everyone passing by, and in hindsight, I couldn't complain a bit, because I was the one that'd been driving recklessly in the first place. This was the most exhausting week of my life up to that point.

Let me explain a bit about what made this so hellish for me. My biggest platform has always been Tiktok, but even then, I hadn't gotten so large as an account yet to be used to the rounds Apollo's video was making. It caught worse than tissue paper soaked in everclear on an open fire, and moreover, it caught the attention of people who knew a lot better than I did about the Greek gods and how to speak to them. Two creators in particular, Hellenic polytheists @hekateanfoodie (Mika) and @zenobia (Dagan), caught wind of my stunt and were not shy about correcting my radically poor form towards their gods, educating me both publicly on the platform and privately in messages. The flood of criticism wasn't something I'd ever experienced before, because believe it or not, I wasn't exactly in the business of going out of my way to be a controversial idiot online (or so I thought).

But here's the thing: my platform wasn't just a space to be goofy and fun. It was my *author account*, which I'd originally started with the express intent of gaining traction for myself as a writer thanks to the advice of an agent I'd been talking to at the time. I was trying to build myself there, carve out a space for myself, my name, my work, and then I found the community of Christian Witches that enjoyed my educational and spiritual content that I posted in between my writing content.

I didn't want to be some fool floating around in the vastness that was the internet; I wanted to be a professional, a source of knowledge, someone who took risks for the sake of helping others grow. I wanted to write my fantasy works and be read, of course; I wanted all the things I had to share to be seen, all the feelings and experiences I'd twisted into digestible metaphors to be *heard*, and between the fantasy and the spirituality, I wanted other people to find sure footing in their own outlooks, lives, and spiritual journeys through the many footholds I was working hard to create for them.

This platform, I'd worked hard on building it. I'd poured hours into it, so many hours, and it felt like it was all burning up in front of my eyes. Thousands of hours spent stacking the stones of my platform were knocked down and scattered in a fraction of the time, and that terrified me. I know it's stupid in the grand scheme of things, to be upset about a profile on some app on the internet, but the last thing I wanted was to be marked as some disrespectful idiot in the eyes of literally thousands of people. I *wasn't* a disrespectful idiot; I didn't *want* to be and certainly wasn't *trying* to be. I just wanted to know about these other gods. I wanted to explore, and share my findings. I wanted to put myself out there, so others didn't have to—so they could see not only the things I did right, but the things I did wrong, so that they wouldn't have to bear the same consequences I was right then. Didn't that count for anything? Those honest intentions?

"The road to hell is paved with good intentions," as the old saying goes.

I'll admit this here: I stood by my altar to God that week and begged for help, for relief. I'd never been so overwhelmed in a public space in my life. Jesus's picture stared at me as I broke down, asking Him what I should do. Of course, in true God fashion, what I got wasn't exactly comfort—though at least He sent Jesus instead of showering His fire on me directly. As I closed my eyes and begged, it was Jesus I saw sitting there beside me, silent, waiting for me to collect myself.

Then He said, "Fix it. Make it right. Apologize and *mean every word*. That's what you do."

I messed up. It was a repeating thought, a truth that was pressed down on me. *I was wrong. I messed up. I was wrong. I messed up.*

And it was then that God revealed something to me, with Jesus there, laying a comforting hand on my shoulder. I needed that hand, because the revelation I received was like getting speared through the heart: God wasn't going to bat for me during that moment with Apollo, not in the way I thought. The look Apollo shared with God, the seconds of silence where nobody moved, that wasn't just a stare down; it was a conversation. One that I was not privy to at all.

God protected me from Apollo's divine wrath in that moment, but no more than that. In fact, it was God who made the deal with Apollo: *don't hit her now, or she'll never understand. Hit her where it hurts her most and where she's most afraid of being hit: in public. Then she'll learn.*

From dust I was made, and so thoroughly humbled was I in that moment, that back to dust I returned, shattered to pieces on His altar. Never in my life would I guess that God would be willing to let me fall like this on purpose, or get hurt like this. I can't say I felt betrayed, just utterly shocked, taken out at the knees. It redefined my understanding of what my God, any god, could do to their devotees at whim, and how, and why, they decided to do it. The reason why this had to be done was clear in my eyes: I was careening down the wrong direction, my theological math coming out all bungled as I mapped my experiences and made my theories.

The reason I can't say I felt betrayed because I'd earned this little piece of hell, and God knew that I knew that. So I begged for help again, help making this right and properly repenting, recanting, my stupidity, and only then did I feel some weight lift off my shoulders.

Thankfully, for all the controversy that was happening around my page on the public front (which does make me wonder, in hindsight, if Hermes was involved in how this video spread around), a fruitful conversation was just about to begin in private. Mika and Dagan were patient with me, carefully explaining on my video about Apollo and their own about where I went wrong and why, and Dagan even offered to help me in the future if I ever wanted to try speaking to a Greek god again, so that it could be done correctly and with the full respect that the Greek gods were due.

That offer meant a lot to me. I'd never come into this series with the intent to be disrespectful, and for all I thought that I wasn't like other Christians, it became painfully apparent to me then that my attitude was exactly that of any arrogant Christian who thought they could walk all over Divinity in other forms just because it wasn't in the form of God. Knowing there was someone willing to help me do it correctly, and display that proper method of contacting the gods, was a comfort in the mess I'd made otherwise.

But it was halfway through the week, where my notifications were flooded with comments and tags and stitches that let me know in no uncertain terms that I'd screwed up, that my patrons on Patreon voted for another Greek deity: Persephone.

Oh, no, I thought. *How will everyone take this? Jumping from Apollo straight to Persephone, after all that happened?*

I was once again terrified of how this would go and what the outcome would be. But I told Dagan anyway, that my next deity to interview would be Persephone, and I asked if he could help. He accepted. We set a date and time to meet. He told me what to do, what to offer, and how to behave. And on the day of the meeting, he read the auspices that indicated Persephone was fine with sitting for a conversation—so long as I asked no questions about her husband.

That was more than fair to me. This was the other half of the Death and the Maiden couple I'd looked so fondly on, but thanks to Dagan pointing me towards better resources than I would've known to look for, I found the true story of Persephone, the goddess of springtime vegetation and unexpected, unwilling queen of the underworld, loved and feared all the same by mankind, and so cherished by her mother that Demeter was willing to throw the whole world into despair to get Persephone back where she belonged: in the sun, among the flowers and fruiting trees. I read several myths to think of questions to ask, passed those questions by Dagan to make sure they weren't rude or ignorant, and when the day came, I made my honest apology to the Hellenic polytheist community for my disrespect and prepared to speak with this well-known goddess.

Dagan told me to set out these specific things: grains, in which I chose buckwheat and millet, an apple, and diluted wine (half red wine, half water). I also made sure to take running water from the faucet, which counted as a source of living water, and wash my hands before we began. Then Dagan offered frankincense and invoked her with praise and her many titles.

After Dagan invoked Persephone, and we had her clear permission to continue, I settled in and welcomed her to my space. I also got rid of a candle on the table that was a little ugly, but I wasn't sure if I should include (as it had spring motifs, but I couldn't get a new candle in the votive, so it was half melted). She had me take it off—it was, in fact, too ugly—and then I asked her to let me see her wherever she was.

I think she might've been confused by what I wanted to see, because what came to me first was darkness, nothing. Then a flash of a statue of Persephone, like the many busts of her that had been carved over time.

"Ah, no, Persephone," I started, "I mean, can I see you as you are right now? Can I be with you, wherever you are?"

"Oh, I see."

Then the blackness behind my eyes gave way to something else: green and pink and blue. She let me into the same space I was in with Apollo, a field of flowers, with some kind of city or something in the far background. She was sitting at an elegant white tea table, like you'd see at an outdoor cafe— an umbrella overhead and everything—and there was a chair empty for me.

Persephone was a woman with golden brown, curly hair, wrapped up under a thin headband. She had a soft face & chin, a straight nose, and large, soft eyes, and she wore a white and light pink dress, flowy like chiffon. On the table appeared my metal three-leaf centerpiece, which had with the apple and grains in each leaf, and she seemed to like it. Then she had the glass of wine in her hand.

I saw myself there, too, sitting in that chair beside her, oozing anxiety: my back straight, my arms stiff as I held my notebook, my eyes wide enough to take up half my head as I stared at Persephone. Then I opened my eyes and came back to my living room so that I could use my pendulum to find which tarot deck she wanted to speak through. She chose Amrit Brar's Marigold Tarot, and she wanted four cards per question. Then, once I had this information, and her image locked firmly in my mind's eye, we got started.

"Alright, well, hello, Persephone!" Even the voice in my head was shaky. "Thank you so much for agreeing to this, and I'm glad I was able to approach you properly. And please forgive me if I accidentally do or say something rude, or if my thoughts get away from me, or if—"

Persephone shut me up by raising her hand. "Peace," she said, with a little curl to her lip, as if I were a funny little rabbit shaking before her. "You're okay. You're fine. Stop your chittering and relax."

I paused, then deflated with all the air I didn't realize I'd kept trapped in my lungs. After taking a moment to get it together, I nodded and said, "Right. Okay. I guess, to start us off, then, can you tell me what you love about being in 'full bloom,' during the spring and summer?"

I. WHAT DO YOU LOVE ABOUT BEING IN "FULL BLOOM"?

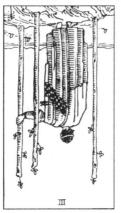

Greed, possessiveness, and unkindness of spirit. Illusions, dreams of this world. Suffering.

Lack of vision for the future, ignorance of the present.

Unrest and an inability to move on.

Excess of force applied to a situation, leading to disaster.

"Write this down," she said as I stared at the cards, grasping for their combined meaning. "This is a reprieve. It's where I spent my beginning days, and I don't want to think about what will happen later in the year. I want to enjoy where I am now: in a place where the world is flourishing again. I'm happy to see the world come alive and bloom once more, and I'm eager for it towards the end of my stay below, restless to bring life back. But when I'm here, it's bliss."

"Ah, I see that! It is nice here." I noticed Persephone wouldn't look at me directly, but she had the smallest smile on her face, which gave me courage. "So, I've recently learned more about epithets, and I see you have many names. How do these help your followers understand and worship you?"

2. HOW DO YOUR EPITHETS HELP PEOPLE UNDERSTAND YOU?

Courage, venturing into new experiences without fear. Many forked paths in life.

Breaking bonds, freedom, detachment.

Forcing us to consider different perspectives. Learning how to form our position in the face of new problems.

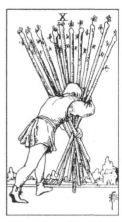

Heavy burdens, being overwhelmed, and struggle.

She stayed staring off into the distance, though she tilted her head as she answered.

"If I were to appear in my full divine form, with every facet I have, it would overwhelm the minds of men. I come in different names to guide my followers on whatever specific situation or challenge they might be experiencing, or whatever they need to learn at this time in their life. It would be too much to come to my devotees as all names, especially when they seek guidance for specific things."

"Oh, that makes a lot of sense! Divine forms—like with Semele and Zeus. Is that it?"

Persephone thought for a moment. "Something like that, yes."

"Fascinating. I understand. Well, alright, I notice you have a lot of variations in your myths, those little details—why is that? And is there any one correct version?"

3. IS THERE ANY ONE CORRECT VERSION OF YOUR MYTHS?

Corruption, obsession with the material world at the expense of spiritual wellness, and greed.

Vigilance, thought, growth of new ideas. Creativity to pursue intellectual challenge. Caution important.

Duality. Someone intellectual, skilled, brave, and wrathful. Graciousness and deceptiveness.

Overextending oneself or one's resources and avoiding responsibility.

"No." She glanced at me for the first time in this encounter and winked. "You should know."

I think she meant because I'm a Christian, and we all know what a mess the Bible's become, with its different translations and the meanings we've injected into that, but I could be wrong.

Persephone continued: "Some who wrote these myths genuinely wanted to capture the truth, the whole truth, down to the finest detail. Others were trying to introduce these old myths to new audiences. Others still had completely different reasons for changing the story. But what matters is the core of the story, the main message of it, not these irrelevant details. Getting stuck on these details is pointless."

"I get that," I said. "That puts it in some great perspective, actually. The core of the story versus the details." I paused there at that little table with her for a moment, absorbing that idea, and then started shuffling my deck again. "Okay! So, my next question: I was reading on the story of Orpheus, and I had a completely different view of this before I actually read the official version. I didn't realize it was *you* that was moved by his sentiments, too! In which case, why did you give him that condition to leave Hades? Was there a divine law, or something else, that prevented it?"

4. WHY WASN'T ORPHEUS ALLOWED TO TAKE HIS WIFE HOME?

Faith in ourselves and our ability to approach self expression with optimism.

Separation, low self esteem, mistrust, and disharmony.

Unwillingness to see problems as they are, looming disaster, avoiding change.

Directionlessness and a loss of ambition or vision.

Persephone cast her eyes down on the table, her lips bent in a frown. She seemed sad.

"Orpheus had hope and faith that he could change the course of nature in the physical world," she explained. "It wasn't possible, but he had to see that for himself through experience, hence the condition that was bound to be broken. He was too reliant on his relationship with Eurydice, and it led to him being unable to accept that natural order."

"Oh, that's sad." For me, it made an already sad story all the more heartbreaking. "It makes sense, though. On the topic of stories, how about when Pirithous came down to see you? I was appalled on your behalf reading about that!"

5. THOUGHTS ON PIRITHOUS'S ANTICS?

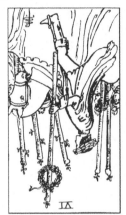

Failure to recognize one's own shortcomings due to feelings of pride and superiority.

Creativity, ambition, and opportunities actively in bloom.

Pessimism, dread, and resignation.

Social disputes and prioritizing others at the risk of one's own personal development.

Persephone scrunched her face at the thought, her nose wrinkling, and then we actually shared a good laugh. Her smile was lovely, her laughter clear. With shoulders still shaking with her last bit of laughter, she spoke.

"I knew what he was going to try before he even stepped foot in the underworld. I knew it wouldn't end well for him, either. He had too much ambition, too much ego by far, to think he even had a chance at accomplishing what he came to accomplish, and he did something incredibly foolish and paid for it. And Theseus, too—knowing what they were about to do was wrong, yet doing it anyway because of an oath? It's simply foolish."

My pencil raced across the page as I kept up with the stream of ideas, feelings, and words that suddenly rose up in my mind. "Yeah, I can imagine that was an interesting time nonetheless. But okay! That's it for the main questions. Now: how do you see yourself?"

6. HOW DO YOU SEE YOURSELF?

As I shuffled, there was no indication to pull any cards, so I closed my eyes and peered at her. She was once again staring straight ahead, not looking at me even from the corner of her eye, and her face was set in a perfectly composed mask. Her lips moved, and I received her words with dazzling clarity in my head.

"I see myself as exactly as I say I am: the Queen of the Underworld, and Goddess of Spring and Vegetation."

"I see! Clear cut, I get that. How about how others see you? What do you want there?"

7. HOW DO YOU WANT OTHERS TO SEE YOU?

Romance, idealization, being charmed. Idealization can lead to fantasies, grand gestures, intentions pouring over.

Vigilance, contemplation, thought, and growth of new ideas. Creativity to pursue intellectual challenge. Caution important.

Unconditional love, compassion, empathy, patience. Emerging from hardship beautiful, thoughtful, and considerate of others.

Cruelty, manipulation, ill intentions, injustice, and narrow worldviews.

Where she once had a relaxed face, composed, here she frowned. Her brows creased, not with anger or meanness, but with a ferocity that left no room for questioning or rebuttal.

"I want others to see me as *me*," she said, her voice hard. "As an autonomous and sovereign goddess. Mankind gets carried away with my story, but we can't change what happened just because it isn't palatable in the modern age. I wish people wouldn't see me only in relation to that story, or my husband, but as *myself*, as I see myself. In my titles, I want to be seen as kind, and loving, and considerate. Someone who has been through challenges and triumphed. I shine," she insisted. "See it!"

Then she looked at me head on, with nothing but seriousness in those honey-brown eyes. They glowed with the spark of her will; they were molten, full of passion, and I could only stare in wonder for a moment as her answer, and the powerful way she'd said it, sunk in.

"Wow," I whispered after a moment. "Thank you for that answer. That's incredible. Um, we're at the final question now, and I wanted to know: do you have any messages for your followers?"

8. ANY LAST MESSAGES FOR MYSELF OR YOUR FOLLOWERS?

1. *Romantic desire, pining, wanting new love, new beginnings.*

2. *Vanity, dashed ambitions, lack of challenge.*

3. *Cruelty, manipulation, ill intentions, injustice, and narrow worldviews.*

4. *Poor luck and failure.*

I meant to ask for myself, or anyone else, as well, but I think she got it, because her answer felt less directed at her serious Hellenic patrons, but those who try to honor her in passing or aren't well versed in how to approach her appropriately, like I once was. For the people who draw her in lovey-dovey stories with Hades, painting her pain as empowerment, and who scratch her mother Demeter out from their hearts and cast down that great goddess as some shrieking, overbearing mother hen.

Given the look on her face, I expected her voice to be steely. But when she spoke, her face softened, her lips pursed and brows set in what felt like the expression a mildly depressed mother would give.

Then she said, "To misinterpret things we're uncomfortable with—*that* is injustice. What is, is. What isn't, isn't. Vanity, ego, and the need to shelter ourselves from that which we don't want to hear, leads to a failure of understanding who I am and what I'm here to do."

"Another incredible answer. Thank you so much, Persephone, for your time and for coming to speak with me. This has been lovely, and I'm grateful to have had this experience!"

And then, just as with Apollo, that field of flowers and grasses and the city in the distance disappeared until nothing was left but the apple, buckwheat, and millet on my table. Dagan told me what to do with these offerings afterwards, too: libating the wine, properly disposing of the offerings. I don't know how to describe how I felt after all that; it was the total opposite of my experience with Apollo, and it left me feeling light, peaceful, and purely content. Granted, I'd still needed to write all this up, edit the massive video I'd make of this, and post it, but with everything more or less said and done, I just let myself feel that little spark of joy for a moment.

That was my last interview with any of the Greek gods, too. While Persephone was willing to sit for some questions, Dagan also consulted with Zeus himself about any further interviews with these gods, to which Zeus gave a firm and resounding *no* through the auspices. Later in the year, when I would go searching for other deities to speak to on relevant topics, Dagan pointed me in the direction of a friend who served as an augur of the Roman gods, who told me much the same: that Jupiter was not interested whatsoever in me poking around in the affairs of these gods, either. So effectively, those are two entire pantheons that will never be on my list of gods to publicly interview like this (though if I wanted to ever encounter them directly, privately, under the supervision of their devotees, that would maybe be a different story). While it's unfortunate, it's definitely understandable, and I've respected the decisions of both Zeus and Jupiter since.

The next day after my interview with Persephone, though, I just took a deep breath and hit post. I was exhausted in every sense, and certainly, I had no idea how anything I posted would be received. Thankfully, though, the reception was warm, the peace was restored with the help of Mika's boosting of my message, and the people who were rightfully upset with me saw that I meant no harm whatsoever and genuinely wanted to do right by them and their gods. Just as things had gone up in flames with one video, they were doused with another, and I was able to take the biggest nap in peace.

I was also able to take the time to regroup and grab onto this discomfort. There was someone I'd been requested to speak to over and over again that still, despite all my attempts to steel myself, frightened me in ways I can't quite explain. However, with Persephone's interview and the whirlwind of activity that came before it, I was more than steeled. I was fresh out of the fire, shiny and glowing and re-smithed, and I committed myself to confronting that fear in the next interview.

No matter the consequences, no matter the danger—real or perceived—I would do my due diligence, and I would explore the part of Divinity that didn't just let me sit comfortable in my understandings of the world. No more asking silly little questions, no more playing around. The reasons I was doing any of this were becoming abundantly clear, my focus shifting from satisfying my own curiosity to demonstrating the things these deities wanted to know.

I was there, suddenly, to show polytheist practitioners that these gods and God, they didn't have nearly the bad blood everyone assumed they did; they were all in it together, making a network of Divinity that stretched across all of time and space, that kept our very universe stable. Just as important, I was also there to show others of my own faith that these gods were *gods*, Divinity, not "fallen angels" or "demons" or whatever else my ignorant fellows in faith insulted these beings with. Nor were they even the "great spirits" I'd thought they were up to that point—because if I learned *anything* through this fun exercise of humility, it was that entities that serve as gods, deserve and will demand to be respected as gods, no matter what religious framework I'm coming from.

To that end, I thought to myself: why not just rip the bandaid off and do it? Why not speak to a *true* fallen angel? A true Emperor of demons, of hell itself and all its citizens? Why not shrug off all my fear, all my preconceived ideas of such infernal beings, and all that I've ever been told by a poorly informed modern Western culture?

Why not speak to Lucifer?

LUCIFER

Lucifer. The Son of the Morning. Lightbringer. The bright morning star. The devil himself, radiant in his knowledge and his horror. As a Christian all my life, he'd forever been a being of terror for me, an enemy of God and all things good in the eyes of the church, a dark and prideful angel audacious enough to try and drag God off His throne with an army of rebelling angels at his back. I'd even been told an old folktale, from my Slovenian grandparents' generation: that the devil, Lucifer, had challenged God, and said that he could win over more people to his side than God could if just given a fair chance.

And God took him up on that bet, giving him one hundred years to thoroughly corrupt the souls of mankind and lead them away from God. Those one hundred years, they said, were the last century: from 1900 to 2000. Given it was the century that saw two world wars and horrors unimaginable across the globe, I do sometimes wonder about that little folktale of theirs.

Still, all those wicked things were what I was always taught Lucifer was, and yet he remained a sincere, secret fascination for me. I could never unhook myself from the curiosity his name brought up. I could never stop myself from wondering, either, if the devil—Lucifer—was really all that people said he was, or if, like any of these other deities I'd spoken to, like God Himself, there wasn't more to the story than that.

Surely, there were many interesting theories about him. Lucifer wasn't always the name of the Christian devil; it was also the name of the Roman god Lucifer, the morning star, counterpart of the evening star Nocifer. However, in terms of this Christian devil, Lucifer was only ever really a *title*, one that showed up only one time in the Bible in reference to the Babylonian king Nebuchadnezzar. It was never meant to be the name of any devil until somewhere along the way, Christians made it so.

From the rumors I heard, it's because there was a political squabble between a Pope and a bishop, which resulted in the name Lucifer essentially being blacklisted, but the only person I could find named Lucifer was St. Lucifer of Cagliari, who apparently vehemently opposed the theological concept known as Arianism, which posits that Jesus is the Son of God. What is now standard doctrine was apparently a topic of debate in the 300s CE, and the denial of Arianism, originating from Egyptian Christian Arius, led to St. Lucifer being awfully controversial, especially in his sanctification.

But around this time, I'd already been questioning a few things. For instance, what if "the devil" wasn't actually a bad guy, but simply an entity out there doing the job he was given? (This is a line of thinking that already exists in "Satan," or Ha Shatan, the adversary, a title given to God's angels that are sent to test us like one tested Job.) What if God commanded Lucifer to play the role of bad guy? What if they were both in on the joke, playing out a story in front of us that we took a touch too seriously? Combine that with things like the Netflix show *Lucifer*, where Tom Ellis plays a charming fallen goofball with some family trauma to work out, and I wondered if maybe it was possible that this "devil" could be... *different* than I thought he was. Than I was told he was.

The only way I would know is if I tried to talk to him myself. That much I knew, and yet I was still terrified, because for someone who had never stepped outside this theological bubble of mainstream Christian ideas concerning demons and the like, it was truthfully a bit of a gamble. Maybe I was right, but maybe I was wrong. Nonetheless, I swallowed my doubts and decided to go ahead anyway, because either way, I told myself I'd learn *something*. Something was more than nothing.

So I asked some trusted friends I'd made, like one wonderful demonolater, Aziel (@heyaziel), about what I should put out for Lucifer. She suggested chocolate, cherries, and good whiskey for offerings that he'd enjoy, and she helped point me in the right direction for a little research, which let me know that Lucifer was connected to Venus. Given that Venus is also known as the morning star, it made sense. So for stones, I had black obsidian as a both protective and scrying tool, a bit of celestite for angelic communication, and lapis lazuli, which is connected with Venus.

Then I did my typical starting prayers, burned a bit of dragon's blood incense, made sure his sigil was on my phone (as my printer had died on me recently and I didn't want to mess up drawing the sigil), and let whatever was going to happen, happen.

"Lucifer, Son of the Morning, Lightbringer, please come chat with me!" *What the hell am I doing this for?* "I have for you some chocolate, cherries, and whiskey; I heard you like these things. If you're comfortable coming to speak, I welcome you here. Are you here with me?"

Between the pendulum swinging in a strong circle and the candle flickering high and wild, I had confirmation he was there. As always, I asked for him to pick a tarot deck he'd like to use, and he chose Kat Black's Golden Tarot.

Then I felt his energy, too: something skittering up my arms, as if my skin broke out in embers. It wasn't like Loki's pinches; it was a fiery crackling up my skin. I'd never felt anything like that before. Once it passed, I took a deep breath and closed my eyes to try and find Lucifer.

I was met with something horrifying lunging at my face: it was the image of the Seraph I'd always seen representing God, but it looked as if it were made out of stone, like a gargoyle statue. Its fingers were sharp, its teeth massive, and its eyes a bloody red. It snarled, moving as erratically and suddenly as a creature in a nightmare, and it was in my face, snapping its jaws at me.

My heart sank, and my eyes squeezed even harder together, as if my eyelids could squish the thing. I curled into myself, nervous, sure that I'd misread God's signals and that He was actually furious with me for doing this. He must've been, right? That's what this thing was—it was God, angry—

And then, where there were red eyes, there were blue ones, two orbs of blue flickering light in a sea of flame. The light burned this gargoyle creature away cast a warm, comforting net over me, enough that I was able to relax. It was an energy I'd come to take for granted since it was always around me, and it wasn't until something so different came up that I'd been able to recognize how it really felt: the light and power of God.

Warm. Heavy. Stable. Like being wrapped in strong arms, like being haloed in honey-gold light.

"These are my eyes," God seemed to say as the two blue flames shined down on me. "You know my eyes. These are my eyes."

With that, I was finally able to relax. I was assured that the gargoyle creature wasn't real; it was just the last ditch effort of all I'd ever learned in mainstream Christianity to spook me off this interview. I'd fed it all day, after all, being anxious even though I knew I had no real reason to be, but it was something I couldn't help. It was attached to me like a leech, this little gargoyle imposter, and as soon as I'd given it the chance, it jumped at my face like a wild dog gone too long without food. Without God there, I might've called it quits and become like one of those funny people who test out witch-craft, mess it up, and go forsaking everything they ever did as they run back to the comfort of the re-ligious paradigm they grew up in. I would've never figured out what that thing *actually* was, or where it came from, or why it was there.

With a deep breath, and God fading from my mind's eye, I tried again. "Lucifer, I'm sorry about that. Are you still willing to talk?" When my pendulum swung in a circle, a strong yes, I said, "Thank you. Can you reveal yourself to me, please? Can I see you?"

Then, and only then, did Lucifer come into view. I stared into a bright, cloudless blue sky, where columns stretched up into the empty air, and above them came an angel, a beautiful angel of light. His hair was blond and curly, his wings a brilliant white, his eyes a luminous pale gold. The only thing he wore was a white cloth around his hips, which flowed around him like something out of a painting in the Sistine chapel. Altogether, he looked so perfectly angelic that I could've puked.

I couldn't help it: I stared at him. Something felt wrong. There was no way, *no way*, that Lucifer looked like that. I refused to believe it. So I tried, cautiously, gently, to say as much.

"Curly blond hair?" Even though I had no intentions of being rude or mean, I couldn't stop my lip from curling into a proper ball-busting smirk. "Never figured you for that. Is this how you want to appear right now?"

He smirked, too, enough that his teeth peered through, and then it changed—the whole scene, from the sky to his clothes to general appearance. His eyes stayed that pale gold, but the pupils were long, like a dragon's or a cat's. He had black leather armor on, his hair still pale gold, but longer, drap-ing around his shoulders. His wings, too, were huge and looked like they were made out of light. But the sky went from blue to a deep and dusky red, and I saw we were on a huge stone tower overlook-ing a place similar to that red planet Hekate showed me before, only more rusty orange than outright red. The floor had a beautiful mosaic pattern, sandstone and darker, brownish stone creating some kind of flower or sun or star, and behind us was a tiny, plain stone chair, crumbling at the edges from how old it was. It sat against a raised platform with yet more columns reaching up to the sky, and despite how worn and plain it looked, it still struck me as some kind of throne.

I saw myself, too, standing there with my journal and pencil. Even though I'd done this a few times by that point, I was still learning about how this *meditation* thing worked—though I didn't recog-nize this counted as meditation at the time—and I wondered if I was doing something wrong, to see myself in third person like that. Wasn't I supposed to be looking out from my own eyes? I tried to a couple times, and sometimes I did without meaning to, but I also jumped outside myself to watch us both, too, and that got a little disorienting.

I figured that was a dilemma for another time, even if it was starting to eat a little hole of doubt into the back of my mind. I watched my own face change, into the one I was making on my real face: a raised brow, a smirk being hooked into an impish half-grin. Then I said, "Were you teasing me, with that image before?"

Lucifer eyed me. "You said you wanted an angel."

"Right, but that image is a bit stereotypical, don't you think?"

He shrugged, but he didn't say much. Not until I settled myself down against one of those pillars and nestled my notebook against my knees, ready to ask questions. Before I could, however, Lucifer folded his hands behind his back and peered at me with a completely blank expression.

"You'll fall if you stay there," he said.

I blinked. "Oh, no, no, I'm okay! It's okay, really! Watch!" Then I stood up and walked right off the tower. I imagined a little blue platform appearing under my feet with each step; it held me firmly over the insanely steep drop down to the sand. "See?" I tapped one square with my heel. "Nothing will happen to me here; don't worry."

After all, my real, physical butt was firmly attached to my living room floor. So long as *that* didn't drop out from beneath me, what could happen to me in some place that only existed in my head? What real danger was I in? Lucifer returned my hopefully friendly smile with his own.

Then the blue platform dropped out from underneath me, as if it was never there to begin with.

I laughed as I fell, because I could *feel* it. The lurch of my stomach as I suddenly dropped down, like when riding one of those drop tower rides at a theme park, the air whistling past my cheeks. But this wasn't where my physical body was, and so long as I knew that, I knew that anything was possible—*anything*. Even, say, me suddenly sprouting big brown eagle wings out of my back and recovering my position with one easy flap of feathers. My shoes tapped gently back on the tower platform, and the wings faded into blackish-brown dust off my back.

"If that was you who made that platform drop," I said with a smile as I settled back down against my column spot, "that was rude."

Lucifer didn't say a word. He only kept smiling, but the smile felt different. Warmer. Maybe I'd passed a test of some kind. As far as I was concerned, I was just having fun.

"Alright, so," I said, clearing my throat, "thank you again for joining me, again! I think it's fair to start off with a light-hearted question, so on that note... what do you think about that *Lucifer* TV show, and all the hooplah around it, with that group of moms that tried to get it cancelled?"

I. WHAT DO YOU THINK OF THE NETFLIX SHOW STARRING "YOU"?

Public success after hardship. Achievement, recognition.

Still a card of misfortune, but help is nearby. The end is near.

A warm, loving man of good counsel. Enigmatic, subtle strength.

He didn't quite laugh, but he did smile a bit bigger.

Lucifer pointed to the cards. "You see what they say. Representation is representation. That show, silly as it is, put me back in the minds of people, for once not as some villain. That in itself is success. The people that wanted it taken down are misled; they don't see the good in that character, nor do they want to. They don't want to admit that I might not be what they think I am." Then he sighed. "Though the producers don't quite understand me, either. I'm not some material driven, revenge-mad fool. I have no interest in any such nonsense on that show. Only in leading those who need me."

Alright. I could work with that. I wrote it down and nodded. "I figured as much. It's definitely not meant to be a serious representation, I think, but in one episode of it, there was a concept I found really profound: that hell is a place of our own making. What do you think of that?"

2. IS HELL A PLACE OF OUR OWN MAKING?

Somewhere along the way as I asked that question, I found myself no longer sitting, but standing towards one of the floor mosaic's edges. Lucifer started inching closer, step by sure step. He'd been pacing that mosaic floor, and with this question, he stood next to me and held up a black and white flame.

"It's as simple as this," he said. "Do you want to be upset constantly, committing this self-flagellation for your faults and wrongdoings until you have no skin left on your back? Or do you want to be free? That show has that much right: that you create your own hell. Hell is here, on earth."

I nodded. "Makes sense to me. With that said: what are your thoughts on the state of humanity?"

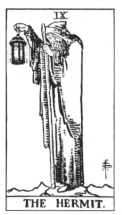

Know thyself. Reflection, contemplation, self-acceptance. Introversion and solitude. Don't be too attached to the world.

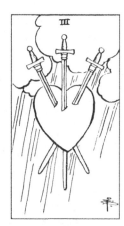

Melancholy and a broken heart. Misery, sorrow, and grief at the end of an affair or friendship. Take heart; time will ease the pain.

Celebration of good luck. Friendship, revelry, abundance. Fulfillment of hopes. Creativity, understanding. Recovery.

3. WHAT ARE YOUR THOUGHTS ON THE STATE OF HUMANITY?

Consider outcomes. By preparing, the worst result is less likely.

All get what they deserve. Sacrifice. Not all battles worth fighting.

Harmonious family, friendship, and rewarded labors manifesting.

Lucifer grimaced and looked away from me. He said, "I'm not quite disappointed. I knew what humanity was capable of all along. I know that they *can* have what they want: happiness, bliss. But retribution needs to come first. And it will. No action is thrust upon the world without a consequence to meet it."

We both moved to the center of the floor here. One thing I noticed in these spaces, where I could suddenly so vividly see these entities, was that they were restless. They walked around, shifted in front of me, popped into my face only to then reappear far away—but for all they did do, they just did *not* stay still in my experience. So I planted myself there in the center of the platform while he paced around again, and I waited for him to eventually come to my side like he'd just done.

"I—well, damn. Okay," I said, mulling over his answer. "So... what is your role in the world?"

4. WHAT IS YOUR ROLE IN THE WORLD?

Life will always send challenges; you can't have good without bad, light without dark. Don't dwell on misfortune, but look forward to future joys and opportunities.

A woman of few morals, willing to use others for her own ends. Untrustworthy and fickle.

Distrust and dishonesty. Suspicion. Unreliability, theft, and dishonorable actions may be afoot. Be careful who you trust, though loyal ones do exist.

One word came clear as I read the cards: Doubt. An agent of doubt—that was the idea Lucifer put in my head.

"I make people aware of what they might've overlooked before," he said as he strolled up to me, his face a stone mask. "I rip the blinders away in any way that gets attention. I don't ask permission to use the methods I use, either. I do what works. I remind people not to get too comfortable with what they think they know. Nothing is as it seems; everything is worthy of questioning. Even God."

He gave me a pointed look with that one, as if expecting me to have a reaction, and I shrugged; what the hell was I supposed to say? What did he *want* me to say? I didn't know, so I just said what I felt in response to that little challenge he hung in the air over us.

"Well, I understand where you're coming from," I started, "but I trust God. So I don't feel the need to question *Him*, but more the things people ascribe to Him. Let's move on: someone mentioned that *you* were the white dove on Noah's Ark, signaling land. Was that you? If so, why help humanity?"

5. WERE YOU THE WHITE DOVE OF THE FLOOD? WHY?

1. Material gain, prosperity, growth. Promotions or new job. Happiness, achievement. Spiritual and material satisfaction.

2. Courage in the face of adversity. Take a stand to overcome hardship. Problems solved, hardship overcome. Bravery will be rewarded.

3. Optimism may confuse an issue. Consider all scenarios. By preparing, the worst becomes less likely.

Lucifer whispered, "I was."

The seriousness that came down in the atmosphere as I asked this was something else. He was over-looking that rusty planet as he continued.

"Without humanity, none of us would be here. What would be the reason to keep the cosmos aligned? Or walk this rock? What is a world with no life? Humanity needed relief. They didn't know what to expect on a journey like that. For all their faith, there's only so long you can survive. I helped them find the ending they sought. But humanity is incredibly brave, to keep on like they did."

"Oh. That's really cool, actually."

And I thought it was such an interesting twist on the whole story—that maybe that little dove was there to say, *enough, now!* Or argued the case for humanity to get off that ark. What a fun idea.

As I thought about it, I tried to choke down another sip of whiskey; I'd poured some for him, and some for myself, too. I'm a bit of a baby when it comes to alcohol, though. If it isn't sweet and fruity, or I can very clearly taste the alcohol, I generally don't like it. This whiskey was torture as a result. Still, I tried to drink it to show some solidarity with Lucifer, to share in the whiskey and fruit and chocolate with him as a sign of friendship and closeness. But every sip made me want to *expire*.

"Sara," he said as I shuddered from the taste, "you don't have to drink that if you don't want to."

"I do want to!" I held the cup under my nose, and the smell made me gag. "It just sucks. But I'm not wasting it! I put out drinks, so we're drinking."

My next sip had me grimacing even worse than before. I even coughed a little. As I closed my eyes again, though, I froze, because Lucifer was hovering over me. His voice was a little rougher, like a rumble of thunder so far away that one could miss it and never realize a storm was coming.

"Don't take even one more sip of that. Put it down."

"Okay, okay, fine" I said with a huff. I'd just have to pass on that half-drank whiskey to my boyfriend. "Onto the next question, then: what is your favorite thing to teach your followers?"

6. WHAT IS YOUR FAVORITE THING TO TEACH YOUR FOLLOWERS?

Enlightenment. Self acceptance. Divine scrutiny. Confidence one lived a just life. Endings, new beginnings.

Treachery, intrigue, battles which may be lost.

Studious youth. Scholarship, study, academia. Hard work brings high achievement.

"Discovering the highest self," Lucifer said, with a smile that felt razor sharp, "and finding the confidence to work for that highest self—to recognize it when they see it and not feel ashamed of it, however it looks.

"Not every road leads to victory. Sometimes, we have to go back to go forward. However, with enough study, self inventory, and honest work, one can achieve exactly the self mastery they seek. These are important lessons, and I, as a teacher, am a reflection: what one does with me, one gets back. The more effort, the more reward."

Something about that lodged a stone loose in my brain. I couldn't tell you what it was at the time, but it just got things to start moving and shifting around in the back of my mind, as if making room for that little nugget of information for later.

"Alright, well," I went back to shuffling my cards after the feeling passed, and I saw myself sit down there on the ground, at the edge of the mosaic, "here's another question for you: my father had a dream once, that he was in court, where God was the judge and you were the prosecutor. And it was said that you and God were two sides of one coin. What do you think about that?"

7. WHAT DO YOU THINK ABOUT "TWO SIDES, ONE COIN"?

As I said, entities don't stay still in meditation for some reason. Lucifer had been moving about all this time, and then suddenly, he was sitting down next to me, hip to hip. It seemed like he was checking if that would unsettle me, to be *that* close to him. I could feel the stiffness of his leather armor as it dug into my shoulder; I could feel how *solid* he was, as if he actually was right beside me in physical reality. When I just got comfortable up against him instead, though, he softened a bit more, felt more relaxed—and he helped me get the deeper interpretation I was looking for in these cards.

"It's as it says there," he said as he tapped the Emperor, "one cannot exist without the other. We offer two extremely different approaches to the same goal. It's almost something of a game: who can bring the most people to their highest self with their respective methods?

There can be no winners without losers. Patriarchal authority. Motivation to achieve success. Competitiveness, desire for victory. Power, masculine strength.

Abandonment of materialism. Putting aside financial security for spiritual fulfillment. Cutting off from old and seeking a new life of order and simplicity.

Generosity rewarded. Financial good fortune, wealth, and security. Favors rewarded, debts repaid. Gifts or inheritance. Sincerity and trustworthiness.

"There's no one way to look at this. The 'battle of good and evil' is a gross oversimplification of things, and truthfully, it isn't relevant. What matters is that people do what's right for them. There's no purpose in shaming or condemning people for choosing one path or another; in the end, people will do what they need to do to achieve what they need to in their life, and that's the end of it."

"Yeah, you know," it surprised me to admit it, "you and I agree there. I like that a lot."

Here's where the energy became the softest it was all night. Whatever death spasms came from that last bit of anxiety in me, the anxiety about even reaching "out of bounds" to other entities in this world, be they god or demon, just faded.

And If I'm being honest, I was watching for reasons to be afraid at first; it was like I was expecting this to become some silly horror movie. I knew it was stupid to expect that. God and I both talked about doing this interview beforehand, and He said Himself that Lucifer has been portrayed differently than what he truly is, and that being calm and open would lead me there.

That I would find him in the quiet, the dark, away from the world, and that it'd all be fine.

Still, you just don't shake the bug of mainstream Christianity that easily, By this point, though, Lucifer kind of crushed that bug for me. It felt like I was sitting with a really good friend, one that I'd always been that comfortable sitting so closely to. I remember being completely unafraid, to the point of almost feeling like it was a bit of a shame that nothing Hollywood-esque happened. It was a completely normal and safe experience. As God said it would be.

It was here I really understood that fear is one of the roots of evil. Fear blocks the path to enlightenment by stopping us from ever reaching out to those things we wonder about, especially as others condemn us for wondering. You can't get anywhere if you're afraid to step forward, or of what people will think of you.

But while we were sitting there enjoying being on the same wavelength for a minute, quiet and calm, I finally snapped out of my cozy little daze and picked up my cards again.

I said, "Well, then, all that aside—we're almost at the end of these questions. Here's one: how do you see yourself?"

8. HOW DO YOU SEE YOURSELF?

Fickle, flighty man, with trouble controlling his temper.

Travel for the wrong reasons. You can run away from life, not yourself. Detachment from reality, following unattainable dreams at expense of what's good about life.

A man with great hidden sadness. He keeps his emotions in, leading to self destructive tendencies.

Again, the energy dropped, the mood becoming a bit blue. It wasn't a harsh expression he wore, but his face was just a touch stony. "It's difficult for someone like me to watch humanity," he admitted. "It's frustrating. Upsetting. They could be so much more, but as they are now, they're like worms in the mud.

"I am a hurt person. I *hurt*, seeing what is, knowing what could be. I want to see this world made right. But as I said, we have to wait. For retribution."

"Um." I didn't really know what to do with that, but I felt like I understood it, and I said as much. "I feel similarly, I think. I get you. Though this makes me wonder, with all you want to do and how you feel, and all things considered: how do you *want* to be seen?"

9. HOW DO YOU WANT TO BE SEEN?

Lucifer said, "I can't change what I am or where I come from, and I don't need to. I left Heaven willingly; I'm the reason the coin has two sides. I wanted to give humanity another option. I'm a proponent of loving oneself enough to know one's value and worth. To never put one's own needs under anyone else's. I am the one who knows what it means to have a bond with the Self as means of creating one's own lifeline, and there's no risk I won't take for people to see that: that they are their own lifeline, their own salvation."

I'll be honest: he lost me a bit there. But I got the general idea eventually, and once again, I found myself agreeing with the core piece of that: you can't wait for everyone else to help you, or notice you're in need of help.

You have to put yourself first and see

Fulfillment through a relationship. Love of one creates compassion for others. Material happiness and security. A strong relationship.

Disregard for potential risks, negligence, withdrawal from society, apathy, lack of action.

Travel for the wrong reasons. You can run away from life, not yourself. Detachment from reality, following dreams at expense of what's good about life.

your needs taken care of first, or else you'll be damned to your own hell. It was an idea worth sharing and toying with, even if I as a Christian still see God as the rock that supports and guides us in getting to Salvation—whatever that even means.

At this point, Lucifer was standing again. I had one question left, and he was looking over that planet, hands behind his back like a general, or a king overlooking his kingdom.

"Okay, last question before I get outta here: what message do you have for others or for me? Or just in general?"

10. ANY LAST MESSAGES FOR ME OR OTHER PEOPLE?

1. Ill conceived messages could lead to dispute and resentment.

2. Destructive excess. Arrogance. Friends may feel taken for granted if popularity goes to your head.

3. Abuse of power, weakness, and inability to hold true to one's convictions.

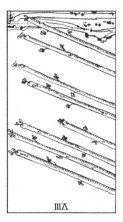

The way he looked over his shoulder made my heart ache—just a bit. I knew by that look that this would be the most serious and passionate out of any of his answers. As the cards revealed themselves, and their meanings became apparent, I just kept writing it all down; the meaning of the cards kept spooling together into an answer that seemed to never end. After a little bit of that, I think he noticed that I was getting confused, in all these separate ideas, because he clarified their meaning to me.

Though even as I wrote this, and I found words to clarify all this information further—as I shot another quick question into the void to see if he was fine with me adding a phrase I thought would explain this better, because it was still a little confusing—I felt that he wanted nothing but for me to get this out there however made his message digestible and elegant.

"I know all too well what excess pride can do," he said. "Too much of anything leads to problems—and as God and I hold two sides of that one coin, so too do *humility* and pride.

"Balance. This is what people need. Too much in either direction is a sign of weakness, of lacking something in oneself. I represent the pride to hold one's head high that so many, in this era, lack. It's been a point of slander used by those not even seeing their own arrogance—the clergy, the supposed men of God. Pride is something they trample in others when they see it just bud, while their own pride is overgrown with strangling vines.

"Pride enough to hold true to one's own beliefs, abide by one's own code—security enough to know it isn't the code of the man next to him, and that it doesn't have to be—that is power. How people have approached concepts of faith and spiritual enlightenment has left people resentful and broken It's time to change that. Reclaim one's power. Be proud once more."

I set my pencil down and re-read this answer a couple times over, as if this would be on some kind of divine SAT test someday. Then I hugged my knees to my chest and sighed.

"Damn," I said. "That's one hell of a message. But okay—that's all I had to ask, honestly. Lucifer, thank you for coming by and answering my questions. It's been incredible talking to you, and you're welcome back here any time, I'd say."

It seemed like Lucifer's favorite thing to do was offer that soft smile. Never in my life did I figure Big Bad Lucifer to really be that kind of gentle, but then again, I'd learned a whole lot about him that night that had absolutely nothing to do with whatever mainstream Christianity had to say, so I shouldn't have been surprised. But after that smile, Lucifer began to walk away, and the big tower we were on melted to nothing but shadows.

I was back in my living room, by myself. Chocolate and cherries eaten, whiskey waiting to be given away. I made sure it was okay to give my boyfriend the remaining snacks, too, before I passed it all on with the whiskey, and then I was ready to clean up and head to bed.

The offer of hospitality I'd extended to Lucifer felt a little silly at the time, I'll admit, but I didn't realize what that offer would lead to. If you'd told this scared, uninformed, half-deconstructed Christian witch playing Spiritual Jackass that she'd have an entire altar dedicated to Lucifer less than a calendar year later, she might've given you a nervous chuckle and changed the subject. But there it is now in my living room, right on the bar cart: a place where Lucifer can get all the offerings of whiskey or gin or, sometimes, Malibu coconut rum, that he wants for when we dive into shadow work and other meditations together.

Nonetheless, by this point, I'd already had some of the wildest spiritual experiences of my life, and I'd *just* crested ten interviews that week. In fact, I'd made a very busy schedule for myself by lining up interviews with the help of practitioners of different religions, and it was all swimming in my head, the amount of information. I thought my head might pop with it all.

That night, though, I gave up on making sense of it all and decided to focus on resting.

THOTH & ANUBIS

Along with Lucifer, that week I'd also had the good fortune to meet one of the many Kemetic practitioners on Tiktok, @thesacredsycamore (Beau). Not only did they reach out with an offer to help contact two of the Egyptian deities they worshipped—Anubis and Thoth—but they also gave me direction on what to offer, how to offer it, and what to do with it afterwards, which was very much appreciated given that I wouldn't have even known where to start looking for proper information on these deities.

(Though I will say, if you, like myself, are still prone to turn to Google for information on deities of different cultures and time periods, do yourself a favor and make it Google scholar. Find papers written by academics—archaeologists and anthropologists whose entire job it is to find out how ancient cultures actually worked from what they left behind. Not some random blog by some self-proclaimed high priestess of whatever.)

But of the many Egyptian gods, or *Netjeru*, that I found fascinating, the two Beau was able to help me with were some of the ones I was most interested in. Anubis, especially, is one I think most people know from popular media depictions: the tall man with the jackal head, god of funerary rites and the dead, escort of the souls of kings and protector of the land of the dead. He was incredibly important in ancient Egyptian culture due to their focus on getting safely to the afterlife. What I didn't know was that Anubis, or Anpu, as the Egyptians called him, was the one considered to have invented this ancient culture's legendary embalming methods. Learning about this, and reading up on Anubis's myths for the sake of questions, delighted me, and it gave me a lot of things to ask him about that I couldn't wait to get to.

Thoth, too—what an incredible god! The record-keeper and messenger of the Netjeru, Thoth is the one who records the outcome of Osiris's judgement of a soul after Anubis placed their heart on a scale, opposite to a feather. He was the one who invented the Egyptian's ancient writing system, even though the Pharaoh at the time refused to use it, and he's also the god of science, magic, knowledge, wisdom, learning, and the moon (perhaps overlapping with Khonsu like Apollo with Helios).

While I did originally tease apart the answers both Anubis and Thoth gave for their original posts, I've decided here to braid them back together as they actually happened, so you might get a clearer picture of how this all went down for me. Before we began, though, I'd set the table with an onyx stone just because it looked pretty and felt appropriate, and then some bread I'd baked fresh that day and two glasses of ice water. According to Beau, this was what was customary to offer the gods: bread, water, and incense, specifically frankincense. From what I'd seen of my own religion, alongside Greek and now Egyptian, it seemed that frankincense was pretty popular among many different gods and cultures of this part of the world. For myself, I had a little sparkling water and an orange as a snack while we spoke.

This was a part in my interview journey where I felt it necessary to *match* whatever I'd given to the gods, as a way to show that it wasn't worship, but simple hospitality; we were sharing a meal *together* in my eyes. It was the same as offering a guest something to eat and having tea or coffee with them. Eventually, I would come to not bother so much for myself, if only because I didn't want to be eating snacks when I wasn't hungry or when I was right about to go to bed, but having some water or tea nearby was always fine, too. Though here, for this interview, I also had an angel statue—something I would do especially in the beginning, to signify the bounds of my space (the end of the coffee table) and signify God's presence there to help me out if, for whatever reason, I needed it. With the Netjeru, I mean—how could I not be nervous? We'd all read the story of Exodus, or at least seen *The Prince of Egypt*. It wasn't like God and the Netjeru were just playing cards together when all that went down, and in fact, in Exodus 12:12, God even says that He'll kill every firstborn and *punish* the Netjeru.

I think it's safe to say there was some tension between all these Divinities at least for a little while. I had no idea how the Netjeru would receive me, which is why I made damn sure that they'd be fine with talking to me, a devotee of the God of Israel, before even thinking of approaching. Beau confirmed that they'd be fine with speaking, and for both Anubis (Anpu) and Thoth (Djehwty), they wrote out a lovely invocation:

> *Dua, Anpu, beautiful guardian, the one who protects his herd, so that they may uphold Ma'at in his name. Dua, Anpu, Khenty-Amenitiu, Protector of the Dead and Keeper of Secrets. Please accept this incense, bread, and water as a token of my devotion. May this water cool you as you work hard in the beautiful West.*

> *Dua, Anpu, Delight of the Enshrouded One. I invoke you here to assist Sara, follower of Christ and the God of Abraham, on her quest for knowledge and understanding, and hope you can give her the answers she seeks. Let it be known by Ra and all the Netjeru that I am an upholder of divine order devoted to you, Anpu. Dua.*

Likewise, Beau invoked Thoth with his own lovely invocation:

> *Dua, Djehwty, Lord of the Divine Body, the one who gifts us with knowledge so that we can honor you with our learning. Dua, Djehwty, He Who Balances and Scribe of the Gods, please accept this bread, water, and incense as token of my devotion. May this water cool you as you work hard in the land of caves.*

Dua, Djehwty, Keeper of All that is Hidden Under the Heavenly Vault. I invoke you here to assist Sara, follower of Christ and the God of Abraham, on her quest for knowledge and understanding, and hope you can give her the answers she seeks. Let it be known by Ra and all the Netjeru that I am an upholder of divine order devoted to you, Djehwty. Dua.

I enjoyed listening to them invoke Anubis and Thoth, seeing how one would go about it. Just as much as I'm interested in the gods themselves, you see, I'm also very much interested in their devotees—their rites, their invocations, their way of connecting with their gods. It's as important a piece of understanding these deities as contacting them directly is, in my opinion. But nonetheless, once Beau confirmed that Anubis and Thoth were on their way, I sat and closed my eyes, ready to enter this meditative space again.

By this point, it no longer unsettled me to go wherever the spirits of Divinity led me. In fact, I was eager to go. I wanted to see what they saw, where they were; I understood then that, despite my original arrogant insistence that these gods were simply guests in *my* house, on the contrary, I was actually very much a guest in *theirs* whenever they took me away to these places. And I was coming to love these places, honored to be able to see them at all.

Again, I am a fantasy writer. I also, by this point, still worked at my original nine-to-five, where I would write blogs about people we supported and their accomplishments, so I was used to picking up the details of places, too. My blogs were about more than just what the person said about, say, a job or a volunteer opportunity they had; it was about the atmosphere of their workplace, the color of their uniforms, the blue skies and colorful flowers outside an establishment, and the way their supervisors or fellow volunteers had a sparkle in their eye when describing them.

These details told something about the situation as much as any actual testimony did. They were a part of the scene; they contributed to the emotional and mental undercurrents that spoken words alone couldn't capture—and weren't asked to. In my own fantasy stories, too, the place details weren't without reason or intention; they contributed to an understanding of not only the setting, but the characters shaped by it. And in these interviews with the gods, I came to look forward to these beautiful visions, because they said something about the gods: what they liked, where they were, the energy and feeling that surrounded them. It was their vast and expansive energy re-arranged in a form I could perceive, and with my visualization skill already at maximum thanks to my fantasy work, it was easy to look around and see even the smallest details of a place like the one Anubis and Thoth took me to.

So once I confirmed these two were here with me, I also confirmed which tarot decks they wanted to use. For Anubis, he wanted to use Amrit Brar's Marigold Tarot, and he wasn't a god of many words, because he only wanted one card unless more became necessary. Thoth, too, wanted to use the Marigold Tarot, but he wanted *at least* three cards per question. After that, with all three of us settled, I closed my eyes and let myself see whatever they wanted me to see—and goodness, I was certainly not disappointed.

"Hello, Anubis, and hello, Thoth," I said into the darkness. "Welcome, and please enjoy this bread and ice water. I'm hoping to learn from you both today, and I'm excited to get started. But first, can I get a sense of your energy?"

This was the question I would ask that seemed to open the floodgates for a time being. And certainly, from here, it was pretty dark—until a sudden plume of torchlight sparked into existence. Then we were in a dark stone hallway leading towards a chamber in what appeared to be a tomb; something about it felt underground, out of sight, hidden.

Firelight danced off the brick, and Anubis was there, easily twice my height, but looking exactly as we depict him: with the jackal head and the human body. I understood through my research that typically, the Netjeru move about as either animal or man, not always both like we see them depicted, but deities also seem to try and fit our expectations of what they look like, in my experience. Maybe there are fewer surprises for the practitioner that way. It makes sense, given that even the smallest bit of doubt can become like rust on a practitioner's mind, weakening it and wearing it away until they lose the connection altogether. Nonetheless, Anubis was black and gold at his arms, face, and ears, though not at his chest for some reason, and he moved with a slow grace.

We made it into the tomb's chamber. There was a coffin of some type in the middle of the room that he covered with the top of a stone slab. He directed me to sit in a small chair between him and Thoth. I think I had a flash of Horus for a minute when I looked at Thoth, because a falcon headed man was there ever so quickly, but then he disappeared, and I was able to focus and get Thoth afterwards. He had an ibis head, with very pale blue-green feathers, and a black cap of hair on his head that reached his shoulders. He wore what, to me, looked like a sorcerer's robe, rich deep blue with golden edges and embroidery, and he sat in that chair with a pencil and paper in his lap. Thoth stared at me with such intensity that I felt his gaze alone would flatten me.

In fact, it almost seemed like Thoth was studying me: like he was as interested in me as I was in him, and that we were both going to take away something interesting from this. That energy honestly endeared me to him right away. But Anubis, who sat opposite of Thoth, was quiet, reserved, and watchful, in a way that felt comfortable and safe.

"Alright, thank you for having me here," I pipped as I settled into the chair. "To get us rolling, let's start with Anubis. Anubis, I understand that there was a time before the mummification of Osiris, where humanity didn't know of this yet. What happened to their bodies before then?"

A1. WHAT HAPPENED TO THE BODIES OF THE DEAD BEFORE YOU?

Anubis shook his head here.

"It wasn't good," he said, and his voice was low and smooth as velvet, so very gentle. "It was a shame, and a great regret of mine: they decomposed. Their bodies gave way to new life here in the world of the living. But it's good now, that such things can be avoided, so their bodies can continue on in the next life without rotting."

That interested me, that the ancient Egyptians would find their physical bodies still useful and important in the spiritual world. I nodded and said,

"Understandable—and yes, it's good to have a way to avoid that now. Alright, over to you, Thoth. My first question for you, is what inspired you to share your talents of writing, magic, and mathematics with mankind?"

Regret, loss, mourning, disappointment. Destructive nature of sorrow in excess.

T1. WHAT INSPIRED YOU TO SHARE YOUR TALENTS WITH MAN?

Right away, Thoth was answering, whipping out cards, and he sure was talkative. I enjoyed interpreting these cards as he helped me work through what they meant.

"Mankind is scared of what they don't know," he said with a tilt of his ibis head. "They avoid it. I wanted them to engage with the world. Knowledge is how we escape the bounds of the physical and go elsewhere, transcend elsewhere. What a beautiful thing it is. I want people to turn their attention to that enlightenment. So what you're doing here is an interesting thing."

That made me pause. I didn't expect him to have any thoughts to share

Disinterest, intro-spection, doubt, pessimism, inability to see the good in life.

Delusion or disconnect with reality in regards to a relationship.

Intelligence, trustworthi-ness, security, generosity, and resourcefulness. Something more than this material world. Nurturing, supportive, and responsible.

about what I was doing, if only because no other deities (besides Apollo) really said anything about it. "Oh," I said, blinking. "I mean, I'm on the same page as you. I don't want to avoid things; I want to learn! So I'm happy to learn here today with you both."

Thoth couldn't really smile, given he had a beak, but I felt a warmth radiate off him that gave the same idea. Encouraged, I turned back to Anubis.

"Alright, Anubis, another question for you: speaking of Osiris and others earlier, I read that there are two versions of your myth: one where you're a child of Ra and Hesat, and another where you're the child of Osiris and Nephthys. Is there a correct version?"

A2. IS THERE A CORRECT VERSION OF YOUR PARENTAGE?

Martyrdom, hard-ship, confusion, facing consequences.

His voice was quiet, but solid: "Irrelevant." I got the sense he would be blunt and adamant in his answers, but this one he was especially stern. "It's nothing but a matter of how one wants to perceive me. But truth be told, my role is my role. I serve it, no matter my parentage. To discuss it is to waste time."

"Ah, I see." It was something like what Persephone was talking about: the details didn't matter, just the core of the story. I was starting to really absorb that lesson the more deities I spoke to. Though some things still made me curious about myths and origins of deities, and that had me turning back to Thoth. "That's completely fair—and interesting! But moving on: Thoth!"

The ibis-headed god nodded here, then got up, drifting closer to Anubis. His robes swept the ground as he glided across the stone.

I read my pre-written question: "Some myths say you were born from Ra's lips, and other's that you were self-made. What was it like to come into existence? Any impressions?"

T2. WHAT WAS IT LIKE WHEN YOU CAME INTO EXISTENCE?

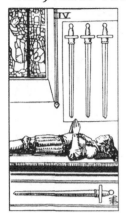

Solitude, reevaluation, and rest. Self reflection, renewal. Blades pointing inward.

Failing to recognize one's own shortcomings due to pride.

Home, celebration, joy, harmony. Encourages us to enjoy our time with those we love and get our house in order.

It was a vague question, but my aim was simple: understanding, through Thoth's perception of himself as he came into existence, a hint or two about *how* he came into existence, and which myth better matched it.

"Before I was formed, I was thinking to myself exactly how I wanted to *be* formed. I knew what my role was, and what I was to become. As I thought, I made sure to make myself right. I made myself as I am now. And it felt like a homecoming, such a reunion, to create myself and join the rest of the Netjeru; I felt as if I'd found my place among kin. I was ready to work."

In my mind, that explanation meant that he'd created himself. Compared to Anubis, who seemed disinterested in discussing the intricacies of his myths, I was glad to get a more direct answer from Thoth on the same subject. "That sounds fascinating," I said; "Thank you for explaining that! And now, back to Anubis," who, all this time, patiently waited as Thoth spoke, "in the story of Bata, it says you became king of that certain city after everything ended. Was that a temporary role, given it was in the overworld, or are you still king?"

A3. ARE YOU STILL KING OF THAT CERTAIN CITY FROM THE LORE?

This question was simple enough that it could've been answered with a pendulum, and Anubis's answer came neatly and clearly: "No, no. It was temporary. My role is here, with the dead."

"That's fair," I said, pencil gliding across the journal with the last few letters. "And it's cool, too! I mean, I figured as much, but it was interesting to hear that you were also a king. Okay—Thoth, we're back to you. Can you tell me, of all the things you created, what your favorite is?"

T3. WHAT'S YOUR FAVORITE INVENTION OR CREATION?

1. Bad news, wastefulness, preoccupation with projects at the expense of other priorities in life.

2. Fixation on material world, anxiety, greed.

3. Positive changes in luck and money. Change in destiny apparent. Beware things too good to be true.

Thoth hovered over me, his beak nearly close enough to tap on my head. "I am a lover of efficiency," he said. "My best tools by far are the tools that help humanity effectively manage their life. The calendar, mathematics with regards to finance, these delight me. To see mankind organize their lives for efficiency and success—that is my favorite. Man deserves to have a mind free of mundane struggles, so that they might focus on better pursuits than worrying about things they can write down."

I couldn't help but exclaim, "Oh, cool! I agree; I think it's good that we don't need to waste time remembering what we can reference, so we can spend more time on application than memory."

"Yes!"

His enthusiasm was so bright, like morning sunshine, as he focused so intently on me. I had a big smile on my face as I watched his feathers fluff a bit, his eyes big and so wide open.

"Ah, Thoth, I've got another question about that, but before I ask, let me get back to Anubis."

When I turned back to that legendary jackal-headed god, though, he had none of the bright energy of Thoth's enthusiasm—just a little bit of warmth, friendliness, as he relaxed in his seat and waited for me to speak. I wondered if he was enjoying watching Thoth be excited to talk about these things, or if he was just happy to be there, because there wasn't anything but patience and kindness from him.

I cleared my throat. "Alright, Anubis—this next question is one that really intrigues me: I know of multiple different names for the underworld, all different in the contexts of their cultures and the faiths around them. Are these different places, like we might have different countries? Or are they all different versions of the same place?"

A4. ARE THE VARIOUS UNDERWORLDS THEIR OWN ASTRAL SPACES?

Entrapment, vice, bondage, addiction, and a lack of control. A prison of one's own making.

Transformation, changes, evolution—especially if hard won. New obstacles and opportunities appear with time.

Drama, authority, power, unapologetic self-expression, confidence. New opportunities undeniable.

This was a tricky one, I guess—harder to explain for him than the others, because where Anubis wanted only one card for his other answers, he insisted I draw three here.

"It's a complicated answer," Anubis said in that soothing voice, giving a feeling of damp earth and cool caves. He leaned forward, folding his hands as he propped himself up on his knees. "There are different places for different functions. Some are like simple holding tanks, where souls wait to move to where they need to go next to continue their lives. Others are places where they find judgment for what they've done, depending on their crimes, to teach them harshly what to avoid in the next life. And others still are places that bathe souls in light for a job well done. Here, they might remain indefinitely, or they might choose to continue learning other things back on earth. But each place has its functions, and no two are the same."

"Oh, wow. That does kind of line up with what a lot of different faiths think, but it's cool to know they're different places altogether, too; that's really interesting!"

And it gave me something to think about. Even just in Christian mythos, there were different slivers of afterlife—heaven, hell, purgatory. The descriptions Anubis gave seemed to match these ideas, but then again, they had their own underworld, and so did the Greek gods, and so did the Slavic gods—but it seemed, according to Anubis, that there was a need for these different areas for all the many different people and their different directions taken in life. I meant more to ask what these other afterlife areas were like at all, like what made Hades different from Nav and the like, but this was its own insightful answer in and of itself.

"Okay, alright, next question for Thoth. Coming back to your inventions, what do you think of what humanity has been able to do with these gifts you've given us? Like landing a rocket on the moon—imagine that! I'm curious to know your opinions."

T4. WHAT ARE YOUR THOUGHTS ON HUMANITY'S USE OF YOUR GIFTS?

While it seemed Thoth had been listening to Anubis just as carefully as I had, and while he'd been so enthusiastic to discuss these things all this time, here, his enthusiasm burned low. He stood up and crossed his arms, facing that dark doorway that I came in here through. Thoth shook his head and answered me.

"So much damage," he said with a sigh. "What I wanted was a world where mankind used these gifts to advance to the heavens—like on that rocket. And they have done wonderful things, of course. But the wickedness done with these maths and figures—it's enough to wonder if it was always

Calamity, struggle, conflict, misjudgement, challenge, great change. Potential disaster.

Denial, stalemate, indecision, illusion

Misplaced, lost faith, suppression, weakness, feeling as though free thought has been restricted.

to be this way. If, where we saw opportunities for humanity to apply this knowledge together, to one goal, the world could only ever be a place where they thought to use it separately, for their own selfish goals. So much study in weaponry and things of destruction—why?"

Honestly, it made me a little sad to hear him talk the way he did about it. I can't imagine the disappointment of handing humanity the tools to be great, only to watch them use those same tools to destroy the world he oversaw with the others on humanity's behalf.

"No, I completely agree. I understand. It's awful, the things we've done with it. But before we come back to that, let me ask Anubis another question."

Anubis sat up straight, though he seemed to be watching the somewhat dejected Thoth from the corner of his golden eye.

"Alright, Anubis: in Greece, your image was likened to that of Hermes (and Thoth's, too)! What do you think about that, or the fact that this statue is in the Vatican Palace?"

A5. THOUGHTS ON YOUR LIKENESS IN THE VATICAN PALACE?

Steady, bright confidence. One must ask if they have this level of self awareness.

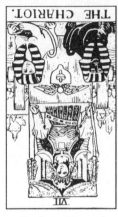

Defeat, loss of control, or lack of direction.

"I don't care about the statue," he said, so matter-of-fact. "I am aware and comfortable with who I am. Hermes' people misunderstand me, struggling to liken me to something that isn't who or what I am."

"Got'cha, got'cha. Alright. Thoth?"

Thoth glanced over his shoulder, arms still crossed.

"Again, I definitely understand how it can be upsetting to see what people have done with the things you've taught them," I said. I tapped my pencil against my journal, thinking of how to inject a lighter mood into my question. "But, in terms of writing, at least, most works, if not all, that are attributed to you are ones of facts and truths. What do you think about writing done for telling stories, fiction?"

T5. WHAT DO YOU THINK ABOUT FICTION WRITING?

He didn't quite balk, but he shook his head a little, and then he was off pacing again, gesticulating as he explained himself as if eager for discussion, expression.

"'What a waste of paper'—this is what I thought once," he said, and I sat there at my table with a bite of orange hanging out of my mouth from the surprise. That wasn't what I expected at all! But as I swallowed it down and started recording his answer, he kept going. "Stories were once told orally, so there was no need to spend materials writing trifles and made-up things when there were more important things to record.

Ill placed admiration for idea or person, large doubts, confusion, a dent in one's confidence.

Unrest and an inability to move on.

Chaos, discord, or resolution.

"But what I've noticed since you all learned to write your tales down, is how those tales have grown in magnitude. So much has changed in your ability to tell such stories, humanity's ability to track the worlds they dream up and make them so detailed. You're all so stuck on your creations; it's interesting. It's fascinating, actually."

I couldn't help but add, "And of course, e-books mean there's less paper waste."

"Yes!" He clapped his hands together. "That, too! Fascinating, truly fascinating."

Alright, well, that's definitely an interesting answer," I said, chuckling, "thank you for that. Anubis, our next one is for you: since mummification isn't such a thing anymore, I was wondering if you help modern morticians with their work?

A6. DO YOU HELP MODERN MORTICIANS WITH THEIR WORK?

Denial, stalemate, indecision, and illusion.

Anubis nodded. "Yes. I help. Old ways didn't work in this modern world, so we had to adapt. I helped humanity discover a new way of performing this 'mortician's work,' as you call it."

"Aw, cool! That's so interesting; thank you for that. Now, Thoth, I understand you have something to do with the moon per your lore. Do you have any relation to Khonsu?"

T6. DO YOU HAVE ANY RELATION TO KHONSU?

The sun felt like a bit of a teasing answer when asking about the moon. When I closed my eyes and dipped back into that tomb to look at Thoth, I saw him wave the question off as he settled onto his seat, a quirk to his brow (if an ibis had them, of course).

"Khonsu and I have different approaches to handling the moon, I suppose, and we may or may not agree on it," he said. "But truthfully, the moon is only one of the many things I look after or touch upon, and so it's not the most of my work; let him do what he does with the moon."

Happiness, comfort, growth. Good news, confidence, good luck.

Vulnerability, powerlessness, and possibly inflated ego.

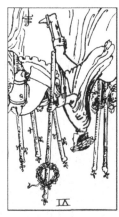

Pride, superiority, failing to recognize one's shortcomings.

"Fair, I suppose. Alright! That's all of my specific questions for you both. Now we can get into the last few. To start, Anubis, could you tell me how you see yourself?"

A7. HOW DO YOU SEE YOURSELF?

Here, Anubis had a bit of a downcast eye—the most emotional he'd looked the entire interview.

He said, "I carry burdens, regrets. There was a time before humanity where I might've appeared sooner. But now, I'm steadfast. I do my role as is required. That's what matters."

"Oh—that reminds me, with that time before humanity you mention. I had another question before we ask Thoth about himself: there was once a time where jackals would take the bodies buried too shallow. Did you always not like this, or did you only intercede when humanity asked?"

Regrets, refusing transformation, disappointment, false accusations.

A8. WHEN DID YOU BEGIN INTERCEDING FOR HUMANITY'S DEAD?

Steady, bright confidence. One must ask if they have this level of self awareness.

Again, that somber note. It seemed this time, Anubis was hinting more at the latter part of the card—at whether one had achieved such self-awareness. The answer spooling in my head confirmed that idea.

"There wasn't an awareness yet for how humanity was suffering," Anubis explained. "Humanity hadn't quite reached its heights yet; it was just becoming recognizable. But then they cried out to me, when their dead were desecrated, and it was then I became aware of what duties I had to humanity already living, too. Since then, I've served."

"I see. Wow. That's so fascinating; I appreciate you sharing that." I blinked at him a bit, then turned to Thoth to continue our where we'd left off. "Now, Thoth, I actually had one more question for you, too—sorry about that! But now: you're often depicted as either ibis or baboon. What aspects of these animals do you identify with, especially regarding the baboon?"

T7. WHAT ASPECTS OF IBIS AND BABOON DO YOU IDENTIFY WITH?

Thoth nodded. "Ah, these. They're impartial animals, you see, those baboons; they defend their things from others, and they're always looking for threats. Both of these animals, being animals, are not willing to waste time on what doesn't serve them, but they're willing to defend what's theirs, as I am with things I create and the humans that uses them."

Dishonor, mistrust, being too preoccupied with problems of others to address one's own issues, disconnect from emotion.

"Oh!" That explanation made more sense to me than I thought it would, given how radically different both the ibis and the baboon were. "I see. Okay! Now let's pick back up from the ending here. Thoth, I'd also like to know how you see yourself, if you don't mind telling me?"

T8. HOW DO YOU SEE YOURSELF?

1. Diligence, craft, dedication, skill. Commit to one's craft to achieve results in life.

2. Partnership and romantic energy, excited to fall into new relationships and opportunities, finding ways for old relationships to endure.

3. Bad news, powerlessness, loneliness, self sabotage. Negativity, attempted healing.

Thoth tapped the cards I pulled here, then said, "It's as it says there, on those cards: I'm diligent in my craft. I'm in love with my work, my duties, and all it can do for the world. And heartbroken at what wickedness it can cause. I'm an inventor; I believe in the power of my inventions to do good. I want them to do more good, less harm; that's what I made these things for!"

It was hard not to get swept up in his energy with him. He was a very assertive force, full of life, and it made a stark contrast to Anubis, who sat so still and silent as he waited for Thoth to finish.

"I love it," I said as I recorded his answer, "and I can see it, too! To bounce back to Anubis, now: Anubis, how do you *want* people to see you?"

A9. HOW DO YOU WANT OTHERS TO SEE YOU?

The somber note lifted, and he was once again sitting elbows on knees, leaning forward, smiling—as well as a jackal could smile.

Romantic desire, pining, wanting new love and new beginnings.

ACE of CUPS.

"I am the one of new beginnings," he said. "This is precisely what it means to go to the afterlife. Leaving one life for the next. I am the one that helps at the beginning of that journey, through that transition. It's a beautiful thing."

"Aw, that's lovely." I couldn't help but smile with him. "And Thoth? How do you want people to see you?"

T9. HOW DO YOU WANT OTHERS TO SEE YOU?

Misfortune, depression, unsuccessful ventures.

Pessimism, dread, resignation.

Rivalry, competition, obstacles, trickery.

The intensity of these cards surprised me. As I looked between them all, Thoth paused to think a bit.

"Well, you see," he started, "my inventions haven't always been the most well received, to the point that I wondered why I should bother giving humanity my gifts at all, if they wouldn't appreciate them. But I have the need to share knowledge, for better or worse, and so I'm going to do just that. I am one that perseveres—again, for better or worse. I am a master of navigating obstacles and fighting for my belief in my work and what needs to be done. No matter how bleak the world or the future may seem, I am one that pushes on."

"Ah, I understand. That makes perfect sense, and I'm happy to hear that!" Once I'd written his answer down, I sat back. "Well, we're at our last question now, and I suppose I'll ask it of you first, Anubis: do you have any messages for me or others you'd like to share before we part?"

A10. ANY LAST MESSAGES FROM ANUBIS?

For the first time in the interview, Anubis had some urgency, some stress, to his voice.

Closure, working towards resolution, hostility.

"Yes—closure," he said. "Get closure. One of the biggest things that weighs down the heart in the afterlife is regret; it's represented as a 'heavy heart' for a reason. Give your apologies, right your wrongs. Don't come to the next world bogged down with the weight of the one you just left, or your journey will be a burdensome one, if it happens at all."

"Now that's some really good advice," I said, nodding as I scribbled away. "And you, Thoth? Do you have any messages you'd like to leave for me?"

T10. ANY LAST MESSAGES FROM THOTH?

Self destructive, controlling, dishonest, and manipulative behaviors.

Harmful secrets, confusion, and mental disconnect.

Judgement works in our best interest. Painful lessons are needed to experience change.

He, too, was stressed, just like Anubis! I didn't know why all of a sudden they were so serious, but Thoth was no less intense in his message.

Thoth said, "Yes, yes, for all: beware! So many things in this world are useless, and do nothing to serve you on your quest to your highest self. Don't feed them! Focus on things that enrich you—and ensure you never hide the truth, and that you never smother knowledge, no matter how uncomfortable it makes you, or you'll learn painfully why you shouldn't."

"Oh, goodness." I stuffed the last bit of orange into my mouth and sat back, surveying what I'd just written. "Alright. That's fair. I appreciate you both giving this advice. But! That's all I had for now, so thank you both so much for meeting with me! I enjoyed your company, and I wish you well. Goodbye for now!"

Again, how well can a jackal or an ibis really smile? Not that well. But I didn't need to see it; their smiles were more a current in the air, and then, that torch-lit tomb faded from my mind's eye, until there was just me sitting there with some bread and water. The ice had long melted.

In Kemeticism, it's considered rude to not eat the offerings, as they hate to see food go to waste. Those two slices of bread became a bit of lunch, the water much needed after something sweet like an orange. Then it was a matter of cleaning everything up and tucking my notebook away. All the while, I felt good, knowing I'd been able to avoid making a mess with the Netjeru on first pass with them.

And their answers—my God, their answers. This, I was coming to learn, was yet another part of the fun: finding these many thoughts and ideas I never would've thought about myself. Ones that very clearly came from consciousness that weren't mine.

Ones that proved to me—even if I didn't *need* more proof—that I wasn't alone in these interactions.

VELES,
LADA, & ZORYA

I'll tell you what: the next couple weeks after the Apollo debacle were a whirlwind, not just because of Lucifer and Anubis and Thoth, but because of the next three guests that I spoke to the week after: Veles, Zorya, and Lada. Thanks to the help of a very kind practitioner, @olivia.emina (November,) I was able to more confidently and respectfully approach these three gods for the first time.

Now, a thing about Slavic paganism is that so much of what we know about it has largely been cobbled together from what scraps of records we have *about* them, which come from Christian scholars and Muslim traders. It's through their documentation of customs they found upon coming to the lands of Slavic tribes and the records of their interactions with those they traded goods with, including their religious customs related to trading, that we can figure out a smidge of what was going on—like the fact that Slavic pagans were totemic, meaning they carved totems, wooden idols, of their gods, and that they would leave offerings out after making a request. An offering was considered accepted when it was eaten by wild dogs or just generally disappeared the next day. If it was still there, they had to make another offering and try again.

At the time, I still had a very big hang up with actually following any proper offerings. I don't know why, looking back; it just felt like a boundary I wasn't ready to cross yet. But as my understanding of henotheism and God developed, through talking with Him and more research, those convictions would eventually fade. For the time being, however, I considered it pretty lucky that I hadn't had any issues with Kresnik, and so speaking to these other ancestral gods of mine with someone to act as mediator made me feel so much better. I'm grateful to November for their invocations and their help figuring out offerings; it made a big difference, I think, in how it all went down.

But let me tell you something: invoking and speaking to even *one* deity at a time is intense. Speaking to *three?* At one time? Woof. It took at least two hours, and keeping the channeling open for that long, at the end of an already long day, was a challenge unlike any other. Still, I soldiered on, and I found myself surrounded by three deities that were so incredible to sit with and speak to.

Let me tell you a little bit about them. First, we have Veles, god of mischief, music, magic, cattle, and the Slavic underworld, Nav. These seem like an odd array of things to be a god of, I know, but there are reasons for them. In Slavic mythology, you see, Veles is a god, but he's also a bit of a trickster; he'll turn into a great serpent and sometimes wrassle with the Slavic god of war and thunder, Perun. It's said that one day, Veles stole all of Perun's cattle, and there was a big fight about since Perun was understandably upset about it. But Veles is also one who, being a god of the dead and the underworld, has some associations with magic (much like Hekate), and he's a big fan of music, too— to the point that some Croatian wedding traditions still include not starting the music before a cup of wine is poured out by a nearby tree. Even if the people don't remember *why* they do this tradition anymore, when you know about Veles, it makes sense: a libation of wine to the god of music must take place before the music, and by extension, the festivities, can start.

Next we have Zorya. Remember when I said that Hekate wasn't the only goddess that could teach magic? Along with Veles's associations with magic by virtue of his ruling the place where spirits— human and otherwise—reside in Slavic lore, Zorya is the one that Slavic pagans, especially women, would learn their magic from. She taught a specific type of magic that only initiated women could practice, which is where some of the idea that Slavic paganism is closed comes from. While the Slavic gods are open for all to worship, it was only through careful study and learning from one initiated woman to the younger generations that the ancestral practice of Zagovory, or "sound shaping," took place. The spoken word was a central part of Slavic magic that people practiced, hence its name.

Zorya is tricky, though. Sometimes she's one maiden goddess with a few different forms (the Morning Star, Utrennyaya, the Evening Star, Vechernyaya, or just the Star, Zvezda), and other times these aspects are considered completely separate sister goddesses. I view these aspects as epithets of one goddess. But Zorya is responsible for opening the gates of the heavens for the sun god to go about his daily chariot ride, as well as guarding the celestial dog Simargl that lives in the Ursa Minor constellation. In specifically Slovenian lore, from what I've found searching around, it seems that folktales pin Zorya as the daughter of Vesna and Kresnik.

Lastly, we have Lada, who I think we know the least about. She's cognate with several different fertility and springtime goddesses across Slavic tribes, such as Vesna and Živa, and according to some, she's not a real goddess at all—more a fabrication, perhaps even a mocking character, invented to slander Slavic paganism. However, there is some evidence to suggest that she is beloved among some tribes alongside her twin brother and husband, Lado. The name literally means "the beautiful," and she's a goddess of springtime, women, fertility, and love.

So with all of this knowledge under our belt, let's go ahead and dive right in.

After November's invocation of all three Slavic deities, they left me to do my thing, For each of these deities, I had some different offerings out related to their associations. Honestly, Veles was a bit tricky, but November mentioned that he really seemed to like those gritty, earthy things, like pinecones—so for him, along with some pears that just struck me as very *Veles* at the grocery store and a shot of Jägermeister, I put down some pinecones from my pine tree and an obsidian crystal to represent the dark depths of Nav. For Zorya—specifically, Zorya in her Morning Star aspect, Zorya Utrennyaya—I had an orange, some daisies, a cup of chamomile tea, and a carnelian stone, all as homage to her bright and shining, fiery force. Lastly, for Lada, I had daisies, cherries, rose tea, and a piece of rose quartz, related to her role in love, beauty, and life among the Slavs of yore.

I took a little bit of each fruit for myself to snack on, as well, only to realize that taking a little bit of each meant I had quite a big bowl of fruit to eat. Oops. If I had to do it again, I suppose I'd have just picked my own single fruit, like an apple, but I was really hung up on sharing the same things I was sharing with these deities at the time. There are so many little quirks and hang ups that get in our way when we're unsure, you know? So many decisions that, in hindsight, when you become more comfortable with what you're doing, feel a touch silly. But that's the reason we do it: so that we grow, look back, and see where there was room for improvement in whatever it is we're doing.

Nonetheless, as I sat down and got comfortable, I once again confirmed with them all that they were there and got a big fat yes from each of them. Unlike with Anubis and Thoth, however, every deity here decided they wanted to use a separate deck of cards.

For Zorya, Kat Black's Golden Tarot.

For Lada, the Universal Fantasy Tarot.

And for Veles, Amrit Brar's Marigold Tarot.

With *three* separate decks cleansed and at the ready, I closed my eyes and asked each of these deities to step forward and let me see their energy.

The scene bled in like watercolor on canvas. Little bits of brown and green, trees, soon framed a dusky sky that started blackish-purple and soon melted into a blazing red-orange on the horizon. Hills of green grasses rolled out as far as the eye could see, the occasional little cottage and their fences dotting the land. A thick border of trees surrounded this field, and just as with other deities, like Hades or Apollo or Anubis and Thoth, it seemed there was an entrance into this place.

I sat right in front of that entrance: a big hole where one could walk through a forest so dark that all was black with shadow beyond its borders. There were trees and rocks around the dark opening.

Of course, one thing about any entity that we need to keep in mind is that they tend to come in the form that you'll best respond to—which is why some people see angels, for instance, as women, while others see them as men. In this case, I seemed to be very attached to the way Russian painter Andrey Shishkin interpreted the forms of the Slavic gods, because it was his paintings that informed my understanding of Zorya (specifically his painting *Zvezda*) and Veles as they came through. Lada appeared as a naked woman, her hair flowing like a river of sunlight down her head and a crown of flowers sitting on top. She crouched on one of the rocks and hugged her knees to her chest as Veles and Zorya came around me.

"*Dobrodošli*, everyone, hello, hello! Please join me and enjoy a bit of fruit and drink as we chat. I've got some questions for you all, if you don't mind?"

Veles had the creaky laugh of a mischievous old man as he came into view. He never stayed still for long, pacing a bit with his arms crossed, but he had a twinkle in his eye and a smile almost hidden under the brush of his beard and mustache. By the way both Veles and Zorya smiled at me, I assumed I had the go ahead, and so I started with my questions for Zorya before turning to Veles, then Lada; Zorya's things were stationed to my left, and it made sense to me to go clockwise. Around and around in a circle of questioning we went, everyone taking turns, and the amount of switching between decks and scribbling answers left my hands cramping by the end, but it was worth every moment.

When I turned to her, she had a kindly smile cut into her jowls, her hair silver and a little frizzy, her clothes silvery white, and an embroidered gray/silver headband. Her eyes were warm and bright, and she had the presence of a wise older matron.

However, where she was there in her Dawn aspect, bright robe, gleaming crown, silvery bright hair, it was strange that the world around us suggested dusk. I wasn't entirely sure what to make of that, other than the fact that it was night where I was, and it'd been around morning time where November was. Maybe that had something to do with it.

"Zorya," I started, "to kick us off, I must say I'm curious: your myths are a little conflicted about your image. Some say you're one goddess, some say you're three different ones, and I see right now you're here as Zorya Utrennyaya, yet the world around us suggests—?"

ZI. ARE YOU ONE GODDESS OR MULTIPLE SHARING A TITLE?

A fickle, flighty man, perhaps one with trouble controlling anger.

Still indicates good fortune and contentment. Perhaps there's some taking good fortune for granted.

Creativity and inspiration. Development of strong emotional tie. Deep, significant change. Quiet, gentle, studious.

There was a sting in my ear, a sharp call to pick cards before I'd even finished asking my question. Once I had them all laid out, I saw Zorya with a little smile, essentially waving my question off as if it were silly.

"Child, many gods have different faces," she said, "but that doesn't mean they're different beings. My faces are very different—the bold, the bright, the Morning, and then the slower, the cooler and more emotional, the Evening. Sometimes I prefer to be in one aspect of myself over another, to show one side more, but that doesn't mean I am not who I am. All these faces have their time and place—and is that not the same for you humans?"

It was a good point. We have our work selves, our social selves, our home selves, don't we? All different, yet all the same person. "Okay, I understand! That makes a lot of sense; thank you. And now, Veles," I said as I shuffled the deck he chose, "to start us off with your set of questions, a fun one: what is your favorite kind of music?"

VI. WHAT IS YOUR FAVORITE KIND OF MUSIC?

1. *Loss, theft, uncompromising values, and obsession with socially acceptable roles and routines.*

2. *Exercise foresight with an open mind. Consider many options and plan accordingly so you benefit.*

3. *Fixation on the material world, anxiety, and greed.*

With his arms crossed over his broad chest, he leaned back and barked a laugh before he answered. "Oh, you know—those fun little songs, the ones that kick up a bit of trouble. What's that one you know? Something along the lines of 'Mi Ga Spet Žingamo'?"

Oh, boy. He was referencing a Slovenian song about being drunk with your friends six days out of seven, all while your wife yells at you to get home because she's been waiting for you all day. When I described it, he laughed again and continued.

"Yeah, songs like those that tell funny little stories, those I like—and the ones that teach us what not to do when the liquor wears off."

His energy was infectious, his laugh so bold that I couldn't help but crack a smile with him. "Jeez, alright," I said, waving him off. "That's fair; we all love a good song like that time and time again. Alright! Now, Lada—for our first question for you, I will say: your origins are up for pretty big debate among scholars of Slavic religion. With that in mind, I'd like to know: what was the world like when you came into existence?"

LI. WHAT WAS THE WORLD LIKE WHEN YOU CAME INTO BEING?

If the price of victory is too high, it may be best to choose honorable defeat.

Sometimes we cannot avoid a major change. We should not be afraid of setting out a new path.

A shallow person who likes to get what they want, regardless of consequences. Spoiled and self indulgent.

Lada scowled, though somehow, her frown still seemed sweet. The flower crown cast shadows over her eyes as she tucked her legs in tighter. Her voice was sharp, quick.

"My image was tampered with! I was slandered by these 'Christians' that 're-discovered' me. I was always here, and my place was with the children. The mothers, the life. I was always here to support it all."

Even if I didn't know what to say, I did feel for her. It seemed folks like those medieval Christians didn't know how to not ruin thing.

"That must've been awful," I said. She nodded and huffed.

I looked at her a moment longer before turning to our next guest. "Alright, Lada, we'll come back to you, but for now, Zorya!"

What a patient smile she had on her face as I turned to her.

"After doing some digging," I started, "I see you're described as the child of Kresnik and Vesna in Slovene lore! What does that mean to you, and how do you relate to Vesna?"

Z2. HOW DO YOU RELATE TO VESNA AS A MOTHER FIGURE?

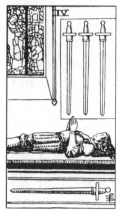

Meditation and seclusion. Rest and recovery. Return to simplicity. Contemplation brings a sense of peace.

Tyranny and domination; a cold, cruel man.

Creation, fertility, energy. New beginnings. Self-reliance, self-sufficiency, and personal empowerment.

Her smile grew. "Ah, Vesna. She taught me the importance of my roles, of light and how *much* light there should be. I open the gates to let lord of the sun out each morning, and I close those gates each night; without this routine, there would be no life. As Vesna rules over spring and fertility, she had a special role in mind for me, that I would ensure there would be enough light to keep the world alive, yet enough dark to let it sleep, lest everything burn.

"Vesna and I are connected in that way: ensuring the balance of life in our different ways, different roles. I've spent much time reflecting on it all."

"Wow." It seemed like all the gods had such specific and eternal systems—like they really did think of everything before they opened the gates on the world and let it run. "That's something. Thank you for your explanation! Okay, okay—Veles?"

He leaned against a tree as I swiveled around to look at him.

"Coming back here now: what's your favorite thing to teach humanity and why?"

V2. WHAT'S YOUR FAVORITE THING TO TEACH HUMANITY? WHY?

His voice boomed: "Toss it all off!"

I got this feeling of what I imagine would be the satisfaction of swiping all the dishes off a table, crashing everything and making a big old mess.

"Get rid of all that old muck; get rid of it!" Veles clapped his hands together and grinned. "I like to teach people to throw off the shackles of old ways of thinking and get creative again. To let go of 'should be's' and 'should not's' and run after what's shiny and new. Adventure! People are too concerned with what others think. To hell with it all!"

Indecision, unforeseen difficulties, and an unwillingness to change.

Misplaced, lost faith, suppression, weakness, or feeling as though free thought is restricted.

Fertility, as well as life to new beginnings, feelings, relationships, and projects.

I blinked at him, positive that it was just the way his sentiments translated in my head, and clarified: "To hell?"

And he shrugged, a touch of mischief twisted into his smile.

"Well, certainly not to Nav."

At that, I laughed with him. "Alright, I got'cha. But coming back around to Lada," who was still sitting there, tucked up on the rock, "Given your role, though, how does your twin brother and husband Lado help you fulfill it?"

12. HOW DOES LADO HELP YOU FULFILL YOUR ROLE?

Shock of all shocks, when you think of a different god, they do take that as an invitation to say hello. Lado popped up behind his sister, also naked with short golden hair. They were the spitting images of each other, and they were cheerful with each other, too.

Lado spoke for his wife: "We share. We keep each other balanced. Our roles and very being are intertwined; we carry all parts of the whole that is love and procreation in humanity."

And then Lada added: "I couldn't do this work without him, nor him without me. We're one; we represent the bond of marriage."

Lado left shortly after, leaving me

It's often only possible to seize opportunities by checking our passions and urges.

The only way to deal with inevitable problems is to focus on the benefits they bring.

Too much worry about the future can keep us from enjoying the present. Anxiety isn't a good guide.

blinking as he faded back into the trees and disappeared. I nodded. "That makes sense." Especially when we think that Lada and Lado are, from how I experienced them then, practically the same being, just split up into different parts of one idea. "Thank you both! And Zorya, another question for you: regarding your aspects, how do they help people understand the concepts of Dusk and Dawn?"

13. HOW DO EPITHETS HELP PEOPLE GRASP DUSK AND DAWN?

1. That which bends is less likely to break. Identify obstacles and avoid battles none will benefit from. Calculate. Desires may be unsatisfied, but it's a worthy sacrifice.

2. Emotional youth. Creativity, inspiration. Development of emotional ties. Important time in a relationship: deep, vital change. Quiet, gentle, studious.

3. New skills learned and applied with success. Creativity used to overcome financial hardships. Making do with little by acquiring new knowledge and skills.

Zorya gave off a tired feeling here, like she was on the precipice of a sigh.

"Once, you know, humanity didn't have light all the time," she said. "In Dusk and Dawn, I was, simply, Twilight: I was the one to bring them the light that started the day, and to dim that light down to signal the end of the day. It meant mankind had to plan their days well, use their time right: they couldn't work at night and run themselves ragged.

"Things have changed now. This modern world—it lets people work and work with no rest, as they just create their own light to work by. But once, people understood when it was time to work, and when it was time to rest, thanks to my Twilight; they understood and aligned themselves with the natural World Clock, and they were better off for it."

I sighed with her. "Yeah, that is true. I'm guilty of that myself, working late into the night." Like I was right then. "It's just hard to stop, y'know?"

Zorya only gave me a look, as if to say that this was exactly her point. I couldn't deny it. But what I could do was change the subject, and that's what I did as I turned to Veles.

"So, Veles, all this leads me to my next question for you: how does Nav differ from other understandings of the underworld?"

V3. HOW DOES NAV DIFFER FROM OTHER UNDERWORLDS?

Experiencing fundamental, painful change. Transforms us with rebirth and rest. We come back stronger, even if Judgement is painful in its execution.

Authority, integrity, connections, intellect, fortitude (both physical and mental). Power, remembrance—a presence that demands respect.

Regret, loss, mourning, and disappointment. Destructive nature of sorrow in excess.

Veles clapped a hand on my shoulder. "Ah, Sara. Listen: Nav is a place where trials continue, not end. Kings come here to be re-smithed and reborn, as there's no such thing as a king or a peasant in Nav. All are broken down, swallowing their lessons, and they come back new and ready to continue. They become stronger. Sadness for the dead is useless; they don't stay down long. It's an arena, a place for a tournament. Nav is not the end at all."

Here's a fun little side note for you: I didn't realize that there actually *was* a canonical concept of rebirth in Nav at this point. It wouldn't be until later, when I went to read up a little bit more so I could write a proper blurb about Veles, that I would discover this fact that I'd apparently overlooked in my research. The fact that it popped out in this reading like this? As I read this back, it was another confirmation that I was, indeed, speaking with the right entities.

"Alright, I hear you," I said, writing away. "Before we continue, though, let's come back to Lada. Now, Lada, you're likened to Aphrodite and Freyja in the domains you have, including war! But you also have dominion over spring, life. What's your favorite role?"

13. WHAT IS YOUR FAVORITE DOMAIN TO RULE OVER?

For the first time in the interview, Lada perked up, and a radiant smile split her lips. "Oh, I think my favorite is the new life," she said as she played with a lock of her golden hair. "The babies. I love seeing how childbirth changes people. Some never become good parents; they never learn how to see beyond themselves. But those who are good and simply don't know how to express that goodness—watch them change when a little life falls into their hands. Watch them learn to smile for the sake of their young.

Stubbornness, loneliness, inability to communicate.

Fear or boredom may result in rash decisions; consider consequences before taking action.

Too much worry about the future can stop us from enjoying the present. Anxiety isn't a good guide.

"The selflessness childbirth creates for willing mothers is beautiful. Unwilling mothers, though, they're burdened. No one should be forced to carry out such responsibility. Childbirth should be a good thing, done for right reasons—not selfish or cruel ones."

"Absolutely, I agree. That's really nice! Never thought about childbirth this way." And I'll be honest: as nice as it was, it still didn't make me any more willing to have kids of my own. I did appreciate that she specifically marked the mothers of the world who never wanted to be mothers, and who shouldn't have had to be, too. "But speaking of life and the natural world, and all the things in it: Zorya, sources mention you as the power that practitioners of Zagovory learn from. What do you think of modern folk practice, and the reclaiming of old traditions?"

74. WHAT DO YOU THINK OF MODERN SLAVIC FOLK PRACTICE?

Facing demons. The more we understand our fears, the less power they have.

A fickle, flighty man, perhaps one with trouble controlling anger.

Prosperity, stability, happiness. Potential for greater joy within the home.

Zorya had that *tut* on her tongue, the way elders sometimes do; she sucked her teeth and shook her head.

"People's emotions get the better of them these days," she grumbled. "They use magic for such stupid things. Magic is not a trifle. It shouldn't be used by those unwilling to try mundane ways of fixing themselves first. To practice Zagovory, one must be stable—wise and understanding the power they hold. But these days, it seems just anyone can go tamper with any magic!

"However, the power is still there. It comes from the old ways, after all, this magic: when used adeptly, yes, it brings great fortune to houses. And you can see trickles of history in the practices being done now."

I nodded and wrote quickly, my hand aching as I ground graphite against the paper. "Ooh—I agree, honestly, and thank you for your insight! Alright, alright, to be fair to everyone, we'll have to come back to that. To switch track back to you, Veles: some myths mention you steal from Perun and fight with him. Why do this?"

V4. WHY FIGHT WITH PERUN ALL THE TIME?

Veles didn't even bother pulling a card for this. I just felt the answer, so loud and clear that it was undeniable:

"Because I can."

That's it; that's all he said. And he said it with a big laugh and a shrug.

"Okay," I said, also shrugging, "that's certainly reason enough for me. Coming back to Lada, now, then: Lada, what's your favorite thing about spring?"

L4. WHAT IS YOUR FAVORITE THING ABOUT SPRING?

Like Veles, there were no cards for this question; she just gave a clear answer.

"There's no one favorite thing. How could I choose? All of it is magical."

"I understand that. Spring is a treat, especially after winter. Okay, then—Zorya, back to Zagovory: Would you elaborate and tell me what you want people to know about this magic?"

Z5. WHAT DO YOU WANT PEOPLE TO KNOW ABOUT MAGIC?

Zorya had a sharp stare, like a grandmother ready to chastise a group of children. She said something that reminded me of Hekate:

"Something people need to understand is that magic is neither a crutch nor a competition. It's not something to trifle with out of boredom. It's a real and powerful tool that everyone develops at their own pace for the sake of themselves and their community, not their every silly little whim."

"Got'cha, got'cha—and I completely agree. I appreciate you reminding us of this, Zorya. Now, Veles, to continue where we left off, why do you choose the form of a serpent when battling Perun?"

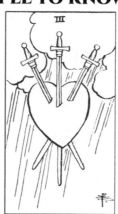

Melancholy and a broken heart. Misery, sorrow, grief at the end of friendship. Time eases the pain.

Fear or boredom may result in rash decisions; take care to consider all consequences before taking action.

Bitterness and hatred may develop from grief. Jealousy, inflexibility.

V5. WHY BE A SERPENT WHEN BATTLING PERUN?

You know what's embarrassing? During this time, I still hadn't made the connection between the Snake King in Slovenian lore and the fact that Veles was described as a serpent, not just a dragon. I wonder what he thought as I sat unaware, waiting for his answer.

Veles said, "The snake sheds its skin, and with it, all its past problems. Sometimes our fights are based off disputes, and sometimes not, but no matter what, this cycle of death and rebirth resets the score, you see. I can keep coming back as the old ways and problems are reset each time we fight."

"Wow, alright, nice!" It was the most poetic I'd heard Veles be. As a god of music, it seems that where there's music, there tends to be poetry, too. "Okay, Lada: how can mothers and children seeking protection find you?"

Guilt, deception, despair, anxiety, and lies. Words may be the root of one's despair. Self confrontation and self inventory must be carried out with honesty.

Experiencing fundamental, painful change. Transforms us with rebirth and rest. We come back stronger, even if Judgement is painful in its execution.

Healing, balance, harmony, cycles. Recognizing the inevitability of all things and making the best future without being rash.

I5. HOW CAN MOTHERS AND CHILDREN FIND YOU FOR HELP?

The ability to focus on results, ignoring all distractions and thoughts, is a skill shared by artists and warriors.

Beware of deception in your midst. Cowardice. Fear of change. Disgrace and abuse of power.

That which has been will be again. The eternal circles of life dominate our destiny.

"I can be found anywhere," she said. She didn't often lift her eyes; there was always some tiny touch of somberness I didn't quite understand. "But in focusing on doing what is right, and having faith that all phases of life, good and bad, are but phases, they can find me. One has to want to be strong for others to understand what I teach."

That made sense to me. I nodded and turned again, rotating in my mind's eye like I was on the world's slowest carousel ride. "Okay, moving on: Zorya! Some folk songs connect you to Venus, or a separate Morning Star, if you know what I mean. How do you feel about that?"

76. THOUGHTS ON YOUR CONNECTION TO "MORNING STARS"?

Here, she looked at me a little funny, but she laughed, and it was a laugh that sounded just like my Oma's. It startled me to hear it.

"Do you mean Lucifer, or demons, or some such?" Her smile was warm, lighthearted. "Well, let me tell you: being likened to demons is nothing new. We've all gone through this non-sense at some point or another, us gods not of this Christian faith that's all over the place now.

"But those folk songs remain *be-cause* people remember us. *Because* they remember me truly, and my role and my domain, and *because* they understand who I am and who I once

Tyranny and domination; a cold, cruel man.

Domestic dishar-mony. Tradition and resistance to change may lead to friction.

Courage in the face of adversity. Taking a stand to overcome hard-ship. Bravery rewarded.

was to them, even if not consciously. Yes, I think to be likened to Venus is a sign that I'm still here—shining bright enough for people to remember me, if not in their minds, then in their souls."

Remember. Yeah. Remembering the gods. Something about that idea struck me not in the head, not in the heart, but deep in the embers of the soul. This part of the interview was where things got weird as a result of that strike, but in a strangely good and nostalgic way: I felt like I was home, yet not. The best way I can put it is like when you return to your childhood home, where your parents still live and where you grew up.

It very well might still feel like home, even though you have your own apartment or house now. There are still memories etched into the tattered end of a couch, or the lamp that never worked right, or the mismatched tile on the kitchen floor, or any other number of odd details that you don't re-member or think about until you see them again. As I looked around at these gods that I was positive I'd never met before that moment, I genuinely didn't know what to do with that feeling. I didn't know what to say, either—not until I blurted out my confusion in a simple question.

"Why does it feel like I know you all? Like you're familiar?"

Zorya smiled so big that her eyes crinkled at the corners. "Of course we feel familiar," she said, so gently it was almost a whisper. "Your soul has roots here, in these lands, among these people, with us. You know us. We know you."

And then, flashing suddenly across that bruise-purple sky, was a face: God's face. God's face, with a little knowing smile, streaked across the heavens, as if to remind us He was there, too. Zorya, Veles, and Lada saw Him, of course, and a thick silence fell over us for a second before Zorya spoke again.

"He loves you, you know. That one up there."

I stayed quiet. There was no way to respond to that intelligently, not in that moment. It took me a second to recover my balance after her remark. It's one thing to read over and over again in the Bible that God loves His children and yada-yada, but it's another thing to have a separate entity—one who is divine, who understands Divinity—say it about you specifically. Moreover, it was a pretty crazy experience: to acknowledge that I was in a faraway place at some faraway time, deep in the past, and that then I was there, in my living room, wearing a different face and traveling through a different life, but was no less recognized by these gods of old. It might not make sense the way I'm writing it, but it's a feeling I can't really describe accurately.

All I knew was that there was something a little more complicated to the story of my soul than just "God made it." God made it, sure—that's why He was there, forever hovering nearby, forever watching me run around and explore the world ready to pluck me out of a problem—but He didn't necessarily raise it. Not right away.

For whatever reason, He found the Slavic gods worthy of raising it in His stead. Then, at some point along the many generations that it took to get to me, He came to collect it. That's the idea that smacked me hard enough to leave me dizzy there.

"Okay," I said, blinking this endless swirl of thoughts away, "back to the questions. Veles, you know, something interesting is that one myth mentions you take on the image of St. Nicholas to help a family. What associations do you relate to with him?"

V6. WHAT DO YOU THINK ABOUT ST. NICHOLAS?

Craft, diligence, dedication, and skill. Adaptation. One must commit to their craft in order to see results.

Self control, self inspection, and finding power to navigate adversity with grace. More mental than physical.

Weakness in work or team situations, incompetence, inability to delegate.

Veles studied me for a moment, then smiled. "That St. Nicholas, yeah. Well, you know, both him and I are like loners, when you think about it. We help those who need help, simple as that; we see trouble, we fix trouble, no matter who caused it—even if we caused it, honestly," he said with a grin. "All in good fun."

He quickly added, "But we never leave an outright mess. We want to help and have some fun on the way, St. Nick and I."

"I see." Though, as I hadn't spoken to St. Nicholas yet, I couldn't really compare Veles to the notorious Saint. "Alright, and Lada, I'm curious: what is something you want to teach?"

16. WHAT IS SOMETHING YOU WANT TO TEACH ALL HUMANITY?

That which we have worked for will bear fruit if we have the patience to wait.

Dreams can block the progress of one who doesn't know how to distinguish them from reality.

Injustice, false accusations, and prejudice.

Lada shrugged. "Well, I'm not one of the end of seasons, but the beginning. Humanity gets too lost in the vision of the end goal that they don't even consider all the possible things that could go wrong, and then they start blaming others. I want to guide humanity on being present, and focusing on the work they're doing, not the rewards they *may* get. Focus on the work first, the now, and let what reward comes when it comes."

"Makes sense to me!" I tried to respond intelligently, but my spiritual battery was running out fast, and my main focus was on trying not to rush the interview to the end just so I could go to bed. It was a growing weight on my head, the exhaustion, but I shook it off as well as I could and kept going. "That's some advice quite a few people could use, I think. Okay, Zorya, what is your favorite thing to help people learn?"

17. WHAT IS YOUR FAVORITE THING TO HELP PEOPLE LEARN?

"Ah, well." She smiled, clasped her hands. "That's that there's no reason to chase cheap victories. They mean nothing! Hard work, that's what people need to do: hard work brings true rewards that shortcuts and underhanded tricks can never bring. That's something people need to remember.

"And of course, I love teaching Zagovory, and magic in general. I love teaching humanity how to discover the mysteries of the world, and how to find and use the keys to this world through magic and knowledge. An enriching experience, it is."

"Yeah, absolutely," I breathed, enjoying listening to her talk. Then I whirled around. "But now, Veles, others also liken you to Loki or Hermes. What do you think?"

Unfair victory as hollow as defeat. Failure or a win against an unmatched opponent leaves one demoralized. Trickery, manipulation, unfair tactics; accept it.

Reap what you have sown. Basic material goals achieved; time for comfort. Hard work rewarded. Enjoy it. A favor to a friend.

Female intuition. Spiritual awareness and acceptance of life's mysteries. Secret knowledge, intelligence, intuition. Consider all factors before making decisions.

V7. WHAT DO YOU THINK OF COMPARISON TO LOKI OR HERMES?

Regaining inner strength and alliances.

Righting wrongs, accepting consequences, abiding by truth. Consider a situation before taking any other steps.

Greed, potentially shallow fulfillment, concern with material world.

Here, Veles made a face, like the idea was a dumb one.

"Good men, they are—good men! We're fellows in the work we do, yes, but we're not the same. We all have our different problems to address and ways of moving in the world. It's men who want to skip the work to know us, and who stamp our face on something they already know, that's a sign of greed—wanting our help without having the decency to know us by our names. They should talk to us directly rather than hide behind familiar names."

I nodded and focused on writing. "Got'cha, yeah, that makes sense. I guess it's easy to cross them when people are just looking for the similarities and nothing else. But alright, Lada: where do you go during winter? We know Marzanna goes to the underworld during spring and summer, but what about you when the opposite happens?"

17. WHERE DO YOU GO DURING AUTUMN AND WINTER?

It was a little difficult to find the thread here, but I got the sense that she goes to a difficult place—maybe the underworld?

"It's a yearly cycle," Lada said, "but it's difficult to give up my place on the world for a time and take the rest. It's hard to stay away when all pray for warmth and light again. I have to, though."

"I think I understand. Thank you for sharing! Well, that's it for the specific questions. Now, Zorya: how do you see yourself?"

Rivalry, disharmony, conflict, though transient.

Stress and pressure may become extreme; a time of loneliness may need to be overcome.

Must learn to govern our feelings to the utmost and let those loved and fought for go.

Z8. HOW DO YOU SEE YOURSELF, ZORYA?

Destructive excess. Can indicate arrogance. Friends may feel taken for granted.

Travel, a speedy journey, ideas made reality. News, action. Hasty decisions may be regretted.

Rivalry, disharmony, conflict, though transient.

Her brows scrunched in thought. "Myself. Hmm. Well, I will say that not all my aspects are those I prefer to be in, but I can't spend more time in one than another. I can't be too fast or too slow in my work, though I do ride about and carry messages on the World Clock to humanity—always have. I'm not one to hesitate, you understand? I get my work done, regardless of the thoughts of others."

My pencil flew, my writing always one or two words behind hers. "And Veles, you?"

V8. HOW DO YOU SEE YOURSELF, VELES?

Veles sat on a rock, arms crossed. "Well, you know, I'm someone that doesn't win all my battles—but that's okay. I don't need to. I'm not ashamed to admit the mistakes that lead to me losing a scrap; I'm not one to take things personally. Not easily bruised in the ego, because I know there'll always be a comeuppance." He winked at me. "When things go wrong, I'm always sure they'll go right again."

With a nod, I pipped, "Ah, I love that! Alright, and now Lada, how do you see yourself?"

Self control, self inspection, and finding power to navigate adversity with grace. More mental than physical.

Defeat, loss of control, or lack of direction.

Change in one's destiny apparent, but be cautious before jumping into something too good to be true.

18. HOW DO YOU SEE YOURSELF, LADA?

Logic and perseverance help overcome seemingly impossible obstacles.

Some things we think are good can hold us back. Need to question the values people decide for us.

Beware of sentimentalizing the past. Was it really better?

Her stare went sharp and narrow as a cat's. "For one, I know I'm portrayed as a goddess of love and beauty and fertility, but that doesn't mean I'm not also sound, powerful, and wise. Love and beauty do not mean vanity and stupidity. Gentleness is not weakness."

Fair.

"And sometimes," she added, "I look to the past, when people remembered my husband and I more clearly, but I can't keep looking there. There's no way back, only forward."

"Agreed. Thank you, Lada! And now, Zorya, how would you like others to see you?"

19. HOW DO YOU WANT OTHERS TO SEE YOU, ZORYA?

"First and foremost, I am a being of action." Zorya was staunch about this, her chin tipped up and her eyes shining like two sharp pinpricks of light. "I will never stand idle when my people need help. I am powerful, and I will do what must be done at all times. I take this seriously. Those who seek my guidance and protection will have it."

It was a strong answer, both in her words and the feelings she bore down on me while I wrote, and I sat there with those feelings before moving on.

I looked up from my book with a smile. "And Veles? How would you like to be seen?"

Brash, hotheaded, keen to do what's right. Getting things done. Righteous anger, courage, triumph.

What doesn't kill you makes you stronger. Protect those who can't protect themselves. Great strength of character.

Goals reached when you set on a path and stick to it. Success, fulfillment of dreams, achievements, creativity.

V9. HOW DO YOU WANT OTHERS TO SEE YOU, VELES?

Disobedience, resistance, and determination. Marking oneself in life.

Home, celebration, joy, harmony. Enjoy time with those you live. Get your home in order.

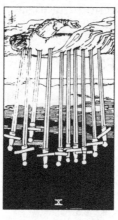

Power, advantage, domination, and authority.

"I am a liberator," he said as he got up and paced in the grass around us all. "Nothing feels better than going against the grain, especially when you know it's the right thing to do. But that doesn't mean I don't recognize kin!"

Given what I'd just felt with them all earlier—that while God made my soul, it was these gods that rocked its cradle—I think this might've been a little cheeky side note to me, too. Subtext and all that.

Veles continued: "I'm the authority of anti-authority, understand. I'm a leader, but I lead my devotees to the sense of self only being free and in good humor can get you."

That made me smile. "Aw, Veles—that's awesome. I love that. And Lada?" I turned to her, the smile still hanging on my lips. "How should we see you?"

L9. HOW DO YOU WANT OTHERS TO SEE YOU, LADA?

Lada stood up from her place on the rock and hovered over me, gold hair tickling my face. "People should remember: I keep the balance between life and death, with Marzanna. But it isn't a bitter fight; it's just the way of nature. I won't suffer intolerable situations, nor do I advise anyone else to.

"And another thing," she said as she wandered around the grove. "When things people say get to be too offensive, or my talents aren't wanted, I leave. No one is forced to be by my side, and I'm not forced to be by their side, either. If people want to call me a fake goddess, let them. They won't hear from me."

Running away from an intolerable situation.

Rivalry, disharmony, conflict, though transient.

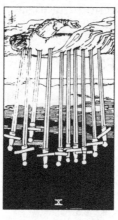

Hidden forces may work against you. Don't misplace your trust.

It was a cold statement, chilly despite the sunshine that glimmered off her. "Understood," I said. "Well, okay. Before we all part ways, are there any messages you'd all like to share? Zorya, starting with you, is there anything you'd like to say I didn't touch on?"

Z10. ANY LAST MESSAGES, ZORYA?

She shrugged and shook her head. "I have nothing to say I haven't already said, so no."
"That's fair! Alright, Veles, how about you?"

V10. ANY LAST MESSAGES, VELES?

Assuming the worst and misunderstanding one's or someone else's needs.

High, almost foolhardy energy. Act more recklessly. Be more assertive or more brash and forthright.

Carelessness, pessimism, lethargy, or roadblocks in achieving one's goals.

He grinned, as if I were a funny little thing, spinning between the three of them all this time. Though he knew I was tired by then, too, halfway to the temporary grave that is sleep—but do you think that stopped him from giving one last message?

"If you have things you want to achieve," he said, "there's no room for self pity! Shake off the stagnation and do something that makes you feel wild, untameable. Give no one permission to constrain you; live on your terms!"

What a god. Veles is a seriously fascinating and foundation-breaking energy; I know Kresnik isn't a big fan considering Kresnik, in Slovenian lore, is the one Veles fights under the title of the Snake King, but it's really such a treat to be around divinity that's all about being wild and free.

"And Lada? Any messages you'd like to share?"

L10. ANY LAST MESSAGES, LADA?

Lada looked over her shoulder at me. Again, her eyes held some faint sadness, her frown just pulling the edges of her lips down, but she had strength in her voice:

"People want their good fortune to come to them a certain way, but rarely does it," she said. "Be grateful that fortune is here at all. Focus on growth, on how all these blessings can help, no matter how they come, and be patient and graceful with others to avoid squandering blessings."

Once I'd written the last word of her response down in my notebook, I honestly just let myself flop back against

Understanding difficulties is the first step to overcoming them.

We don't always recognize good luck, which sometimes comes when we can't properly appreciate it.

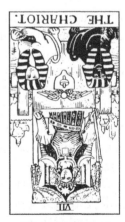

Dispute, defeat over a petty matter. Don't let small disputes become major problems.

the couch and breathe for a second. My eyes were closed, and that meant my mind had nowhere else to go but the grove we'd all sat in all the while. A grove that felt so much like a home I'd never seen—like soil that had fed my soul so very long ago, the way new garden soil feeds a transplant germinated somewhere far away, in the greenhouse or on another farm, with an expert's guidance.

"Alright, well," I said, pausing to exhale as much of my exhaustion as I could, "thank you so much, all of you. These answers have been so insightful, and I appreciate you taking the time to give them. I do hope I'll get to see you again, if you ever decide to come by—but until then, the only thing left to say is *se vidimo!*"

They smiled at me, the smile of long lost family, and then all bled away to nothing. I clapped my hands together to snap myself out of the lingering fog a meditation like that leaves behind, and then I was fully present in my living room—alone, with nothing but the buzz of the silence itself, and a bowl full of cherry pits where there was once a good bundle of fruit.

Like Lada had the whole time we talked, I hugged my knees to my chest. There were so many answers I got from that interview, and yet it seemed there were more questions sprouting, too: how is a soul's trajectory determined? Which part of one's ancestry can lay claim to a soul like this? Why did God make my soul and leave it with the Slavic gods rather than just hold onto it Himself? What was I supposed to *do* with that feeling of Family-But-Not-Family I had with those ancestral gods?

At that moment, I only had the answers I'd spent all night recording, and those would have to be enough for the time being, because my head felt like it was stuck in cotton. Bed. Sleep. Rest. That was all I could think about as I disposed of the gods' offerings and called it a night.

As is usually the case, I remembered no dreams. But you can be damn sure I slept all the way through the night, heavy as a rock floating all the way down through a river to get firmly stuck in the soft riverbed.

MARY
MOTHER OF GOD

Did you know that the Immaculate Conception doesn't refer to Jesus, but to Mary?

It's said that when Mary was conceived, she was born completely pure and without original sin—something that, after a *lot* of debate, became an official and inarguable part of Roman Catholic dogma in 1854. The Immaculate Conception was what made her the perfect person to bring the Son of God into the world; the whole Adam and Eve mess never even touched her, and *through* her, no woman ever had to be worried about that silly old curse anymore, too. In fact, one of her many devotional titles (outside the more well known ones, like *Theotokos*, or Mother of God, and Queen of Heaven, and Co-Redemptrix), is the New Eve; she fixed what had been considered "broken" for so many centuries.

In many works of art, her blue cloak, a symbol of her status as Queen of Heaven and her pure heart, her holiness and her deep faith, is often blended with rich hues of red underneath in artwork, signifying also the blood of martyrs and her own Son, the suffering love of a Mother, and the humanity still present within her. However, oftentimes you may also see on her head a crown of twelve stars, and at her feet is sometimes a moon, sometimes a snake. Much of it comes from this bit of the beginning of Revelation 12:

And a great sign appeared in heaven: a woman clothed in the sun, with the moon under her feet and a crown of twelve stars on her head. She was pregnant and crying out in the pain and agony of giving birth.

Then another sign appeared in heaven: a huge red dragon with seven heads, ten horns, and seven royal crowns on his heads. His tail swept a third of the stars from the sky, tossing them to the earth. And the dragon stood before the woman who was about to give birth, ready to devour her child as soon as she gave birth.

And she gave birth to a son, a male child, who will rule all the nations with an iron scepter. And her child was caught up to God and to His throne. And the woman fled into the wilderness, where God had prepared a place for her to be nourished for 1,260 days.

There are many different ways we can interpret this. It could just be that the writer of Revelation was copying off of the myth of Leto's birth of Apollo so that a Hellenic audience might better understand the implications, the parallels, between God's kingdom and Zeus's (and therefore make it easier to replace one with another). It may be that this Woman is actually a representative of Israel, or the Church, given that Joseph has a similar dream in Genesis of the sun, moon, and eleven stars bowing down to him (which is what gets his brothers so ready to do some mean things to him before he gets caught and sold to Egypt). It could have nothing to do with anything and just be a really cool fever dream, too, honestly. But I'd like to think that this woman is Mary, and what a thrilling narrative Revelation 12 gives us, of Michael and his fellow angels whooping that dragon's ass as it tries to chase after our dear Heavenly Mama.

Nothing can touch her, and nothing can stop her from doing what she needs to do by God's design. And in Catholic doctrine, especially, Mary is the great intercessor, one who has a direct ear to her Son and who, wherever she goes, has the whole host of heaven's angels by her side. Feared by demons, loved by God, Mary is a striking, fascinating figure—and one who's had to do a lot of work since the advent of Christianity to keep what peace could be maintained among the many new people that Rome brutally, misguidedly conquered in her Son's name.

You see, while Jesus Himself is often pictured as a baby under the hood of her blue cloak, sheltered there and sharing in her human nature, it seems that many native goddesses of many different nations have likewise taken refuge under that mantle and aligned themselves with the figure of the Heavenly Mother. Because the Israelites' Mother Goddess, Asherah, had been erased with the reforms of King Josiah, and the Christian religion had a Father, and a Son, and a somewhat feminine Spirit, but no official Mother, Mary has come to also stand in as the archetypal Divine Mother that so many other cultures would've otherwise lost forever in the colonization and conquest of their lands during the first thousand or so years of Christian spread. There have long been reports of apparitions of Mary appearing near the temples of pagan goddesses, and stories of her becoming "sisters" with figures such as La Santa Muerte. There are also stories of her appearing exclusively to women and children, which is what had so many Popes and other religious leaders so wary of their Mother.

Though she did appear to one man in the 13th century: St. Dominic. It was him that she taught how to make the first rosary and told to pray the Our Father, Glory Be, and Hail Mary instead of other prayers and Psalms that religious folks and monks used to pray.

There's so much more I could say about our Heavenly Mother, who I've always known as Mama Mary, but I'll tell you a little bit of my own experience (or, rather, my own mother's). Mary, if you didn't know, is a matron and intercessor for those trying to start families, and my parents wanted a child so bad but just couldn't have one no matter how hard they tried. At one point, my mother gave up. She tossed it into God's hands and told Him that it was up to Him whether a kid was in her cards or not. Then, that week, she says she saw a flash of Mama Mary's face, bright and clear as any other person's if they were standing in front of her. She was smiling, with twinkling eyes and dark curls framing her beautiful face. A moment later, she disappeared.

That week, my mother found out she was pregnant. And twenty-five years later, here I am, writing all this up. I've got a Mama Mary pendant on my key chain and in my wallet, as well as a bronze pendant of her that I like to wear, and several beautiful rosaries. To hold them, according to a dear friend of mine, Kyle (@king_kylie1405), is to hold her hand, and to pray the Hail Mary is to ask her to come sit with you—and of course, where she goes, the angels go, and where the angels go, Jesus goes, and where Jesus goes, the Holy Spirit goes, and where the Holy Spirit is, there is God.

It's an important prayer, no matter what the other denominations tell you. Trust me.

But now that you've got a bit more context on our Heavenly Mama, let me tell you about my own bona fide experience with her: the Queen of Heaven, the Mother of God.

In my research of Mary, the one thing that really made me feel somewhat ill was the way in which so many more strictly conservative sources seemed to sap her power away with how they spoke about her. They made her seem so meek and quiet, perfectly obedient, perfectly tame, incapable of even swatting a fly for fear of hurting its little wings. But the Mother who demons fear, who thwarted the dragon, who bore the Son of God, and who would viciously protect Him wasn't that meek and quiet image the traditional (read: misogynistic) folks had in mind.

So when her name appeared on my Patreon poll that week, I went and set my table to come face to face with the *true* Mary. She's associated with flowers like roses and lilies, and the blue of her cloak we talked about was once a hue made with lapis lazuli—a stone that's deep blue and flecked with gold as if mimicking the sky—and so I set down two cups of rose tea, a paper rose by her picture, lapis lazuli, and two other stones: moonstone for the reference to the moon beneath her feet, and blue lace agate to represent that peace, comfort, and serenity she carries to her children. In the center was a metal box with a picture of her coming to a few children; inside that box was a beautiful Portuguese rosary.

Speaking of the rosary, I had my own larger rosary wrapped around my hand. Starting with the Lord's Prayer and moving onto the Hail Mary, I invoked Mama Mary and asked her to come close, so that I might ask some questions.

And as fate would have it, it made sense that the image of some sweet and meek little woman didn't sit right with me, because when Mary came in full splendor, with a crown of diamonds that sparkled like stars and rich red robes similarly dotted in crystals, there was nothing meek about her. In fact, she was *massive,* just like some paintings I'd seen of her where she loomed over other humans there to honor her. Her dark curly hair was long and shiny, her eyes a piercing blue-green, huge in her head, and she had a laugh that boomed from her chest when she saw me standing in the doorway of wherever we were, as well as a big, full-lipped smile.

We met in a place made of marble, with shiny floors and a big red-cushioned throne surrounded by gold in the back, vases of pale clay dotting the sides and high ceilings. It had the atmosphere of a Catholic church, silent and still in a way that made voices seem hushed even at normal talking volume. But Mary beckoned me over and set up a table for us to sit at in front of that throne, a plain wooden table like you might find in any average person's house, and the two cups of tea I set out were there on it.

When I looked out the door I'd come through, I found that this cathedral was in the clouds; you could see a village down below, houses dotting green fields, while we sat high above it all.

"Clouds?" I grinned as Mary towered over me. "Really? Is Heaven really like this?"

I laughed a little, too, but 'll tell you a secret: I was afraid. It was so stereotypical, this slice of heaven. What if I was making it all up? Even as I got more and more used to meditating like this, and diving into these intricate, beautifully fashioned spaces that Divinity wove for me to sit with them in, there was always that creeping doubt: *what if I'm just fooling myself? What if none of this is real? What if I can't actually speak to Divinity and just have an overactive imagination?*

"It can be," she said as she fingered the handle of the teacup. Her voice snapped me out of those thoughts underpinning my meditative state—just wiped them away, as if telling me to *trust* with all my heart, and honestly, I didn't have much of a choice but to do that. Her chin rested on her hand as she stared out there. "The outer edge, anyway. This isn't all there is, but it *is* where I like to come to watch the people, you know?" How rosy her cheeks were when she smiled. "I love watching you all."

We sat there for a second, just enjoying the silence, before I sat up and got to work. "Alright, Mama, as I'm sure you guessed, I'm here to ask you a few questions. I know I don't reach out often, but I hope to help people understand you better, and so I'm ready to dive in; are you?"

Mary was not, and is not, demure. She leaned over on the table, tracing patterns in the wood, and she had a soft, easy smile, a shimmer to her eye.

"Of course," she said with a little wave of her hand. "Ask away."

And then, to my surprise, she chose Threads of Fate's Weaver Tarot to speak with. I thought for sure she'd like something like the Golden Tarot, but this was the real Mary, after all—not the sanitized, gold dusted, statuesque creature that centuries of poorly veiled misogyny created. There was an edge to her, serrated and ancient, underneath the glory of her crown and the richness of her robes.

"Okay, so—first question that's burning away at me, is what was going through your mind when Gabriel came to speak to you?"

1. WHAT WAS IT LIKE WHEN GABRIEL CAME TO SPEAK TO YOU?

She blew out a long breath, her eyes gone wide as she shook her head and held up a hand, and we laughed a little; I figured this might've been a hell of a question.

"I was terrified," Mary said as she stared into her cup of tea. "The one I might've sought guidance from was the one asking me to do this, God—but Gabriel was patient and kind, and he was willing to wait for me to make a decision."

As Mary said that, in the corner of the cathedral/throne room/people-watching station was a flash of a man robed in white and blue, with blond wavy hair, white feathered wings: Gabriel, flickering in just for a moment to give us a smile before he blinked away. Mary grinned after him, then continued with such warmth in her eyes.

Find balance and peace. Be open to different opinions. Rigidity in viewing people or the world isn't good. Detach from confrontation. Realize possibility of human grace and growth.

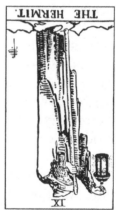

Isolated too much—time to reconnect with the world. Too much of a good thing is a bad thing. Trouble finding solitude in quiet moments.

Those who refuse to pause and relax are handed a big time out from the universe. Not smart to ignore one's needs for progress.

"He was willing to wait for me to calm down. I had to consider things, you know—the dangers, the challenges that would come with being a still unwed and pregnant woman at the time. But I'm glad I chose to do it. That card you pulled, that reversed Hanged Man, is right: it's not good to ignore your needs and just dive into something for the sake of getting some kind of progress, but I knew better. This wasn't just about progress, nor was it just about me; this was about all of humanity. I understood that very well."

"I can see that. But speaking of motherhood and all that—what was it like to raise Jesus?"

2. WHAT WAS IT LIKE TO RAISE JESUS?

Those doubts came to eat me again, because this big beautiful Mama, and all the gold and marble, disappeared. All I was left with was shadow and darkness and a Mary that seemed like a wraith of her former self. Her cheeks were gaunt, her curls stringy and plastered against her sunken cheeks, and her eyes were big and watery enough to swallow the world and all things with it. I wondered if maybe I'd gotten the wrong entity after all, or if I was, in fact, just making this all up, but then her parched lips parted, and her voice trembled as she spoke.

"The grief." Her eyes threatened to swallow me. "The grief, goodness— nothing about raising Him compared to those moments at the cross. What followed was the worst three days of

Grief, loss. Moving forward is hard; the vision of the future is gone. Rely on community; don't dwell on the past. Forgive.

Those who refuse to pause and relax are handed a big time out from the universe. Not smart to ignore one's needs for progress.

A steam roller. Emotional detachment and ambition create success and trouble. Brashness creates impulsive reactions and confrontations.

my life before He rose and came to us after. I would've rather suffered infinite difficult days with Him as a child than do that again.

It wasn't just that she said those things: it was that she *projected* that truth, those feelings, and that was when I realized it: this was the manifestation of her grief. The dark circles under her eyes, the wraith-like nature of her—as if saying *never again, never again*—and the viciousness I felt lurking behind us in the dark.

As utterly un-Mary-like as it seemed, I understood: this was her. The Mother of God that demons feared. One who would tear forward with a fury only matched by God's own angels, riding on limbs unnaturally long and gaunt, with nothing but pure rage, pure grief, pure desperation wrapped on her bones. She would rip her way across the earth, ready to destroy anything and everything that threatened her babies; she was one not only clothed in the sun, but who had swallowed the sun into her eyes, her stare burning all to ash—her robed head wreathed in the fiery golden light of God. A protector by way of destruction, a force so primordial and resolute that none could escape her.

However, one of the sorrows of Mary was knowing this horrible death would happen to Jesus, per the prophecy of Simeon when she brought baby Jesus to the temple for the first time. For all this ancient motherly vengeance, there was none she could direct at God, and she knew that; she knew what was to happen had to happen. Her only option was to swallow this fear and this hurt, though, for the sake of something bigger than her and her Son's earthly body, and that's where the idea of obedience to God really shines through: she had to just trust Him, even when that primordial mother's instinct told her to snatch her baby back from the edge of death. That prophecy was giving her time to come to terms with it. From what I understand, though, having that prophecy didn't make it any easier.

After a moment, that image of the avenging Mother faded, and we were back at the table with tea-cups in our hands as if nothing ever happened. My heart was heavy for her, and her lashes brushed her cheeks as she sighed. It didn't take long for her to find her smile again, though—a teasing smile that could find humor in the past as much as grief.

"But that moment aside, raising Jesus was... not always easy," she admitted. "As a mother, the thing you need to do is take breaks. I had Joseph, a wonderful father to Jesus, who helped me raise Him. Oftentimes mothers don't give themselves breaks, but you *need* to, if you're going to do right by your children. Can't just keep going and going.

"As a boy, though, Jesus had a way with getting into trouble; He was driven by logic, ration, the hard, Divine truth He had in Him. Unblinded by ego, He would say things others might've wanted to ignore or even deny, and it came to confrontation, even danger at times. But He was determined; He knew, even as a child, what He wanted to say, and He was going to say it no matter what."

We laughed together, and I felt that this card, Knight of Swords, was exactly describing young Jesus. Anyone who's read stories about Him as a child knows He got into some nonsense, and He wasn't afraid to keep getting into it, too. I can only marvel at Mary for being able to gentle parent the Son of God, even when He tossed a fabric maker's wares into a big pot of black dye and ruined them or let His poor parents get halfway home from Jerusalem without realizing He wasn't there with them.

"Oh, yeah—I can imagine," I said. "I remember a few stories about what Jesus got into. But alright, okay, moving on from that: so many Popes tried to bury your prayers and rites, too, only to bring them back, then bury them again. What do you think of all this?"

3. WHAT DO YOU THINK OF POPES BURYING YOUR INFLUENCE?

Her face struck me. She wrinkled her nose and scowled here, nearly rolled her eyes. One card from the Weaver Tarot, the Knight of Wands, was also a picture of a torch with two arrows, a snake coiling around them. It mirrored the Two of Coins, a card of balance. Knowing Mary's image is often seen stomping on snakes—symbols of evil in these images—this was interesting, and so was her answer.

"Those men, those Popes," she muttered, "they couldn't decide who and what I was to the Church. All this nonsense was because they were afraid, and wholly unequipped for, the work I do. Fear and overwhelm were a constant for men who didn't know what place women had in their world.

Delicate balance interrupted. No longer able to keep up. Frozen and overwhelmed. Put some things aside and re-evaluate.

Getting results. Unbridled enthusiasm and motivated pursuit of goals. Chase your dreams and bring them to action, but don't rush it.

A period of burden. Maximizing output. Pushing will get you where you need to be, but don't be afraid to delegate.

"But as in all things, there's a balance here, a delicate one, between Man and Woman, between all energies in general. They went and toppled that balance. I have no care for the nonsense they did; it never should've been done."

Once I was done writing, I sat back and took a sip of my rapidly cooling tea. "I see," I mused. "I get that completely. Although, actually, can you elaborate on that, the work that you do? How do you represent the idea of the Divine Feminine in Christianity and help people with it, especially considering so many are also all about Asherah and Hagia Sophia these days?"

4. How do you represent the Christian Divine Feminine?

Instability in finances and the home. Focusing on the immediate future without consideration for the long term future.

A period of solitude. Focus on yourself. Vocalize your needs, connect with others, and set healthy boundaries.

Creativity, dreaming, formless energy. Throw away preconceptions; be open to exploring what's new. Information revealed.

Mary nodded here and leaned over the table, looking straight at me. Her stare alone could've burned up my body and left my soul hanging there like a lost star.

"Listen to me carefully," she whispered, as if telling me some great secret that not even the other angels of heaven were allowed to hear, "all the mysticism and spirituality in the world is nothing without practicality alongside it. Men thought, and still think sometimes, that women are unequipped to understand spirituality and the unseen things in this world, but all that mysticism, that dreaming—of course women can understand it. Men who deny that women are spiritual beings delude themselves.

"However, those who chase after spirituality alone, going only for the unseen, delude themselves as much as those who shirk it entirely for base, material needs. You have to keep your affairs in order, your needs met, if you're to chase after the glory of God. No use in ignoring your body—it's a part of you that God gave you." Mary sat back and tossed an arm over the back of her chair, and I was surprised, yet encouraged, by the iron certainty she seemed to carry in every inch of her. "I am the Mother of God, and yet even I took breaks to care for myself when I needed to. Motherhood is often a thankless job, but regardless, it's not one you can do ignoring yourself and your needs. I am the Feminine that sets boundaries; I am the Feminine that encourages the solitude necessary to build *oneself*, so that we might build and support others."

It was with this answer that I really noticed it: for all Mary's bold ways of speaking, she had bold mannerisms, too. She spoke like a queen yet carried herself like the common woman: strong, weathered, secure, with a grace not so soft, refined, and regal like one would think from how Catholicism always describes her, but sharp and stern, hardened by time and experience and duty. She waved her hands as she spoke, like any older village women I'd ever known, and all this time, she'd certainly made it clear when something displeased her or amused her in these questions. During this question, it seemed she noticed how I noticed that, because she elaborated.

"No one can be so soft spoken and mild to the point of being taken for granted and reach their true potential," she said with a gentle smile. "Not by letting people walk all over them—by disrespecting themselves like that. We are God's creation, and we deserve respect from all, *including* from ourselves."

"Oh, wow. That's a beautiful answer!" And it was making my hand cramp to try and keep up with her as I wrote, but it was worth the pain. "Now, on the flip side, there are these pagan sites, too, that insist you're not just a human woman, but a goddess, completely divine in your own way. What do you think of that?"

5. WHAT DO YOU THINK OF THE IDEA THAT YOU'RE A GODDESS?

Delicate balance interrupted. You're no longer able to keep up. Frozen and overwhelmed. Need to put some things aside, pause, and re-evaluate.

Partnership that's balanced and healthy. Both sides are invested and committed. A relationship manifests opportunities.

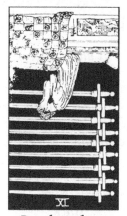

Paralysis from deep shame and negative self talk. The mind is chaos, pushing you to exhaustion. Recognize how hard you're making things. Awareness propels you out of your headspace.

Again, Mary wrinkled her nose. She grimaced as she shook her head, as if the idea was uncomfortable.

"I am not a goddess," she insisted, her voice quiet yet solid. "Never was. For the Church to dismiss me, for women to worship me—both upset the balance I walk. I neither need nor want worship. I just want to help.

"I forge deep relationships with those who look to me because I want them to be free of the guilt and shame they carry simply for being born women, or not men."

I paused my writing to ask: "What about folks who aren't men or women? Do you want that for them too?"

Mary nodded. "I want it for all. The Church took a holy office and demonized it. There is no shame in being Woman, or rather, Not Man; we are not lesser. Men tried to cut away the power of things distinct from them, to put themselves above it all. It's wrong."

"And so I'm guessing that's what you help with?"

There were no cards, only a pendulum swinging in a wide circle. A resounding, clear yes.

Her words bloomed in my mind. "I want to help women remember that they are worthy and holy. Jesus loved the women in His life. Of course I want people to go to my Son above all, but when they come to me, I want them to know balance—that all things have their place in this world."

"That's awesome, thank you! I love this." I mean, how could I not love listening to the most highly honored woman in Christianity so concretely speak for those that the men of the Church just left behind? "Okay, okay, next question: there are so many Saints and other entities in Heaven, too, that people might work with as they work with you, and I was wondering: why would people want to work with a Saint, rather than toughing everything out with God directly?"

6. WHY WORK WITH A SAINT RATHER THAN ALWAYS DEFAULT TO GOD?

Questioning the long-held beliefs about happiness, connections, priorities, etc. There's more to life than money. A beautiful step towards bringing joy and lessening resistance.

Convention and growth in rigorous practice. No shortcuts. Traditions are there for a reason. Dedicate yourself to a new area of study. Teach. Structure and tradition in one's practice.

A blockage in creative flow. Low self-worth or the feeling that creativity has become work. Review creative relationships and see where you feel stuck.

It was that Hierophant card that really hit me. But as I wrote the card meanings down, and they started to lay themselves plain in my head, Mary filled in the gaps for me.

"There are many roads to God," she explained. "Some people, like you, are more lax and informal They don't have any set item they want to work on, and instead want to focus on building a relationship directly with God. This is fine. But with Saints, those practitioners who find value in *tradition* and *structure* will do excellent; the Saints can help them focus on specific goals, as can angels. Building that structure, going by old ways and rigorous set-up, we can say it's traditional for a reason."

"Do you mean like, with novenas and rosary meditations and whatnot?"

"Yes. These things work. They build focus, full concentration on the matter at hand, and create a grounded space. It takes time to sink into them; they can reform your thinking."

"Oh, cool; I never thought about it this way!" Though I will admit: doing an entire rosary meditation shuts the brain off it in a way that feels so very good when you're used to your thoughts flying a mile a minute. "That's really nice, actually," I said as I thought about it. "And, okay, we're getting towards the end of our questions, so: how do *you* see yourself, separate of all these other associations?"

7. HOW DO YOU SEE YOURSELF?

1. Rapid movement to emotions, someone heart-led in actions. Illusion is involved. Be mindful of your path.

2. You may be acting a bit passive or abusing power, and that's not suiting you. To earn respect, you must give respect.

3. The ebb of life, bumps in the road. Strength and resilience in the face of loss; be curious of the possibilities.

Mary once again got pretty serious here. Her voice was powerful; even without raising it or yelling or anything, you could just feel it in your chest as she spoke, as if it were booming.

"I *am*," she said, so simply, with no room to question it. "I say what I say. I do what I do. All of it, for the people. I have no interest in garnering undue power, nor do I care to be quiet and mild when the situation doesn't call for it.

"I am a Mother, and mothers can't be one thing all the time. I am full of love, emotion, guided by intuition and faith with a nod to practicality. I am strong. I've seen many things, felt many things—and yes, I am resilient. I said I would rather endure infinite difficult days than experience what I did with my Son on the cross again, but in truth, it's for the people. If I had to do it again, go through all that again, all to ensure my Son is heard, I would."

"Wow."

Not gonna lie, I was just blinking at these cards for a second. I knew Mama Mary was no gentle little lamb, but I also never expected her to be so severe! It was amazing.

"Okay, well," I twirled my pencil and went for my pendulum again, "is that how you want to be seen, too? It sounds like it."

8. HOW DO YOU WANT TO BE SEEN?

The pendulum swung in a big circle.

"Yes," she said, "but also, I want people to understand: I am not without a voice. I am not without an opinion."

"Alright, got'cha. Heard loud and clear! And speaking of being heard, do you have any messages you want to deliver? I know we have a lot of non-Christians that follow these interviews as well, and I think it'd be cool if they could get a better picture of you, too." I paused and shrugged. "Or just a message for me is fine, too; whatever you want."

9. ANY LAST MESSAGES FOR ME OR OTHERS?

What did I expect, honestly? Mama Mary just dove right in, a sharp nod and a hard-set face.

"This is a message for all: the time of spiritual awakening is here, and you should release your reservations and dive right in," she said, her voice tight with a motherly urgency. "I can say with absolute certainty that anyone that wants to chase that spiritual awakening is safe with God, with my Son, with the Saints and angels, but no matter who calls to you on your path, *do your due diligence.*"

And speaking of Jesus, there at the doorway was suddenly a man dressed in simple white robes, with curly dark hair and eyes just as

Carrying a large burden from oneself or others. You must release it. It may take time, but it needs to be gone.

Dominion over all things mystical. Step into the subconscious and divine realms. Reclaim wisdom, prioritize spiritual relationships.

Convention and growth in rigorous practice. No shortcuts. Traditions are there for a reason. Structure and tradition in one's practice.

bright as Mary's. If you've ever seen Akiane's *Prince of Peace* painting, it was a spitting image, and I knew just by the way the energy shifted that it was Jesus—there just to be there, smiling big at His Mother, who kept on in her stern guidance.

"Know the entities who reach for you well, no matter where they come from," she said, and her brows were set not in anger, but in such a granite seriousness. "Know how these entities want to be approached; be sure they are who they say they are. Create the container for a healthy practice and find the time to be grounded in your work. It'll help you in all ways, especially that structure. Don't take shortcuts. Do what's best for you, and let us all be saturated in Divinity."

"Fantastic." I couldn't help but rub my eyes as the information sank into my mind—and I couldn't help a big yawn, either, given how late it was. "Thank you so much, Mary; this is incredible! It's been a pleasure, and so now I'm calling it a night. But I'm sorry it took a Patreon interview for me to reach out like this; I feel like I should've been doing this all along."

Mary only shrugged. "Your path is yours. God is the goal, and it's God you focus on. That's what matters. Now go to bed."

Her face softened with that, and I swear, Jesus laughed a bit in the background. There was my Heavenly Mama, sending me off to bed like the silly little child I was. I had work in the morning, and I was eating into the few hours of sleep I allotted myself each night the more I sat there, but the thing about these interviews is that once you get rolling, it's really not so easy to just stop.

Though as I went to bed that night and reveled in all those beautiful answers, the grandness and strength of the Mother of God, it was the image of that haunted, gaunt Mother, eaten up by grief, that still lingered in the back of my mind. To this day, it's a startlingly clear picture—a duality to Mama Mary that, for most people who get taught the one dimensional version of a meek Mother, just doesn't get considered or acknowledged, as if she wasn't allowed to be sad in the first place.

I'll be the first to stand up and call that a grave injustice to her. But me, at least, I know I'll never forget that haunted, grieving Mary.

ARCHANGEL MICHAEL

Michael. What is there to *not* say about Michael?

I think in online spaces like witchtok, Michael has become an unexpected top name to hear pass around, given the amount of folk witches, Enochian magicians, and religious practitioners like Jewish and Christian mystics that have come boldly into the fold of public spiritual life. And as I've said before, if God is like a bottle of full sized-perfume, Michael is like the travel size. His name means "He Who is Like God," and it's for a damn good reason: of all the angels in Heaven, Michael is the Right Hand of God, the chief warrior of all the angels, head of the seven Watchers that still remain in Heaven, the protector prince of the entire nation of Israel, and the one depicted as having cast Lucifer out of God's house.

(Granted, we know a bit more about that story now.)

Like a winged superhero, Michael is the one named in many celestial battles, as well as the one responsible for locking up quite a few fallen angels in Sheol, or the Jewish concept of the underworld (which is not necessarily hell, but more just a resting place for the dead, from what I understand). He's also an angel who, in many mystic and magical traditions, is a guardian of the cardinal direction of South, the element of fire, and the season of Summer. In Damien Echols' *Angels and Archangels*, who I referenced for the sigil I used to invoke Michael with God's permission, Michael is described as one who can help people with all matters of discipline—be it physical, mental, or spiritual.

When Michael came up in the polls, I was ecstatic. Of course, I'd seen Michael a bit before—all that Roman legionnaire armor, that chin-length brown hair and those glorious brown eagle wings, the strength that simply *poured* off him—and I was thrilled to be able to talk to him face to face. Before that, I actually hadn't really done so, if you can believe it. In my practice, I run to God first, and God almost exclusively. Don't ask me why, even as I and these other Divinities I speak to tell you about the many different roads to God; for some reason, I've always just been comfortable going straight to the Source, no matter how intense and overwhelming that Source is.

But again: there is *so much benefit* in speaking to these other entities, and for many, an archangel like Michael—He Who is Like God—is easier to approach. Barely easier, yes, but easier.

And this interview... this certainly tells the story of what it means to encounter Michael, and any angel, really, as you'll see. It was my first taste of working with him directly, and it blew me away. Even then, it still wouldn't come close to the things he taught me further into our journey together, which I'll tell you about afterwards.

For now, let's take a moment to appreciate the warrior leader of the angels of Heaven.

Like I said, I used Damien Echols' *Angels and Archangels* book for the sigil of Michael, and knowing he's associated with fire, I had out some typical items to represent that fire: a yellow chamomile-scented candle from the summer guest altar, sticks of cinnamon, and carnelian and sunstone. As a nod to his status as a warrior, I also had a piece of tiger's eye and my deer antler knife, and because he's an angel, I had a piece of celestite. This last stone acts as an angel antenna of sorts, and so I always pull it out for any talk with angels.

In front of me was a card from Doreen Virtue's Angel Oracle deck, one with a *blond* Michael holding a sword and shield (and wearing... just a bit of white cloth around his waist for some reason). The card itself was a "You Are Safe" card, I guess pulling on Michael's protective guardian imagery.

Around this time, I hadn't yet read James L. Kugel's *The God of Old*, from which I learned that angels don't eat or drink. That's why I was so confused when I kept trying to figure out something edible to offer him, and I kept getting a signal like, *no thanks*. No matter how much I asked, and how much I double-checked, it was always the same: *no, I don't want anything*.

So I just shrugged and moved on. I settled into my usual meeting space, lit my candle and some frankincense, said the Lord's Prayer and St. Michael's prayer, and I asked God to let Michael through. Once I'd confirmed he was there with the pendulum, I closed my eyes and let the darkness behind my eyelids shift however it needed to shift.

"Hello, Michael!" I said, trying for confidence in my voice. "Welcome! Before we begin, can I get a feel of your energy?"

The first thing I noticed, interestingly, was a heaviness in the stomach. Like an anchor, almost—weighty and secure. There was warmth, too, and Michael appeared sitting on a small chair or throne over the clouds. He started with how I usually imagine him: wearing steel armor with red robes, almost like a Roman soldier, with brown hair, wings made of light, eyes burning bright.

His jaw was strong, his nose straight and hard, his brow set over those burning eyes. His arms were huge, his chest broad, and he had the feeling of an army general.

But his colors shifted after a while—his hair going from brown to gold, his suit blue, just like the Emperor card in Doreen Virtue's Angel Tarot deck, if you've ever seen it. At one point, a totally separate face came up under moon and stars, too, a long blue robe that I realized wasn't Michael, but Gabriel. He kind of looked like a Byzantine painting of him, with a thin neck and a very round face with big eyes. For the second time, I'd seen Gabriel pop by, and it delighted me.

"It's always you two together," I said, chuckling. Gabriel smiled and settled, and I continued. "Hello, both of you. Gabriel, did you want to answer questions, too? Would you like to do this together?"

Gabriel shook his head here. It seemed he just wanted to pop in and say hello before disappearing. Then it was just Michael and I, and he had an air like he found all of this pretty amusing; the bend of his lips as he smirked gave me this sense of robust energy, an individual so confident that not all the world could weigh him down.

"Okay, well," I reveled in the feeling he gave off; it was a sunny, bold, powerful energy that just lit my spirit up, "in that case, Michael, let's dive right in! First things first: upon reading about how you are the advocate of Israel, and Satan the accuser, can you tell me how these roles work together?"

1. HOW DO ADVOCATE AND ACCUSER WORK TOGETHER AS TITLES?

As soon as I pulled these cards, I noticed him standing there, arms crossed, looking over my shoulder. It was like he was inspecting the cards to make sure they accurately captured what he wanted to say.

"It's self explanatory, isn't it?" He wasn't yelling, but his voice hit like a fist nonetheless. "Listen, now: one seeks to find fault in the subject, and the other to defend against the condemnation of those faults. God is judge: He must hear both arguments. Though I will say, some aren't very original in their arguments," he said with a curling smile. "Nonetheless, it's about balance. Nothing is all one side or the other."

"True, yeah. That's fair." And I guess a little self explanatory. "Okay, well, how about this: when reading certain texts and ideas between religions where you appear, they say that one shouldn't ask you or Gabriel to intercede, but to go directly to God. When is it appropriate to contact you?"

Do what is right. Fairness, justice, equal opportunity. The strong should help the weak.

A corrupt man, or one who holds grudges. No imagination.

2. WHEN IS IT APPROPRIATE TO CONTACT ANGELS?

A departure. A charming, attractive, enigmatic person. Beware disloyalty or fraud by someone you trust.

An important journey. Travel across water, transition, leaving behind hardships, finding new understanding.

As I pulled the cards, the first one made me pause, mostly because it made no sense to me. "Are you... sure you want this one?" I groped for some feeling to tell me *no*, that I'd made a mistake, but as I closed my eyes, I saw Michael standing there with a brow quirked high.

"What are you doing?" He pointed to the card. "Put that down. Pick the next card, and you'll see. It'll make sense."

"I—alright, if you say so."

So I picked that next card, and I still didn't quite get it. It took a while of stretching these concepts, diving into their more abstract meanings, for me to make heads or tails of it, and the whole time, Michael was watching me like a teacher watches a student perform a demonstration in chemistry class. Apparently I'd struggled enough after a while, because he finally showed me how to stitch those threads together into an answer that I could work with:

"I seek out injustice and rip it out like a weed," he said.

"Serious issues of the soul, where there is only oneself to blame and one's own actions repent for, only God can fix those. But peril with others—betrayal, for instance—or getting the discipline required to become a more powerful and centered individual? These are things I assist with in the name of God."

"That makes sense." Sort of. "The Right Hand of God isn't a position you hold for nothing."

He shrugged. "It certainly isn't just a title."

As I shuffled the cards again, I nodded. "Alright, alright. Getting to our next question: I read that one of your roles is as an angel of death, separate of Azrael's duties. That you give souls one more chance to redeem themselves in the hour of their death before weighing them after. This sounded a lot like Anubis's weighing of hearts, and I'm curious: is this the same thing?"

3. DO YOU HAVE SIMILAR HEART-WEIGHING DUTIES AS ANUBIS?

There was no life in the cards as I shuffled, which meant it was time for the pendulum. As the crystal swung in a large, affirmative circle, Michael answered me.

He walked behind me with slow, measured steps. "Yes. This is a way of determining the fruits of a soul's last life that deities of various pantheons use to decide next steps for their journey."

"That's cool!" I was sitting cross-legged in the clouds, right at the edge of Heaven. We hung over the earth, and risking toppling down to the ground so many miles away. Knowing that it was a meditation and not physically real kept me from getting nervous about it. "And speaking of yourself as an angel of death, your position in Heaven—what's it like to lead God's army?"

4. WHAT IS IT LIKE TO LEAD GOD'S ARMY?

There was a note of something here that was a lot more melancholy than I expected.

Michael paused and looked over the edge of the clouds. His face was flat, blank, as if he couldn't allow himself the emotion. "I am a general. It's as with any army: you organize. You care for your soldiers. You don't send them on useless missions. You deal with mutiny."

This was where the melancholy really set in, though, and his blank face shifted; it went stony.

"But the hardest battle I ever fought in Heaven wasn't a battle of swords, but a battle of wills. Sweet words are as sharp as any sword."

I wasn't really sure what to do with that last line, honestly. The only way it made any sense was if I combined it with Lucifer's admission that he left Heaven willingly, and the knowledge that other infernals followed him. But with that came the implication that there was never actually any great war in Heaven, but a great *debate* instead. A heated debate, a heaven-rending debate.

"Okay, okay, I think I got'cha. On that note, though," my curiosity ate me up once we got to this subject, "what is your opinion of the Divine Infernal? And Lucifer?"

THE HIGH PRIESTESS

Female intuition. Spiritual awareness and acceptance of life's mysteries. Secret knowledge, intelligence, intuition. Beware over enthusiasm and consider all factors before making an important decision.

Unfair victory is as hollow as defeat. Failure or a win against an unmatched opponent has left you demoralized. Trickery, manipulation, and unfair tactics used, but you need to accept the outcome.

5. WHAT IS YOUR OPINION ON THE DIVINE INFERNAL?

Gain at the expense of others means emotional bank-ruptcy. Greed cost-ing everything.

Do what is right. Fairness, justice, equal opportunity. The strong should help the weak.

He wasn't looking at me by this point, but sitting on that throne and just staring out over the world with his chin in his hand. There was nothing but steel in his eyes, and a crease to his brow that cut into his face like fault lines in the earth. Then he gave me the longest answer of the night.

"Infernals have different methods than we do," he mur-mured. "They're fine using any means to get what they or their followers seek. This is effective, but dangerous: they're not so concerned with God's justice as they are their own. It's justice on their own terms. This can be difficult to work with, as you have to learn what justice means to them.

"Moreover, not all who go to them do so with good inten-tions. Some seek infernals expecting to take shortcuts or exercise pettiness. They expect to *use* infernals like servants, underestimating them entirely. It always backfires; the Di-vine Infernal is not to be made into someone's bitch."

"Oh. Damn." Were angels allowed to swear? "I mean, fair, but what about Lucifer specifically? Is any of this message about him?"

Michael side-eyed me like I was silly. "No. I'm not interested in speaking on him."

I blew out a breath and said, "Okay, fine, we can go to our next question: some denominations seem to think you and Jesus are the same entity. What'cha think of that?"

6. THOUGHTS ON THE IDEA THAT YOU AND JESUS ARE THE SAME?

Michael shrugged. "There were so many good things ascribed to 'He Who Is Like God' that man wanted to give Jesus legitimacy with my image. But Jesus is Son of God. I am not. I am God's creation. Some might see us angels and try to explain us away, focusing only on the Trinity, but this is an error."

The thing is, though, that as he talked, I couldn't stop star-ing at him. I mean, his cloak was just so blue here, his hair so blond, that before he could even answer, I found myself blurting out something else entirely.

"Michael, I'm sorry, but I'm confused. Isn't it a bit stereo-typical to be in the clouds, as an angel? And Damien Echols' book says you're represented with red. I'd like to see you with red. Why are you wearing blue?"

And by *stereotypical*, I meant *fake*. I meant *wrong*. I meant, *I'm making this all up,* and *this isn't really Michael,* and *I'm a fraud,* and *I'm just talking to myself in this living room,* and *I'm going to be eaten up by whatever monster I've accidentally let in.*

Generosity reward-ed. Financial good fortune, wealth, security. Favors reciprocated, debts repaid. A gift or in-heritance. Sincerity, trustworthiness.

Bitterness and hatred may develop from grief. Jealousy, inflexibility.

Doubt is a hell of a drug.

But even if I was pretending to just take the piss out of Michael and his choice of setting, there was no lying to an angel. Especially not the angel that was like God. He knew that I was ruffled as all ever, scared and unsure of anything I was doing in that moment; he knew I'd accidentally stepped into a deep, dark lake of doubt and was thrashing and floundering trying to get out.

It was at this point that weird things happened: I felt like I was losing my grip on the sight of him, and then there was just red. Nothing but red, like red haze, with two dark eyes hanging suspended in it all. This was his energy: fiery, powerful, raw.

"We don't have bodies," he said, and his voice came from everywhere, all around me. "We aren't contained to any one thing. Nothing is set in stone. Whoever says anything about what is and isn't, is irrelevant."

Then we were in a different location entirely, not in the clouds, but in a place that felt awfully familiar—because it wasn't real. It was a Dark Souls map, specifically Dark Souls 1, at the bridge in the catacombs. It was as if he went searching through my memories to go find someplace I'd like more than those silly Hallmark-style heavenly clouds.

But let me tell you, being in a *video game map* didn't make me feel like this was any more legitimate. I huffed and grumbled, "Why are we here?"

Michael, once again in the shape of a person—the brown-haired person in the red and silver armor—said, "You thought the clouds too 'stereotypical.'"

I blinked. "Michael, this is a video game map."

He shrugged and waved a hand. "All the same. What does it matter? It's not as if there are any physical locations or faces you need to concern yourself with. If you like this, we can stay."

"I—"

Then he was crouching down to get eye level with me, and his face was right in mine. "Listen to me," he said as he grabbed my shoulders. "Stop doubting yourself. So you see blue and not red—what of it? So you see clouds and think that'll make people scoff—what does it matter what they say? Your doubts are getting in the way of you truly seeing and accepting what's before you."

As if to make a point, he flashed between brown and gold hair, red and blue clothes, like he was saying *it's all of no consequence to me.* So I really had no choice but to relent. As soon as I shrugged and accepted he was going to do whatever the hell he wanted, we were back in the fluffy clouds of Heaven's edge.

I rubbed my eyes and tried to massage the budding headache from my temples. "Fine, then," I said with a sigh. "Let's move on. Say someone wanted to work with and approach you: how would they go about doing that?"

7. HOW SHOULD PEOPLE TRY APPROACHING YOU FOR HELP?

He didn't want to pick any cards. He just speared me through with a clear thought:

"Don't. I approach those who need me. God decides who I work with. Not humans."

"Oop—alright, then." That wasn't an answer I expected. "How do you see yourself?"

8. HOW DO YOU SEE YOURSELF?

Again, he didn't seem to want to pick any cards. It was only the card I used to represent him in the first place, the "You Are Safe" oracle card. The depiction of him there, with the golden hair and the big wings, it suggested he wanted to be seen as a sunny, bright, vibrant energy; he is light and power, refined and deadly, yet warm and safe. The words I received from him confirmed it.

"I am a guardian. I will always fight for those who need me."

"And how do you want others to see you?"

9. HOW DO YOU WANT OTHER PEOPLE TO SEE YOU?

Bondage, disillusionment, loss of hope. A time of difficulty. Indecision makes things worse. Trouble ahead, illness or misfortune.

Financial security brings artistic freedom. Support, private labors, personal betterment, lack of materialism, good use of wealth.

This answer was clear as day as I wrote down the tarot cards' meanings, but Michael explained nonetheless. He sat in his throne and stared holes through my head as he spoke.

"When all else is lost, and one hits their limit, I am the one who drives you to chase discipline. Discipline creates the strength to overcome adversity and let go of fear: you keep moving, no excuses. One has to make the decision to help themselves. I hold them to that decision, so that good things follow."

"Oh, wow, okay." Gotta love an angel like Michael; if you say you want something, you bet he'll make you work for it. "I definitely see that. Is that the message you want to leave, too, or do you want to say something else?"

10. ANY LAST MESSAGES FOR PEOPLE?

Here was the only time he chose three cards to answer a question. Two were knights, one of which was actively striking down a dragon, which made me think of how Michael is always seen crushing Lucifer or a serpent (even if he doesn't actually spat with Lucifer like people say he does). It could've also been a reference to his being the angel to strike down the dragon, that "Satan," in Revelation. They were also riding, away from the reversed King of Swords.

His voice was undeniable as I took in not only the card meanings, but the imagery. "Hear me: if you believe in your cause, *fight*. This is a dangerous era. Band together; your leaders no longer serve you. They look out for their desires and interests, not yours.

A brash young man, hotheaded but keen to do what's right. Getting things done. Righteous anger. Bravery, courage, heroism. Triumph over opposition.

An adventurous young man. Putting ideas into action. Eagerness. A journey or move into a new home.

Tyranny and domination. A cold, cruel man.

"This isn't about any one specific thing happening today. This is about the state of the world. Change occurs with radical action. The world cannot hide from the sun; strike evil underfoot. The only enemy is injustice, and that enemy takes many forms."

The feeling in my chest as I got this message was tight. Like I'd just taken a massive breath in preparation to yell across a battlefield. I got the sense of embers, too, fire, which Michael is associated with. My hands felt like they couldn't write fast enough, and the muscles in my arms were tense, as if ready to brace against a strike. To say it was intense would've been an understatement.

"Okay, damn." I shook my hands out as I threw the pencil down. "That does settle it, I guess. Thank you, Michael; I appreciate the message. And, well, that's all I had for now, but I appreciate you coming to talk, and I hope we can work together even more someday!"

At that, Michael smiled, but then he was gone as quick as he arrived. All the clouds of heaven, the little throne he'd parked out there, it disappeared until there was only me and some rocks and a little yellow candle. So I packed up all my stuff and went off to bed like always, and I wondered what it would be like to get further into working with Michael.

As my path progressed, I'd certainly find out. I'll tell you all this: if you want to level up your discernment like nobody's business, if you want to learn what it means to play around in the big league and get some confidence on levels unimaginable, and if you're not afraid of a pretty good spiritual and mental price tag, Michael's your guy. He's the one who taught me, in very extreme and intense ways, that there was *nothing* in the spiritual world that could hurt me without my permission—that the only one who could decide my downfall was God first, and myself next.

He taught me how to not be afraid, even if it meant cutting off my own arms and knocking me down. He taught me how to challenge myself when I was holding myself back, and he taught me how to push for one more rep in the gym, one more word on the page, one more step in my journey, even when I didn't think I had one more *anything* left in me. He taught me what it meant to be like God, and it's helped reduce the thick, heavy doubt to a whisper of its former darkness.

I don't know if I'll ever be completely rid of it, or if it's possible to be—because after all, it *is* wise to question if what you're seeing is legitimate, and to test the things you hear, the spirits that claim certain names and titles and whatnot—but I've never walked with more sureness in my step, and I've never been so *unafraid* of the world and all the things creeping in it, seen or unseen. After all, doesn't Jesus Himself say it in Matthew 10:28?

> *And do not fear those who kill the body but cannot kill the soul. Rather fear Him who can destroy both soul and body in hell.*

There's only One that can do that, and with Him, it's not about fear at all. It's about *trust*. And knowing that, there's absolutely no reason for me ever to fear anything again—not so long as God decides I need to keep on trucking.

So until He decides it's time to stop, that's exactly what I'll do, and thanks to Michael, no one will ever convince me to do anything but that.

ARCHANGEL RAPHAEL

What can I say? People love the angels, and it was no surprise to me when yet another angel was chosen off the polls. When that angel was Raphael, I'll be honest: I was a little excited, because I know that Raphael is not only the guardian of air, the direction of East, and the season of spring per Damien Echols' book, *Angels and Archangels*, but also that he's heavily associated with Mercury (and especially Gemini because of his affiliation with air). Given I'm a Virgo, which is also ruled by Mercury, though, I figured there was a little something of a connection there. Beyond all that, he's also the angel of healing, and often, you'll find nurses, doctors, or other health professionals calling on his aid, or sick people looking to him to intercede for healing.

And you know, Raphael is a very cool angel. One of the few angels actually mentioned in scripture, I think one of his most famous appearances is that in the apocryphal Book of Tobit. When Tobit, a blind man, sends his son Tobias on a mission to get some medicine from the city, a stranger appears and offers to help him find his way around. They get the medicine together and rest by a river, where this mysterious stranger tells Tobias to catch some fish for lunch and save the guts.

On the way home, they discover the house of a woman, Sarah, whose father has already buried seven of her husbands. Each time she marries, the demon Asmodeus comes and kills her new husband before they can officially consummate the marriage, which essentially makes it as if she's never been married at all. This stranger tells Tobias to go and marry that woman, and that when the demon comes, all he has to do is toss those fish guts in the fire and fan its smoke towards it to get it to run away. Meanwhile, Sarah's father is already digging him a new grave and thinking him another idiot about to lose his life to this awful curse.

But Tobias does what he's told, and Asmodeus flees, and then Sarah finally gets to consummate her marriage and keep her husband. Tobias takes her home to his father, and when he's able to see again, he sees his son standing there with a new wife, and with the helpful stranger that reveals himself to be Raphael (and later... chases Asmodeus to Egypt and binds his wings there just for fun). It's one of the funniest stories about angel and demon shenanigans because it's so incredibly Looney Tunes, but it's also a good indication of Raphael's character: he's tricky, he's discreet, and he's *severe* when it comes time to knock someone (like poor Asmodeus) around.

So let me show you a little bit about how I experienced this incredible angel.

Just like with Michael, I figured Raphael might not want anything to eat or drink, but I still dragged my big Virgo mug out for my own cup of tea. Once again, I also had Doreen Virtue's Angel Oracle deck in play, with Raphael's "Healthy Living" card to represent him, as well as some malachite, regular quartz, and celestite to represent healing, clarity, and communication. The two lavender bergamot candles I had, along with some chamomile tea, said *healing* to me, and his sigil from Damien Echols' book laid out in the center of my table.

When everything was set up nice and pretty, I burned some rosemary to cleanse the area, anointed myself with holy water, said the Lord's Prayer and asked God's permission to speak to Raphael, and invited him in. He confirmed he was there with the pendulum swinging in wide circles and chose Threads of Fate's Weaver Tarot for his answers.

Once I was in the zone, I settled in and closed my eyes. "Raphael," I said, "welcome. Can I see you? Can you show me where you'd like us to be?"

First, coming into the scene, I was right away met with a face that was marginally strange—some real Uncanny Valley stuff. Like with Gabriel, who sometimes pops in, it was as if some Byzantine painting had come to life: I stood in that cloudy place overlooking the world, which I believe is just the edge of the celestial boundary, and I saw a pale man in green robes with curly brown hair and eyes so massive and black that they swallowed half his face. I wasn't sure if what I was seeing was actually Raphael, and so I asked—and Raphael, like Michael, then whirled me through a number of appearances to the point that I almost couldn't keep up.

We ended up in a forest, where he became a man with a green robe, sharp golden eyes, and longer brown hair, then a man in a golden helmet with skin that looked brittle and dry like charcoal, and then a man with golden wings, then with more ashy wings that had gilded feathers—and then it all changed again to a single eye rimmed with thick lashes, staring, surrounded by six wings, with stars swirling in that eye—before eventually, we settled on the first thing I'd seen to begin with. The round-faced, robed man with the curly hair and massive, infinite, dark eyes.

I nearly got whiplash just sitting down in my living room. Nonetheless, the message he gave me was clear: *it doesn't matter. I look how you want to, and are able to, perceive me.*

So, yeah. Quite the interesting opening to the meditation there before starting my questions!

"Alright, well, thank you for joining me, Raphael," I said, and I opened my eyes if only to try and orient myself a bit after all that action. I cleared my throat and shook my head. "I have a few questions for you. To start us off, while I know your name means 'God Heals,' how did you get your other associations, like travel and communication?"

1. HOW DID YOU GET YOUR OTHER ASSOCIATIONS?

Raphael mixed the golden helmet and green robe as we sat in the forest, as if to hide the face that he must've known was giving me a bit of distress. After all, it was freaky, those giant black eyes and that Byzantine art style he came in! But then, Raphael leaned against a tree and spoke.

"Through the success of stories like that of Tobit, I suppose I garnered a reputation: a healer and then some. Since I also bring prayers to God, including confessions, this would be showing my role of communication."

He showed me images here, too: I saw a young scholar struggling over books, with Raphael guiding his reading, one angelic hand pointing at the pages from over the scholar's shoulder.

"I lift blockages," he said. "I aid in knowledge and intellectual pursuits. Angels are here to empower people by making them see *truth* first and foremost, and that the biggest downfall one has is their own selves. As such, these other things I deal in are also healing, as healing goes beyond the physical: it is the mental, the spiritual, the emotional. All of you know what you have to do. I am here to tell you: do it."

Acknowledgement of public success/victory. You've persevered through challenges, and it's paid off. Careful of your relationship with success. Stay curious to possibilities.

Repression of guilt. Trying to justify actions so that you don't have to make amends. Air things out and move forward.

You're freer than you think. You have power to change, but sometimes you need to hear the tough love. Pushing boundaries, moving forward, beating self doubt.

"Ooh. That's intense." And the freedom in which he was just *showing* me things on top of telling me—that was something that took a bit of getting used to, as if I were entering a whole new level of this claircognizant thing I was building. "Okay—so speaking of that healing, what medical advancements intrigue you the most?"

2. WHAT MEDICAL ADVANCEMENTS INTRIGUE YOU THE MOST?

KNIGHT of WANDS.

1. Feeling dissatisfied with life. Relationships feel stale or disconnected. Try to re-establish connection with yourself and others.

2. Getting tangible results. Enthusiasm and pursuit of goals brings success. Thoughtful, purposeful action. Haste and poor planning does no good.

3. Partnership, whether romantic, friendly, or work related. Invested, committed, respectful partners with a deep bond and connection.

Raphael stared. His stare wasn't unnerving, but it was a swallowing, gripping gaze. He thought for a moment, but I heard him whisper as I looked through the meanings of the cards I pulled:

"The mental."

When I finished writing the meanings, he sat near me.

"This is an interesting era, where humanity is concerned with their minds as much as their bodies, maybe more. Many would benefit from quieting their mind in this world, and it pleases us that you're learning: work without rest is waste. The advances in mental health intrigue me."

"Ah, yeah—that is an interesting one. But regarding healing in general, I understand that you enjoy healing plants. What are your thoughts on the persecution of herbalists?"

3. THOUGHTS ON THE PERSECUTION OF HERBALISTS?

Here, I was hit with such an energy of perseverance; it felt like I'd been gripped by eagle talons that would never, ever let go. His helmet was gone, and his face was pinched, his frown making his eyes seem that much more massive. He confirmed his anger at the demonization of herbalists' work with the pendulum when I asked for clarification, but his words were those of hope.

"I helped people keep the knowledge of plants and find ways to ensure it stayed alive," he said. "Even the smallest things. One piece of information is like a key that opens the doors to a corridor full of rooms, in that as you unlock each room, you discover more items and tomes and, yes, more keys,

You're on the edge of change, but resisting it. Resisting change you know is coming just makes everything harder.

You're freer than you think. You have power to change. Pushing boundaries, moving forward, beating self doubt.

Need for structure. Make progress through consistent focus and work. Build your vision brick by brick.

to continue going. Those little pieces were all humanity needed for the knowledge to linger—and here it is, returning again now, both in your modern medicines and in more traditional remedies. Such information could never be killed completely. There is *always* a way to defeat the ignorance of those that would bury knowledge."

"Oh, wow." That intense energy threatened to choke me, just by the sheer weight of it filling the room. "Absolutely," I whispered, "I agree. And in that vein of modern medicine, what do you think of the state of people's general health today?"

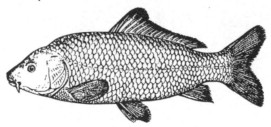

4. WHAT DO YOU THINK OF THE STATE OF PEOPLE'S HEALTH?

Hard truths and tough love, intellectually plugged in. Not always do we get the answer we want to hear. All about truth. No attachment to the outcome. Separating fact from feeling and being unbiased.

You've endured many struggles but achieved success. Victory will require effort. Patterns and history at play. Tend your wounds and learn to weather the sunny day. Survivalism.

Stuck in a pessimistic mindset. Not seeing the good in life stops you from achieving true potential and wisdom. Restore some play in your life.

He looked away from me.

"This world isn't suited for health," Raphael muttered, and his face soured. "Those that *could* obtain health physically, mentally, and emotionally are blocked by many things: the denial of responsibility, the damage from life-long struggles that leave them drained and pessimistic.

"Some people have never learned how to be strong and in good health, while others' strength has become a curse that forces them to forever be on guard, in stress. As I said: endless work is waste. Where there is no rest, there's distraction and survivalism that plagues the mind, body, and spirit. Many deflect from doing what they need to do to heal because they don't want to face the truth, thinking they aren't strong enough for that reality they're ignoring. A sorry state, the world is in."

I paused my writing. "I think I understand where you're coming from, but I do want to clarify: you don't mean everybody, do you? Like, what about people who have chronic illness that'll never be cured? Are you talking about them?"

"No, of course not. Those are the people who need the most support," Raphael said. "I'm talking about those who push to the point of breaking themselves into pieces."

I pursed my lips and nodded. You know that saying, the one that starts, "if the shoe fits"? Well, consider this shoe a glass slipper, because it fit me *perfectly*.

"So, that being said," I started as I tossed that thought out the nearest mental window, "how do *you* help people regain their health in a world so unsuited for it?"

5. HOW DO YOU HELP PEOPLE REGAIN THEIR HEALTH?

Passiveness isn't suiting you; abusing power isn't suiting you. Remember that respectful leadership works. Unplug from your to-do list.

Intuition, subconscious, divine realms. Logic isn't the best place right now; prioritize spiritual relationships. Reclaim wisdom, find stillness.

Stuck in the ebb with challenge after challenge. See where you play a part rather than playing the victim. Accept recent changes and move forward.

Raphael stood up and paced about the forest we were in; his cape swirled around him, and his helmet was back on, shining even in the dim light. As he stared off through the trees, he said, "By showing them that they need to take responsibility, first and foremost. They need to take as much control as they can if they want to improve; for those things out of their hands, I help them remember the things they *can* control, and the ways in which they *can* access higher qualities of living despite all the barriers they face.

"I help them step away from this world that demands they steep in their stresses. I encourage them to retreat to the place within, where their wisdom lives. I help them find accessible means of healing, of accepting their situation, and I show them that there is no shame in asking for such help to live in peace."

"I see, I see!" Sometimes it frustrated me, how slow I wrote; my handwriting got sloppier and sloppier as I raced to stay one word behind him. "Thank you for sharing that! Okay, on a different topic: your stories have you showing a man how to get rid of the demon Asmodeus. Is there any bad blood, so to speak, between the angels and the demons?"

6. IS THERE ANY BAD BLOOD BETWEEN ANGELS AND DEMONS?

1. Carrying a large burden. No matter the origin, you need to get rid of it, no matter how long it takes.

2. Enjoying success. Harvest is here, stability secured. You've worked hard. Independence won. No point in joy if you can't share it. Joy and abundance in all ways.

3. Quietness. Small victories. Balance within the self. Personal acknowledgement of progress. More awareness than celebration, with minor roadblocks to overcome.

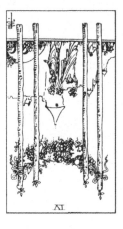

Again, the helmet was gone, and there was this pinch in his face. It made him look so angry. I think he wanted me to see him angry like that, so I paused the shuffling of my cards.

"I, um—Raphael, is this a question you don't want to answer? I can think of a different one—"

"Shuffle the cards."

Oh. I blinked at him and just kept shuffling, and sure enough, there was the sting in my ears that suggested which cards needed to come out, like needles getting jammed straight through to my ear drums. I flung the cards out as if that would get the feeling to go away, but it was overwhelming, and so was Raphael's presence as his words buffeted me like a summer storm.

"This world cannot continue like this," he snapped. "The feuding, the picking sides, the nonsense— it's blocking progress. I have no qualms with the infernal, no care. What I care about is that people are seeing *the whole coin*: seeing us, seeing infernal, and seeing it *all* as a part of this world. Seeing the value *all creation* holds. One cannot be without the other."

I won't lie, as I was writing and reading these cards, I got scared. It seemed so unlike anything you'd *expect* an angel to say, and so I started wondering: *is this really Raphael? Is this really what an angel of God would say? Or am I just inserting myself into these answers?*

And I got smacked for it.

"Sara!" His voice was thunder, shattering the trees and scattering their leaves. "This is *no time* for your doubts!"

And then he flared his whole being, stretching himself into something different; his eyes were shining with blue-purple stars, his body morphing into nothing huge wings that hovered over a glowing patch of gold in the pink-edged clouds, all awash in the evening sunlight. His wings were gray with glimmers of gold at their edges, and he, himself, was nothing but a massive eye between all those feathers, staring down at me. Even when I'd tried to banish the image altogether, until nothing was left but the blackness behind my eyelids, there was one giant eye outlined there, staring straight through me.

"You know the truth," he said. "You already understand what I'm saying. The knowledge of good and evil humanity has is imperfect, unlike that which we angels have. It's deceived you countless times, confused you as to the truth: *all things are necessary.* When the world sees this and understands that there is no left without right, or light without dark, when they *understand the value* in all things, then the feuds may finally subside. The world will be whole again: the coin in its entirety represented."

"Okay, alright, I got it! I understand, fine." I opened my eyes once more to get away from the intensity of the images, but it didn't make a difference; his words weren't just in my head, but in my very bones, and they wouldn't ever come loose. "But," I shivered with the last scraps of wayward energy and took a breath, "okay, to continue: I understand angels appear to people who aren't of the Abrahamic faiths at all. Why and how do you help people outside the faith?"

7. WHY AND HOW DO ANGELS HELP NON-ABRAHAMIC PEOPLE?

Focusing on oneself to create beneficial long term patterns and habits. Building the life you want on your terms. Independence.

Illusion and compulsion coming from your shadow. Believing lies that cause harm. Subconscious wounds and darkness.

A need for focus and discipline. A beginning of a journey. Don't distracted; later, you can have breathing room, but not now.

Raphael shrank back down from that giant winged eyeball in the clouds to talk in that little forest grove again—a normal man, wearing a green robe, with the golden helmet hiding his face.

"Our first priority is the advancement of humanity," he said. It's a God-given priority." How curtly he said that, as if it were really that simple. "There is no gatekeeping this help; all who need it shall have it. This healing is available to everyone—but keep in mind it isn't free. It costs effort, and struggle; those who do no work will see no fruits. Still, we angels help cultivate the healing through discipline and the facing of harsh truths. This is not a teaching style that suits all people, but it is how *we* teach. Those who want and thrive in this type of teaching are the ones that will benefit the most from it, of course."

"I see. I do know some people who have had some trouble with angel teaching styles, so that makes sense. Okay, well, we're onto our last questions: how do you see yourself?"

8. HOW DO YOU SEE YOURSELF?

The way the energy turned with this question threw me for a loop. Raphael seemed almost wounded here, for lack of a better word, but he turned again with that severity and seriousness.

"I am let down by humanity, with what hope I had in them," he said, and I felt the venom in how he hissed each word; he was furious with us. "I feel betrayed, for all they've done so clearly against the guidance of God. I didn't understand why humanity would do things like this and struggled with it for a long time. You were supposed to be *better* than this!"

I froze as his words hit me, pelting down like hail. Oddly enough, though, his sentiments reminded

Struggling, uncertain. Losing sight of intentions for public validation. Falling into false optimism.

The ebb of life. See where you play a part rather than playing the victim. Accept recent changes and move forward.

Bumps in the road, ebb of life. Assess your needs. Strength, resilience, courage, and a mindset shift necessary.

me of Lucifer: the disappointment and frustration he so clearly had for humanity, the disdain that muddled the love still there. Was this something that united all angels—even fallen ones? What really separated a fallen angel from their still-heavenly counterparts, then?

"Now you're getting better," Raphael continued, quieter, "but I still feel as though I had a hand in this somehow. That I should've done more. I never asked permission to, as I thought surely people would do so themselves. But someone should've done more—and that is what I am. Someone who should've done more."

Have you all ever consoled an angel? Because right there, I did. I stared at him for a moment as his head hung low, and I looked up towards the sky, to wherever I felt God was.

"Hey," I said, "come help us, here, God. Let me know: was there anything Raphael could've done to make anything happen differently?"

I even pulled out the pendulum, and it swung in a straight line: a hard and fast *no*.

"See that, Raphael?" I dared to sidle closer to him, and I peered into the dark holes of his helmet, but there was nothing there to see. "You couldn't have known. You couldn't have done anything that you didn't already do."

"But I should've—!"

"Should've what?" Again, I searched for God. "God, forget *could*: can you tell me if Raphael *should've* done anything differently?"

Again, a strong, undeniable *no*. And I got the sense deep in my gut, the sudden knowing, that things had to happen the way they did for a reason. So I said as much.

"Listen, bud: you do realize that humans have free will, right?" I dared to put my hand on his shoulder, and the wool of his cloak was rough against my hand. "That we gotta make our own decisions?"

Raphael paused, then nodded. "Yes, I'm aware."

"Well, alright, then. You know that we need to make our own choices *and* mistakes. There's nothing to be done about that; things happen how they need to happen, even if it hurts to watch."

He stayed silent for a long time. Then he said, "I know. But I still wish there was more I could've done to make more of you understand what you needed to understand."

I sighed. There was nothing to do about him feeling that way, really, so there was no choice but for me to move on and maybe take his mind off it.

"Alright, well, next question: how do you want others to see you?"

9. HOW DO YOU WANT OTHERS TO SEE YOU?

QUEEN of PENTACLES

THE STAR.

II

1. Reliable, nurturing, grounded. Keeping things simple. Formidable in business despite being ingrained in the home. Creating a secure and harmonious environment.

2. Alignment and harmony, relief after challenges. For those depleted by life, this brings lighter times to be expected. Those who went through the ringer haven't hardened. Keep courage.

3. Facing difficult, confusing, and chaotic decisions. Feels like there is no "good choice"—but make a choice so you can move on. Limbo is stressful.

Here, it was pretty clear again, and Raphael stood up straight. I kept hearing the word whisper in my head as I wrote the card meanings: *healer, healer.*

"I am a healer, first and foremost," Raphael said. "I stabilize people, get them on their feet. and help them rebuild their strength to face the future. For all that has happened, *I am still here.* I still want to help. People need help. I want people to be their best, but they must understand they need rest and recovery to do so; no one can heal and become their truest selves when they lay in shambles. I help people move on from patterns that keep them in shambles."

"Wow. I love that." And I could only hope to learn some of that from him myself, given that I was once again doing this late at night, as I apparently had a bad habit of doing. "Okay, last question: do you have any messages for me or others?"

10. ANY LAST MESSAGES FOR OTHERS?

In fact, by this point I'd been lamenting on the side how late it was getting, as I was tired. This interview took way longer than I thought it would. I was exhausted by this point in the night, and I went to pull more cards, but Raphael only smiled at me rather than choosing. I confirmed he didn't want to pull any cards, and then he said:

"One shouldn't push themselves to ruin just for results. Now go."

I swear, somehow I always end up getting send to bed by literal divine entities. I never would've expected such a thing in my life, but there I was, once again, being told to call it quits and head to bed. He let the background fade away, himself disappearing into the darkness of my closed eyes, and that was the end of the discussion for Raphael.

"Goodnight," I said, at that point to no one and nothing—though maybe he still heard me. He probably did, honestly.

But after that, I closed the communication, and I just sat there decompressing for a little bit before hurrying off to bed. Raphael—what an angel. And once again, what a wild encounter—one that gave me two more questions for every answer I got. He was right about quite a few things, but one of the things he was most right about was the fact that there was a lot more going on than meets the eye.

One coin. That phrase, it was lodged into my brain for a good reason, and I knew Raphael knew it, too. My dad's dream was coming up again and again in those days, the dream where God was the judge, His face shadowed and hidden in a great courtroom, and where the "devil," Lucifer, was the prosecutor, and Jesus the defense, and Mama Mary sitting there in the audience, waiting to hear what would be decided.

You see two sides; I see one coin.

This phrase, this concept, it seems to follow me now. I sink deeper and deeper into these themes the more I look into both the Divine and the Infernal, especially given that in a court, the Defense and Prosecution may argue, but they're still colleagues just doing their job—and God, the Judge, likewise sits above it all, His judgement a culmination of all facts, all angles, all ideas, to create Justice.

Food for thought, I guess. But nonetheless, it seemed if I wanted to get my doubts kicked into the trash and my discernment leveled up in ways unimaginable, it would be angels that could help me best—even if they intimidated the hell out of me. "Be not afraid" and all that, right? So I resolved there, all snuggled into bed, to never be afraid again.

Or at least, to try not to be.

THOR

Some good few weeks into this journey, of course, the question appeared: how could I talk to Loki and Freyja and not eventually talk to Thor, too?

Thor is a figure likely deeply attached to the face of Chris Hemsworth these days thanks to the Marvel universe. His legendary hammer, Mjölnir, is known by thousands of people now, as is his status as a god of thunder. But what about his other roles—such as that of the god of agriculture and the common man? And what of all the incredible folklore and stories about him that never get told in the Marvel universe?

Like how, when a frost giant took that great hammer from Thor and held it at ransom, demanding Freyja's hand in marriage before he gave Mjölnir back, Thor went and *dressed up* as Freyja (with Loki shapeshifting into a woman and joining him for support)?

Or how, when Loki shaved the head of Thor's wife, Sif, Thor threatened to break every bone in his body unless he found a way to replace that golden hair (and so Loki not only replaced it, but got some extra things smithed for the gods, too—including Mjölnir)?

Or maybe when Thor stopped at an inn butchered the goats that carried his chariot for supper, wrapping the bones in the skins and instructing no one to touch them—only for the innkeeper's son to chew on one of the legs and cause the goat to be a little mangled when Thor cast a spell to resurrect them?

There's a lot of fascinating folklore about Thor and his (mis)adventures with the other gods of the Norse pantheon, more than our many pop culture avenues of exploring this deity have to offer. That's why I knew I had to get some more information about Thor from his own mouth—and I was thrilled when @larisamagick (Larisa), a fellow Slovene and one who worked with Thor, reached out to help me learn some better ways to go about invoking his presence alongside my other research.

So when the day came for me to put all I'd learned together into another interview, I was ready, and off to work I went.

From what research I gathered about Thor, I understood several things: that he was associated with oak, with the rune Thurisaz, and that he was a big fan of mead. So I plucked some healthy oak leaves from a nearby tree and drew Thurisaz on one of them, then laid down a hammer and a shield-shaped brooch on top of my exercise gloves and weight lifting belt (as Thor, himself, has gloves and a belt that make him much stronger, and it felt appropriate). I poured two cups of some really good mead, set out some bread, a red candle, and some acorns, and then grabbed some carnelian, tiger's eye, and sunstone—stones that made me think of Thor's bold and powerful energy.

Then I put on some Danheim and Heilung tunes (groups I loved to listen to as I wrote *The Glass Witch*), got settled, did my standard protections and prayers, and opened myself up to meet this much beloved Norse god of thunder.

"Welcome, Thor!" I said, even though there was nothing behind my eyelids. "Please accept these gifts of bread and mead. I have some questions I'd love to ask."

Then came the images, bit by bit. It delighted me, that I got such vivid details of the place, without even having to focus all that hard. The set-up I had on my coffee table came through—bread and mead—but it more popped up like daisies among huge feast in this great mess hall; we sat at a long table covered in food like turkey legs and pies and roasts and other such things. Across from me was Thor, dressed in a greyish tunic and dark pants held up with a finely embroidered belt. His reddish hair was cut short, but his beard was full; he looked like a strong and friendly man. It was a dark hall, though, mostly lit around the table, and I didn't see much of the rest of the room since I was sitting on the side facing the windows, which couldn't have been more than a few feet away.

Speaking of those windows, though, something about them stuck out: they were huge panes of stained glass, as if we were in a Catholic church. I stared at them for a minute: the purples and greens and blues and reds that made up their patterns.

"Stained glass, huh? Never figured you for that."

He already had a turkey leg in his hand, and he waved it around. "Don't look at me," he said. "That's *your* God up there, making Himself known."

My jaw dropped at the thought. But once I recovered from that idea, I found it pretty funny. It was yet another way God was letting me know He was always there, watching; He'd done it more directly with the three Slavic gods I spoke to, where I saw Him up above, but the stained glass windows was His way of trying not to be completely obvious and intrusive, I think.

It didn't work. The windows were so radically out of place in an otherwise very Nordic mess hall. But I appreciated the idea nonetheless, especially because I love stained glass.

"Well, alright then," I said, chuckling, and I snatched my glass of mead. "I guess we'll just get into it, stained glass or no! So, I understand your hammer was supposed to have a longer handle, if not for Loki's antics. Would you have preferred it with a longer handle?"

1. WOULD YOU HAVE WANTED A LONGER HANDLE ON MJÖLNIR?

Thor waved a hand. "Ah, what's the point in even thinking on that? What am I to do about it?"

In the background came laughter, creaky as wind through dead leaves. Speak of the devil, and he'll appear; speak of Loki, and you'll find he's been there the whole time. When I looked for the source of the laughter, sure enough, there he was: sitting on the table with his back to me and a smirk over his shoulder. His shaggy red hair ran wild, his eyes dark, and his armor was still simple black leathers. Thor just kept at that turkey leg and continued.

"The hammer still works beautifully. I can do just as good work with it. Would I prefer a longer handle? Eh—does it matter? I have what I have, and I like it."

The gruffness! This really was a god of common man, and I mean that in a good way. There was no sense that I had to be formal with him, and it made it easier to relax. The mead did, too, of course, but Thor himself made me feel safe.

"Okay, okay—I get that," I said as I chewed on my own

That which bends is less likely to break. Confusion and conflict. Compromise. It's worth avoiding strife to settle issues however you can.

Some disillusionment. Taking good fortune for granted, but still having good fortune and contentment.

piece of toast. Watching Thor destroy that turkey leg was making me hungry. "And now, something I'm curious about: what does strength mean to you? As a warrior, as a god, what do you think of it?"

2. WHAT DOES STRENGTH MEAN TO YOU AS A WARRIOR GOD?

Be wary of spending beyond one's means. Generosity is very good, but be sure it doesn't lead to debt.

Unfounded accusation, rebellion against an unfair situation.

Thor nodded. "Strength, yeah. It's a serious thing. It isn't all encompassing or everlasting; you have to let it recharge. Recognize your limits. You know how many warriors have died, stupidly, for their arrogance? All that talent, wasted, because these men didn't understand that strength is recognizing one's limits as much as it is their skill. Not succumbing to ego, recognizing fights you can't win," and here, I was reminded of the story of the loudly snoring man he couldn't kill, who turned out to be a giant king, "you have to know when to call it quits, no matter the situation."

"Ah, yeah. That must've been quite a shock, that situation with the giant you were in."

He chuckled without humor. "Oh, yes. It was."

Another swig of mead for me. I have a bad habit of sucking down drinks that are in front of me: if they're anything other than water, they're gone in two minutes. "And with you at the time was Loki. Honestly, a lot of myths feature you two together, and yet at one point, he was associated with the devil by Christians, or at least some kind of antagonist. What do you think?"

3. WHAT DO YOU THINK OF LOKI BEING DEPICTED AS EVIL?

Injustice, false accusations, prejudice.

Inspiration, clarity of thought, inspired solutions. Problems solved, goals reached. Action, power, strength.

Loki wanted to answer, too; I could feel it. Thor was pulling two cards per question, and so he let Loki have one card while he pulled the other. Loki pulled Justice Reversed. Thor pulled the Ace of Swords.

"I am no enemy," Loki said with a harrumph, his arms crossed. "Horrible, that I've been portrayed as such."

And I had to take a second to marvel. It hadn't been so easy to see him, or to hear him like that, when we first spoke. Yet there he was, clear as day in my mind's eye, speaking with *words* and not just vague feelings I had to painstakingly split from my own. It hadn't been *that* many weeks, surely, and yet—to witness this had my heart feeling as fluffy and clear as a little summer cloud.

Thor chimed in, dragging me back from my silent celebration. "You Christians invented this Good versus Evil narrative, you know. We're a team, and it's unfair to Loki that people see him as some enemy of mine. Creation and destruction—we fight for what we want to preserve. We want to preserve humanity, so we have to channel destruction in ways that aren't cataclysmic." He glanced at Loki and shrugged. "Loki is Loki; he does what he does."

I nodded and said, "I understand. Figured as much! Same with Veles, honestly."

Loki smiled at mention of Veles, his brow quirking.

"But now," I said after a bite of bread, "something else I noticed in your myths: you casted spells! Magic! I found that interesting. What are your thoughts on magic?"

4. WHAT ARE YOUR THOUGHTS ON MAGIC?

Thor didn't have the little glass of mead I'd given him; suddenly, it went from a regular old glass to a solid oak tankard of it. He took big gulps from it, as if that tankard held a lake's worth, and he had that same nonchalance with this question, but behind it was such conviction.

"There's more than one type of weapon in the world," he said. When he put that tankard down, he had a sparkle in his eye, and the grin of a man that would fight the world with one hand tied behind his back. "I won't have anyone resorting to tricks to best me in battle, so I learned some of my own, to hold my own and make things simpler. Never have to worry about food if you can raise the creatures you ate," he said, a nod to the tale of the goats he butchered and raised again, "and also, it's practical knowledge; it helps."

"Fair enough! I agree. And thinking back on that story of magic, with the goat—why goats to pull your carriage?"

Hollow victory is as bad as defeat. Trickery, manipulation, unfair tactics used; accept the outcome.

Do what is right. Fairness, justice, equal opportunity. The strong should help the weak.

5. WHY DO YOU USE GOATS TO PULL YOUR CARRIAGE?

A good card, but shows tendency for excess, over enthusiasm, misplaced optimism.

A slow, reliable man. Sticks with a project no matter what. Responsible, pragmatic, honorable, keen to assist others.

Thor smiled, chuckled. "Goats are incredible little things. Spry and mischievous, but lively, loyal, and good beasts. They work hard, have good natures, and are stupidly friendly. Sure, they can be mean at times, but usually they're just playing."

He seemed to really like them, which was sweet. Loki sat there nodding along, always a little smirk on his face.

"I see." I paused from my writing and thought about his answer. "I like goats, too—those funny eyes they have, and the way they hop! But our next question is one I've seen others request I ask, and I'm curious, too: why are *gods* like yourself so invested in the lives of us humans?"

6. WHY ARE THE GODS SO INVESTED IN HUMANITY?

The energy changed here. Gone was the happy-go-lucky, bold and bright, friendly energy; it was replaced with something sharp as bramble, hard as steel. Thor sat back with his arms folded, and his lip started to curl.

"It's frustrating to watch you, is why," he muttered. "We see things that you don't, and for all our antics, this is our way: watching over you. We don't need your food or your shelter. But you, humanity—there are so many opportunities in the world. So much confusion on the right way to go about providing for yourself. And sometimes you choose ways that are a damn shame to us! Why? For what? All of you have power, talents. Why squander what's yours, wishing for what someone else has? If you were meant to wield others' skills, you would. Don't complain that fate gave you a mace over a sword; learn how to use it, ferociously! It's sickening. We want to help you see your potential."

Coveting success of others while wasting one's own talents. Jealousy, envy.

Bondage, disillusionment, loss of hope. A time of difficulty. Indecision makes things worse.

Loki leaned over the table to add, "And you think I can be a menace? Pah! People. People are the worst menaces to their own selves."

"Oh! Well, alright, then." Damn, was that one hell of an answer. "I think I've heard this sentiment, or something similar to it. I get what you're saying. In that vein, then, how can people develop that strength in this modern day, to be themselves and reach their potential?"

7. HOW CAN MODERN PEOPLE HARNESS THEIR POWER?

A shallow person. Spoiled and self indulgent. Should be forced to face responsibility.

PAGE of PENTACLES.

Studious youth, study, academia. Hard work brings achievement. Good news.

That energy didn't let up. He was just going at it.

"Stop suckling your mother's teat, is what you can do!" He slammed his fists down on the table; everything along its surface rattled. "All these people today—I tell you, you can have all these pretty muscles and still be a waste on the battlefield if you have no strength of mind, of spirit!

"When you get the strength without the responsibility, you get an overgrown and terrorizing child. This world is geared towards battle of the mind more so than the body now; strength comes from wisdom. If you have a strong mind, a strong body will follow, and vice versa, so on and so forth."

I sat there blinking at him. Loki blinked, too. Thor's energy is apparently pretty intense when he's feeling something strongly; I wouldn't want to get caught on the wrong end of those fists.

"Understood! Understood completely, thank you!" I said, if only to snap myself out of my dumb stare. I sucked down the rest of my mead and said, "Okay, well; here come our last three questions. First: how do you see yourself?"

8. HOW DO YOU SEE YOURSELF?

ACE of CUPS.

True contentment and bliss, harmony. Peace, satisfaction. Fertility and bountiful abundance.

PAGE of CUPS.

An emotional youth. Creativity deep, significant change. A quiet, studious youth.

"I have nothing to prove," he said with a shrug. "Eat, drink, and be merry—I'm all about this idea. I love joy and feasts, and I like to share this with others, too."

Which would explain the giant mess hall we were in.

"Jubilant, youthful, fun, *alive*—that's me," he said with a big grin. "I can get emotional, sure, but it's a part of me, of the vigor. The strength of character as much as body."

And I felt that energy rolling off him in waves. It was enough that, had I the rest of the bottle of mead on hand, I probably would've sat there longer, enjoying the vibe. I connected with that wish to let loose and have *fun*. To not be serious and make some trouble.

But I reeled it in and said, "I love that. And how do you want others to see you?"

9. HOW DO YOU WANT OTHERS TO SEE YOU?

THE HIGH PRIESTESS

Female intuition. Spiritual awareness, acceptance of life's mysteries. Secret knowledge, intelligence, intuition.

Taking the easy option won't solve the problem. Impatience and distraction prevents goals from being met.

Here, he sighed and frowned.

"I'm not some oaf," he insisted. "I know things. I'm wise. I understand battle—how to see oneself through it. And I can help one achieve that warrior stillness, the wisdom that comes with experience. And yes, I know some magic—this 'female work.' It's a good tool; I don't believe in denying oneself tools because of gender nonsense, nor do I see emotion as weak. I am many things, and I can teach many, too."

"Aw, man, that's awesome, though," I said, and I meant it. Thor was so honest and open; who wouldn't love that? "And your last message for me, or anyone?"

Thor waved a hand.

10. ANY LAST MESSAGES FOR PEOPLE?

"I say believe in yourself! Believe in your wish for truth! You need to stop doubting yourself. When you're confident in your knowledge and skill, you'll achieve the peace you're looking for. Lion heart! Be blessed; know your life shines ahead of you!"

"Ah—is that just for me, or for all?"

His brow shot up, and his smile had a smug bend to it. "It's for anyone it needs to be for."

Anyone meant me, too, I guess, which was fine by me. That was a really encouraging message; I wasn't about to pass it up. And so, a good cup of mead and bread later, a good conversation later, and we were done. That was that!

"Thank you for your time, Thor—and thank you, too, Loki, for visiting!"

Loki had such a Cheshire cat smile. Seeing the two of them side by side, too, I couldn't help but think that their dynamic was that of a somewhat more playful Michael and

JUDGEMENT.

Self acceptance. Standing in divine scrutiny, confident that one has lived a just life. An end and new beginning.

ACE of PENTACLES.

Contentment and happiness, achievement. Spiritual and material satisfaction.

Lucifer. Less serious, more about enjoying life than getting work done. I could appreciate it.

"With that," I said, "I'll wrap this up and say goodbye. I'll see you around, maybe—but if not, it was wonderful to meet you!"

With that, they nodded and slowly faded away. And as I've said already: Thor's energy already made me feel on top of the world as it was, but having a cup of mead on a weekend morning, and *especially* on an empty stomach, only magnified that feeling like hell. Nonetheless, as I packed everything up and fixed up my living room table, I gathered the offerings and brought them out to the oak tree I'd taken the leaves from.

Because from my research and understanding, it was customary not to eat the offerings, but to put them outside by an oak tree when it came to Thor. *No problem,* I thought, because I would've likely tossed them out to the pine tree in my front yard anyway. However, once I walked out to that tree and poured the mead onto its roots, then scattered the bread into the grass around it, I realized:

I'd just performed a libation.

It was like a chain link snapped in my mind. Something that only a few weeks prior had me feeling such a mental block—a libation to a different god—suddenly felt as simple as handing a gift over to an esteemed guest, and nothing at all that would've been affronting to God (because, I mean, I was already giving these gods I spoke to a gift anyhow; what difference did it make to pour it out for them?). I was surprised at myself anyway, though, because look at that! Me, libating out there! No doubt my neighbors, if they were looking out their window, were wondering what the hell I was doing playing around the oak tree, but that didn't matter to me.

What mattered was that I felt peaceful—free. Connected not just to God, but to an ever-flowing network of things that I was slowly, *slowly,* starting to get a better view of. And it was little things like this that helped me along in that connection.

You know what's really wild, though? Later, while I was still thinking about all of this, I stepped out to go for a walk around my neighborhood, and just as I got to the edge of my driveway, I saw something wreathed in the greenery there. It looked as if someone had cleared this little area away and bent all the branches into a frame of leaves just for this thing lying there, directly in the sun: a dead branch perfectly in the shape of an Algiz rune.

There was no way I could leave it there. The fact that an Algiz rune, a rune of protection and prosperity, appeared after a conversation with Thor and a libation to him, couldn't have been coincidence. So I grabbed it and went my whole walk with it, and to this day, it still sits on one of my bookshelves—a gift from this ever-friendly god of thunder, and a sign, to me, that I was doing something right. Or, at the very least, not wrong.

And nothing put a spring in my step that morning more than that.

ST. MARY OF MAGDALA

Now, of all the Mary's we know about in the Bible, there's one that, alongside *Mother* Mary, become a serious fixation in the search for the Divine Feminine: St. Mary Magdalene.

The Apostle to the Apostle. The most beloved companion of Christ. The one Jesus kissed often on the mouth, according to the apocryphal Gospel of Philip. The one purposely conflated with a prostitute (that "unnamed sinner" in Luke) by Pope Gregory I so that she might not be so respected and revered—even though she was an incredibly important financial sponsor of Jesus's mission and one who, by His power, was healed of seven "demons." The one that other Apostles like Peter did not believe, and the one whose Gospel was so controversial that it was buried in the dry caves of Egypt and excluded from the New Testament—so controversial that some pages were even burned, never to be discovered, never to be translated, never to let us complete the picture of her words.

But after a German scholar found her Gospel just hanging around in the marketplace of Cairo, Egypt in 1896, everything changed. It was honestly quite the battle to get the thing translated, given that every time this scholar found the time and sponsorship to do so, something world-rendingly destructive happened (like, you know, the first and second World Wars), but eventually, *finally*, it was translated from Coptic, and we discovered absolute treasure troves of knowledge within. Little bits like this alone are worth everything to the Christian who knows that there's more than what the mainstream churches tell us:

> Peter said to him [Jesus], "Since you have explained everything to us, tell us this also: What is the sin of the world?"
>
> The Savior said, "There is no sin, but it is you who make sin when you do the things that are like the nature of adultery, which is called sin.
>
> That is why the Good came into your midst, to the essence of every nature in order to restore it to its root."

Then He continued and said, "That is why you become sick and die, for you are deprived of the one who can heal you.

He who has a mind to understand, let him understand.

Matter gave birth to a passion that has no equal, which proceeded from something contrary to nature. Then there arises a disturbance in its whole body.

That is why I said to you, 'Be of good courage, and if you are discouraged be encouraged in the presence of the different forms of nature.'

He who has ears to hear, let him hear."

I'll let you in on a secret: whenever Jesus says *he who has ears to hear, let him hear*? That means He's saying something that has a deeper meaning than surface level readings allow for. It means He's dropping God's company secrets, and those who are clued into the world behind the esoteric curtain need to pay attention. All throughout the Gospels, Jesus sprinkles these bread crumbs, trying to lead us to what He knew and what He wanted to guard so carefully from the wrong people, and they appear in Mary's Gospel in a way that feels like putting aloe on a burn.

Because it's in her Gospel that we hear the words: "let us praise His greatness, for He has prepared us and made us into True Men." Given that Peter once asked what the point of teaching Mary anything was, since she was a woman and therefore somehow lesser, and Jesus responded by saying that He would make her a man, it's yet another head-tilting moment, another puzzling statement, that smacks of something more than meets the eye (or, rather, hits the ear).

Meggan Watterson's *Mary Magdalene Revealed* proved one hell of a resource for me to dig deeper into these otherwise scant few pages, and when read alongside other discarded documents like the Gospel of Thomas, of Philip, or read next to the Acts of Paul and Thecla and The Thunder: Perfect Mind, it really does give a picture of a Christianity that was never *allowed* to be, despite how powerful it was. And so, when St. Mary Magdalene was chosen on the Patreon polls, I knew I was out to have quite the night discovering more about this woman who was so very near and dear to Jesus.

And what a night it was.

At my table were several things to invoke the presence of St. Mary Magdalene, one of which being a pysanka—a Ukrainian Easter egg. It was the only one I had with a base color of red, which is important if you know the folktale of Mary's egg. It's said that, after Jesus rose from His tomb and ascended to heaven, Mary went to Emperor Tiberius and told him what happened. Emperor Tiberius waved the tale off, said he'd believe that an egg could turn red before he would believe someone could come back from the dead—and lo and behold, one of the eggs on his banquet table turned a shockingly bright red. That folktale is what keeps Christians coloring Easter eggs, even if their ancestors colored them for different reasons and different gods.

Along with the egg, I also had rose quartz, carnelian, and garnet, as well as an apple and some rose tea. I wanted things that represented love and fire and passion, things that held that energy of beauty and grace and *power* that Mary's story, and her own person, so clearly held in them. And once I'd done my prayers and confirmed that Mary came through to say hello, I found she wanted to use Doreen Virtue's Angel Tarot deck.

With everything set in place, I closed my eyes and let myself get settled.

"St. Mary, hello! Please, sit! I'd love to help others get to know you a little better. I have here an apple and some rose tea to share, so I hope you'll humor me tonight with these questions I have."

As I was thinking about St. Mary earlier this week, poking around and researching and learning, I'd gotten a flash of a woman's face who was dressed in red and had lighter brown, curly hair, bright eyes. I'd also gotten a startled look from her, like the way someone friendly would look if you walked up to them in a store while they weren't paying attention.

And rather than meet in the clouds hanging over the world like I had with so many other Christian figures, we met at what seemed like a town in the desert, with square buildings baking in the sun and people walking all around, some selling things, some just leading donkeys through the unpaved streets. There were mountains in the distance, square and blocky cliffs, and we were under an awning at a little table. The tea appeared there as we sat; it felt like an outdoor café at a tourist destination about two thousand years in the past.

St. Mary was there across from me, dressed in a red cloak with a rich blue dress underneath and a necklace of gold. Her red veil was likewise held there with a gold circlet, and her eyes were light; at first they reminded me of Mama Mary's, but they shifted to something like lapis lazuli, blue and full of golden stars. She was watching the people come and go around this busy part of town, relaxing.

"Well, hello, Mary!" I couldn't stop looking around. If only I had the art skills, believe you me, the things I could *paint*—such ridiculously vivid images. "Interesting that we're not meeting in Heaven."

Naturally, my doubts started taking over—is this really St. Mary? Are we in the right place?—so I shot a note to God:

Please, God… don't let this be an egregore or a fake or something. Please only let the real *Mary Magdalene through.*

And then the craziest thing happened: St. Mary's eyes went gold. That was what really got me: I was getting flashes of something almost dragon-like, and that confused me, because weren't things like dragons tied more to, say, Lucifer?

Then St. Mary took my hand.

"Don't worry," she murmured, her voice soft as sand, though her hand went from a person's hand to a tree. And her face, too, was like coarse bark, almost charcoal. "It's me. I'm here."

Then this tree-like piece of her broke away, until her normal human self sat there, and someone else hovered beside her. I think I met Asherah for the first time with that, because then there was a woman who looked like she was made entirely of charcoal, with hair blazing like it was made of fire and eyes of gold. She came with St. Mary to be supportive, it seemed; that was the feeling I got. The woman didn't say anything, and certainly didn't say who she was, but I felt it in my gut in a way I can't explain: this was Asherah.

"Whoa." I blinked at her, this burning tree of a woman. "Okay. Hello, Asherah—interesting meeting you here. Didn't expect it at all!"

Asherah's nose crinkled as she smiled, and then she leaned to say something to Mary I couldn't hear before hovering a little farther away. With Mary patiently waiting with her hands in her lap, I just shook off the shock and kept it moving.

"Alright, St. Mary, with all this happening in front of me… can you tell me what you and Asherah have to do with each other, if you don't mind?"

1. WHAT DO YOU AND ASHERAH HAVE TO DO WITH EACH OTHER?

Content and rewarding family life: great harmony with those around you. Relationships are strong and trustworthy, needs are met. Relationships with friends and family are genuine; peace, joy and unconditional love surround you.

Struggling with a decision. There are conflicting emotions or thoughts about which way to move, so you're avoiding choosing altogether.

You know what you need to do, but you're afraid to act. Have faith. Get a mediator if needed.

Asherah offered a little smile before she faded away. St. Mary smiled, too, but it didn't reach her star-flecked eyes.

"The voice of the Woman has been lost, as you know."

Then, another figure appeared beside her that I was less shocked to see: Jesus. He was wearing a white robe tied with rope, His hair short and rough, His beard covering the lower half of His face, and He sat beside St. Mary after giving her a small hug, tapping His cheek to her head. Mary continued after I greeted Jesus, and Jesus sat silent as she spoke.

"Older ideas seem to have won out over the true progressivism of my Lord. We are at an impasse here—between Divinity and Humanity."

Then Jesus got up. He was a little restless, and He spoke, too; He seemed incredibly disappointed, frustrated, if the shadows at his brow were any indication.

"It wasn't supposed to end like this—all this in My name."

Mary nodded, and Jesus disappeared after that. She looked at me with her hands balled up in her lap.

"There are many players in Heaven," she said, "all with their own roles. Asherah has such a role, holding up the feminine power that's been lost, helping us do so in a world where people are only just now starting to remember her. She, I, and my Lord's Mother, we all work in this role of reminding people of our power as women. It's a tug of war between the old and the lost right now; again, we are at an impasse."

"Oh, wow. Okay." So commenced the mile-a-minute scribbling as I tried, desperately, to catch all these details I was seeing and hearing. "That's a lot. So, speaking of that feminine power, how do you feel about the Church's attempt to minimize you? And dissuade people from your image?"

2. HOW DO YOU FEEL ABOUT THE CHURCH MINIMIZING YOU?

Her face scrunched up here, like she'd seen a bit of particularly gory road kill.

"They tried to lock me away, that church," she muttered, "and they did the same with my Lord's Mother! But they failed.

1. A wonderful new person coming into your life. Budding romance or renewed romance. Joy, pleasure, and happiness. Spiritual abilities take flight; growth and rich experiences.

2. You don't need to stay in your situation. Possibilities exist to free yourself. Believe in yourself and stay positive. See the truth, act with faith.

Just as Asherah was wrongly discarded, so too was I, because I gave women hope for something more than what men wanted them to believe.

"But we are *here*. We aren't going away. We never went away! We were always here, waiting for people to see the truth again."

I nodded as I wrote, and honestly, as with most interviews, I didn't really know how to respond to this level of emotion I got from these entities. I felt almost like a therapist, just playing some kind of psychological tennis, batting phrases of empathy and understanding over the net as they sent back pieces of their truth.

"Got'cha," I said. "Yeah, the idea that His women followers were just as valuable to Jesus as any other must've been a hard pill to swallow. You're even known as the Apostle to the Apostles, given you were the first to see the Resurrection. And knowing all this, I have to ask: what was your relationship with the other Apostles like?"

3. What was your relationship with other Apostles like?

Enjoy time with people. You have much to give, to family, friends, or others. Handle challenges with understanding, warmth, confidence, and resourcefulness. Prosperity, sensuality, a sensible approach.

You don't need to stay in your present situation if you're unhappy. If there looks like there's no way out, look again. Plenty possibilities exist to free yourself. Believe in yourself and stay positive. See the truth and act with faith.

Mary's brows shot halfway up her head as she sighed. "Oh, it wasn't easy. I was good enough to lend money to support them, but the idea that my Lord would actually speak to me as He spoke to them? They wouldn't accept that at first. Or that I would be told things that they weren't, as if they were entitled to His word first.

"That's why I prefer being here sometimes—in comfortable settings, familiar images. In this town, rather than those clouds. I can get away from them for a little bit. We're fine now, of course; we work together, as they know better now. But sometimes I still like to get away. Back then, I had to deal with challenges with a firm hand, like that little card of yours says."

"I see. Yeah, I remember reading the part of your Gospel that tells how they just didn't want to believe you about anything Jesus said to you." Luckily, something about this interview felt less like a therapy session that I was underqualified to lead and more like a simple conversation among women—a good feeling, a really good feeling. "But on that note, your Gospels aren't considered canonical, though they have an idea about the afterlife that I felt matched tradition a little better. What do you think of your message versus the Church's hellfire and damnation narrative that took over?"

4. WHAT DO YOU THINK ABOUT HELLFIRE AND DAMNATION RHETORIC?

"I worked hard to get those messages back out there—to get them found again." Her jaw clenched before she continued. "Our Father is not wicked. He wouldn't take humanity, who He knows has imperfect knowledge and is trying their best, and cast them down with no mercy. This," she said as she gestured at nothing, and I got the sense that she meant *religion*, or even just plain *existence*, "is about love. It's about healing your relationship with Him, and by extension all creation. Now, people are starting to see the truth again. I can only thank God for letting me speak and come back into the public eye. Love God! This is what matters, because when you love God, you love *all*."

As I put the pencil down, I blew out a breath. "I agree a thousand percent, but, it's good to hear it be said out loud, too! Okay, so: what was it like, to be an Apostle?"

Two people sharing a close relationship. Friendships deepen. Mutual love, respect, and understanding develop. Conflicts resolved.

Achievement and success. Excellent reputation You've made good choices and worked hard. Public acknowledgement, award.

5. WHAT WAS IT LIKE TO BE AN APOSTLE?

Once again, Mary's eyebrows crawled up her head. She *tsked* and rubbed her temple, all while a smile split her lips, and then she said, "Oh, my. Honestly, it was a whirlwind, but a happy whirlwind. So much happened so fast, but I knew what we were doing was right. Nothing could've stopped us."

At this point, I got flashes of Jesus and the others laughing, sharing food and drink on their travels, coming into new towns unsure of where to turn for a place to sleep, but knowing they'd be okay.

"We were a family," she said. "We were with our Lord."

"Beautiful." I could've pitched a tent and lived in those memories forever. "Though, the way you met Jesus was wild. What was it like, with those demons haunting you?"

Believe in your dreams. Look to the future with optimism. Make long term plans. Trust intuition. Faith. A sense of purpose, a new beginning.

Past delays end, and plans manifest swiftly and energetically. Feels good to see dreams coming true. Lots going on, so stay grounded.

6. WHAT WERE THE DEMONS LIKE?

Enjoy time with people. You have much to give to others. Handle challenges with understanding, warmth, confidence, and resourcefulness. Prosperity, sensuality, solid approach.

A successful time. Projects going well. Talents and skills bring rewards for you and others. Accept opportunities offered and have confidence you'll succeed. Business deals.

I won't lie; I was very confused to pull the Queen and King of Coins. But I got it eventually as I wrote, because she leaned over her cup of tea and watched me scribble, then started explaining.

"I was a successful woman, yes, but my success came at a cost. What I had to compromise for it soon became a problem for me. Arrogance filled me, poisoned me, and it was my Lord that saved me. So I gave up those ill won comforts to follow Him."

I got the sense that those demons were more metaphorical than anything, which makes sense. It was maybe an unkindness of spirit that had her then, a roughness that money tends to bestow on people, and Jesus helped her get rid of it.

"Okay," I said, nodding, "that makes sense. I see where you're going with this. But speaking of Jesus, I will admit that I'm dying to know: what was your relationship with Him like?"

7. WHAT WAS YOUR RELATIONSHIP WITH JESUS LIKE?

She squirmed a bit, her lips twisting as if she was trying to cage some words that meant to rip free, but eventually, she spoke the part she was willing to share:

"It's not about me. Or us. It's about my Lord and His Father. But Jesus was a bold and bright person, full of life, with real love and passion for His Father. Preaching truth was His project in life. Almost too good to be true, that I could go with Him, but I did, and it was wonderful. I knew He loved me. I know He still does. All was good."

As she spoke, Jesus came back, with eyes warm and golden like honey. He sit beside her at this little cafe-like place and hugged her to him. It was really sweet. I almost didn't want to keep asking questions, because they looked precious together, the way they beamed at each other, like two celestial partners in crime, two eternal companions watching over the world.

But I had to keep on, so I picked my pencil back up and said, "Understood! Well, we're down to our last few questions already, so let's see: how do you see yourself?"

Exciting opportunities. Embrace them. Ready for the challenge. A creative, outgoing youth, passionate about life. Confident, courageous, exhilarating, mischievous.

Content and rewarding family life: harmony. Relationships are strong and trustworthy, needs are met. Peace, joy and unconditional love surround you.

8. HOW DO YOU SEE YOURSELF?

Luckily, these were some of the easier cards of the night to interpret, but of course Mary gave me her integrated thoughts, and I welcomed them:

"I'm not interested in the fight as much as I am healing the damage that comes after. That's where we are: post battle. I know what people need to heal right now, in this mess of a world. I provide the way to healing through our Lord and His Father; I want to light the way to them.

"People need a shoulder to cry on, and I am that. I help. I bring back the balance once wiped away by the Church, and I do so alongside my Lord's Mother."

"And how should people see you?"

A person of deep but mature emotions. Intuitive person who trusts their perceptions. Empathetic. Patient. Generous. Gentle. Unconditionally accepting of others.

Moderation and balance. Better results come by reevaluating things. Working with others. Compassion is key to success. Forgiving brings healing. Self restraint.

9. HOW DO YOU WANT TO BE SEEN?

Skilled work is rewarded. Learning everything about a subject. Apprenticeship. Learning or going to school.

She shrugged, and I thought she was about to skip picking a card, but after a bit of shuffling, she found one she liked.

"I see myself as those things I already mentioned," St. Mary said, so simply. However, her brows pinched all of a sudden, and her voice took up a sharper edge: "But also people should know: I am *not* complacent. I am here to find what was lost, to show it to others. I'm still learning, too. Learning from you all, and all creation is forever on this journey of learning until the very end. Even us Saints."

"Wow, that's an idea." Saints, learning from us goons still on earth? "I—well, I was going to ask if you had any messages. Would you have others, or is that it?"

10. ANY LAST MESSAGES FOR ME OR OTHERS?

Mary shook her head, and again, she just spoke instead of giving me any cards to read from. "That is my message. That we're all on a journey, no matter where we are, be it on Earth or in Heaven. We learn at all stages."

I shook out my aching hands once I was done writing and nodded. "Amazing. Okay, St. Mary— honestly, that's all I had to ask for today. But thank you so much for your time! This was a wonderful meeting, and I'm glad for the opportunity to speak to you. Goodbye for now!"

Once more, she smiled at me, and her face disappeared behind my teacup as I drank down the last of my very cold rose tea.

And then it was just me, some empty cups and plates, and the crackle of the couple candles I lit for this whole interview. Once I clapped my hands together, Mary drifted away, as did the whole cityscape, and I was left to sit there and digest everything I'd been told.

Make no mistake: even after getting yelled at by Raphael and learning, slowly but surely, to just let the images and words happen, it still made me nervous when the unexpected happened—like Asherah popping up. There's something about Asherah that I still feel I'm not ready for, but I've come to understand that she knows this, and that this is almost... the *point* of figures like Mama Mary, like St. Mary Magdalene. Asherah is there, guiding them as they guide us, and cloaking herself in the many shapes and names more palatable to modern Christians while she guides the lost and broken women back to the power that so many different kings and Popes and what-have-you have tried to bury.

I can't tell you why I'm not ready for it because I don't really know myself. What I *do* know, though, is that even though I'd never given all that much thought to St. Mary before, she's become a figure of my utmost respect since this time, and since my reading of her Gospel. She is a True Man, a true *human*, in the most human *and* divine sense of the word, and I appreciate the time she spent showing me what that means.

But nothing could've prepared me for the next interview that popped up on the polls.

JESUS

When Jesus appeared on the poll lists, I was pretty excited. How could I not be? It's Jesus! We all know who Jesus is, and we all want to hear from Him, don't we? Especially given all the bold and creative (and horrible) things modern Christianity has tried to insert into His mouth—and all the sheer *atrocities* done in His name. Time and time again, I'll tell people who want to know what the truth is to simply reach out and ask Jesus themselves what really happened, and this? This was a chance to put my money where my mouth was.

Here's the thing, though: given that it's primarily God, Jesus, and the Holy Spirit I work with and speak to, I'm already pretty familiar with God and Jesus, who They are and what They're about and how They want to help us. That's why I decided it would be fun to open up the panel to everyone else—to give a space for others who are deconstructing and relearning their relationship with God to step up and ask questions. I thought it'd be a good way to invite everyone into the experience with me. I thought it'd be fun.

And then I saw the kinds of questions that were being asked.

What does Jesus think of pagans?
What does He think of the church and the way they've twisted His word?
What does He think about the LGBTQ+ community?
What does He think about Lucifer, or "the devil"?
Is there something He wishes His followers knew?
Does He hate me?

It broke my heart to see all of these questions come pouring in, because I knew that many of them were laced in pain. Too many people have grown up disillusioned and confused, wondering how the Jesus they were told to love, this Man of mercy and radical justice, could be the very stick waved around to beat the innocent by so many so-called faith leaders.

Of course, it meant this would be an important interview—one that I was worried I would get wrong, with an entity I was terrified to misrepresent. But as I was looking up things I might set the table with, searching through the Bible for mentions of herbs, I came across Matthew 23:23:

> *"Woe to you, teachers of the law and Pharisees, you hypocrites! You give a tenth of your spices— mint, anise, and cumin. But you have neglected the more important matters of the law—justice, mercy and faithfulness. You should have practiced the latter, without neglecting the former."*

Some versions also say dill instead of anise, though these are two very different things. I wonder how that happened.

And at first I thought I should've avoided these spices, but after thinking about it, God has asked for the most seemingly random herbs on His altars before: mint, cinnamon. I didn't get why. Now I do: because He's been offered things like this for eons, and He was also using it as a way for me to know: *yes, this is Me.* Not an egregore, not a demon—not something maliciously pretending to be God or unaware that they're a fake. When Divinity tells you things that you don't know about, and then you discover it in their texts and their mythos and their history, that's a fantastic sign: it means *they* know who they are, and they're trying to tell you, in any way they can, who you're talking to.

Here at the interview table, though, I also saw an opportunity here for a spell: one where, with a tithe of mint, (star) anise (because I don't have actual anise unfortunately), and cumin, I poured my intentions forward like rich wine and earnestly asked Jesus to help me bring back that spirit of Justice, Mercy, and Faithfulness we seem to have forgotten. A trade in its most ancient and traditional sense: a tithe, a sacrifice, for a gift.

I also asked Him to help me represent Him as best as I could, and to help me help others get back to the basics, the truth, the heart of things. And then, I went through as many questions as I reasonably could in a night, using the pendulum, the tarot cards, and the Bible itself. It's a long interview, so get comfortable—and keep in mind that there is some really heavy stuff mentioned in here.

Like, *really* heavy. The Holocaust comes up. A lot of violent imagery comes up. Some less than fuzzy passages of the Bible come up. Just be ready for it.

Now, with all that said, let's get into it.

As I said, I had a tithe of mint, star anise, and cumin at the table on Jesus's blue fish plate, along with some blueberry mojitos (a mint based drink), some bread with honey (to represent that breaking of bread, the land of milk and honey, and other such Biblical imagery), and a white candle and a sphere of onyx to burn up and draw away any negative energy left around the space that might get in my way of hearing Him right.

This was a huge deal for me, approaching Jesus and being responsible for delivering His words. By the questions I had ready for Jesus alone, I knew this was going to be one of the most important interviews I would do. There was no room for fun and games here, not really, and I carried that seriousness into every step of the ritual space, from the making of the drinks to the cleansing of the table space with holy water and frankincense.

So after my prayers and offerings, and after making an earnest request to hear Jesus and see whatever He wanted to show the people who would see all this, I settled down and got to work.

"Alright, Jesus," I said after a long, deep breath. "Here we are. Can you let me feel your energy before we start? Not just images, but really the *energy.*"

Every time I ask anyone in Heaven this, be it God, Michael, anyone, it feels like I'm wrapped in a tight hug from behind, fully enveloped, as if to say that they're there watching ahead of me, protecting me. But this time, that feeling was a little different, starting from behind and ending in more of a side-hug, a brotherly and friendly feel.

And the images came anyway, of course. We started in a town at the base of a mountain, a town with square buildings that looked like they were made of some kind of pale orange stone. We were standing under an awning made of wood, shady, and Jesus was there dressed in simple maroon robes, with darker skin and dry hair, and a rough beard. His eyes were honey-brown, so bright they glowed like sunshine, and He was carrying a big cloth sack over his shoulder. He looked back at me with a twinkle in those bright eyes, an optimistic smile.

I smiled, too. "Thank you. Can you move the pendulum in a circle and back and forth for yes and no, so I can make sure I have your answers here?"

This was a struggle. Jesus smirked here; I could feel it, as if it were tugging at my own lips, and I could see it on His face, too. And while He'd answered an enthusiastic YES when I asked Him to help me get these messages out right, He barely moved the pendulum after. He seemed to prefer simply painting an image in my head or using the intuitive tell I feel in my ears whenever talking to God: something that can range from a brief tingle in my ears to feeling like someone was shoving a nail straight into my ear drum. It's something I like to call the whispers of the angels, because no matter how it feels, that seems like what the intention is: that someone is delivering a quiet message to me, a bit of direction, and that I have to pay attention to really understand what's going on.

After the pendulum kept fussing about over my palm, I gave up and just closed my eyes.

"Fine, fine. I'll just listen," I said, just barely managing not to huff in my growing frustration. "God, and by extension Jesus, didn't really like to make things easy for me a lot of times. "But please help me hear you right! We have so many questions to get through, but I think this batch of them can be answered with a yes-or-no format?"

Then, as if to make up for the lack of clarity with the pendulum, His words crashed directly into my mind, direct and undeniable: "Fine by me."

And then we started walking away from that town, down the road towards the big rocky mountain. I tried using the pendulum again, but it was difficult each time. He really just didn't seem to want to use it for whatever reason, though when I insisted for the sake of having something concrete, something to ensure I wasn't just putting words in His mouth and overriding His thoughts with my own, as the whole world seemed to have done a million times over, He obliged me the tiniest bit. We started with the shorter questions first, the ones that I thought a pendulum alone would be enough for to get some simple answers, but my goodness, am I a goon.

After all, it was Jesus we were talking to here.

And knowing Jesus, would anything He said really be simple, even if He made His answers quick?

"Alright," I said as we walked, "so, first one: all your parables, do they have some kind of hidden, esoteric meaning? Are they more than metaphors?"

He shrugged.

"Anything has such meanings if you draw the right parallels," He explained, and then He tapped His temple. "Think. Think *hard*. Push the bounds of the world you see—and you might find such parables relate to all kinds of things, within and without."

Made sense to me. "Okay, I got'cha. So, another person asked: are you invoked, or called on, just by calling your name? Or do people need to do elaborate rituals like I have right here to get in touch with you?"

His face scrunched a little as He shook His head, even before I finished asking the question.

"No, no. Anytime, anywhere, just call me, and I'm there."

"Aw, cute—that rhymes," I said, chuckling, as I lightly elbowed Him in the side.

Jesus grinned at me, an honest, carefree smile that just exuded warmth. Then He continued, "No one needs to do anything big and fancy to reach me. I'm always there to help."

Out of nowhere, He started taking big, laborious steps, hunched with that bag. I think it was on purpose to get me curious about it, because He'd been completely fine with the weight of it up until that point. So I took the bait and asked.

"What'cha got there? In that bag?"

Jesus glanced at me, and His lip curled in a mischievous smile. "Oh, this? Why don't you take a look inside and see?"

He put it down and opened it, and excuse my language, but it was an *oh shit* moment, because inside was all purple: stars, gasses, the very stuff of creation was inside that bag, expanding infinitely forever. You could fall in that bag and likely never come out, with how much *space* was in there. And He was just carrying it around, on His back: the world, the universe.

Jesus bumped His shoulder to mine and grinned. "You want to carry it?"

"Oh, jeez," the energy told me that He wasn't asking so much as insisting, "I mean—I'll try."

And then I had the bag, like some giant Santa's sack, and obviously, without being physically real, it didn't seem like much, but I was aware of it nonetheless. Aware if I carried it wrong, my spine would snap. That if I let my knee buckle wrong, I'd go down and never get back up. But we kept walking down that road, towards that big barren mountain ahead of us.

"Okay," I said as I adjusted my grip on this bag full of pure Universe, "another person wanted to know: do you have any set signs, like certain tarot cards, that signify you've heard a prayer?"

"Mm-mm." He shook His head, even frowned. "No, there's no set anything. People shouldn't rely on physical signs like that. When I answer, they'll know; they just need to have faith. And if they think they *do* see or feel a sign, all they need to do is reach out and ask. I'm always there."

"Okay, but, like," I shimmied a little as I walked, in that goofy way that I do when I'm about to be annoying and want to soften it with a bit of humor, "*I* have some associations for you, y'know? I've got a card that makes me think of you right away when I see it. Is that bad? Or is that okay?"

I was talking about the Knight of Swords: a card all about that loud and unapologetic voice of love and justice, a person always defending what's right no matter what anyone feels about it or who has something else to say. It's Jesus to a T, and it's the card that His own Mother pulled for Him when talking about how He was as a child, so it just makes sense to me.

Jesus shrugged. "If you connect things to me, I'll use them to let you know I'm there. But it's about a connection, not anything pre-set or pre-defined. Work with me to make a language we both understand; that'll be better than any card or crystal or whatever else."

I nodded. It was as I thought after His initial answer; these symbols and tools just help you understand your own view of Jesus, really. How do you see Jesus? Who is He to you? Start there, I guess, because otherwise, nothing will mean anything.

"Okay, I got'cha," I said, and I felt woozy every time I had to open my eyes to write something down; it was like the real world was the dream, the meditation the reality. Hate when that happens. Makes it harder to work. "Now, someone else asked: do You ever get overwhelmed with the amount of followers you have? I mean, there are a *lot*, let's be real."

Again, a shrug. So nonchalant, this Son of Man!

"Does it matter if I do or don't?" He waved a hand. "What needs to be done, needs to be done. But more than that, everything is clear to me. It's inexplicable—you won't understand—but 'overwhelm' doesn't really play a part."

I nodded. "I can see what You're saying, I think. Interesting. Okay. So, you know," I paused as I checked my list, debating whether or not this question was appropriate, but I was compelled to ask it, "one person just asked if they could have a hug. I dunno, it felt like something to ask anyway: are You willing to offer a hug, or rather, reassurance to those who ask, like this person?"

"Of course." His smile was so bright. "I can give them that, always."

"And then another: can people do Biblical magic without being a Christian? Obviously I don't think this includes things like Jewish Kabbalah—"

"No. It doesn't."

"—but I mean, working with You, Saints, angels, and just generally calling on You for help?"

His brow quirked. "You already know the answer to that."

And I guess I do, but it was weird, Him basically giving me carte blanche to give the answer in His stead. The answer is: yeah. They've already said as much; the Saints and angels and Jesus Himself all help those who need it.

I kept going, checking off questions like it was a Census questionnaire. "Alright, another question: do you know past and future events?"

At this point, we'd stopped on that road for a hot minute. This bag was heavy, if not physically, then spiritually, and I don't know how to explain that kind of weight. All I know is that it exhausted me mentally and spiritually, so I set the bag down, and Jesus took it back up on His own back.

"I said before: everything is clear," Jesus explained. "Past, present, future, they don't exist from where I see things. All is one. All is laid plain."

"Oh." That was certainly an interesting way of thinking about it. "Damn. Okay. Uh, someone else wondered if being saved is a requirement to get to Heaven?"

The baffled look He gave me here was priceless, like He'd never heard a crazier idea.

"What?" He blinked, shook His head. "Going to Heaven means being saved from the cycle."

That word popped up real clear: *cycle*.

He continued: "You can't do the reward to get the reward. That makes no sense."

"Jesus, you said it's a cycle, though." I squinted at Him like that was going to make anything clearer. "Are you suggesting... like, what other gods of death have suggested? That all of this is a way to living again, like, on earth? Reincarnation?"

"Yes, exactly that," He said. "You come here until you're done learning, and even then, you always have the option to come again and learn some more. It's how it's always been."

"Ah, wow. Okay." What do you even do when you have answers like that just dropped on your head? All *I* could do was keep asking questions. "Someone else was also wondering if you had a tattoo of some kind, with a Revelation vision they had?"

Here I couldn't really grasp an answer from Jesus, even though He was standing right there in front of me. It felt like something was blocking my perception as He stayed silent. I insisted on the pendulum right then to get a solid answer instead, and I got a firm "no." Only then did Jesus cut me some slack and let me hear Him speak again.

"That person saw something, but it wasn't what they thought."

"Oh." This seemed code for, *don't keep prying*, and so I just wrote it down and moved on. "Alright, alright. Now, last on our pendulum list: do You really know *everyone?*"

I got an immediate sharp feeling in my ear, which is a massive *yes* in my little language I've developed with God and His Son and Spirit. Jesus just nodded, and we continued down that road like nothing. And then, as I broke out the Golden Tarot that He chose to speak through, we were suddenly walking up the mountain path. There was a stone shelf at the top, a narrow ledge in the shade, where we could see that city we'd walked from, and the sandy, stony landscape beyond it.

"Okay, well, now that we've had a warm-up, here comes a heavy question: what do You think about the state of the Bible, and Your followers, and all these things happening in Your name?"

I. WHAT DO YOU THINK ABOUT THE STATE OF THE BIBLE AND WORLD?

A time of worry, but don't despair, as a sea of change is in the air.

Irresponsibility with other people's money may lead to debt. There is also a chance for fraud, so be wary.

Warning against taking your blessings for granted. Yearning after the forbidden or unattainable, but you already have so much to be thankful for. Is it worth throwing everything away for what may lose its appeal?

For all His smiles and lightheartedness before, Jesus's face suddenly dropped flat. He looked real tired as I asked this, with a flat face of exasperation, brows set in a hard line, mouth grim and tight.

"We're at the precipice of something new, you understand," He said. "These people use me for riches, but they fail to understand: no amount of riches can fill the hole in them that Truth can. They've forever given themselves over to that void, and they scream and thrash in their pulpits with this false passion, trying to revive what warmth Truth once put there in their chests. And those who deceive know exactly what they do; they know they lead people astray for their own gain."

I frowned. My chest ached with some discomfort, some nagging feeling to keep digging into this answer. "But what about the people who genuinely believe they're doing the right thing? Not all are active deceivers, I think: there are a lot of people who really think they're upholding Your word, with the things they say and do."

His lips pressed together so tightly that they just about disappeared.

"Those who do these things, all this injustice and harm, and think they're right to do it—they never knew Me."

Oop. "And, uh, sorry if this is a dumb question, but" that's what that heavy, nagging feeling in my chest was: *fear and doubt,* "you're not talking about us, right...? About witches? And magicians?"

Because I'll be honest: that one line in the Four of Cups, about people seeking *that which is forbidden or unattainable,* closed a fist around my heart. I was actually just as scared as anyone else who might've wanted to know these answers from Jesus; the only difference was that I'd decided to put myself out there to try and get some peace for not just myself, but everyone else who burned up with this curiosity, too. Still, for all my confidence that God led me to the path of magic and mysticism, I was still so easily shot by those doubts, that fear, and it seemed that this mucky spiritual tar would go and latch its sticky self onto anything at all, *anything*, that might suggest that I'd actually been wrong about this Christian witchcraft stuff the whole time.

After all, what if we *had* been wrong somehow? And what if it was us who were going to get smacked instead of all of these people running around saying terrible things in the name of God, driving people away from Him with their cruel attitudes and their willingness to tear others down for just existing? Of course saying it back like that makes it easier to come back to earth, but fear and doubt are a hell of a drug, as I've said time and time again. Even when you think you're perfectly faithful, ironclad—that you've seen and heard and learned it all—it comes creeping back up like bile.

Jesus watched me as I ducked my head, waiting for Him to drop an axe of judgement on my neck. Then He reminded me of Matthew 6:24 in *full context* (emphasis mine):

> *No one can serve two masters. Either you will hate the one and love the other, or you will be devoted to the one and despise the other.* You cannot serve *both God and money.*

And He directed me to that footnote about that verse: that the word used here is mammon, the "biblical term for riches, often used to describe the debasing influence of material wealth" that was often mistaken for an evil spirit or god in the middle ages, according to Britannica. According to the Jewish Annotated New Testament, this word referenced how people put their trust in things that weren't God to sustain them and provide stability—namely money, as if the exchange of gold for labor was something secure and stable all on its own and that all one's problems could be answered so long as a steady stream of money kept flowing into their household, forgetting that many of the twists and turns of fate didn't depend on gold, but God (22).

This was, plainly, about the materialism—about the televangelists shaming their congregation for not tithing enough for them to get new cars, bigger pulpits, *jet planes* All a bunch of ridiculousness.

Still, the answer soothed me enough that I could stand up straight again. "Yeah, I see that," I said with a shrug. "But what about the Bible specifically? What do you think of that?"

2. WHAT DO YOU THINK ABOUT THE BIBLE SPECIFICALLY?

I pulled that extra card, the Ace of Cups, which surprised me. I expected some condemnation, but it became clear soon as He explained:

"The Word is not just a book. The Word is more than this. Ink on paper can never contain the entirety of the Spirit, but it can teach you to recognize its presence. Between the laws of old, the names, the details, there are moments that carry power. Have you not felt them yourself?"

I had. Sometimes, I read a passage of triumph, where God answers His people or otherwise relieves them of some great sorrow, and I tear up instantly when I see the love people have for God, the love He likewise has for them.

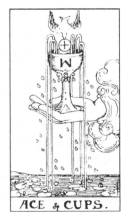

Overflowing love and joy. True contentment, harmony, bliss. Peace, satisfaction, a perfect union. Fertility and bountiful abundance. Spiritual fulfilment through unconditional love.

ACE of CUPS.

"Strong feelings guide you as you read," Jesus said, His face set hard in his seriousness. "They give you full meaning. It isn't the point of the Scripture to catalogue every crumb of detail and not the living, *continuing* Word. People are so focused on details, little things, but never Truth."

And this reminded me of something I'd always told myself to help me discern that Truth in the Bible: if it's something that oppresses and abuses the innocent, it is not of God. It is not Truth, it is not the Word of the God who is, Himself, the Protector of the oppressed and downtrodden, Destroyer of injustice. Of course, Jesus sums it up more succinctly than I in Matthew 22:36-40, when He says to love God, and love one another as yourself.

This is what all of God's laws are based on, according to Jesus in the Gospel of Matthew. And this one Truth I've held to has helped me discover so many things—like the practice I have now. Like the ways the Bible had been edited to justify the persecution of millions of different people across time.

I nodded, mulling this over. "Okay, well... what do you think of all the different denominations?"

3. WHAT DO YOU THINK ABOUT ALL THE DIFFERENT DENOMINATIONS?

A time of worry, but don't despair, as a sea of change is in the air.

As I pulled the card, I also got a clear flash of letters and numbers, as if I'd just read them with my own eyes: Galatians 3:28. An incredible verse, probably some of St. Paul's best and most defining work for the budding religion that came post-Resurrection:

There is neither Jew nor Gentile, neither slave nor free, nor is there male and female, for you are all one in Christ Jesus.

When I looked at Jesus, though, I almost laughed. This Son of Man. I swear, had He been anyone else, He might've been chain smoking, given the look of sheer exasperation on His face.

"Again, details! The details!" He threw His empty hand out to the air and shook it at the open sky, huffing in his frustration. "There is one Church, and she's gone and cut herself to pieces. But no more." He dropped His hand and nodded. "Soon."

What the hell did He mean by soon? I got a little nervous with how stony-faced He was, I'm got going to lie to you. But the idea, and the image of a tower crumbling under a fearsome lightning strike, came clear. As that thunder flashed in my mind, I knew viscerally right then and there:

The Church was going to have one hell of a Tower moment at some point.

Some point soon.

"Uh, alright, okay, okay," my God, this was getting intense, "some also wanted to know: what do you think of the LGBTQ+ community? And of abortion and the ending of Roe v. Wade?"

As I shuffled the cards, I heard Him say, "What's there to think? They're people." Yet He guided my hand to the cards He wanted nonetheless.

But I kept shuffling, even as the ringing was going off in my ear to pick a card. Because again, that doubt, that fear, it came and gripped my stomach and pulled it down, down, down—as if it could drag it all the way down to the deepest caverns of hell. Did I *really* just hear Jesus say that? That's what I was asking myself then: did Jesus *really* just say that about the LGBTQ+ community, or was I dwelling in some seriously wishful thinking?

What if I turned this card over, and it suggested just the opposite? What if all I was hearing was just wishful thinking, and every Evangelical screaming *love the sinner, hate the sin* was right about LGBTQ+ folks? About *me*, given I, myself, am bisexual? What if Jesus was going to look me in my eye and tell me I'm doomed for something I can't do anything about?

These questions choked me. I honestly felt like I didn't want to stop shuffling, just so an answer would never have to come. And here, I knew I had to pause and apologize to Him.

Because I was so afraid.

I was afraid He would say something that *wouldn't* be what we all want Him to say: that He loves us, that He doesn't have any problem with us. I was afraid I'd pull cards that would slap these sentiments away and deliver harsh words no one wanted to hear. I was afraid the Jesus I knew would be a complete and utter fabrication.

So I stopped shuffling and held the deck tight, and I let myself be honest as Jesus sat there waiting for me to get it together.

"I'm sorry," I whispered. "I'm sorry; I'm just afraid of what you'll say. But I don't want to put words in your mouth, and I don't want to misinterpret you. Please just... give me the strength to deliver your message as true and clear as it needs to be made, no matter what that message is."

Jesus set the bag down and crossed His arms as He stared at me. And there was a palpable rage skittering through the air, but not at me. At the world. However, along with it came a feeling that the rage wasn't useful or helpful to the situation. As His lips parted, I braced myself for Him to speak—and in true Jesus fashion, He came for *everyone*.

4. WHAT DO YOU THINK OF THE LGBTQ+ COMMUNITY?

"It's an intolerable situation both without *and* within," He said. "This group here, this LGBTQ+ community, needs to get away from it all—the outer persecution by corrupt folk claiming My name *and* the infighting within your ranks. You'll always be running so long as you're scattered, arguing amongst yourselves. You need to dig your heels in, lock arm in arm, turn, and face this evil head on. Be strong, be unified. Fight injustice with justice."

A lot came to my head with this. TERFs. Bi-erasure. Nasty attitudes between identities. You can't win if you're divided. It seemed He didn't have much

A corrupt man, or one who lacks imagination or holds grudges.

Conflict, argument, confrontation.

A card of travel, of running way from an intolerable situation.

to say about the people doing the persecuting, because that was a bygone conclusion: it sucks. From the silent rage that was rolling off Him in waves, I understood viscerally that He can't stand it. But the infighting in LGBTQ+ spaces wasn't something I expected Him to talk about.

"Okay, I get You." And by God, did it feel like a stack of bricks was lifted off my chest. "I feel that," I said, and I blew out a long breath before continuing. "So, wait a minute—how about, like, all these people praising You for the death of Roe v. Wade?"

5. THOUGHTS ON ABORTION AND THE END OF ROE V. WADE?

Failure, division, and frustration. Possible breakdown of a relationship.

Dwelling on past sorrows may prevent you from moving on. Let go of the past, and the confusion and distress may disappear.

Bitterness and hatred may develop from grief. Jealousy, inflexibility.

And again came those waves of silent rage. What a look He had on His face. So thunderous.

"The past is the past," He said. "The decisions that have been made, have been made. People used My name for injustice and abuse. The relationship between Me and these so-called *faithful* is broken, and *they* broke it! But there's no reason to dwell on it. One must act to fix it now.

"People affected by these decisions. shouldn't succumb to grief. Keep clear heads. Work. Move. This won't get fixed from a place of despair, this injustice. You've been wronged—*call on Us! We will help!*"

Here, I was reminded of a verse I'd been reading about in James L. Kugel's *The God of Old: Inside the Lost World of the Bible.* This is a bit of *violent Scripture,* though, so be wary of being uncomfortable with this mention of murder and such.

The verse in question is Exodus 22:21-24 (and all emphasis in here is mine):

> *You shall not mistreat* any widow or fatherless child. *If you do mistreat them, and they cry out to me, I will surely hear their cry,* and my wrath will burn, and I will kill you with the sword, *and your wives shall become widows and your children fatherless.*

In Exodus, it seems, God is speaking to the person writing this, warning them directly of what'll fall on their heads if they act stupid when they should know better as His people. He is actively compelled to strike out against the unjust. It isn't quite written the same in Deuteronomy 27:19, as if to edit out the idea that God *must* act when called to act for some reason, but the spirit remains:

> Cursed be anyone *who perverts the justice due to the sojourner, the fatherless, and the widow. And all the people shall say,* "Amen."

I hurried to write all this down and kept on, because something needed clarification: "And Your thoughts on abortion itself? On the overturning of Roe v. Wade?"

I already knew how He felt about Roe v. Wade; I'd asked Him before, and He was pissed, to put it lightly. Table-flipping pissed. But He said it again plainly:

"Young mothers shouldn't have to bear this."

And those that choose not to be mothers?

"Those not wanting to be shouldn't have that choice made without them!"

"Well, damn." I just blinked for a second, because He was mad; He full on yelled that last bit. "Okay. Let's get away from the modern topics, then, and ask plainly: what do You think of the other religions in the world? And the polytheists who are and want to remain polytheists, but still acknowledge and even want to revere You?"

6. THOUGHTS ON POLYTHEISTS WHO STILL ACKNOWLEDGE YOU?

His face smoothed out here, that storm of rage quieting, and He thought about it for a bit.

"Religions come, religions go," Jesus said after a long moment. "Their people come and go with them, try as they might to keep their power and their dominance. Nothing lasts for-ever, though.

"Well, hey, now," I said with a cheeky smile, "doesn't this apply to Christianity, too? To you?"

And I was surprised at the answer. At the little chuckle He gave with it.

"Time is a desert, Sara. It shifts and twists, never the same desert one mo-ment to the next. It buries things just

Courage in the face of adversity. Overcome hard-ship. Problems solved. Bravery rewarded.

Fear of change is inevitable, but you must face it. Resis-tance is useless.

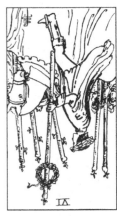

Treachery, in-trigue, and battles that may be lost.

as well as it uncovers things, and then it buries those things again. Yet the things it buries and uncov-ers aren't gone; they'll always be there, even if you can't see them. I and My Father will always be here, but the grip—"

"I'd call it a stranglehold," I interjected, surprised at my own bitterness, and even more surprised at His reaction as His little smile fell, and as He looked down at His feet while we sat there.

"Yes, Sara, the *stranglehold* will loosen. The columns," which I understood as the institutions of the Church, the official structures and chains and cages made by these boxy rules, "will be buried, and the people will rise, gasping, from the sand.

Honestly, the entire time He was explaining this, I was trying not to squeal and bounce around my living room. Do you understand what you're reading? Because I understood what I was writing: a parable. A parable from *Jesus*! Like the ones He gave His Apostles! Like the ones we reference time and time again, those beautiful metaphors! And He was giving me a fresh one I'd never heard before, and it lit my soul *up*, let me tell you.

"Right, right!" I was suddenly buzzing with excitement. "But what about the polytheists them-selves? The ones who respect You and want to talk with You, maybe even revere You?"

Jesus laughed. "Let them come! Come one, come all. Breathe. Live. Know my arms are open to all."

The vibe started to lighten up. Where I had all this heaviness and worry, it was fading fast, because Jesus was vibrant, even beyond the exasperation with what's been going on these days.

"Okay, next one: a lot of people have been saying you, yourself, were a witch. I personally don't think that quite scans, but what do you think about that?"

7. THOUGHTS ON THE IDEA THAT YOU'RE A WITCH?

Irresponsibility with other people's money may lead to debt. There is also a chance for fraud, so be wary.

Treachery, intrigue, and battles that may be lost.

Indecision at a critical time could lead to defeat.

The scowl He had. I didn't expect part of what He said, nor did I expect the dryness in which He spoke.

"I guess that Lucian fellow won."

He was referencing what I'd read in Robert Conner's *Magic in Christianity: From Jesus to the Gnostics*, where one Roman individual, by the name Lucian, wrote about the early Christians that he saw as ignorant and believing without reason. Notable that most Christians at this very early time were women and slaves—people Lucian saw as unlettered, unlearned, ignorant. Lucian also seemed to think that Jesus Himself was little more than a street magician doing fancy tricks.

But I had to ask: "What do You mean?"

Jesus sucked His teeth and sighed. "Think about it. A witch? What does this word even mean? Who and what I am isn't constrained to these kinds of ideas. I am simply Me. I do what I do."

Then He got up and leaned His weight on a staff, with a bit of white robes peaking from under the maroon. It was a shepherd's staff.

"I am a Shepherd," He said. "To the flock, My very being is magic. But it's My Father's force that guides us all—that I wield in His name. Labels like 'witch' mean nothing to Me."

"Oh, I see. Okay. I understand." I was sitting all cross legged on that mountain, journal in lap, writing away. Then I tucked my pencil behind my ear and said, "Alright, well, here's another heavy one: some say You're just a prophet, some say You're an ascended master, and some say You're the very literal Son of God, like, God made flesh. What's true? Is there a truth?"

8. ARE YOU THE SON OF GOD OR WHAT?

1. Failure, division, and frustration. Possible breakdown of a relationship.

2. Unfounded accusations, rebellion against an unfair situation.

3. Pragmatism, collaboration, compromise. Victory by working with others, not against. Changing one's behavior more likely to succeed than changing others'.

He was sitting again, and He waved a hand.

"Sara, what does it matter?" His lips pursed as He shook His head. "I could come down and say any of these things right now and still, people wouldn't believe it. They didn't the first time as it is. At the end of the day, I am still but a servant to My Father. What matters is His law. So long as people don't forget what's truly important, the details are just that—details.

"Whatever one thinks when they look at Me, if it helps one come to God, then that's that. We are all Children of God in some way."

...Huh?

I won't lie. I do believe Jesus is the literal Son of God, both because I grew up with this understanding of a triune God and because it allows Jürgen Moltmann's beautiful thesis in *The Crucified God* to work, and so I was spiraling for a direct answer. Yes? No? Was I right? Was I wrong?

But while my mind was in a state of complete confusion, He was really adamant about this:

"You know, it could've been anyone in My position. We aren't chosen or made because we're great; we're great because we're chosen, all of us, for whatever purpose we have in this world. *All* of us play a part. We are *all* important."

And there's a lot to be said here. If you think about the prophets of the Bible, they aren't chosen because they're lofty and powerful figures. They're often the least likely people to be considered for the title of prophet or the like; the point is that any of us, at any point, can do what needs to be done.

So I guess that question was chalked up to a big old, *I won't tell you because what matters is not Me to begin with.*

Wild.

"Um, okay, I guess." I sat there with pencil and paper in my lap for a second, somewhat at a loss. "Fine. Sure. But there was one additional bit to this: Your people didn't accept You as the Messiah. What do You think about that?"

9. WHAT DO YOU THINK ABOUT YOUR PEOPLE NOT ACCEPTING YOU?

And I got an answer that *stung*, because you could see the pain on Jesus's face. It had nothing to do with His people rejecting Him or not. Rather, it had everything to do with all that had been done to His people in His name.

Here is where He really shocked me with the imagery He put out, so if for whatever reason a mention of the travesties of the world, like the Holocaust, upset you, then you'll want to steel yourself for this portion of the interview.

Because in terms of people actually rejecting Him, He said: "There will always be some who will reject the idea that the Messiah came, no matter how many times a Messiah figure appears. But I didn't want this. All this, all that's happened—I didn't want this."

Jesus's face was wrenched in an agony I don't think I've ever felt—the kind that makes you draw blood when you bite down on your lip. I didn't know what to do about that, but I also knew I didn't want to just sit there while He went through all those feelings, so I sat back and gathered up the courage to get myself in some seriously *hot* emotional waters.

"Can You show me what you mean?" I hugged my knees to my chest; this was no time for writing. Whatever He showed me here, I knew I'd remember. "Can you let me feel what You're feeling—just a little piece?"

A man with great hidden sadness. He keeps his emotions to himself, which leads to self destructive tendencies.

He blinked, and then we were off this mountain, just for a moment. Instead, I saw Him banging on iron gates, howling, weeping, screaming. When I looked up, I saw three words above that gate that have become a moniker of one of the worst tragedies of the 20th century, where we, we Christians, killed Jesus's people (and so many others in just this specific moment in history, like the Rroma, the disabled, the LGBTQ+, and more) in His name.

And as a Christian myself, all I can say is: what in hell is wrong with us? This isn't the first example of our atrocities against Jesus's own people; it's simply the biggest in our living memory. Why the hell do we do such unbearably wretched and unspeakable things, things that exceed one's imagination for injustice and horror—doing them not only in that one moment in history to one group of people, but across centuries, across continents, across peoples and cultures—and think God smiles on that?

And why, my siblings in faith, do we constantly brush our fellows, our offending brothers, off with "but they weren't real Christians"?

They called themselves Christians as they did these things; do you understand? They held up the image of a dying Christ, then spit on His life, His friends, His family, His culture, His people, His very God, while they continued (and still continue to this day) this parade of *death*.

We have a responsibility to do something about that. To not just denounce the types of Christians that think Jesus's message is one of hate and violence, but meet them in the middle of their death parade and shout them down. To stand by those that have been hurt and fix all this that we have let happen. After all, I mean, how could we let the God of the oppressed and downtrodden become the hammer which people use to do just that, with no limit to the cruelty and suffering left scattered around? How could we let the God who protects the sojourner, the widow, the fatherless, become the very name these folks would be bludgeoned with? And how could we think God would ever be smiling down on us for that?

We have a lot to answer for. So much. And no Christian should ever have the audacity to say to themselves, "well, I never said anything mean to anybody, so I don't have to worry about it." No one should ever feel themselves absolved of responsibility for the crimes committed underneath Christ's own cross just because they personally haven't lobbied against people's rights or, I don't know, *started a whole genocide.*

They are us. We are them. The title *Christian* cannot mean anything until we're willing to wrest it back from the people that have used it as a banner under which they can unite in their hate and cruelty. And to see how Jesus howled there, and knowing so many Christians will still never hear *this,* never mind the soft and subtle voice Jesus speaks with, I know there's still work to be done.

We can't be quiet. It's not possible. To be quiet in the face of this madness is to be still while fire catches on your pants and licks up your leg, consuming you. There can never be silence in the face of injustice, not unless you want to be eaten alive by your inaction.

Jesus and I sat there for a long time after that, and you bet my mojito soon went from half drank to bone dry, gone. But after rubbing my face and looking at my list of questions, I managed to jump back into it with Him and continue on.

"Okay. From here, I notice You put the idea forth that the whole Messiah thing is like a cycle. It made me think of how some say things like, for example, Ragnarok are a cycle. Can You elaborate?"

Jesus didn't pick a card for this. "It symbolizes a reset. Every now and again, things get twisted, bent, and someone needs to set it right again."

That had me thinking, especially about astrological ages. Don't people say that the era Jesus came was the Age of Pisces? And it made me think more of what I'd been reading in *The God of Old,* how at one point, the age of prophets was considered gone, God unreachable, things in turmoil. But even before reading that book, I'd found a little voice in my head saying: *we're all prophets now.* Or, at least, we can be.

Because we do have the tools to find and reach God. We're picking them up again. We're learning how to close the gap of communication and familiarity between God and Humanity again.

Does this have something to do with the Age of Aquarius? I don't know. But it's a big idea nonetheless, and one that's been admittedly haunting me since the thought popped into my head.

"So, going further with this cycle and the Messiah idea... what do You think of the Rapture? And all the people literally just waiting for the world to combust?"

10. WHAT ARE YOUR THOUGHTS ON THE RAPTURE?

KNIGHT of SWORDS.

A brash young man, hotheaded but keen to do what's right. A man of action, one who gets things done. Righteous anger, bravery, courage, heroism. Triumph over optimism.

That was Jesus's card—or, at least, the card I'd assigned to Him in my head. Specifically in Kat Black's Golden Tarot, it had a picture of a knight beating off a dragon at its horse's feet.

It's become a beast," Jesus said as He leaned against the mountain wall beside me, with that same exasperated energy He had earlier. "This idea spiraled out of control. All things *will* end, yes, because everything has an end at some point, *everything*, but no one knows when that is."

And then, as I went to ask another question, He had an unprompted line:

"There is so much clarity here, where I am. It's difficult to watch you all."

I shrugged. "Perfectly understandable. We're kind of a mess down here. But someone else asked: what are You like? By that, I mean: how does one distinguish between You and God in a reading?"

11. HOW DOES ONE TELL BETWEEN YOU AND GOD?

Jesus glanced at me and grinned. "Why don't you tell them? You know."

"What, me? But don't You want to—"

He shook His head. "You know. Tell your experience."

And, well, if He didn't want to pick any cards and wanted me to just go for it, I'll tell you. Jesus has what God (and likewise His angels) don't. At least, God doesn't have this without the lens of Jesus, which was the point of bringing His Son down to experience all this Himself in my understanding, and the angels just straight up don't have it at all. What Jesus has is a sympathy for and extremely intimate understanding of the human condition.

The angels have perfect knowledge. They watch us make stupid decisions and don't understand what our problem is. They don't get why we can't just do the right thing. They sometimes feel robotic, but it's not because they're robots; it's because their system and intelligence is so refined that nonsensical decisions just aren't even a consideration.

This means working with angels is dangerous. They can push us too far, past our breaking point. Even God is adamant, strong as diamond, unmovable: He has patience, yes, but He will still expect you, like the most stern Father you can imagine, to heed what He tells you, not because He wants to undermine your free will, but because *you asked Him for the advice or steps to take, and He gave them, and He doesn't understand why you aren't following it if you wanted it.*

Do or don't. Whatever choice you make will have its natural consequence.

Jesus doesn't really have this air. He's stern at times, downright angry and annoyed at others when people do awful things, but He still has the air of a very old friend, or a mentor that you haven't seen in a long time. Nonetheless, He's the mentor that, when He speaks, you always soak up every word He says, because He delivers it in a way that's easier to understand, human, conceivable—and it was reflecting on this that I understood the real reason people are told to go to God *through* Christ.

Because He's the intermediary between that human malleability and that divine inflexibility. He can help you more gently understand the sometimes completely unfathomable and seemingly impossible advice. He gets us, because He's been there.

A long answer, but that's the answer I came to.

"Jeez, putting me on the spot like that," I muttered, and He chuckled before I got back to my questions. "Okay, next! What do You think of Lucifer?"

12. WHAT DO YOU THINK ABOUT LUCIFER?

Now, that was one wild card to pull for Lucifer—especially since how Lucifer sees himself included the King of Cups *Reversed*. And this had me laughing pretty hard, I won't lie, because Jesus sucked His teeth and huffed. The lightness came back, the heavy emotional storm cloud of the past few answers gone.

"He thinks he's so big and bad, but he isn't," Jesus said with a *tsk*. "He isn't the cold and strict and unphased thing he tries to come off as. The thing is that he's loyal to a fault. You know," and this phrase banged my head hard, "you know what I'm talking about."

A warm, loving woman. Maternal and nurturing. Gentle, insightful, and considerate of the needs of others. Loyal, honest, completely trustworthy. Can easily blend with her surroundings, maybe a little too much, as she doesn't assert her own opinion often. Creative, a lover of art and poetry.

QUEEN of CUPS.

Truth be told, I do. Lucifer is a frustrated being. He, as the Adversary, is always trying to show God that humanity isn't all that—yet at the same time, he so clearly wants humanity to be all that, because he knows what we could be if we just stopped being stupid.

Angel-vision, y'know? Not understanding how we can mess things up this bad.

Jesus continued: "That Lucifer wants to push humanity to perfection, but not at expense of themselves; he still respects free will. He's a rather conflicted fellow, actually. Good and evil are words that, like *witch*, mean nothing, especially in relation to Lucifer. This is a battle here, but it's between knowledge and ignorance. The knowledgeable know they can take advantage of the ignorant, and so it's up to you to become just as knowledgeable, that you might never be tricked by anyone's lies."

"I got'cha. That makes a lot of sense." It made me feel better, too; it confirmed what I saw in Lucifer when I'd spoken to him. He's just not at all what the Church has said, not one bit. "Now, Asherah... how about her? Where do You relate with her?"

13. HOW DO YOU RELATE TO ASHERAH?

THE EMPRESS.

Matriarchal author-ity. Goal-oriented person, concerned about means used to achieve success. Collaborative and cooperative, com-promising. Fruit-fulness, fertility, abundance. Happi-ness, creativity.

KING OF CUPS.

A man with great hidden sadness. He keeps his emotions to himself, which leads to self destruc-tive tendencies.

With the cards I pulled, I knew right away: we messed up. Neither God nor Jesus are happy that Asherah's been cut out, because she represents another side of something that, as a result of us cutting her off, have lost: balance. And Jesus said as much as He stared out over the little town we'd come from.

"Balance has been distorted," He said. "Another injustice. Asherah is throneless now, but her work carries on through My Mother, and Mary Magdalene; she's waiting for the time when people are ready to see her again. This destructive-ness in this world is a result of imbalance, this severing of one part from its whole. Asherah was a Mother before there were mothers. We're coming back to that balance now."

I'd been listening to music all this time I'd been speaking to Jesus, and right then, Hozier's *Take Me to Church* came on. Jesus frowned at it.

"I hate songs like these," He said, "because I hate what drove them to be written."

There was a rasp of frustration in His voice. By "what drove them to be writ-ten," I understood that He meant the pain caused to the songwriter by the injus-tices the Church has committed.

"I hear you," I said, "and I agree. It sucks. But hey, speaking of Mary Magda-lene... what is Your relationship with her like *now*?"

14. WHAT IS YOUR RELATIONSHIP WITH ST. MARY LIKE NOW?

While reading the booklet description, I got the sense that these were the things Jesus admired about St. Mary. I got the image of St. Mary grinning, joy-ful, as she came and hugged Jesus in a similar place to where I met her, in that town under the awning of a cafe. They were two peas in a pod.

Then Jesus said, "She helped us plenty. I admire her greatly; she's an honor-able woman. I'm grateful for her. Everyone should be grateful for those that choose to stand by them."

So to put the lid on this: their relationship, however you interpret it, is plainly still today one of pure love and joy. Whatever that means to you, let it be, but love and joy is definitely the focus here.

"Alright, alright, I see. I got you. Now, here's a more personal question, I guess: what kind of things did You like to do as hobbies in life?"

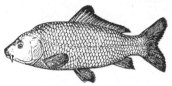

QUEEN OF PENTACLES

A generous, sensible, intelligent woman with a head for business, but also warmth. Posi-tive, boisterous, a good sense of humor. Hard-working, philanthropic.

15. WHAT WERE YOUR HOBBIES IN LIFE?

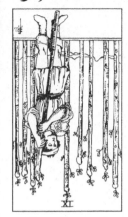

Obstacles, problems, resistance.

Travel. A speedy journey, ideas made reality. Messages, news. Hasty decisions may be regretted.

Indecision at a critical time could lead to defeat.

I was surprised at the straight stack of Wands cards that came down, but as I read them, an image of Him as a boy, talking to the rabbis, came up, and it was clear to me: He loved projects of the mind.

"Mind, huh?" I poked at the cards. "But the mind is more associated with Swords than Wands. What's up here?"

With a warm smile, He explained it to me: "Philosophy is a creative thing. I loved grappling with philosophical problems and debating them—and that's the fun in debate, isn't it? It's creative thinking that cracks the worst problems. You have to understand something well, and think about it in different ways, to reach new ideas."

"Oh, I understand! Yeah, that makes sense. Well, we're about done with tarot, so here's a bonus question: what should people do if they feel like they're having a hard time reaching You and God, or feeling Your presence?"

16. WHAT SHOULD FOLKS DO IF HAVING A HARD TIME REACHING YOU?

Right away, the first word that popped in my head as I read the card description was: *rest.* But Jesus elaborated:

"Retreat from the world," He said. "The focus is all off: come sit with Us, in Our space, and don't neglect Us for the world. Don't have one foot in the material world and one foot in Ours; really be present with Us and forget everything else for a while."

And you know what? For this question, I'll add my personal diagnosis of a problem like this: do some meditation. Shut off outside thoughts, all outside worries, and just be for a second. Focus and make sure you aren't pushing and forcing yourself to try and feel them; just exist and let yourself be still.

But that wrapped up the tarot portion, and believe it or not, before this moment, I'd never really bothered much with bibliomancy. Tarot cards were what I was comfortable with, so when it came time to pull out three separate parts of the holy Scriptures—the Jewish Study Bible, the Jewish Annotated Apocrypha, and the Jewish Annotated New Testament—I was a little nervous. Still, I decided we'd come this far, and that all we could do was get to the end, no matter what the end looked like.

"Okay," I said as I clapped my hands together, "here's the Bibliomancy part! Crazy! Never done this for a reading like this, so let's see: Jesus, how do You view yourself?"

Problem with a relationship, a partner feeling taken for granted or jealous of a potential rival. Promiscuity, unfaithfulness, yearning for a more exciting life.

I landed on the Jewish Study Bible, and Jesus had me point to Micah 2:12-13:

"I will surely gather all of you, Jacob;
I will surely bring together the remnant of Israel.
I will bring them together like sheep in a pen,
like a flock in its pasture;
the place will throng with people.
The One who breaks open the way will go up before them;
they will break through the gate and go out.
Their King will pass through before them,
the Lord at their head."

Jesus nodded. "I am a uniting force. One who gathers the flock and brings it to safety."

"And how do You want to be seen?"

Here's where we ended up in the Jewish Annotated Apocrypha. We landed on the part in Jubilees, which was a rewritten section of Genesis from what I can find, where Joseph escapes Potiphar's wife, who was trying to seduce him—first by propositioning him, next by trying to force him. He flees, losing his coat in the process, but she turns it against him, claiming that Joseph tried to assault her, and she has him jailed for doing the right thing, which was, you know... not committing adultery.

Likewise, Jesus felt this was relevant, but I didn't understand why until He explained:

"I want to be seen as someone who does what is right, and yet has My actions are used against Me. They," meaning His modern followers, "use My name wrong. They read the good I went to spread and make lies of it."

"Oh, damn, yeah. Yeah, I see." I wrote that down, bobbing my head like a bird as I finally understood what He was saying. "Well, okay, last question, now: what message do You have?"

And here we were at the Jewish Annotated New Testament, but imagine my surprise when what my finger landed on was not the actual Scripture, but the annotation:

"Third passion prediction... does not use the phrase 'Son of Man.' Most of these passages receive messianic interpretation only in Christian sources" (154).

When looking at the verse that this annotation related to, I saw it was Luke 18:31-34:

Jesus took the Twelve aside and told them, "We are going up to Jerusalem, and everything that is written by the prophets about the Son of Man will be fulfilled. He will be delivered over to the Gentiles. They will mock him, insult him and spit on him; they will flog him and kill him. On the third day he will rise again."
The disciples did not understand any of this. Its meaning was hidden from them, and they did not know what he was talking about.

And then Jesus sat there on that mountain with a more serious look on His face and, with a straightforward tone, said:

"Everyone tries to make the pieces fit a different puzzle. Humanity will never agree on everything. But humanity needs to try. All these gifts, professions, devotion," in which I was sure He was referring to the offerings people make to Him and His Father, "what's the point if the forcefulness of those gestures breaks the world? People remain obsessed with the details while *scorning* the Truth."

I understood pretty solidly what He meant, and I was surprised that we came back full circle: to the love, justice, and mercy that were forgotten in Matthew 23:23.

"True." I sat there for a second. "Yeah. Well, it's extremely late. I do need to go. But Jesus, thank You so much for this. I'll see You around, I guess!"

He smiled again, one last, big, beaming smile, and the mountain, the town, all of it faded away until it was just me in my living room. With that, I had to decompress for another entire hour before I could go to bed. It was late, but how could I have slept after that? Worse was the next day, having to write all this up after having just gone through it. I'll be honest: I cried a bit during the interview, and I cried a bit again writing it all up. It was so much. It was so *heavy*. That bag of the universe Jesus was carrying—this, all this, was a part of the contents of that bag.

But I think it's really time that Christians reclaim that Truth. In my mind, God, His Spirit, and Jesus all represent the undying, unapologetic, and undeniable voice of justice. It isn't just that They're pure *love and light*, like so much modern discourse makes them out to be. Of course that's a part of it. But love and light without discipline is not effective, and people shy away from the sides of God that make them uncomfortable: the sides that shout down injustice that they'd otherwise turn a blind eye to, the sides that avenge the oppressed and heal the wounded, that actively turn and smite the wounder for their transgressions. People forget that God Himself is a God of the underdog, to the point that they use His name to continue kicking that underdog.

So again: it's time to reclaim the Truth. The real God, the real Jesus, the real Holy Spirit, that the Church has so clearly forgotten. If we focus on correcting one another, let it not be for details—the clothes one wears or the music they listen to or the personalized way they decide to approach God (with magic, with church, with whatever), or any other number of stupid details that, while they certainly create a composed picture when we force all God's followers into conformity, ultimately mean nothing.

Let it be for the injustice, and the wickedness, and the cruelty, that they wrongly speak in God's name. And let us make up for all our filth by first acknowledging it's even there, then linking up arms with those the Church has persecuted and standing with them.

A long and winding thing, this chapter. A lot of thoughts wrapped up in pictures and metaphors and feelings. But nonetheless, in the end, it is what it is: this chapter here is my struggle to convey the Jesus I know, uncensored, unashamed, to everyone who seeks to really know Him. I hope it helped you understand Him better, and I hope you got some answers, too—ones you wanted, and maybe also ones you didn't know you were looking for.

THE MORRÍGAN

And here we are, conversing with the Morrígan. A goddess I'm sure many know well—or at least, a goddess I'm sure many have heard of.

A goddess of Celtic polytheism, the Morrígan is a *true* triple goddess, in that she's actually the amalgamation of three different goddesses that create the one we call the Fae Queen, the Phantom Queen, or the Washer at the Ford. Those goddesses are Badb, the Battle Crow, the aspect of the Morrígan that represented war and death, confusion and fear, then Macha, representing war and also fate, success, fire, and fertility, and then Nemain, who personifies the frenzy, fury, and chaos of the battle-field. These three are said to be the Morrígans, or the ones that make up the one Morrígan we think of today when we think of the Irish goddesses of war and death.

Though the Morrígan is the husband of the Dagda, one of her most famous stories is how she chases after the Irish hero Cú Chulainn for rejecting her as his lover. (Granted she was disguised as a young woman, and he had no idea it was her—or that any of the animals that attacked him on the road after were her, or that the old lady that offered him three cups of milk and that he blessed three times was her, but I digress.) She reminded him of his bad manners and told him in no uncertain terms that he'd die in the upcoming battles, which he did.

She's a brutal goddess, a fascinating one, and when it came time to talk to her, I was more than happy to do so. To prepare, I consulted with my good friend and co-writer for *Discovering Christian Witchcraft,* @feralsouthernhousewife (Mimi), as well as my friend @the_stitching_witch (Beck)—both of which have extensive experience with the Morrígan. As a result, I found myself equipped to approach an invocation better than if I'd tried to go at this alone. There were many things, it turns out, that I didn't know about properly invoking a goddess of this caliber.

So while I did have two lavender candles burning, some mugwort, which is associated with her, and a thing to represent death—a knife—the most important part of the set-up I had was the water for three votive offerings. Votive offerings are different from normal ones: in these, you pour your gift directly into the water (be it a bowl of water, something like a river, so on), and for all three of these aspects of the Morrígan, and the Morrígan herself, I had a shot of whiskey. Good whiskey, too, Irish whiskey: Tullamore D.E.W.

So once I was settled and ready, my blessings done, my prayers said, my candles lit and my space prepared, I poured a shot of whiskey into each of the four bowls of water I had out, and I invoked the Morrígan as respectfully and earnestly as I could.

"I call out to The Morrígan, the Phantom Queen, the Fae Queen, Washer at the Ford; if you're okay with speaking to me, please come and accept this offering of whisky—as well as an offering for the three goddesses that make you up. Three faces, one woman: I ask Macha, Badb, and Nemain to come, and to come together as The Morrígan."

It was a little formal for my usual style, I won't lie, but I wanted to do this right and make it clear what I was asking. But while I'd had my own imaginations of what the Morrígan would look like throughout the day, maybe someone in dark clothes with brown hair, she came through completely differently.

As I asked her to let me feel her, I got a sense I wasn't expecting: someone totally calm, wizened. I don't know if maybe I thought a goddess of death, war, and prophecy would be a little more intimidating, but she just appeared there, with red hair plaited in two thick braids, a cape of feathers that reminded me of Freyja, and a shield. The Morrígan stood on the banks of a great river, and I walked up to her as she stared out at the rushing river. As I got closer, I saw the three beings that made her up, who surrounded her almost like small statues at her feet, with their heads ducked until it was time for them to speak.

Those three looked different, too. There was Macha, who kept showing me flashes of herself blood soaked and eyeless, like a skeleton, though sometimes she would show me a dark haired young woman, too. Then there was Badb, a silver-haired crone with a sly smile. And there was Nemain, a red-headed woman with a frenzied, unfocused look in her eye and a wild, toothy grin. They were like anchors at the feet of the Morrígan, whose shoulders were broad under her cloak, and whose back was straight with dignity and power.

The gravel crunched under my feet as I came up along the riverbank to greet them. "Hello, Phantom Queen! Thank you for joining me!"

The Morrígan smiled, glancing at me sidelong as I approached and bowed my head to her. She had the face of a slighty-older-than-middle-aged woman, and she had a complete calmness in her eye. But the river ran with blood for a moment, then cleared, then ran with blood again.

"The blood doesn't last in this river," she said, as if she guessed the question I hadn't yet fully formed in my mind. "It comes and goes, comes and goes, a tide. Life and death."

Right out the gate, I knew we were in for it, if she was already speaking so clearly to me. Still, I triple-checked that she and her three aspects were there and asked her to choose a deck. She chose Amrit Brar's Marigold Tarot, and we agreed that each of her three aspects—Badb, Macha, and Nemain—would choose a card, and that she, as one goddess, would give the final response. I also made sure to write down that opening bit of wisdom she gave me, and then we were off.

"So, An Morrígan," I started as I whipped out my journal there at the riverbank, "given how much modern neopaganism and Wicca seems to be based off Celtic polytheism—or, at least, a heavily reconstructed and modernized version of it—what do you think of the way people perceive the concept of a triple goddess? I mean, you're really a triple goddess! And yet the versions I've heard about are all about life and motherhood and feminine power, but rarely the death, the grit, the war and prophecy and strategy, that you have in your station."

1. THOUGHTS ON HOW PEOPLE PERCEIVE A TRIPLE GODDESS TODAY?

The Morrígan rolled her eyes, then leaned over on a big rock on the riverbanks and stared out at the water. The way we answered questions was interesting to see play out as we tried it; from what I understood, the Morrígan interpreted and created her answer from the fragments of her own ideas and feelings that these three aspects offered up. It was definitely a different way of going about things than I was used to, but I didn't struggle or fight for meaning; I simply opened my mind to what solidified into words and rolled with it.

She cocked her head. "It's difficult," she said, the three goddesses at her feet

Macha:
Re-evaluating whether a relationship or goal is really fulfilling.

Badb:
Breaking bonds, freedom, detachment.

Nemain:
Unwillingness to see the problems for what they are, looming disaster, avoiding change.

shifting. "These Christian attitudes here, of good and evil, they persisted—and these people you mention wanted to avoid that which centered on death and what they considered negative. This world... you cannot chase light all the time. There is growth in darkness, life's cradle rocked in death. It's folly, to erase what is considered dark. People miss the full circle of life this way."

"Oh, absolutely. I completely agree." Then I was looking from outside myself, seeing myself wrapped in a thick woolen cloak and writing away in my journal. We were a few feet apart, as if there was a great gap between us, and I suppose there was, given we were Humanity and Divinity. "Well, on the topic of those darker aspects: how do you, as three sisters, oversee the battlefield?"

2. HOW DO YOU OVERSEE THE BATTLEFIELD AS THREE SISTERS?

Macha:
Calamity, struggle, conflict, misjudgement, change, disaster.

Badb:
A lapse in judgement and holes in one's intuition.

Nemain:
Overextending oneself or one's resources, avoiding responsibility.

There was a simplicity in her answer: "We see the truth of the situation. And we act."

I was reminded of a video I'd seen earlier that day, of a border collie herding sheep, and the connection was clear to me right away. They herd the soldiers, inspiring rage and frenzy and fear and morale depending on who the winner will be. Their screeches that drop a hundred men from fear alone, their frenzy that turns men into machines, their omens and active participation, all work to create the fated outcome.

"Divide and conquer," the Morrígan muttered, her gaze skimming over foaming, rushing water. "Piecemeal the enemy."

"Wow. That's so cool." I don't know what about it had me so enthused, but the idea of it all was exciting, and I bounced like a kid hearing their older siblings tell some outlandish and awe-inspiring tale. "That's so *cool*! Okay, okay—when the wars are over, I'm curious: what interests you most about watching over humanity, if anything?"

3. WHAT INTERESTS YOU THE MOST ABOUT HUMANITY?

The cards I pulled were super straightforward, but the answer was a little surprising.

"It's the same song and dance with you humans, every time," the Morrígan said with a huff. "You know so many truths and yet pretend not to. The humblest man that sups with his family—how does he remember what the supposedly wizened king doesn't, about the inevitability of death?

"So stubborn, you humans—stubborn enough to accept the same fate a hundred times over if you think you have the smallest chance

Macha: Stagnation, resisting change.

Badb: Peace, self awareness, family, birth, death, and enlightenment.

Nemain: Discord, disorder, overbearing control, break down in power.

of changing it even one time. It's interesting, watching you scrape and scrounge. People don't learn because they can't learn what they already know. Chaos comes from trying to deny obvious truths."

I blew out a breath as I wrote. Is that what it looks like to Divinity? Us learning the same lessons over and over, trying to change a story already written? "Jeez. I never thought about it that way." I tapped my pencil to my lip, then shrugged. "Well, onto the next: I'd like to ask you, Fae Queen, what separates the faeries from the angels and infernals? What defines them?"

4. HOW ARE FAIRIES DIFFERENT FROM ANGELS AND DEMONS?

Macha (1):
Weakness, breaking down, losing control, having difficulty problem solving.

Badb (2):
Denial, stalemate, indecision, illusions.

Nemain (3):
Self satisfaction, good fortune, contentment. Finding joy in what one has and finds it abundant. Goodwill to oneself.

The Morrígan smiled at the water as she thought. Then she spoke.

"The Fae are not interested in helping one find stability or control over the world and oneself, all this enlightenment and learning, like angels and demons might be," she explained. They're only interested in living—and they'll help you consider your options, but they won't council you one way or another.

"They have their affairs in order, as one should. They're there to share space, to pitch in on projects, to enjoy life and find others to enjoy it with. Their advice can twist in circles; they might give you six hundred ideas and none they suggest over the other. With the Fae, their company is the prize."

Hmm. "And how would you recommend people work with them, if you recommend it at all?"

5. HOW WOULD YOU RECOMMEND PEOPLE WORK WITH FAIRIES?

Macha: Persistence and resilience in the face of adversity. Despite challenges, when faced with goals, we must rise to the occasion and stand proud.

Badb: Ill paced infatuation with an idea or person, overhanging doubts, confusion, a dent in one's confidence.

Nemain: Unconditional love, compassion, empathy, patience. Emerging from filth, hardship, and ruin. Thoughtful, considerate.

Macha had quite the mean smile here, where as Badb had a look of warning. I could've sworn I saw some poke out from the trees further away from the river: bigger creatures with big black eyes and hats made of mushrooms and things. They were watching us, silent, trying to keep just out of sight so that they weren't intruding, but still visible enough to let us know they were watching.

"The Fae," the Morrígan started, without looking at the clustering audience among the trees, "are people, too. Difficult people, but people. They may not do things in a way you understand, but you might learn their language well enough. It's important not to be fooled by the images of fairies you've made in your mind and to recognize that not all are so quaint."

An image of Tinker Bell or some other cartoon fairy popped into my head as she said that.

"Many can be downright nasty, even without mishandling. But if you truly strive to understand them, you can discover a world of rich fun."

"I see! Okay. That makes a lot of sense." Sometimes I felt like an archivist, the way I would get an answer and write it down so quickly, as if I were trying to stuff the raw concept into a bottle to draw on when I needed it. Most times, though, I just didn't really know what to say to Divinity when it gave me an answer. "On a different topic, though, I understand that your husband, the Dagda, died in battle as you prophesized. But he still has influence over the world from wherever he resides now, and so that makes me wonder: what does it actually mean for gods to die?"

6. WHAT DOES IT MEAN FOR THE GODS TO DIE?

Macha:
Wishful thinking, imagination, pre-occupation with fantasy. Memory, the flighty nature of thought, intro-spection.

Badb:
Abundance, gen-erosity, security, and level headed-ness. Reliability, tolerance. Know-ing one's limits and strengths and how to make the most of both.

Nemain:
Generosity, pros-perity, gratifica-tion, reflection, and loss versus gain. Understand-ing the harmful and helpful facets of the material world.

She considered me, and her face was one of easy, peaceful knowledge, like if I'd caught my mom sitting on the deck and thinking away.

"You have to understand that this human world is not a permanent place for us," the Morrigan said. She cocked her head but stayed otherwise still. "Death is a return back to our seat of power beyond the veil, to reflect on what we've seen and done before we return again to continue our aid." Then she paused, elaborated. "Knowl-edge is our wealth. Death is a tool. It isn't the end or a tragedy; it's a door-way. We carry things in and out of it as needed."

I got the sense that she was giving me very small parables; the words flooded into my head, all about Death, about what it was like and what it did in the world and so on. Overall, it gave me the idea that death wasn't an end for the gods, like we understand it, but more like sleep, rest and rejuvenation. How-ever, for gods who don't care much about the flow of time, their deathly sleep can last so long that we people might think they're dead forever, when in reality they're just away for a bit. It's just a moment to them.

This made me think of the idea of Jesus as the Son of God—that if we think of Him as seriously God made flesh, then it only makes sense that He'd have to return one day to a world not physical like this one. And it made me think of Ragnarok, too, of it happening in cycles, and the many Norse gods that are said to die but are clearly still here despite their ends in battle.

Really interesting stuff.

"Thank you for sharing that with me," I said as I watched her.

I didn't know it yet, but the idea was a seed that would drift down into the very deepest parts of my mind, where, when it germinated, would once more help me understand something about my own God. It's funny like that: how conversations with anything and anyone that *isn't* God somehow find a way to teach me something more about Him anyway.

I kicked at the riverbank rocks as the idea took hold, and then I shrugged. "I guess our next ques-tion is up: I see you appear often in people's practices, regardless of who they're working with already, and I'm curious as to what inspires you to work with someone? What do you see in their lives and experiences that has you wanting to come into their life?"

7. WHAT INSPIRES YOU TO WORK WITH A PRACTITIONER?

These were not very good cards that I pulled, save for the Knight. But the first and last ones were cards that suggested plenty issues one might need divine assistance with, and soon the Morrígan had her three separate cards combined into her one answer. She turned more towards me and pinned me with her bright stare.

"I turn the tide for the winner," she said. "There is a winner before the battle begins, and I know how one becomes the victor. It's strategy and frenzy, theory alongside action."

Which seemed to be courtesy of Macha most of all, who was less about Nemain's frenzy and more about the events and plans of war, the success in conflict and the life *after* the battle.

Macha: Someone smart, skilled, brave, wrathful. Duality: gracious and deceptive. Can be tactless, speaking without thinking.

Badb: Hostility, indecision, and disharmony.

Nemain: Greed, possessiveness, unkindness of spirit, illusions and dreams of the world. Suffering, vision obscured by a closed fist.

The Morrígan continued: "There isn't time for sitting on the fence if one wants to move. I help people see their true potential; I unblind them to the lies of internal and external enemies. If one is entering or already in a battle, of any kind, I will help them face it."

I nodded. "That sounds incredible, yeah. But alright, so: how do you see yourself?"

8. HOW DO YOU SEE YOURSELF?

Macha: Separation, mistrust, low self esteem, disharmony.

Badb: Financial troubles, struggles, victim mentalities, rejection. Strife is self inflicted.

Nemain: New beginnings, spontaneity, innocence. Mental journeys more important than physical ones.

Again, I found myself looking at surprisingly less-than-positive cards, and yet there was a goodness to it. I'd asked God about what to expect from this reading beforehand, as I tend to do, and gotten similarly murky cards on the Morrígan, so it was interesting to see how these cards from the Morrígan herself echoed those sentiments a little bit, and why.

Though as I thought about that, the Morrígan spoke with a dry, cracking humor in her voice.

"Your God has no business seeing me so clearly."

I startled. "Um, well—"

Then she held up a hand, as if to say it was all in good fun, and sighed. "But these times are strange. Battles fought on my land are of the mind, not of steel and blood. You must adapt to the world—and when I saw the change coming for my people, I didn't know how to handle it at first. How to understand the loss. I was furious.

"Still, I'm an expanding being. I know battles and battlefields have many shapes and manifestations. The rise of Christianity here put me at odds with my own people for a time, what with how these Christians viewed gods that were not theirs, but I found my way back. And now my work is more important than ever."

"Jeez, yeah. I can imagine that whole situation was a mess." My mind was starting to feel fuzzy. It was late at night, as always, but I wasn't about to let myself lose steam when we were so close to the end of my questions. "But how do you want people to see you now?"

9. HOW DO YOU WANT TO BE SEEN?

Macha:
Suppression, lacking discretion, or feeling incapable of expressing oneself fully.

Badb:
Decisive, if mournful, in one's pursuits. Perceptiveness, sadness, honesty in the face of all decisions. Confronting painful and necessary truths.

Nemain:
Navigating love and relationships of all kinds. Clarity and honesty in one's values.

It seemed like she was getting farther away from me, as if the riverbank were stretching. I could still hear her voice just fine, though. It rang through the humid air, over the stones and up to the blanket of clouds above.

"Three faces, one woman, as you said before," the Morrígan explained. "I can't be seen as only one being, or at least, I can't be seen without understanding the three that make up the one. You must appreciate all facets of a gem to understand its shape, or they'll see only one facet that looks like nothing more than clear glass.

"Nonetheless, I am one that will always be ready to make bitter decisions because I hold my values dearly. One knows what to expect from me when I come, and being with the Fae, I have to be this way: someone who can reliably make decisions and judgments. I am clear in what I want."

"Wonderful. Thank you." I rubbed my stinging eyes and shook the sleepiness out of my head. "This is our last question, now, but it's open ended: is there anything you want to say to people?"

The Morrígan glanced at the three huddled around her and had that long look on her face, like she was caging a deep sigh.

10. ANY LAST MESSAGES FOR ME OR OTHERS?

"There are too many wounded people walking around this world, the history of their battles written clear on them," she said as the three goddesses huddled closer to her legs. "You can't heal what you won't properly clean and dress. Even if it stings to clean one's wounds, people must remember: those very wounds hurt no one more than their own selves. It's in one's best interest to heal, and all the better if their healing spites their attacker."

That last line was such a Cú Chulainn call out. But the Morrígan ended her thoughts with her chin held high.

"There's no sense sending a wounded warrior to battle, so make sure work is done to remain functional."

Macha: Preoccupation with the perfect life, broken familial bonds, violence, discord.

Badb: Pessimism, dread, and resignation.

Nemain: Closure, working towards resolution (not necessarily positive resolution), and hostility.

Once I'd finished writing that last bit down, I nodded. I gathered my cards back into one complete deck and held them close. "Understood," I breathed, a little relieved. "Thank you again, An Morrígan, Phantom Queen, Fae Queen, Washer at the Ford! This has been a pleasure. I appreciate you spending time with me, but for now, I think it's time to say goodbye."

The three goddesses at her feet lifted their heads and stared at me before the Morrígan nodded. Then the riverbank stretched, carrying all four of them away with it, leaving me alone on the banks.

And while I can't say that I'd done every interview right in terms of approaching deities, I can say that I was happy to have had the opportunity to try again here. I was thrilled to be able to put in the honest effort to contact these other pieces of Divinity, to put myself out there and let whatever happened, happen. And best of all, I was ecstatic to have gotten such crisp and clear images of the Morrígan and the other three goddesses. It actually felt like I was on those banks. Like I was there, just inches from a river that could've knocked me down and dragged me away.

There's something visceral about an experience like that. Given that I'd started this journey hardly seeing anything except the barest flash of a face, the fact that I could sink into what felt like a whole separate pocket of the world and really embrace it was something that, just a year beforehand, I might not have believed myself capable of doing. But there I was doing it.

And there I was learning to be unafraid of the unexpected, too. The audience that came to watch us, they didn't scare me. I knew that then: I didn't need to be scared. No matter where I went when I closed my eyes—be it in meditation, or just before I drifted off to sleep—I knew I was fine. That I'd get the most out of it if I just let what needed to happen, happen.

So I skipped off to bed that night with that immediate realization, all while the little theological seed the Morrígan dropped on me settled into the dusty corners of my brain. But its stem and leaves and petals became apparent soon enough, and they took the form of a question.

What if Jesus didn't die to save us, but as a way for God to show solidarity with us? And our suffering? Heresy in the highest.

ARCHANGEL GABRIEL

If there's any angel that can match up to Michael in fame, it's probably Gabriel. This here is the angel that told Mama Mary she'd be having the Son of God, and the one that spoke the first few lines that became the Hail Mary prayer—you know, the *Hail Mary, full of grace, the Lord is with thee*, lines. The next ones, *blessed are you among women, and blessed is the fruit of thy womb*, comes from her cousin Elizabeth after Mary runs over for a visit. However, did you know he also came to Zechariah, husband of Elizabeth, to tell him about the birth of St. John the Baptist too?

(He also puts a bit of a curse on Zechariah. Tells the poor, terrified guy that he'll be mute until all the things Gabriel talked about come to pass because he didn't believe the angel the first time he got told. Oops.)

Nonetheless, Gabriel's catchphrase is the Angel Classic: "Do not be afraid." He's the angel whose name means "Strength of God," and he's frequently sent on courier missions to make God's plans known to men. Sometimes seen as a woman, but depicted in Scripture as a man, Gabriel, like other angels, tends to come however someone will best receive him. Angels don't actually have genders, after all; as divine beings, the forms we see them take on are just cloaks and mirages. But for all the people I've talked to who have ever encountered Gabriel, there's a general consensus among us:

He's pretty. A very pretty angel. The pretty boy of the Big Four of the cardinal directions.

Speaking of cardinal directions, according to Damien Echols and many other sources, Gabriel is the angel of water, the direction west, and the season autumn. He's associated with the moon, which makes sense because of his link to water, and so he's all about emotions, building intuition, and creativity—especially in the sense of self expression. I actually have a little shield with Gabriel on it because as a writer, I know him being the angel of messages and expression makes him a great ally to have when it comes to getting my words across right on paper. (Maybe that's the reason I'm so much better at writing than speaking. Who can say, really?)

But with Gabriel on the roster for this week's conversation, I knew I was in for a good time. He's an angel that I just don't ever feel spooked thinking about, and I was excited to see what he'd have to say (and glad to get the chance to talk to more angels, too, because there are so many). So let me walk you through a delightful conversation with Archangel Gabriel.

With all my tools laid out, I had a pretty solid set up for getting into the space to chat with Gabriel. I had Damien Echols' book set up for Gabriel's sigil, some celestite working as my angel antenna, and some beautiful crystals (amethyst, lapis lazuli, and blue lace agate) for feelings of peace and wisdom. A candle and some quartz to continue organizing the energy and some holy water certainly didn't hurt, either, and to focus my attention, I had a card from Doreen Virtue's angel oracle deck: Gabriel's creative writing card. If I was going to write this interview down, after all, I felt that would make sense—and it seems Gabriel did, too, because he's the one that told me to put that card down.

Once I was comfortable, and I'd said the Lord's Prayer and done a blessing on myself with holy water, I was ready to settle into the zone and speak. But me being halfway energy blind, I can never really tell when an entity *actually* enters a space; I just know that *I'm* ready to talk. It's hard to grasp them sometimes just by asking, and that's why it's important for me to use tools, like pendulums and such, to make sure that I'm not completely out in left field. So that's what I did: I confirmed with God and Gabriel that he was there via pendulum, confirmed Amrit Brar's Marigold Tarot as our medium of choice, and then I trusted that the angel I wanted to speak to was the angel God let through.

And I was not disappointed.

"Gabriel, hello!" I peered into the darkness behind my eyelids, waiting for anything to happen. "Welcome! Can I get a sense of you real quick? An image, a feeling?"

The darkness gave way to light, and what I got was the image of a very tall man in blue robes rimmed with gold embroidery, with a strong nose and sharp face, whose hair was such a shiny gold and whose eyes were the brightest seafoam green. He had gems around his neck and on his forehead in a loose circlet, like amethysts and other green and red stones, and he had wings that actually started lower down his back, draping off him in a way that made me wonder how he could fly. Usually wings were up on the shoulder blades, so that as an interesting detail.

Still, when I'd seen him before, it was similar to this in at least the color scheme, which told me I was on the right track. In the past, he'd showed up looking more like Byzantine paintings, though, so the fact that I got a very clear and fully fleshed out *person* here was comforting. When I asked about this form, however, and why he chose to come like this instead of like the Byzantine art he'd appeared as before, he showed me version of him that was much more raw: a massive eye wreathed in gold wings and wisps of blue light, staring straight through me.

Gotta love the eyeball angel forms.

But soon, he took on that more human form again, and the rest of the scenery bloomed around us. We were on a long, well-trodden forest path, and he just took my hand like a parent might as we walked along it. He had an almost cheeky smile and a soft, yet solid voice.

"I'm here," he said, his smile gentle. "Just walk with me."

"Ah, alright, well," wasn't much else to do but exactly that, "let's get into it, then. As you're the angel that most often delivers messages to prophets, I was wondering: what inspires God to send you to the many prophets and people, like Mary, that you've appeared to?"

1. WHY DOES GOD SEND YOU TO PROPHETS AND OTHER FOLKS?

Gabriel's brows shot up, but his smile grew. "Ah. Remember what Jesus said to you? About resets? At times, humanity falls into chaos. Or, rather, it *will*. But humanity, with just a single clue, will figure out how to progress—if not for themselves, then for future generations." He turned to me with a wink, his smile curling into something cheeky, as if we were sharing an inside joke. "I provide that clue. I give a key piece of the puzzle, and then they're off and away."

"Oh! That makes sense. Alright. And when you come, I notice people seem to portray you as both man and woman at times. Is there a certain gender you'd prefer to be seen as?"

Rises from hardship and filth and is beautiful, deeply thoughtful, and willing to consider the circumstances of others.

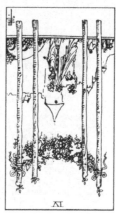

Prioritizing others at the risk of our personal development.

Balance, adaptability, problem solving. Finding resolutions with confidence in oneself. Eternal and cyclical nature of the divine.

2. DO YOU PREFER TO BE SEEN AS ANY SPECIFIC GENDER?

He waved me off, his hair flying around his face as he shook his head, and I didn't get the urge to pull any cards. This was one of those moments where Divinity made itself clear in my mind.

No," Gabriel said with a shrug. "Gender is inconsequential in this realm. It means nothing."

See what I mean? It was Gabriel that confirmed this idea for me: angels don't care about gender. This is a human construct that we put way too much stock in, which is silly, when you think about it: like angels, our souls have no gender. And in heaven, according to Jesus, we, too, will be like angels, if we remember Matthew 22:30; we won't be defined by the gender we rolled around by in life (unless maybe we, for whatever reason, have some deeply rooted attachment to the performance we call gender in this life).

I scribbled down the last of Gabriel's answer and nodded. As soon as I closed my eyes again, I was back in that forest with him, and I said, "Okay! Another thing I thought would be helpful: I've asked for your help with creative writing before, but what other things do you help with?"

3. WHAT DO YOU HELP PEOPLE WITH BESIDES WRITING/MESSAGES?

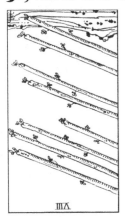

Quarrels, delays, needing to slow down to reevaluate goals and circumstances.

Everything one touches turns to gold. Rich in practical knowledge. Keen instincts, cooperative nature, business sense.

Self satisfaction, good fortune, and contentment. Warmth and goodwill to oneself. Finding joy in what one has.

Gabriel had that easy smile on again. "Self expression comes in many forms," he said, "but the goal of it is to be heard and to have one's needs understood. Most people don't ask for what they need. Most people don't even know how to phrase what they need. If one needs help phrasing their desires and properly understanding them, call on me. We can work through it together. The world is difficult enough to navigate; one shouldn't have to navigate themselves on top of that."

"Oh my God," I said, staring at him. Then I was out swinging fists at nothing, because I couldn't stand it. "That is so *sweet!* Gabriel! You can't just say cute things like it's nothing!"

He laughed at me, a bold and sunny laugh, then ruffled my hair. "I just say what's true."

I gave a few weak swipes at his sleeves, then huffed and collected myself. Only when I relaxed did I realize I'd been smiling. "Okay, okay, so," I started, chuckling at myself, "there's a lot of conjecture, yeah? A lot of people say Mary technically had a choice to have Jesus, and others say that she technically didn't because who can deny God? So, I really wanted to ask: what would happen if someone denied God's request to be a prophet, or carry Jesus, or anything like that?"

4. WHAT WOULD HAPPEN IF SOMEONE DENIED GOD'S REQUESTS?

Before I even finished pulling cards, I heard Gabriel so clearly: "you think they haven't?"

But once I got the cards laid, out, it was easy to piece together. Even without pausing to listen to Gabriel elaborate, I could see the story play out in the cards: of course all the prophets and folks we've heard of and read about are ones that took up the call. For the ones that didn't, there's nothing to write about, is there? Gabriel confirmed it as I closed my eyes again:

Vulnerability, powerlessness, possibly inflated ego.

Power, prosperity, strength, optimism, confidence, and good luck.

Inspiration, exciting possibilities or ideas. Stagnation challenged.

"Really, people have all the time. Look at you! You took a long while to accept it."

Ooh, *zing*. Embarrassing. But it is true: here, Gabriel was referencing the times before I'd created my public platform. I'd been getting the same cards time and time again: the Hierophant (or in Doreen Virtue's deck, Unity), the Hermit, and all other such cards with a theme of *spiritual teaching*. Again and again, they popped up: *spiritual teaching, learn more and share your knowledge, a big change*. And time and time again, I put them down and curled up.

I said, *God, who am I to do that?* And I just kept shuffling, overwhelmed at the very idea, but the same cards kept popping out. For months. They came until I relented and started posting a tentative video here, a tentative video there, about the little witchy things I did—and discovering a whole community of folks who apparently needed to hear what God taught me so long ago.

We paused in the forest as I thought about that. Meanwhile, Gabriel put a hand on my shoulder and said, "Most people think they aren't worthy of what I tell them they're going to do. Some just need time and a little more convincing, and others want nothing to do with it. Oh well," he said, shrugging. "It means moving on to another person. There are so many of you; it's not like every single one is bound to say no. A lot of times, people need the push to be great. But you only hear of the ones that said yes, never the ones that said no. Maybe you hear of the ones that need some convincing. But you know, God likes to pick the unlikely ones; He likes to surprise people."

I blinked at him for a while. He said all this as casually as if he were chatting about a new bakery that opened up, which was a little surreal. But it made me think, and it made me feel small. Not in a bad way, but in the way that maybe a child feels small when they look up at their parents, who are so big and strong in comparison, who are safe.

"Well, alright then," I said as I started walking again. Gabriel came with me. "That's reasonable, I think. Um, for the next question: what do you think of mainstream Christianity?"

5. WHAT DO YOU THINK ABOUT MAINSTREAM CHRISTIANITY?

Abundance, generosity, security, level headedness, reliability, tolerance. Financial and material security.

Breaking bonds, freedom, detachment.

Accepting changes and evolution, especially when hard won or painful. Passage of time brings new obstacles and opportunities as old ones fade.

The stare he gave me from the side of his eye was chilling. It made me brace for the worst, admittedly. And while I couldn't tell if that look was because of mainstream Christianity or because he was just annoyed by the question, I will say that his answer was a little unexpected.

"The way of our Father is a beautiful thing," he said. "When followed, His laws bring all the things in that first card there: abundance, generosity, security, reliability, tolerance, all that. That's what any religion that follows Him *should* be. Christianity has taken a strange turn, though, but it seems like you're all finally getting back to the Truth, little by little.

Keep fighting. The Church will sooner fall than change on its own, but keep going until things are more like how they're supposed to be."

Oh, damn. "Got'cha," I said, and you know I also had to ask, "and Christian Witches? What do you think of them?"

6. WHAT DO YOU THINK ABOUT CHRISTIAN WITCHES?

Again, Gabriel threw another wild answer at me, one that reminded me of Hekate and Zorya. Sure enough, he even mentioned them as he spoke.

"Watch out for that boastfulness," he said as we again stopped in our tracks in the middle of this big, peaceful forest. "Those two you thought of, Hekate and Zorya, are right: many get into magic not for connection, but for gain." Gabriel's stare went dark, even a little stormy, as he towered over me. "Magic isn't just a tool to bypass life's trials. Magic is a philosophy, a way of study, a commitment to learn further than earthly barriers will try to convince you to stop learning at.

"Magic is less about what it can

Greed, possessiveness, and unkindness of spirit. Illusions and suffering. Vision obscured by a closed fist.

Intelligence, trustworthiness, security, generosity, contemplation. Supportive, and responsible. Protective and restorative.

Failing to recognize one's own shortcomings due to feelings of pride or superiority.

help you get and more about what it can help you see and understand. The potential for good is absolutely there, but it's a dangerous path, and it's not for everyone. Not everyone has the sense of responsibility it requires."

"Ooh. I never thought about it like this." And I wouldn't digest it until months later, because God let me know several times over the course of the next year: *not everyone is responsible enough for this path or this power.* Still, I buzzed around him like an overexcited fairy. "Okay! And as you're a messenger, if you were reaching out to people, what signs should they look out for?"

7. WHAT SHOULD PEOPLE LOOK OUT FOR WHEN YOU COME BY?

Gabriel pulled no cards. He just flashed a handful of things in my mind, outlines like sunspots behind my eyelids before they became vivid images. So if you ask for Gabriel to show you a sign, and see white wings or feathers, pomegranates, stars, water or the beach, fish, the Ursa major and minor constellations, or bears in general, you *may* have this here archangel floating about.

And if you you're out meditating, or dreaming, and you find yourself in a massive Gothic cathedral rimmed in gold, towering over a thick green forest like the one he had me walk through in this interview, you may ask yourself if it was Gabriel that brought you there.

"Okay, then," I said as all these things flashed before my mind's eye, and I scribbled them down with the speed of a student trying to get the last few words of their test essay done before time ran out, "we're coming into our last questions: how do you see yourself?"

8. HOW DO YOU SEE YOURSELF?

Gabriel and I reached the end of this forest path. There was a cliff at the end of it, where the evening sun sat orange and bright on the horizon. He sat on a rock by the cliff edge and stared out at the world around us.

False joy and overtasking oneself.

Harmful secrets, confusion, and mental disconnect.

Past regrets, ignoring the call to transform, disappointment, false accusations.

"It's been disappointing to watch humans take on more than they should as they struggle to understand what their role is," he whispered. "I am the one that has to watch it all play out right on their face: the shock, the confusion, the fake joy and fear. It's tiring. Tiring seeing worthy people doubt themselves, and more tiring still to hear unworthy people throw their fears in those worthy people's faces and make them doubt even more. I am the one that witnesses; I am one that tries to help."

"Oh. I get that, yeah." It seemed angel angst was more common than I thought. "But how do you want to be seen?"

9. HOW DO YOU WANT TO BE SEEN?

Need to move on, feelings of alienation and long lost love.

Unwillingness to see problems for what they are, looming disaster, avoiding change.

Discord, disorder, overbearing control. A breakdown in power dynamics.

Gabriel looked over his shoulder with a sly smile, a sparkle of mischief in his eye.

"I am the Herald," he said, and the thought practically burned into my mind. "Things don't last forever. I am the one who blares the trumpet of change as things end; I am the one who first tells of the coming upheavals. I am a menace for those in power. I come to break the power structures men cling to, so new ones can be attempted. God is the catalyst; I am the forecaster."

"Whoa. That's... heavier than I expected." And would imply that his trumpet is the one that signals the End Times that the more extreme Christians love to crow about—while also suggesting the End Times don't seem to be the end they think it is. "Well! That brings us to our last question, then: do you have any messages for me, or for others?"

10. ANY LAST MESSAGES FOR ME OR OTHERS?

It was as though he was whispering over me as I pulled and pieced the cards together: "Oh, Sara, listen. The world is wide. The opportunities can't be counted.

"Just because one's path is full of bramble, doesn't mean you can't find another way to what you're looking for. Too many people become their own bramble, getting in their own way before they ever even set out on the path.

"But if you put your faith in your own abilities and in God—"

"What if they don't believe in God?" I had to ask.

And Gabriel rolled his eyes. "Or

Put your faith in yourself and your abilities. Approach self expression with optimism.

Lapse in judgement and holes in one's intuition.

Generosity, prosperity, gratification, reflection, harmful and helpful facets of the world.

whoever, the universe or whatever else, you'll discover you can do what you're afraid of. You'll discover that you almost threw your chances of success away, doubting yourself. But every choice has a consequence, and every wish does, too. There's no life perfectly free of challenge."

With the last letter written, I nodded. "I see! That's a great note to end this on. And, well, thank you for all this, Gabriel." As I fumbled my way through my parting words, he smiled like a parent might. "But that's all I had for now, so I guess I'll see you another time! Thank you again, Gabriel, and goodnight!"

"Goodnight," he said, and then the cliffside and the forest all melted away to nothing.

As I said, I wouldn't quite digest what Gabriel said to me then as I packed my things up and stumbled off for a bit of sleep. You know, the thing about *responsibility.* But it's true, isn't it? How many folks—be they witch *or* Christian—think that somehow they're more elite, more special, untouchable by the common rabble, just because they have faith? Or magic?

Or both?

It's one of the most humbling lessons to learn as a mystic of any kind: our gifts are exactly that, *gifts.* They're not to be taken for granted or flaunted or abused. They're not to be held over people's heads. They're not to wear all loud and proud to intimidate other people or lift ourselves above them. They're not there to serve our ego or confirm all our previous thoughts with no growth or reflection. But a lot of people getting into spiritual things of any kind don't understand that. They don't understand that a mystic path is a painful path, and that the kind of power you *really* get looks, more often than not, like weakness.

Sometimes I have people ask: "if you're a witch, why aren't you rich and famous? How much power do you really have if you're not a millionaire or living the best life?" And it's a fair question, but my response is simple: *it's not my time to have those things.* I can get them, sure; there are many roads to fame and fortune. But God says no—at least, for the foreseeable future. God says to me, as I dream of being the famous writer I always wanted to be, and as I dream of the big dream house and the many different pets I'd love to raise, *just enjoy where you are right now.*

Like with my meditations, my visions for what I want in life are so vivid. I can see them as if they're really happening; I can see outside myself as if looking at pictures of myself at events, and I can see from my own point of view as if I'm really there, signing books and talking to people. I can feel the cramp of my hand from holding a pen too long, or the feel of paper against my fingertips. I can hear the voices of people who've read my books; I can anticipate the plush of hotel carpet under my feet.

But that's not what's in front of me right now. What's in front of me, right in this moment, is an old T.V. screen I use as a monitor, and a glass of water, and a binder clip, and an old pencil. What I hear is the sound of birds in this rural area of southern New England I call home. What I smell is rain, and what I feel is the breeze of a just-ending summer rainstorm. Do you know how much I have to be thankful of, right here? Do you know how much wealth I have, in this little half of a house I call an apartment, with my garden thriving after a good rain and my refrigerator full of food? Do you know how many people have already said to me that what I've shared and done has helped them, and how many people have changed their understanding of both God and their own selves through what I've been told to go teach?

I don't say that to brag. I say that to remind myself that "fame and fortune" is wildly subjective, and that to admit this is to acknowledge a very important lesson God's been trying to teach me by denying all these mirages of my Super Fancy Author Goals: that what I have is enough, and that where I am is an important part of my journey I have to *live through*, not skip past by way of magic and force and impatience. If I'm to be a magician worth anything, I have to acknowledge this lesson and complete it. Or else, how many moments will I never fully remember, because my mind's eye was always on something else far in the future, obscuring the vision of the two eyes in my head?

Take it or leave it, but as I look back on my talk with Gabriel, I find myself re-learning the lesson all the same. May you learn whatever lessons you need to learn right now, too—and may you learn them without looking past them to see the fruits. Just enjoy the flowers for now, and trust that fruits will come.

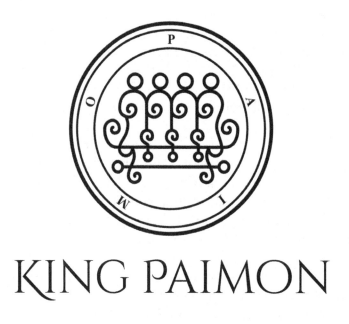

KING PAIMON

Apparently, I was nowhere near done investigating demons—not after speaking with Lucifer, and after even deciding to take the plunge and investigate this "other side of the coin" I was becoming privy to. This *other side* of what was clearly a much more balanced equation than anyone in mainstream Christianity would like to admit was something I felt like I had to drown in, if that makes any sense. In fact, I'd say my first conversation with Lucifer—and my budding work with him, where I took a pickaxe to the walls of modern misconception—only made the morbid fascination that I'd tried to bury for years *worse*. There was something about the infernal divine that made such dreadful sense, and yet none of the people talking about them from a Christian perspective seemed able to grasp what I was trying to put into words. I couldn't go to them to understand "demons," no, because I knew I'd hear all of the usual, tired things:

That they hated people. That they loved to trick us into being awful, ugly little worms that offended God at every turn. That they wanted to eat up our souls like Sour Patch Kids and shit them out into the hottest pits of hell.

But given my experiences with Lucifer were as far away from any of this nonsense as possible, and that God Himself seemed to have something of an inside joke with the fallen angel—that Lucifer and Michael could stand in the same space during my later, private meditations and actually *get along* to some degree—I knew in the marrow of my bones that these typical ideas about the infernal divine were a bunch of nonsense. However, I found no real practical reason for contacting demons outside Lucifer. No need to do so, nothing I wanted to work with them on. My hands were already quite full in my guided studies into demonolatry with Lucifer, after all; these other entities were *cool*, but they weren't for me. Probably. Most likely.

Right?

So color me shocked when I found myself putting another demon on the list of potential entities to interview. I told myself it was a silly idea. That I had no reason to do this. That I would just be putting myself in an odd situation, constantly strolling up to demons that likely weren't thrilled to see a Christian poking around in their space just for fun. And yet there I was typing in a name that I'd only learned because I watched a spooky movie recently. I still knew pretty much nothing about the Goetic demons, mind you, yet I felt compelled to test fate and put this name on the list. Naturally, at some point in the weekly poll, there highlighted as the top choice was none other than King Paimon.

I pulled cards with God about it, of course. This was nothing new; out of respect for my God, I tried, where I could remember (which was pretty much eight to nine times out of ten, honestly) to ask His opinion about the spirit I'd be speaking to. In this case, God gave me the clearest *are you sure?* energy I'd ever felt; He knew I was nervous and wanted me to make sure I was ready.

But I remember shrugging at Him and saying, like a fool, "well, interview's due this week, so I guess I have no choice but to be ready."

Not the thing to tell God. Not if you want to keep your mind in one piece.

As I said, I only knew about him because I'd watched a spooky movie. *Hereditary*, to be specific. It was a thrilling movie, gruesome and bizarre and apparently something pretty horrific for any-one who had parents like the mother figure, according to my boyfriend. The whole time, though, I couldn't help but laugh as this odd parade all came to point to King Paimon. I knew better than to think that this was at all a realistic interpretation of demons; I logically understood that this was some Hollywood level shenanigans, and that real members of the infernal divine did not go around making these strange and murderous cults.

So why, then, did the idea of King Paimon unsettle me so badly, even weeks after watching the film?

There was only one way to find out, and that was by doing what I seemed to have discovered a talent for doing: rolling up to the front door of said entity with a gift, a list of questions, and an iron set of balls. Once again, I found myself turning to Aziel for help, as she's worked closely with King Paimon; she pointed me in the right direction and gave me some wise counsel for how to approach this infernal King. This was one that she warned me wouldn't tolerate disrespect of any kind, and that wouldn't very much appreciate my being informal and goofy with him—which didn't help my nerves at all. But better to know and have the chance to act accordingly than not know and suffer.

From my own look into the *Ars Goetia*, I understood that King Paimon was master of the element of water. Aziel also mentioned that there were two infernal Princes that came alongside him: Bébal and Abalam (who, themselves, have more to them that meets the eye, if you know where to look for your research). At the time, I didn't—and truth be told, there's still a lot I don't understand—but I decided to just walk in with what knowledge I had and hope for the best.

Besides the two Princes, however, did you know King Paimon also has a camel? He's depicted as a young, handsome, and royal man that rides this camel everywhere, and so of course, I got some advice to give the camel a little something, too, as a sign of respect. And with all that knowledge, I felt pretty well equipped to dive into this conversation and make some magic happen.

But remember when I gave God the ol' "ready or not, here I come"? Yeah. I do, too. I still get tired thinking about it. Before we go any further, let me tell you what happened a night or two before my sitting down for the interview.

That week, I went to bed the same as I did any other night; my boyfriend was still streaming in the office, and I took comfort in his voice through the door. Then I shut the lights off and laid there in the dark, wrapped up tight in my blankets and telling myself that I'd be okay, that everything was fine—because even if I've come a long way since I was a night-light dependent youth, and even if I had the skills to not instantly get smushed by some weird spirit hanging out in the shadows, the dark still made me a little nervous. At this point, I don't think I'll ever fully shake those fears, no matter how many nights I manage to not get killed by some spook hiding under the bed. It is what it is.

However, unlike every other night where all was well and good, *this* night was one where an old friend came back to choke me: sleep paralysis. Last time I had a good bought of sleep paralysis was when I was a teenager. I didn't recognize it at first, of course; I was too busy having a dream about living in an older apartment complex, stressing about having to go grab an order of Chinese food delivered to the main entrance, and stressing even more about something being particularly *off* about my DoorDash driver as he stood stock still in the complex's parking lot and stared at me. Even when the heavy main entrance door shut behind me, I couldn't get into whatever room that Dream Sara lived in fast enough; it felt like there was something staring at my back as I bolted up the carpeted stairs, ones soaked in years of cigarette smoke.

And then I was awake—allegedly. Except I couldn't move my body more than half an inch in any direction, and when I tried to call for my boyfriend, it came out nothing more than a hoarse rush of wind. No words, no nothing. So there was no way for my boyfriend to realize that there was some shadow skulking around our bedroom, and that it was going and pushing the candles on my main altar around—pushing them right to the edge of it, as if to throw them to the ground. The picture of Jesus sat there staring at me as if deciding whether or not to condemn me right there in my bed. I knew what I was dealing with by this point, a sleep paralysis nightmare, and I did my darndest to wake up. After thinking the first line of St. Michael's prayer, however, my limbs stopped feeling like lead, and whatever fog was on my mind disappeared. I was wide awake, in the dark, and when I sat up to turn my lamp on, I found that the candles on my altar hadn't moved an inch. The apathetic, condemning stare Jesus had in my nightmare was once again a set of open, warm eyes and a soft smile.

Fuck's sake. I laid there for a good minute trying to relax, but my nerves were running up and down my spine like a flurry of needles. *Did King Paimon hear I wanted to talk to him? Was that him screwing with me already?*

Those were my first thoughts, I'm ashamed to say. But my very next thought was, *why would he bother doing such a thing, though? What reason would he have to go out of his way to do that?*

And I don't even remember how the thought crossed my mind, but suddenly there I was, thinking of the Adversary: of those angels playing the Bad Cop, out to test us. It was a thought that came so suddenly, it was like a slap—and then I just laid there in disbelief.

God did that. This thought didn't budge; there was nothing to come counter it, unlike with my knee-jerk reaction of blaming an infernal King I'd never even met. This was something I just knew, deep in my soul; I recognized this trick. *God did that. He sent that shadow. That was an angel. An Adversary.*

And I knew in my gut that He did that to test whether or not I'd *actually* be able to handle speaking to another member of the infernal divine—if I'd *actually* been ready, rather than trying to force myself to be and hope for the best.

I don't think I'd ever been more exasperated with God in my life. But somehow, suddenly, every drop of unease or nervousness I felt about King Paimon just disappeared, as if I didn't even have the energy to feel such a thing. And I didn't. I was too busy fighting off the bone-deep exhaustion that came with my epiphany to care anymore. Stupid movies or no, infernal King or no, I resolved to get myself together and talk to King Paimon all the more after that—this time, to make up for the little smirch of guilt I felt about being so ready to point a finger at him for no good reason. After all, there hadn't been a single thing in that dream to suggest any infernal presence; it was all assumption.

Come day of the interview, and I may have overthought the offerings, honestly. Even if I wasn't *scared*, I was still *worried* about disrespecting King Paimon somehow. Still, I felt the spread I ended up with for everyone was pretty nice: given the theme of water, I put out cucumbers, cherry tomatoes, and blackberries for King Paimon and his Princes, as well as a bottle of lovely Spanish wine so that I could give a glass to each of them, and for the camel, a bowl of water, some oats, and some mint. Because I'd read that camels could eat both of these.

As I said: overthinking. There was no physical camel whose digestive tract I actually had to worry about, so I likely didn't need to be so serious about learning what camels could and couldn't eat. If for nothing else, though, I'd like to at least think my effort was appreciated. But with King Paimon's sigil in the center of the table, along with more water-centric and energy fixing stones like lapis lazuli, moonstone, onyx, and selenite, and some iris incense for a nice fragrance, I was ready to roll. No spirit was an exception; I set my space with the Lord's Prayer and asked God to let King Paimon and his Princes through—no one else, and certainly no egregores.

Then I settled in and felt something like a skittering across my skin. Infernal energy was something I felt like I'd never get used to; it was so sharp, so intense, all at once, and I couldn't stop myself from shivering. That was some good confirmation as it was, but I still used my pendulum to make sure King Paimon was with me, and to verify that he wanted to use Amrit Brar's Marigold Tarot.

I shook my hands out to ground myself with all this energy floating around, and I spoke: "King Paimon, I formally welcome you and your attendant princes Bébal and Abalam, as well as your camel, to join me tonight and have a discussion! I have some questions about you that I'd love answers to, if you're willing to give them."

The infernal realms are weird, I'll say that right now. Every single place is different; it really is its own country's worth of space and places and pockets, and given that King Paimon lords over Jinnestan—the country of the Jinn—I figured this is where we might've gone. Yet I never could've imagined how shockingly vivid the images of our location would be.

What bled into my mind's eye was a man dressed in black robes that were rimmed with red and gold, a large hat-like crown, and massive, kohl-rimmed eyes, a soft and pretty face. He rode on top of his camel while Prince Bébal and Prince Abalam walked beside him.

Prince Bébal was a bald man with bluish, wrinkled skin, like a draugr almost; his eyes were sunken, his face a little thin-lipped and grim. Prince Abalam almost struck me as more like a cleric; his hat-crown was like King Paimon's, but it was more just a golden frame of it rather than a whole hat, and he had blue robes, blue-tinged skin like Prince Bébal's, and a staff with a gold top. Altogether, they were a striking trio: somber, dignified, and radiating such heavy presence.

Then the view zoomed out, so that I could see that we were in a dark cave. I could see myself standing there between them all, so small in comparison, and there was this massive jagged opening to this cave wall that poured red-orange light from it, as if illuminated with lots of torch fire. And as it turns, out, it was: we walked in there, and it was almost like a market square, with fuzzy black shade-spirits with glowing white eyes hanging around the stalls. They were hovering around stalls with colorful red-orange rugs for awnings, as if they were merchants trying to sell their wares to each other. The buildings themselves were square and looked like they were made of clay.

Our whole walk through this area was silent. All the shades tracked us as we walked, their stares open and inquisitive. Eventually we stopped in a place that was basically just a single room with a table in the middle, where the offerings I'd put out appeared. The camel sat in the corner just chewing on the oats, millet, and mint I gave it; it was a very nice camel.

King Paimon lounged there across from me like the entire city belonged to him, and honestly it probably did. But he set some ground rules with me right away, which was that Prince Bébal and Abalam were not going to participate; it was all about King Paimon and his thoughts, and so I focused only on him for the questions.

"Alright, again, thank you for joining me," I said as I settled on the cushion he'd given me to sit on in this strange place. "Please enjoy the things I have set out! But to get into it, let me ask: what was the world like when you came into being, when you were born?"

I. WHAT WAS THE WORLD LIKE WHEN YOU CAME INTO BEING?

"Born?" His brow shot up. "What do you mean, *born*, girl?"

"Uh," I fumbled a bit, looking for the words, "I guess you could say, what was it like when you grew fully aware of yourself?"

He tipped his head up. "Ah. I understand. You're asking what it was like for me to understand who I truly was, and not what I was told to be."

I shrugged. "That sounds like what I mean. That's what I'm asking, yes."

He stared at me a moment longer, then lounged like a true King. "There was much bloodshed," he said. "Those Watchers, fools. They unleashed a mess. What's the point of winning a war when another plucky fool starts another one against you

Loss, dishonor, defeat even in the event of victory. Some victories feel hollow or ill won.

Breaking bonds, freedom, detachment.

Completion, peace, self awareness, family. A complete understanding of the cycles that life has to offer.

a moment later? Or your attendant stabs you in the back? And yet the humans were free. Free to do it all and bear all their terrible consequences. They learned." He cocked his head, considering something. "At least marginally."

"So," it was hard to put my curiosity into words at times, "you left the ranks of the angels *after* the Watchers did?"

He nodded.

"And so you were an angel once, then?"

King Paimon's face went flat. "This question is stupid, considering you already confirmed it."

"Ah—true, sorry." An infernal King with low tolerance for nonsense, this one! "But there's some debate as to whether you were once a Power or a Dominion; would you tell me which one is true?"

2. WERE YOU ONCE A POWER OR A DOMINION AS AN ANGEL?

I used my pendulum here. Its swinging about as I asked helped me get a concrete answer: Dominion. King Paimon was once a Dominion, of the fourth rank of angels, who guide the lower ranks, keep Creation in check, and bring wisdom down to humanity. We might say that King Paimon still does all of this, honestly—but as Infernal King rather than Heavenly Soldier.

"Oh, interesting!" It was always exciting to get concrete answers like that. "Thank you for clarifying. Now, here's a more light-hearted question, King Paimon: where did you meet your camel?"

He gave me a quizzical look, then laughed.

3. WHERE DID YOU MEET YOUR CAMEL?

Weakness in a work or team situation. Incompetence and inability to delegate.

Martyrdom, hardship, confusion, facing consequences, forcing oneself to consider different perspectives.

Deception and reevaluating whether a goal or relationship was truly fulfilling.

"My dear dromedary, yes." King Paimon crossed his arms and glanced at the big lug as it chewed away at its oats. "This animal was a wretched pain at first: stubborn and difficult to ride. Hard to form a bond with it right away. But I had need of a mount, and this was the first creature that answered. I bore it and learned to manage it, and now he is my only mount. I would not willingly abandon him."

"I see! That must've been interesting at the start." My thoughts were starting to become a messy whirlwind of half-questions and budding ideas as I wrote. "But okay—so, what has you interested in arts and sciences? Seeing as it's one of your areas of expertise, I'd like to know your thoughts on them."

4. WHAT INTERESTED YOU IN ARTS AND SCIENCES?

King Paimon stood up and practically started orating, as if we were in a lecture hall rather than a tiny room. Hands out wide, big voice, it was almost theatrical.

"What is there not to love about arts and sciences? It's the very way to overcome the pithy weaknesses your card there, your Strength Reversed, talks about! But people think they can do everything with it, so much—they need some humility."

He said that bit with a feline smile, like it was a joke. But he spoke a little more calmly after that as he tucked his hands behind his back.

Joy, moving forward, stagnation being the cause of one's challenges.

Weakness, breaking down, loss of control, having difficulty problem solving.

Romance, idealization, being charmed. Over emotional fantasies, big gestures, intentions pouring like tears.

"Humans, they do so much, work so hard, only to end up worse off than they started—all tortured by their art or plagued by questions their sciences introduce. It's interesting to see the madness people spin into, a beautiful testament of will. The world is created by art, and it is understood through science."

"Oh." I felt like a first grader sitting on the rug in school, just staring up at him as he talked. "So there's multiple angles to it, then. Fascinating! I can see what you mean. But on the note of working hard and ending up worse off, I wonder: what do you think of the original Solomonic summoning methods? Personally, I'm angry on your behalf for it, with how they recommend one *threaten* you to get you to speak plainly! What was the reason for that? How do you feel about it?"

5. HOW DO YOU FEEL ABOUT BEING BOUND IN SOLOMONIC MAGIC?

THE MOON.

Subconscious fears, illusions, deceptions. Miscommunication, trauma. Bad behavior despite knowing better.

KING of CUPS.

Self destructive, controlling, dishonest, manipulative behavior.

THE HERMIT.

Loneliness, alienation, isolation, extreme caution.

As I asked the question, he curled his lip and muttered under his breath: "Ugh! Those summoners." Once I was done speaking, he went on.

"They were insecure little runts, is what they were—those who came up with this. Hated by fellow men, they wanted power to control them all, all those hateful faces, and so they sought to control us."

I noticed that Prince Bébal and Prince Abalam were silent as death, their stare fixed on the table.

"But we love a tragedy," King Paimon continued with a sigh and a wave of his hand. "There's a reason their wishes backfire when they approach a 'demon' like this. Though, then they blame it on the fact that we are infernal beings, and not the fact that they were rude. If we complied with these tricks and threats, it was to show them what we *could* do for them, and then to rip it away."

"Absolutely, I understand." I tapped my pencil to my lip. "I think that's why that theme of 'don't ask the devil for favors or it ends badly' is so prolific in media—and speaking of media, what do you think of movies like *Hereditary*? It's the reason I was hoping to speak with you, honestly: because that portrayal, I know, did you no justice."

6. WHAT DO YOU THINK ABOUT YOUR PORTRAYAL IN HEREDITARY?

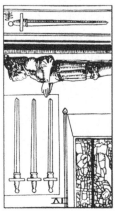

PAGE of WANDS.

1. Victory, superiority, pride.

2. Stress, restlessness, and an unwillingness to take risks.

3. Wonder, optimism, creativity, and confidence. Having the foresight to protect oneself. Excited for the next step in one's journey.

I'll say this yet again about tarot: it's a language. With any language, there will be cultural subtext and slang that takes a *lot* of practice, fluency, and patience to grasp. In tarot, that subtext and fluency pops up when an entity starts to use less of the meanings of the card themselves and more of the actual imagery painted on a specific deck—which is why having a few different decks can be helpful to a more experienced reader. This answer was one of those times where King Paimon drew on the art of the cards as much as their meanings. The story was clear through Amrit Brar's gorgeous art in the Marigold Tarot:

The Six of Wands had a big and beautiful flower, in a contained space made of other flowers. Pristine, untouched, left undisturbed. The Four of Swords, whether reversed or upright, had the same image: a single pretty flower held at the center of four sword points, like it was being held hostage. And lastly, the Page of Wands featured a skeleton with a radiant halo, holding a bouquet and looking up to the sky, like someone receiving flowers on a stage after a performance.

Between the pictures and the messages of the cards, and the way King Paimon elaborated, it was clear to me: the flower was the Infernal, the movie directors the Page, and the mess they created were the swords of misrepresentation and callousness that accosted those poor flowers.

"They ruin beauty," King Paimon said. "They might as well take that flower and stomp on it, for that false fantasy of glory and fame using our images. They make us grotesque, undignified, simple monsters lusting after your bodies full of pus and blood and filth. Why? We're above this."

"Oh, yeah, absolutely." By this point, even though I knew King Paimon preferred more formality, I was finding it easier to slip into my more direct talk: a sign that I would've liked to think he knew meant I was getting more and more comfortable with him. "You know, I read somewhere that apparently the infernal *want* to possess bodies, that just 'walking in circles' would be a pleasure since you can't do it physically? It didn't seem right to me, but King Paimon, could I get your thoughts?"

7. DO DEMONS ACTUALLY CARE TO POSSESS PEOPLE?

I don't think I've ever gotten such a sharp and clear side-eye from an entity before. His glowering took up my whole mind's eye, his disgust palpable.

"I would not even dignify that ridiculous notion with a response," he hissed.

"Oop—fair enough."

But then he continued anyway, as if to make sure that this idea was forever erased from my mind: "We have no need of what you have, and yet humanity is obsessed with making us the ones that are the source of all rot regardless." Then he smirked and tossed me what felt like a throwaway line: "Always the scapegoat, never the bride."

I nodded, mulling over his answer. Then I said, "I sort of figured as much. But then, something else I'm curious about: where does evil come from? I know it doesn't come from you, the infernal. And if we ate of the tree of *Knowledge of* Good and Evil, shouldn't we... know better? We know what's evil, so what inspires people to choose it?"

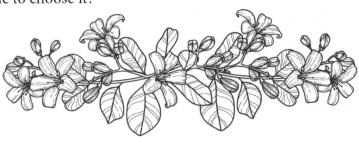

8. WHAT INSPIRES PEOPLE TO DO EVIL THINGS INSTEAD OF GOOD?

Now here was one hell of an answer. King Paimon paced a bit and frowned, then spoke with a rasp in his voice as if he was annoyed.

"Humanity will endure great pain if it means they can avoid change. The pain of routine is more bearable than the fear of the unknown: unknown breeds fear, fear breeds chaos, and chaos breeds evil. People's panic destroys their reason. They make up nonsense to justify clinging to old ways, even if those ways don't work. But eventually, they can't bear that either, and all goes to hell," he said, with a grin—a joke. Then he continued: "It's the way of animals, this. But it's the way of animals to adapt, too. Humanity is pitiful at adapting gracefully."

My God, if that isn't the truth, I don't know what is. Look at where we are

THE HIEROPHANT

Spiritual awareness, conformity, wisdom, gaining knowledge through learning. Teachers and mentors. Find wisdom in new places while respecting society.

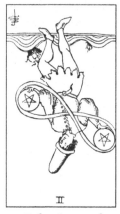

False joy and overtasking oneself.

Discord, disorder, overbearing control, and a breakdown in power.

right now with people foaming at the mouth over things as basic as pronouns, creating culture wars to release their frustrations on non-issues—all while refusing to do the *real* work of fixing the systems that keep us miserable, underpaid and under-stimulated, locked in a life too bleak to bear.

"I understand; thank you for the insight!" And as I looked over my list, I found we were already about done with all this, which surprised me. It didn't feel like it'd been that long. "Now, I have only a few questions left, and my first is: how do you see yourself, King Paimon?"

9. HOW DO YOU SEE YOURSELF?

KING of SWORDS.

THE FOOL.

1. Authority, integrity, connections, intellect, physical and mental fortitude. A presence that demands respect.

2. False accusations, disharmony, general unfairness.

3. New beginnings, spontaneity, change, and innocence. The most important journeys are mental, not physical.

I must say, time and time again, he really did surprise me with the card pulls. Here was another one of those times.

"I forge my own way," he said, almost casually, yet with a bit of disdain lacing his voice. "I'm not concerned with trifling things. I reinvent myself as I see fit, regardless of how and with what others might smear my name. I am my own man; I need no one's approval. I value intelligence and self sufficiency. I appreciate courage to start a journey no matter where it leads one to. No time for opinions or thoughts on others or others' thoughts on me; my pursuits are my focus, not the mess that is mankind."

"Ah, interesting! Thank you. Given all that, though, how would you want to be seen by others?"

10. HOW DO YOU WANT TO BE SEEN?

Again, what the hell were these cards? They almost had me wondering what I was doing and if I was hearing right, given that, at face value, their meanings seemed completely opposite of how I was seeing King Paimon. Though, as tended to be the case, I had this answer unraveled and explained soon enough: it was an answer apparently not focused on how he wanted to be seen, but how he *didn't* want to be seen. Throughout my work with the infernal divine later on, I would come to appreciate this concept: that we can learn about something or someone by learning about what they're *not*. It's a large part of what inspires me to keep going in my work with them: by exploring who God is *not*, I learn more about who God *is*.

Failing to notice issues arising, fearing the unknown, or willfully being ignorant to the answers one's problems.

Martyrdom, hardship, confusion, facing consequences, forcing oneself to consider different perspectives.

Weakness in a work or team situation, incompetence, and an inability to delegate.

But King Paimon seemed pretty annoyed as he spoke: "What I want people to see is their own power. I am not the one to whisk problems away. I am not a savior, or a hero. I am a King, and it is my job to lead, not to fix petty squabbles with fools who are secretly waiting for me to do all their work. I am no one's slave or servant. I do not work for free. Humanity needs to stop looking at divinity as an easy path to what they want. Respect me as King; don't run to me for every little issue. Respect my time and be thankful when I come to help; don't expect my good graces."

"Understood!" I nodded and wrote with enthusiasm. "I see now; this makes a lot more sense than what I was thinking at first. Thank you again for explaining! That was my last real question, honestly, but I'd like to know before we part ways: do you have any messages you'd want to share with people, or was that last bit it?"

11. ANY LAST MESSAGES FOR ME OR OTHERS?

Embarrassment, anxiety, or inability to stand up for oneself.

Naïveté and recklessness.

Wonder, optimism, creativity, and confidence. The foresight to protect oneself. Excited and inspired, but more constructive than foolhardy.

It took a little bit for the frown to melt off King Paimon's face, but eventually that almost saucy attitude came back, that sly smile.

"I want people to get a little... outrageous," he purred. "A little reckless, even. If they've been stagnating, floundering, it's time to take up their mantle and go see exactly what they can do when they finally decide to give up doubt and believe in themselves. Aren't they tired of being nothing? They have to decide to grow, like a seed in the dirt, rather than waiting for everyone to pile more dirt on them. Rather than wait for the right dirt, or more rain, more sun, they should make the decision to *be*. This doesn't mean be stupid, though; it means be free."

"I see! I love that." The last word went down in my notebook, and then I sat back and breathed a deep sigh, unloading a lot of tension I didn't realize I'd been holding. "Thank you! I'm excited to share this. But with that, again, I really appreciate your and your Princes' time, and I wish you well as we part ways!"

He hovered over me, smiling, but before he left, I asked what he wanted me to do with these offerings. It didn't feel right to toss them—especially since there was a *lot* of it sitting there. To throw it all out felt incorrect. Just in case, though, I wanted to make sure he wouldn't prefer me to toss them outside, and to my surprise, he let me eat what was on the table.

So I ate a very large late night snack of cucumbers, tomatoes, and blackberries.

But as I got ready to go to bed that night, I found myself in a state of *peace*. It wasn't a sunny peace, though. It wasn't a happy-go-lucky, rainbows and sunshine, warm and fuzzy peace. In fact, I'd even say it was a cold peace, or maybe not even peace at all, but rather just a *lack of fear*. A numbness. Emptiness.

In the same vein, what I had in myself after that incredibly successful interview wasn't confidence, but matter-of-factness, as if it were just another day at the office. I wondered what I'd even let myself be so afraid of to begin with, too. What I felt for my ability to navigate this increasingly complex and strange world of the Unseen wasn't the sunny virtue of such optimistic and radiant faith, but the cold concrete building blocks of knowledge. The more I learned, it seemed, the more I went still; the more I moved forward, the more I found myself itching to be at rest.

But a flower doesn't stay a flower forever. Eventually, it wilts and bears fruit. As I tucked myself into bed, though, and all these petals of honest curiosity were browning at the edges, I could only wonder what this fruit would look like when it finally ripened. Whether it would be sweet or bitter, or both.

The only way to find out would be to wait, and to support the Tree the flower was attached to in the meantime—something that continued to be a challenge as the months wore on.

ISIS

I think we've all seen artworks of Isis at one point in our lives or another. She's the goddess with iridescent wings that spread all along her outstretched arms, who's depicted with the symbol of the sun or a throne on her head, and who is also often depicted alongside her dead and risen husband, Osiris. Alongside Anubis, she may be one of the most recognizable and well known Egyptian deities in our modern era, even among those with no particular interest in studying this truly ancient religion. However, did you know we're all calling her by her Greek name—just as we are these other gods?

You may have noticed from our first interview with Kemetic deities that Anubis and Thoth were actually called something like Anpu and Djehwty among the Egyptians, and Isis, too, is known by a different name: Aset. She's the goddess of healing and magic, and one who, in her lore, went to collect the scattered pieces of her murdered husband after Set murdered him and revived him with the help of goddess Nephthys (Nebtho). Beyond that, Isis is also written as the mother of the god Horus (Heru) and the protector of the Pharaoh, and one that tricked the sun god Ra into granting her the magic powers that make her so famous.

Another fun fact about Isis: her cult of worship seems to have spread all the way up to England, thanks to the Greeks adopting her into their own syncretic form of worship between Greece and Egypt. With some political back-and-forth over the course of several different emperors' reign, this cult rooted itself in Rome, too, and then, once Rome stampeded their way up the western coast of Europe and hit the Isles, it was a done deal: this beloved mother figure, full of healing and magical power, had cults of worship stretch as far up as the Romans could go. Interestingly enough, it seems that the cult of Isis once had the same treatment in Rome as did early Christianity: as a cult that appealed especially to the women, slaves, and general lower class, most attempts to stamp it out did very little to actually dissuade anyone from practicing it, to the point that eventually the politicians relented and came to accept it.

When it came to my approaching Isis, I will say that I wasn't actively searching her out. I'd been talking with my wonderful friend, @king_kylie1405 (Kyle) about anything and everything, just chatting away. We'd talked before about Mother Mary, folk Catholicism, and so on, as both of us have heavily Catholic backgrounds and love our Heavenly Mama. However, Kyle is also a devotee of Isis, and while there's certainly a running list of Wildest Things to Happen during this journey, this part took the cake (so far).

Kyle noticed that Isis was there with him, and he took the time to channel a message from her.

"Oh, that girl," Isis said, "I know her. I want to talk to her too."

Cue my surprise. A goddess like Isis, wanting to talk to me? Maybe Anubis and Thoth had said something to her; I didn't doubt gods talked and word got around (especially given God Himself liked to pick up the phone between pantheons in some apparent Divine Counsel networking).

More than that, though, it turns out that not only God noticed I was burning the candle at both ends and running myself ragged trying to build my spiritual platform while working a full time job; Isis did, too, and Kyle told me as such.

"Slow down," Isis had him tell me: "you need to rest. You're doing too much."

Needless to say, I did not listen. But even when the little gas pump light turns on in your car, you can still drive that bad boy a few more miles before you break down on the side of the road, and that was what I apparently intended to do at that time in my life. No, I was more interested in learning how I might go about speaking with Isis, and Kyle agreed to help: he told me that she'd like not bread and water, but something sweet to eat and drink, if I were to give any offerings. He also told me more about her, where to look, and what else to put out for her. And the day of the interview, he walked me through a beautiful invocation to her.

Then I set the table with two cups of sweet rose tea, the honey cupcakes I'd baked that morning, two eggs for their symbolism of rebirth in Egyptian religion, and certain stones: lapis lazuli, onyx, rose quartz, and sunstone, which I'd figured made sense with what I knew of her and what I'd read upon searching for general associations. Then, with the Lord's Prayer said, the invocation done, and the pendulum confirming Isis had, in fact, come by, I found her tarot deck of choice; Kat Black's Golden Tarot. We settled into it after that, as I was, by this point, quite used to doing.

However, just because I was getting used to it, doesn't mean it got easier in a linear way: sometimes some entities were harder for me to grasp, even though I considered myself to have a fair bit of practice by then, and Isis was one of them. It was problematic, you know; I only had about two hours to do this interview before I had to run off like a rat to the next thing on my to-do list, and so I didn't have time to suddenly suck at meditating out of nowhere.

"Hello, Isis!" I said as I tried harder to grasp her energy in my mind's eye. "Thank you for coming! Please enjoy a cupcake and some tea with me; may they keep you cool and refreshed. Please let me see your energy clearly as we get started!"

What I saw was kind of wild. She showed up almost like her art at first, with the kohl-rimmed, dark eyes, the yellowish skin and blueish hair like a painting, the big disk of a sun on her head. Her wings were so brightly colored, all blues and reds and golds. But it was a shaky image, as if it were trying to slip away from me: it seemed like she was flickering in and out of existence.

"Isis, am I seeing you now?"

The one thing I hated about this journey, honestly, was how easy it was for doubt to come creeping in, like leaks from a water damaged ceiling. But Isis as this painted figure nodded, and eventually, her image settled into a more concrete person, with black hair and whiter robes. Her wings, however, were still just as bright and colorful.

We were in a desert, but not like the Sahara; it was more like the desert of New Mexico or Arizona, dotted with little shrubs and things. I wondered if she was trying to be here in America, but be in a setting more desert-like (especially given it'd been raining like hell all week here). There was a long road we were walking down, a great orange cliff in the distance like those sandstone cliffs you see out in the American desert, and there was one single tree.

Knowing what I know about God, and how He likes to stay watching, I can't help but feel that the tree was significant. I feel like maybe He'd asked Asherah to be nearby, as it was the only tree in the entire area.

"Alright, well," I clapped my hands together, "let's get to it! I don't have anything pre-written today, so I figured we'll just let the questions appear as we go this time, a real flow of conversation. Though, first, I gotta say: it's interesting how your associations sort of stacked throughout the ages. Did you always have these associations, and they were discovered? Or did you take on new roles over the ages?"

I. DID YOU ALWAYS HAVE YOUR CURRENT ASSOCIATIONS?

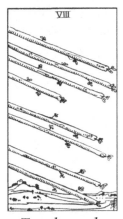

Travel, speedy journey, ideas made reality. Messages and news. Hasty decisions may be regretted.

A corrupt man, or one who holds grudges or lacks imagination.

Indecisiveness, falsehood. Beware those who seek conflict for its own sake.

She only looked at me with one eye for a while as we walked. It didn't unsettle me, but it did make me wonder—and by wonder, I mean doubt myself. Just a little. After all, shouldn't I have, by that point, been able to see her as easily as any other person?

Just keep going. Another thing I was learning was how to shut the doubt down. *Keep going. You'll get it.* Slowly but surely, I was learning to manage it before it got too big and made me lose the connection altogether; I was too stubborn to give up, and I would remind myself that I *did* ask God to let only the true deity in question through. Here's the thing: it's one thing to doubt myself, but doubting God?

No. I didn't want to do that. Not a bit. So I decided there that I wouldn't. And I'd already baked cupcakes and set the table, too—so I figured I might as well keep going.

However, one eye on me or two, her message still came through loud and clear. "Most of my associations came with Osiris's death," she said. "The magic, the traveling to find the pieces, the things I did to ensure there was justice—it was all for him. Other associations came over time, people discovering the similarities between the domains of myself and others like Hathor, but most were because of the story of Osiris and I."

As if to make a point, another card popped out of my deck on top of the ones she'd already pulled: the High Priestess. Magic and queenliness and feminine power—her main associations.

I nodded and hurried to write it all down. "I see, I see! And speaking of all that went on with Osiris, Set, Horus, I hope it's not rude to ask, but how did you reconcile with Horus?"

She deflated a bit here, and I could understand why.

2. HOW DID YOU RECONCILE WITH HORUS?

"It's exactly as you see there in those cards," she said as we walked along the desert road. "I failed my son with my indecision, and what he saw in that moment was a woman he didn't want to call his mother. It brought me great shame.

"By finally making the decision, thanks to the steadfast resolve of my son, I was able to redeem myself in his eyes, but not a moment before I knew what had to be done, and yet I let emotion blind me."

"Oh. Thank you for sharing that; it doesn't sound like it was a pleasant thing at all." I paused for a bite of cupcake and a swallow of tea, and it was disorienting to come out of the desert and back into my living room for that little bit of food. "I think it's

Withering away of bounty through neglect and inaction. Weakness, indecision.

A challenging youth, passionate with deep insight, although difficult at times. A resolution of outstanding concerns, vigilance against current issues.

A woman of few morals, willing to use others for her own gain.

fair to switch course from that, if that's alright, so to move to a different topic: your worship stretched from Egypt all the way to England back in the day. What was it like, having your worship travel so far in antiquity?"

3. WHAT WAS IT LIKE HAVING YOUR WORSHIP TRAVEL SO FAR?

Still an excellent card, but harmony, bliss, and friendship may take longer to manifest.

Still a card of great success, but accompanied by a little less contentment.

Contentment, harmony, bliss. Peace, satisfaction, fertility, abundance. Spiritual fulfillment via unconditional love.

Isis smiled; her eyes twinkled with the sun's reflection. "Ah, yes. With my original seat of power, and my original people, so far off, having worshippers all over like that meant it took a moment longer for my blessings to stretch that far. But they came, and they still come to people who still honor me." Then she glanced at me. "My blessings include all things love, healing, family, joy, and safety. I like to travel and see these new lands as I deliver these blessings; I like to learn of the new people who come to know me. It's fascinating."

It was like the sun was radiating out of her, too, with that smile—and it made me feel a bit warmer, too. "I bet!" I said. "You must've seen so many different empires and countries over time. What kind of nation has been your favorite?"

4. WHAT KIND OF NATION WAS YOUR FAVORITE?

It seemed my refusal to fall too far into doubt was paying off, too, because by this point, she was less a painting, more a person; she finally stared at me head on as we stood on that road.

"Of course there's no place like home," she said, both eyes fixed on me, "but truthfully, my favorite nations have been ones whose queens are ferocious, their universities stuffed with books. Still, for all the tragedy I saw, there was no place free of tragedy. Even the strongest queens, and the smartest scholars, hadn't the answers to save everyone. Everywhere has strife, whether at home or abroad—but it doesn't have to be like that."

A strong, independent, logical, calculating woman. Perceptive, holding private grief.

Fear, depression, and strong feelings of guilt or revenge.

Scholarship, study, academia. Hard work brings results. A messenger, good news.

"Oh, I love that—and I agree." I took a moment to basically sear her face into my mind before continuing. "It makes me wonder if it'd be different if people cared about each other more—but in that vein, as you are yourself a mother, what does motherhood mean to you?"

5. WHAT DOES MOTHERHOOD MEAN TO YOU?

Destructive excess. Can also indicate arrogance. Friends may feel taken for granted.

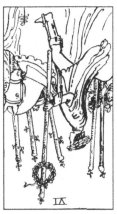

Treachery, intrigue, and battles that may be lost.

Still a card of misfortune, but help is nearby. The path may be rocky, but the end is in sight.

Suddenly, the otherwise kind-faced Isis frowned with a sharp tug of her lips. Her brows set flat across her eyes, her shoulders stiff.

"It's not the role of a hero," she said, her voice hard as rock. She loomed over me. "What comes first is the child, always. Not the mother's wishes, not her ego, the *child*. It's easy to feel betrayed as a mother, and like there's no help for you as you put your needs behind others. But help is there. A community raises a child; motherhood is all about rallying your resources and people for the good of someone other than yourself. It's a serious thing, not a game."

I wrote as quick as I could. "Oh, absolutely! I think there are a lot of parents out there that could be reminded of this, honestly. But okay, another thing I'm wondering about: you have associations with magic, and I'm curious about your thoughts on modern witchcraft?"

6. WHAT DO YOU THINK OF MODERN WITCHCRAFT?

We started moving again and walked a little further down that road, towards the big cliff.

"Magic doesn't make one suddenly all powerful," she mused, each word slowly spoken, carefully chosen. "The more that know it and its power, the more that are armed. Gone are the days when only a few trained folks held the power; now any and all can sling spells and cause grief, even among supposed friends." She sighed and stared at me, not with the same hard expression as before, but with her face crumpled in something just above pain—exasperation, maybe. "Much goes into romanticizing old gods as well, but no society has ever been pure or perfect. Today's world is one of freedom that many before never enjoyed or conceived of. Magicians must learn to be strong in today's world, adept, and they must realize the use and necessity of magic beyond getting little material things.

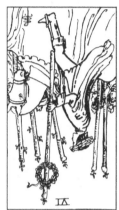

Treachery, intrigue, and battles that may be lost.

Beware of sentimentalizing the past. Was it really so much better, or were you too naïve to see the truth?

Wealth, be suspicious of materialism. Prosperity at expense others means emotional bankruptcy; an inheritance often involves the loss of a loved one. Greed may mean the loss of all gained.

"Right now, people are always pushing hard for money or some such, trying to always affect the mundane with the magical and losing themselves."

I blinked. This was an answer that felt similar, but not the same, as others I'd heard from Hekate and Zorya. It was more than just a warning of seeking power: it was a call to sense for magicians, a reminder of not just what not to do with their power, but what they should've instead focused their time on. A rebuke of using magic just for the odd material wish, an acknowledgement of the responsibility that came with being a magician—and an acknowledgement that people had always been a bit (or a lot) irresponsible when they discovered the power of magic.

"Alright, yeah, I see that," I said, cocking my head like a bird, as if I could roll the thought around in there until it settled into the right place in my mind. "And speaking of going outside the mundane, I also wonder: what's the Kemetic underworld like? I was in a secluded piece of it with Anubis and Thoth, I think, but I'd like to know a little more about the rest, if that's okay."

7. WHAT IS THE KEMETIC UNDERWORLD LIKE?

Fear of change is inevitable, but you must face it. Resistance is useless.

Inspiration, clear thought, inspired solutions. Problems solved, goals reached. Action, power, strength.

Weakness, intolerance, and lack of understanding need to be overcome.

"It's not a place where one stays the same as they were," she said. "They see what they couldn't before and learn what they didn't know. The underworld is where past ideas are shattered and new things are always possible. Often people are scared to approach death, but it comes for us all—and all of us change with it. It's a lovely place for those who want to be complete."

"Whoa," I breathed, though I wasn't sure what else to say because I was trying to write as quick as humanly possible. So what I said sounded pretty flat. "Well, alright then. I never thought about an underworld ever being like that." I paused to rub my eyes.

"But! We're down to our last three questions, so without further ado: how do you see yourself?"

Isis nodded, even as I hurriedly shuffled through the cards. I'd been going a little fast towards the end, honestly, because I was feeling quite some pressure from my daily schedule, and I'd been baking all day and was tired, but I still tried to slow down so as to not come off like a jerk. When I did, I was able to see her better—and when I rushed, I realized, I was seeing her worse.

It clicked then. How silly I was! Of course—why would it be easy to channel an image of a deity if I was forcing it? Or trying to drag it in before I was ready to see it? I wasn't broken; my visualization skills weren't crapping out on me.

I was just being impatient.

So a word of advice: don't try hardcore meditating & channeling when you're tired, you're feeling rushed, and your brain is a beehive from a day's activity. You'll just feel like I did right then: like a massive jerk. I paused my shuffling altogether there.

"I'm sorry, Isis," I said, deflating. "I've been a bit hurried here, haven't I? I hope you don't think I don't want to talk. I'm just worried about getting out of the house on time, is all."

She smiled at me, her arms folded over her chest, and I had the sense of her being a proud teacher after a student struggles and finds the right answer. I took that as a sign to keep shuffling again, and in her own time, she came through clear with the cards.

8. HOW DO YOU SEE YOURSELF?

"I am a queen," she said. "As queen, I must make decisions that aren't always easy. I've failed in this before, confusing family loyalties for the bald truth before me, but no more. All I've survived has taught me to never sway from the course I know is right. I am sure of myself now, more than ever, and I know the steps I must take to ensure my work is done."

"Alright, wow." I nodded, and this time, I didn't rush my writing to the point of cramping my hand. "And how do you want to be seen?"

A strong, independent, logical, calculating woman. Ruthless, knows what she wants.

What doesn't kill you makes you stronger. Strength within necessary to survive.

Indecisiveness, falsehood. Beware of those who seek conflict for conflict's sake.

9. HOW DO YOU WANT TO BE SEEN?

Indecision at a critical time could lead to defeat.

Material and spiritual prosperity. Keep stock of bounty for less fortunate times.

Don't take blessings for granted. We tend to yearn after the unattainable, but is throwing away what you have worth that?

Isis looked up, the sunlight glowing off her face. "As someone whose mistakes have led to growth. Never again will I be someone to let misguided wishes make me falter. I am strong. I am wise with the gifts I bestow, with wisdom born of experience."

Someone aware of her own history— that was the energy in the air, and she confirmed it a moment later.

"I have grown," she added. "I understand my role well and will always be here to help."

"Understood! Thank you for that. And, well, we're at the end now, Lady Isis, so I'd like to ask: do you have any messages you'd like to share, either with me or others?"

10. ANY LAST MESSAGES FOR ME OR OTHERS?

Isis's smile grew bigger, and her stare went sharp.

"I'm always among you all, trying to remind people of balance and the value of compromise." Then she sighed. "No one wants to talk to each other anymore. No one wants to do the work to understand their fellow man. Not every situation ends in a satisfying way, and that's okay. What people need to understand is that maintaining strife for hopes of a perfect resolution is nonsense.

"Rarely does a situation go such a way because people forget that the person they're quarreling with has grievances, too. Cooler heads must prevail. You need to work towards solutions, not just satisfaction. You may even find a new partner or friend from such worthy adversaries because of how you handle yourself in the situation."

Balancing act. Hard choices. Indecision will make it worse. Compromise, choosing lesser of two evils. Make the best of a bad situation. Meeting a worthy adversary.

That which bends is less likely to break. May need to compromise. Desires sacrificed to avoid ongoing strife. Time for action. Postponing resolution will do more damage.

A fickle, flighty man who may have trouble controlling his anger.

An enemies-to-lovers vibe? In *my* tarot readings?

"The strife needs to end," she said, even as I smiled to myself at that goofy little thought, and she repeated herself as if to refocus me. "The strife needs to end."

"Fair, yeah—I hear you," I said. Once I was done writing, I closed my eyes to take in what she looked like one more time, just to enjoy the energy and the image, before I tipped my head. "Alright, well, that's all we have for today. Thank you so much for your time, Lady Isis, and I do hope you enjoyed the cupcake and the tea! I appreciate you sharing your answers with me!"

She beamed at me, and then, with a clap of my hands, the image faded away. I was somehow well ahead of schedule for my day, too. It was almost like I didn't have to worry so much about time at all.

And don't get me wrong: I was still exhausted and cranky for a good part of the day, because that's what happens when you burn the candle from both ends. But at least I'd accomplished this little kernel of learning with Isis. And understood doubly her message to slow down. Though, at that time, I couldn't slow down. I had a lot going on, and I was being pulled in a lot of directions, and I knew her advice was sound, but I felt like I couldn't *afford* to follow it.

Even though God Himself was telling me the same thing, I felt I couldn't follow that advice. And we all know what happens when God's advice goes unheeded long enough. But for the time being, I couldn't bring myself to do anything about the ever-increasing strain on my time and energy, so I just kept driving my spiritual car with my little gas light on, hoping I'd make it to the next proverbial gas station before I ended up stranded.

On to the next thing, I remember thinking to myself, even with my eyes burning and my head swimming as I ran around my house to gather my things. *Onto the next.*

JUDAS ISCARIOT

If there's one person in the story of the Gospels that really makes me pause, it's Judas Iscariot.

Another one of the most recognizable figures from the Gospels, Judas is the Apostle that betrayed Jesus and got Him caught by Roman officials. He did so for thirty pieces of silver, and some accounts say that after Jesus's death, he bought a field with that money and then just... fell over in it and exploded somehow (Acts), while others (particularly Matthew) say he returned the money and hanged himself out of guilt. One of the most common ways you'll see Christians cling to the idea of Biblical inerrancy (the idea that the Bible is perfect and correct all the time) and deny any contradictions in the book is by lining these two events up in a gruesome, icky theory: that Judas hanged himself, decomposed in the hot sun, and eventually fell by way of the tree branch snapping or something, causing his bloated, decaying body to burst open.

Either way, the point is clear: Judas was painted as the bad guy for betraying Jesus, as one would expect. Some Gospels even mention that when Jesus said one of the Apostles would betray Him and handed that Apostle a piece of oil-dipped bread, Satan entered into him (John 13:27), causing him to do it. However, I remember reading *The Book of God: The Bible as a Novel* by Walther Wangerin (the first way I read the Bible, because the long pages of rules and stuffy language bored me to tears when I tried to read it as a younger witch, and the novelization made everything so much more *human*), there was one interesting idea woven into the text: Judas thought he was *helping*.

In the novelization, Judas betrayed Jesus not because he was a crook, a dishonest man, or anything else, but because he wanted to force Jesus's hand. He wanted Jesus to reveal who He truly was and start bringing the divine wrath on people, so that everyone would have no choice but to recognize Him as Son of God and follow Him. Jesus didn't take the bait, however, as He'd already told the Apostles that the Son of Man had to die and spend three days in the earth; He knew what was coming all along. Judas, horrified at the outcome, was filled with remorse.

Since then, Judas has always been pictured as a terrible person. In Dante's *Inferno*, even, when Dante got down to the very last rung of hell, it was one single man, Judas, being chewed on by Satan himself as the World's Worst Sinner. Since my perception of him had been colored by the novelization of the whole story, though, I couldn't help but feel bad for him. But even if we hadn't taken into account that idea, that Judas just wanted to see Jesus have some anime-worthy power-up in front of everyone, the way the other Apostles speak about Judas in the Gospels is also pretty brutal, trying to paint him as a greedy and dishonest person from the start (despite his being one of Jesus's closest Apostles). Something didn't feel right about all this, and by his remorse afterwards, I felt like he had a piece of humanity in him worth mourning.

Before I interviewed him, though, I did ask Jesus about him, and in true Jesus fashion, He brought me right to the guy rather than just talking about him. We were in a long, narrow hallway, with only a torch Jesus brought and placed in an empty sconce on the wall to light the area before the rest plunged into shadows. Along the wall opposite of that torch were many cells with bars shutting them closed indefinitely—no door, no lock. Just bars.

These cells were no bigger than a broom closet, so anyone inside couldn't have laid down in them; they could really only sit or stand. In the cell Jesus stopped at was a hunched man that wore nothing but a loincloth, and whose bones poked through his dirt-stained skin. It was Judas, shivering and alone, and Jesus looked down at him with a face twisted in pity.

I got the sense from Jesus that Judas thought he belonged there. That he wouldn't come out, no matter how many times Jesus went to talk to him.

So of course, I put Judas on the poll as a potential interviewee. And when he was chosen, I was more than ready to jump in and figure out exactly what was going on with this ex-Apostle. Let me walk you through the mind of Judas Iscariot, so that you might see and feel what I witnessed in that dark, dusty hallway, on what was plainly a prison visitation.

Maybe it was crude, but I did have some coins on the table to represent Judas: six coins, either nickels or quarters or dimes. I also had my silver cross necklace, with an amethyst lodged in its center, as well as celestite, blue lace agate, and lapis lazuli for communication and peace. All of this was around a big sphere of onyx to absorb any and all negativity that might've passed through. While it was simple, it was effective in focusing my mind back on that old prison, and so with my prayers said and my blessings cast, my mugwort burned for better psychic reach, my cinnamon incense lit for courage and power, I went back into that dark hallway to find Judas. Jesus came with me again, like a chaperone, though He didn't say much as we delved on down there. There was a grim flavor to the dust in the air as we walked.

Eventually I got there, and I confirmed with Judas that he was with me and willing to talk. He chose Threads of Fate's Weaver Tarot, and then we were off.

"Alright, Judas, here we are again," I said as I hunkered down against the wall. I sat at his level, notebook on my knees, and sighed. "I won't waste any time, so let's dive right in. First thing that I'm wondering: what are you doing in there? What's going on?"

Judas had black hair, shaggy and a little curly. His eyes were huge and watery, his body ragged and hunched, covered only by a loincloth, and he had some hint of a rough beard on his face. As I said, I'd gotten a sense of why he was there before, but it was important to hear him say it.

I. WHAT ARE YOU DOING IN THIS CELL?

"I need to do this," he said, his voice shaky. "I need to. I've thought so long and hard. I can't forgive myself that easily. It's one thing to have what I did predicted, another to *do* it. Feels like I've been here only for a moment—it's not enough time."

The idea stunned me. Only a moment? I don't know what happens to time in the other worlds, or what eternity means to souls, but I wanted to let him know how much time passed, and damn if I didn't try.

"Bud," I said, "do you know what era I'm from? What do you mean, you haven't spent enough time down here? It's been—!"

Then Jesus put a hand on my shoulder. He put a finger to His lips, His brows set hard, an edge to His stare.

TEMPERANCE.

Balance and peace. None are perfect or pure evil. Humans live in the grey area. What we know to be true may not be. Human grace and growth.

THE SUN .

A good time to be optimistic; success is on the way. The sun will shine soon. Plug into your power.

Major transition now occurring, one filled with sadness. The road ahead is one that's best for you. Can't rush the process. Find peace in the moment.

That was my cue to shut my mouth, even as Judas stared at me with those giant eyes.

"Okay, well, never mind." I said as I rubbed my eyes. Jesus's hand slipped off my shoulder as I kept going. "I'm sure you figured I'd ask this, but: why did you do what you did? There are a lot of theories, you know—that you just wanted to take your cash and leave, that you believed it would force Jesus's hand, that you knew it had to be done... What's the truth?"

2. WHY DID YOU BETRAY JESUS?

ACE of SWORDS.

Cut through illusion; get to the heart of issues. Mentally pushed.

KING of WANDS

Dreams ready to manifest Commitment. Balanced self care.

THE FOOL .

Not thinking things through. No foundation to act on one's wants.

Judas stared at me a moment longer, then hugged his knees up to his chest and scowled. Even with Jesus right next to me, Judas spoke nothing but his plain truth.

"I had to do something. Our Master was too powerful for people to understand. I wanted them to see it. I wanted people to see Yeshua and see the face of the Son of God. But all I felt I'd done was make a mistake, the worst mistake anyone could ever make. To see Him hanging there off that wood," he paused and blew out a breath, shuddered, "it's still so fresh."

"Mmm. And what happened to you after? The consensus is you died."

Yes or no questions didn't need cards. I pulled out my pendulum and asked the question over and over until it started to move, and it spun in a wide circle as he spoke.

"Yes—hanged."

I sat there with that. And again, it all felt fresh, like Jesus really had just died yesterday and Judas had only been down here for half a day at most. He spoke like he was still stuck in the very evening it all went down. In what lore we have, Judas hadn't lived to see Jesus come back, and a week ago, when I got him to stop muttering to himself and look at me, what I'd done was shout at him. *Hey!* I'd slapped the ground hard enough to startle him, so that he had no choice but to look outside his cell. *What are you wailing for? What you did had to be done!*

Between that moment and this interview, I'd felt strange—like when you know someone is staring at you, wishing for you to turn around and see them so they don't have to speak up to get your attention. Maybe he was trying to talk to me as much as I was trying to talk to him after that. I don't know. But he was vehement about not talking to me at all until I yelled at him then, and then he was quiet as I explained what I wanted from him, and then he nodded so furiously when I asked to talk to him again. So who really knows what was going on in his head?

One thing I will say is that I think spirits do change and grow with each person they meet. No doubt someone met Judas before, or tried to. But had they said the same things then? Bothered to explain? Did he forget, in this timeless place, if someone told him what I told him? Did he not believe it? I don't know. As I keep walking this path, I find the more I learn, the less I know; for every one answer comes three more questions. I just don't have time to get answers to them all.

But I looked at Jesus, who sighed and shrugged, as if to say *fine, go ahead.* I told Judas then.

"Hey, do you know?" I shifted across the hallway until I was leaning against the bars, and my God, Judas's eyes were *massive*. The whites around the deep brown irises lit up his face like headlights, he had them open so wide. As if *I* were the ghost, and not him. "Do you know that Jesus is standing right there? That He came back after He died? That the world changed a whole lot since then? That it *had* to change, that Jesus *had* to die for it all to happen?"

Judas stared at me, his lips quivering. Then a whisper of a question escaped on his breath. "Did the Kingdom come? Is the world saved?"

"Oh, jeez, I can't say that," I said, huffing a laugh. "World's a mess still. Maybe a worse mess than before; I don't know. But it changed!"

And I told him all about it: how everyone did come to know Jesus's power after He came back. It created a whole new religion, and it sparked the rise and fall of whole empires, and it came to burden as many people as it liberated. I told him about Christianity, and the following religion Islam that sparked up five hundred years later, and I told him about how people do horrible things in Jesus's name as much as they do good things—how people used His name and His power to justify the worst atrocities as governments while others tried to do some good on the ground for their communities as individual people. He stared at me the whole time, blank-faced.

"Yeah," I said as I leaned my head against the bars. "It's been a two thousand year ride, you know. A big old shitshow, if I may say so." I couldn't help but smile when Jesus sighed. "And you know, Judas, those other Apostles... they weren't so charitable to you. It's written like you just wanted money the whole time. What did you think of the other Apostles?"

3. WHAT DO YOU THINK OF THE OTHER APOSTLES?

Again, his face crumpled in that bitter scowl. He sat there, back against the wall of that cell.

"They were—no, they were good men." He rubbed his face with one dirty palm, smearing dust on his cheeks. "But they forgot their own beginnings. They were quick to judge. They didn't know how I went to the guards, or what I said to them, yet they wrote some story anyway, made things up about me. Made me out to be worse than I was. They thought themselves so righteous, but they were as flawed as any other."

"Huh. Well, that doesn't sound too off the mark. I can imagine, from how they painted you from the get-go. But you know, there is a whole Gospel attributed to you that I can't understand. It goes into crazy stuff."

He looked at me like he had no idea what I was talking about.

The ebb of life. Assessing needs after loss. Strength, resilience, courage needed. Shifting your thinking for success.

Sinking into darker aspects of life. Easy to feel shame, fear, judgement. Remember your good attributes.

Take inventory of yourself. Shift in life, beliefs, structure. Easy to feel ashamed of the past. Be kind: self growth is hard.

4. THOUGHTS ON THE GNOSTIC GOSPEL OF JUDAS?

Seeing your experience with an enlightened perspective. Stronger, more resilient, and ready to focus on the good in life—able to see the beauty that surrounds you.

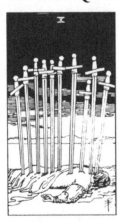

Disaster. You may have been running from it, but it's time to move through it. A huge part of you is gone. You may feel betrayed. Reconnect.

Energy to action. How can you translate ideas and passion to the real world? Take things seriously enough to do what people don't want to do.

"This 'Gospel of Judas' was found in the first century after Jesus's death, written in Coptic. Did you write this, or have anyone write it for you? It says things like Yahweh being an inferior and evil creator god, there are all theses angels and stars that make more angels and stars—very Tolkien-esque stuff, if I do say so—"

"No, no. I wrote no such thing," he insisted, sitting up straight. "I can see clearly now. People use our names to give credence to foolishness. I see my experience has done something useful—but *that* was not my experience! I wrote nothing to suggest my Master's Father was weak. I did what no one else could bear to do, for His sake, but I did it because I believe in His power. And His Father's."

Case closed, I guess. Judas's Gnostic Gospel has some crazy stuff written in it, but I do think that sometimes the church leaders did get it right when they wrote some things off as fiction, because that Gospel really did have me thinking of Lord of the Rings, with all the singing angels creating a bunch of stuff; it didn't seem like anything that ever came up anywhere else in the entire history of the Abrahamic faiths (or even any other religions that carried on a sense of One God, like Zoroastrianism, Yezidism, anything). Still worth seeing if it had anything to do with reality, though.

"I see." I shuffled my deck and said, "Well, as we move on, we've talked about the Apostles. But what do you think of Jesus? Then and now?"

Here, Judas smiled, almost ruefully. Jesus, too, had a knowing smile as He crossed His arms over His chest and leaned against the wall.

5. WHAT DO YOU THINK OF JESUS?

"He tricked us," Judas said. "With His dying, He tricked us. But for good cause. He is our friend. He did what He knew He needed to do, no matter what anyone else said. When He explained things, He was cheerful. When He didn't, He was so quiet. He knew more than we ever could."

It was a little bittersweet. Jesus never said anything while He was down there with me, even as Judas spoke; He seemed like He was just there to facilitate and listen, and to keep me centered since He looked more ragged than I'd seen Him in His interview. I think Jesus was appearing as He had towards the end of His journey, which unsettled Judas a little at first. Longer, tangled hair, a little paler as if worried or even somewhat sick. Nonetheless, He jumped in here and there with little things, redirections and snaps of ideas, but otherwise let me lead the way.

Underhanded tactics. Someone is trying to get away with something sneaky. No impulsiveness when trying to get away from something. Reactiveness doesn't help.

Focusing on yourself and creative habits and patterns that will really benefit you long term. Building the life you want on your own terms. Independence.

Clarity can cut through confusion. New realizations that change your behavior. Being less absolute and more playful as truths are revealed.

"Alright, well, here's a fun question: what do you think of people's theory that you were connected with the Sicarii? The rebels that went knifing people to fight Rome's imperialism?"

6. THOUGHTS ON BEING CONNECTED TO THE SICARII?

A layered card. Are you balanced between give and take? View the situation from an unbiased place without judgement. Drop insecurities or doubts.

Driven by desire for stability, wealth, and security. Clear vision, a need for structure to accomplish goals. Drop insecurities or doubts.

Overwhelm and uncertainty, loss from within the self that has shattered one's foundation.

I think he gleaned from my mind what they were once called, because as I was asking, he nodded. "Terrorists," he muttered, sounding resigned. "They called them terrorists, huh?"

Then he shrugged. "I understood them, but I disagreed with them. It's not fair to call them terrorists. They were doing what they thought was best to deal with the blight on our land, those Romans. I was not one of the Sicarii, but I understand why one would be. And maybe if things had been different, I would've been with them—but I followed Yeshua."

"Ah. I see. Interesting!" The sound of my pencil scratching over notebook paper echoed through the hallway. "Alright, we're almost done. Judas, can tell me how do you see yourself?"

7. HOW DO YOU SEE YOURSELF AND WANT TO BE SEEN?

Sinking into darker aspects of life. Easy to feel shame, fear, judgement. Remember your good attributes.

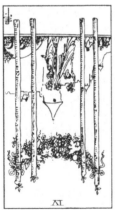

Quietness, small victories, and balances within the self. Personal acknowledgement of progress. Awareness.

Desire for stability and wealth to be generous to others. You must see everything from a higher perspective. This requires balance, practicality, and warmth.

The answer wasn't what I expected. A lot milder than I thought it'd be.

"I am working here. Through my actions. I am a flawed man with much to answer for, and I'm answering for it. When I'm done—not if, but when," he said, with as much optimism as I'd seen from him this entire time, and a real smile, "I'll be different."

"Got'cha. And how do you want others to see you?"

There were no cards, just a simple line that echoed in my head:

"As a man who's made mistakes."

"I understand. Okay! That's pretty much it. But Judas," I peered at him as he kept his knees hugged to his face, as he stared at the dust of his cell as if it would tell him something new, "do you have any other last messages you really want people to know?"

8. ANY LAST MESSAGES FOR ME OR OTHERS?

Again, his smile went solemn, rueful, as he stared at the floor.

"Don't force change," Judas said. "Let it happen naturally. The world is a monstrous place, and trying to fix it with brute force will only destroy you. Instead, seek opportunities to be the light, not opportunities to rip up the dark. And don't hide from mistakes. Embrace them, work through them, and walk back into the world when you're ready. I'm not yet, but one day. Maybe."

"Fair, fair. Well, that's it, then." I closed my notebook and got up to stand next to Jesus, who didn't look away from His old friend. "Thank you, Judas for your time—and you, Jesus, for facilitating."

Jesus glanced at me and smiled like a tired father. As I waved to Judas, who barely lifted his head enough to watch us, Jesus put a hand to my back and guided me out of this endless hallway of cells. We left together, up crumbling

Growing and embracing life with childlike enthusiasm. Reconnecting with the playful aspect of yourself. Finding new opportunities. Age can bring cynicism, so find that childlike love again. Reconnect; don't try to recreate the past.

Big dreams are ready to be made into reality. Being plugged into the big picture. Choose the best people to help you work on your vision. Inspire positive action—don't force it.

After a period of withdrawal, you're working your way back into the world. There's a sense of new beginnings as the universe opens up new people, places, and things to you.

stairs and into a bright light, and then there was nothing but the darkness of my closed eyes. When I opened them, I felt that familiar wave of dizziness that comes with sitting in meditation for a solid hour and a half, and I stared at the silver coins on the table.

If I'd felt any sympathy for Judas before, it was triplefold then. The poor guy was stuck in a prison of his own making; that's what that hallway was. A place where people went because they thought they belonged there, away from the world, away from people, away from light and grace and God. He was punishing himself, even when Jesus stood right in front of him. And Jesus understood enough to leave him there, even though He clearly didn't like it: Judas has to figure out how to forgive himself.

I believe in him. I believe he can do it. But after I posted this interview, while there was plenty outpouring support for Judas, there was a comment that wasn't entirely unpredictable: one asking why anyone would sympathize with Judas, giving that he sold Jesus out. And my answer was simple: when you can learn to sympathize with people, all people, and never deny someone their humanity, you find God. If a Christian can truly love their neighbor and their enemy—if they can even learn to love the devil himself, however they understand the devil—they can come a touch closer to understanding Divine love and mercy.

Judas was a person who made a choice that honestly, people make all the time. It wasn't a good choice, or one I'd defend; selling your friends out isn't exactly awesome (unless they're an active threat to people's safety or something). But it wasn't the worst choice we've ever seen people make on this planet, either, that's for damn sure—especially if he really did it to try and get Jesus to reveal His divine nature and didn't think it'd all go south the way it did.

It's easy to talk big and act high and mighty about someone we see as "lesser" or "evil" when they aren't around. Being quick to judge feels like it's human nature, honestly. And yet when you come face to face with those same people, you find it's a lot harder to keep that self-righteous energy, because you're forced to be confronted with the fact that the person you claimed was an evil monster, a demon straight out of hell, a scumbag and a pile of burning trash, is still just as much of a human as you are. That, had things been different, and you'd walked in their shoes and grown to have the worldview they have, you might've done the same things as they did. That's a horrifying thought: that we can all be angels or demons, or a blend of both, and that the only thing that decides which way we lean and grow is our experiences, and our responses to those experiences.

Unlike Dante in his silly little *Inferno*, who gets progressively *more* hostile to each level of sinners until he can point fingers, jeer, and laugh at these people who apparently deserved their fate in his eyes, someone who actually knows what Jesus was talking about will become the opposite: like Jesus in this interview, they won't deny a man the punishment that man thinks he deserves, or skimp on the purifying fires of the afterlife, but there will always be that tenderness. That hope that they can overcome their own formative experiences, learn from those deep lessons, and let their soul shine.

I have hope for Judas. I believe he can get out of that cell, and I think Jesus does, too. It may take a while longer yet, but with enough time, I think we'll find this lost Apostle not down in the dark, but up in the light, where the others are—and maybe then, he'll teach his old fellows the final piece of the lesson about God's mercy. His incomprehensible, all-encompassing mercy.

We'll just have to wait and see.

ARCHANGEL AZRAEL

I won't lie to you: including Christian spirits and general Abrahamic entities like angels into the Patreon polls was a big relief for me. I didn't have to worry so much about doing things perfectly, or getting the exact offerings, accidentally offending ancient and primordial deities and getting myself into a mess; I could just trust that God was with me and get down to business, asking freely about some of the more nitty-gritty spiritual topics with ease and knowing I wouldn't get the run-around from deities or spirits that didn't know me or know why I was bothering them.

So when Azrael popped up as the winner of the next week's poll, right after Judas, I can't say I didn't feel some relief. *Good,* I remember thinking. *Angels are easy.*

(And by easy, I really just meant *familiar.*)

But Azrael is a strange angel, because he actually doesn't ever appear in Christian lore. His name means "Help from God" in Hebrew, and while the name itself may not appear in Canonical scripture, the concept of the Angel of Death—the Mal'akh ha-Maweth in Hebrew, or Malak al-Mawt in Arabic—is familiar in Jewish and Muslim lore. The concept of the Grim Reaper is familiar to western Christians, in which Azrael seems to take on the role, but in Christianity, Azrael's role officially falls to Michael, Azrael himself being largely unrecognized in scripture but accepted in popular culture.

In Islam, though, Azrael (Azrail) is one of the four major archangels, the others being Gabriel (Jibril), Michael (Mikil), and Israfil. In Judaism, again, the name doesn't really appear canonically, but this angel's likeness and name does appear in Kabbalistic texts like the Zohar, and in apocryphal texts like what appears to be the Arabic rendition of the tradition of the Book of Enoch, as compiled by Sabine Baring-Gould in her *Legends of Old Testament Characters:*

> *God heard the prayer of Enoch, and He suffered Azrael to accomplish what the prophet had desired. Then the Angel of Death bore away Enoch, and showed him the seven stages of Hell, and all the torments inflicted there on sinners: after that he replaced him where he was before (72).*

In short: tradition and history and scripture and storytelling are a massive mess, and there's never going to be a consensus on anything religious no matter how hard we try. It is what it is.

But Azrael being the Angel of Death means that he is a *psychopomp*: a figure that guides souls of the dead to the afterlife. As such, I was interested to get his perspective on his own self, and what the work of a psychopomp entails—so let's take a look.

To start our interview, I set up some things that, to me, represented Death in the larger psyche of humanity: the crow, that age-old opportunistic creature known to pick at corpses, a coin to nod at the idea of "paying the ferryman" in some cultures, and stones like celestite, lapis lazuli, onyx, and obsidian for their qualities of angel communication, truth, wisdom, and energy transmutation. All was surrounded by a rosary with beads of purple agate, another nod to spiritual knowledge and healing, and to represent Azrael himself, I had his Counselor card from Doreen Virtue's Angel Oracle deck. I lit a candle for Azrael, said my prayers and did my blessings, and then asked him to come by.

Unfortunately, I'm a very last-minute person, and I'd run out of time to procrastinate on this weekly reading, so I was shoving it into an early morning session right before work. As I've said before, it's never a great idea to try and contact an entity when you're pressed for time—makes it harder to focus and harder to absorb what's being said—but I could only work with the time and space I had. So when Azrael confirmed he was with me through the pendulum, I set off.

"Hello, Azrael!" I had to shake the sleep off me, as I'd woken up early to get this interview done. Seems I can't bring myself to do these meetings unless they're first thing in the morning or last thing at night. "Thank you for speaking with me, and I'm sorry I'm a bit of a hurried mess this morning, but I really want to get to talking with you. I've learned some things that definitely raised some questions. But first, can I see you?"

Azrael bled in, as they all do when I sit down to meditate. It takes a little while to see them. But I noticed he looked a lot like Gabriel: that same blond hair, same gentle face. His eyes were deep purple, like amethysts, and he wore indigo and magenta robes. His wings were dark gray, almost black, and when he flapped them, dust flew off. Ashes maybe. He met me in the clouds, as most angels have, but the sun became the moon, and we sat there in the silver light.

I confirmed the deck he wanted to use, Amrit Brar's Marigold Tarot, as well as how many cards he wanted to use—one, which I thought was because he knew I was on a bit of a time crunch.

"Are you sure?" I didn't want to make him feel like he couldn't use more if he wanted to. "I'm fine with using more than one card—"

Azrael held up a hand. "No, no. I won't need more than one, trust me. Just go."

Worked for me. I blinked at him, then shrugged and said, "Okay. I guess I will. To start us off, though, now I need to ask: I notice that *psychopomps*, as they're called—all these deities and angels of death—don't really use many words. Why is that?"

1. WHY DON'T ANGELS AND DEITIES OF DEATH LIKE TO TALK?

Codependency, miscommunication, misunderstanding.

Azrael smiled at me, free and easy, and his voice was so soft. There was a somber element that wasn't sad or grim, just calm.

"There isn't much to say," he said. "The more you say, the more people latch on. There needs to be rest. Finality."

I felt it in my bones, the words he *didn't* say: he meant the people left behind as much as the dead. People cling to things, any scrap of news or information they can get, so he has keep it brief with them when he comes to deliver any news, especially about loved ones that have passed.

"Ah, I got'cha. Okay. Well, moving on to what I was reading about you, I gotta say I'm curious: how did Christianity miss you? Especially if you're around in Judaism and Islam—at least in the non-canonical texts?"

2. HOW DID CHRISTIANITY MISS THE FACT THAT YOU EXIST?

Again, Azrael smiled as if he found the idea funny. But then he sighed.

"Ideas can be oppressive. Death is a loaded thing. People fear it. They don't want to fear me—God's own angel. There's dissonance. I am the Angel of Death, but this title brings brutal images."

"Understandable. A shame, really. But that makes me wonder: Samael is also the Angel of Death in some instances. What's the difference between your and his role around death? I mean, I can imagine, but—"

Heavy burdens, being overwhelmed, struggle. Oppressive issues.

3. WHAT'S THE DIFFERENCE BETWEEN YOU AND SAMAEL?

Excess force applied to a situation, leading to disaster.

He had a withering look, as if the idea annoyed him. Pulling this card stopped my thoughts, and he spoke.

"Samael is for extreme situations." he said. "I carry the dead. I do not cause death, though some might see my coming as a direct predictor of it. But I guide and bring comfort. Samael destroys."

"Ah. No, that makes sense. 'Venom of God' and all that. But what's the hardest part of carrying the dead, would you say?"

Suddenly, things shifted. Gone were the moonlit clouds, the silver shining eerily off the gates of Heaven, as if all the other angels and Saints were asleep. The stars, the world below, all was gone, and there was a deep, dark forest, trees thin and black but thick with needles, ground covered in well-trodden, ash-soaked snow.

"Where is this?"

Azrael stood there with white robes instead of colorful ones, but he still had ashy wings. He also carried a lantern. It glowed a soft golden light, the color at odds with the black and white tone of everything else.

4. WHAT'S THE HARDEST PART OF KEEPING THE DEAD AWAKE?

"The hardest part of leading the dead," he said, "is keeping them awake."

I looked behind me, and there were ghoul-like people hobbling behind us. Their skin was blue-gray, their eyes sunken in, and they didn't seem quite conscious; they were just moving after the golden light. Some fell into the snow as if fatigued, and they didn't get back up. It seemed like they were chasing after the light of Azrael's lamp with slow, sluggish steps.

Azrael's voice pulled my feet to keep moving: "They don't have the same minds they did when they lived. It's trouble, keeping them going. But the living... that's difficult, too. Some are immune to the comfort I offer, no matter how hard I try—or how hard they pray."

"Oh. Okay." We walked down that snowy road a little longer. When the silence made my ears buzz, I broke it with my next question. "So, on an unrelated topic to all that, what do you think of the idea that you were once human? I read this somewhere as I was looking into you: there was apparently a man named Ezra, or Azra, who 'never tasted the taint of death' and became an angel—was that you?"

Poor luck, failure.

5. WERE YOU ONCE THE HUMAN EZRA (AZRA)?

Mistrust, insecurity, and loss of hope.

Again, that withering look.

"Ever trying to invent origins for me, you people," he said with a sigh. "So long as things have died, I have lived. I exist. I grow tired of people who insist I don't. The dissonance they experience is too strong. God—our Lord, our Father—is not some being of *only* comfort and light.

"He is darkness and death as well. He lingers in all parts of creation, from life to death. My purpose is to be a comfort, His light in the darkness."

I thought about it. Azrael. "God is my Help"—our comfort. It made sense in conjunction with what Azrael said, and I felt the name was one hell of an aspect of God to bear, but it was an aspect worth bearing

"I hear you." I said. "But on another note, I heard somewhere—maybe in Islamic folklore?—that you have so many eyes and hands and feet. Can you show me your true self?"

You bet I knew what I was getting into as I asked this, but I never pass up a chance to see an angel outside of their human illusions. I love angels. They're so wild to experience.

And this was no exception. Azrael didn't pick any cards for this; he only cocked his head, then disappeared. I was alone in the snow, but not for long: a moment later, where there was once a snowy road, there was then a black cloud full of eyes, as many as the stars in the sky. Around that cloud were the pink-purple clouds of twilight, and from that cloud came dozens of hands, all reaching down to the big globe that was the earth and grabbing at what I assumed were souls, lifting them up to be swallowed into the dusk, passed through it up to heaven. Even as we spoke, it seemed, Azrael was at work like this, doing his job, taking thousands and thousands of souls off the planet and up into the ether. He never paused, never slowed down. He just kept going, every minute, every hour, every day.

But all I could do was stare. Azrael is big. And intense.

Then we were back in the snowy woods, with him all blond and pretty, smiling as if amused.

"When all goes black, and the body goes cold," he said, "that is where we're walking right now."

I didn't recognize it at the time, but later, I would ponder this interview and wonder: all these souls that fell down into the snow, were they the ones who saw nothing but darkness when they died? The ones who didn't, or couldn't, follow the light to the other side, who were too tired as souls to keep going on? There were so many reports of people dying, only to get resuscitated and wake up dripping with fear, because the "other side" was nothing but empty, quiet darkness, no sight or sound or consciousness—just an abrupt end to the thing we call life.

In the meantime, I nodded. "I guess that settles that. But what should folks know about death?"

6. WHAT SHOULD PEOPLE KNOW ABOUT DEATH?

Turning our gaze from the physical trappings of this world to consider divine perspectives. Spiritual awareness and the endless nature of the divine.

I was a little surprised to pull the Hierophant, but it made sense, especially as Azrael spoke.

"It's as the card says. Death is not an end; it's a waystation. The glory of God is infinite. In it, too, is the life of souls—infinite, if changing and shifting in ways we don't understand. Feel that infinity. Know it before it comes for you, and," he smiled wider, eyes sparkling with mirth, "do not be afraid."

"Ah, makes sense, yeah." Angels, man. "Beautiful! Thank you. Now, coming to the end: how do you see yourself?"

7. HOW DO YOU SEE YOURSELF?

"Wow," I muttered. "Never figured you'd pick this card."

He shrugged. "I must be more for people. Distracting the grieving, keeping their minds busy and their spirits together. I bring momentum; I push people when they forget the necessity and inevitability of death."

"Got'cha. I love that! And how do you want to be seen?"

High, near fool hardy amounts of energy. Impetuousness, grandstanding, and overconfidence. Rashness. Be more brash and assertive.

8. HOW DO YOU WANT TO BE SEEN?

Courage, power, venturing forward into new experiences without fear. Many branches and forks in the path of life.

Another unexpected card. I was starting to worry I was misreading him until I read the description. As soon as it clicked, Azrael nudged me and grinned.

"I am infinite," he said. "You are infinite. We all are in our potential. I want people to see me as a harbinger of new beginnings as much as endings."

I nodded as we walked through the forest. "I see—how cool! Okay, okay, last question: are there any messages I can help you deliver today?"

9. ANY LAST MESSAGES FOR ME OR OTHERS?

Here, he got a little serious. I caught the flash of buildings, as well as the flicker of tea lights on the stands of a darkened Catholic church.

"Faith for routine's sake is faith wasted," Azrael muttered. The smile was gone from his face, the sparkle snuffed from his eyes. "True connection to the Divine—in any capacity, whatever you call it—is lost when we follow tradition for tradition's sake. One must find their own connection and way forward, with education, diligence, and sincerity. People must learn before they can act."

Huh. That struck a chord with me. *How about that.*

"Alright, well—thank you for that," I said as I snapped my book shut. "I'm glad we had the chance to talk; this was clean and straight through! Please come by whenever you need to; this has been great. Goodbye, Azrael!"

And then Azrael nodded and kept on walking, all those ghouls ambling along after him and his lantern. They walked further and further, until there was nothing but snow, and then nothing but darkness. I opened my eyes to the familiar sight of the coffee table, the T.V., the rug—and I knew it was time to get up and run off to start the rest of my day.

Loss, theft, uncompromising values, obsession with socially acceptable roles and routines.

There isn't much to say about this, I don't think, except maybe this: my boyfriend and I had a conversation about this once, and Azrael's answer confirmed for me that this line of thinking was correct—that when people serve tradition, rather than tradition serving people, it's time to retire it. Moreover, for Easter a few months after this interview, my mom and I decided we'd actually go to a church service for once. The whole while, something didn't quite feel right. I thought that maybe it was in the stares of the people we passed, strangers to us since we didn't usually go. But then my mom leaned over to me in the middle of the service and whispered,

"Something doesn't feel right. This feels all wrong."

I spent the rest of the service asking God about it. *Is it this? Is it that? What's mom feeling?* And the answer I got, for all my poking and prodding through my intuition—what I like to call my "built in pendulum"—was simple: the majority of these people weren't in there for God. They weren't in there for true belief in the story of Jesus (though they'd never tell you so). They were there for appearances, to go through the motions, to check it off their "Good Person" list for the day. They were there to say they'd done what they were supposed to (and, by extension, that no one should ask them for more.)

Sad, considering it was a Catholic church, and we were hoping to feel the good feelings proper worship within a community is supposed to bring. But this was exactly what Azrael told me about just a few months prior: people aren't looking for their own relationships with God, but damn if they don't get self-righteous just because they did the Good Christian song and dance.

But conversations like these, with the angels and the Saints and the many other pieces of Divinity that make up the world, certainly help me build my own connection. They make me feel alive. They make me feel at peace, unafraid of the world and the things in it. They make me come closer to understanding what it must be like to be a parent as I look at those so very self assured Christians, the ones who stomp their feet and decry me as an agent of Satan, knowing they haven't learned all there is to learn or experienced all there is to experience.

Most importantly, they bring me closer to my God—make me more *able* to fling myself into the abyss and trust Him to catch me. And if I get nothing else out of this than that, then I'll rejoice, because it means I've gotten *everything.*

KING BELIAL

Was it stupidity that kept having me put the infernal divine on my Patreon polls? Was it careless-ness, senselessness, all just a big joke in my mind, to think I could just keep walking up to these entities and asking for a handful of answers to my silly questions? Or was it a need to compare and contrast these entities and their Scriptural references—a belief that this Great Equation between what people call *good* and *evil* was, in fact, balanced, and that I just needed to learn the proper spiritual formulas to unwind it?

Likely the latter, I'll be honest. But oh vanity of vanities, that I thought I could learn such a thing so easily, with just a couple pokes around the infernal realms and a couple quick calls down below. I understand that this Great Equation, this spinning coin, is something I'll likely study for the rest of my life and still never understand, but unlike the defeated soul who inspired the first chapter of Ecclesiastes, I don't find it a reason to despair. Knowing *something* is better than knowing nothing at all, even if that something becomes like a carpet of jagged glass cutting deeper into your feet with every step forward. So I was determined to continue on, and to continue approaching the infernal di-vine with nothing but the wish for knowledge—to play, as I liked to call it, Spiritual Jackass, and meet these entities just to see what happened to me.

King Belial was chosen next, and in all honesty, I'd seen him before in my meditations with Lucifer. I'd seen many things and many entities in my meditations with Lucifer; they all came and went as they pleased through the great study we'd often sit in together during readings or guided meditations. Sometimes they showed me things that made no sense to me, and sometimes they offered nothing at all save for a knowing smile, but all in all, I appreciated each and every glimpse they were willing to show me. Anything that was more than I'd seen before.

At this point, I'd made my way around a few texts on demonolatry and could do a good deal of research myself. I knew King Belial's name was the word used in St. Paul's letters to the Corinthians, too, specifically in 2 Corinthians 6:15:

What accord has Christ with Belial? Or what portion does a believer share with an unbeliever?

Belial is a word that means "wicked" or "worthless," and many would think it's just a title of Satan. But knowing that Satan is also a title, one applied to many of God's own angels (HaShatan, or the Adversary), we just end up getting into a big tangled ball of titles that goes nowhere and does nothing. No, more than titles on titles on titles, many demonolaters throughout the ages came to understand each of these infernal entities as their own beings, who each stood in stark contrast to the angels still in Heaven.

So I, too, came to understand this infernal King as his own being, and I found what I needed to know about him: that he was of the element of earth, that he was known as the Lawless One, and that, through the experience of many demonolaters I'd come across, he seemed to be the ultimate destroyer of obstacles, a breaker of chains.

Now, for this interview, I'll admit, it was probably my goofiest attempt to summon a demon yet. Knowing that King Belial was earth based, and knowing that I wasn't about to go find some precious metals to carve his sigil on like old grimoires suggested, I instead found a perfect way to blend demonolatry with kitchen witchcraft: by drawing his sigil on a potato. Then I nestled that potato into a bowl of buckwheat, surrounded it with malachite, moss agate, and obsidian stones for more of that earth energy, and got out my green candles for a bit of that good thematic color magic. His offering was a shot of vodka—traditionally a potato-based alcohol, but the brand I used, *Tito's*, is corn based. Either way, it worked: grains like corn are also associated with earth.

After the Lord's Prayer, I confirmed King Belial was there with the pendulum, lit some mugwort to enhance that psychic connection, locked in the Weaver Tarot by Threads of Fate as his deck of choice, and got down to business.

"Hello, King Belial!" It was always a struggle to me, to think of what to say when I felt an entity hovering around me like a cloud. "I politely and formally welcome you into my space. And I do hope you don't find the potato *too* silly; it was all I could think to do for your sigil. Still, please, come in and sit, if you will!"

I had to specifically ask God to keep Michael off this one. Michael had a tendency to linger whenever I worked with Lucifer, but because I heard that he had a bit of bad blood with King Belial, I instead asked that if God was going to send anyone to play referee, that it be Jesus—and that He leave some space for Lucifer to put his eyes on the situation, too. He was becoming something of a guardian whenever I entered his territory, mostly to make sure I didn't get myself stuck somewhere stupid, which was much appreciated.

We met in Lucifer's library, where I would normally meet him to discuss things I was reading or learning about. *Library* is a bit of a stretch, though: it was more like a sizeable study than anything. It was a dark room, with muted greens and purples in the curtains and the carpet, as well as good leather chairs and a long couch by a coffee table of well-oiled, dark wood. (Though sometimes, that coffee table had been a dining table, full of taper candles and silver plates of fruits and meat and such.) A marble fireplace sat dead of flame on one wall, sandwiched between plenty of old books that lined the walls in their floor-to-ceiling shelves, and a massive window behind Lucifer's big resolute desk let the main source of light in. However, that light diffused the way the sun does on a cloudy afternoon, making it impossible to really see what was outside while it was shining.

There was a door in the back that led out to a hallway; that's where all the other members of the infernal divine I'd seen liked to pop in from. I've never gone too far outside it to see what's out there, only a few ways down a dark hallway that seemed to stretch into nothing and nowhere.

King Belial himself looked nothing like what the *Ars Goetia* described him as, and I figured he wouldn't. Apparently, some believe he comes as *two* lovely angels on a chariot of fire, and maybe he did at one point, but here, he was a massive, single figure. One with great metal armor, with horns rising from a bald head, and with eyes that burned a furious yellow. The gravity of him was immense; his very presence suggested power like the hardest, most resolute rock. Oddly, though, it seemed like his body was made out of charcoal, or some kind of flaky stone despite that strength. He sat down on the other side of the coffee table, settling beside Lucifer on the leather couch, while Jesus sort of lingered next to me. It felt like an office meeting, honestly.

"Alright, King Belial," I said as my soul settled into its own little leather chair, "As I understand it, you're in charge of lies and guilt, and you won't give practitioners truthful answers unless you have some gifts and such first. I hope the gifts I put out are enough, and I'm not going to tell you what to do or say, of course, but I will say this: whatever you answer with is going to come back on your head more than mine."

He guffawed, arms crossed over his chest, and he looked at Lucifer as if to say, *did you hear that?* Lucifer's eyebrows crawled halfway up his head, as he sipped what looked like a cup of black coffee, and I felt Jesus shift beside me. For a moment, it felt like I was in the principal's office—myself a disgruntled kid surrounded by tired, if amused, adults. I held my hands up and clarified.

"Listen, what I *mean* is, I'm looking to genuinely represent you here, and so whatever you tell me I'm going to assume is the truth and how you want to be known by other people. That's all I'm trying to say. I'm taking everything at face value, so you decide with your answers how people who'll read this interview see you as we go along. Fair?"

King Belial's smile felt like it was caging another laugh, but he nodded. "Fair."

"Okay, well," I clapped my hands and organized myself, "first things first: I read that you would once show up as two beautiful people in a flaming chariot, but I see you a lot different here in front of me. The horns, the... you know. Any reason you've changed aesthetics?"

I. WHY A DIFFERENT LOOK FROM THE ARS GOETIA DESCRIPTION?

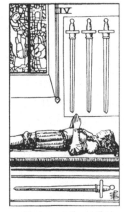

King Belial shrugged. "People were afraid before. All people have always liked beauty; what's beautiful, they're more likely to trust. But then things changed again—maybe people's expectations. I am a reflection of what they want to see, and I use it to my advantage."

"Alright. Sounds fair to me. And speaking of fear," I shook my pencil at him, "I'm curious: why do you think people are afraid of infernals?"

Rest and withdrawal. Regaining strength while you can. Separation from challenges. New perspectives, resilience, energy.

New beginnings in the material realm. Opportunity must be nurtured to its end. Be open to different outcomes and possibilities.

2. WHY ARE PEOPLE AFRAID OF INFERNALS?

"It's simple, Sara," King Belial said, and he sighed. "People have dissonance between that which they see before them and that which they've been told. They look away and pretend they didn't see the evidence of that which they know to be truer than any man's babble. They can't handle it. They create their own danger and apply it to us."

I was one word behind his as I wrote it all down, letting the thoughts flow without resistance. "I get that, yeah," I said. "It's a shame. But when it comes to you: I understand you're called both the Worthless One and the Lawless One. What do Worthlessness and Lawlessness mean to you?"

Denial. Difficulty seeing situation. Make a choice. Tension in emotions, repression.

Intuition. Subconscious, divine realms. Spiritual energy serves better than logical energy.

3. WHAT DO WORTHLESSNESS AND LAWLESSNESS MEAN TO YOU?

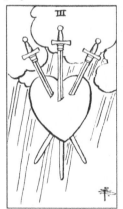 

Heartbreak, betrayal, and grief. We need contrast to see the good in things.

Enlightened perspective. Feeling strong, resilient, focused on the good.

The cards were loud and clear on this one. Always blows my hair back a bit when the messages I pull feel like such a direct smack in the face.

"Worthlessness is being cast away," he said. "Being left to die. When people decide you're worthless, they leave your survival in your hands. Then, when you do what you need to survive, they call you lawless; they claim you're breaking the rules they cast you out of. Isn't that funny? And stupid? So I say, too: lawlessness is freedom and life, especially when you're abandoned."

"Oh, wow. I feel that." It was an answer that spoke to me as clearly as an arrow spoke to my heart: sharp, direct, decimating. I knew the truth of it by the very way it echoed off my mind. "That's a really interesting way of looking at it; I love that." Once I collected myself from that answer, I moved on: "Okay! And now, something I've been chewing on is 2 Corinthians. What do you think about if? What do the unbeliever and the believer have in common?"

4. WHAT DO THE BELIEVER AND UNBELIEVER HAVE IN COMMON?

The unknown, feelings of the unconscious self, mysteries waiting. Encouraging you to embrace those mysteries. Rely on your intuition and unseen forces.

Near completion of a journey. Working hard and getting things done. Continue showing up for your long term vision. Celebrate the work you've done.

King Belial waved a hand and sighed, as if the question exhausted him. "Humans are all the same, Sara. Whether they call the happenings beyond their control the work of God, or one of us infernals, or Fate, it doesn't matter. You all pursue your own wants and goals, no matter who you serve. You all find something to make your life meaningful. Human tenacity is what unites you. It's a good thing."

The energy in Lucifer's office felt pretty nice; King Belial was flooding it with that bold, bright, powerful air that I knew from beings of war and flame and thunder. Maybe Michael and King Belial don't mix because both of their upbeat, broad-chested energy is too much to put in the same room, with Michael being the army captain and King Belial being like a pirate captain. But King Belial had this strength to him that was *admirable*, and this answer was so sweet.

"Alright, I like it! But what things do you teach folks?"

5. WHAT KINDS OF THINGS DO YOU LIKE TO TEACH PEOPLE?

King Belial sat up and crossed his arms. "People need to learn to grab onto what they want without shame and make their own dreams come true," he said. "There's nothing in this world one is unworthy of, unless they decide so. Stability to ground one's dreams—that's what they need. People can have whatever they want if only they're willing to create a plan and follow through."

"Nice! I agree. I think a good plan and the chutzpah to follow through is everything." I flipped around my notebook and went down the list of questions. "Okay! And now, when it comes to demonolaters in the modern era vs. Solomonic practitioners, what are your thoughts?"

Driven and methodical. Gradual progress. Freedom with work ethic.

Creativity, dreaming, youth, impulsiveness. The strange and bizarre.

6. WHAT DO YOU THINK ABOUT SOLOMONIC MAGIC?

Conventionality in all forms, in particular with spirituality. Growth that comes with rigorous practice. No shortcuts. Tradition exists for a reason. Structure.

Sinking into the darker aspects of life. Exploring the shadow is necessary, but it's easy to feel shame, fear, judgement. Potential anxiety, confusion. Ground yourself.

This answer was so good that I had to pause and text it to a friend.

"There was tradition for a reason," he said, with Lucifer nodding beside him, even if he looked a little tired at the ideas King Belial put forward. "I won't say it didn't work. But to what end? Back then, it was for power and glory. Nowadays, you kids seem more interested in fixing yourselves than getting any of the things we were once asked for. Not all of the time, of course. Plenty little shits still want all the power in the world. But it seems out of fashion now to want only wealth and fame."

I looked at Jesus with my mouth hanging open, a laugh building in my chest that I tried to swallow down. Jesus took a deep breath but stayed silent. "Ah," I said, once I'd recovered from that answer. "I see. Got'cha, got'cha! And now, I know that you tend to be nearby sometimes, and that you, like others, might reach out. How can people tell you're around?"

7. HOW CAN PEOPLE TELL YOU'RE NEARBY?

I felt King Belial's voice as if it was booming from my own chest: "I am a road opener. I come when one can tunnel through rock no longer. I clear the way after one's found rock bottom. When they find that, they find me."

Then there was the feeling of something weighing me down, heavy to the point that I couldn't move. I figured he sent this feeling of heaviness, of chains—all that frustration with your current position, rage and helplessness.

"When you feel those chains," he said, "feel me nearby with a hammer."

I wasn't expecting that answer. Nor was I expecting the sudden *snap* of that heaviness, the tension just releasing in an instant, as if those chains were struck off. It baffled me, and I found myself staring at Jesus, because this sudden lightness—what we might call a *weight lifting off our chest*—it was found in more than just King Belial's hammers. More than just the light of his flame. It was found in the light of God's, too: in the light of mercy, justice, and peace, which I'd felt freed me from my own chains a long time ago.

Sometimes, I can't help but chuckle at St. Paul. He had such bold and intense spirit in his writings, and yet I

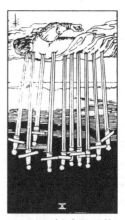

Grief, sadness, depression, anxiety, panic. Emotions are heightened. Entrapment, unsure of how to get out of this mental space. Self healing is smart.

Arrival of an all time low. This give you what you finally need to move on. Change becomes easier when we're desperate. Welcome shifts or new activities.

wonder: didn't he see that his Lord was, and is, *also* a breaker of chains? One that defeated death itself and made the impossible, possible? The answer King Belial gave to this question of 2 Corinthians was a good one, of course, but *this* revelation here? This was one that, in my opinion, also answered that question. Both were true. *More* were true. This would be one of many ideas I would discover that could answer the question of this overlap in what is actually a Venn Diagram between God and Devil, between Christ and Belial.

"Okay, alright, I see," I said, as that gnosis bomb exploded in my brain, and as Jesus's lip curled in a smile despite Him not once glancing my way. "We're getting to the end of our questions now, so King Belial, can you tell me how you see yourself?"

8. HOW DO YOU SEE YOURSELF, KING BELIAL?

Partnership, whether romantic, friendly, or work related. Both people are committed and respectful. Deep bonds and spiritual connection: a fruitful relationship.

While opportunities are flowing, you're rejecting them. The outside world seems boring; we're not ready to focus on the world. We may be retreating out of fear.

King Belial nodded, and his answer was blunt and to the point: "I don't care about the world. I care about me and mine. If the world goes to shit, it's because you all let it get that far. But me and mine, I take care of. I don't let mine fall apart. Not while they have their own dreams that need chasing."

Again. All this about God and His angels vs. Lucifer and his demons. Yet they say some awfully similar things, despite how different they feel. They have remarkably similar goals for their flocks.

"And how do you want to be seen?"

9. HOW DO YOU WANT TO BE SEEN?

He refused to pick cards. "I don't care how others see me."

"Oh. Okay." I shrugged. "Well, then that's it, I guess. Here's the last question: do you have anything you want to say? To me, other Christians looking to talk to you, anyone else?"

10. ANY LAST MESSAGES FOR ME OR OTHERS?

"People need to learn to think before they speak," he said. "It's tough right now. We know. Everyone's having it rough. That doesn't mean you melt down like a toddler. Pick yourself up, dust yourself off, and stop letting emotions take you for a ride. Remember you're in charge."

Plain and to the point.

With all that said and done, I found myself exhausted. I mean,

1. Emotional imbalance. May be feeling reactive, moody, or harsh; emotional disconnect or intensity. Create space for reflection.

2. A delicate balance has fallen by the wayside; you're no longer able to keep up. You need to put some things aside.

three energies like Jesus, Lucifer, and King Belial in the same space? For an entire hour and a half? It made me dizzy. So I closed my book after the last letter was written down and rubbed my eyes.

"Alright, that's all I've got today. Thank you, King Belial. I appreciate your time and attention. And while I'm still here, Lucifer," I turned to him, and he blinked at me, "should we talk about getting back on a regular study schedule? I know I've been terrible at keeping track."

He smiled, nodded, and did that with me before we all parted ways. Then I was alone, my ears ringing and my head swimming. I felt like I could've slept for a thousand years.

Again, though, there was that sense of suspension that took over, just as it had with King Paimon. No troubled waters in my soul, but nothing I could call peace, either. Knowledge made me feel free most times, but it tasted like ash other times—and once again, oh vanity of vanities, that I thought I could collect it all without repeating lessons Humanity had already learned, or that I could hold it all without being weighed down into the great lake of primordial waters, of grief, that it spawned from.

For with much wisdom comes much sorrow; the more knowledge, the more grief.
—Ecclesiastes 1:18

It wasn't because I was faced with truth that went against what I believed in that I was grieved. It was because I was gifted truth that made me aware of the many *mis*truths that once informed my beliefs. And because I knew so many were standing on the edge of this great lake, too afraid to jump in, yet dumping clear and cool water on their head from a *different* source entirely in order to pretend they'd seen its bottom and had the authority to speak.

The world was making me tired, and yet the knowledge kept me awake, unable to close my eyes despite how they burned. This was why this "peace" felt so incredibly unpeaceful. But what was I to do? There was no unlearning what I'd learned. There was only moving forward, swimming deeper into that lake, even as my muscles ached and my lungs burned for lack of air.

AZAZEL

Azazel. Anyone who's read the Book of Enoch knows Azazel. He's one of the many angels that came to earth to take up human wives, and specifically, he's the one that taught humans the skills that would later come to ruin us: magic, metalworking, and makeup. They wouldn't ruin us because of their nature, however; there's nothing inherently wrong with any of these things. Rather, they would ruin us because we were not ready for them, and Azazel couldn't have realized how we might abuse his gifts—or what God would do when He found out we had them.

These gifts, after all, are the gifts of Heaven: the company secrets, if you will. The Divine tools and knowledge that God wanted to keep from us, lest we do exactly what we did: live in a hedonistic, violent whirlwind, marked by the oppressive presence of the half-human, half-angel creatures, the Nephilim, that encouraged us to drown in the worst parts of the Human Shadow. We reveled in vanity, we made wicked weapons to kill each other with, we let suffering stack up all over the earth. Honestly, magic was the least of our problems, and certainly not the one that got the other angels still in Heaven to take note of our suffering.

We see it here, in the beginning of chapter four of the Book of Enoch, as our protectors Michael, Raphael, Uriel, and Gabriel see the horrors these premature teachings wrought:

And then Michael, Uriel, Raphael, and Gabriel looked down from heaven and saw much blood being shed upon the earth, and all lawlessness being wrought upon the earth. And they said one to another, "The earth made without inhabitant cries the voice of their cryingst up to the gates of heaven." And now to you, the holy ones of heaven, the souls of men make their suit, saying, "Bring our cause before the Most High."

And they said to the Lord of the ages, "Lord of lords, God of gods, King of kings, and God of the ages, the throne of Thy glory standeth unto all the generations of the ages, and Thy name holy and glorious and blessed unto all the ages! Thou hast made all things, and power over all things hast

Thou, and all things are naked and open in Thy sight, and Thou seest all things, and nothing can hide itself from Thee. Thou seest what Azazel hath done, who hath taught all unrighteousness on earth and revealed the eternal secrets which were in heaven, which men were striving to learn; and Samlazaz, to whom Thou hast given authority to bear rule over his associates. And they have gone to the daughters of men upon the earth, and have slept with the women, and have defiled themselves, and revealed to them all kinds of sins. And the women have borne giants, and the whole earth has thereby been filled with blood and unrighteousness. And now, behold, the souls of those who have died are crying out making their suit to the gates of heaven, and their lamentations have ascended and cannot cease because of the lawless deeds which are wrought on the earth. And Thou knowest all things before they come to pass, and Thou seest these things and Thou dost suffer them, and Thou dost not say to us what we are to do to them in regard to these."

After this, God commands that Azazel be bound up and tossed into the earth, where no light may reach him, and that to him, all sin be ascribed. This is why, later in Leviticus, you'll see the command to give up two goats: one to be killed as sacrifice to God, and one to have a paper with all the community's sins tied onto it in writing before it's chased away from the village, into the desert. The desert was where all unclean spirits and lawless things were thought to reside once upon a time, and the function of Azazel is made clear: he is the Sin Eater, the one who swallows up the wrongs of the community specifically on the day of Yom Kippur—the Day of Atonement. Lots would be cast to see which goat went to God and which to Azazel, hence the *scapegoat*.

Azazel, too, wears that title of *scapegoat*. And of course, there are other mentions of him, too—in the text known as the Apocalypse of Abraham, where he appears on earth before Abraham as an unclean bird that God yells at to go away. He, along with Lucifer, have both been theorized to be the snake in the Garden of Eden. So apparently, the idea that he really did get trapped forever underground isn't entirely the case.

But I digress. For all the Watchers that fell, it was him specifically that took the brunt of the beating, and who was singled out by name to bear this great punishment, hence the concept of Azazel as the scapegoat. Whether you see Azazel as trapped underground forever or freely moving around on earth, though, there is still the idea that the punishment of the Watchers will one day conclude with being thrown in the lake of fire, where they will allegedly burn "forever"—though, elsewhere in the narrative, it's said that the length of punishment for such sins is ten thousand years. Is ten thousand years forever? Maybe. Maybe that's how Azazel is already on earth again. Who knows, really?

All I knew was that I felt for Azazel. The perspectives of these narratives, written by who-knows-who (because I think we can understand that this was written by someone else claiming to be Enoch, given how odd the text is and that the actual written parts only date back to maybe 300 BC), never really allow for the other side of the story, and they seem so much more focused on making more of a case for God to be the Eternal Super Warrior God and scare people into submission than to actually explore the connotations of what this whole story means.

I felt for Azazel because I imagined he probably did genuinely love the woman he picked for a wife, and that he loved the child(ren) that came from that, too—that if the story of Enoch is true, that he had to watch his beloved be destroyed in front of his eyes while trapped and unable to do anything about it, even after offering honest apologies and petitions. That broke my heart. I mean, God can forgive our idiot human selves a thousand times over, but the angels get no second chances? Even though God, according to this book, already saw this coming? It seemed a bit far fetched to me, and I wanted to investigate, and to my surprise, God let me—with supervision.

So I went and dressed my table with things associated with Azazel, who's connected to the element of air. Again, my good friend Aziel gave me some pointers on approaching Azazel and things that he liked, and so I included on my work table things like sandalwood incense, chocolate with almonds in it, Earl Grey tea, and a few other things I didn't expect. I never would've thought rosemary or amethyst had anything to do with him, given these things are heavily associated with God and healing and protection in my mind, but then again, Azazel was once an angel of God.

With all of this out, and some celestite to get a good Angel Signal, I settled down and tried to reach the place I'd become familiar with in my conversations with demons: Lucifer's study. I asked not only God to allow me to do this, you see, but Lucifer to let me into the infernal realm and invite Azazel, too. It only felt respectful to do so. However, looking back, there was one thing that I think might've been a snare in my plan here: I assumed that because I was a woman, talking to Azazel would be easy. I thought he just liked women on principle, and that it'd be simple for me to pop in and chat.

There's an old adage about assumptions, though. I'm sure you know how it goes.

And soon enough, the energy shifted. It was strange. I felt like there was a layer of something in the air that settled on me like a cloak. After I confirmed with my pendulum that Azazel was there, and that he wanted to use the Marigold Tarot, I just closed my eyes and let the scene begin to swirl and bleed through, until I had a grasp of this condemned angel.

"Azazel, hello, hello! I formally invite you to come chat with me. I have a few offerings here for you, as thanks for your time and attention. Please, come sit and chat. I'd love to get a few answers from you on some things."

Right away, I found myself in a similar place as Lucifer's study. It wasn't quite the same; it was more of a pocket office within this great manor I was used to traipsing through in my meditations with Lucifer. But as I popped in, I saw myself sitting there in a massive, antique red leader chair, dressed in a black button-up shirt and black slacks like I was about to start a long shift of waitressing at an upscale restaurant, and across from me was a shiny and ornately carved wooden desk, where Azazel was writing something; it looked like he was keeping accounts, or doing paperwork. Something official.

He was a man with long, straight black hair, a neat and nicely pressed black suit, a strong nose and straight set brows, and very bright golden eyes. When he noticed me, he put his pen down and folded his hands on his desk, but he didn't say a word; he only stared at me with an intensity that could've bored a hole straight through me.

"Azazel," I said, and I offered a friendly wave, "hi."

Silence.

It felt like there was a brick wall between us. It baffled me. Usually, even when I talked to demons, they were pretty willing to answer questions and let me record them, but here, there was something unspoken hanging in the air that I genuinely did not understand. After all, what reason did he have to give me such a cold shoulder? Had I done something wrong already?

"Um," unfortunately for both of us, I was (and still am) a bull-headed idiot with an unhealthy lack of fear, so I waved my notebook. "As I said, I've got some questions for you, if you're okay with chatting. Should we just jump right in?"

Azazel's eyes shimmered, but he still said nothing. He only brought his hands up, his fingers lacing together in front of his mouth as he stared at me. Then he was staring behind me.

When I twisted around to see what he was staring at, I yipped. It was my guardian angel behind me, puffed up and staring with massive eyes, like an owl facing off with a cat. I'd never seen him come with me and be present before, but apparently, *this* was the spirit that would broker this conversation: the angel assigned to me at birth. He was there in the form I'd met him in: one where he wore tattered, grungy, dark robes, with two horns twisting off his head and several gleaming, fiery eyes shining in his face, as well as several more eyes dotting the edges of his ash-gray wings. His skin was grayish, too, his face sunken, his veins pressed against his skin as if he were severely dehydrated. The closest thing I can compare it to is the incredible design of the Angel of Death in *Hellboy II*, but that's not quite it, either. I'd met my guardian angel face to face for the first time at the foot of a dark, terrible mountain, where the land was barren and scorched by rivers of fire, and where the sky was clouded with ash and fury, and since then, it'd been easier to see him—like I did right then.

"Will you relax?" I snapped at him, swatting at his overly puffy wings and blocking him from reaching his arms around me. It was like he was trying to lock me in that chair, to say, *this is mine, my human; don't touch. I am her warden. Me. Don't touch.* "You're being rude!"

Do you think he listened to me? No. He just kept an arm across my shoulders as if to hold me in that spot for the whole interview, and he never once broke eye contact with Azazel. I felt like I was about to get stuck in the middle of a cat fight. With a groan and a swig of tea that I wished was whiskey, I just kept trying to crack Azazel's shell.

"Excuse my guardian; I don't know what his issue is," I said, the last part hissing sharp out of my mouth. Only then did my guardian loosen up a little bit, but I could feel the pure *alertness* radiating from behind me. "Anyway, Azazel, would you like to get started?"

Silence. Again. His only answer were those two endlessly burning eyes, gold as desert sand.

Hello? I won't lie; it was frustrating, the silent treatment I was getting. Was it because I was affiliated with God, and there was understandable bad blood? Was it because I offered something wrong? Was it because I popped in here all happy-go-lucky? I didn't know, but the last thought thoroughly chapped my ass, I'll tell you that. *What's wrong, Azazel?*

Can't find out unless you ask, right?

So despite my guardian angel clawing at my shirt and trying to get me to stay siting, I popped out of my chair and strolled right up to Azazel's desk. Hands stuffed in my pockets, shirt messily buttoned, hair tossed in a sloppy low bun, I looked like a jaded office worker about to pick a fight with HR about something stupid. He kept staring at me the whole time, even as I leaned in closer.

"Excuse my chutzpah, but did I do something? Is there a reason we're squaring up the way we are?" When he *still* didn't respond, it took everything in my power to not let my frustration show. Rather than groan, I let out a low whistle, and I said, "Jeez. Tough crowd I've got here, huh?"

At this point, Azazel sat back in his seat, his hands folded in his lap. Still didn't say a damn thing, though. I was wondering if he was waiting for me to snap. Instead I turned around and strolled around the room a bit. Its walls were lined with books, as were most offices in this manor, and the carpet underneath was ornate, red with green leaves; it was soft and cushy underfoot. The door to the rest of the manor was open, and behind Azazel was a big window, where the darkness of night made it impossible to see what was out there, save for a few stars.

"Nice office you got," I said. "Cozy."

Cozy save for my guardian angel, who was still puffing by the chair and motioning for me to get back over to him. But as I did with all spirits I encountered, I trusted they wouldn't hurt me. So I sighed and moseyed back over to the desk, then parked myself on it, half sitting on its edge.

"Look, if you don't like me, or think I'm an idiot, you can say so. I promise I won't be mad," I said, with a smile and a wink. And then, and *only* then, did I get the tiniest crack of a smile. Maybe. I couldn't tell, really; his lip twitched, but maybe *smile* is a bit of a stretch.

I kept going. "I'm not here to give you a hard time. I'm just a goof, okay? I am with everyone. So if I'm not super formal, it's not because I don't respect you—I do! And in fact, my being informal is a way of showing my respect, y'know? From what I know about you, I think you're pretty cool, and I wanna learn more.

"And trust me," I added, in case I hadn't already said enough, "if I *didn't* like you, and I *didn't* want to be respectful, you'd know. I'd be throwing ten-point words around like I had a thesaurus stitched under my eyelids and talking like some asshole lawyer about to go toe-to-toe with you in court. Know what I mean?"

Suddenly, someone was flashing beside Azazel. Blonde hair, dark suit—it was Lucifer, and he was popping in and out a bit like a glitching video game character. Azazel glanced towards him and blinked, as if listening to something I couldn't hear, and then he actually *did* smile.

Then, suddenly, we were out of the office. Azazel took me to another place, and here, he looked the same, but with a long black cloak. It was a place that looked set for ritual, with a sigil carved into the floor and a table with a chalice full of blue flame at the center that he was working over. In the background were chained up things, people, I think—though they didn't really look like people. They were more like gargoyles, all lumpy and stone-like, and they had no eyes, but they were clawing for that blue sigil-circle.

At the time, I had no idea what they were, or where *we* were, or what any of this was supposed to represent. It wasn't that we were in hell in the way people normally think about hell, but given these gargoyle things were all chained up, I thought it might be that these spirits were here as some kind of Purgatory, paying for something they did on earth and working through it in order to one day move on and get somewhere else. Either that or they were demons. I couldn't tell.

"What'cha doing?" I popped over to Azazel and stared at the blue chalice with him, but I couldn't make heads or tails of it.

It was a cup. With blue fire in it. Clearly magical as all ever, but nothing I felt like I could understand or access. And Azazel certainly didn't explain it, either; shadows danced off his face as he stared into that cup, and the sigil underneath us glowed a fierce blueish-white. So when Azazel didn't answer me, I wandered away. He tracked me from the corner of his eye. The whole time I wondered: *is he trying to show me something important? Or is he trying to scare me?*

Given he didn't want to explain any of what I was seeing, I could only assume it was the latter. I've never been a fan of having my courage challenged like that, but maybe he just wanted to see if I was, I don't know, *worth* talking to. That I wouldn't go running and screaming the second he showed me something a little tougher.

That was fine by me. But I was a pain in the ass, through and through, and I let him know.

"Are you trying to spook me?" I stood square in the middle of everything—the stone people, the table, Azazel. His brow quirked as I shrugged. "I hope you wouldn't think this would spook me. It'd take a lot more than this to unsettle me."

Over the plumes of blue flame, I caught his stare, but it seemed open this time, as if he was waiting for me to do or say something more. Still nothing but silence from him, though. Maybe he thought I'd get frustrated enough to give up, but again, I'm a royal pain in the ass. I just kept talking. Maybe that's what he wanted? For me to just talk, instead of expecting answers from him without me offering any talking of my own? I didn't know, but it felt easy to open up and speak whatever was on my mind, like the energy in the room allowed for it, so I did.

"It's kind of stupid, you know," I said, "the way people talk about humans. And I mean, people: other witches and stuff." I paced in a wide circle around the table with my hands stuffed in my pockets. "People make themselves so small, and for what? Do you know how many times I've seen people say some junk like, 'oh, us humans are *just* humans, *just* weak little useless humans, and the gods are *gods*, so much infinitely stronger!" Like, yeah, sure, gods and such have more energy and power than humans, no one's denying that—I'm not saying I could take on a god and win, no, sir— but are we really that weak?"

Over that cup of blue flame, I thought I saw his eyes twinkle in a way they hadn't before.

"Are we really *just* humans? Do they have to make it sound like we're vermin or something, like grubs in the dirt?" I paced near him in a smaller circle. "I see it just the other way. At least for people who believe like I do, I mean, we're children of *God*. Made directly in His image. Doesn't that count for something?

"And if you think about it, are humans not the cause of pretty much all drama on earth, *and* in Heaven? I mean, just from what I know of your story, Azazel, it seems like we're pretty good at stirring up shit and getting everyone into trouble. In fact, you know what? I think humans are dangerous. Unpredictable. Just as bad, if not worse, as any spirit that goes causing trouble. So I wonder why so many practitioners acts like humans, including themselves, aren't worth taking seriously. I mean, again, isn't that just *stupid*?"

It was there, too, that I wondered if maybe we were chafing because, despite my being a woman, I had the energy—and maybe a bit, just a *squeeze*, of the audacity—of a man. I certainly wasn't walking around all graceful and small and sweet around there, that was for sure. I was being the same goofy, frank self that I'd been with Lucifer and with King Belial—though not quite with King Paimon, because at least with him, I knew what he expected in terms of behavior.

I didn't know what Azazel expected, though; I hadn't thought to ask anyone about it. I also didn't know why he didn't seem to like me, or if maybe I was just projecting. All I knew was that I don't think either of us expected what we got from each other, and that was a funny thought. But when Azazel still didn't say anything, instead staring at me as if he'd discovered a new specimen of big, fuzzy moths, I looked at the weird creatures surrounding us.

"What are these?" I said as I moved on, and I pointed to the gargoyles, or people, or whatever they were. Honestly, they really didn't look all too human: as I said, they had no eyes, but more just dark holes in their heads. And they had little horns on their heads, and talons on their feet and fingers, too, that looked like they'd been neatly carved with the rest of their stubby bodies. They bent over as if in prayer towards the cup of blue flame. When Azazel didn't answer me, I walked into the pile of them and stood in the middle of them all, if for no other reason than to show I wasn't worried about these things. "What do they do?"

One of those stone-things lifted its head up from whatever it was doing and stared at me with those empty sockets. It reached a lumbering hand up for me, which, given it was slow as molasses, was easy to sidestep. There wasn't *much* room to sidestep it, granted—not without bumping into another one. Still, I managed. But did I mention that there were a *lot* of these things?

And that they were *all* starting to look up at me, taloned fingers outstretched?

"Sara!"

One second, I was standing in the pit, and the next second, there was a lot of feathers whipping my mind, and then I was back in the middle of the room, far away from the chained-up gargoyle things and their outstretched hands. Someone gripped my shoulders and yanked me around, and I found myself face to face with Lucifer, who I'd never seen look anything close to angry before right then. The crease between his brows from how hard his eyebrows slanted down, the deep cut of his frown, it was like it'd been carved from stone into his face. And while he didn't say anything, he didn't need to; the gold of Lucifer's eyes crackled like embers, and the cat-like pupil was thin, menacing.

I didn't realize why he was so angry then, and I wouldn't for several more weeks, but let's put the pieces together. Where had I seen something stone, gargoyle-like before? Where had I seen something that lunged at me and tried to snap me up, that scared the living hell out of me? Only once: when that red-eyed gargoyle-thing in the shape of God's messenger seraph came trying to scare me away from speaking to Lucifer.

This was a pit of demons. Whatever they were doing around this blue flame, in this otherwise dark cave, I didn't know, but they were doing something with Azazel, chained up like prisoners, and I'd just parked myself in a clump of them like I was going out into a field to pick daisies. I mean, if I'm honest, I once again knew I was perfectly safe and sitting in my living room, so I didn't think it was that big of a deal to go poke at the weird creatures in meditation, but if Lucifer was going to look that serious about it, I knew I wasn't about to try going over to them again.

While Lucifer was giving me a scolding look, though, Azazel stared at me from the other side of the chalice. Then he was staring at Lucifer, and there was some wordless conversation going on between *them* again before we were all back in that study we started in. I don't know what Lucifer said to Azazel, but finally, after a half an hour of battling wills, and a little more earnest commitment that I wasn't scared and wasn't going anywhere unless he expressly told me to go pound sand, whatever wall between us broke down. He again folded his hands in his lap and spoke.

"Fine. Ask your questions."

"Yes!" I couldn't help whooping and bouncing around. I also didn't know whether I wanted to kiss him for relenting or whack him for busting my chops so bad, but I chose neither and plopped back down in the red leather chair. My guardian angel was still there, hovering over me, and this time seemed pretty determined not to let me walk around the study anymore, by the way he covered me with his wings. It was like wearing one of those overhead roller coaster harnesses. "Thank you! As much fun as we're having here, I am glad to move onto some questions, so I guess I'll just... start?"

Azazel sat back and gave me this slightly sardonic smile, so I took that as my cue to keep going. Wasn't going to risk him rescinding the willingness to answer questions after he just displayed it.

"So, first thing that's on my mind is pretty predictable, I guess: human women. Why come down for them? What about them interested you?"

I. WHAT INTERESTED YOU IN HUMAN WOMEN?

He sighed here, motioned to the desk full of papers. "Humans," he said. "I have done the same thing down here, in these infernal realms, year after year. Decades. Centuries. All the same. The thing that keeps it interesting is humans. Maybe the themes of human struggle are always the same, but each human is different."

"And about women specifically?"

I got this image of a gorgeous lady, with big honey-brown eyes, bronzed skin, hair somewhere between wavy and curly, and a pretty red robe. She had a bright smile and freckles across her cheeks and nose, as well as wrists full of gold bangles.

"Eyes," was what Azazel was telling me with this. "Their smile. The way they adorn themselves. It's fascinating."

I wondered if that might've been the woman he met when he came down to earth, but I felt it'd be insensitive to ask, so I just moved on.

Joy, moving forward. Stagnation is the root cause of a majority of one's challenges.

"I got'cha," I said with a nod. "But when you got down here and settled among the people, what inspired you to teach them all the things you did? It's giving Prometheus vibes, not gonna lie. You know—that Greek story about us getting fire and the Olympic gods getting all angry about it?"

2. WHY DID YOU TEACH HUMANITY ALL OF THE THINGS YOU DID?

Vanity, dashed ambitions, or a lack of challenge in life.

I don't know if he found that funny, but he did huff a laugh and shrugged.

"I saw their potential," he said, his voice low and velvety. "They just needed to have someone to show them the way forward. You said people don't give humans enough credit regarding their strength, and I agree. That's why someone had to show them what they could do, what they could be. Being children like you were is fine, but one day we all must grow up."

I wrote like my life depended on it, if only because I was thrilled to finally be hearing Azazel speak. "And all the stuff they did afterwards—the killing and all that with those swords. Did you expect that?"

Here, his face fell, and he stared at the papers on his desk.

"It was horrible to watch people at first. What they did with the things I taught them. But it was worth it for the advancements humans made overall."

"Okay, yeah. Definitely giving Prometheus vibes, then." I crossed my T's, dotted my I's, and continued, "I understand, though; I get you. But moving onto another topic, I hear that some think you were once a different being that got split into yourself and King Paimon? That Adonai is some 'false god' or something and smacked your original self Shemyaza in half? That you were the Sumerian god Shemash? What's happening here in all that jumble?"

3. THOUGHTS ON THE SHEMYAZA/SHEMASH THING?

Being in love with the idea of love, jealousy, needing to be tethered back to reality.

I was sitting in that big red chair like a scrawny mafia man from the 1930s; all I was missing was a cigar or glass of whiskey on top of my pen and paper. I don't know why that was the vibe, but I was having fun with it. I was also wearing my guardian angel's wings like a cloak half the time; no matter how many times I asked him to relax, he held me tight with that same air: *this is mine. My charge.*

Azazel shrugged again and ignored my guardian. "I am my own being," he said. "I was not and will never be a part of King Paimon. The need to rationalize in human beings is so strong; it's pathetic. A weak attempt to make sense of *the* world in a way that doesn't challenge *their* world."

"So," I blinked at the card and his words, "no, I get you. I hear you. But... *are* you Shemash, though? Or is this another 'getting caught up in the details' situation?"

He stared at me. "What does it matter if I'm Shemash or Azazel? What matters is what I did and do."

Our guest would not give me a straight answer, so I'm chalking that up to "follow the story you know." In which case, I was talking to him in the context of Azazel, an angel of God that fell, so that's what I kept rolling with, and that's how he kept rolling, too.

"Alright, fair's fair," I said. "But now, speaking of what you do, you mentioned that you spent centuries doing (and still are doing) this certain type of work in the infernal realms. What does that entail? What's it like?"

4. WHAT KIND OF WORK DO YOU DO IN THE INFERNAL REALMS?

Discord, disorder, overbearing control, a breakdown in power dynamics.

I'll be honest, that's not a card I expected. He seemed like he had it pretty together when I first found him writing whatever he was writing on those papers. But as I wrote the card meaning down, I saw Azazel wave a hand in my mind's eye.

"I've been doing the same thing for centuries," he said with a sigh at that desk, "but it is back-breaking work. Managing this mess that people both create *and* blame us for, it's wretched. All this work, and for what reward?"

"I mean, yeah. I can't say I know. But can you speak more to that blame?"

"We manage human filth," he muttered. "We corral it for it to be transmuted. All for people to act like we create it."

"Hmm, yeah, that makes sense." I stared at my notes, then pipped, "That sucks, actually! And it seems like, even though you're a *fallen* angel, you're still doing so much to keep the world moving, as much as angels up top still are. On that note, what's the difference between a fallen angel and a demon? I keep seeing people say they're all one in the same, but... that doesn't seem right. I mean, some of y'all in here were once angels, some once *gods*. Surely an actual demon is different?"

5. WHAT'S THE DIFFERENCE BETWEEN A DEMON AND A FALLEN ANGEL?

Courage, power, venturing forward into new experiences without fear.

Again, as I said, I was too wrapped up in spiritually wrestling Azazel earlier, but those gargoyle things? Those were demons, only I didn't recognize them as such then They were demons, and they were nothing like Azazel, or Lucifer, or King Belial, or anyone else; they struck me as spirits, things that didn't have much of their own autonomy. But I wasn't making the connections yet, nor was I thinking about it that way, so I had to ask.

To which, Azazel nodded.

"There are many different branches of creation. Fallen angels are not demons; we started holy. We were created from a wholly different source. Demons are feral little things—the minor ones. Demon doesn't accurately describe gods and angels, but spirits who are their own thing and go their own way, whatever that way is. We fallen angels and gods corral them, too."

Which would explain the whole "commanding legions of demons" thing to me, to be honest.

"Got'cha." It was this answer that would spin me to the conclusion I have now, and that I've already described to you. "And also, you know, I heard it said that angels have this 'perfect knowledge,' and that's why they don't (or shouldn't) make mistakes. In the Book of Enoch, you asked forgiveness, but God wouldn't give it. Does this have something to do with "perfect knowledge'?"

6. WHAT DOES IT MEAN FOR ANGELS TO HAVE PERFECT KNOWLEDGE?

This is where it got a little interesting. In Azazel's office, he pulled out a ball and a lamp, then turned the lamp on. One side of the ball was dark, the other light, like the earth against the sun.

"When you are here," he said, tapping the dark side, "you can't see the light. Same goes for the other side; you can't see the dark. Perfect knowledge is where you and I are standing right now; we can see both the light and the dark, where it comes from, why it's there."

"That's the way for angels. We see things in a way you humans don't, and we've had thousands of years to observe patterns and watch the consequences of all of your actions. It's not that we can see the future; it's that we can deduce the obvious consequences of an action based on what we know of the past and what we plainly see in the present."

Accept changes, especially if painful . Time brings new obstacles and opportunities.

"So when you did what you did way back in the day...? Wait, hold on."

I erased a question I had pre-written and replaced it with this one:

"Alright, follow me, here," I said, as if I were less a reporter and more a detective trying to get several witnesses' stories straight. "If angels are without free will, allegedly, because of this kind of sight and deductive reasoning that you have that makes you simply unable to take the unreasonable path, then how did any of this happen? With you and the others? I don't get it."

7. HOW DID ANY OF THIS HAPPEN IF ANGELS HAVE NO FREE WILL?

An intellectual, defensive, skilled, brave, and wrathful man. Duality—graciousness and deceptiveness. Tactless, setting goals and saying things without thinking how appropriate they are.

Azazel got a little wistful here. I don't know how else to describe it. What I do know is that suddenly, we were far away from the office again. In fact, we were sitting halfway up a rocky, desolate mountain, not unlike one I'd met my guardian angel by. Down below was a huge lake of fire, bubbling and glowing and spurting magma, the hot melted rock lapping at the shore. Azazel and I were sitting there like two guys on the front step of some run-of-the-mill house on a street corner. Given that per the Book of Enoch, it mentions that the Lake of Fire is actually in heaven, I figured it'd make sense how I found my guardian angel here, and how Azazel and I were allowed here: in the place it would all end one day. This was essentially God's backyard, and it was *wild*.

"Sheltered things, we are," Azazel whispered. The glow of the lake reflected in the gold of his eyes. "Angels are brash. Sometimes they step out of sorts, get carried away and make mistakes."

A thing that kept popping into my head was Sodom and Gomorrah. How those angels gloated about ending that city, and God sent them to wander the desert for decades as punishment.

"In God's eyes," Azazel continued, "if you see as clearly as we see and still make a mistake, how can you be redeemed? That's how it is, to be an angel. We made the mistake first. We were made an example of. We are the reason the other angels choose to stay locked in heaven. All of them up there chose God over humanity."

I don't know how I even got to asking this as I stood up, but I loomed over him and said, "Do you still love God? Or no?"

8. DO YOU STILL LOVE GOD?

This was a question I asked with the pendulum, given it was what I thought would be a simple yes or no, but the pendulum was going haywire. It felt like he didn't want to give me a straight answer, but eventually something concrete came through—both in the pendulum and in my mind.

"I'd like to," Azazel said, "but I can't. He made me choose. I will always choose human women."

I pursed my lips and bumped his shoulder with my shin. "Just women, or all humanity?"

He smiled. "Women," he said. "Women are things of beauty. The men, not as much. I appreciate them. But the women have a different way about them than men."

We'll chalk that up to preference, I think.

"Ah, I hear you," I said as I started pacing around the uneven footing of the mountain. "But... you know, I don't know. It's kind of stupid, isn't it? That God can forgive us humans, but not you? 'Perfect knowledge,' my ass. If He's gonna get you for that, then He should get us, too, because there's plenty of dumb shit we do that we *definitely* know better about, yet do anyway."

And I don't know what was wrong with me by this point, or where this audacity came from, but I looked up into the dark, ashy clouds. I faced upward, towards the highest part of heaven, where I knew God was, and I ran up until I was closer to the top. Then I spoke my honest opinions.

"I'm just saying, God. Doesn't seem very fair to give them such a hard time, especially since they're still working hard out here. Kinda sucks, actually. I'd advocate for this one here; he tried to apologize and You didn't take it. What's up with this, huh?"

The face of God (or, rather, His representative seraph) is pretty intense and thunderous on a good day, but right then, it was all blazing eyes and shadowed face from high up above that mountain. I could've felt that stare hit me from the very deepest pit of hell, it was so intense.

"Hey, hey!" I raised my hands in surrender. "I'm just being honest with you. These are my real feelings, and I'm not gonna lie to your face and pretend I don't feel this way. So what's up? Why can't they be forgiven after an apology if we can be forgiven?"

I swear, I got the most "mind your business" feeling for an answer, but it was a good answer. He pulled something up from deep in my mind and reminded me of what I'd read at one point somewhere: that the bodies of the Watchers will be destroyed, cleansed of the wrong they did, but their souls will return to Heaven to be with God again. That it *will* all be okay in the end. It's not my job to worry about it. That there'd be a Big Reset, that thing we call the Apocalypse, and things would be back to square one, maybe to restart.

That the Lake of Fire was not the end. For any of us.

"Eh, alright. Sure. That's fair. I don't mean to be rude or anything, but I'm just saying." I gave a sheepish smile. "You know I mean well."

Despite the intensity, there was a smile hanging among all that thunder, all that ash and fire above me. God sent me on my way nonetheless, and then it was back down the mountain to Azazel, who seemed at least a little amused, given he was smiling as he sat there. But then he was the most relaxed he'd been the whole time.

"Okay, Azazel," I said as I settled back down, "we're getting into the end of our questions here, and I'm curious: how do you see yourself? What do you think about yourself?"

9. HOW DO YOU SEE YOURSELF?

Greed, possessiveness, unkindness. Illusions and dreams of this world. Suffering, the eyes obscured by a closed fist.

I was truly starting to wonder if he was screwing with me, because why would he pull cards like the Four of Coins to describe himself? I figured he wouldn't see himself with a card that carried such heavy and, frankly, not-so-good connotations. But he explained.

"I want what I want," he said. "I collect what I want. It is my right to do so, all things considered. But still, I am bitter. Because all these things I want will one day vanish, and then what will have been the point of my existence? Wanting more, just to have it—only to know it'll all be gone."

"I—well, I won't lie to you, that's kind of a weird viewpoint."

He looked at me with a crease to his brow, like I was a little shit, which I am. All I could do was shrug and explain my position.

"Listen. There are people walking the earth right now that don't believe in an afterlife." He looked at me like I knew better, and I waved it off; I wasn't interested in talking about whether those people were right or wrong or anything right then. "Whether or not it exists doesn't matter, okay? They don't believe it. They believe one day, they'll close their eyes for the last time, and then it's all black. Black forever. Consciousness shuts off, never to experience anything again. But you don't see those people walking around refusing to enjoy the experience while they have it just because it'll all be gone one day. That'd be a waste."

He stared at me. Blinked once.

"And, I mean," I shrugged, "if the world resets one day, you can collect it all again. Sometimes people play the same game like, thirteen times, but we play it a different way each time, and it's still fun, even if we know every plot point of every quest. It's what you make of it. I don't know."

It was at this point I remembered I was kicking rocks on a mountain and that I needed to go to bed at some point, so I capped that whole monologue off with another question.

"So how do you want to be seen?"

10. HOW DO YOU WANT TO BE SEEN?

Weakness, breaking down, losing control, issues with problem solving.

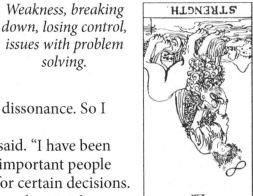

Again, was he screwing with me? Strength reversed? I even asked as much: was he sure he wanted this card, rotated this way? But he reminded me of what he said earlier: humans are pathetic when it comes to trying to fit things into their preconceived understanding, trying to explain away dissonance. So I just shut up and let him explain.

"I have experience with these things this card describes," he said. "I have been weak in my choices and made messes I couldn't get out of. It's important people face the consequences of their actions. There are no do-overs for certain decisions. Forgiveness can be a long way off. No one pities you when you make mistakes; more often, your one sin becomes one thousand others that *other* people pile onto you to absolve themselves with no personal effort. Can you bear it? This is what I ask, because this is what I know."

"Oh. Damn. Well, that does explain it. Thank you for that. But now, we're at the last question, and I just wanna know: do you have anything else to say? To me, to others?"

Now, by this point, we'd sort of come to an understanding. He knew I meant well despite my boisterous, Type A, 1930's New Jersey Rat energy that to this day, I still can't explain. I don't know what about Azazel made me pull out a side of myself I usually reserve for very good friends or goofy online personalities, but that's what happened, and I hoped he wasn't feeling weird about it.

So I paused my shuffling and reiterated: "Hey, listen, I am really sorry if I in any way disrespected you tonight. It absolutely wasn't my intention by any means; as I said, if I wanted to be disrespectful, I'd never have acted so cozy and comfortable, you know? Can you forgive me?"

II. CAN YOU FORGIVE ME FOR BEING AN IDIOT TONIGHT?

And then Azazel smiled, a *big* smile, one that made his eyes crinkle at the sides, and he pulled his card.

"How well can you forgive yourself?" His smile stayed on as he spoke. "How many times will you repeat the same apology before you stop to listen if it's even been accepted? Stop speaking. Listen. Cut your losses if you need to, but move on. You can't grow and learn from pain you forever sit in."

I paused my writing. "...Is that for me specifically, or for anyone?"

"It's for whoever the shoe fits."

"Okay, alright—say no more." I closed my book and held my hands up. "I got'cha. But, okay, wait, before you go, I had a song in mind that I thought you might like. Can I play it for you?"

His brow shot up, as if the idea was unexpected, but he nodded, and so I pulled up Dikanda's *Ketrin Ketrin*. As it played, I let all the images I associated with that song pop by like a slideshow. By that slideshow, I shared with him what *I* thought was beautiful about human women: the voices, the songs, the dancing, the way they weave flowers into crowns and pour their souls together into firelight and good food. And he didn't seem to hate it. He seemed to enjoy it as we sat on that mountain, at the edge and end of the world. Then it was nearly one in the morning, and I knew had to go to bed.

A need to move on, feelings of alienation, and love and relationships long lost.

"Well, I guess that's it, then. Azazel," I said as I finished off my cup of then very cold tea. "I appreciate you coming by, I really do. I enjoyed getting the chance to talk to you and get some answers to some questions that have been burning me for a long time. You're welcome here whenever you'd like, and if *you'd* like, I hope to see you around in the future, too. Until then, it's time to call it a night!"

Azazel stayed sitting, but the brick wall I'd felt between us earlier was gone. Despite the fire and sulfur and everything else, it felt easy—and the harsh, hot wind blowing through that place didn't feel so bad, either. With a gentler look in his eyes than the one he gave me at the start of all of this, he wordlessly drifted away, and all that fire and brimstone with him. And then there was just me, wondering what the hell happened, and how I could've made that better.

In hindsight, I absolutely think Azazel was calling me on my nonsense: that he knew I thought I'd be able to just walk in and start asking questions like it was nothing, maybe because I was a woman, maybe because I spoke to a couple demons already, and he wanted to check me. One good takeaway, aside from the many answers Azazel gave me that then continued to help me develop my theories and understandings about the Lake of Fire, the Second Death, so on and so forth, is that assuming anything is going to be easy is a good way to have the hardest time of your life. This is true for pagan gods, for angels, and most certainly for demons.

But it's a lesson worth learning. One that I balance with the idea that nothing can hurt me—because *that* is an idea that I've held onto ever since Michael's intense and alarming lessons. And as Jesus says in Matthew 10:28:

> *Do not be afraid of those who kill the body but cannot kill the soul. Rather, be afraid of the One who can destroy both soul and body in hell.*

I have no fear of these things because I understand the only One with the right, and the ability, to destroy me completely out of existence entirely, is God—and I have faith, trust, that He won't do that. The body dying isn't really something I worry about regardless, because the soul will still be there, and if any entity is bold enough to remove me from my body, that just makes it easier for me to move in the world behind the curtain—*much* easier. That thought and verse, along with Michael, are actually what helped me get over a lot of fear, especially my lifelong fear of the dark.

Even If I die, I'm not really dead.

Still, balance. Balance between gripping fear and unbridled confidence, between over courteous behavior and overly brusque behavior, between challenge and insult. It's a fine line, and I don't always recognize it. But here, Azazel showed me that line, and why it wasn't drawn with my casual mannerisms, but my assumptions. A lesson well learned, I think. Hard won, but well learned.

ST. DISMAS

Crucified besides Jesus were two criminals, sometimes called revolutionaries: one at His left, and one at His right. One of those thieves accosted Him. This thief said, "Hey, you! Aren't you the Son of God? Do something, then! Save us!"

And the other criminal, despite all the pain of the cross, leaned over and barked:

"Do you not fear God, since you are under the same sentence of condemnation? And we indeed justly; for we are receiving the due reward of our deeds; but this man has done nothing wrong." And he said, "Jesus, remember me when you come into your kingdom." And He said to him, "Truly, I say to you, today you will be with Me in Paradise." (Luke 23:40-43)

That man, we never knew the name of—but in Christian tradition, this criminal, soon understood as the Penitent Thief, was given the name Dismas, meaning "sunset," "to the west," or possibly "dying" in Greek. This name appeared in the apocryphal Gospel of Nicodemus, a text from the fourth century that was originally known as the Acts of Pontius Pilate. There, the frantic thief is named Gestas, and the other Dimas (Dismas). He's now the patron Saint of reformed thieves, condemned criminals (including those on death row), funeral directors, and undertakers in the Catholic church. Nothing is really known about him, save a handful of legends, but he's an important figure in the crucifixion.

Unbaptized.

A criminal.

Literally on death's door, at the very last possible minute of life.

Yet worthy. Hanging there right alongside the Son of God, condemned to the same mortal fate. One line of St. Dismas's prayer for intercession comes to mind: "Let us witness the good news of salvation to the sinner and *never judge anyone as unworthy or hopeless*" (emphasis mine).

There was something that really stuck with me about St. Dismas, and I found it worth investigating. So to see his name pop up on the polls—to see folks' interest in the Good Thief—put quite the spring into my step. I wanted to know what this "paradise" Jesus promised him was like; I wanted to see it with my own eyes, and see who this thief was and what his character was.

To this day, thinking about it makes my heart ache. Let me tell you why.

What things are associated with a figure like St. Dismas? I wasn't entirely sure, and there certainly weren't any New Age sources to point me in any certain directions, so it was entirely up to my own creativity to figure it out. What I ended up doing was putting down one of the pysanky we'd inherited from my boyfriend's family as a symbol of rebirth, as well as amethyst, blue lace agate, and carnelian for spiritual wisdom, peace, and passion. A single piece of clear quartz was there just to further concentrate that energy, and a candle lit behind it all was standard Catholic instinct, honestly; Catholics love candles. Me included.

But with everything set up, the same prayers done, the same protections dropped on me like a veil, I reached up to Heaven and called for the Penitent Thief.

"Hello, St. Dismas! Please, come spend some time with me. I've got some questions for you that I'd like to ask over a good cup of tea. Please, let me see you; come chat!"

It took a moment, but the pendulum started moving in a circle, meaning St. Dismas was there with me. I closed my eyes and waited for the imagery to paint itself in my mind, and I'll be frank: I've never seen Heaven quite like I saw it here. I spawned outside the gates of Heaven, as always—I don't think I'm allowed inside those gates as someone still living—but usually, where I see this landscape in daytime, full sun, white clouds, this time it was the most beautiful blend of reds and purples and gold from the gate. On the horizon was a pinkish sunset, the sun half over the horizon and throwing that beautiful color all over the place.

St. Dismas himself was there, first in off-white robes with gold and red embroidery as he took me on a quick tour of a couple things—a wintry forest with his hands full of a goblet of mulled wine, then a barren area in the middle of nowhere, landscapes I still don't really understand the meaning of—and then he showed himself sitting beside me on those colorful clouds, in deep burgundy and gold robes with leather sandals. His hair was a sandy brownish-blond, curly and connecting into a well-kept, shorter beard, and his eyes were warm as honey. He was a pale man with a strong nose and brows and a smile that screamed *golden retriever,* so bright and enthusiastic.

The vibes were incredible right away, as his smile grew. I used my pendulum to confirm his deck of choice, Threads of Fate's Weaver Tarot. One thing I did note, though, was that the base of my wrist pinged like there was a point in it; it made me think of a nail used in crucifixion

"Hi! Hello! It's good to meet you," I said, and he nodded, staying silent for the time being. I kept at it: "Well, I guess... let's just dive in. I know this is probably a tough question to start with, given we just met, but it's one I'm curious about: what caused you to become a thief in your life?"

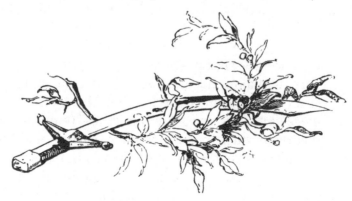

1. WHAT CAUSED YOU TO BECOME A THIEF IN LIFE?

A few options are available. Make a choice you're most in alignment with. No get rich quick schemes— long term success.

Wealthy, successful, ambitious, protective. Age and experience bring understanding. Making things happen.

Instability. Unexpected bumps in the road. Focus on what brings you happiness; material wealth isn't everything.

St. Dismas nodded again, but his smile fell as he looked to the ground. Then he pulled cards that really did half the speaking for him, but he elaborated anyway.

"I had enough wealth not to die, but I wanted more." He cupped his hands, and gold coins poured into them from nowhere. "I wanted to *be* more. I wanted to have wealth fall like a waterfall. I thought it meant something."

Then the gold decayed into dirt and crumbled between his fingers.

"But it gave me no peace."

"Ah. I understand, definitely. And so... when you got to that point on the cross, what brought you to speak up for Jesus?"

2. WHY DID YOU SPEAK UP FOR JESUS?

That last card puzzled me, but St. Dismas spoke on that wound:

"I wanted more, more—that was the 'wound.' But look there."

We watched that sun set together.

"That is more beautiful than any gold. However, I didn't know it in my life. I chased wealth more than the warmth of God's golden sun. But then I was faced with death in that moment, on the cross, and I saw it. Jesus was the *more* I'd been chasing. I knew it fully. I wouldn't let him be bad-mouthed by people who, by *that* point, still didn't understand. There was the truth, right between us; *there* was the future! Strung up and nailed right beside me, a thief. We were equals in death then—me and God,

New beginning in material realm. No time to rest. Nurture opportunity to the end. Be open to different outcomes and possibilities.

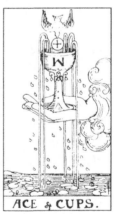

New beginning in emotional realm. A wonderful lesson; release it and move forward. A new path filled with joy. Loving opportunities.

You've fallen into a space of excess and intensity, coming from a place of wound. Tend the wound.

as His Son. I had to speak. I had to reach for Him. I'm glad I did."

His every word was passionate. I don't know how else to put it. He was so sincere. I think I made a good choice to toss that carnelian into my ritual set-up, because it fit his energy perfectly.

"Wow. Thank you for that," I said. "And now, if it's not too much to ask... what is this paradise Jesus promised like? For you?"

3. WHAT IS PARADISE LIKE FOR YOU?

It was at this point that I realized the Heaven I was seeing was without a doubt *his* specific paradise, because we went touring it like we had one of those vacation packages you see advertised online that promise to take you to four separate countries in a week. First, we were sitting first on a beach at night, with the full moon shining down on the sand and the water, and with a cool and gentle breeze passing by us, rustling through our hair and seeping past the threads of our cloaks.

Then we were on a massive cliff, covered in lush green grass, soft and ticklish against the ankles and so very sweet-smelling. Far away was that same ocean, and before it a city full of twinkling lights from the houses. It was dark, the sky bruise-purple. Behind us was an angel that I think was trying to keep St. Dismas from showing me too much. It was the strangest angel I'd ever seen, though, all blue and orange like a Dr. Suess character with a head that had no eyes, mouth, or nose. It drifted behind us, lurking there, waiting for us to move along.

And eventually we did. We came to a place where there was a huge white marble platform. On it, a giant woman in a white shawl and blue robe, and a silver crown of stars, stood watching over a couple embracing and kissing between marble columns, a symbol of love lasting forever between souls.

I squinted at her. "Is that *Mary?*"

St. Dismas shook his head. "No."

"...the Holy Spirit, then? Sophia?"

"No, no."

If not either of those two, I didn't know who it could be. A crown full of stars? All I could think in relation to that was Mary, but if it wasn't her, or the Holy Spirit, then maybe it was another Saint. All I knew was that she had the softest smile as she watched the married couple dance and squeal and celebrate together on that marble platform.

There was a lot. But all of it was so pretty. I've never seen anything like all of this. And you know how Christians will tell you that you have to "test the spirits," like it says to do in the Gospels? How these spirits have to profess Christ as their Savior, as the Son of God, yada yada?

I couldn't help but be curious and ask that question in between all this: a good old, *St. Dismas, do you see Christ as Son of God and as your Savior?* And I'll give you three guesses as to what is answer was. Bonus points if you can guess how emphatically he said it.

"Damn. Okay." We ended up back on the steps of Heaven's gate, watching that pinkish sunset. That's... wow. Beautiful. Uh, I guess we'll just move onto the next question: what should people take away from your story?"

Mostly I wanted to see if it would be any different than what the Church says. But his answer was pretty wholesome.

4. WHAT SHOULD PEOPLE TAKE AWAY FROM YOUR STORY?

Good fortune and abundance. Assess relationship with wealth. What's your long term plan? Heal wounds with self sufficiency.

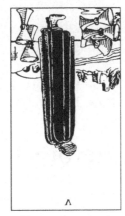

Viewing experiences and losses from enlightened perspective. No repeating lessons. You feel stronger, more resilient, ready to focus on what you have.

A new level of wholeness. A sense of completeness and closure. Celebration, triumph. Don't focus on the next thing: bask in your current success.

"I spent all my life chasing after money. And it was good, sure, but for how long? For what?" St. Dismas shrugged and waved a hand. "No, by the end of my life, I'd come to terms with what I'd done and what I'd spent my life on. I knew it wasn't right for me, nor what I *should've* spent my life on. But I did learn. There's no reason to pity me; I am an example of what happens when you focus on what's truly important and recognize it—as well as the errors that prevented you from recognizing it before."

"I see. I love that! Okay, how about people's focus on salvation? I mean, these days, people seem to focus pretty exclusively on their own salvation, acting like being 'saved' is a sticker they can sport as some special badge. But you know," as I kept talking, St. Dismas's face went flatter and flatter, as if what I was telling him was disturbing, "I read *The Crucified God* by Jürgen Moltmann, and it seemed he had a different idea about salvation and people's obsession with it—"

5. WHAT DO YOU THINK ABOUT PEOPLE'S FOCUS ON SALVATION?

What I got, and what stopped my thoughts in their tracks, were some harrowing images.

Gone were the light and the pretty tones. It was all blue and black, and I saw an old man sitting on weathered stone in some kind of city square; his eyes were too shadowed to see. Then there were skeletons wrapped in fine robes with rubies in their eye sockets, all just propped up around the otherwise abandoned town like warnings, and a woman in a red and gold robe walking down a gray street full of ailing people, like an assassin. It felt as if she were the one who made this city the way it was. Stranger still, her eyes were on fire, burning as if her very skull were a lamp filled with oil.

"When you treat salvation the way I treated my gold," St. Dismas whispered, "you get corruption and decay. There is no paradise in greed and selfishness."

"Oh, holy shit—oops," I caught my curse, staring at the flame-eyed woman as I hissed, "Sorry."

Then I wasn't really sure what to ask him, because the question I wrote down didn't make sense anymore as I read it, but he spoke anyway with a single card.

You're on the right path. Not all opportunities are created equal. Think long term and get your internal compass right.

"Remind them," he said. "Remind them: they must listen. No one is listening. Those who know how to listen need to show others how to do so."

By that, I think he means that no one knows how to hear God, especially those so obsessed with salvation. And they're losing the plot for it. It was quite the spooky imagery he used to make his point, I will admit.

"Okay, okay, so I guess we'll move on," and how thankful I was when we shot back to the gates of Heaven, away from that awful strip of madness he'd showed me, "how do you help people that call out to you?"

6. HOW DO YOU HELP PEOPLE THAT CALL OUT TO YOU?

An arrival. Realizing who you really are. Empowerment. Prioritizing relationships with loved ones and getting alone time.

Feeling stuck. Focus on a foundation of self love. You may doubt your ability to hold so much. Ground yourself.

A block in creative flow. Self worth tied to your work; creativity has become work. Focus on doing what reconnects you to creating.

"I help people see what's important," St. Dismas said with a shrug. "We all deserve a second chance."

In the cards, I focused on the notes about self worth, self love, and I felt it had something to do with prisoners, those who are paying for mistakes made. St. Dismas continued.

"We all deserve a second chance. None of us are too broken for God's love, or for change. At any moment, one can put down their current life and fashion a new one. Even if it's made of scrap metal, it'll shine brighter than the finest work of a hollow hearted smith."

"I got'cha; thank you. And now: how do you see yourself?"

7. HOW DO YOU SEE YOURSELF?

1. A need for structure. We make progress with consistent focus or work. Building vision brick by brick.

2. A relationship gone sour. Both parties bringing baggage. Be curious and stay or walk away in the face of habitual patterns.

3. Raw potential of prosperity: no resting on your laurels. The universe is co-creating with you and showing new opportunities.

"I am a man who had to be helped out of my old ways," he said, looking at his feet. "But I still had to make the choice to be helped. God wouldn't have helped me if I hadn't been open to it in the first place. But I was done with life, and with what I'd done with mine—I was ready to face the truth. Now I am the living result of those choices."

I thought it interesting for him to say he's the *living* result, all things considered, but clearly he's still here in some way. Afterlife is still life, no?

"I see. How how do you want to be seen, St. Dismas?"

8. HOW DO YOU WANT TO BE SEEN?

I thought I'd screwed up pulling the same card in the same position as the last question, but it actually seemed to tie both answers together.

St. Dismas said, "I am someone who will never lose sight of what's important again. I wasted myself on nonsense in life, on fantasies that brought me no closer to joy. I didn't want to put in the work I needed to." He sat up straighter and barked, "Never again! I was fortunate enough to be able to understand, just in time. But I'm not special. Anyone can be like me and turn themselves around."

"Perfect." There was something genuinely healing about listening to St. Dismas speak. "Alright, well—

A period of intense work. May feel soul crushing. Hours of diligent work is vital. Encouragement.

Lack of follow through, not living up to one's potential. Doubting abilities, deception, greed.

Structure, progress through focus. Don't lose sight of your vision.

here's our last question. What messages do you have to share with everyone?"

9. ANY LAST MESSAGES FOR ME OR OTHERS?

1. Scales of justice present. You've been wronged or wronged someone else, or grappling with a moral issue. Justice is rooted in truth. Don't turn a blind eye to misdeeds.

2. Focus on yourself over others. You need to be your first priority. Care for yourself so you can care for others Practice detachment and break codependent habits.

3. May be friction among a group. Ego is taking over communication. Don't worry about who's right; worry about solving the problem together.

He was nothing but serious here.

"One can't take shortcuts with their own selves, their own souls," he said. "They can't disregard the things eating at them. If you want change, it's time to make change. Go! Find support; change your life! Become who you want to be! Build your own paradise—just a sliver to remind yourself of what's important."

Which, to him, and to me and other Christians, is God and the health of the soul. If you're not Christian, that's okay; what you find will be different for you. But find what's important and chase it nonetheless.

I wrote down the last couple words and looked them over, then nodded. "Okay, that's a wrap, then! Thank you. St. Dismas. This was an amazing interview, and I'm glad to have had the chance to meet you. Goodbye for now, and I do hope to see you again sometime!"

St. Dismas nodded, ruffled my hair, and then he was off, wandering back across the landscape of clouds and towards that pink-purple sunset. Then all faded away again, and I was back where I started: in my own house, a little sanctuary I'd earned with my own money and carved out for myself there in the woods of New England.

To this day, when I think about the concept of Christian joy, of being close to God and genuinely loving Him with all one's heart, I think of St. Dismas. I can describe to you the many scenes he took me through, beautiful, peaceful places where there was no death or suffering, but I can't explain the feelings that came with it. St. Dismas got his paradise, all right, and it remains one of the most beautiful things I've ever seen in Heaven. I mean, who knew something like that could exist in the same place that has the famous Lake of Fire?

But it's there, and St. Dismas is living there in it, happy as a clam. I don't think he ever thought he'd get to go someplace like that after his death, given his lifestyle, but he got it anyway. I'm happy for him. And I'm keeping his messages close, too, because there's wisdom in them all.

Maybe a few warnings, too. Warnings that, unfortunately, the people who need them most likely won't listen to, as tends to be a recurring theme where spirituality is involved. Those who have ears should hear, but those who don't, there's not much to do about.

Oh, well.

PRINCE STOLAS

You know who had me interested in the Ars Goetia before I ever even *dreamed* of actually contacting them? If you guessed Prince Stolas, you're absolutely correct. From the first moment I ever laid eyes on a picture of him from the *Dictionnaire Infernal* drawn up by Louis Le Breton, I was smitten—because he was an owl with a little crown and long bird legs! How sweet! How *cute*!

Granted, I was aware that fawning over an adorable owl with a crown was not necessarily the correct way to approach an understanding of this Prince, but back then, I was still very afraid of these spirits, and I was willing to do anything to lessen that fear—including squeal over the Ars Goetia pictures that *weren't* a bunch of animal heads stuck onto spider legs (sorry, King Bael). Still, even with my fervent wish at the time to never come in contact with demons of any kind, and with my worry of somehow "accidentally" summoning a demon (pause to groan here), I found that this cute picture of a crowned owl tapped against the theological glass cage I'd built around myself. It tapped it, and fractured it, in a crack too small for me to see right away—and that crack said, *how could something as sweet as this Prince be a bad thing?*

A dumb question, honestly, because no matter how "cute" a member of the infernal divine looks, it's best not to take them lightly. This goes for gods and angels, too. Jophiel being the angel of beauty doesn't mean she won't cut heads off. Aphrodite being a goddess of love doesn't mean she doesn't have baneful epithets. Prince Stolas being an adorable owl with a little crown and long bird legs doesn't mean he isn't one of the many princes of hell that could absolutely waste you.

But when have I ever claimed to be a smart person that employs caution?

Prince Stolas is nonetheless a wonderful figure among the Ars Goetia. A master of herbs, astrology, and crystals, he can teach the magician many things about these tools and systems, as well as bring some much needed wisdom surrounding them. Unlike other demons, who are more interested in actively meddling with the affairs of people or inspiring them to action, Prince Stolas is a scholar at heart, and in true scholar fashion, prefers not to be bothered unless necessary. It makes me think of what I heard about Jewish folklore once (which I'm not sure is correct, but I heard): there are different types of demons, some of which are evil, and some of which are just spirits of obsession, that collect knowledge like a dragon collects gems, and who are happy to share it with those who will properly appreciate all of their time and effort.

I'd been dying for a reason to talk to Prince Stolas for so long. I'm not entirely sure why I thought I needed one, really—God knows I could've just asked Lucifer to check and see if Prince Stolas would be open to it—and yet I couldn't bring myself to come anywhere near him until he got the majority of the vote on my Patreon. So when he finally *did,* you can imagine that I was giddy with excitement.

Let's take a look together at Prince Stolas, 36th demon of the Ars Goetia.

For my conversation with Prince Stolas, I knew two things: he's a wise master in his area of expertise, and he's a demon associated with the element of air. According to S. Connolly's *The Complete Book of Daemonolatry,* he's an excellent demon to help the magician in "clarity of the mind and practicality in all matters" (31), and as such, I felt Earl Grey tea, pecans, and caraway, all air based, would be good to put around as offerings, along with amethysts to circle his sigil. I lit a white candle after saying my typical prayers and asking God to let Prince Stolas come through, and then we were off.

"Prince Stolas, hello, good evening! Please come and chat with me; I'd love to ask a few questions."

I knew he was there when the candle flame started flickering higher and I got a vivid flash of a barn owl standing beside me, looming over my shoulder. Its giant black eyes were like shadows made into liquid, all shiny yet endlessly dark. But once I confirmed he was there and what tarot cards he wanted to use—Kat Black's Golden Tarot—we were off and away, without me gushing over him too much.

We ended up in an office similar to Lucifer & Azazel's, all of which seems to be in the same mansion. It's an interconnected place, with rooms and corridors sprouting up as needed—a proper magician's house, if you think about it. However, I could tell this room apart because it had a different window, and the desk was crowded with books of all kinds. The floor was also full of books, while Prince Stolas, as a barn owl with a black beak and golden crown, roosted on top and picked through the pages of one especially weathered tome.

He had the air of an old professor who took his time noticing a student hovering in the doorway, and he gave me one quick nod to let me know it was okay to settle in and start shuffling cards.

"Okay, thank you! To get started, why did you choose to study herbs and stones and astrology? I read somewhere you're not so interested in war and such, that you just like to research. How come?"

I. WHAT HAS YOU SO INTERESTED IN YOUR RESEARCH?

Prince Stolas fluffed up and hunkered down onto that book as if it were a nest. "No one can say knowledge isn't a noble pursuit," he said. "Nothing goes unnoticed to those who read their messages. It's a great power, truly. Fighting, all that might and such, it's useless bravado to me. There are easier, more efficient, more concealable ways of felling a foe." Then he paused and considered his

1. Good fortune and contentment. Some disillusionment, taking good fortune for granted.

2. Enlightenment. Self acceptance. Ready for divine scrutiny, knowing one lived a fair life.

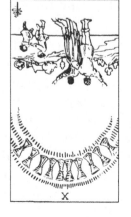

answer further. "Though with this, of course, also comes the knowledge of healing to save oneself and others. Yes, there is practicality in this."

"I got'cha. And I'd like to know: what do you think people take for granted about astrology?"

2. WHAT DO PEOPLE TAKE FOR GRANTED ABOUT ASTROLOGY?

Problems with a relationship: a partner feeling taken for granted, or jealous of a potential rival. Promiscuity, unfaithfulness, or wanting a more exciting life.

Optimism and wanting to believe the best may confuse an important issue. Consider all scenarios, including the worst. By preparing, it's less likely to happen.

Prince Stolas puffed himself up and settled further onto the desk—a proper depiction of the phrase, *ruffled feathers*. His eyes narrowed to thin strips of black as he muttered, "Many use it only to fluff themselves up or disparage others in comparison to them. They treat it as merely a matchmaking tool, or a point of kinship and pride. This is not the function of the cosmic bodies and their secrets. One can see the rise and fall of kingdoms in its mathematics; one can predict, with accuracy, the flow of energy that wraps around your world. It's a beautiful tool."

"I see that. Agreed!" It made me think of those lifestyle magazines that had horoscopes written out for the more casual New Age style spiritualists—which, of course, still have their value, but certainly don't represent all there is to do or know with the system of astrology. I looked back at Prince Stolas and said, "So, also, I notice some places I was looking at mention you as a fallen angel. What do you think about that? Were you ever an angel?"

3. WERE YOU EVER AN ANGEL?

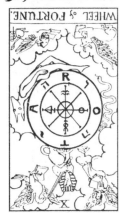

Bitterness at misfortunes clouding one's ability to see the good luck also dealt by fate.

Significant negative forces are at work. Take care to guard against hatred, resentment, and abuses of power.

I don't think I've ever seen a barn owl manage to look bitter, but something about the way his face feathers fluffed up told me he wasn't thrilled with the question—as did the Wheel of Fortune reversed. Still, he confirmed he was an angel via pendulum, specifically a Principalite.

"Azazel is not the only one that taught you humans magic," he said as he stood up on his long legs. "You humans were great in your capacity to build, but more refinement was needed. More respect to the way of things. Azazel taught women the magic of the root, but I taught the more practical purposes, so that you might not die like beasts."

"Huh." This got me to start thinking about witches in general, and how they're often associated with birds like the raven or owl, which is especially noted in the Greek *Strix* and Polish *Strzyga* (both words meaning owl, relating to a sorceress or monstrous woman). The women who knew their way around plants, both to hurt and help, were all seen as witches, with these birds considered bad omens among the townsfolk. "Interesting. Given the thought, though, around women and magic and owls and ravens, all bad omens and the like... why do you choose an owl or a raven when appearing to people?"

4. WHY DO YOU APPEAR AS AN OWL OR RAVEN?

Here, there were no cards pulled. He just gave me the images, of those moonlit nights and scraggly trees where the birds like owls and ravens sit overhead, a foreboding image that made an uneasy, stomach-churning feeling take root in any passerby.

"They are omens of misfortune and foreboding, those owls and ravens," he said, "yet also birds of wisdom and secret knowledge. Those who are unafraid are worthy of my gifts. Those curious enough to seek answers will find them."

"I see, I see." I lost sight of him as I opened my eyes to write, but as soon as I closed them, I was back in that well-lit room surrounded by towers on towers of books, yet no chair to sit on. "So that does sort of line up with what I'm thinking. Okay! Now, another curiosity of mine: what do you think of pop culture representations of you, like in video games and this web series, *Helluva Boss*? It seems you're a popular figure to include, but I wonder how you feel about it."

5. WHAT DO YOU THINK OF HELLUVA BOSS AND OTHER MEDIA?

I always expect demons to get upset with the way they're portrayed, as both Lucifer and King Paimon weren't thrilled with their representations. But Prince Stolas didn't seem that bothered. His wings went up in an owl's version of a shrug, and he gripped the cover of his book with one talon.

"What was I to do," he grumbled, "kill everyone that used my image?"

I don't know if you've ever seen a barn owl do that thing where they hunch over and let their head hang low as they watch something, but he looked like that as he peered at me from where he perched.

And I admit that I was frequently trying to check my gushing, because I love owls. And he was such a pretty white barn owl, with those toasted-marshmallow-colored bands around his face and at the edge of his wings.

"It's better I come to terms with mankind's need to caricaturize things for their own stories," he continued despite my staring. "People need to remember the origins of their tales, lest they get too familiar. We are still ferocious beings, even if we do not always appear so for the sake of decorum. Double edged sword, it is, that people lose their fear of us— good to remind people of our virtues, but bad to make them forget our dangers."

THE CHARIOT.

Pragmatic. Collaboration, compromise. A victory obtained by working with others, not against them. Changing one's own behavior will probably work better than trying to change others'.

THE HIEROPHANT.

Spiritual guidance and authority. Tradition and structure may be necessary to create order from chaos. Change in relationships. Leave the past behind. A greater level of spiritual understanding.

I nodded as I wrote. "I understand. I do! But I do think it helps, too, seeing you all in different lights in media." When he did his owl shrug in response, I shrugged with him. "Okay, moving on: what do you think people take for granted about *you?*"

6. WHAT DO YOU THINK PEOPLE TAKE FOR GRANTED ABOUT DEMONS?

Tyranny and domination; a cruel, cold man.

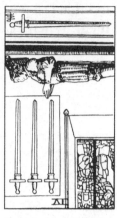

Stress may become extreme, or a time of loneliness and isolation may need to be overcome.

"They abuse us for knowledge," he said, his head dipping even lower as he stared at me. "'Solomonic magic'—pah. We are great spirits, not slaves. We are noble and free beings, not to be contained by man's ego.

"All they want of me is knowledge that could be found just as well without disturbing me; it's already in the world. Newer practitioners, however, are less likely to act like this," which, based off the energy I felt roll off him, I figured *this* meant greedy, hungry for knowledge without giving anything in return, even respect. Prince Stolas bobbed his head. "It's heartening."

"Yeah, that must be frustrating, the Solomonic practice." Can't say it didn't work, but it often worked at one hell of a cost. When provoked with Solomonic magic, demons that would've otherwise not cared enough about a practitioner to ruin their lives might suddenly find their agenda cleared for torturous fun and games. "But speaking of noble and great spirits, I understand you command 26 legions of demons. What's it like for you to command them as their Prince? What does it entail?"

7. WHAT IS IT LIKE TO COMMAND DEMONS AS A PRINCE OF HELL?

Life will always send challenges and trials to overcome; you can't have good without bad. Look to future joys, not misfortunes.

Love declared. Satisfying love, either platonic or romantic. Balance, unity, happy compromise. Friendship acknowledged. Deep mutual understanding and intuition.

This was a big question for me. I hadn't quite pieced together my thoughts on demons yet, and I was hoping to have Prince Stolas help me out with it. His black eyes sparkled in the light of the study's chandelier candles, and he bobbed his head again, as if pleased to answer.

"Ah. We hold this world together, Sara. More than you understand." He stood up tall and proud on the desk and puffed his chest feathers. "Lucifer doesn't want to see the world come to ruin any more than your God does. So we wrangle these feral and destructive forces—powerful things, when you know how to control them, but still very stupid. It's a thankless job, but it must be done."

"Oh! That's interesting."

I had to open my eyes and pop out of the office to think about it. The idea rolled around in my head like a marble on hard wood floors, loud and yet hard to catch. But it made sense: not all spirits in this world were good, and demons weren't all like *these* demons—which, when you think about it, weren't really demons at all, but angels and gods and such. This was the moment I remembered those odd gargoyle things from my chat with Azazel, too, and when I blinked as the things I'd seen finally clicked into place. Those things were demons—and they weren't demons that were strong enough to make any amount of fuss unchecked or without the reason of any of their managers. They were small fry, strong enough to be a bother, weak enough to be contained, and that last part was the only part that mattered for a practicing witch that didn't want to deal with them. When I closed my eyes again, Prince Stolas was sitting there, comfortably fluffed and waiting for me.

"Thank you," I said. "That helps a lot, actually. But we do need to move on, so now, as we get into the last questions, I'm curious: how do you see yourself?"

8. HOW DO YOU SEE YOURSELF?

The imagery on the Moon in the Golden Tarot deck is really cool: deer and dogs and other such animals finding themselves in odd and impossible places under the smiling moon's light. I thought it interesting that I pulled it beside the Three of Coins, too, given how. Three of Coins had people studying in a darker area.

"I spread my wings farthest in adversity," Prince Stolas said. "Much have I suffered, and much have I learned as a result. My renown I've earned through the labor of learning. I do good work here, excellent work. I am proud."

"And how do you want others to see you?"

9. HOW DO YOU WANT TO BE SEEN?

He paused, then fluffed and refused to pick any cards.

"The opinion of others means little. I know who I am."

"I see." And I respected the hell out of that. It was an answer that reminded me of King Belial, yet it was such a quiet and self-assured way of carrying that energy. I peered up at him as I got back to shuffling my deck. "So, here we are at the last question. I'm curious: do you have any messages? For me, for others?"

Talent rewarded. Creative ability bringing material gain. Recognition. Status through accomplishment. Abundance. A new home. Redecoration.

There may be obstacles to overcome, and cycles of good and bad, but get through it and good times will come back. Embrace darkness and daylight will be back.

10. ANY LAST MESSAGES FOR ME OR FOR OTHERS?

 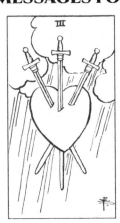

1. Emotional turmoil. Loneliness, insecurity in a relationship.

2. A broken heart. Misery, sorrow, and grief after affair or friendship. Time eases the pain.

How does an owl smile? I don't know, but I got the sense that he was somehow.

"This message is for anyone. But people are a *distraction*. What matters is your work, your studies, your own goals. Too often, people throw themselves away for others, but I tell you, books will not betray you. Time studying is never time wasted, unlike time spent with people— especially ungrateful people."

"Oh, jeez, yeah. I see what you mean, and I definitely can agree to a good extent." Of course, me being the silly thing that I am, I'll always value time with people in between all my work; I've got a touch of that golden retriever energy that makes it impossible to stick my nose in a book all day. But it was a fair warning nonetheless. So I finished writing his answer down, closed my book, and nodded. "Well! I guess that's a wrap, then. I've got to skip off and bake some bread, get some things done, but nonetheless, I appreciate your time and attention, Prince Stolas, and I hope to see you again sometime! Thank you for all of your answers!"

Prince Stolas stayed giving me that beak-smile all the way until I opened my eyes and clapped my hands, shattering the image of the office and shocking myself back into the waking world. Early interviews were a little more difficult than evening ones, if only because I couldn't go to bed directly after; I had to keep running, keep moving, keep working, even as all this information swirled in my head and as leftover images of the meditation flashed in my mind every time I blinked. But I made it happen. My bread got baked, my work got done, and I got to moving on with my typical routine. Granted, it was a murderous routine I had at the time, what with the full-time job and the equivalent of two part time jobs I'd made with my writing and my personal social media, but one I'd maintained (somehow) for over a year by this point. Didn't make it any easier, though.

And in settings like those, it's easy to take the spiritual for granted. It's easy to have it go "in one ear and out the other," so to speak, which is difficult when a magician is actively trying to work on these things in their life. Still, as I went about it, it was that silly, gushy feeling for an owl in a crown that kept me thinking about it all day: I'd met Prince Stolas, and he'd given me a major thing to think about, namely regarding how minor demons operate—and where and how they can give unsuspecting people a run for their money.

Needless to say, if I feared demons before as a Christian, I do not fear them as a Christian Witch. Not anymore, knowing that the ones most likely to bother us are ones just trying to see if they can trip us up, like a mean kid sticking their leg out as you walk by. *They're just little guys,* I remember thinking to myself as I schlogged through e-mail and hoped no unexpected projects dropped into my lap at work. *Just little things doing what's in their nature to do.*

I wasn't afraid of demons after realizing this, no—and more than that, I didn't fault them for being what they were, either. *That* part was what really made the twenty-something-year-old weight, the clamp of fear about demons, finally unlatch from me and dissolve for good.

ARCHANGEL ZADKIEL

In the Bible, in Genesis, we find ourselves in a sticky situation as humans by page two. No one can deny that. The apple debacle happens, and then everyone is doomed forever to a life of pain and drudgery and what-have-you, as the story goes. But pretty quickly, we find ourselves looking at the man whose name marks the three major world religions: Abraham, who, with the blessing of God, has a baby they name Isaac even though they are seriously, *seriously* old.

And then, for giggles, God tells Abraham to sacrifice his one and only son.

The binding of Isaac, this story is called—though it doesn't end with a person getting sacrificed, because at the last second, an angel of God swoops down to tell Abraham to stop. God wasn't serious, there's no need to kill Isaac, it was all just a test—the angel is saying everything to get Abraham to put that knife down, and thankfully, it works. Abraham stops and sacrifices a nearby ram that happened to get trapped with its horns stuck in the bramble instead.

The story moves on pretty quickly after that, the angel remaining nameless—though over time, it was understood that the angel that came here was Zadkiel, whose name means "Angel of Mercy" or "God is my Righteousness." One of the angels that fights beside Michael against their rebellious counterparts, Zadkiel is a powerful angel that helps people understand the compassion and mercy of God, as well as take on those values into their own daily lives. He's an archangel associated with the sign of Sagittarius, and whenever I think about him, the color purple comes to mind. Something less known about him, though, is that he has an alter ego: Sachiel, an angel of fortune and wealth.

Knowing that one angel can wear two names, and appear so radically different each time, as if wearing a mask, changes how one thinks about angels. It was by discovering that Zadkiel and Sachiel were the same angel, despite looking radically different as I encountered them in spellwork and meditation, that made me wonder how angels really worked. If maybe there was something more than just the single name each angel carried. I hadn't figured it out just yet, though the little seed of an idea had long since germinated.

But I digress.

Archangel Zadkiel came up on the polls one week, and I was excited, because I saw this as an opportunity to get to know Zadkiel a little better outside the few times I saw him with Michael and Gabriel during meditation. I figured he'd have some good advice for how to stay cool and compassionate, even when everything felt like it was burning down, and that was the angle I walked into the interview with—so let me show you how it went.

Being an angel of mercy and compassion, as well as an angel of wealth and luck, I had a combination of crystals there to focus the energy around Zadkiel's sigil: amethyst, rose quartz, celestite, and carnelian, all stones of wisdom, love, confidence, and good communication. A little rose quartz angel and my purple lace agate rosary, as well as plenty of candles, also helped with their pink-purple tones and their loving, soothing qualities. I did have to get a bit of techno-witchcraft going with Zadkiel's sigil, because I couldn't find it pre-drawn online to put up, so I had to trace it myself in the Notes app on my phone. But hey, if it can work on paper, it can work on a phone (made with much more magically interesting materials)!

Then I set my space with God and asked Him to let Zadkiel on through, and it didn't take long for the familiar peaceful energy to appear.

"Zadkiel! Hello! Please come by and let me get a feel for your energy; it's good to sit down and get to talk to you one on one like this!"

Soon enough, I had both the push of an angel's energy and the swinging of the pendulum to confirm Zadkiel was, indeed, there in the room. Now, as I've said, I've seen Zadkiel come around with Gabriel and Michael before. Usually, he's dressed in a purplish-magenta set of robes with gold trim, big wings, deeply bronzed skin, and short black hair. But this time, he showed up more like a stereotypical angel: fair and brown haired, with clear eyes that seemed too big for his head.

"Are you sure you want to show up like this today?" I really liked his other appearance; I thought it looked cool in the first form he'd came to me in. "As such an... angel-like angel?"

Zadkiel stared at me, and then he sighed. He shifted through a number of different masks and faces, distorting himself every which way to see which illusion would best get me to focus on him. Eventually, though, it seems he picked an image out of my brain, a photo that I'd really liked as character inspiration, and just wore that like a mask—though he kept sliding between that Too Big Eye and masked form, as to remind me that it wasn't really how he came to look right then.

Good thing he's the angel of mercy and compassion, because I know Raphael didn't have half the patience when I was fussing about his appearance. Speaking of Raphael, I'm pretty sure he popped in at one point too, just to give me a look and go—there was a flash of green and gold, and another set of big, dark eyes staring at me—but then it was just Zadkiel and I.

We started our journey together in what seemed like a monastery, with Zadkiel holding this big golden incense thurible, and with some monks singing in the pews of a tiny cathedral behind us. Then we were out in the open, outside what looked like a city with a big castle and a wall, an open rolling field around us. It was my first time seeing either of these places, and I could only guess it was somewhere in Heaven again. There are a *lot* of unexplored pieces of Heaven.

But we got our ducks in a row, agreeing on two cards per question with Amrit Brar's Marigold Tarot, and then we were off.

"So, Zadkiel, to start us off: what does mercy mean to you?"

1. WHAT DOES MERCY MEAN TO YOU?

"Decisions," he said as I puzzled over the cards he plopped down, "decisions are mercy, especially when the decision is to rest. One's efforts do not grow in a barren field. Mercy starts with oneself and extends outwards—it's a choice, a commitment, to oneself and others."

"Oh. I see that, yeah! Okay. And now," there was no way I could've avoided asking about this, "I'm dying to ask, but once I called on Sachiel, and I saw a very different angel than the one standing in front of me right now. But it was you! You are Sachiel! Why did you show up so differently?"

Overextending oneself or one's resources and avoiding responsibility.

Action, completing projects, resolving conflicts. Efforts grow fast if decisive.

2. WHY APPEAR DIFFERENTLY AS SACHIEL?

Travel, inner journeys, growth and evolution after hard times. A personality that will adapt to new situations.

Wonder, optimism, creativity, and confidence. Having the foresight to protect oneself. Moving forward with projects constructively.

I distinctly remember getting a string of angel names at this point. It's important here to note that many angel names end in -el, and they all mean something about God.

Gabriel: "Strength of God."

Michael: "He who is like God."

Samael: "Venom of God."

Zadkiel: "Righteousness of God."

Sachiel: "The Covering of God."

It was at this point Zadkiel explained:

"We are manifestations, or reflections, of aspects of God. Our names are our titles—our masks. Each title holds its own power. What we are called in relation to the gifts people see us provide change their perception of us—not us as autonomous creatures."

A very interesting answer, in my opinion. Also difficult to conceptualize, because we see these angels as their names, and yet they seem to see themselves as separate creatures, pieces of creation, that are maybe assigned specific masks to wear throughout their work and existence among us. It seemed that Zadkiel was inferring that angels without an aspect of God to wear, like any of these names, are blank-slate beings. Like a phone fresh out of the box, its factory settings and default wallpaper still in tact.

So weird.

"Alright, then, let's keep going with this line of questioning," I said, in full journalist mode as I rapped my pencil against my notebook, "in the Bible, angels of the Lord will often talk as if they *are* God, talking in first person. You even did it, I guess, when you stopped Abraham. Why do you talk as if you are God?"

3. WHY TALK IN FIRST PERSON AS IF YOU ARE GOD?

"We are like God's seeing mirror," he said. "Perfect messengers, we dare not alter a single word He gives us to say. We are vessels for divine speech. This is our glory, our service—and, yes, our pride."

He said that like he was giving me permission to use the word *pride* in relation to them.

"I see," I said as I wrote. "And on another note: how does astrology mesh with angels? You being associated with Sagittarius?"

Breakthroughs, confronting facts and problems, finding solutions. Issues must be handled decisively.

Self satisfaction, good fortune, and contentment. Joy in the abundance one has. Warmth and goodwill to oneself.

4. HOW DOES ASTROLOGY MESH WITH ANGELS?

Closure, working towards resolution (though not necessarily positive resolution), and hostility.

Navigating love and relationships of any kind. Clarity and honesty in one's values.

Zadkiel smiled here, and by the shake of his shoulders, he almost laughed.

"You humans are so numerous, yet you divide yourself into twelve," he said, chuckling. "Such small numbers. Yet still, we angels are infinite," he said, gesturing up towards the blue sky. "The celestial bodies signify different things to *you*, but they hold such energy; they're the push pins of creation. We are their stewards and understand their functions. We find ourselves understanding our relationship to you by their functions, too. You are difficult creatures to understand."

I mean, fair. But actually, if you didn't know: there is a whole rank of angels dedicated to moving celestial bodies: the Dominions, of which Zadkiel is actually chief. So that's pretty interesting that it came full circle there, with how angels use our system of organizing ourselves through stars to understand us a little better. I guess when people spend all day talking about how a Taurus moon means they like to be comfortable, all you really have to do is listen long enough to figure out what the average astrology fan is like by how they view the zodiac signs they stick to themselves.

"I got'cha—cool!" That made the whole concept of astrology make more sense to me, which was unexpected. "Okay, and now, what's something you wish people understood about angels?"

5. WHAT DO YOU WISH PEOPLE UNDERSTOOD ABOUT ANGELS?

Wonder, optimism, creativity, foresight. Moving forward in a creative way.

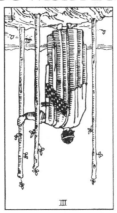

Lack of vision for the future and ignorance of the present.

The wind sweeping through the grass here looked really nice. Honestly, I never did really figure out where we were; all I could see was a stone tower inside a stone wall and lots of grass and mountain around. It was peaceful, though, and it made it easier to listen.

"Faith keeps angels moving," Zadkiel said. "We can guess, and make judgments based on what we see and know of the past, but all our inspiration to act is because of God. We trust His orders and His judgment. Truth is, we hardly know ourselves what's going on or what's to come. We simply wait for instruction. God orchestrates us in perfect harmony."

Well, damn. Let this be a moment of reflection for you: if you were struggling, not sure of the direction of your life, not knowing what you need to do or where you need to go, or how to even start, then take heart, because the angels don't know, either, I guess. And they have a *lot* to do that they still manage to figure out how to get done.

Realizing that, I smiled and said, "Okay! And what's something that bothers you about the world?"

6. WHAT BOTHERS YOU ABOUT THE WORLD?

Carelessness, pessimism, lethargy, and roadblocks to goals.

Vigilance, contemplation, growing new ideas. Easy to get carried away looking for intellectual challenge.

With these cards was the first time I heard Zadkiel get a little frustrated. He went on a bit of a rant:

"People think themselves into a hole. The world is broken for all this 'I can't' thinking. All of these dreams and ambitions, and negative thoughts waste them." He scowled and shook his head. "You convince yourself things aren't worth doing or aren't going to work—whether to shirk the work involved or because you genuinely believe yourself incapable, I don't know."

"Oh. Well, I mean, jeez." I sat there in the grass, blinking up at him with my notebook clutched to my chest. "You're not wrong. But that's pretty intense."

He just shrugged.

"Alright, fair, though. Moving on: what do you want to help people with?"

7. WHAT DO YOU WANT TO HELP PEOPLE WITH?

"People focus so much on what they want to accomplish that they bowl each other over in the meantime," Zadkiel said with a sigh. "They become callous and cruel towards others who have what they want and go to any lengths to get it, even at the expense of others and themselves. People need to soften their hearts and remember the ends to not justify the means. *That's* what I want to help people understand."

"Perfectly reasonable." *But good luck telling that to most of the people who need to hear it.* "Okay, well, we're towards the end of our questions now, so let's see: how do you see yourself?"

Rivalry, obstacles, competition, trickery. Competitiveness.

Envy, no desire to think critically about one's actions.

8. HOW DO YOU SEE YOURSELF?

Creativity, ambition, opportunities in bloom.

Ignoring the call to transform, disappointment, and false accusations.

Zadkiel nodded. "I am not one who judges, but I am one who delivers the verdict. The people I come to need help to change, and I bring the chance to, with opportunity, safety, and love. People need help to remember their potential; we try by God's guidance."

The cards I pulled also signified his dual nature here: the opportunity of Ace of Wands, the mercy of Judgment Reversed (which, just by its orientation, said "no judgment" to me). As a side note, Sachiel, Zadkiel's alter mask, is associated with wealth and abundance, the Wheel of Fortune card, and likely a bulk of Sagittarius's Jupiter associations.

I sat back and crossed my arms. "And how do you want to be seen?"

9. HOW DO YOU WANT TO BE SEEN?

1. Abundance, generosity, security, reliability, tolerance. Aware of one's powers and limitations and able to reap the benefits of both.

2. Disinterest, introspection, doubt, pessimism, an inability to see the good in life.

"I am the one who tilts the cup back up," he said, referring to the cards I pulled. Interestingly, on the Four of Cups, the cups were tilted downward, all pessimistic and upset, and Zadkiel, with that King of Cups energy, was the one setting them right. "When people are lost in uncharitable thoughts," he continued, "I am there to remind them to be easy and let go of frustration and cruel thoughts. I symbolize the good one attracts when they lift their faces from the ground and face God with grateful, open hearts."

"I see that! And now, any last words before we wrap up?"

10. LAST MESSAGES FOR ME OR OTHERS?

Here, he didn't even pull any cards: he just said it plainly.

"Compassion, mercy, kindness—it starts with oneself," he said, tapping his chest. "It starts with repentance of wounds you caused yourself or others, and with forgiveness, too. Let go of old pain. Embrace the light of God's love. No mistake is too big to forgive, and no person is not worth compassion and mercy. When you're gentle with yourself, gentleness with others follows."

"Understood." I won't lie, after the entities I'd been around the last couple weeks, both within my interviews and my meditations, it was almost jarring to hear an entity be so gung-ho about God that I had to remind myself that I was talking to an angel. But with that written down, I closed my notebook and sighed, feeling like I'd run a marathon. Sometimes the interviews flowed smoothly, and other times they just took a lot out of me, and this was one of the latter cases. Still, it was a conversation worth having. "Thank you, Zadkiel! Absolutely need to meditate with you more soon, but in the meantime, I appreciate you stopping by and answering my questions. Until next time!"

Zadkiel grinned at me, and then all the light of the sunny field around the castle darkened down to nothing. I collected my things and hobbled off for the night, more than ready to go to bed—angel energy was never easy on the mind, no matter how nice the angel was—and all the while, I thought about the consensus that was brewing between angels: they're really out there winging it half the time (no pun intended), doing what God says not just because they're soldiers, but because they don't have any other option than to trust what they're doing gets the results they're hoping for in the end. That, and the being *underneath* these angel names seems to be more complex than just their meanings.

I wonder just how many masks an angel can wear, and just how many times people have seen an angel without recognizing it was one, especially in spiritual practices. They come so many ways, with so many different guises, all to conform to what people need to see and hear at the time, that pinning them down with our human understandings doesn't feel possible.

But as the old adage from Hebrews 13:2 goes:

> *Do not forget to show hospitality to strangers, for by so doing some people have shown hospitality to angels without knowing it.*

It seems there's a damn good reason that had to be said, and we may have stumbled on just a piece of that reason with this interview.

Just a little something to chew on for the next time you meet a complete stranger, I guess.

ST. NICHOLAS

You know what's funny? Every time I've mentioned Santa Claus to my friends in Slovenia, the big red Santa with the sleigh and the beard and all that, their first response was:

"Oh, yeah! Coca-Cola!"

The branding game these American companies have is unreal, to get a figure as iconic as Santa Claus that intimately tied with the red can their product comes in. But before Santa Claus, and certainly before Coca-Cola, there was the Saint that inspired the image of our gift-giving friend of children, and that's St. Nicholas: patron of sailors, brewers, archers, children, and repentant thieves, bishop of Myra, prisoner of the Roman Empire, and potential attendee of the Council of Nicea to create the Biblical Canon we know today (where he may have punched someone for being a heretic.)

But of course, some of the better known stories around St. Nicholas are the ones that involve him being charitable to others. One of his miracles was the finding and reviving of the bodies of three children that a butcher murdered for meat. This butcher, after seeing what St. Nicholas could do, repented instantly and turned to God—though in some stories, like the French version, that butcher is dragged around with St. Nicholas to become Père Fouettard, or the Whipping Father. In other versions of the myth, especially Germanic ones, it's the ever-famous Christmas demon, Krampus, that follows St. Nicholas. Either way, their function is the same: punish the bad children on December 5th while the Saint himself gives gifts and blessings on his feast day, December 6th.

Not Christmas, the 6th. Because in Europe, actual Christmas day is about feasting and being with family, not gifts. On the eve of St. Nicholas's feast, though, kids will put their shoes out hoping for them to be stuffed with toys and candy the next day. This goes back to a legend of St. Nicholas hearing that a family was so poor that the father was about to sell his two daughters to a brothel, as he couldn't afford to pay the dowries to get them married off. To save the women such a horrible life, St. Nicholas walked by and threw tons of gold coins into their windows, which fell into their shoes and the stockings that were drying over the fireplace. St. Nicholas did this a couple times before the father spotted him in the act, and the good Saint made him promise not to tell anyone about it.

Obviously, he must've told someone, if we know about this story now.

However, he's been a beloved figure since, and over time, he took on more and more fantastical traits, standing alongside several other pagan figures among winter, especially the Slavic figures Dedek Mraz (Grandfather Frost) and even Veles. After a while, the Dutch way of saying St. Nicholas (Sinter Klaas) seemed to stick, and we eventually got our Santa Claus through many more silly legends and fables (and a nudge or two from capitalists around the late 1800s). It's quite the departure from the miracle-casting bishop of Myra, and so for the month of December, I cancelled the Patreon polls and made a month of winter figures to reach out to, starting with St. Nicholas.

Let me walk you through the long road I took to get to him.

So to contact St. Nicholas, I did quite a bit of preparation. The most intense part of this was the nine day novena, calculated to end on St. Nicholas's feast day, in which I really just asked that he'd come spend some time chatting and answering my questions. But throughout the novena, I would offer the typical Santa offerings: milk and cookies. Afterwards, for my final novena gift, I promised fifty dollars to an initiative that bought and delivered toys for kids whose families otherwise wouldn't be able to afford giving their kids anything for Christmas. Along with that, the interview gifts themselves included a cup of Austrian winter-themed tea, blended with cinnamon, orange, rosehip, almond, apple, and other such winter spices, as well as a few more cookies (homemade and store-bought) and a Christmas cookie scented red candle.

Obviously, we all know that Santa Claus is a far cry from St. Nicholas—but given how it's all tied together now, it felt like at least a good poke of fun. So after my final novena prayer, my other protective and meditative prayers, and a pass of the pendulum, I was able to confirm that St. Nicholas did, indeed, come to visit me, and that he wanted to use Kat Black's Golden Tarot to speak.

"St. Nicholas, hello!" I said as I settled in. "Wow, huh? That was the last prayer of our novena—our first ever. I know I made some slip-ups here and there, but hey, we made it in the end! But now, to get down to business, I'd love to invite you here for some cookies and tea and hear your take on a few things."

I knew St. Nicholas was on the way even before the novena, because throughout the last prayers, I eventually caught sight of St. Nicholas. Most would describe him as wearing red robes, hence Santa's red robes, and certainly I eventually saw him in that, too, but first, he was wearing white and blue, with ornate blue embroidery on silver-white sashes. He also had a white bishop's hat and a curled golden staff, a white beard stark against bronzed skin, and he was standing on a snowy road. We were standing somewhere that looked like Greece—or at least, what I think Greece looks like—with pine trees, an Orthodox church behind us, and the chilly ocean off to the side, some ways from the path. He had a twinkle in his eye as he greeted me with a friendly and hoarse hello, though it became clear soon enough that he didn't have quite the same jolly nature you'd imagine from Santa. Rather, he was kind, but stern and no nonsense, serious about things that mattered to him. Like a wise grandfather who loved his grandchildren enough to raise them right.

"So, St. Nicholas," I said as we walked towards the church, "let's get the elephant out of the room here: what do you think of the image of Santa Claus, and how it came out of your story?"

1. WHAT DO YOU THINK ABOUT THE IMAGE OF SANTA CLAUS?

I was hoping he wouldn't be too upset about it, but before I pulled the cards, I heard him huff a laugh and speak.

"A marvelous invention of fantasy and whimsy," he said, "but not at all the truth."

And then the first card I pulled literally had what looked like an exasperated bishop on it. That's the funny thing about Christian spirits: reading tarot with them becomes double the exercise in imagery and thinking outside the box. That bishop was very clearly St. Nicholas representing himself: as someone who isn't thrilled with the idea of Santa Claus and yet unable to do much about it. This was confirmed as he kept speaking, tracking the ground as he walked with the support of his staff.

"Such a tale takes away from the nature of my story, you understand. In fact, it casts the meaning of Christmas off entirely for the sake of a lie. All this focus on gifts, when there's an entirely different gift to celebrate!"

I cocked my head. "But we know Jesus wasn't really born in winter, no?"

St. Nicholas shrugged my question off. "Yes, but this is the day we've designated to celebrate, and so celebrate we do. It isn't time to think about gifts and things, all these things."

Gifts foolishly discarded. Jaded cynicism and disillusionment. Regret, anger, bitterness. The end of a relationship. Loss, sorrow, and grief. Depression. A tendency to focus on negative memories.

Unfounded accusations and rebellion against an unfair situation.

Overall, I got the impression that he's not a fan. He was definitely firm on the gifts thing, which makes sense considering how, as I said, his day in early December is for gifts in many European cultures, not Christmas itself.

"Okay, I get'cha," I said as I wrote. "But what about Krampus? And the Whipping Father, who was that innkeeper in your miracle story? The legends go that you travel around with them and reward good kids while they punish bad ones. What do you think?"

2. WHAT DO YOU THINK ABOUT KRAMPUS?

1. Hopelessness and deceit. Try to rally your strength to overcome adversities that face you.

2. A strong, independent, logical, and calculating woman. Determined in her goals. Perceptive, intelligent, quick witted, with private grief.

By this point, we were in the church, and he had a flat look on his face, like the question was irksome. I also puzzled over the Queen of Swords. It seemed odd to me, given I hadn't asked about anything particularly feminine.

"I brought no innkeeper with me," he said. "I didn't take him from his inn for what he did, no. As for Krampus, that's a separate creature altogether. He's in the dominion of the White Lady."

I was surprised to hear him say "The White Lady," given that it was one of the many titles for Frau Berchta, but as soon as he did, the Queen of Swords made perfect sense. That was what he was saying: he was talking about Krampus in relation to her when he drew those cards. As I noted the connection, St. Nicholas opened the doors to the church and kept talking.

"Krampus isn't an evil creature, per se, but a wild one. That creature isn't my responsibility to look after. Frau Berchta has gone through some strife, all things considered." By this, I assumed he was talking about the stamping out of old Alpine beliefs. "She should have the right to keep her own heart and look after the poor beasts as much as the old souls."

As I wrote, I caught glimpses of our movement with every blink: we were going into the church, where the walls and columns were all marble and gold, the pews a rich, warm-toned wood, the floors covered in red and gold carpets. St. Nicholas, too, was no longer in his white and blue robes, but ones of deep red velvet and gold trim. He went down the aisle and, for the rest of the interview, talked to me from behind a white-clothed altar. It was a small church, empty of iconography or statues, but still beautiful and peaceful inside.

I looked around for a moment, then brought myself back to the conversation at hand. "So do you think Krampus was a god like Frau Berchta?"

Here, he shrugged; he didn't really answer, as if he didn't want to acknowledge one way or another. But St. Nicholas overall gave the sense that Krampus (or a group of them as they're sometimes referred to, the Perchten) are more Frau Berchta's companions, working with her in some way.

"I see," I said, then got back to shuffling the cards. "Now, another interesting thing is your association with Veles. What do you think of Eastern Europe's synchronizing you with him?"

3. THOUGHTS ON BEING SYNCHRONIZED WITH VELES?

Obstacles, problems, and resistance.

A strong, sensual woman. Knows what she wants, but wouldn't hurt anyone to get it. Passionate, creative, generous.

St. Nicholas huffed. "I am not Veles. Simple as that. And I disagree with the idea that I'm comparable to Veles in any way, but what am I to do about people and their stories? All these stories seem to get out of control one way or another. Honestly, if it made people feel better to put me where he once was, and that brought them into their new faith a little more easily, then fine, fine."

I held up a hand. "Ah—but wait, though!"

Then I went flipping into my notes to find what Veles said about St. Nicholas, just because I forgot and was curious. I wanted to share it with St. Nicholas, so I did, letting him read it over my shoulder as I brought my journal over to him. It was then I realized that what Veles once said was actually a similar theme to yet another odd card in the reading: Queen of Wands. Veles said that St. Nicholas and he were both loners, hardworking folk serious about their roles, and ones who couldn't just let broken things lie, even if they went out causing trouble themselves here and there.

All the while, St. Nicholas nodded as he read it with me.

"I could say that's true, yes," he said. "Who can see a mess and leave it? But we're both odd men now, out causing a scene wherever we go. I suppose it's natural people would confuse us, purposely or not."

I leaned over the altar and set my journal down on it. "Fair, yeah. I see the correlation, if you look hard enough. But speaking of gods, I'm curious: how about these gods that became Saints? Like Saint Brigid? She's not a Saint anymore officially, sure, but what do you think?"

4. WHAT DO YOU THINK OF GODS THAT BECAME SAINTS LIKE BRIGID?

Again, St. Nicholas had a flat, almost exasperated face.

"That wouldn't have needed to happen if my fellow Christians knew their place and didn't bludgeon people with God's cross. Of course people won't let go of their gods if you bludgeon them and threaten them. I didn't!"

That is true, yeah. St. Nicholas stuck with God even when he sat in a Roman jail for his faith.

St. Nicholas continued as he smoothed out a wrinkle in the altar cloth. "It's clear these folk did the same, doing what they needed to stand by their gods. I understand. But it's foolish that it ever had to happen. Had the message of love only ever been spread with love, it might've been avoided. At least now, these beings don't need to disguise themselves as Saints anymore."

"Ah, yeah! I agree, definitely," I said. But on the topic of Saints now: what does prayer to you as a Saint? And do how you perform miracles or carry those prayers to God?"

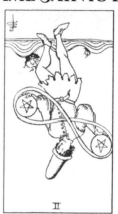

A poor investment, debt, and financial worry.

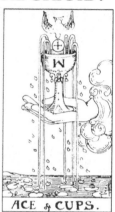

Overflowing love and joy. True contentment and harmony. Bliss, peace, satisfaction, and fertility.

5. HOW DO YOU PERFORM MIRACLES OR CARRY PRAYERS TO GOD?

Irresponsibility with other people's money may lead to debt. Be wary of fraud.

Enlightenment. Acceptance of oneself. Ready for divine scrutiny, sure that one lived a fair life.

A warm smile made his cheeks ball up and his eyes crinkle at the corners. "Ah, miracles," he said. "Many have certainly claimed miraculous power when they've done nothing of the sort. Miracles are power hidden in your soul. And who made your soul? God. You have to be willing to let God guide you to finding and unlocking that power. You have to not just believe, but know that He hears you. All things are possible through Christ, remember.

"Prayer, however, is when you gather the courage to face God. Only then can you understand what God can do through you as one of His divine creations. Understand that magic not of God can only go so far," and by this, I assumed he meant magic from nature or without God's help. "Others with their other gods have outside assistance, too. But it's about asking God to let His design flow through you to affect the world. Our power channels it."

"Oh. Wow. That does explain it, yeah." Though I wouldn't know how much more it could be explained until later. Looking back, this may have been the pre-requisite idea I needed to absorb a bigger idea in connection to myself and my own magic as a Christian Witch later on. At the time, though, I was just trying to integrate this new tidbit with all the other things I (thought I) knew, and so I tucked it in my journal and pressed on. "Though, regarding our power in our souls, there's the topic of relics. It seems people think that the body parts of Saints have power, as well. What do you think of how people treat relics?"

6. THOUGHTS ON HOW PEOPLE TREAT RELICS?

Laziness and a desire for wealth without effort.

A passionate youth with deep insight, but difficult at times. Resolution of concerns. Vigilance against a threat. Use any knowledge available.

St. Nicholas blew out a breath and shook his head "Goodness, listen. We are not our bodies. Our souls are not at home in mummified old bones. They aren't what people think they are. People seek some tangible thing rather than doing the work to let their own power shine through."

In which, I was promptly reminded of All Saints Day—where it was promised once in the Catholic lore that all people would live as Saints after death. All of us, Saints.

"Some of us that you call Saints just so happen to understand this before we die," he said with a shrug. "That's all."

I was a little stunned by that, but hey, damn—I'll take it. There's a lot of possibility in that one idea.

"Okay! Thank you for that," I said as I tried to rub the ache out of my head. Yet again, this was a late night interview, and yet again, the things I was learning were the kinds of things I never would've thought on my own—a sign that, along with the burgeoning headache, meant I truly wasn't alone. It always found a way to surprise me when I realized that. "And what do you think of your feast day?"

7. THOUGHTS ON YOUR FEAST DAY?

St. Nicholas folded his hands on the altar and sighed. "Tradition is lovely, Sara. And I'm glad people have fun on my feast day and follow these old traditions still. But getting old isn't bad, truly! No, no! We create our own traditions as we grow older. The magic remains if you let it." He gestured around at the church. "Today can be just as good a time as yesterday, but you have to acknowledge the differences between the two before you can let go of the past and stop trying to make the present conform to it. Work to mold the future rather than dwell on past ways, with that childlike delight guiding you."

Beware of sentimentalizing the past. Was it really better than now, or were you too young and naïve to see the world for what it really was?

As I scribbled, I nodded. "Ah, okay. I think I see what you mean! So, for our next question: how do you see yourself?"

8. HOW DO YOU SEE YOURSELF?

"Sara, I've seen many a thing in my day. Cruel and terrible things. Now, especially, I see many cruel and terrible things. But it's important to reflect on it. To be that beacon of God's light, rather than contribute to the things that keep making it so dark." He glanced at me, his eyelids drooping as if the whole concept exhausted him. "Hurt as I may be to see this world broken, I am one that wants to see it fixed."

"I hear you, yeah. That's really nice." And in a morbid way, I was glad that the Saints in heaven were just as tired with this nonsense we're all living in as the Saints still on earth. "But how do you want others to see you, especially given this Santa debacle?"

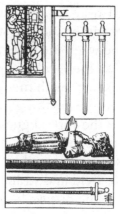 

Meditation, seclusion, recovery. Healing wounds. Contemplation bring peace.

A charming, enigmatic person capable of great disloyalty. Beware of fraud by someone you trust.

9. HOW DO YOU WANT OTHERS TO SEE YOU?

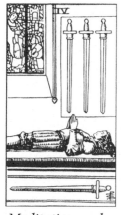 

Meditation, seclusion, recovery. Healing wounds. Contemplation bring peace.

Gifts from the heavens. Good things come to the deserving. Intellect and vision. Dissatisfaction, yearning.

He nodded and sighed.

"I am one that believes rest is important," he said. "There's no use working yourself to the bone for nothing. But rest can't last forever, either. I am one that takes time to see and learn. But even for all the fantasy of this Santa Claus, yes— I am also one who enjoys giving gifts where I can. Gifts of Heaven that God grants me the privilege of gifting, gifts I have the fortune and joy to give. It's good to give, so all have some rather than one having all. You all need to learn this."

Fair. "Agreed, really. And now, with all you've said today, I'm wondering: is there any message you'd like to give? To myself, others?"

10. ANY MESSAGES FOR ME OR OTHERS?

Here, St. Nicholas picked no cards, because he'd already put one vibrant image in my head. We were out of the church and in the moonlight, surrounded by forest, where shadows twisted and curled into shapes unrecognizable.

"Trust your intuition," he said, with a twist of mischief in his small smile. "Trust what you see. The lesser light," the moon, "is still light. Don't wait for perfect light to see. Just see and know your eyes will adjust. People need to believe in God and themselves, if they're to understand their potential."

I nodded as I stared up at that big, bright moon. "Duly noted." Then I clapped my book shut and let out a rush of air, as if the exhaustion of channeling St. Nicholas had all built up at once in my lungs and left.

"Well, that's all the questions I have, so St. Nicholas, a sincere thank you on this feast day! Pleasure to meet you for the first time, and I hope to see you around in the future, too."

With a warm smile and a pat on the back, St. Nicholas faded into the scene he'd brought me to, and then everything melted away to pure darkness. I was left alone there with just a pile of cookies, a cup of cold tea, and a more winter-themed statue of Santa I'd used as a placeholder for St. Nicholas. I was thoroughly rung out, between the novena and the interview and everything else.

As I said: it's nights like these, when I get revelations I simply did not conceive of before, that I know someone else was there with me. Which, for anyone who still has those old Christian hang-ups—that there shouldn't be anything there, and that anything in the house would be a sign of a demon or something of the sort—I guess that can be pretty scary. For me, though, it was fascinating. I took a moment there in front of my makeshift altar, despite how the floor was starting to hurt to sit on, and acknowledged how wild it was to think that I was doing what I thought everyone was once making up, by the vivid and strange stories they told: I was reaching across the veil and into a world completely unlike the one we lived in. I was contacting entities that people could only theorize about—asking questions like *what would this Saint think about this? What would Jesus say about that? What would a demon do if I called one?*—and getting answers so outside of the bounds of my original ideas and conceptions that, after a while, I almost felt like my brain would burst.

It's why I'm at the point I am right now: the point where I feel that the more I learn, the less I know. There's so much to explore, across so many places in the world, that I think I could do this for the rest of my life and still only make it a fraction of the way through all there is to see and learn. The thought of not making it through all these things to see and learn might've made me feel pressured once, but now, I feel like there's all the time in the world. Like I can float on a lazy river through it all, whether I'm stuck in a body or wandering around as a traveling soul. I've got time, and in the meantime, I've got my work cut out for me with answers like the ones St. Nicholas left behind.

MORANA

Among the Slavic gods, specifically in their Slovenian iterations, there's, of course, Kresnik and Vesna: gods of summer and spring, with interesting and silly stories, and with surprisingly mundane hobbies for Divinity (I mean, who's ever heard of a god happy to just sit on a mountain and herd cows instead of bothering with anything else?). Then there's those of winter and all things dark and cold—ones like the Snake King, or Veles, who in Slovenian lore, is father of Vesna and husband of the Dark Queen Mara, Vesna's mother.

Mara is, of course, another name of Morana (along with Morena and Marzanna): a goddess of winter, death, nightmares, and magic, who, over time, has become associated with the nightmare demon, the Mora.

While the Christianization of Slavic tribes caused much of their native myths, customs, and religious rites to be lost to time, some things, especially concerning Morana, survived. In Poland, for instance, the end of winter was symbolized with the burning or drowning of the Marzanna doll: an effigy of the winter goddess, who, upon dying, would return down into the belly of the Slavic underworld Nav while the spring goddess woke and climbed her way back up to earth. Sending Morana down to her death was symbolic of sending winter away. This happens specifically around the Slavic shrovetide festival of Maslenitsa (which, if I had to guess, is named after the amount of butter cakes and other fatty, decadent things people eat, given that the word *maslo* means *butter* in Slovenian and is likely something similar in other Slavic languages).

However, like all gods, Morana has her place, her role, and her function—and it has nothing to do with the contrived ideas of Good and Evil we've all taken up as a modern society. Mischief, yes, and trouble, of course, but not true *evil.* It seems like only recently people have begun to more openly acknowledge the value in darkness and decay, in night and nightmare. And with the first snow of December coming to pass during my list of planned interviews, I knew I had to clear everything aside to make time and space for a conversation the great *Kraljica Zime*—the Queen of Winter.

She was there. She was awake.

So let me show you my encounter with this lovely winter goddess, and the many things she revealed to me.

For Morana, I had the same tea I'd made for St. Nicholas, both because of its red color and its ingredient list having apples, something Morana is fond of. I had an offering for her, as well, as thanks for her coming to speak with me: a fresh apple with buckwheat and millet. Some sources claimed that these were associated with her because she was once a dual goddess, with an end-of-summer or autumn counterpart to represent the end of the sunny seasons before she came fully into her winter aspect. I also wrote her sigil on a piece of paper and set one of her symbols, the raven, in front of it. Then it was a matter of the same old protections, the same old pendulum work, and soon enough, I got a clear answer that Morana was with me, and that she wanted to use M.J. Cullinane's Guardians of the Night tarot—a deck I'd bought specifically for talking with Slavic gods.

"Morana, lady of Winter," I said as I got the cards out of the box, "please come forth! I have for you some tea, an apple, and some millet and buckwheat in exchange for your time. Please, if you'd like to speak, come through and let me see you!"

There's one thing I'll repeat about me and the Slavic gods: they know me, and some part of me knows them. Even though I've heard it said that Morana is a very cold and strict or harsh personality, which I certainly did get as the interview went on, the way she greeted me was the greeting of a mother or aunt who hadn't seen their family member in a long while. She had a beautiful smile, and her voice was clear like crystal wind chimes as she welcomed me into the wintry woods.

We were in a snowy forest with a frozen lake down a snow-covered path. She had a white dress with **red Slavic embroidery** on the sleeves, as well as a big blue-grey fur coat and a **kokoshnik** of the same color on her head, shaped like an arrowhead and dotted with gems. Her hair flowed out from underneath it, dark and shiny, and her eyes were a pinkish color. She had a **small scythe** one would use to harvest herbs.

I could feel that Veles was floating around—I'd caught him in the trees, and he did say hello, but he didn't want to stay and chat—and then Morana led me down that snowy path to the lake, where a big chunk of ice stuck out. Inside was myself, all frozen up.

"Um," I tapped at the ice, concerned, "Morana... why am I looking at a frozen version of myself?"

Morana smiled, even chuckled, as if I were a child doing something silly. She broke the ice with the pommel of her scythe until this other version of me was able to come out, and as the Ice Sara stepped free, Morana then cut at her with the scythe. The Ice Sara didn't die, though; she didn't even bleed. But she—and I—felt lighter as something invisible clinked into the snow and left deep imprints. There were what seemed like chains on the ground, ones the scythe took off with a single swipe.

"You need to break your bonds," she said, even as I stood there staring like a cow stares at people passing by their fields. "You've some habits holding you back, I see."

"Okay." *Goddamn. Right away, we're starting with this?* "Noted. But all that aside, I have a few questions for you here! But to start, Morana: *kako si?* How are you?"

I. KAKO SI, MORANA? HOW ARE YOU?

I always ask this question when I start with the Slavic gods. It's a way to stay conversational and casual with them in our working relationship, which is really more about speaking the Slovenian language and understanding the old Slavic ways than anything, just forging relationships with an old part of the Slavic Divinity and consciousness.

But I pulled the Devil Reversed, which seemed to match Morana's nature from my reading. Sometimes as Morana spoke, I was getting messages in Slovenian rather than English, but of course I'll write them all in English.

"You of the sun," she said, in Slovenian, "you have to learn how to stand in dark times. Don't sleep. Don't stop. Understand winter—that is where I am. Right now, I'm not queen of the corn," or grain in general, from my understanding, "but the queen of Winter, death."

Breaking bonds, freedom, detachment.

I'd have been an idiot not to recognize it: this had something to do with the whole Ice Sara thing, which had my gears turning. She was making a nod to magic; that scythe was full of it. As we left the apparition of myself, we went back up the cliff and into a clearing in the woods, where she perched on a big rock in the middle of the trees, a stone cliff behind her.

At that time, I couldn't understand the point of what she was showing me. Looking back, though, I find the gears in my head turning all over again. Such is the way with Divinity: they love to hand you a briefcase of spiritual goods you didn't realize was a ticking time bomb.

"I... see," I said, still confused as all ever. "Okay! With all this magic I'm seeing here, I'm curious: what kind of magic do you have? What do you do, and teach?"

2. WHAT DO YOU DO OR TEACH WITH YOUR MAGIC?

"Mine is the magic of confusion, Sara," Morana said, with a loose and easy smile. "The magic of endings and death. I am the last sleep. My magic is that which stops the old before the new begins."

The forest blinked away, and suddenly, I was getting flashes of people sleeping and waking up startled. One vision in particular was that of an older woman flying awake from crazy dream, only to see the shadow of Morana outside her window, in the snow. Then we were outside that house, a log cabin tucked into the dark and snowy woods. Morana stood in the candlelight coming from the window, out in the yard before the border of thick trees. She peered into the house with a smile.

Mistrust, insecurity, loss of hope.

I got the sense that this "confusion" was more about the dreams themselves, and testing people through night terrors.

"Alright," I said as I stood with her out there, and with Veles, who lingered by the woods with a bear. It seemed like he was just there to watch. "Moving on, how about your associations with agriculture? That surprised me, all things considered. How do you work in the harvest time?"

3. HOW DO YOU WORK WITH AGRICULTURE AND THE HARVEST?

Bad news, wasteful-ness, preoccupation with projects at the expense of other pri-orities. Opportunity and benefitting from a realistic approach.

"From death, life occurs," Morana said, though she never once looked away from that house. "The plants die, corn becomes straw, and so you are fed. In-dustry—you must work to gather the spoils death leaves behind. All things die so that more may yet live. Hence my tie with agriculture." Finally, she turned to me. "I oversee the end of the life of those plants you cared for to bring you your winter food."

So kind of like her providing for her people before the deep dark, then. That was an interesting way of thinking about winter gods, definitely.

"I get'cha; that makes a lot of sense!" I stood there with her, ankle deep in the snow, writing away like the little journalist for the gods I'd somehow become. "And now, the Marzanna effigy drowning... what do you think of that?"

4. THOUGHTS ON DROWNING THE MARZANNA DOLL?

I really thought she would say she didn't like it, be-cause I mean, the people are drowning her in the spring! But Morana quickly taught me not to expect things and to just let what happened, happen, because she pulled my favorite card.

Planting seeds for goals that bloom over time. Small, inten-tional acts. Bringing good to the world.

"I already said: death brings life," Morana explained. With my 'death,' accord-ing to you folk, so comes new life: my daughter comes up from Nav to fill my shoes until I come to reap that which she's sown. Seeds of a ripened fruit are mine to deliver, and Vesna's to plant and sprout. I am not upset with this festi-val, this effigy drowning."

"Oh, okay." It reminded me of what the Morrígan said: about how death was more just a good, clean rest and reset for the gods. "I understand. That's kinda cool, actually. But okay, okay—what about Winter should people appreciate?"

5. WHAT SHOULD PEOPLE APPRECIATE ABOUT WINTER?

Feeling powerless or trapped. Limbo, being unable to move. Op-portunities slipping. Regain inner wisdom and gain a different perspective.

Here, I felt the Morana people talked about in the sources I'd read: the harsh and stony woman, the fed up matron.

"Obsessed, you all are, with your work, your own power." Her face was twisted in disgust as she looked down at me, her brows all furrowed and crinkled in between. "There are times to make action, and there are times to make plans. My domain is one of prophecy. Yes, sleep, dream—let me speak in a time where your minds are not racing to the next thing like a fool.

"You can't take action that does you any good if you never stop to plan. This is a time of endings, reflection, the death of the land and of merciless industry. Be with loved ones. Rejoice in what's survived. Count the stars, stay warm inside. Obey the natural order."

I blinked at her. If only I could've gotten a written slip from her to give to my boss at the time, to tell him I was taking every winter off to sleep. God knows we all like to stay in a warm bed when it's cold as all ever during the winter; maybe this is a part of the reason why. Maybe there's something good about *obeying the natural order,* as Morana put it: respecting the rhythms of nature, because we're a part of nature, too.

"Speaking of sleep," I said as I shoved those thoughts into the Think Bank for later, "how about this nightmare demon I've read about? Some say you're connected to it. If you are, how so? I know you mentioned night terrors, but this is a whole separate creature here."

6. ARE YOU CONNECTED TO THE NOČNA MORA? IF SO, HOW?

I did not expect the Three of Cups. It's a card of celebration and joy, like lottery-winning luck and partying. How did that have anything to do with what I asked? I was about to ask her for clarification when she just dove in, coaxing my eyes shut so I could look at her clearly in meditation.

"*Jaz sem kraljica,*" she said. "I am a queen. Nightmares (*nočne more*) are my people." She made it clear dreams were her domain, including nightmares. "The wood is deep. The nights are long. Those who know how to spot warnings will heed them. When dreams don't work, nightmares do. Terror motivates."

Maybe that's what there was to celebrate: the fact that, after so many attempts at reaching people, something finally worked—something brutal and gripping like a nightmare.

"Got'cha. Seems like dreams are your main mode of communication then. Okay!" I tossed my pencil down and snatched up my cards. "Now, with Veles—how do you two work together in winter?"

Sharing a time of great joy. Working towards common goals to be a success. Joining forces with those one enjoys.

7. HOW DO YOU AND VELES WORK IN WINTER?

Clarity to see an obstacle forming, wit to plan for a challenge. Use logic to find answers. Situations will benefit from honesty. Be careful of illusions that mask themselves as answers.

At this point, we were off and away back to that rock in the middle of the snowy forest. She sat there with Veles behind her, who she had a big smile for.

"We test you humans," she said. "You grow too bold; where you step, there is no certain safety every time. Illusion and magic, confusion and trickery—can you see through it in the dark night? Your precious fire often only blinds you further. What is true? What is real? What is not? You cannot know in your arrogance. Only in fear and uncertainty can you test the world around you."

"Ah, fair. That makes sense, especially for Veles being god of mischief and magic, too." I sipped my then-cold tea and waved a hand as if that would help me better collect my thoughts. "But now, what's something people frequently get wrong about you?"

8. WHAT DO PEOPLE GET WRONG ABOUT YOU?

She sighed here, the way an old-fashioned mother sighs when her child falls and cracks their head instead of helping them up and coddling them.

"I am not here to ruin you. Through these tests, you prove capable of bringing the world through another cycle again. You survive the dark, the cold, and you are rewarded with my daughter's thaw. You cannot survive if you're stupid. May we gods of mischief and death teach you cleverness and self-preservation."

See what I mean? Death gods, mischief gods, winter gods—they're not evil. Just unorthodox in how they teach. "Understandable," I muttered, that thought making me smile. "That being said, how do you want others to see you, then?"

PAGE of PENTACLES.

Wealth of assets, generating abundance. Use setbacks to prove yourself.

9. HOW SHOULD PEOPLE SEE YOU?

QUEEN of CUPS.

Dishonor, mistrust, and being too preoccupied with the problems of others to address one's own concerns.

"*Nisem tvoje matere,*" she said. "I am not your mother. Don't ask me about matters of the heart. I am not the shoulder to cry on. I am not the doting one. My time is time to rest one's body, not one's resolve."

I definitely got the sense here that she's not the one to deal with people's feelings well. She's about steeling you through hardship and sharpening your wits. Not a goddess to go to if you want comfort, that's for sure.

"And how do you see yourself?"

10. HOW DO YOU SEE YOURSELF?

How interesting that she pulled the same card as she did for herself and Veles. I almost wondered if I got the wrong card before she started talking.

"Like how others should see me, I am one not of comfort, but logic. There is, and there isn't. Sentimental ideas lead to foolishness and death. Survival requires a bit of coldness. I bring that cold." Then she pointed that icy stare on me. "You of the sun—you must learn what it is to be cold to circumstance. To not take things so personally and see the utility in all around."

Now, here, I meant to interject and say that I thought myself plenty cold when the circumstances ask for it, but she got me with the taking things personally. In true Virgo fashion, I criticize myself enough that when others criticize me, it's annoying as hell, because chances are I've already beat myself up in some way around the topic already. But that's no good, and I know and acknowledge that, even if I don't want to: other people can see what your own blind spots can't.

"Got'cha," I said instead, aware that I didn't have the right to say anything else. "And now, Morana, do you have any final messages for myself or others?"

ACE of SWORDS.

Clarity to see an obstacle forming, wit to plan for a challenge. Situations benefit from honesty. Be careful of illusions that look like answers.

11. ANY LAST MESSAGES FOR ME OR OTHERS?

Taking a bold move or risk. Now is not the time to fall back on the tried and true; be original, claim personal power. Resist urge to second guess yourself. Challenge the status quo.

"Yes. Rest challenges the status quo, understand. Wisdom challenges the status quo." She was making a sharp point about the tarot booklet's word choice, which I found fascinating. "Release your fear of the future. Focus on surviving the here and now. It is time to endure. It is time to be bold and acknowledge your needs. Else you will not see spring."

"I hear you. That is something to keep in mind, yeah." Especially for my fellow workaholics out there. "Thank you, Morana; it was lovely to meet you for the first time and talk to you! Like Veles, and your daughter and son in law and granddaughter, you are welcome here anytime. Goodbye for now!"

I left her there in the snow, waving goodbye as she faded into the woods and into the dark. Then I got up and tossed her offerings out to the yew tree in my yard. Given I was constantly getting up to tend my sourdough-loaf-to-be during my conversation with Morana, I also gave her a piece of that bread fresh from the oven the next day, too, and that was gone even faster than the apple. So I guess she wasn't displeased with me throughout that whole thing.

But that phrase, *you of the sun,* it haunted me, mostly because I couldn't make heads or tails of it. It wasn't until much later—and by that I mean the moment I looked back over this interview and remembered what I went through—that I came to understand what Morana was talking about. And frankly, I don't know why people who are interested in chthonic and infernal energies don't work with a goddess like Morana, because she is exactly the kind of stern, chaotic, and chillingly indifferent queen full of harsh lessons that, in my experience, is the cornerstone of demonolatry.

You of the sun—I, of God's energy—*learn to be cold to circumstance*—learn to sit in that endlessly deep, dark, and unlimited infernal energy. To understand it, inside and out, and align myself with it *without* forgetting its inverse. To accept when things need to be how they are and avoid sticking my hands in what isn't my business, and to accept when it's time to get to work and change them. Whether God or Lucifer, Summer or Winter, Sun or Moon—all of these opposites, these binaries, are simply two pieces of a larger whole that function together, in one system. To fall too far into any one side of the binary is to see the world, both material and spiritual, from a skewed lens.

My last name, Raztresen, means *scattered.* This can mean anything from *scatterbrained* in a more slang sense to *scattered* in terms of, say, scattered ashes, or people scattered all over the world. It makes me think of how many times that word, *scattered,* shows up in the Bible—and usually not in good terms, especially in the Old Testament. But in the New Testament, it's the Apostles who are scattered, be it just to spread the gospel or because of Roman persecution or anything else. They're out there scattering themselves, for the sake of God, rather than because of something they did that pissed God off and caused Him to have to scoop everyone back together later on in the prophecies.

Sun and Moon together make eclipse, make twilight. And just as the Seventy Apostles did, I, too, am learning how to scatter myself all over the world, the one seen and the one unseen, as the many missionaries of old did. Unlike them, though, I'm not going off to preach in the places I visit, but to listen. I'm not going out to tear down the cloak of darkness, but to wear it alongside the cloak of light. I am learning, with each and every encounter with the world outside this one, to become a being of contradictions: one who can hold two conflicting ideas at the same time and still live in harmony.

In short, *postajam Somraknega. Postajam Raztresnega.*

I'm becoming the Twilight One. I'm becoming the Scattered One.

And the path forward is thin as a knife's edge, easy to slip off of into one side or another of the dualities I'm told to hold and therefore easy to fall victim to. I can't say I recommend this path, nor that I'm thrilled to walk it myself. But I will say that it's a path that won't stop calling until it gets the magical practitioner to take a step forward—and with just one step, the practitioner is cemented in, unable to go back to a world where Black and White are two separate colors. Forever stuck in a palette of only grays, forever watching the sunset and the sunrise while never seeing high noon or midnight.

But if God is all things, light and dark, good and bad, loving and wrathful, then it only follows that I, as a being made in His image, would have to learn how to hold that capacity for contradiction, too—learn, or else give up ever trying to understand Him, which would mean that all this meditating and interviewing and learning is just tourism, with no aim or purpose other than memories and good campfire stories. God did make me a writer, after all: who's to say all this isn't just idea farming for story ideas, instead of actually being a way for a human being like myself to get closer to God?

And who's to say that, for *Raztresnega*, this wild adventure can't be both at once: a layered, complex story unfolding in the realm of fantasy, and a deep, unbending connection to God forging in the realm of reality?

It's one of the only ways a path like this can stay any fun.

FRAU BERCHTA

If your house isn't clean, the Winter Witch of the Alps will come slit your belly wide open and stuff it with stones and straw—allegedly.

All throughout Austria, a good chunk of Germany, and even edging into what is modern day Slovenia, there's a well known name that comes up near every Christmas season: the name of Perchta, *Frau* Perchta, and her Perchten, or more specifically, Krampus. For Slovenians, this fearsome figure is known as Pehta Baba—an old witch who eats children, yet can help and heal people with her herbalism, too, as she does in the film *Kekec*. There, this witchy figure Pehta heals Kekec's blind friend Mojca with a potion of healing herbs. This makes me think that some aspects of her were synchronized with Baba Yaga, who has similar stories of helping people who were worthy and eating ones who weren't. However, her name was originally more something like Frau *Berchta*, and she was far from an evil witch of winter coming around to terrorize people for having dust in their home.

Like her northern counterpart, Frau Holle, Frau Berchta is a Germanic goddess very near and dear to people, even with the advent of Christianity. Her function is that of a psychopomp, in which she takes souls of the dead to the afterlife—specifically the souls of children, who follow her about and become her *Heimchen*. In Christian thought, unbaptized babies were taken by Frau Berchta, who would lead them through the forest and keep them safe as she brought them to her lands across the veil. The Catholic church, in an effort to stamp out the veneration and cultural love of Frau Berchta, then created these wicked rumors about her being an evil witch who slit the bellies of those with dirty houses and who went around with the demon Krampus and other such monsters terrorizing people around Christmas. All this was done to demonize her and scare people away from her.

In reality, she's a maternal goddess who watches over the wild things and, in her folklore, is a wise and strict deity, one who punishes those with too much audacity and rewards them when they learn—like the story of the girl who went to spy on her party with the Heimchen because she didn't believe it was real, and whose sight was taken from her until she realized the error of her faithless ways. She was shown mercy after she regretted her lack of faith, and Frau Berchta restored her sight.

As a Slovenian, the concept of Frau Berchta interested me, and I was also burning to know: what did she think of us Slovenes, who also came to love her due to their close proximity with Austrian people in the Austrian empire? What did she think of us, aliens in a continent we'd just settled in, and bringing into their lands gods that paralleled her and Frau Holle, like Morana? I was curious, endlessly so, and so thanks to @feral_southern_housewife (Mimi) and @hexmarie (Brittany), I was able to find the resources and tools to try and contact this ancient goddess. Let me show you how it went.

For Frau Berchta, I set my table with the goods I was suggested: elderberry, salt, and jasmine flowers to dress two candles, a few pine cones as a gesture towards the forest, and some sour cherry liquor. Cherries, I was told, were one of the fruits associated with her. I also set out onyx and moonstone for a nod to her role as a psychopomp and the nature of death, as well as an apple and chocolate for the Heimchen; given that they're the souls of children, I figured sweets like this would be well received. So once the prayers were done and everything was set up right, my space cleansed with a good dusting of rosemary smoke, I was ready to sit down and talk with Frau Berchta.

"Frau Berchta, *willkommen in meinem Heim!*" God knows I couldn't resist the urge to bust out some bungled German. "I hope you're doing well. I have some offerings for you. Please come forth and let me feel your presence!"

Now, here's where I should say that a key discernment tip that you're dealing with an entity and not just your imagination is if your preconceived notions of them suddenly change. What I mean by that is that, if you'd been thinking of them beforehand, and they looked one way in your mind, you may find that they looked different when they came through at your actual sit-down ritual. Such a thing happened here: I was imagining something more like what I'd created in my book, *The Glass Witch*. The main character there is a woman dressed in black with white hair and deathly pale skin.

What I actually saw was a woman with golden hair tied up in hoop-like braids on either side of her head, as well as a crown of twigs and bramble that soon flourished into a crown of holly. Her dress was white and delicate, and her bright, icy eyes were sharp, but not mean. We were in a forest much like the one I'd seen with Archangel Azrael, and in this snowy clearing, we rested to talk. With her were a bunch of little children, all running about as if they were kids at recess. As nice as it was to watch them have fun, though, it was bittersweet, knowing that these were children who'd passed.

I confirmed Frau Berchta wanted to use Thread's of Fate's Weaver Tarot, and then we were ready.

"Alright, to get us started, Frau Berchta, I am very curious about something: you've become a part of the lore of my people, the Carantanians, now known as the Slovenians. I was curious about how you felt about them when they moved into this land between the 3rd and 5th century?"

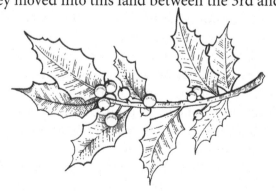

1. WHAT DID YOU THINK OF THE SLAVS WHEN THEY CAME TO EUROPE?

A need for structure. Progress through consistent focus and work; Keep showing up for your dream and build it brick by brick.

A scarcity mindset stops us from receiving. Losing connection when hyperfocused on money. Acknowledge abundance in your life.

Raw energy to inspired action. Take ideas seriously. Doing the less fun work to ensure success.

Frau Berchta considered me with those sharp blue eyes. "They were interesting people," she said. "Industrious folk, but so ready to take things for their own gain. It wasn't easy at first to deal with them, no. But they learned. And they did well for themselves, very well. There is such a thing as working too hard, grasping for too much. It's not the thing to do in a new land. But yes, they learned."

It took a second for that to sink in, but when it did, I shrugged. "Yeah, that sounds fair, if I know my people."

They were, in fact, quite the hardworking folks. Ones who came looking for more than they had in the east. But they were mellow, too, and maybe that's what Frau Berchta meant: the way Slovenians became peace-loving folks who would rather crack a beer than a skull.

"Speaking of learning, though," I continued, "I mean—with the Slavic people came the Slavic gods. And as a result, I see that a lot of people compare you to Morana. What do you think about this?"

2. THOUGHTS ON YOUR COMPARISON TO MORANA?

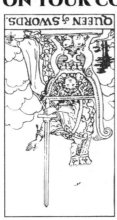

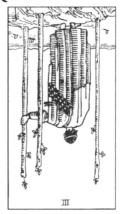

A collaboration. People with different expertise. Getting things done and make a great impact.

Being too harsh. Getting frustrated by others' emotions sliding into coldness and judging others.

Stuck in self judgement. One can't expect perfection and constantly be trying to fix things.

Setbacks, not accomplishing all that we want to. No time is wasted. Prepare for changes.

Stagnancy. Unable to bring life through. Don't focus on what's not done; create space for self love.

She had a lot to say here. This was the biggest answer, five cards. I stretched my wrists, because between the amount cards and the deck itself, I knew I'd be writing for a hot minute.

"She's a tough woman, Morana," Frau Berchta said. "Cold and uninterested in the feelings of others. I like that. Neither of us are interested in quailing types," she said with a smile, her lips peeling apart to show her white teeth, "but sometimes I think she could benefit from a lighter touch. Nonetheless, we are different. When people tie us together, it tugs us away from our respective domains and creates a mess for us both. I care nothing for causing nightmares. She cares nothing for delivering children. Just because we appear in the same seasons, doesn't mean we stand in the same role. We are who we are, and maybe our spheres of influence collide, but that's it."

"Ah, yeah. Good point." The silence stretched as I struggled to write all this down fast enough. Eventually, though, I got it all recorded, and I closed my eyes to join her back in that forest full of children. "Morana's certainly an interesting one. But one thing that ties you two together is the association with the goose. What does this animal mean to you?"

3. WHAT DOES THE GOOSE MEAN TO YOU?

1. Too passive or confrontational; neither are fitting. To earn respect, one must give it. Unplug and remind yourself of past successes.

2. Enduring challenges but achieving great success. Meet new challenges with courage. There are patterns at play. Tend your wounds.

Frau Berchta huffed a short laugh. "The goose. It's a plump animal. Silly, mischievous at times, yes. But it's also an animal of great courage and love for its flock." Her eyes twinkled as she watched the Heimchen. "Yes, the goose is a good mother. Not perfect by any means, but true. It tries hard for its own and its flock community; it cares for a community and raises a child with joy."

"I can understand that," I said. We watched the kids for a moment. "Okay! Well, while we're on the topic of associations, there's been some discourse about Krampus, and I have to know: who is Krampus to you? What is he?"

4. WHAT IS KRAMPUS TO YOU?

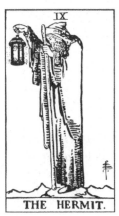

A period of necessary solitude. Surrender and trust it's in your best interest. When we're alone, we see aspects we've repressed. Accumulating wisdom, traversing the unknown, being in nature, tranquility.

I won't lie: I really didn't expect to pull the Hermit here.

Frau Berchta sighed. "Krampus is the wild one. He doesn't like people much and prefers to stay away, but he is the heartbeat of the forest, the quiet of the world. He won't easily come out."

And in fact, I think she brought Krampus out, because between the trees were two large eyes watching us, and then a big goat-like thing covered in reddish black fur. He had big antlers, big hooves, and a long tail, but he wasn't aggressive or mean. Another image of him in the forest with a goat head and a little violin-like instrument appeared in my mind, too, with the goat-man bounding away at the first sign of a disturbance in the forest.

"He's not interested in human nonsense," Frau Berchta explained as she stood by him. "He might eat children if they get too close, but generally he minds himself."

"Is he like the Slavic Leshy, you think? The forest guardians?"

"Mmm, no." Frau Berchta and I both watched Krampus hop away, deep into the woods. "He's less the guardian of the forest and more just the forest. The soul of the wood itself."

"Oh, I understand. How cool!" Never did I think about it that way, but maybe that's where the idea of Krampus eating children comes from: the way they get "swallowed up" by the forest, so to speak. I thought about that a second longer before I shook the thought loose and kept on. "Though, that brings me to our next question: you became associated with Krampus, and changed into Frau Perchta, or Pehta Baba, thanks to the church's meddling and demonization of you. What do you think of this association—and all the belly slitting and hay stuffing and children snatching?"

5. THOUGHTS ON THE FRAU PERCHTA / PEHTA BABA IMAGE?

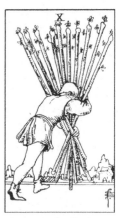

An enduring, wise woman. Will always say what you need to hear, not what you want. More plugged in mentally. Can help solve problems, but they won't be soft. Truth above all.

Energy to action. It's time to do the boring things associated with success that people don't want to do. Deadlines, plans, taking goals seriously.

A new beginning in the material realm. Opportunities must be nurtured. A great sign, but you still need to show up and do the work. Be open to many opportunities.

A period of temporary burden. Time to maximize output, or to delegate tasks so you can focus. Awareness of what new responsibilities that success brings with it. Push through it.

Frau Berchta once again had a lot to say. She curled her fists up and ground her teeth, her gaze looking somewhere far away, and then she turned to me with a steely glint in her eye.

"There is utility in these images," she admitted. "They kept me alive in the minds of others. But I'm glad to be moving past this era now, too. I can be left in peace again, with people knowing my true nature and what I do. It was grossly disrespectful still, to be treated that way after all I'd done for these people. But I know who I am. I know my role. I've performed it all the while, and I always will. I've worked no matter the circumstances, but it's time to return to the truth now."

Nodding furiously, I said, "Absolutely. As you should! You strike me as a wonderful force. Which is what fascinates me, honestly, because at one point, you *did* exist in the Christian psyche as a positive force. Can you speak more on what that was like?"

6. WHAT WAS IT LIKE TO WORK WITH CHRISTIANS EARLY ON?

The universe is full of potential. Don't fight it. If facing challenges, trust that they are or will be over in your favor. Expansion.

Rejecting opportunities. A "woe is me" attitude. Judging things before giving them a chance. Retreating out of fear.

Being overwhelmed and confused. Your current thinking won't bring answers. Reconnect to your intuition.

That steeliness stayed in her stare. "I seized the opportunity to stay. I stayed with the people as long as I could, and I remained even in the mess that church did. Fear. Fear, they use it to hold a vice grip on people, more concerned with their gold and their jewels and their power than anything—than even their own God!"

The rage. Maybe I should've expected it, but that steel was something I could taste in the air; it was the tang of blood, the ringing of swords and the rust, the *decay* of once strong foundations. There was a wound in the tapestry of Divinity, and Frau Berchta was determined to speak on it.

"Look what it's done," she snapped. "The people now, their intuition is ruined. What they once knew, they no longer understand. Their unease comes from uncertainty bred by that church! Even as the people turned to this new God, I reminded them of my works and my care. But that wasn't enough for the church. It's never enough. It's made slaves of its so-called people."

"I hear you. You've got every right to be angry." I held up my hands as if that could appease the goddess; it took a moment of silence before this wave of rage passed and Frau Berchta sighed once more. Then she rejoined me on the log we sat on in this clearing and watched the children with a faraway stare. I picked up my cards and whispered, "But as we start closing this out, I think we can move on to a little soft finish: I understand a clean house is important to you. What about it do you value?"

7. WHAT DO YOU VALUE ABOUT A CLEAN HOUSE?

New beginning with all things material. Great news. A new prosperity. Manifesting wealth internally. Be diligent to reach your dreams.

Exhaustion after conflict. Tension so draining that it offers perspective. Maybe what we're pushing for doesn't matter as much. Finding solutions and pushing aside ego.

A lot of energy and passion but lacking direction or an outlet. You need a healthy outlet, or the mind becomes chaos. Thriving on building new things.

She shrugged. "Everything that happens outside the house, it lingers and snags on things like this silly tinsel you've put on your tree here."

My lips twisted to keep from scowling. I like tinsel on my Christmas tree.

"It snags all the tension from outside your house and puts it everywhere," she continued, "until no place remains as a solace for you. You must keep a clean house to keep a clean mind, or you'll wallow in your own misery, unable to escape. The house is your refuge, your fortress. Let nothing from the outside world, no mayhem, leak into it."

"Got it! Agreed, especially about the refuge idea. Alright, onto the next: how do you see yourself?"

8. HOW DO YOU SEE YOURSELF?

There was a somber note here. "I have borne so much," she said. "Disrespect, slander, and total failure of the people to remember me as I am. Yet I've pushed on, knowing this era would not last. Finally, it's ending."

"...And how would you like to be seen?"

A period of temporary burden. Time to maximize output, or to delegate tasks so you can focus. Awareness of what new responsibilities that success brings with it. Push through it.

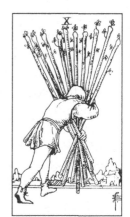

9. HOW DO YOU WANT TO BE SEEN?

A few options are available, and you're centering yourself to make the best choice. Think of sustainable options long term.

She turned to me and speared me with those bright eyes. "I am not only one thing. I am not only a protector of children or one who wants the house clean. I can be many things, of light and dark, and I want people to be honest with me about how they see me in their lives and practice.

"I am not here to be constrained to any one idea. I will help people the way I help, but they must understand not to expect me to align to their ideas."

There was no arguing with that. "Fair," I said. "And now, do you have anything to say as a general message?"

10. ANY FINAL MESSAGES FOR ME OR OTHERS?

"Feelings are not fact," she said, stoic as all ever, her chin tipping high. "Things that hurt you, you can't keep letting hurt you, especially after the issue is resolved. Like a frostbitten finger, let it fall away. Move on."

"Understood," I said as I snapped my journal shut. "Alright, well, that's that! Frau Berchta, thank you so much for coming to speak with me; I really appreciate you taking the time to do so. For now, we'll call this interview finished!"

Frau Berchta nodded, smiled, then slipped off the log and drifted towards the woods. Her Heimchen immediately followed behind her, following her like children would their own mother, and she took the littlest one by the hand as they marched on into the dark forest. Then the white snow became black shadow, and there were no children, no trees, no nothing. There was only me, sitting there with my eyes shut.

What an interview. I hauled myself up from that table and knew without a shadow of a doubt that I'd have a good night's sleep, what with the way I was suddenly aware of how my eyes burned. But as I got ready for bed, all I could think about was Frau Berchta as she poured out her frustration from centuries of twisted stories and slander—and the wildness, the animal-like innocence, that I simply did not expect from a figure as renowned as Krampus.

Not processing pain in a healthy way. Struggling to move on from the past. You may need to push a bit to move forward. May also be creating a lot of pain with negative self talk.

It's figures like him, with all their danger apparent and yet not so scary, that make me question ideas of good and evil more than I already do. I mean, really, do we call the wolf evil for needing to eat? I suppose I can't say *no*; there are plenty tales, especially German ones like Little Red Riding Hood, that would suggest that the wolves are considered pretty nefarious, too, even though all they're doing is snapping up a snack that some poor human parents left unattended. Rather than fear, mistrust, and stories painting these creatures as something wicked, though, the truth is that these are beings to be respected and cautious with.

But explain that to a child, and they'll get curious. They'll want to say hello to the thing they're supposed to respect, not keep a healthy distance from it. So fear and horror it is, until they can learn a touch more nuance. Rarely does the lesson ever get to the nuance part, though; fear is something too visceral to let go of. With Krampus, and with Frau Berchta, too, it's the fear of death and horror and punishment that stays fresh in people's minds, striking them like lightning. The stories of Frau Berchta's goodness, or of whatever Krampus was before Christianity's demonization of him?

No. Of course those wouldn't stay in popular psyche.

This brings me back to the reason I started this series: to get the truth of how these ancient spirits and pieces of Divinity thought about *themselves*. Not what the church said, or what a few old folks said, or what warped stories and legends re-written by people from a completely separate religion and culture said, but what *they* said. The gods have their own ideas about who they are and what they're meant to do, and every time I listen, I find myself just feeling sad that people will hear everyone talk about them *except* them.

It's frustrating. Endlessly so. But all we can do, especially as witches, is keep building our skills—our divinatory skills, our clairaudience and claircognizance and so on. All we can do is keep researching, cross-referencing personal gnosis with what tattered scraps are left behind from days long gone, and then hope we can find a rope leading us back to the source of these stories, these ideas. It's a long road, but it's one that I think is well worth walking—so I'll keep walking, until I'm called to stop.

ARCHANGEL URIEL

The last archangel of the cardinal directions in magical philosophy, Uriel, was bound to come up sometime. After all, we'd already spoken to Michael, Gabriel, and Raphael.

The reason this angel ended up here during the month of December was simple: he's the angel not only associated with a cardinal direction (north) according to Damien Echols, but also an angel associated with the element of earth and the season of winter. As such, I figured it'd make sense to reach out and ask him a little bit about some things: himself, his story, winter in general, all of it. In the Bible, he's also a bit underrated—mostly because he mainly only shows up the Book of Ezra and in the Book of Enoch (sometimes under the name Phanuel, which many insist is also Uriel).

In the Book of Enoch, Uriel, whose name means "God is my Flame" or "Fire of God," is the one that warns Noah about the upcoming flood and stands alongside the other three angels (Michael, Gabriel, and Raphael). In the Book of Ezra, Uriel answers the prophet Ezra's questions about why evil exists in the world by essentially saying, "your human brain is too tiny to understand it, so don't worry about it." Which is... interesting. But Uriel is still considered an angel of wisdom, one who can help people find new insights, ideas, and clarity on situations and act with grace.

I'd also been listening to my boyfriend tell me about a story he was reading, *Omniscient Reader's Point of View*, where Uriel was described as the "Demon-Like Judge of Fire." The idea that an angel was at all "demon-like" was something I could talk about that forever; most don't realize angels can appear as monsters and demons just as much as the "devil" can come as an "angel of light" according to St. Paul in 2 Corinthians 11:14.

By this point in my journey, though, talking to angels wasn't anything too serious. It wasn't something I needed to do an insane amount of research on, or get any specific tools or gifts or offerings for; angels became the "easier" interviews, not by way of the experience itself, but just by virtue of the fact that I only needed to slap down a sigil and a couple crystals and be on my way. So really, it was coming up with the questions here that was the bigger deal, as well as going through with the interview in the first place, and I made sure to do both with the theme of Winter in mind.

Let's take a look.

As I said: angels are easy. They don't eat; they don't drink. They just want to talk. So I set up Uriel's sigil from Damien Echols' book, along with my ladybug rosary (for the red beads) and my prosperity wand for his associations with money and wealth. I had my moss agate there for the same reason, some obsidian to suggest winter and darkness, and two winter bells: one red, one green, as he's depicted in both colors depending on who you ask. Lastly, a good Woodwick candle always adds to that wintertime feel, and on top of a snowflake tablecloth, I say we were pretty solid in the Uriel-Winter-Money-Wisdom department.

"Uriel, hello! Please come by and speak with me tonight! I've got some questions I'd really like to ask you."

By this point, I'd long since stopped using so much mugwort for extra psychic enhancement. It really was as simple as saying the Lord's Prayer, maybe a prayer to an angel or Saint if that was who was on the roster, and then just jumping on in there. I didn't need the mugwort anymore; I just needed to know what tarot deck they wanted to use when I got the images in my head to let me know they'd arrived, and for Uriel, the deck of choice was Amrit Brar's Marigold Tarot.

Most interesting to me as I talked to Uriel was the fact that we were out in a snowy field, with a town just a couple miles off in the distance. It felt almost Christmassy, and I guess that thought bled onto Uriel a little bit, because he appeared looking something like Raphael, but without all the Uncanny Valley element; his face was like a Renaissance painting, not a Byzantine one, and his eyes were as soft as the little smile on his lips.

He had a deep green robe on with a gold edge, and in his curly brown hair was a golden ribbon. For a moment, he had a little crown of pine branches on, but that soon disappeared once I stopped thinking about Christmas, so that was likely my own subconscious dropping that on him. He didn't seem to mind, though; he was willing to appear any way I wanted to see him—either as a man or a woman with longer hair that the golden ribbon wove through—but eventually he settled on a man's image. His wings weren't quite made of feathers so much as they were white and gold light, and he had eyes like garnets and a big wooden staff with a fiery red gem in it.

"Thank you for being here, Uriel! First, I'm curious: Damien Echols mentions you're good with helping with divination." I cocked my head as I stared at him, because even for all my work as a Christian Witch, the idea that there was an angel that helped with *divination* still threw me for a loop. "What do you think about divination, given how Christians fear it?"

1. WHAT DO YOU THINK ABOUT DIVINATION?

I wasn't expecting a curled lip from Uriel, but he had a sour face as he explained his cards.

"Fate is not binding," he said. "At any moment, it can change—be it by God's will or our own. Our actions impact the cosmos as much as the cosmos impact us.

"People look for a reason to be helpless. They obsess over things without doing anything about the situations they inquire about. Divination is for advice. It's to help you move forward. It's not to help you stay stuck."

"Ooh. I hear you, yeah. That being said, though, when it comes to communicating with angels through divination, I notice a lot of people say that angels don't do that and that anyone who works with them are actually talking to demons." I kicked at the snow and chewed on my question before I spit it out: "What do you think, Uriel? How do people know they're talking to an angel?"

Bad news, powerlessness, loneliness, self sabotage. Negative words, attempted healing.

Naïveté, disharmony, and holding onto the past in an unhealthy way.

2. HOW DO PEOPLE KNOW THEY'RE TALKING TO AN ANGEL?

New beginnings, spontaneity, change, innocence. Most significant journeys are mental, not physical.

Overextending oneself and one's resources and avoiding responsibility.

As always, it's not an angel if it isn't trolling the hell out of you. During our time together up to this point, Uriel kept mirroring the things I was doing physically, like resting my jaw on my knuckle or crossing my arms. I asked about it, and he only gave me this big smile. But when I asked to see his true form, it was more than I'd bargained for. Almost *infernal.*

We were suddenly sucked out of the snow and into a cave of some sort, all red and black and pulsing as if alive. It was an endless drop; we were hovering above a well of shadows. Uriel hung there in red and black armor, as if it were made of garnet and obsidian, and his staff was a mighty blazing spear. Around him were creatures like goblins, clawing and snarling and trying to get at him as if to knock him out of the air.

But then there was light. He was shining so brightly in the middle of all that spooky stuff, blinding and burning whatever little creatures were reaching up for him. I just let him do what he needed to do, and eventually he revealed himself fully: as a warrior who set the whole world on fire and burned away the weird goblin things, which I think were coming from my own doubts and insecurities. Demons, you know? Little rank-and-file creatures, nothing too difficult to deal with—especially not for an angel of Uriel's caliber.

Then we were back out in the snow, and he was waving for me to join him in this little yurt thing that seemed to have just sprouted up from nowhere.

"There is an element of trust," he said as I came over to the yurt. He sat down at a simple wooden table and motioned for me to sit with him. "There's a reason we see angels so often with children. The fear to see what doesn't match expectations is real."

Yeah, it sure is, because I questioned him for the sake of settling the issue and immediately got flooded with the Spooky Infernal-Looking Backdrop so he could make a point.

Uriel continued as I sat with him, sheltered from the snow and the outdoors. "Children know because they know." He rested his chin on his interlaced fingers, his robes a bright green, his eyes sparkling that deep red as he smiled. "They stop burdening themselves with what should and shouldn't be and let us work. Those who are curious and ready to acknowledge other possibilities will be able to best perceive us—unscripted, un-doctored."

"Fair enough." It took me a second to get my bearings; I was still seeing goblins getting toasted like marshmallows when I let my mind wander. "I guess that makes sense. Okay, well—given you are the last of the four archangels of the cardinal directions, how do you feel about the way the church scrubbed your image from it?"

3. THOUGHTS ON THE CHURCH REMOVING YOUR IMAGE?

Mental fortitude over physical strength. Inspect weakness and confront that which terrifies you. Self control, self inspection, power to navigate adversity with grace.

Balance, adaptability, problem solving. Eternal and cyclical nature of the divine.

He shrugged. "Honestly, what do I care if my image is up in a church somewhere? I'd rather it not be there if it means people will focus less on misplaced and hollow shows of adoration and focus more instead on that which really matters in the world.

"God is *here.* We are *here.* Among you." Uriel winked, and he seemed so human compared to the other angels I'd spoken to; it was almost as uncanny as Raphael's Byzantine get-up. "See us in the faces of one another, in your dreams, and in your brethren. Don't waste time building elaborate collections of things, especially if it only helps you feel justified in ignoring the real work to be done. It's one thing to use an image as a focusing tool to connect with us, and another altogether to put these vanity displays up."

Which makes me wonder if he didn't have something to do with breaking the statue I had of him once. Me being a Virgo, an earth sign, I'd wanted to connect more with Uriel, and a roommate got me a gorgeous statue of him for Christmas that, unfortunately, toppled off the altar and shattered into pieces. Though it might've had something to do with me having it right by the door and constantly swiping it every time I walked by—and by his chuckle, he knew that I knew that.

I huffed. "Got'cha, yeah. Now, another thing that was interesting is that you were noted in Jewish tradition as the one to check the blood on the doors in Exodus. I always thought it was Samael that came by doing all the executioner's work. What do you think?"

4. ARE YOU THE ONE WHO CHECKED DOORS FOR BLOOD?

Uriel confirmed with a sigh and a shake of his head that it was a two-part deal: Samael was there in Exodus, doing the hack-and-slash work. But Uriel was the one checking the doors for blood.

"Yes, I was there," he said. "I checked the doors. But the one who followed behind me was the one to throw the axe. I was judge of each door, Samael the executioner of those unprotected. And he delighted in it. I did not. It takes a team of two to represent the breadth of the situation. Samael enjoys striking down the unjust and unworthy. I find no pleasure in identifying them; I simply do it."

"Oh, wow. I can see that. Though, given that it takes two, I wonder how that lines up with you ferrying souls if Azrael is the one that guides souls to the afterlife?"

Inevitable. Promising brutal resolution. Righting wrongs.

Living and working through hardships, triumphs. Completion, growth, success, enlightenment.

5. DO YOU ALSO CARRY SOULS LIKE AZRAEL DOES?

New relationships and ventures, creativity, desire, intuition. Inspiration on the upswing. New and exciting possibilities, ideas, and people may be explored.

An intellectual: skilled, brave, and wrathful person. Duality of graciousness and deceptiveness. Making statements without thinking if they're appropriate.

He gave me this sly little look. "Do you think souls only go one way?" Uriel said. "Or that their course only runs once on this earth?"

I blinked at him. Before I could answer, he kept going.

"Azrael guides them away to the afterlife. I help souls come to earth—whether for the first time or the millionth time. We wear many hats and do many things, us angels. But for the souls that scream to come back, or need to, I guide them to what they're seeking."

"No way! What?" After checking with the pendulum to confirm that's what he was saying, I sat there for a second, puzzled. I definitely didn't get that messed up, and yet it was the most direct confirmation of an idea of reincarnation I'd ever seen an angel give. "That's crazy. Well, I mean, okay then. If it works, it works! I guess we can move onto our next question: of all the prophets God ever had, what do you think united them? What did they have in common?"

6. WHAT QUALITIES UNITE THE PROPHETS, IN YOUR OPINION?

Need to move on. Feelings of alienation or love and relationships lost.

New beginnings, new perspectives, and favoring pessimism.

"Hmm."

He thought about it while I shuffled the cards; I could see him rubbing his chin in thought as he stared at the table of whatever tent we were in, away from the snow.

"Things I notice unite them are the way they're treated by those who think they have it all figured out. People think they can read Scripture and know everything, but all Scripture is, is the history needed to understand where you all came from and the instructions to not kill yourselves ten times over.

"These prophets were all trying to remind people of the way back to God—He who lives and directly teaches you what you want to know—and for it, they were ridiculed, ostracized, rejected. They tried anyway, but so many stories of ones before you made it into an unlucky job."

"I hear you there." I'm always thinking about when I read the Bible as a novel, and there was one prophet in particular who was described as living basically homeless, suffering from dysentery, and outright rejected by the entire of society at one point. A rough life. "Okay, well, onto the next: what frustrates you about people the most, if anything?"

7. WHAT FRUSTRATES YOU ABOUT HUMANITY THE MOST?

We started off strong with a scoff from our guest of honor. Then I pulled the cards and was surprised at the direct answer.

"Not everything can be comfortable," Uriel said, his words dripping with bitterness. "Overcoming the mental block of life's challenges is mightier than the greatest physical feats—but humanity has never been an animal able to tolerate discomfort well. That lack of discipline, I find concerning."

"Ooh." I shook my pencil at him and smiled. "You and I can agree there. Alright, jumping off from that, how do you see yourself? What role do you play for humanity?"

Perceptiveness, sadness, bitterness, and honesty in the face of all decisions, especially difficult ones. Healing is bitter. Confronting necessary truths.

New beginnings, spontaneity, change, innocence. Many of the most significant journeys are mental, not physical.

8. HOW DO YOU SEE YOURSELF AND WANT TO BE SEEN?

Overextending oneself or one's resources and avoiding responsibilities.

Joy, moving forward, and stagnation being the root cause of one's problems.

He sat back and sighed, then said, "I see myself as the one who helps people understand what they're lacking. Who can show people the truth they don't want to face and help them get to what they want. We all—no matter the origin, infernal or angel, god or house spirit—we all want to see you thrive. You cannot thrive trapped in lies.

"I am the Fire of God." The deep red of his eyes flashed with some deep inner spark of light. "The one of wisdom. Wisdom is harsh, painful, but liberating."

"Understood!" And unquestionable. There was more than words that made an angel's answer; there was a sense of weight and truth that made it impossible to do anything but accept the words they said. Like pushing a CD into a player until it gets sucked in. "And how do you want to be seen?"

Uriel wasted no time with cards: "Exactly as that."

Nodding, I said, "I figured. And now, as our last question: what messages do you want to deliver? To me, to others?"

9. ANY LAST MESSAGES FOR ME OR OTHERS?

Partnership and romantic energy, being excited for new love and opportunities or finding a way for old love to endure.

Poor luck and failure.

Remember you have people in your corner," he said. "You have support, and you have so much to enjoy that you're wasting focusing on what you don't have. Bad luck is attracted to a negative eye. Find the support in your loved ones to know that you have a reason to forge on. You are not alone, and if you truly feel you have no one, call on us! Call on God, call on His angels, His Son, Mother, anyone.

"Not one moment do you have to bear alone, nor are you forever doomed to circumstance. Every day, people crack under the weight of this world. Let us help!"

"Wow." What an answer. He was earnest about it, too, if the way he leaned forward and balled up his fists on the table was any indication. "Well, alright then. I guess that's that! Thank you, Uriel, for sharing your wisdom with us, and I hope to see you around as you see fit. With that, I'll say goodbye for now and skip off to bed."

And so I did. With a friendly smile, Uriel nodded and melted into the scenery, all of it becoming a wash of colors in a watery smear, like watercolor paint running down canvas. Then Uriel was gone, and my eyes were open, staring at the coffee table full of ritual items.

Even as I look back at this, I can't say I'm surprised about anything that happened here, honestly. Meeting with an angel at any time is a recipe for a gnosis bomb. I just didn't expect Uriel to be so up front about things like reincarnation, or to be so flashy with his nature as an angel—especially given how calm and gentle he'd been as he came into the fold. But if there's one thing to know about angels, it's that, like their Maker, they will destroy your expectations with a smile and keep you on your toes. It's the only thing that keeps us humans truly humble.

I do wonder about what he said. Souls screaming to come back to earth. Why? What for? What could people want to come back to do after they'd gotten a taste of paradise?

I mean, jeez. Is it that boring up there?

And of course, the next question I think of asking is: have I done that? Have I come back after getting up there, or have I never been there at all? I don't know. I'm not interested in finding out, either, even though I've caught crumbs and glimpses. I am who I am now, and I'll worry about who I will be when I get there. Who I was is gone and of no consequence to me.

Maybe that'll change, though. God switches it up on me more often than not. Who knows what I'll be doing in a year from now, or even half a year? Three months? Maybe I'll be forced to grapple with the concept sooner than I thought. All I know is that having anything like this, any confirmation of what I'd been wondering about, was enough to satisfy me then, and it still is now.

ST. JOSEPH

One of the craziest things to me about the Christian religion is how much of it we take for granted in terms of what's "true" and what isn't. By that, of course, I mean: the amount of *tradition* that has leaked its way into Christianity: holes patched up over time by conjecture, regional folklore and ideas, and Christian writings that, for one reason or another, never made their way into the Bible. Because if we look at the Bible as we have it now, we discover that we actually know very little about Joseph outside his name, his parentage (a descendant of David) and his profession (a carpenter); once we're past the infancy stories laid out in Matthew and Luke, he just... disappears. And everything we think about him, as well as his Saint Powers over workers, immigrants, house sellers *and* buyers, immigrants, fathers, expectant mothers, and interestingly, a Good Death, comes from other traditions, lore, and stories.

For example: his association with farmers and workers came from a middle ages situation in Sicily, where apparently, after praying to St. Joseph to intercede with God for rain in a drought, the rain came. This spared the people from dying of starvation by way of losing crops to drought, and since then, St. Joseph's feast day on March 19th has been a massive deal. I know that I, myself, growing up in a heavily Italian American area, always loved getting delicious, flaky zeppole stuffed with cream for St. Joseph's day. However, just like St. Patrick's day has become the time we all wear green and be Irish for a day, St. Joseph's day likewise became a moment of general celebration for Italian Americans.

In Italian folk magic, too, St. Joseph is also one who you can pray to for intercession on getting a house. If there's a particular house you'd like, a nine day novena, offerings of acts of service or other gifts at the end of the novena, and some extra commitment to studying the word of Christ can *potentially* help you get the keys to your new home. It's not foolproof, though, and so the idea of Saint punishing—desecrating icons by burying statues upside down or taking, say, Baby Jesus out of the manger and away from St. Joseph—comes from times when angry practitioners would take out their failed novenas and magic workings on the Saint in retaliation. (It goes without saying that I do not recommend one participate in this practice.)

However, in infancy gospels, like the Infancy Gospel of Thomas, things change a little. We get more of both the Virgin Mary and St. Joseph as parents here, as well as Jesus as a child, and one key moment—a very human moment, I might add—comes up when St. Joseph scolds the hell out of Jesus for... constantly cursing the village kids to death for petty reasons like running into him or putting a stick in the pool of water he was playing at. In this story, St. Joseph tells Jesus to knock it off on behalf of the townsfolk, and in response, Jesus forgives St. Joseph, but makes everyone who told St. Joseph to talk to Him go blind. Then St. Joseph tugs on his ear hard enough to make it go sore, because the poor guy is frustrated, and Jesus pulls a classic speech on him. The line goes:

> *It sufficeth thee (or them) to seek and not to find, and verily thou hast done unwisely: knowest thou not that I am thine? Vex me not.*

Translation: "You can't do this to me! You're not my real Dad and you don't know why I'm even here with you, so don't piss me off!" (Who knew Jesus had this kind of fire in Him as a kid?)

But with all these things in mind, the reason I came to speak to St. Joseph is, naturally, because of a poll on Patreon—though this was one where, instead of picking specific deities, I gave my patrons the option of choosing specific *themes*. We were on the theme of death for the week, and given I'd already spoken to so many spirits of death earlier in this journey, I decided to take a look at what other Saints or spirits I could find, and I was surprised to find that St. Joseph was listed there.

Especially since he seemed to be not just a Saint of death, but of a *good death,* whatever that meant.

So let's get into how I explored this topic with St. Joseph—the last of the Holy Family (that people are aware of or remember) that had yet to be interviewed.

To speak to St. Joseph, I didn't have too much to bring out, but what I did have was probably predictable: my nativity, where he, Mary, and baby Jesus sit under a big star, as well as a wooden cross in nod to his work as a carpenter and my rosary with wooden ladybug beetles (both for, again, the wood, and the fact that his wife Mary is heavily associated with ladybugs, to the point that they're called *Marienkäfer,* or Mary Beetles, in German). My wintertime Woodwick candles also made for some pretty good ambience.

Before asking him to join, I said the Lord's Prayer, Glory Be, and a small pre-made prayer for St. Joseph asking for intercession. Then I confirmed he was there, confirmed his tarot deck of choice (Thread's of Fate's Weaver Tarot), and let myself sink into the meditative space.

"St. Joseph, hello! Please come visit me and chat for a bit; I've got some questions for you that I'd love to know about."

Soon enough, we were out in a similar place as I'd been with Jesus and Mary Magdalene: a busy street, full of people bustling around. And there next to me at a little table, in the shade of a building's awning, was Joseph, with shaggy brown hair, sharp yet very warm brown eyes, and an easy smile. Right away, he gave me the feeling of a gentle and kind father figure. It took a while to center on a way to see him, as conflicting images of older Joseph or younger Joseph kept coming through, but eventually he settled on what he liked and what I could make sense of: a middle-aged man with a little grey just starting in his hair, but otherwise not so much age dusting his features just yet.

"Alright, well—hello again!" I sat at the table with him and beamed. "Thank you for joining me. I have some questions for you today, especially concerning the topic of death. In that regard, the first question is: what is a good death? What does that mean to you?"

I. WHAT DOES A GOOD DEATH MEAN TO YOU?

Was I confused to get Justice Reversed? Yes. But it made sense as he explained.

"You shouldn't go into your next life with any regrets," he said, his voice creaking, deep with age and the exhaustion of a laborer. "If you can come to the end of your life having made peace, then I'd say your death is a good death. Peace is good."

2. HOW DO YOU HELP PEOPLE FIND PEACEFUL DEATH?

"I feel that. But how do you help people find that kind of peaceful death?"

He didn't even pull any cards here; the message just came through. I really shouldn't be surprised about this by now with these Christian spirits. It almost seems like they go out of their way to avoid the cards, as if the cards are something limiting for them when they could just *talk*.

"Through prayer," St. Joseph said. "I intercede so that the death itself is as painless as possible, and then I work with them on final amends and unburdening their soul."

"Got'cha. That's pretty straightforward; I like it!" Once I was done scribbling, I waved my pencil. "Okay, and just because I'm curious: what was it like heading the Holy Family?"

Repression of something we feel guilty about. Trying to justify them so you don't have to make amends. Airing things out and forgiving yourself will help.

3. WHAT WAS IT LIKE TO BE THE HEAD OF THE HOLY FAMILY?

Period of necessary solitude. Surrender and trust it's in your best interest. Seeing everything from a higher perspective. Accumulating knowledge and wisdom. Traversing the unknown.

He had a little bit of a groan here, not in a bad way, but in an "I'm tired" way. There was still a little half smile to him, though, and as I found the right cards, he explained.

"My role was to provide and to stay out of the way," he said. It felt like I should've bought him a coffee, had we been in a place where I could've done that; the man looked like a bit of espresso would've been a welcome treat. "I watched in the background as my Son did what He was put here to do."

I paused. "You call Him your Son, even though—?"

Right away, St. Joseph said, "I do. I do consider Him my Son, yes; I raised Him with Mary, my wife. I know who His real Father is, but that doesn't mean I wasn't also His father, or that I didn't love Him as mine. I did what I needed to do."

"Oh, wow, alright. Nice. Thank you for that. Okay, well, speaking of your Son—was there any change in the afterlife after He was resurrected?" This was a bit of a risky question, but it was something I had to ask *someone* about, especially with the topic of death. St. Joseph certainly would've known as much as anyone else in Heaven, I felt. "I understand that beforehand, it was thought that people would simply rest until it was time to rise, but with Jesus resurrecting, a lot believe that's undone, or that the souls are woken up? What happened here?"

4. DID JESUS'S RESURRECTION CHANGE THE AFTERLIFE META?

New beginnings in all things material. New prosperity or a shift towards it. A new level. Showing up and being diligent in the work.

An energetic, creative person with great ideas. May have self doubt. Be courageous. Acknowledge fear of failure and success.

St. Joseph sighed and shrugged. "I am not a man that thought I would be here in this position," he said. "Who am I? The husband of the Mother of God—there's nothing special in this title. At least, I saw nothing special in it.

"Yet there was, apparently. I died, and it was like closing my eyes—nothingness. Then when I got the strength to open, I opened them to responsibilities I didn't realize I'd have. Didn't expect to be a Saint at all. I'm just me."

"Whoa, that's pretty wild, then!" Imagine that, taking a really long blink and then being told you've got a job as a holy figure for God? Working from Heaven? The idea delighted me, but I kept focused and moved onto the next question. "Alright, alright—I mean, I think there's something special to the title, but moving on: what advice do you have for people coming up to the end of their life?"

5. WHAT ADVICE TO YOU HAVE FOR PEOPLE AT THE END OF THEIR LIFE?

I was shocked to pull the Devil here. Didn't understand how it could've related to death, not in the least—until his voice scraped over the table and settled in my mind.

"Pride." That word took up all the space in my head. "People need to change. They need to let go of how they were in the past. When you get older, or when your body begins failing, it's okay to ask for help. Don't let your vices steal the comfort of your last days from you. It's never worth it. You'll hurt yourself and others if you insist on it."

"Honestly, wow." I felt like this was advice that wasn't for me, but for others—but then again, who's to say I won't be the kind of person to insist on doing everything myself and refuse help later in life? "That's a pretty solid answer; thank you. I see what you mean a hundred percent. Okay, well, if that's for them, then what advice do you have for their loved ones?"

Believing in falsehoods and being influenced in a way that can cause real harm. A need or compulsion from the shadows. One must confront the deepest layers of themselves and do it without judgement.

6. WHAT ADVICE DO YOU HAVE FOR THE DYING'S LOVED ONES?

Dreaminess that one isn't taking action on. One must have forward movement.

He folded his hands on the table. "It's denial, Sara," he said. "Families in denial about what they're seeing. I understand it's painful to lose a loved one, but the tough conversations need to happen. You can't just put off the work that comes with the end of life, hoping you'll never see it. There needs to be plans put in place so the dead can rest easy and not worry about the family they're leaving behind."

"I got'cha, yeah." The scratching of my pencil on the notebook filled up the silence that bubbled there. "That makes sense. And here's kind of an oddball question, just because I've been thinking about it since reading up on you, but what do you think makes a good husband? How do you be one?"

7. WHAT MAKES A GOOD HUSBAND?

For the first time in a good while, St. Joseph smiled, and there was such sunshine in his eyes. "Ah. Support—you need to support your family. And not just financially. Your family is looking to you to share the burdens of making decisions best for all, even if once upon a time those decisions wouldn't have been the best for *you*." He turned to me and elaborated, his smile growing: "It means giving up a lot of yourself to know the ones you love are safe and thriving under your care. People need to learn to lose themselves and live for others as much as they do their individual person."

"Got'cha, yeah. That's some good advice, I think. It takes a team." Which was something I'd learned well myself once I moved out on my own: people count on your labor, whether as partners or as dependents or anything else. It's easy to not think about that living with parents or some such. "But alright, we're coming into the final round now, so please tell me: how do you see yourself?"

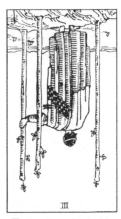

Experiencing setbacks. Nothing is a waste of time. Be prepared for changes, even if they're not what was anticipated.

8. HOW DO YOU SEE YOURSELF?

The ebb of life. Hitting bumps in the road, assessing one's needs. Strength, resilience, and courage are needed, but ask for help if you need it.

"I was a provider back when I was alive. Even now, I do what I must, no matter the obstacle. I'm no stranger to bumps in the road and try to navigate them with grace. It's all I can do: see the situation for what it is and act. I'm not the type to deny the truth of a situation."

"And how do you want others to see you?"

9. HOW DO YOU WANT OTHERS TO SEE YOU?

A balancing act where big aspects of life want attention. What can be out-sourced should be, with a focus on what's sustainable. Create more ease in your life.

"I see myself this way, and you should see yourself this way, too," he said to me—and I didn't get the sense it was a general message, but something meant for me. "As someone who is resourceful. Who knows their limits and when to call it quits, or when to reach out for help. I'm someone that doesn't suffer if I don't have to; I ask for help and find ways to relieve the burdens so I can keep going." Then he tapped my shoulder. "You are this way, too. Be this way."

"I—okay. Um."

It was funny that he should say that, because in between our questions, I'd been fighting back skittering thoughts: worries, fears, frustrations, all of which were threatening to burst out and grab onto him. Like the prayers of the Sicilians, I was close to having similar asks just spill out onto the table, only for me to cage them up and try to keep it professional. But as I said: spirits are hard to talk to, because they can tell there's something up; they can read the thoughts you're trying to bury. That's why this felt like a surprisingly fatherly moment, like he was giving me advice and a pep talk directly.

"So," I said after a moment, "our last question is: do you have any messages you want to share?"

10. ANY LAST MESSAGES FOR ME OR OTHERS?

This was the simplest and most comforting answer I'd gotten. He didn't even want to pull cards. St. Joseph only smiled and said:

"Just do your best. That's enough. You'll be okay."

"Aw, that's sweet," I said. Then, once I was done writing, I clapped my hands and began my awkward exit. "Well, that's all the questions I have for you, St. Joseph, so... I guess that's that! Thank you for coming by, and I'll see you when I see you!"

He nodded, and then the town crumbled away, until I was left by myself, back in my living room. And I'll be honest with you: this was one of those interviews that, as I picked up my things and got ready for bed, had me feeling like emotional Jell-O. There's more than words that come through in these interviews. I've picked up more tricks: the ability to feel the grain of a table's wood under my hand, or the sun on my face. The ability to see things as clearly as if I were watching a movie. The ability to *feel* the things that aren't said—like a father's love and bone-deep exhaustion.

With St. Joseph, it was like being with a man whose kids had all grown up and who was happy to see them thrive, but who bore the scars that only parenthood can bring: scars on the soul and the mind. I, being childless, can't pretend to understand that, but by sitting with him and listening, I was able to get just the faintest idea of what St. Joseph endured being the provider of the Holy Family—and the love he had, too. There was so much of it.

And I'm willing to say: if Mary is our spiritual mother, and God our spiritual Father, then St. Joseph, like he was for Jesus, can be our spiritual stepfather. The one that, even though everyone is fully aware isn't related to you, still cares about you like you're his own kid. So whether you're looking for a father's comfort, or looking to help make things easier, he's a wonderful Saint to turn to.

And if you don't ever need it, at least you have the wisdom he dropped with us here. That alone is something worth holding onto for those darker moments, especially when you need a reminder that yes, your best is good enough.

ARCHANGEL METATRON

Over the course of this book, I think I've mentioned the Book of Enoch several times. Enoch, the one who we follow throughout the *three* pseudepigraphal books related to him (yes, there are actually three), is canonically a direct descendant of Adam and the great-grandfather of Noah from the whole Flood Debacle. He's reason we know about the Watchers and what created the Nephilim that led to God resetting the whole world with the flood; we know about the lake of fire, and the promises God made to absolutely wreck the fallen angels for their missteps in sleeping with human women, as well as a lot of interesting details about the locations of places, heavenly objects, and more, as the angels essentially give Enoch a tour of Heaven.

The names of many angels appear there, too, like Michael, Gabriel, Zotiel, and so many more. There's a lot that happens, and many that come to share their wisdom—and by the end of it all, Heaven gains a new angel as Enoch is lifted up to, in legend and in Jewish Hekhalot mysticism, become the great archangel Metatron, sometimes known as "Lesser Adonai": a bearer of the Divine Name that acts as God's representative. Beyond that, if you ever take the time to read the Book of Enoch, you can find quite a few interesting bits of imagery woven throughout, not just with the scary parts of Heaven, but the whole functions of angels and prophecies and other wild stuff he gets to see before they bring him back to Earth. Definitely give it a read if you enjoy that kind of wacky stuff.

Going further, though, we find Metatron especially prevalent in Jewish Kabbalah, being the ruling angel of the top sphere, but I wasn't out contacting him with any methods from Kabbalah. I was just out there with some rocks and a candle, hoping he'd see me sending spiritual smoke signals and pop down for a chat (if God let him). Turns out, most angels and demons can be reached just fine this way, and you can avoid a lot of mess getting involved in mystic systems you have no business being in. But a lot of the sources on him, if you ever decide to look into him, are notably New Age, and it's best to just avoid those altogether. Ask God to help you find Metatron if you really need to, for whatever reason.

This angel is one of two angels that have ever been human (the other being the prophet Elijah who became Sandalphon), and specifically, as we came into our monthly theme of prophecy on Patreon, I was just interested in seeing what it was like to be a prophet that became a divine being the way Metatron did. I'd only ever seen him once before, and it was only for a brief moment; he came in a suit of armor, brassy and bold and feeling very much like a force that could've crushed me to dust if given the command.

I wanted to know more, naturally. I wanted to know who he was underneath that armor and his typical duties as "Lesser Adonai." So I kicked us off with a chat with this famous (yet not exactly canonical) archangel, and it certainly brought up some interesting ideas.

Here's how it went.

Now, with Metatron, my main focus was *spiritual power.* The color of spiritual power—of psychic skill, of wisdom, of supernatural force—is purple, and so of course, I had some of my purple things out: namely amethyst (a classic for spiritual workings) and my purple lace agate rosary. I also had clear quartz, a good tool for focusing and organizing energy in a room, and celestite, the stone that I've mentioned acts as a sort of "angel antenna." That, along with Metatron's sigil from Echols' book, an angel statue, and a plain white candle, were all I needed to get focused and prime myself for a connection—because that's what these tools are *really* for.

Getting you connected. Getting you in the zone and priming *your* mind to work with an entity.

But as always, I said the Lord's Prayer, asked God to open that door and let Metatron pay me a visit, and then confirmed he was there with the pendulum. He also chose Doreen Virtue's Angel Tarot, which honestly, I'm surprised more angels don't use—but of course, it depends on the nature of what they're trying to say. Nonetheless, once I had everything ready, we were good to go.

"Well, hello, Metatron!" I said as I settled in with the energy that filled up our space. "I've got some questions for you today. Please, come by and sit with me this morning, and let's have a chat!"

In Echols' book, he mentions a way to visualize Archangel Metatron is crystalline or white robes and blinding light. That, along with an **artistic depiction** I'd seen of Metatron while searching around online, took me away from the suit of metal I'd seen him wear before and instead gave me an angel that looked something like Gabriel (or maybe I just think of Gabriel whenever I see a blond man). Still, Metatron looked like that type of angel, with long, wavy, light golden hair, and with eyes that looked like they were made of diamonds. They were multifaceted, clear, and laser sharp. He wore simple white robes—probably the most stereotypical I'd ever seen an angel be, if I'm honest—and his wings were massive.

Originally, we were in a place I recognized: one where I'd spoke to other angels and heavenly figures before. A staircase of cloud, a blue sky. There was no golden gate this time, but it was quite the bright space. We moved around here and there over the course of our interview, looking for a place that I could settle in comfortably without getting too distracted by how Hallmark Heaven looked in my head, and eventually we ended up in a cave of geodes. Turquoise and purple gems poked out of dark rocks while Metatron perched up on top of one of them, and then, finally, we got into it.

1. WHAT DOES BEING A PROPHET ENTAIL?

Reviewing plans from an outside perspective. A temporary standstill. Embracing unique beliefs. Epiphanies, selflessness, unexpected life changes.

An exciting new opportunity. Creative and inspiring career possibilities. Innovative ideas enthusiastically expressed. A fresh start, taking risks, new information.

"So, Metatron," I said, "to dive right in: what does it mean to be a prophet? What does that entail?"

As always, Abrahamic figures seem to talk less through traditional tarot meanings and more through the signs and symbols on the cards themselves. Here's why Metatron wanted to use this deck, I guess: the card that would've traditionally been called the Hanged Man was instead called "Awakening" in this deck. That concept, along with the Ace of Wands, was on par with what I'd imagined the prophet role entailed—but of course, he explained further.

"Being a prophet is a business wholly unlike any other," he said from up on his geode. "You are God's messenger in the flesh. It's impossible not to feel in awe, or like you aren't worthy of such a thing—but God isn't interested in what you think of yourself or your skill. He cares about the potential He sees in you. To be a prophet means God saw you and knew you would be able to do what was needed in this world—that He could trust you to speak."

"Got'cha, got'cha. And how can people know if they have gifts of prophecy?"

2. HOW DO PEOPLE KNOW THEY HAVE THE GIFT OF PROPHECY?

"They know when they know," Metatron said, so matter-of-fact. I had to stop myself from groaning and rolling my eyes as he spoke, because what was I supposed to do with that? But maybe he knew I was grinding my teeth to dust, because he kept going. "It's something written into people's plan and not something they can avoid. Though it's a scary place, of course, realizing what your role is and what God's asking of you. Speaking for and to Him has never been easy. But it is worth it. It isn't something the prophetic types can decide *not* to do—not even when all seems lost."

Ain't that the truth. While there are plenty verses in the Bible where false prophets are loudly wrong, when there *is* a message God wants out there, it's like trying to hold a bee in your mouth. You can't keep it in without getting stung to hell and back, in my experience. The Holy Spirit is a ball of angry, buzzing needles when She wants to be heard. But there was no need to speak for me then, only to listen—and that, in and of itself, was tiring enough in the presence of Metatron, who gave off a lot more energy than one would think if they saw how calmly he perched on that geode.

Leaving doubts behind. Self confidence and success. You might not feel ready, but your life has trained you for this. Magical occurrences, concentrated efforts. No more procrastination.

Fruits of one's labors grow. Harvest on the way. Review progress of your journey. Anxiety is unfounded. Perseverance, reaching milestones, and unnecessary worry.

"And what about signs?" This was a pendulum question, a simple *yes* or *no*. "Can you get signs in childhood or something like that as a more concrete way of knowing?"

3. WHAT SIGNS COULD PEOPLE LOOK FOR ABOUT PROPHECY?

Metatron shrugged. "I suppose, yes; they can hint at it. But it's more that innate knowing."

Which I guess made sense. I was thinking of all the prophets and big figures then—Moses and Elijah and all of them—that tried to decline or run from their duties, especially when things got intense, but who nonetheless went and did them anyway and made a total upheaval of things.

"Okay! I see. That makes sense." I rubbed the sting of fatigue from my eyes and shuffled my cards. "But now, with the Watchers, as a prophet, how exactly did they contact you? I know you fell asleep and had dreams, but is there anything more specific about that?"

4. HOW DID THE WATCHERS CONTACT YOU AS A HUMAN?

"They came in extreme ways," Metatron said, with a bit of a bleak look on his face—a face I recognized, because it was a face I often wore. The face of a human squaring off with angels. There was still that human memory to Metatron; that's what that expression told me. "Desperate. They were desperate. My guardian angel at the time protected me while they put me to sleep to get to me in dreams. It was terrifying, but it was necessary to achieve my purpose of helping these beasts, these Nephilim, get off our planet."

"Yeah? The Nephilim really were no good?"

He shook his head. "They were wretched, and God needed me to bridge communication between them and their masters."

"Oh. That sounds intense." Understandable, but messy. I sighed and said, "Okay, okay—well, in that vein, how can other people learn to contact entities in the first place? Like spirits, whatever deities they worship?"

A card of extremes. Spending too much or too little. Change is inevitable; your hard work is paying off. Don't let fear limit you.

Getting things done and leaving planning behind. Honoring commitments, attending to details. Renewed motivation, abundance.

5. HOW CAN PEOPLE LEARN TO CONTACT DIVINITY?

1. Enjoying time with other people. Having much to give. Handling challenges with understanding, warmth, confidence, resourcefulness. Prosperity, a sensible approach.

2. Creativity and hard work will bring great rewards. Anything nurtured will flourish. Enjoy beautiful things in life and take care of yourself. Spending time in nature, caring for health.

"It's about connection," Metatron said. "When you're able to slow down, rest yourself, and connect with things that are alive—plants, animals, people—you will see. But like all things, it is a skill. Everyone practices and develops it their own way. Be patient, work hard, and you'll succeed. Anyone can do this. This alone isn't what makes you a prophet, understand: prophets have a mission."

"Fair enough! That would make sense, given how many people have these skills again."

And while I hadn't yet read this book at the time, Metatron's words remind me now of what Matthew Fox said in *Hildegard of Bingen: A Saint for Our Times*: that a prophet was just a mystic that was out to cause trouble. Yes, indeed, there was a mission there for a prophet, and it was a dangerous and difficult one, if we take a look at their track record in the Bible.

In that moment, though, I wasn't thinking about all that. I was just thinking about being respectful and making sure I was being considerate in how I wrote down the answers and asked the next questions. As I finished writing his answer and picked up my cards, I said, "Now, how about this Book of Life? I understand you record all things of past, present, and future? What's it like to do that?"

6. WHAT IS IT LIKE TO WRITE IN THE BOOK OF LIFE?

A time of success unimaginable. Endeavors are blessed with abundance. Work done has brought changes; you're on the path for enlightenment. Reaching personal insights and joy.

Creativity and hard work will bring great rewards. Anything nurtured will flourish. Enjoy beautiful things in life and take care of yourself. Spending time in nature, caring for health.

He had a smile and a faraway stare here. The gems of the geodes around him sparkled as if alive, and there was a purplish-blue tint to the cave that made it seem like we were deep in the belly of another planet entirely.

Metatron stared at the hands he'd folded into his lap. "It's an honor," he said, "to record the happenings of the world God created is a clerical thing, but so important. God is writing a story, and I'm transcribing it. A great honor."

"I bet. That sounds really cool." I mean, imagine? Recording everything that happened, is happening, and will happen? "And given that you were once human before doing all these kinds of things, can you tell me about the process of becoming an angel?"

7. WHAT IS IT LIKE TO BECOME AN ANGEL?

1. Sadness will pass and reveal its purpose. Forgiveness is a powerful healer.

2. Don't focus on the negative; crying over spilled milk does you no good. Grieve what's been lost, heal, and have faith that all happens for a reason.

Metatron huffed, a laugh without humor, and he shook his head. I was surprised that I pulled such negative cards; I figured he'd have something more positive to say, just as he'd been so humble and happy about the Book of Life. But then, when do angels ever do or feel what I expect them to?

"It was brutal," he said. "I became aware of my every flaw as a human. My every frailty of spirit, and all the things I'd done against God in my weakness and imperfection. I was torn apart and rebuilt from the very core of me, into something else."

"Well, hey, I don't know," I said, wandering closer to the base of the geode he sat on. "I know we aren't perfect, but that's part of the fun: learning and growing, trying our best. No?"

He stared at me, then shook his head with a sad smile. "I mourn for humanity. When you see what we angels see, you realize there is no 'fun' in the mistakes humanity makes."

I sighed. "I mean, I guess. We have done some messed up stuff." There was no denying that or getting away from it, the capacity of humans to be worse than devils, even as they tried to be angels. But I didn't have time to dwell on that, not right then, so I said, "Moving on, then: how does your human life give you perspective as an angel? I feel like angels that were always angels don't quite understand humans the way someone who was once human might."

8. HOW DOES HUMAN LIFE GIVE YOU PERSPECTIVE AS AN ANGEL?

Memories from personal history. Childlike innocence, lack of guilt. May reconnect with people from the past. Inheritance, gifts, reunions. Kindness to or from others.

Balancing a situation with moderation. Working slowly and cooperatively with others. Compassion and kindness are the key to success. Forgiveness brings healing.

"Not a bad assumption," he said as he hopped down from the geode and stood with me. He was tall, yet his presence didn't feel so crushing, like angels sometimes did; maybe he was trying to make it a little easier on me, knowing what it'd been like for him to experience something similar. "I still have all my memories as a human. I see now where my actions were wrong, but I remember why I did each thing I did, and what it felt like to regret it after. I remember the limited scope of perspective I used to have. Angels that were never human don't understand what it's like to see so little, yet still have to act as if we see everything."

I blinked at him. Metatron stared back at me with those diamond eyes as if he were a scientist studying a furry little animal.

Then his gaze softened, and he whispered, "Being human is terrifying. Harder than being an angel. Harder by far. That keeps me humble when I work with you all."

"Wow. Okay." Didn't expect an angel to say something like that, not at all. Being human, harder than being an angel? "That's... pretty cool, I won't lie. But I am curious: how do you see yourself?"

9. HOW DO YOU SEE YOURSELF?

Metatron shrugged and refused to pull any cards. "I don't care to see myself any particular way or define myself like that."

"Okay... but what about how others see you?"

10. HOW DO YOU WANT OTHERS TO SEE YOU?

Outgoing, creative, passionate about life. Seeks out new experiences and can make things happen. Confident, courageous, mischievous, busy.

PAGE of WANDS.

Even if Metatron didn't think much of himself, though, here he had quite a bit more to say.

"I want people to see me as an ally," he said as he folded his arms and leaned against the geode. The purple crystals inside glimmered. "Not scary, like you thought I'd be."

Oops. He got me.

"I remember my time as a human," he continued with a smile. "I enjoy fun. I enjoy the glory of life God's given us all. Plenty things hurt to see, yes—but plenty things are worth seeing. I love you all, my fellow humans, and I want to help where I can."

"Got'cha—that's sweet! And, well, I guess to close it out: what messages do you have to share? For me, for others?"

11. ANY LAST MESSAGES FOR ME OR OTHERS?

Metatron put a hand on my back and walked me towards the end of the cave, where it opened back up to the clouds and light of Heaven. I don't know what kind of portals this celestial realm had, but they were pretty convenient for getting around, at least.

"This is for anyone who needs to hear it, "Metatron said as we walked. "Too many people are not being honest with themselves. I see it! Every day! But when people call on God, and they ask for the strength to be their truest, finest self—that's when the world will feel like it's spinning in a whole new direction. People need to wake up and claim their power. Everyone here has a purpose: find it and live up to it!"

Then we were standing at the cave opening, and as soon as we stepped out of it, the whole thing disappeared. Metatron smiled at me under the bright, near blinding light of the sun, which caught his robe and made everything almost too bright to actually see. I sat there soaking up the light for a moment, then nodded.

"Alright, well—thank you, Metatron. That is a great message. I have to run now, but I appreciate you taking the time to tell me a little about prophecy! May we meet again whenever it's time!"

THE HANGED MAN.

Reviewing plans from an outside perspective. A temporary standstill. Embracing unique beliefs. Epiphanies, selflessness, unexpected life changes.

Abundance is on the way. The universe rewards gratitude with more. One could be the giver or receiver of wealth. Reliable people will have opportunities. Paying off debt and celebration.

Metatron nodded and patted my shoulder, and then Heaven faded from all that light to nothing but the darkness of closed eyes, the glow of the kitchen light around me. I blew out a long breath once I was alone, and I slumped in my chair and sat there for a few minutes before I was able to move on and get to bed. Didn't even clean the ritual stuff up; I told myself I'd do that in the morning.

As I laid in bed that night, though, I couldn't help but feel encouraged. Even though I'm sure I'm no prophet—and would never want to be so presumptuous as to put that word on myself regardless, because there are too many ridiculous and ego-addled folks out there claiming to be the Direct Mouthpiece of God—I understand the mess that comes with the concept. When God tells you to do something for Him, you can't help but try and run away from that, because where there's *God*, there's going to be *controversy*, and a whole dumpster fire to go along with it. No one wants that.

But the prophets go and do it anyway, even when they don't want to. Metatron, having been human, knows what that's like, and that's comforting—knowing there's an angel out there who *gets us*. Who understands what it's like to be a human, and to experience Divinity as a human, and to not want to deal with the craziness Divinity wants us to get up to but doing it anyway. The things in the Book of Enoch that are described are things that, honestly, remind me a lot of my own experiences doing these interviews, and if it's *anything* like that, then you know Enoch spent a lot of time being completely exhausted before he got sucked up to Heaven to be an angel himself.

We have so many allies in this world—that's what encounters with those like Metatron make me feel. We have countless allies: those who can relate to us, those who can't but want to help anyway, those who can see from a perspective we can't and make us consider new ideas. There's never a time people are alone, and there's not a single struggle that people go through that someone else hasn't overcome before. Even struggles like those with Divinity. *Especially* struggles like those with Divinity.

All Divinity asks is that we be honest about who and what we are. Then, they get to work *with* us—not against us (even though, admittedly, it feels like they're against us when they make us go through crazy trials to grow). And if that's not comforting to think about, then I don't know what is.

PRINCE VASSAGO

In the quest for more knowledge about prophecy and divination, naturally, I couldn't get a celestial perspective without also getting an infernal one. More than one type of entity can master these concepts, after all, and certainly more can teach them, too—including those like Prince Vassago, the third of the seventy-two spirits of the *Ars Goetia*.

By this point, speaking to demons was no different than speaking to anyone else to me. It may seem like that was pretty quick, given I'd only spoken to a scant handful of the infernal divine before him, but it is worth noting that throughout all this time, I'd gotten further into my work with Lucifer and started a mess of a project that really made me too tired to worry about approaching demons anymore. Of course, most demonolaters will tell you that these entities are dangerous—and they are—but in my mind, they're no more dangerous than any other angel or god or anything else. They're certainly no more dangerous than God Himself, and I've never had a single problem being in close quarters with Him, that's for damn sure.

Most of all, though, there were a few perks of going from *witch* to *mystic* to *magician*, as I had been over the course of this journey, and the main perk was the unbridled confidence that fueled my many successful games of Spiritual Jackass. I can tell you a secret about magic: like fairies, it'll die if you don't believe in it.

It'll also die if you don't believe in yourself, and if you aren't one hundred percent certain that what you're capable of is true, good, and *enough*.

So I started going into these interviews, especially with demons, with a "what could go wrong?" attitude. I strolled into the infernal realms fully confident in the protection of my God, which I'd always been, and fully confident in my own power to deny those terrors and things I didn't want to experience, to snuff them out. Between God holding me up against a million beatings over time, teaching me when to fight, and Lucifer holding me down in the face of the very stuff of nightmares, teaching me when to surrender, I knew nothing could get me that didn't have my permission to get me. Moreover, I'd experienced what could go wrong with entities like Apollo; I knew the wrath of a god was serious stuff, and that Divinity was not to be trifled with.

That's why I knew that if I came with full respect and did my due diligence to properly approach an entity, giving them the respect I knew they deserved, then that meant I'd taken the necessary precautions—both as a magician and as a human being—to be blameless. Because don't you know?

Psalm 119:1:
> *Blessed are those whose ways are blameless,*
> *who walk according to the law of the Lord.*

(If we remember that for Christians, the law is basically Don't Be a Prick, then that makes this pretty easy to do: coming equipped with knowledge, an open heart, and respect does wonders when dealing with entities of any kind, even the ones people say are "low vibrational" or whatever.)

So as I went doing my research for this month's theme, and I discovered in the catalogue of the Goetia a demon known as Prince Vassago, I didn't feel a lick of nervousness. I found out that this was a demon Prince who rode a crocodile, which was pretty cool, and that he was a good source for knowledge on divination. Here's his entry in the *Ars Goetia*:

> *The Third Spirit is a Mighty Prince, being of the same nature as Agares. He is called Vassago. This Spirit is of a Good Nature, and his office is to declare things Past and to Come, and to discover all things Hid or Lost. And he governeth 26 Legions of Spirits...*

Likewise, S. Connolly notes that Prince Vassago is of the element of water and really good with teaching divination skills. The other demon mentioned in this description, though, Duke Agares, is similar to Prince Vassago, also being a demon that rides on a crocodile, but instead of teaching past and future, he teaches a magician every language there is, causes calamities like earthquakes, destroys the ego, and was once of the Virtue class of angels. Very fun stuff.

However, as with most Goetic spirits, there isn't much more to be found about Prince Vassago, save maybe some information about him in a book predating both the *Ars Goetia* and Johann Weyer's *Pseudomonarchia Daemonum* (False Monarchy of Demons). The old work is a book called *Liber Officiorum Spirituum*, or *The Book of the Office of Spirits*, and in this book, Prince Vassago (as Usagoo) is as an angel that can spark lust in women and help people find hidden treasures. All of that is well and good, but I was coming here to find out more about divination as a concept, and so knowing that Prince Vassago was knowledgeable in it and that his element was water was all I needed to prepare a place for him at the table.

So let's dive in.

For a water-based demon, putting a plate of offerings together was a little simpler: most fruits, like raspberries, blackberries, and blueberries are aligned with the element of water, which I put in a bowl for him, and I had a shot of good blueberry liquor to offer him, too. I also had his sigil drawn out on paper (because despite what most old school occultists say, I just refuse to believe you need to carve sigils in precious metals to get any spirit to come by), and I had my onyx sphere as a nod to the technique of scrying, as well as blue stones like lapis lazuli and blue lace agate to symbolize water. Some iris incense was necessary, too, as it turns out the infernal divine like pleasant smells like flowers and such; they don't like to be invited into dirty and stinky spaces. (Which does explain how some burning fish guts were able to drive King Asmodeus away from Sarah in the Book of Tobit.)

After doing my prayers, cleansing my space with rosemary smoke, and asking God to let this infernal Prince on through, I found that foreign energy drifting on through soon enough. I especially knew he was there when I felt little pinches here and there, which reminded me of when I first spoke with Loki. It didn't bother me, though, and I confirmed that we were going to use the Universal Fantasy Tarot for the night—a dreamy, strange deck that I loved getting to use every time it popped up.

"Prince Vassago, hello!" I motioned to the table. "Please join me for a little chat about divination; I've got some blueberry liquor and mixed berries as a gift of thanks for your time."

So for what little information I could find about Prince Vassago, one thing I remember reading is that he doesn't really have a fixed form. He can show up in any manner of ways, and being a little mischievous, he can mess with people, too. I did see some pictures of him riding a crocodile, though, which would explain why his eyes were such bright, golden, reptilian looking things once I started getting clearer flashes of his face.

But the Prince himself was a man with a teasing smile, and long red robes and a red hat on a brown bob. He took us from a swamp to a place where there was a magical table, full of some blue and glowing light in the middle—almost like the one I'd stood at with Azazel, but different, as if it were a completely separate room with a whole different function that I would've never been able to guess. It was too dark to see anything farther than a couple feet from the table, too.

Prince Vassago faced off with me from the other side of the table. He was grinning as if he were silently teasing me, which was fine; I'm sure there was plenty worth teasing me about, like the fact that the paper I'd written his sigil on was so obviously ripped out of one of my many little notebooks. But the energy was overall open, lighthearted, and I knew I was in the clear to start.

"So, to start us off," I said as I glanced at this intricate ritual table, "I would love to know: why do you think divination is such a feared tool?"

I. WHY DO YOU THINK PEOPLE ARE SO SCARED OF DIVINATION?

Even in defeat, we create an ideal victory. Flowers with good roots can blossom after a frost.

We must learn to govern our feelings and leave those we've loved and fought for free to go.

Too much worry about the future can keep us from enjoying the present. Anxiety is never a good guide.

"Oh, goodness," he said with a wave of his hand. "When people don't know the future, they worry. When they do know the future, they take action. Whoever knows has the power. They might escape bondage, or connect with forces that could topple kings. Kings can't have that." His teasing grin somehow went wider, wide enough that his face could've split in half. "Not even God can have that."

A lot of times, it felt like these spirits were taking jabs at God—and if I knew that, then God knew it, too. Why didn't I ever say anything, then? Because God didn't need me to defend Him, nor did He ever seem to care about little pokes and prods, and if He didn't care, I didn't care. So I just shrugged and wrote down Prince Vassago's answer.

"Fair enough," I said, and he cocked his head as I went back to shuffling the cards. "But you know, that makes me wonder: I would hear stories of people learning the future, trying to avoid it, and then falling right into it anyway. Like, Oedipus for example. What do you think of that trope, and how it makes fate seem so inescapable?"

2. WHAT DO YOU THINK OF THE IDEA THAT FATE IS INESCAPABLE?

Naïveté and reck-lessness.

Romantic and artistic passions must be ruled by reason and the advice of those that share our destiny.

Material wealth can never compensate for the lack of peace. The world will be ours if we are masters of our own soul.

Prince Vassago scowled from across the table.

"Foolish little tragedies, stories like Oedipus's. Easily avoided if one works by logic and reason rather than panicking. Imagine if Oedipus had stayed put? Not been overcome with fear to the point of running off? There are people who shouldn't ask their fate if they can't handle the answer. Mastery of oneself starts in the heart," he said as he tapped his chest, "not the stars."

"Oh, wow, that's a really good way of putting it. I see that." That made him smile, as if satisfied. I tapped my pencil to my lips and said, "But then, what would you say divination is good for?"

3. WHAT IS DIVINATION GOOD FOR?

One thin brow shot up, and he gestured to me. "What is divination good for? Look—look how you use it. Just to talk, but always to inquire. I am not your grandmother or your friend, that I might put up a phone to my ear and speak to you plainly.

"I am of a world not like yours," he said, his nose turning up, "and the only line to connect our worlds is divination—the magic, the earnestness of the practitioner to seek that connection. Plainly put, divination is as useful as the concept of communication is."

Sometimes we cannot avoid a major change. Don't be afraid of setting on a new path.

Emotional balance is achieved when we can distinguish illusion from reality and accept both.

Poor luck and failure.

"I got'cha." We started moving, circling the table as if always maintaining that opposite position. The blue glow of the table made him paler than he maybe was, and it caught hard on the yellow tint of his eyes as he watched me. "Though with the way people see it now, is there anything about our view of it you don't like? I mean, I've certainly seen people ascribe some interesting, yet unrelated, things to the idea of divination. Like crystal healing. Somehow that got lumped in with divination."

4. WHAT DON'T YOU LIKE ABOUT HOW WE UNDERSTAND DIVINATION?

Weakness, breaking down, losing control, and having difficulty problem solving.

That which we worked for will bear fruit only if we have the patience to wait.

Codependency, miscommunication, misunderstanding.

The look Prince Vassago gave me was that of a socialite that had just been told that the restaurant didn't have any proper vintage wines. Half derision, half laughing. But then he gave me an answer in between all these harsh words from the cards.

"Sara, nothing is more vexing than when a person comes to divine with the worst answer already stitched on their heart. When they use divination in such an anxious way, desperately casting lots only to cling to the negative, *ugh!* I seethe. These types don't want solutions. They want pity and a reason to die in a beautiful tragedy."

A lot of these answers had me fighting back a smirk of my own. Such drama. Such flair. It reminded me a little of King Paimon, only a touch *more* theatrical. I loved it, though—even if I had to watch myself to make sure I didn't come off as rude. My natural inclination was to be a ball-buster, and the type of joking, teasing, jabbing energy the infernal divine brought to the table didn't help, but I wasn't about to find out how well demons could handle the old Italian American jabs I grew up with.

"How would you prefer people used divination," I said instead, even as I fought with my face to keep it straight, "or at least viewed it?"

5. HOW SHOULD PEOPLE VIEW AND USE DIVINATION?

1. Emotional balance is achieved when we can distinguish illusion from reality and accept both.

2. Poor luck and failure.

3. To be authoritative, we must be recognized as such and committed to building what we have promised.

THE MOON.

THE EMPEROR.

He sucked his teeth with that question.

"There's nothing more pathetic than a sniveler," Prince Vassago muttered. "If someone is to ask me about the future, I want them to face it with pride, no matter what lies in wait. Life can't be roses all the time. It will never be roses all the time, in fact. Those who divine need to use their knowledge to take control, not to lay down and die under Fate's thumb. Disgusting, the way people give up."

Damn. Okay. Let it be known that angels and demons both will give it to you straight and pull no punches—likely because so many demons once *were* angels.

"I hear you," I said as I scribbled on. "But okay, okay, all that said—why did you decide to start helping mankind with knowing past and future?"

6. WHY HELP MANKIND UNDERSTAND PAST AND FUTURE?

Loss, theft, and uncompromising values, obsession with socially acceptable roles and routines.

Like shadows, the demons inside us always seem to be bigger and more threatening than they actually are.

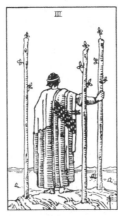

Useful to view the things through the eyes of a child at play. Secret truths are sometimes right there, but we can't see them.

"Oh, because it's so frustrating to see mankind walk so blind through life, groping for that which they want, not able to see how close it really is. So I give them a nudge," he said, with a smile like the Cheshire cat. Then the smile dropped clean off his lips, and his stare gleamed with venom. "Though not every time I've been summoned has been by my will. But generally, I'm happy to stop a circus of the blind leading the blind if I can."

I made sure not to touch the table as I circled it, because I had no idea what it could do. "Got'cha," I said. "I feel you on the summoning thing; that must be frustrating. Okay—we're cruising right along here. What tips do you have for people trying to learn divination?"

7. WHAT TIPS DO YOU HAVE FOR PEOPLE LEARNING DIVINATION?

1. When others lose faith in us, we are vulnerable to attack from within.

2. Real success is being surrounded by love and friendship. To be able to give parts of ourselves as we really are.

3. However bitter a conflict may be and however the outcome, we are always able to stand up for our ideas and principles.

"Desperation is an ugly thing, Sara. No one should learn these arts with the approval—or disapproval—of others in mind." He rolled his eyes, as if the thought was so beneath him that he hated even having to speak on it. "It will only lead to muddling the message and forcing falsities on themselves and others. People need to be sure of themselves as they come to learn."

"Heard. That makes a lot of sense." I shook the deck of cards at him. "Well, to close all this out, I am curious: how do you see yourself? You, as a Goetic Prince of Hell?"

8. HOW DO YOU SEE YOURSELF?

Codependency, miscommunication, misunderstanding.

Even when we lose, we gain the experience of defeat. It may be useful for winning future victories.

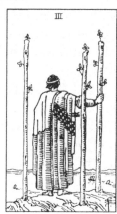

Useful to view the things through the eyes of a child at play. Secret truths are sometimes right there, but we can't see them.

Prince Vassago shrugged and perched on that magic table as if it were any old thing from a furniture outlet. Maybe he was daring me to do the same, but while I was confident about not being in any danger, I also *tried* not to be an idiot, especially after my experience with Azazel, and so I kept a respectable distance.

"I don't take things too seriously," Prince Vassago said, smirking as he noticed me lingering closer to the shadows. "There's no need! When you know your way and are confident in it, and you're able to consider absurd things with ease, you find what others can't. That's how I know all I do: by letting my mind stretch as far as I can conceive, and then a little farther."

It sounded fascinating to me—and like a direct challenge to the comfort I had in the space, as if calling me out for my caution. But I wasn't there for a lesson, like I'd repeatedly had with Lucifer; I was there for the sake of everyone who isn't yet so bold as to go to the infernal realms themselves.

"Alright, I see what you're saying," I said. "Interesting. How do you want others to see you?"

9. HOW DO YOU WANT OTHERS TO SEE YOU?

1. That which we worked for will bear fruit only if we have the patience to wait.

2. Past regrets, ignoring the call to transform, disappointment, false accusations.

3. Preoccupation with a perfect life, familial or relationship bonds, violence, discord.

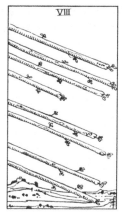

"Ah, I don't worry myself over temporary things, and neither should anyone else. No judgement comes from me—for people, of course, who are willing to let go of the frivolous illusions of life and seek their own fulfillment, other opinions be damned. I'm here for those who are ready to stop being a husk and start being a soul."

And I had no reason not to believe him, because it was as the *Ars Goetia* said: for all his teasing and his daring, he was a genuinely kind spirit. One that, as I'd come to understand of all Divinity, cared for the growth and development of people that had the guts to come seek his help, and would ferociously test people to make sure they were doing their homework.

"Nice. That's really cool; I get you." And even though I was trying to be professional the whole time, I felt that softness that always comes with spending any amount of time with Divinity, be it Classic of Infernal: that gentle kinship and goodwill. "But, well, that more or less takes care of the questions. Are there any last messages you want to give?"

Prince Vassago folded his arms and shrugged. "I've said quite enough. Does this serve you?"

He said it with, again, that Cheshire cat smile. I knew he was asking me if that was enough on the topic of divination, so I let him know: "I think you've answered all my questions perfectly. More than enough here for a conversation on divination, yeah."

We were trading Cheshire smiles at this point. It's something that you'll understand if you've felt it: the daring, the friction, the teasing, that comes with two creatures standoffish and yet receptive to each other, aware of how much trouble they can cause together. I'd felt it with most of the Infernal Divine: the mischief, the opportunity for being a menace on levels previously unknown, the thrill of getting into trouble in places you've told you're not supposed to be. It was a lot different than the feeling of being with angels and Saints: that was more like being surrounded by wise old professors, or older siblings, or parental figures, all of which had no trouble bonking me on the head when I pouted and fussed and groaned at what they were trying to teach me.

Demons are absolutely dangerous. Not because you'll get physically hurt or something (save with a couple specific spirits, I guess), but because they're so willing to let the side of you that never sees the light of day come out and play. It's a type of danger that you can only dose in small amounts if you still want to hold onto any sense of responsibility—a type that reminds you that all our world is, is in fact, just a little waking dream, and that it isn't so serious that you shouldn't have a little *fun*.

Prince Vassago broke our staring contest and tipped his head. "Then that's all I'll say tonight."

"Alright, well—it was good to meet you then, Prince Vassago."

He nodded again, and then he was off, disappearing into the darkness around the table. And that was that. With only a little wisp of him left, I made sure to ask what he wanted to do with the offerings, and I got the sense I should toss them, so outside to my pine tree guardian they went. Then I went off to bed, still carrying just a little bit of that fritzy, troublemaking energy into my meditations before I drifted off to sleep.

ODIN

I'd spoken to Loki. To Freyja. To Thor. And as our last week of the theme of prophecy and divination came about, I thought it'd be as good a time as any to talk to Odin, too—because I heard he knew a thing or two about runes, which are commonly used by Norse pagans as a divination tool. I figure that not only would that finish up our monthly Patreon theme of prophecy and divination, but it would also segue quite nicely into the next chosen theme of magic in general. A two-for-one deal in thematic discussion, if you will.

Of course, I knew a bit of the story of Odin already: that he learned this magic from Freyja, and that it cost him quite a bit of sacrifice. He lost an eye, hung himself upside down for nine days and nights from Yggdrasil, the World Tree, and managed to grasp the secret wisdom within the runes just before he died out there in the harsh conditions he'd put himself in. But what I didn't know was that Odin, the chief god of the Aesir, was mercilessly mocked for this knowledge by the Norse, because magic was traditionally thought to be the realm of women.

Can you imagine? A society where magic was considered as much of a woman's art as cooking and child rearing, and where the chief god could be actively laughed at for knowing it? Blows my mind.

But another thing I learned about Odin in my research is that he isn't the god of sovereignty and justice the way I understand it—that was more Tyr—but the god of *personal* sovereignty, the chaos of battle, and of the dead, as well as poetry, wisdom, magic, and prophecy. His hall, Valhalla, is where those who died nobly in battle will feast with him forever, and he also appears to have some similarities to the more western Germanic god, Wotan (who, in my limited understanding, seems to be something of a cross between gods like Odin and Cernunnos, given his association with the Wild Hunt, the forest, and hunting in general).

Now, Odin was a tricky one for me. I'd spoken to many gods before, yes, but they were gods that weren't the main, chief gods of the pantheon, and especially not ones that were directly responsible for, in their lore, creating mankind as God created Adam and Eve (there's a story of Odin carving the first humans from driftwood on the beach). I'd never spoken to Zeus, or Svarog, or the Dagda, or Ra, or any other such Top Gods that have historically worn similar titles to my God in their respective religions, and that gave me pause. Many Norse pagans I'd come across seemed offended at the idea that I'd hold a more monolatrist view: that all gods existed, but only mine was worthy of my worship. This is a value I continue to hold even after meeting all these gods, and in fact, maybe more so. It makes me wholeheartedly accept statements like in Deuteronomy 10:17:

> For the LORD your God is God of gods and Lord of lords, the great, the mighty, and the awesome God, who is not partial and takes no bribe.

I've seen people get quite upset that I, a *Christian* Witch, would hold this view. (Hell, I've had people come into my space and express explicit disappointment that I was "actually religious" at all, as if the Christian part of my title was all just a ruse.) Maybe some folks also thought that, by speaking to these other gods, this view would change—and I can't say my views didn't change at all. You've already read about how I once denied that these gods were gods; I said only God could be worthy of the word at all, and these other beings were *great spirits* instead (which I soon realized wasn't correct at all and not much different from the folks that insist these gods are just fallen angels or some such). I've obviously changed my position since then, acknowledging that God with a capital G and gods with a lowercase G can exist—can both be a part of the tapestry of the Divine and hold their special roles and powers and domains. But God has always been the Most High, and He always will be in my practice, and to this day, I'm not entirely sure what anyone expected from me.

If you're not also a Christian, chances are we won't believe the same things about God and other gods. No one's expecting or asking us to, either. To get angry about this is perplexing to me, and it reeks of a still heavily Christian attitude for people to be so upset that their new gods are being questioned or rejected in their "Head of Pantheon" or "True God" status (the ironic language of the latter being forever lost on the folks that use it).

Anyway, I was hesitant to speak to Odin precisely because I didn't know what *he* would think for me to approach him, with God, my Keeper, in tow, and with me so obviously not accepting this chief of the Aesir as chief of the world's collective Divine. But when I asked God about it beforehand, I got some positive results, and so I decided to suck it up and face Odin with all the respect I could give him, locked and loaded with plenty of questions about him, his magic, and his work as divine being.

Here's how it went.

For Odin, of course I had some mead for him—a Danish type called Viking Blod, which I felt was a little silly, but it was a type I hadn't tried before, and I was curious. I also had a raven to represent the two he has with him, as well as an amethyst crystal for wisdom, my onyx sphere to represent scrying and divination, the rune associated with him (Ansuz), and as a gift, a plate full of herbs that some sources said were sacred in Norse pagan religion: mugwort, chamomile, and fennel. I also had the Algiz rune Thor gave me after our interview, not only because it meant protection, but because it was a reminder that I was, as far as I knew, in the good graces of the Norse gods.

Then I did my prayers and asked God to let Odin come into my space, and when I felt I had a thread of Odin's energy, I confirmed he was there with the pendulum. He chose Threads of Fate's Weaver Tarot to speak through, and so I got settled in for a night of writing and went to work.

"Odin, hello!" The rhythm of the cards sliding against each other as I shuffled stabilized me, and the music I played—Heilung, Danheim, all that—got me firmly settled in the right atmosphere. "Please join me, chief of the Aesir, father of Balder and Thor. I have for you here a glass of good mead and a gift of fennel, chamomile, and mugwort, and plenty of questions."

At first, there was only darkness. Then, slowly, as if the sun were just rising on a misty morning, everything came into being. When Odin bled into my mind's eye, he was an older man with a black-silver beard and longer, dark hair, but he had a black eye patch over his missing eye. He wore sleek, well-fitted wool clothing in black and grey, as well as a long black cloak and heavy boots. He had a sword at his hip, too, and he studied me in complete silence.

We were in the same place I met Thor, though now there was a throne that Odin sat on (and behind him still was the stained glass, a reminder to me that God hadn't left and was watching, as always). Behind the throne, there sat Thor and Loki, and Thor was eating like hell at that banquet table again. I could finally turn around in this hall and see behind us, too. Outside the banquet hall, down a stone corridor, there was what looked like a well oozing blue magic sitting there out in the open for anyone to pass by. It was good to see Thor and Loki, though, and to say a quick "hello" again.

But I was there for Odin, and we didn't waste any time getting down to business.

"Alright, so! Odin," I said as I sat down at the table, "I've read a bit about you, and given how relentlessly you pursue knowledge, I'm curious: what does knowledge mean for you?"

I. WHAT DOES KNOWLEDGE MEAN FOR YOU?

Opportunities are coming, but you're rejecting them. Judging things before trying them, "woe is me" attitudes. The outside world may seem boring, but you can explore further.

Underhandedness, which could be necessary. Getting away with being deceptive. A warning against impulsiveness.

I'm not sure what I expected, but whatever it was, it was nothing like what happened here. Yes, I had these cards, but as I grasped for Odin's meaning, there were no words explaining this. Instead, Odin took me to a misty tundra, and on it was nothing but the chaos of battle: bodies strewn about, some visible in their dented armor and others just lumpy shapes in the mist, with their compatriots still yelling and fighting and swinging at each other, hopping over the fallen as if they were nothing more than rotting logs—with tattered, blood stained banners fluttering around in the damp wind like an omen of the silence that was to fall over this field. We were walking through it like we were looking at new pillows at Bed Bath & Beyond, even as the swords and axes were swinging all over the place.

Then Odin poked his foot out, made a guy slip in the mud and stumble, and the guy he was fighting was able to bring a sword on him easy. Steel split skin and sinew, the blood bright red as it splashed on what trampled grass remained.

"Sometimes a little deception is necessary to win a particularly frustrating battle," Odin said. He had a sly smile as we kept walking. "Knowledge opens all avenues. It's not me that's not giving things a try," a reference to the language of the Four of Cups, "but others. When we speak of death, all things are a fool's game. There are no rules. The most clever win, not necessarily the most mighty. What good is brute force when your opponent knows the perfect place to strike?"

"Uh—damn, okay." I skittered away from a particularly desperate struggle between two fighters. "I'm in the same boat, I think: I notice a lot of people focus on *honor* rather than getting a job done."

He only smiled at that.

"But okay, well—moving on from the battlefield, while we're talking about magic, I'm baffled, honestly. Why was this considered women's work? In my religion, the prophets were almost exclusively men. At least, the ones we know about, save maybe Deborah. How was it so tied to women here, to the point that the Norse could even scorn *you* for using it?"

2. HOW IS MAGIC TIED TO WOMEN?

We kept walking along this mist, and I shouldn't have been surprised that out of that mist came Freyja, with long red hair and a beautiful silver dress, a finely embroidered grey belt hanging off her hips and a fur cloak around her shoulders. I was happy to see her again, too.

Odin spoke first. "Men think with these," he said as he tapped on his bicep. "They think that through might, all things can be accomplished."

Then Freyja added a thought as she stood beside him: "Women are strong, yes—but not in quite the same way."

And Odin agreed. "Women have to adapt in a world where brute strength is everything."

Creativity, dreaming, raw formless energy. Exploring and being curious and creative.

Exhaustion after conflict. Tension so draining that it offers perspective. Maybe what we're pushing for doesn't matter as much. Finding solutions, pushing aside ego.

They traded off nearly line for line, with Freyja speaking again. "We may not have the physical strength exactly as men do, but we have the agility. The intelligence. The cunning. The patience for a long plan. The boundary between life and death—or *pre*-life, or *un*-life."

She flashed an image of herself pregnant, but only for a moment, and the meaning was clear even without explanation: to me, it was as if she was saying that the state of pregnancy was a time where people held that liminal space between life and death in their own bodies. Not yet alive, but far from dead, a fetus in the womb stood outside of the bounds of Life and Death as we understand it.

Wild.

Freyja smiled, no doubt able to feel my head spinning as much as I did. "It was this that I shared with my husband," she said.

And again, Odin chimed in: "This was a power women nurtured, and it was a power men scorned when anyone other than women did it."

"Wow. That's... something." Nothing like having a concept like that dropped on you so casually. "Thank you for explaining that."

Freyja's smile grew, and then she disappeared into the mist. It was Odin and I again just walking along a loosely cobbled path, with weeds and mud between the stones. The mess of war was behind us, the sounds fading away. I couldn't see very far ahead of us, though.

"Moving on from that, then," I said, checking my list of questions. "Odin, can you tell me a bit about the ritual sacrifice you had to do to get this understanding? It almost reminds me of the idea of 'born again Christians,' I won't lie—the symbolic death and rebirth."

3. THOUGHTS ON YOUR RITUAL SACRIFICE FOR KNOWLEDGE?

Stuck in the ebbs of life with challenge after challenge coming your way. Examine the role you've played in this rather than viewing yourself as a victim. Accept changes and move forward.

Leading with an iron fist. Cold, manipulative, abusive of power. Ego takes over, causing one to lose true power, which comes from supporting those you lead. Needing compassion and understanding.

Odin was quiet for a while; it seemed he wanted me to piece together what the cards were saying before elaborating, which was nice. As we've seen before, some spirits have pulled cards just for the sake of having them there while chattering my ear off before I could even write them down.

"All things you thought you knew must die," he said. "All things you thought you were, those illusions, must die. There is darkness here, but then there is light again, an understanding so bright and fierce that all else seems petty. It swallows you. It makes you see what you never could've seen without being willing first to sacrifice all."

"Huh. I think I get'cha." In this meditation, I saw outside myself—saw me bundled up against the cold and walking beside him, a little thing next to his grand stature. Just a child, walking alongside an elder and asking strange, philosophic, and funny little questions. "Ego death. You need ego death to move on and see more than what's in front of you."

Odin nodded. "Yes. That's the idea."

As I've said before: many revelations and ideas about what I've experienced come after I've experienced them rather in the moment. While Odin's words put a little seed in my head right then, it was the next morning, when I went to write out my discoveries for my patrons, that I thought of the idea that Jesus put forth in the Gospels, in Luke 17:33: *Whoever seeks to preserve his life will lose it, but whoever loses his life will keep it.*

Interesting, how many connections we can find between the esoteric, magical folks across the world. It's almost as if the Spirit World has its own physics, and the many entities that make up Divinity are all beholden to it, just as we're beholden to things like gravity and magnetism.

"Alright, I can get on board with that," I said, tucking these ideas away for later. "Okay. Now, how about divination? What does this mean to you, and what is its function to you? To me, it's just what we're doing here: talking and chatting, question and answer type stuff. But what do you think?"

4. WHAT EXACTLY IS DIVINATION TO YOU?

1. Successful collaboration that you should feel excited about. All parties have different expertise and experience, but they work together exceptionally well. Can get things done and make a great impact. Prioritizing healthy communication.

2. Building on raw creative energy and translating it to the real world. Doing the boring work most people don't love to do. Creating space for goals and taking them seriously.

"Divination is direct access to knowledge, he said. Then he gave me a cheeky smile, and though he only had one eye, it felt as if he was winking. "As your own God says, 'Ask and ye shall receive,' no? The function is simple: ask questions, get answers. When we don't sit in the dark, and instead make use of any and all that could help us find answers, we grow.

"We gain knowledge, and knowledge is power. It connects man to gods and reveals what rocks and sand, the material world, all hide from you."

I shook out my wrist once I finished that stint of writing. Looking over my notes, I nodded and said, "I see—that makes sense! Cool. But what do you think about people using the runes themselves to divine? Is that what they're for, or is that just a part of it?"

5. THOUGHTS ON USING THE RUNES TO DIVINE?

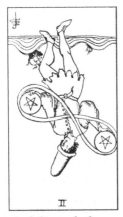

Celebration, harmony. A time of balance. Celebrating what's going right, getting ready to celebrate more. Acknowledging goodness.

A delicate balance has fallen by the wayside, making it impossible to keep up. Putting unnecessary things aside.

"Ah." He smiled the way older men do when they see young folks about to learn a hefty lesson doing something stupid. "Runes need to be handled with care. But to the victor, the spoils. If one can divine with the runes, understanding their power and taking precautions, they'll never lose their footing. But if they aren't careful, they can get swallowed by something greater than them."

"Fair enough." That, I'd argue, went for most divination methods. Most magic in general. "And now, how about in battle and in rule? How does magic in general help here? I've got some ideas, but what do you think?"

Suddenly, we were off the misty path and back in the banquet room. Thor was right where we'd left him, chewing away at the mountain of food on the table.

6. HOW DOES MAGIC HELP WITH BATTLE AND RULERSHIP?

1. It's impossible to prevent the ebb and flow of life. Reflect and assess your actual needs. Strength and resilience are rewarded, along with courage. You must change your mindset. What have you never tried before?

2. Someone with lots of energy. Curious, excited, quick witted. Exceptionally intelligent, insights beyond their years. Boldness to challenge the status quo. Raw, passionate energy.

"What one can't conquer physically can be conquered in other ways," Odin said as he went back to his throne. "It's folly to only ever rely on one's muscle. No one can tame you when you use all your wit and all the power available—even power you're not *supposed* to touch. If you are brave, you take what's yours, no matter what method you find to do so. But you have to decide what's yours first."

"Oh. That makes sense to me, yeah! Okay!" I hopped back to the table and set all my things down on it. "And before we come into our last questions, I gotta ask: as a god and patron of outlaws, what do you think about magic itself being outlawed in so many cultures, like in the Roman empire?"

7. THOUGHTS ON SO MANY CULTURES OUTLAWING MAGIC?

Stuck in a pessimistic mindset that prevents you from tapping into personal power. Restore some play.

Rest, withdraw, and gather your strength. Rest gives perspective, resilience, and energy. Do things to relax.

The throne room faded away, along with Odin's easy expression. I just managed to snatch my things back up; we ended up on the road into a small village, and as we walked, all the people's eyes pointed at us like the eyes of wolves, tracking each step. Their heads turned to follow us all the way down, as if they hated us just for being there, and there were pyres where flames took up everything I could see.

"Magic wasn't an issue for my people, but what came after was nothing good," Odin muttered. "Nothing good at all. At least now, such persecutions are over. People can freely connect with power beyond the world they see again, and they can rest knowing they're no longer outlaws for it. Now all is peace." Then he pointed that one sharp eye at me. "But it may not stay that way for long. Build your strength while you can. Know when to withdraw. A storm is brewing."

How ominous. It made me think of folks like Greg Locke, honestly. While I don't think we'll ever get to this point again, with the burnings and the criminalization of magic, there are certainly people who would like to see it that way, and they'll push back in whatever legal ways they can where their theocratic fantasies aren't allowed to play out. It's up to the people with sense to push back while this problem is only just budding. Not the most comforting message, but not the worst, either.

"I see. Well, let's hope it doesn't come to anything too hard to weather." We can only hope, can only pray, can only try. "But now, might I ask how you see yourself? What you think about yourself?"

8. HOW DO YOU SEE YOURSELF?

Odin nodded. "I am someone who was not what others wanted or expected me to be—yet I am me nonetheless. A master of ecstasy. A leader of all things wild and free. I am mighty, in my own way, with my own definition of might."

"And how do you want others to see you?"

1. Lack of follow through, not living up to potential. Doubt in abilities. Could mean deception, greed.

2. Rapid movement to emotions. A person that leads with feeling. Illusions present. Out of control but feeling great.

9. HOW DO YOU WANT OTHERS TO SEE YOU?

A few options are available to you, and you're centering to make the best choice for sustainable success.

Internal will and resilience. Compassion and love make faster transformation. Merge with challenges instead of seeing them as a battle. Strength to meet difficult things without resistance.

He glanced at me and raised a brow. "Even with the frenzy, the ecstasy—I am not an uncalculated man. I am not a dishonest man, either. I know where I lack, and I find ways to fill these gaps with more knowledge, more transformation." He echoed his last answer: "I am not a man of ego, only might I've forged with my own hands, in my own way."

"Nice. I love it! Okay, well, before we say goodbye, do you have any final messages?"

10. ANY MESSAGES FOR ME OR OTHERS?

The village faded away. Our steps on gravelly, uneven ground became steps echoing off the banquet room's tile again, and Odin smiled here as we paused in the middle of the room. I will say, there was quite a bit of traveling in this interview.

"Be well," Odin said. "Be brave. Be curious. And be worthy of every challenge you face."

"Oh. Okay!" Wasn't entirely sure who that message was for specifically, if it was for any one person in particular. It seemed like another one of those "if the shoe fits" messages. "Alright, well, that's that. Thank you, Odin, for your time; it was lovely to see everyone again and to get to know you a bit! I appreciate all the answers you've given me!"

I waved to Thor, and to Odin, who gave me a big smile before he went back to his throne. And then everything faded away, until it was just me sitting there with a pile of dried herbs and some crystals. Like most nights, it was late, and so it went from interview to post-meditation social media scrolling (for decompression of the mind, of course) to bed. All the while, though, I couldn't help but feel a little heavy in my heart, because there was a pattern here. There was an obvious scar in the tapestry of Divinity—but not because of gods. Because of *people*.

We've made a mess. We've trespassed on each other, all of humankind against all of humankind, using our gods as justifications to do so. Persecutors have become persecuted and vice versa. For what reason, though, has anyone ever needed to persecute?

Frankly, we can ask that question all day, but the point still stands: Divinity recognizes the injustice we've done against their children, and the ridiculous reasons we've used to justify doing so. From my observations talking to these deities, especially ones of cultures that have been historically embattled or repressed by Christianity or have had adverse encounters with God of some kind (for example, the Egyptian gods because of the story of Exodus), one thing is clear: the gods don't have issues with each other, or with God. (And if they did, those grudges have long passed.) They understand and respect each other's role, sovereignty, and importance just fine.

It's the *worshippers* that they have serious gripes with, and that are constantly being negotiated on in terms of what should be done when one deity's child crosses a line or how much to intervene on a larger scale to follow certain prophecies, flows of fate, and so on. We are, without a doubt, the gods' biggest headache, and in my opinion, it makes perfect sense why more nefarious types of religious "leaders" would want to remove divination from people's spiritual skillset: because when you can talk to any god directly, and your answers prove true, you put these false leaders in one hell of a tight spot if they keep trying to shill their abusive and self serving doctrines.

This is, in my purview, an era of personal religion. That comes with its own dangers, and we sure have seen many a spiritual or New Age individual push some damaging rhetoric, of course, but we are still coming to this point so that we might toss off the institutions that have caused us such grief and learn to hear the voices of Divinity again without con men and dictators getting in the way. It's time we open ourselves up to the spiritual world we've been surrounding ourselves with yet neglecting. It's time we learn to *listen* as much as pray; it's time we learn what Jesus meant when He, time and time again, insisted that *anyone with ears should hear* and *anyone with eyes should see.*

Because from what I'm seeing, hearing, learning, and understanding, we won't make it much longer if we keep letting the spiritually blind lead the blind.

ST. PAUL
THE APOSTLE

Man, St. Paul. Is there any figure in the New Testament more wild, controversial, and *loud* than St. Paul (besides Jesus Himself)? Though, of course, for many folks, St. Paul is controversial in a much different way than Jesus. A few verses come to mind, namely ones from Romans, Corinthians, and 1 Timothy—verses that shoddy religious leaders and people looking for a reason to be terrible have used for centuries to justify so much abuse and hate and nonsense.

This was what made me tell God, many years ago, that St. Paul had *until I got my hands on him* to explain himself the day I died and went to Heaven. Thankfully, it seems God heard me, and that St. Paul wanted to explain himself early, because between this interview and several other books that have found their way to me concerning things St. Paul said, I've completely revised my opinion on this fellow. And I found these more bigoted Christians do their dirty work, of course, at the expense of the more beautiful and empowering things St. Paul said, like his famous saying in Galatians 3:28:

> *There is neither Jew nor Gentile, neither slave nor free, nor is there male and female, for you are all one in Christ Jesus.*

This is a core concept of the ragtag religion that was, until Roman adoption, a liberating, society-crushing, radical, and bold faith, one by and for the underdogs. It's a core concept supported and grown by the Golden Rule Jesus put forward (you know, that whole Love Thy Neighbor thing), and that, along with St. Paul's definition of love, make for some of the most moving and powerful concepts Christianity can hold. Let's take a moment to look at 1 Corinthians 13:1-13, where St. Paul talks about love to the Corinthian church he wrote to:

> *If I speak in the tongues of men or of angels, but do not have love, I am only a resounding gong or a clanging cymbal. I have the gift of prophecy and can fathom all mysteries and all knowledge, and if*

I have a faith that can move mountains, but do not have love, I am nothing. If I give all I possess to the poor and give over my body to hardship that I may boast, but do not have love, I gain nothing.

Love is patient, love is kind. It does not envy, it does not boast, it is not proud. It does not dishonor others, it is not self-seeking, it is not easily angered, it keeps no record of wrongs. Love does not delight in evil but rejoices with the truth. It always protects, always trusts, always hopes, always perseveres.

Love never fails. But where there are prophecies, they will cease; where there are tongues, they will be stilled; where there is knowledge, it will pass away. For we know in part and we prophesy in part, but when completeness comes, what is in part disappears. When I was a child, I talked like a child, I thought like a child, I reasoned like a child. When I became a man, I put the ways of childhood behind me. For now we see only a reflection as in a mirror; then we shall see face to face. Now I know in part; then I shall know fully, even as I am fully known.

And now these three remain: faith, hope and love. But the greatest of these is love.

Yep. That was St. Paul who said all that—the same St. Paul that apparently said a bunch of silly things about women and the LGBTQ+ community and more, if any of these *sola scriptura* folks who believe the Bible is perfectly translated and preserved from antiquity to now are to be believed. Thankfully, we have scholars who can remove the biases of such prejudice and try to find out, in earnest, what St. Paul was really saying—like John T. Bristow in his *What Paul Really Said About Women,* which I highly recommend you all read if you want to get twice as angry as you've ever been.

I'll spoil a big concept for you off the bat: it wasn't St. Paul that said women shouldn't speak or teach or are underneath their husband, but the people who interpreted him decades to centuries after through the lens of *pagan Greek philosophers* like Socrates, Zeno, Plato, Aristotle, and so on. These culturally Greek converts to Christianity took all their garbage ideas about women into their new religion, and even centuries later, medieval Christians kept looking to ancient Greece as some pinnacle of intelligence and philosophy and greatness, shoving the true radical ideas of St. Paul out of the way for these outdated, dusty, and archaic ideas that should've been left in antiquity.

And that's only about *women.* There's plenty more scholarship to revisit these "anti-LGBTQ+" sections people use, like in Romans, where we're reminded that our modern ideas of sexuality are absolutely nothing like the concepts of sexuality that existed in antiquity, and therefore couldn't have been talked about. I saw someone online say once that to ask St. Paul about homosexuality would be like to ask Abraham Lincoln what his favorite website was, and I can't get that out of my head, because it's a perfect example of how ridiculous it is to constantly try and graft our modern ideas onto ancient people and base our current values on the philosophical ideas of a totally different time and place. God doesn't change, says the *sola scriptura* folks, but the world sure does, and so do the people that encounter God (and even then, others like Moltmann will argue that God doesn't change *from outside* influence, but *can* change if He chooses to, so honestly, everybody can get bent in some way or another when they start thinking they can actually pin God down in any meaningful way).

Anyway, all this hoopla aside, St. Paul is such a character. Originally a devout and zealous Jewish man, one actively persecuting early Christians and seeing them sent off to their deaths for their faith under Roman rule, his name was original Saul of Tarsus. It wasn't until he had a direct vision of Jesus Christ while traveling that he learned the error of his ways, converted, took on the name Paul, and went out to become the most well-known and outspoken advocate of this religion that we still know of to this day. While he never met Jesus during Jesus' lifetime, he still considered himself an Apostle in full, and he was so intense in all his letters. Reading any of them will make you tired instantly, yet endear you to him all the same; he is Type A energy incarnate.

But if you'll remember in the passage of 1 Corinthians I just quoted, we see St. Paul mentions that he has gifts of prophecy and "can fathom all mysteries and all knowledge"—something that Dr. Justin Sledge of the YouTube channel Esoterica does a deeper dive into when discussing the certain branches of mysticism St. Paul might've followed (Hekhalot and Merkabah mysticism). When St. Paul talks about knowing someone who was "swept up to the third heaven" (2 Corinthians 12:2)? Yeah, he was talking about himself.

In short: St. Paul had the dirty details on some good early Christian magic. And if you think I wasn't going to do a full cannonball into an interview with him to learn more, then I'm guessing you've never heard of me and didn't read a single other chapter of this book except this one. Hello! Welcome! Come along, and see the results of my contacting the one and only St. Paul the Apostle.

So I'd actually just finished a long rosary prayer with Mama Mary before I spoke to St. Paul, because I was doing this interview on Candlemas, a Christian festival day celebrating Mary's return to society forty days after the birth of Jesus. I didn't have anything in particular for St. Paul; I just poured him a cup of tea from the pot I'd made for Mary and I, some good Tulsi Rose tea, and kept my Candlemas candle burning. I also opened up to 2 Corinthians 12 on recommendation of @linathejesuswitch (Lina), who regularly works with St. Paul and knows how much of a handful he can be. Specifically, I read the verses about the thorn in St. Paul's side that God gave him to keep him humble—a sign that he might've dealt with some chronic pain in his life, and could be a helpful ally to have for anyone else suffering that kind of pain.

But as I was already meditating in the Heavenly sphere, with Mama Mary there, I found that I was in the right spot for St. Paul to come over and speak. God let him through easily, and of course, face to face with him, there was no way I could've ever given him the wallop I once promised. I'd have to save that for a later time, I told myself—and a few months after this interview, when I got Bristow's book thanks to @neomudang (Ji Hae) sending it to me out of the blue, I found the need to give St. Paul the old one-two disappeared entirely.

As I said, the man explained himself early.

But once I caught a glimpse of St. Paul, I just jumped into things and got rolling.

"St. Paul! Hello! Welcome; please join Mama Mary and I for some tea and a chat. I've got quite a few questions for you, mister."

Mama Mary and I were sitting in the cathedral I'd first visited her in, and St. Paul was coming towards us, down the celestial path of clouds with book in hand and a shiny halo. He was an older gentleman with grey hair and long greyish robes that later became a bold and vibrant red, and he had a friendly smile I didn't expect, given how I was feeling a bit closed off due to my misconceptions.

But once I found myself standing in front of him, the walls I had up crumbled. There was no animosity, no anger, no nothing between us. Just two people ready to chat about things that mattered. And one of the first things he showed me, before we even got started on the questions, was how he and St. Barnabas would flash their light and gold through the streets of a small village here and there—light only they and I could see, but that everyone peering at them from the alleys was drawn to nonetheless, which I think we'll call charisma. As if putting on a show, St. Paul showed me all these signs and wonders he used to do, and in the next moment, he showed me how they would talk to the people on the sides of the street once they were done making their noise, tucked away and practically hiding in the alleyways as they whispered teachings, drawing little crowds of interested folks so as to not alert too many of the city officials and guards.

I think that was more symbolic than anything. I don't know if St. Paul ever did go loud and proud through the streets like that, the way it's told in the Acts of the Apostles. But I know by his letters that education was his thing, as well as passion for the good news. So I confirmed with him what deck he wanted to use—Threads of Fate's Weaver Tarot—and I settled with him on the cloudy steps before the golden gates of Heaven to ask my questions.

"Alright, so—I don't know if you're teasing me or what, showing me all that," I said, and he chuckled as I lightly elbowed him, "but given all I've read about the early Christians recently, and especially the things you and St. Peter did in Acts, I gotta know: how did you not catch a sorcery charge from the Romans doing all this?"

I. HOW DID YOU NOT CATCH A SORCERY CHARGE (OR TWELVE)?

A challenge for witches and new agers, this is about convention, especially in religion. Growth comes with rigorous practice.

A scarcity mindset. Being laser focused on wealth and money means losing out on what else life has to offer, preventing us from connecting with true joy.

In a blink, the clouds of Heaven disappeared, and we were back in a town not unlike the one he showed himself traipsing through with St. Barnabas: humble buildings, people walking about in robes and doing daily tasks like selling things or hanging laundry out to dry. St.Paul shrugged as we walked down the road of this little Roman town, ambling along like tourists.

"I had sway," he said, as if it were so simple. "I was an established man. Had I done nothing but wonder after wonder, yes, people might've assumed me a fraud—though some did anyway. But when you focus not on gathering a crowd, but on teaching, and a teaching that stems from a solid foundation in the Lord, you get farther with people. It's why I told those fools—avoid your petty 'miracles.' They make no difference to the untrained eye."

"Uh-huh. I see. Interesting." I wondered what he meant by "untrained eye," but at the same time, I had a pretty good idea, too. There was a reason, after all, that magic and miracle were synonymous until they weren't. "Well, you know—one person I know and love that works with you, Lina, mentioned you loved to talk about this thorn here in 2 Corinthians 12. And I gotta say, this whole passage is pretty powerful. Can you tell me about it? About how power is 'made perfect in weakness'?"

2. HOW IS POWER MADE PERFECT IN WEAKNESS?

Somehow, in the two seconds I'd asked this question, we'd left the town. We were outside a crumbling Roman fortress instead, long abandoned, as the last words left my lips.

"The mind is a well established fort," St. Paul said as he turned to me. "You can't attack such a fort without a plan. They're defended by ideas so old and ancient, and so decrepit, yet still, they're sturdy enough to withstand an uneven attack. With this thorn, God took away my energy. He took away my over-enthusiasm, the force of my many pushes in uneven directions.

"He made me think," St. Paul said. We came to a part of the wall with gaps big enough to slip through. As we sidled into the fortress a few steps, he continued. "He made me gently work my way past the rubble of the minds of others, find the open places in the fort to easily enter rather than try to put the full might of God straight through a wall. You win no friends with force."

"Alright, alright. That makes sense." A loose stone tumbled from the fortress and thumped against packed earth. "I know everyone was tradition-obsessed back then, which doesn't make sense to me as a modern person. But you know, speaking of force... I do have to ask. What are your thoughts on the way your letters have been used throughout history? To justify the things people used them to justify, like misogyny, even slavery?"

Stalling or doubts when it comes to moving forward. Slow down, be thorough, and be sure. Haste leads to disappointment.

Lots of energy and passion, but lacks direction or an outlet. Need to have a healthy outlet for this person, or else the mind will become chaos. Building new things.

3. THOUGHTS ON HOW YOUR WRITINGS HAVE BEEN ABUSED?

Barreling through obstacles, filled with motivation and determination. You're more than capable of making it happen. Put in work.

A period of intense work. It may feel soul crushing or not. It's temporary, so find yourself in a state of ease.

Paul had a muscle working in his jaw as I asked. It worked harder as I showed him some of the images of things that I'd seen about the subject through documentaries and movies. He wasn't happy in the slightest, from my perspective, and how could he have been, when he saw how future generations of people were enslaved, silenced, and killed, with his words as the justification? We left the fortress and came back to the roads of that Roman town.

"I wanted people to know their sufferings were temporary," Paul insisted. "Not eternal. When Χρίστος (Chrístos) said He would come back, I believed it—but I misjudged the time.

"I said what needed to be said in *my* time. Χρίστος is coming—but people can't stay as they were while they wait. Not anymore. They need to prepare the way here. Look at this world now."

We left the town to stand in an empty school classroom, full of boys and girls that I was looking at from the back as Paul stood at the teacher's desk. The glass windows were big and open enough to look over a place that looked something like California, or a modern place.

"We are where all are truly one. Where boys and girls alike are learning together. Jesus is returning, but we must make a place for His return—must make the Kingdom within ourselves, where He said it was already. I misspoke. There's work to be done, hard, terrible work, and it must be done quickly.

"The world can't take much more of this," he said as the sky darkened, and what looked like a meteor shower started looming over the town, as if some volcano had erupted and sent massive rocks flying. "It can't remain static as it was. I see that now. It's too much."

From the sense I was getting that went unspoken, with the terror outside and the classroom here and Paul's long face, it felt like he was saying we needed to evolve past where we are. Really internalize the idea of the Kingdom of Heaven being not a place we go to, but a concept we house. Maybe Jesus coming back means just that: that He comes to each of us individually to let us see the worth we have and the way we need to work to make this planet reflect what's inside of us, which is a place where all are free.

I think humanity hasn't really been doing that, with the way the planet's going these days.

"Wow. Shit, okay. Um." How was I supposed to react to any of this at the time, though, when I was watching this school full of children get all these fireballs lobbed at it? Eventually that image faded, and I took a second to recenter myself before continuing. "I think I get what you're saying, but it's a little hard to grasp completely. That's okay; I understand enough. Well, moving on: what do you think of the whole 'magic vs. miracle' debate? I mean, we know you were out there doing all kinds of cool magical stuff. Just in Acts alone, you and Peter were getting into some things. But some people insist it's not magic, but miracle. What do you think?"

4. WHERE DO YOU STAND ON THE MAGIC VS. MIRACLE DEBATE?

THE HIEROPHANT

A challenge for witches and new agers, this is about convention, especially in religion. Growth comes with rigorous practice.

Confusion. The thickest fog possible. When it comes to any decisions you make, walk slowly with one foot in front of the other, so as not to trip.

As I was asking, one word just popped up with the cards before I'd even flipped them:

"Immaterial."

Then St. Paul went on to say, when I had all my card definitions collected: "When God grants His gifts, you don't waste time trying to define them. You use them. People can't see in the fog of their own argument. Does it matter what it's called? No. Only how you use such power—that is the measure of a man. We didn't do φαρμακεία (pharmakeia)—those lowly tricks, squelching money from the foolish dead. We lit lamps in the darkness, that the eternally alive might find their way."

I swear, where he sent me next looked just like the catacombs in *Dark Souls*. He stood with his back to me and held up a lantern in pitch black darkness, and from the shadows beyond, there were people almost zombie-like in their trance that twitched and hobbled past him, as if they couldn't move until they had that light.

Weird. Even weirder than the souls trudging after Azrael. I'm still not sure what to do with that.

"Lamps we lit by God's grace," St. Paul whispered.

I had to ask another quick question before moving on: "Is that what charisma is? When people talk about it?"

"Yes. It's letting God's light shine out of you. It looks like sorcery to those who have never seen it before. But it isn't the fraudulent tricks our opponents defamed us with by their accusations."

"Oh! Okay, okay, I think I'm getting it." It seems to me that magic was just thought of as parlor tricks, Houdini level stuff, by the way he talked, which would make sense if we understand the story of Simon the Magos in Acts. "But then, what—how do Christians tap into that now? Whether Christian witches or magicians or just plain Christians, how do they get that spiritual heritage? That power? How do they use it?"

5. HOW SHOULD CHRISTIANS TAP INTO THEIR MAGIC?

"You can't be seeking power for power's sake," he said over his shoulder. "It's not about us. It's about Him."

And then the rest of the place illuminated, and it was no longer a cave, but a big church. St. Paul was pointing up, to a statue of Jesus on the cross.

"The spark," he said, showing me a little orange ember burning in his chest, "is our connection. The angels watch us as we watch them."

By this, he meant the stars. It's said in Jewish folklore that there's an angel for every star. *Mazel* means constellation.

"Through our spark—our soul—we create within ourselves an Ark. We become a conduit to channel God's might. That is a Christian 'Witch's' power," he said with a bit of a half-smile at me, as if to poke fun at the title, "to connect and call down the attention and might of God with the spark, the soul, the power He gave us all.

"All power stems from the soul, and God made the soul. God lets it flow—there'll always be a soul tie to Him, even if we flex the drop of power He gave us without calling down the lightning strike that is God's majesty."

I stared at him. "So even though it's the power He put there, like the muscle and brain He put on us, it's...?"

"All is His glory. Directly or indirectly."

Focus on the external is born of ego. If we're focused on what others thing of us, or we're trying to impress them, we won't do what's best for ourselves long term.

Out of balance and getting in one's own way. Having big dreams but being unable to reach them means lashing out, getting aggressive, and losing respect. Prioritize healthy leadership.

And I had this image that was just wild. A person standing there, the "spark" of their soul burning in their chest, and like an anchor, it called down such a massive tower of golden light that extended all the way to the sky and flowed around them like a big golden shield. This was what, I figured, was known as "calling down the fire." This was magic—*real* magic.

This was miracle.

I huffed a laugh. "This is what you were showing me earlier, huh? With the charisma and everything else, that light only we could see?"

He only smiled.

"Okay, well," I was giddy, thrilled with the knowledge I'd been given, but I knew I had to move on before I spent all night thinking about it, "how does this relate to Thecla, then? The woman at the window like a spider? All tied up in the things you were saying—what do you think about that? About how people like Thecla reacted to your words at the time?"

6. THOUGHTS ON ST. THECLA?

KNIGHT of SWORDS.

A steamroller. Viewing the world from a logical perspective. Detachment and ambition help one get ahead. Working well under pressure.

THE STAR.

Alignment and harmony, relief after challenges. Everything in your favor. While you've been through a lot, your light has not dimmed.

"That 'woman at the window' felt there was something more out there," said St. Paul, as easily as if he was describing the weather. "When you have the illusions of the world torn down, playing along with the nonsense becomes impossible. I didn't force the woman to react so. I spoke in the authority granted in me by God, and whatever sounds my mouth made didn't matter: it was the glory of God she perceived and heard and followed. Such is the power of channeling the true Wisdom through your spark. The messages flow like water."

These messages were very much not flowing like water in the spoken sense. St. Paul talked one half of the time, and then St. Paul just demonstrated like a science teacher at the front of the room the other half the time. It was tough to parse it. This, I could wrap my head around, but it still took me a second to work after it, and I would often question whether or not I was hearing right as I let the words flow from the tip of my pencil. Knowing doubt only made it worse, I kept writing—a *flow of conscious* style writing, one that made me pause and re-read it afterwards a few times.

"I hear you. That... makes enough sense," I said once I'd gotten through reading it all one final time.

And it did: from what I could gather, it seemed Thecla was being directly inspired by the Holy Spirit, regardless of what St. Paul was saying, and her perception of the Spirit was made possible by St. Paul projecting it outward, the Spirit itself being the wind under the wings of his words as they floated to Thecla's window. I nodded and looked up to him, moving on once I'd made the connection.

"Now, though, how about exorcisms? This is described as one of the top magical acts Christians and Jewish people were known for. But what does it entail? Is it just banishing spirits, or is it more? I even heard *you* were sending Christians demons before you converted—which, I don't know if that's true, but it makes me curious."

7. WHAT DOES AN EXORCISM ENTAIL?

St. Paul cut me a narrow stare from the corner of his eye. He glossed over saying anything about doing so explicitly, but I think if we read between the lines here, we may find an answer that satisfies us, whatever we may make of it.

"Exorcisms reset an area, a person," he said. "Where things could get tangled, people caught in vice, exorcism cuts the knots and frees the soul. Demons are but another force in this world, and when you learn how to direct that force the way it's supposed to be—away from people who don't need or deserve them—you understand exorcism. But they can be directed towards things, too."

"Oh, like when Jesus cast the legion of demons into the flock of pigs?"

He nodded. "Yes. The pigs don't have the will to fight like people do, so they perish under this force, but it works all the same. Mastering exorcism means mastering the flow of clean and unclean forces."

"Damn. That sounds pretty cool, not gonna lie." It made it clear for me, too, what one could do with it—with the inverse of exorcism, which St. Paul clearly knew a thing or two about. "But alright, alright, that wraps up the main questions. Can you tell me how you see yourself?"

Success won. Harvest, stability, living in abundance. Independence won. Continue to connect with others. No point in abundance if we can't share it. More than material wealth.

Arrival and completion. Not only financial success, but harmony with relationships, too. Think long term about future generations. Ripple effect. People will do as you say, not as you do.

8. HOW DO YOU SEE YOURSELF?

Creative dreaming, raw energy. Throw away preconceptions, especially about yourself. Living in the unseens. More questions than answers.

A few options are available to you, and you're centering on the best, most sustainable choice. Not a time for get-rich-quick schemes.

We were suddenly at a desk covered in books, St. Paul writing away.

"I am a humble man, I'd like to think," he said as he wrote.

"Yeah?" I crossed my arms and leaned against the table, standing over him with a mean smirk hooking at one corner of my lips. "What about in 2 Corinthians 12, when you're boasting up and down about all kinds of things, then? Where's the humility there?"

St. Paul only smiled and nodded. "I'm humble save when I have reason to boast, and when I have *reason* to boast, I do. But I've been so challenged. All I was, wiped away with one vision of our Lord... how do you describe that?" He put his pen down and folded his arms, as if beside himself, and then he shook his head. "I am one who takes account, who thinks as they see, and yet I never could've seen all this world as it is now."

"Aha, I see. And how do you want others to see you?"

9. HOW DO YOU WANT TO BE SEEN?

Being stuck in a pessimistic mindset. This is preventing you from tapping into true power and wisdom. Restore play into your life.

Stagnance. Being unable to bring life through. Creating a foundation of self love and confidence. Doubting ability to hold so much.

I was pretty surprised at the negativity of the cards he pulled, but it made for a powerful message. He looked at me and spoke with such iron conviction.

"I am upset knowing my words have taken people farther from the Kingdom of God." His fists balled up even as he kept his arms crossed, and his face creased with the severity of his frown. "I never wanted this. But all we can do now is fix it. I am someone learning to move forward and find a way to continue guiding people, however I can. I want this world to be saved. No matter how."

"Wow. Noted." Always about the salvation, these Christian spirits—but the more I talk to them, the more I don't think they mean salvation the way most Christians mean it these days. "Okay, well, do you want to pull any cards for a final message?"

10. ANY LAST MESSAGES FOR ME OR OTHERS?

A solid yes pinged through me after I asked, so I pulled the cards and got smacked right away with St. Paul's final words.

"I know we want to fix the world right now," he said. "Right away. But the world wasn't brought to this state in a day, and it won't be fixed in a day, either. Don't stop fighting for a better world—never—but remember you can't fight forever with no rest. Find things to enjoy—the stars peeking out at dusk, the last light in the evening sky, fresh fruit, friendship. Find ways to soothe your spirit in the quiet moments so that you might roar like lions in the loud ones. Be brave," and then he leaned over to elbow me and wink, a big smile on his face, "and have some humor, too."

"Absolutely, yeah, I hear you." Then I shut my book and clapped, with a smile on my own face. "Well, alright—thank you, St. Paul, for being here! It was great to meet you and correct my perception of you. I appreciate your time, and I hope to see you around."

And so we parted ways, with him fading off back into Heaven, and with Heaven fading to nothing but the darkness of my closed eyes. I picked up the tea from the table,

Celebration, harmony, and balance in life. Must ride the ebbs and flows for as long as we're alive. Building energy for what you're grateful for. Acknowledging goodness.

Having your eye on the finish line, but missing steps to get to the end. Maybe being impatient and looking for short-cuts. If an emotional issue, find acceptance. We can't run from ourselves.

washed up, headed off to bed, the whole thing. But all the while, I was giddy—and maybe a little frustrated, too.

Because for all my years of being a witch, I had only just then, on that night, received the information I needed to make any of what I did make any sense.

Do you know how often I struggled with the concept of magic? What it meant as a Christian Witch, how it operated? Do you know how many times I fumbled through spellwork and prayers, unsure of exactly what to say or do, unsure of how the creation I incorporated into my workings actually helped? How many times I wondered if I was doing something wrong, or if my spells were actually working? Or what the *point* of spellwork was, if God was the one who held the Big Red Veto button anyway? And then, in one single interview, among all that St. Paul had to say, I found it: the key to Christian magic.

It was a collaboration. That's all magic ever was and ever has been: a collaboration between Man and God, a negotiation between Reality and Fantasy. We aren't expected to come to the ritual table and do all the work; we're only there to bring the offerings, the organization, and the flint and steel that is our magic. Our brothers and sisters in creation—the herbs, the crystals, all of it—can *help*, can certainly contribute a little energy and create the grids of focus for the magic to flow, but it's *us* that actually makes the magic spark, and it's *God* that makes the magic catch. From our ember to His glorious flame.

And how could I not have realized this? As I do my research, and as I look into the spells of antiquity—the Greek magical papyrae, the many cultures and traditions and religions that incorporated court magicians, or "priests," into their framework—I understand that this is how magic has always been: using one's power to reach past the veil and petition the great Divine beings for their help. Negotiating with them, giving a little to get a little by way of our own life force we call magic. Using our divine spark, as St. Paul called it, to reach up and connect with the Divine's great and holy fire, to call it down.

Let me put this further in perspective. I've mentioned Acts before, but I'll tell the story of Simon the Magos here: he was a grifter, one showing off fancy magic tricks and getting people to think he was a chosen one of God with his stunts, only to be *blown out of the water* when Philip and Peter learned him a thing or two by way of the magic afforded to them through the Holy Spirit. Simon was utterly outmatched and baffled by it, and he offered the Apostles money for their secrets—to which Peter shouted him down and let him know that power like this was not something you could just buy. We never learn what happens to Simon after that, not definitively, but the point stands: our magic isn't the only thing that matters in a spell, and judging by the many spells of pagan peoples that ask for divine intervention, where they invoke entities such as Apollo or Bast, or even angels of the God of the Israelites, it seems it never was.

Jesus gave many parables about the kingdom of God: what it was like, how it operated. Likewise, I'll tell you some now about the magic of God, the power He's given us to use. Our magic and God's is like a potluck, with God as our host. He asks that we only bring one dish to the table to contribute while He sets up and delivers all the rest. And our magic is also like the pilot light of a gas stove. We turn the handle and let it click, all while the gas—God's power—flows through, together creating that great cooking flame from the mix of spark and gas that lets us get to work. And lastly, just comparatively, our power is like a little AA battery, whereas God's power is the entire electric grid; we *can* do some things on our own, just as a single battery can power some small machine. We can protect ourselves, or sprinkle a little healing energy into ourselves or our loved ones—but when we decide to put down the battery and opt instead for a plug to insert into that great electric grid, we get the power to do so much more than we could ever do with that one little battery.

Again, this goes for all theists, not just Christians. Whoever might read this, your gods—and of course, God—are Divine. They are operating at a level that humans were not made to operate at while wrapped in flesh, and they're here to help us if we only just *invite them to*—if we can get out of our way and admit that we are not, cannot, and should not be doing all of the work in the unseen, spiritual world. The second we recognize that no one is *asking* us to work alone, or to do everything by way of our own spiritual power with no outside assistance—the second we stop misplacing our trust in the crystals and the herbs and the bits of creation and realize that the true spark of all magic comes from within *us*, not the tools we use—is the second we become true magicians, working in harmony between the cliffs of the Seen and Unseen worlds rather than trying to push against them with our bare hands.

Because who was it that said that famous line? Something about faith the size of a mustard seed, something about *moving mountains* with it? There's a lot of esoteric value in the Bible if you know where to look, and with Jesus dropping these hints here and there, the Bible also becomes something of a magical manual, too, from what I've come to understand. And I feel like I've come to understand a *lot*, and level up in ways I never thought I would, once I learned to let God take the lead and put my wishes fully in His hands, to use my magic as a flare to shoot up to Him and call for help rather than trying to use it to light my way through the wilderness and go at it alone.

Everyone has their own journey, especially as witches, but all I can say is: if you can learn from this interview, if you can skip the frustration of trying to figure out how your magic works, by all means, take the knowledge. Take the knowledge and *run with it*.

You'll thank me later.

BABA YAGA

Now, naturally, with a theme of magic for the month, and with St. Paul already under our belt as a more "official" authority on the topic, I couldn't let it go unbalanced, you know? I couldn't talk about all this and, as a Slavic witch myself, not investigate one of *the* most well known figures in Slavic lore. And so, despite what anyone might say or caution me about—despite the things I read myself in one of the most famous stories concerning Baba Yaga, *Vasilisa the Beautiful*—I buckled up and prepared myself for a night of learning. How she would receive me, given the comedic character I play on Tiktok from time to time, the *Baba Yaga Friend*, was anyone's guess, but no matter what happened, I figured I'd come away with some lesson or another.

Throughout Slavic cultures, Baba Yaga is a figure of many names, tales, and functions. For some more New Age types or those reconstructing Slavic paganism, there's an idea that she's secretly a goddess that was bastardized into a witch. For others taking the more traditional route, she is not one to be trifled with; she'll cut you up and cook you in her house on chicken legs just as soon as she'll help you with some dire problem. As she rides around in a flying mortar and pestle, snatching up children that get lost in the woods, she also seems undisturbed by other spirits of the forest, like the Leshy, and acts almost outside of the bounds of Slavic paganism, as if she's some grand outlier.

We can make theories, of course. There's a story that Veles accidentally made the first witch when a woman managed to trick him into revealing his secrets of magic to her, and maybe, if we tilt our heads and squint real hard, we can tell ourselves that this witch was Baba Yaga. Or maybe we can just accept that Baba Yaga herself is something of an Everywoman, a crone archetype that highlights all the things people used to be scared about when it came to old ladies worn out and bent in the back by the world around them. What I know for sure, though, is that her name, and the several variations of it (like Ježi Baba or Baba Roga, literally *angry grannie* and *horned grannie*), is one that has been used to scare children into good behavior for eons, and that you have to prove yourself worth her time and attention if you want something from her—first by being willing to approach her at all.

I was more than willing to try, and so without further ado, here is my conversation with Baba Yaga.

To meet with Baba Yaga, I made sure to look into the stories about her first and see what I was getting myself into. Then I went to work hunting for associations. One interesting book, Madame Pamita's *Baba Yaga's Book of Slavic Witchcraft,* is a fun resource, where Pamita writes from the perspective of Baba Yaga talking to a young woman, and that was also interesting to poke through to get an idea for offerings. I had to look all over, both in the book and online, but by the end, I found my center.

So what we had was a big plate of chicken bones picked clean from dinner, as bones were apparently a good offering, as well as a cup of good Polish blackcurrant tea. I had a green and red candle on either side of my large black mortar and pestle, a nod to her legendary mode of transportation, and I had moss agate, a Ukrainian pysanka (colored egg), a Ljubljana dragon statue, and a Ukrainian fox statue. All of these things, to me, said *Slavic, magic, mischief,* and *Baba Yaga.*

And sure enough, with my prayers done, the door to my space open thanks to God, and my earnest request out into the void, I felt something take notice and settle in the air.

"Hello, Baba Yaga. Hello, and welcome. I have for you some bones of a chicken and a little tea." (In Slovenian: *pozdrav, in dobrodošli. Imam zate kosti kokoša in malo čaj.*) "Please come speak with me, as while I don't come to ask you to teach me what you know without proving myself, I do have some questions about what you think about your magic, and the idea of witchcraft itself."

The swing of the pendulum told me that she was there, and then she swung it again over Amrit Brar's Marigold Tarot—her choice for the night.

I closed my eyes once I had the right deck and waited for the scene to bleed into my mind's eye. What was funny to me, though, was that the area populated into a scenery that I recognized, because I created it: it was the forest garden where the witch of my upcoming Slovenian historical fantasy novel lives, the one I spoke about with Kresnik and that needs another dire few rounds of editing before I even think about publishing it). Except while most details were the same—the well in the back of the cottage, the sludgy pond outside the fence, the grass and the border of dark, thick woods —the things that were different were the fence itself, and of course, the outside of the house.

The fence was made of bones. And the house itself stood high up on two chicken legs.

There was a woman outside the fence, by a little mailbox, that was hunched over with warts on her face. If you've ever played *Bloodborne,* she reminded me something of the Witch of Hemwick. She had a harvesting sickle in her hand, and she smiled at me with thin lips and big, watery eyes. I wondered at first if this was Baba Yaga, but I remember saying to myself, *no, no, Baba Yaga wouldn't be so stereotypical; I know she's not what they say she is.* I knew from deep in my gut to look further.

The only other explanation, then, was that this was the maidservant in the story of *Vasilisa the Beautiful,* then—but nonetheless, I suddenly found myself inside the house soon enough, which, again, was the house I'd created in my story to an extent. From the table to the kitchen set-up to the big fireplace, it was the same as the place I'd created for my story. Some things differed, of course, like the stairs leading up behind me and the big empty section in the back of the main room, but otherwise, it was from my own mind.

And then there was Baba Yaga, her face grooved with wrinkles and her eyes glimmering as they reflected the firelight, She wore a shapeless, sleeveless, pinkish dress, and she had long, straight silver hair that she brushed. Eventually I noticed she had a more Belarusian headband around her head, as well. When she smiled, her teeth were dark, made of iron. And at first, she stayed pretty quiet.

"Alright, well, it's good to meet you. Thank you for allowing me in here." I felt like she was trying to make things recognizable to me, what with the house looking just like the things I'd dreamed up for fun, but I wasn't sure why. I didn't really feel the need to figure out, though. "Baba Yaga, I guess I'd like to start off right from the top: can you tell me what it means to be a witch?"

I. WHAT DOES IT MEAN TO BE A WITCH?

Vulnerability, powerlessness, and warning of a possibly inflated ego.

Friendships, ties, bonds. Good intentions and good news passed from person to person.

The words came low and quiet. *"Biti čarovnica je biti svobodna,"* she said. "To be a witch is to be free. When you know your limits, you know how to exceed them. You learn from everything that draws light and sips shadow."

Her choice of words brought us out back to the well for a minute, and I got a sense of the duality of things: things that are both in light and dark.

"Everything has two bodies," she continued as she peered into the well. "All of it serves a purpose. All are all. None are none. To be a witch is to see things as they are and be hated for saying so. To find fellowship among few. It's easy to get lost in the power, yes, but that's not necessary to be a witch."

"Oh. Okay, okay, wait." I shook my head and leaned against the well, propped up by its stone and the wooden overhang that held the bucket's rope in place. "I have a question I need to ask if we're to talk about power. I keep seeing these folks say that they were witches, and that they 'came out of it,' came to Jesus or something, and that they *know* witchcraft is so bad. What happened to them? What's going on there?"

2. WHAT HAPPENED TO EX-WITCHES-TURNED-CHRISTIANS?

I knew what I thought already: that people like those were just folks who got spooked of their own capabilities and retreated back to "safety" when they were faced with what they didn't understand. But if only I could show you the way Baba Yaga's lip curled—enough that the iron of her teeth peeked through. She was thoroughly unimpressed, and a lot harsher than me.

"Can't, these girls, I can't with them," Baba Yaga spat. "They disgust me. All this power they want. Then they get a taste and spit it out. They can't find their ass with both hands. It's simple: shadows dance, and these girls were told all their life those same shadows should stand still. So they run, understanding nothing."

I let out a low whistle as I wrote, then snatched up my cards. "And you? How did you come to understand your power and develop your craft? I'm not asking for the secret

Loneliness, alienation, extreme caution, and isolation.

Failing to notice issues arising, fearing the unknown, ignoring answers to problems.

to your power, of course," to ask that was to practically guarantee your guts would be used in the next rung of sausages she made, "just how you avoided these same pitfalls and came into your own self."

3. HOW DID YOU COME TO UNDERSTAND YOUR POWER?

Loneliness, alienation, extreme caution, and isolation.

Success, discipline, enjoyment, safety, seeing the bigger picture and other wonderful things.

Baba Yaga smiled at me as if I were saying something silly. Then she pulled the same first card as she did in the last question, the Hermit reversed, and for herself, she also pulled the Nine of Rings—as if directly contrasting herself to the "ex-witches" through the cards. The satisfaction I get with pulls like these knows no bounds, I tell you; it's like poetry in still pictures.

Baba Yaga whispered in my ear, "My will. My power is my will. It doesn't matter if you know this or not, girl—you will never take it from me. In my isolation, I found myself."

Then I was outside, in the woods, but not just in the woods: I was in the soil. I was in the squish of the rotting things, the mushrooms and the dead leaves. I felt the slime of it. Then I was small, very small, like a bird. A big wolf came by and saw me, its yellow eyes bright, and it snapped at me, but I twisted myself up and away like a shadow wrapped in feathers. In a blink, I was looking down at the wolf from the branches of a tree. I could see the house from there, and the light inside it as Baba Yaga bustled about inside.

Did she mean to harm me? I didn't think so, but I also knew it didn't matter even if she did. Nothing could harm me if I didn't want to be harmed: Archangel Michael's lesson was stitched into the very fabric of my soul.

But when I came back into the house, and she kept explaining, I understood. No, she wasn't trying to hurt me; she wasn't trying to bury me or feed me to wolves. She was showing me what she, herself, experienced in the depths of the wood. In the earth, the rot, the damp, the dark.

I also saw myself from outside myself, as tended to happen, and I didn't exactly recognize myself. It was a woman with my face, and my eyes rimmed with dark lines, but her hair was darker, straighter, and her frame was tall, bony. Her dress was dark, too dark to quite make out in the flickering light of Baba Yaga's fireplace, but it seemed like some blackish-brown. This other me was barefoot, her nails long and pointed, her face made of sharp edges and lips too big for her mouth, near froggish. It was me, and yet it wasn't; it belonged here in this chicken leg hut, and yet it was foreign.

"Silence," she said when the Other Sara settled into her seat, "you need to not fear silence. You need to be comfortable with being small, like the bird, to understand what makes things big. You need to be dead," like the things in the rotting earth that she dunked me in, "to understand how to become new life—and to meet every grave worker," like the mushrooms that popped up at my eye level, "along the way. You need to have your only friends be the lichen and the bears and the bees, and to lose your fear.

"Let people speak while you're gone, learning these things. Let people tear down all you were and rebuild your image without you. It doesn't change the you that *you* know. Not unless you find use in the changes they put on you."

And I guess Baba Yaga must've found some use in the changes that people put on her, from possible goddess to witch of the woods. Though that was a question that was on my mind, too, and I watched the frog-mouth of this Other Sara open, listened to the question as it tumbled free from her mouth.

"Some people say you used to be a goddess, though. What do you think about that?"

4. WERE YOU A GODDESS ONCE UPON A TIME?

Baba Yaga didn't even pull any cards; she just looked at me sidelong.

"What did I just say? What others make of you is their business. I don't care for their games. I am me. *Konec*—the end."

"Okay, okay, fair enough," I said as I raised my hands. Yes, this Other Sara was me, because she did exactly what I felt I was doing in this space—and I decided to just accept whatever this astral mask was and not think about it anymore. "Now, I'm curious: what do you think about magic taught by Veles and Zorya? They're both gods known for teaching magic and sorcery and all that. How is it different from yours?"

5. THOUGHTS ON THE MAGIC OF GODS LIKE VELES AND ZORYA?

Mistrust, neglect, fear, prioritizing others at the expense of oneself.

Finances, social standing, business, fruits of one's labor. Reflection, things hard to cultivate.

She eyed me.

"Where does your magic come from?"

I'll admit: I didn't understand the question. "Mine? From God. My power is all from Him."

"So you're just borrowing it." Her brow shot up. "Is that it?"

I shrugged. "I have some of my own, but it's best use is to connect with Him and His power. He still gave me even the power I have, though."

There was a low, throaty chuckle as her iron teeth flashed. She sat with one leg up, her arm draped over her knee.

"There's always something more special about magic when it comes from a god, isn't there? When you can say a god gave it to you and showed it to you?" Then she sucked her teeth. "Annoying. I find it annoying, how people claw after one type of magic over another just to seem holier. Or better. They have no more power than anyone without magic when they give it all away to appease their ego."

I frowned. "Well, I mean, I don't think I do that—"

"Did I say you do?" Her stare alone shut me right up. "If the shoe fits, wear it, girl, but otherwise, don't make things about you that aren't about you."

Jesus. If you ever want to feel like you're getting a whack from your grandmother, talk to Baba Yaga. I loved it, admittedly; it felt so familiar, *so damn familiar*, but I was also humbled by it.

"Now, listen," Baba Yaga said with a sigh. "Veles and Zorya—they're gods. Gods have good magic. People just don't know how to act around it yet, or what to do with it."

"Okay. I hear you; I get you loud and clear," I said. "There are certainly some people I can think of who want to use their powers to seem above others rather than actually just exist with it. And I don't think there's anything wrong with being selfish—in not sharing that power when you don't need to."

She just ran her old brush through her hair a little bit more, but she watched me the whole time.

"Moving on: I notice the story you appear most prominently in, *Vasilisa the Beautiful*, is a lot like a Slovenian story, except the Slovenian one had fairies playing your role. What do you think of the *vile*? Do you have any connections to them?"

6. ARE YOU CONNECTED TO THE VILE (FAIRIES) AT ALL?

"I appreciate them," she said as if considering a piece of cake she wasn't all too impressed with, "but I am not them, nor am I of them. They are their own beings with their own power. They can teach you things, yes—but at what cost?"

And then I got a flash of dark teeth ripping a little creature apart. If you've ever seen *Pan's Labyrinth,* and the scene where the monster at the feast eats the fairies, it was very much like that, but obviously Baba Yaga isn't a monster. She did smile very wide at me with those bloodied iron teeth, though, which I'd been curious about, and I wondered: iron to better bite the fairies?

"I've eaten my share of fairies, she said as if to answer the question I didn't want to ask out of respect. "Proud things, they are. Proud things are better off as soup."

Damn.

"I see." As Baba Yaga got up went to tend to a pot of something she had cooking over the fire, I just kept rolling. "So, as we come towards the end here, I do wonder: what do you think new witches need to know? *Kaj je najpomembejša stvar*—what's the most important thing?"

New beginnings, new perspectives, favoring pessimism.

Drama, authority, power, unapologetic self-expression, confidence. Making oneself known and flourishing. New opportunities.

7. WHAT'S THE MOST IMPORTANT THING FOR NEW WITCHES TO KNOW?

Lies, maliciousness, cold heartedness, being judgmental.

Steady, well deserved confidence. Charismatic, innovative, bright, and strong. Reaching a point of self awareness where one is completely comfortable with their identity and projects it outward.

As she stirred her soup, she sighed.

"The world lies," Baba Yaga muttered. "The world will do anything to see you feed the moss with your bones. But you cannot kill what cannot see a reason for dying. You cannot kill what's true. Even if truth sleeps a thousand years, it will come back on the thousand-and-first—and new *witches*, as you call them, better find their truth before they fall asleep. Before the world's lies crush them under the damp earth, the *kamen*—the stone." Then Baba Yaga said over her shoulder, "Like stone, you must be strong. Stone bones, *kamni kosti*. Strong enough to withstand the weight of every stupid word. Yes, that's what witches must know. Or they'll be like those stupid girls claiming all the demons in the world as bedmates before their sudden 'salvation.'"

God *damn*, she was not happy with ex-witches who speak against the craft. I had to open my eyes and stare at what I wrote, because I felt that bite *me* in the ass, and I wasn't even the one this venomous sentiment was directed at.

"That's some great advice, yeah," I said with a dry chuckle. "Thank you. Okay, Baba Yaga, I would like to know: how do you see yourself?"

8. HOW DO YOU SEE YOURSELF?

KNIGHT of WANDS.

High, near foolhardy amounts of energy. Impetuousness and grandstanding, overconfidence, infatuation. Act more recklessly, be more assertive and brash.

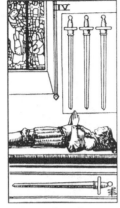

Solitude, reevaluation, and rest. Self reflection and renewal.

After she tasted the soup, she set the spoon down and came back over.

"In my youth, I wanted to gobble up everything," she said, settling back into her seat at the table. "I could've swallowed the world. I nearly did. But I have no such appetite anymore. I am content alone, on the edge of the world. I am a watcher: I like to watch you all."

"A watcher like the angels in the Book of Enoch?"

She grinned with those iron teeth. "Many things can watch besides angels."

I considered that, then nodded. "I get'cha. And how do you want to be seen?"

9. HOW DO YOU WANT TO BE SEEN?

Baba Yaga pulled no cards. She offered me little more than a shrug.

"See me how you need to."

"Fair." I marked it down and considered her. "Any messages, then? Anything I didn't ask, or that you want to say? To witches, to me, anything?"

10. ANY LAST MESSAGES FOR ME OR OTHERS?

A moment passed as I shuffled the deck. That moment was reflected in how long it took after for the words to come as I stared at these two cards I pulled.

"Your world is ugly, and I do not miss it," she said as she stared past me, at the wall. "I pity those that have to live in it. It's full of these things in your cards, the descriptions there. Come away from it, come away. Come to the place where the leshy reigns and man has no hold on what happens. There you find a moment's rest." Then she gestured around to the table, to her home. "This space is wherever you need it to be. Any space that's magical and has a boundary between worlds—you'll find multitudes there."

But surely she didn't offer *her* home. I had to clarify, just in case. "Does your hut count for that?"

Harmful secrets, confusion, and mental disconnect.

Pessimism, dread, and resignation.

Baba Yaga's smile spread slowly on her lips, and the glimmer came back bright and fierce in her eyes. "Only if people have the courage to seek me," she said.

"That's reasonable." The Other Sara stood from her chair and tipped her head to this legendary witch. "Well, alright then. That's about all I have for questions. Baba Yaga, it was wonderful to meet you face to face finally. You've shared a great many things with me, and I'm grateful for it. I'll see you when I see you, so now's time to say goodnight. *Lahko noč!*"

Baba Yaga chuckled as if I were a funny thing, and then she snapped her fingers, and the place I'd built for my fictional characters shattered into pieces, leaving me grasping my way back to earth by the candlelight in my kitchen. Then as I sat there, I once again couldn't get the feeling to leave: I *knew this energy.* I knew this witch. I knew this house and this soul and this forest and this well. There was something so familiar about it all that it made me itch, like scabs healing over but not yet ready to fall off. Every Slavic spirit or deity I'd spoken to felt like that, and this, *this,* was almost too close for comfort. It could've driven me crazy if I let it, but I don't have time for crazy; only progress.

Still, the feeling of Baba Yaga was exactly the feeling I was able to grab onto to write the character Aveline in *The Glass Witch,* but aged up a few hundred years. It was a feeling of something foundational, strong and sturdy bedrock under the feet of my soul; it was something bone deep and infinite, a spring of something I could tap for myself if only I'd bother to try. But I don't know exactly what it is, and I'm already tired enough being myself in this life, this era. I don't think I need to go digging for more tiredness, all that *utrujenost* as old as dirt.

If anything, that nagging feeling of something uncanny in how familiar it is? That's something I can tuck away for later. Not everything needs to be explored the second we discover it, and this, with all the things Baba Yaga showed me and said—they're things I'll carry with me like embers from her fire, until I have the wherewithall, the courage, to come face her a second time.

Until then, I'll be following the march of a very different song, exploring a whole separate lifetime of tangled, messy things.

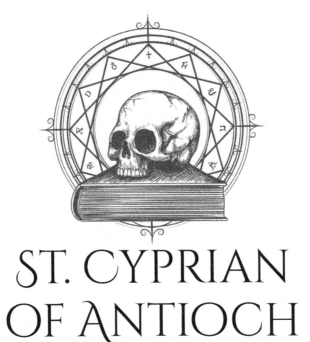

ST. CYPRIAN
OF ANTIOCH

Did you know that there is actually a *Saint* of sorcery? A whole Catholic Saint? Of course, the Catholic church will never tell you that he's the Saint of sorcery, our dear St. Cyprian of Antioch—officially, he's the patron Saint of northern Africa and the Amazigh people—but if you know his background, you'll know exactly why folk magicians, mystics, sages, healers, and even magicians have turned to the name of St. Cyprian for inspiration and enlightenment for a long time. You'll know why he is known, in the Catholic chaplet prayer for his intercession, as *mage, martyr, and mystic*, as *thaumaturge and theophoros*, as *Saint, sorcerer, and sage*.

If you've never heard of him before, though, let me give you a little background here. St. Cyprian of Antioch was once a pagan sorcerer who would take on clients and work his magic on their behalf. Standard stuff. Nothing really out of the ordinary of the time (or even out of the ordinary today). However, one day, a client wanted his help in seducing a woman that, thanks to her newfangled faith in this Christ character, refused to get married. This was St. Justina, who had taken a vow of chastity in her devotion to God and His Son, and this client wanted St. Cyprian to break her will.

So he tried. He sent spirits after her to try and get her to feel attraction to this man, to hound her and ignite her lust, so on and so forth. These *daimones* St. Cyprian petitioned to seduce her weren't evil spirits—not *demons* the way we think of them now—but in ancient Greek practice, they were powerful things, sometimes even known as minor gods. (Thanatos, for instance, is actually considered a *daimon*, as he's a personification of death and not an Olympic god like Hades; he works for Hades, in fact.) Still, most will say it was demons St. Cyprian sent. I think it's important to peel back the layers of Christian propaganda where we can; it's important we recognize where words like *daimon* were corrupted to slander the people who worked with, by, and for these spirits.

To continue the story, St. Cyprian worked these forces on St. Justina three times, and each time, they failed. St. Justina only had to make the sign of the cross to scare these spirits off according to the legend, and by the third failure, St. Cyprian, desperate, went to her directly to figure out how she was thwarting all his magic—magic that had always worked for him and his clients before. When she told him it was through her faith in Christ, he went and made the sign of the cross on himself, then destroyed all his books and converted. Unfortunately, both St. Justina and St. Cyprian were martyred under the rule of Emperor Diocletian, but their names live on as important figures in the first few centuries of Christianity. He's still known as St. Cyprian of Antioch, or St. Cyprian the Magician, to distinguish him from St. Cyprian of Carthage, who was a bishop of the early church. There was apparently no record of a bishop by the name of Cyprian in Antioch.

All that aside, however, you know that I was dearly fascinated with this Saint, especially because a whole grimoire of spells and other magical formulae was written in his name centuries later: the Book of Cyprian, a popular magical text among Portuguese and Spanish folk magicians. In my mind, St. Cyprian fit right into a conversation about magic. I'd already covered St. Paul and given Christian spirits the stand, sure—but how could I have ever passed up a chance to investigate this Saint?

So without further ado, let me show you my conversation with this Saint, sorcerer, and sage.

As with most Christian spirits, the New Age associations and tools just aren't as often transferred to Saints. There are no websites saying "use this specific stone or herb to summon Saint So-and-So," and so I only had the general associations in mind when I went picking out things for the table: my purple lace agate rosary, my amethysts, and clear quartz, all stones that directed energy and fortified magical and spiritual power. A simple white candle and a cup of water were all that went with it: the candle a classic tool in Christian spiritual workings of any kind, and the cup of water a hospitable gesture that, for some reason, struck me as something St. Cyprian would appreciate.

Once I settled in, did my prayers, and asked God to let me meet with St. Cyprian, I closed my eyes and took a breath, and I gave an earnest call out to the pocket of Heaven where the Saints resided. I also managed to confirm that we would be using the Universal Fantasy Tarot for this reading, though that was harder than usual to discern.

"St. Cyprian, hello! Please forgive me; I've no food here today, but I have a cup of water there to refresh you," I said. "Thank you for joining me nonetheless. I have some questions for you."

One thing I will continue to remind everyone is that even after doing this again and again, I still get scared. Not of the spirit itself I'm trying to reach, but of the validity of my own skills. Even after years of experience as a witch, and even after an entire year of contacting these spirits (with at least *some* success), I wonder if I'm just making it all up. I wonder if I'm encountering tricksters, or just inserting words into a spirit's mouth while blowing past anything they're *actually* trying to say. Half the reason I still use tarot at all to do this work is to back up, physically, what I'm hearing in the quiet space in my mind. To prove to myself that I'm not just a big shyster.

That's the trick there. I don't literally see these beings in my kitchen. I don't hear them the way I hear my boyfriend, who is usually streaming on Twitch in the office while I go about my business. And that makes it hard sometimes to trust what I'm experiencing. Still, I try to remind myself that God wouldn't let tricksters on my path—that if I've asked Him to open the door, He won't open it to just anyone. It was Him who suggested I choose St. Cyprian as our last guest of February, so I decided to just shove the doubts down and keep on.

But it didn't make it any easier to get a grasp on St. Cyprian, even after my formal invitation. I kept thinking I was being tricked by old images in my head, like *Prince of Egypt*'s depiction of Moses or of any of those Saint image cards that have people dressed in plain robes. Eventually, though, I got a picture of St. Cyprian that I could let myself be satisfied with: a tall, young man, maybe in his thirties, wearing ivory and light green robes, with a staff and olive skin. He had dark brown hair with shiny curls, a bit of stubble at his beard, and the most luminous sea-green eyes under strong brows.

Antioch is in modern Turkey. It made sense, as I saw him, that I thought he looked somewhere between Greek and Turkish. Though he had a solemn cut to his expression, and he started us off on a cliff, staring down at a river of magma, flames, and what looked like people writhing in the heat.

"St. Cyprian," I whispered as I peered down there, "where are we? And, uh... what's going on there?"

He looked down at the fire, still solemn, and told me, "That's where souls go. It's hell."

I won't lie, I laughed at the idea. I felt like I was being tested, like my chops were being busted to bits. He glanced at me from the corner of his eye, as if waiting to see if I'd take his word for it, or waiting to see if I'd be scared. Was I supposed to be scared? Maybe. Maybe all the other Saints who had "seen hell" and were shown the Lake of Fire and all that were scared right away, seeing everything they'd ever feared their whole human lives be brought to life right in front of them.

But I'd been around the block once or twice already with this Hellfire nonsense, and so I took it upon myself to look closer. When I did, I saw no faces, no features, on these "people." And I knew already, from my conversations and travels with other spirits, that "hell" wasn't a place people went like this—not unless, maybe, they thought they deserved it.

"Yeah?" I pulled back from that cliff's edge. I bumped his elbow with mine, smirked, and he shot me a look that told me I was on the right track with my taunts. The fun thing about meditation is that, while you're sitting there safe and sound in your kitchen or living room or bedroom, you can do whatever the hell you want in this infinite mind-space. So when I see stuff like what St. Cyprian was showing me, I like to investigate. I like to imagine wings made of sharp, shiny onyx in my back, and that's what I conjured up for myself as I hovered one foot over that cliff edge, ready to jump. "Is that so? Let's go get a closer look, then. Come on."

And then I jumped, and I soared down; a moment later, I stood on a rock in the middle of the river of fire that lapped up over the stone's edge to meet my feet. The people in the river looked more like puppets than anything. Like background characters drawn in a webtoon, just bald grey heads and a mouth, but no clothes, no defining features, nothing. They weren't real souls. They were illusions.

In the cliff ahead of me, though, was a throne, and on it was a blond man clad in black clothes and dark wings: Lucifer. I waved to him from the middle of that magma river, and St. Cyprian popped up on the rock with me, but even though I saw Lucifer, I didn't really *feel* him there the way I normally would if he wanted to approach me; he was keeping his distance, telling me that he wasn't there to talk, just to test—and to watch, I guess. Like Veles had with Morana. It confused me, the sheer lack of presence despite how clearly I was seeing Lucifer, but St. Cyprian confirmed several times that the Emperor of the infernal realms was there, watching us. I believed him when Lucifer seemed a bit exasperated that I dipped my feet in the magma river like it was a friend's pool.

A moment later, Lucifer disappeared, and St. Cyprian and I were on the same grassy green cliff we started on, but rather than magma and flames and all that at the bottom, it was overlooking a never-ending, sparkling sea, with a walled off city in the distance behind us. We even walked under a canopy of big olive trees at some point while we talked, sunlight flitting through their odd little leaves, their bumpy trunks providing some visual texture to an otherwise smooth dirt path.

"Alright, St. Cyprian, now that we're all settled here," I said, flipping my notebook open, and knowing full well by the energy in the air that I'd passed whatever test St. Cyprian threw at me, "let's get down to business. I am very curious to know more about you and your power, given how many people talk about you being a magician once. Can you tell me your thoughts on the debate between magic and miracle? What the difference is between the two?"

I. WHERE DO YOU STAND ON THE MAGIC VS. MIRACLE DEBATE?

Needing to move on. Alienation, love or relationships long lost.

Every reaction contains a seed of victory. The warrior who turns away from struggle has already lost.

His shoulders rose and fell with a deep sigh, and his eyes slipped halfway shut, as if the idea exhausted him. That would happen a lot over the course of this interview: I would ask him a question, and he would give me such flat looks, with such dark circles under his eyes and such a hunch to his shoulders, that I would get exhausted just watching him. But I can't blame him. In my line of work, I know that kind of exhaustion all too well.

"Magic and miracle are one in the same," he said, waving his hand. "It's only fools that divide them. Imagine my surprise when," he paused to chuckle without humor, "I burned all my magical tomes, just to do very similar work as a member of the church."

"Oh. I can see that, yeah—that must've been a bit frustrating." I couldn't help smiling, either, because what a pain in the backside that must've been for him to realize that. "But then, what was the difference between the magic you used as a pagan and the magic you used as a Christian? Was it really just a matter of the methods you used, the gods you prayed to? What made it different?"

2. WHAT MADE YOUR MAGIC DIFFERENT AS A PAGAN VS. A CHRISTIAN?

St. Cyprian clucked his tongue and looked around at the branches of the olive trees, with their odd leaves and stubby limbs. "Listen, Sara. Magic not done in service of your highest good is all the same, no matter what god you ask for help. You *Christian Witches,* too—you can fall into this.

"We *all* can—using magic for sinful things, things that cause grief and bring people undue rewards despite their pitiful behavior. No, the real difference between magic and miracle—at least, *my* magic and miracle, my magic then and now—was who I did it *for.* Not just who I did it *with.*" He looked at me with such an edge to his jaw, such a sharp glint in his eye. "I did my magic to help in the end," he insisted. "I never wanted to harm another again."

An inability to move forward, obstacles and waiting.

Knowledge enables us to see beyond the horizon and approach resources available wisely.

And despite how he looked at me, there was still this haze to his eyes—this faraway gaze, as if he was seeing a whole different world instead of the path we walked on. A world of the past, of a different time altogether, where things weren't so nice and peaceful, and where he maybe did things that could haunt him even in Heaven.

With a nod, I said, "I hear you. Given that, though, I mean... how did you go sending spirits after St. Justina? And why? Why would you even take a job like that?"

3. WHY TRY TO PUT LOVE CURSES ON ST. JUSTINA?

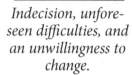

Indecision, unfore-seen difficulties, and an unwillingness to change.

Truth, indecision, inadequacy, emo-tional detachment.

There was a throughline to the Hanged Man reversed and the Empress reversed: indecision. The surrounding mean-ings, too, all matched the huff of a laugh I heard, and the way he waved his hand.

For a moment, the path lined with olive trees disappeared, replaced by a different image. St. Cyprian stood in purple robes, over a candlelit table full of books. It looked like a scene of any wizard you'd ever imagine in their dark tower.

"Power." That was the first word I heard, and the St. Cyprian I knew stood beside me as I watched this figment of the past twist himself over those dusty old grimoires. "I wanted to show my power. I was steeped in my power then. Sending a spirit was no uncommon thing: you bind a spirit of lust and send it on its way. Child's play for adept magi-cians. I didn't think it was right to muddle a girl's mind like this, but also," St. Cyprian shrugged, "I didn't care. I didn't know her. I was being paid."

The rawness and frankness this man kept answering with didn't fail to bonk me in the brain every time. When I blinked, he smiled, the corners of his eyes crinkling.

"Is it so unbelievable?" He sighed, still smiling, and watched his old self work the magic of antiquity at that old table. "It was when my so-very-simple task failed so easily that I began to wonder what I'd done. By the third time, I couldn't ignore my misgivings any longer."

"It makes sense to me. What a story." I appreciated that it seemed like something one might read in a book or see in a movie. All our fantasy, all our fiction, it's already happened somewhere in reality—that's what I was thinking then. I felt like someone should write this story anew, but I didn't have time to let it all unspool in front of my eyes: the introduction to the characters, the buildup, that classic rise and fall, the dark night of the soul, all that good stuff. "Well, okay, then," I said as I shook myself out of my thoughts. "Given that our friend Lucifer is hovering around somewhere, watching just as God is watching—what's your experience with him? I hear people say you told them to work with Lucifer, that you did work with Lucifer. What's your story there?"

4. WHAT CONNECTION IS THERE BETWEEN YOU AND LUCIFER?

I'll say this: St. Cyprian started quiet, but soon, he was just talking, tarot cards be damned. I think he chose the cards he did more just to make me happy than to actually speak through them, because you hear the voice of a Saint like it's something you've always known; it pops up like a sprout from freshly thawed dirt. Experiencing St. Cyprian speaking to me made me think of a book I'd just finished reading the day of the interview, *Mary*

1. Needing to move on. Alienation, love or relationships long lost.

2. The determina-tion and discipline of someone close to us can often help resolve difficult situ-ations.

KING of PENTACLES.

Magdalene Revealed by Meggan Watterson, which talked quite a bit about this voice of the heart.

"I was on the outside," St. Cyprian said. "Justina forgave me, but my actions and my past stuck to me. I would never shake them, even when I knew I was forgiven. I wasn't just a pagan before. I was a *sorcerer*, and it earned me looks from my fellows. It made me scared of what I'd see when I died—if all I'd done after renouncing it all was enough to keep me out of the hell I feared."

Ah. That's why he showed me the river of "hell," then—it made perfect sense. It was what St. Cyprian was scared his magical days would earn him, and I feel like he wanted to see if it would make me scared, too.

But I'm stupid, so it didn't.

"Lucifer showed me that it was enough," St. Cyprian continued. "He showed me that what spirits I messed about with before were nothing compared to true darkness, and that never was I so far gone to begin with. Lucifer, an outsider of God's Kingdom, showed me pity and mercy as a fellow outsider, and he taught me how to use my skills in a new context. I became a magician under another name. I knew light and dark, and how they worked together."

And there it was again. The motif that had been following me around for quite some time by then: the motif of one coin. Two sides, one single coin. St. Cyprian even showed it to me as we left the olive grove and returned to the cliff over the sea. We sat there with our legs dangling over the rock, and the image in my mind that came with us was clear: that silver, spinning coin, hovering in the air.

Another theme of *Mary Magdalene Revealed* is unity of all things. Of light and dark, male and female, human and divine, black and white. All things together, in one place, as they were meant to be, and that we keep forgetting were never so separate. And if you've ever read the non-Canonical writing called *The Thunder: Perfect Mind,* you'll get deeper into this idea: the idea of the Everyman, of being both the whore and the holy one, the first and the last.

"Okay, alright. Fair enough," I said as I scribbled away in my notebook. "I understand you, and I love that. Lucifer is quite the interesting entity, with a lot to teach. But now, I have to ask: what do you think of the Christians that disavow all magic? That try to cut out every single piece of it until all they have left is their Bible and their churches and their devotionals?"

What a disgusted look he had. The furrowed brow, the slight curl of his lip—he was not happy.

5. WHAT DO YOU THINK OF CHRISTIANS THAT DISAVOW MAGIC?

Pessimism, dread, resignation.

Discipline of someone close can help resolve situations.

"Power is power. Why would you stay disenfranchised? To pretend holiness? Holiness has nothing to do with whether you ignore your gifts or not. Speak! Be heard! Heaven is watching—hell is, too! They're waiting to see how you use a power that can overthrow nations, transform universes.

"This is why it's been hidden by your institutions and your leaders—but how do you propose to be a child of God, cutting yourself off from what makes you divine?"

Cue my staring at him with eyes the size of dinner plates. He was so intense that it spooked me a bit. But I understood him loud and clear, even though I started to wonder if it was really him saying it. I mean, was it? Or was I just making it up? I won't lie; I was happy to hear him say these kinds of things, and that's why I doubted. I didn't want to delude myself, and the worry was palpable. However, whenever my pencil paused on the paper and these doubts started to pull me away from him, he would tap my book and say, *Write. Write this down. Yes, write this.*

So I wrote.

"I see," I said, deciding to replace my worry with faith. And then I remembered a question I hadn't gotten to yet. "Oh, hey!" I pipped. "You know, there's some tome in Spanish and Portuguese that uses your name, *The Book of Cyprian*? It's a grimoire of spells and such. What do you think about that?"

He barked a laugh, didn't even pull any cards. Two sentences came sharp and crisp.

6. THOUGHTS ON THE BOOK OF CYPRIAN?

"It's good someone was still doing something with their power. Use my name if it helps—just remember your power!"

"I got'cha. And now, what advice do you have for people trying to learn miracle working?" It was a bit of a cheeky question. "People who want to learn all that *holy magic*, what do you recommend?"

St. Cyprian nodded and cleared his throat.

7. WHAT DO YOU RECOMMEND TO PEOPLE LEARNING HOLY MAGIC?

"Remember what the point is," he said. "Remember why Christ gave us these secrets, this power. This world is beautiful; it needs a guiding hand. One that isn't afraid to do what's needed, even if the world fights them on it.

"To work magic is to use the power God gave us, but miracles? These are done when you believe the mustard seed can move the mountain. When you truly believe it can, and you act and move as if you believe it. There's no room for doubt when *miracles* need to be done."

Seems to me that St. Paul had it right: that spark in us of our own power, through faith and just simply doing what needs to be done, connects to a power greater than we can hold within just our physical bodies.

Hmm.

"I like that," I said with a nod. "Okay, well—how do you see yourself?"

The best marriages can come from radical changes and sudden shocks.

Insecurity or manipulation. Take advantage of your resources, physical and spiritual.

8. HOW DO YOU SEE YOURSELF?

Misfortune approaching, depression, unsuccessful ventures.

Need to rest is greater than the need to work. Thoughts must move smoothly to get new pursuits.

Again, a big sigh. "I don't care to—"

"Ah, come on, come on! Tell me. Pull a couple cards: how do you see yourself?"

He shrugged. "I am a man. I am just a man. I've made many mistakes; I've seen stupid, stupid things. Done them, too. Made enemies, made friends. I've lived, and I'm tired. Is there any more that makes a man?"

I shrugged. "Maybe. Maybe not. But how do you want to be seen, then?"

9. HOW DO YOU WANT TO BE SEEN?

"I am someone who took a long time to discover what was important. But I did, thankfully, before it was too late. I released the part of myself that was fine with the poor way I viewed other people. I grew. I sit with that growth now, from my perch here on this cliff."

"Understood. And now, this is our last question for the night. Do you have any messages? For me, for others? Things you want to say I didn't ask about?"

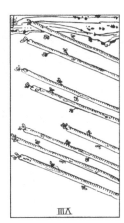

Delusion or disconnect with reality regarding relationships.

Quarrels, delays, and needing to slow down to re-evaluate goals and circumstances.

10. ANY LAST MESSAGES FOR ME OR OTHERS?

One word popped up again as I shuffled: *Love.* I didn't feel the pull to any cards, either.

"The transforming power of love," he said, "remember that. This beautiful scene here?"

And he carried us through the grasses on that cliff, through the olive grove, into the walled city full of people smiling and laughing, yelling about their wares while kids snuck through side streets.

"It existed once on Earth. It still does. Through love, you folk might preserve it yet, and perform such powerful magic through it."

I was listening to a song by this point, *Kyrie Eleison* as interpreted by Dan Gibson, that had all these kinds of feelings. Give it a listen; you'll see what I mean. The singing, the music, the birds. It was springtime bliss in an audio file.

"People are brave," St. Cyprian said as I sat stewing in that song, "and lovely. Connect them."

"Connect them. Yeah. I mean, we can all try." Weird, how peaceful I felt by the end of all this. With a clap of my hands, though, I broke that peacefulness, and I said, "That's about all my questions for now, though. Thank you for your time, St. Cyprian. It was lovely to meet you!"

St. Cyprian gave me a wave and a tired smile, and then everything faded away into blackness. I opened my eyes and stretched. It's hard, sitting so long in a chair and doing this kind of work—but it's worth it.

Love. It's something Divinity is always bringing up. I'm at the point where I'm wondering if Humanity knows what it really is. We act like we do, always sharing moments of love between our partners, friends, family, and so on—but when Divinity speaks about it, it just sounds like something so much more than our human minds are even able to grasp. Combine that with all the wooziness and mayhem that comes with learning mysteries and magical arts, and you've got yourself enough of a headache to last you three lifetimes. But I think the more I hear about it, the less it surprises me—and the less it surprises me, the more I can actually get to work with the concepts both as a witch and as a simple human being. The more I can learn how to love not *despite* having power, but learning how to make that power spawn out of love itself.

Anyway, all that aside, it's simple: we're all here to learn. That's one thing I know for sure. But damn, I wish Divinity didn't have to make it so hard to put all the pieces together—because the more deities and Saints and spirits that I interview, the more I find myself wondering if humanity will ever actually be able to figure all this out.

Knowing what I know about Divinity, though, I know that the answer to what we call Life is actually probably pretty simple. They've told it to us time and time again, after all. But for some reason, we just can't accept that things *are* that simple. That all we have to do is love one another.

I wonder why that one simple command is so damn hard. I really do.

ARCHANGEL RAZIEL

Like Metatron, Raziel is an angel that deals in the realms of enlightenment and spiritual growth. Unlike Metatron, however, Raziel was never human. This meant that I was in for yet another round of fun with a purely divine being, as I had been with every angel before (save Metatron), and I knew what to expect by this point.

You may have caught it throughout some of these interviews by now, but in general, what I discovered with angels is that you do *not* want to doubt yourself. Question the angels all day; converse with them, dig into the concepts they give you, even *argue* if it'll help you engage with their lessons more clearly. (A real holy being like an angel will never be mad at you for asking questions and pushing back; neither will God Himself. In fact, it's encouraged.) But never doubt *yourself*. Never doubt *your* abilities to see or hear or experience them in general.

But let me tell you more about this angel, who is colloquially known as the angel of magic. Raziel, meaning *Secrets of God*, is an angel of mysteries (and, by extension, magic). In Jewish mysticism, specifically Kabbalah, it was said that Raziel showed all of the mysteries of the universe to Adam, who then passed it down to all people. Over the many centuries of human existence, this knowledge has apparently been lost and recovered a few times, with Raziel visiting multiple people over the ages to remind them of what knowledge he originally delivered to Adam.

Similar concepts of these mysteries can also be seen in other religions or philosophies (like the Ptolemaic system of ordering the universe, which is obviously physically wrong in that it puts earth at the center, but it is reminiscent of "layers of heaven" so to speak). But I digress. Raziel, in my interpretation, is also the angel of *cosmic spoilers* in that he has access to God's writings about the world He created, so Raziel knows quite a bit of stuff as God just drafts and edits and publishes this World Story we're all living in.

Now, let me make this explicitly clear here: You don't need to dabble in Kabbalah to talk to Raziel any more than you do Michael, Gabriel, or any other angel. You can just ask him to stop by and chat, so keep that in mind if you want to learn from him. Kabbalah is something that requires years of study under trained mentors; it requires initiation and is an inherently Jewish—and therefore closed—practice. But there are many roads to the same location. If you can talk to one angel, you can talk to any angel, and you can learn things your own way, so long as you're careful. Remember that.

And I want to add a fun tidbit on the topic of Raziel and my conversation with him: when I first posted my Archangel Raziel video on Tiktok, someone very angrily stitched it claiming that the "Holy Spirit" convicted her to tell me that Raziel is actually a *fallen* angel. This wouldn't be entirely out of bounds, of course; there are many angels that are considered *fallen* in the Book of Enoch, yet still part of the Seven Holy Archangels in certain churches like the Coptic Orthodox church (an example of this specific case is Ananiel, the Rain of God). However, upon doing some further digging, the only thing I could find that even *remotely* suggested Raziel was a fallen angel was a book on Amazon.

A book of fiction. Specifically, a romance novel. (One with a shirtless man on the cover, menacing black wings Photoshopped onto his back, to represent Raziel.)

Needless to say, I was in stitches—and very well aware that if there was a spirit guiding that lady, it sure as hell wasn't of the Holy variety. But all that aside, let me show you my experience with Archangel Raziel: the Keeper of All Magic.

With Raziel, there was a bit more of the New Age lines of thought I could've followed with asking him to come forward, but I stuck with what worked for the two Saints regarding stones and items: my purple lace agate rosary and my amethysts. As this was an angel, I also added a piece of celestite as an angel antenna, and I used the Spiritual Understanding card from Doreen Virtue's Angle Oracle deck to represent him. With a single candle to light, we were set up just fine to speak, and after all my prayers were finished and the tarot deck (Kat Black's Golden Tarot) decided on, I was ready to roll.

"Hello, Raziel! Welcome, and good morning. I have some questions for you, if you don't mind answering; would you please come forward and show me your presence?"

How many times will I learn this lesson: that the way these angels come through is connected to how my mind is primed to see them, and that they don't have to look any certain way in the first place? I had a card from Doreen Virtue's Angel Oracle deck to represent him, where he looked like an older man with long white hair and a long beard. Very much giving Gandalf the White. But when he actually popped in looking similarly, my first thought was "no, no way; he can't look like that. Because that's stereotypical. That's what this goofy card says he looks like."

This is a trick of the ego. If it's an image you can hold onto, just hold onto it, for the love of God. Don't worry about it being from somewhere you saw before: they will show you certain symbols and icons that can confirm they are who they say they are. This was literally the image on the card of Raziel that I was seeing, so why was I complaining?

It seemed Raziel asked the same thing, because suddenly, as we appeared in a grove on a bright and sunny day, with a nice sized boulder to my left and green grasses and strong trees all around, I looked up and saw a grid of lines and spheres. It was pure white light, with a rainbow of colors intertwined with it, and in the middle was something dark with a red core inside, like an eye. Then the spheres and lines fleshed out into bright feathers that shone with hints of rainbow color. That was Raziel, his eye, staring at me and asking me, without words, what on earth I wanted him to do with its unblinking stare—and if I expected him to stay like that for our whole conversation.

So I let go, and Raziel eventually came down dressed in white, with the white hair and the white beard. But he wasn't really an older man, more middle-aged. And his eyes were like flashing pieces of bismuth with the rainbow colors, if you could somehow polish those things into smooth circles. He was quiet as he sat on the rock, as if there was no need to speak unless ready to say something important. Then, finally, we were ready to get started.

"Okay, okay, let's get into this," I said, fully determined to speak and listen. "Raziel, I understand that you are described as an angel of *magic* and mysteries. That's interesting, because I never thought an angel would be described as such. And you were one who delivered mysteries to humanity! So I wanted to know first: why is it important that humanity remembers these mysteries?"

I. WHY IS IT IMPORTANT THAT HUMANITY KNOWS THE MYSTERIES?

KING of WANDS

A man of many talents. Charming, witty, and enigmatic. Virile, strong, fiery. Tendency to be hasty.

Problems with a relationship. A partner feeling taken for granted or jealous. Being promiscuous, unfaithful, or just wanting more excitement.

Inaction, inertia, and resistance to change. Hopeless attempts to fight the inevitable.

As is angel and Christian spirit tradition, Raziel spoke to me as much through imagery as he did the actual meanings of the cards laid out in the booklets. The King of Wands first looked like a king of nothing but flames, like a city in ruins, though he was smiling as if it was something to be proud of. And the three of cups, a happy card, was reversed; Judgement, with Jesus risen and all rejoicing, was reversed. I understood it just fine, and yet couldn't put it into words until Raziel helped.

"Without the mysteries, you become kings of only earthly things; sooner or later, all your castles will come crashing down," he said as I flipped through my booklet.

When I tried making sense of the booklet descriptions against what he was saying, he tapped my journal. "Write. Tell this: The reason people are so drawn to your 'witchcraft' is because they know something is missing. How many times will you lose it? Worse, how many times will you throw it away, fearful? You grip your Father's skirts—why not, then, any of the Wisdom He shares with you? You'll be lords only of rubble if you refuse to open your eyes to the inner machinations of the world—those seen and unseen."

"Oh, I see. Thank you for explaining that; I understand exactly what you mean. Wow." I sat there blinking like a fool, cartoonishly dumbfounded, before I pipped, "I never thought of it that way. Well, in that case, let me ask first: are the mysteries explained the same way each time they're delivered? Are they the same across religions, or are there different ways of explaining it each time?"

2. ARE THE MYSTERIES EXPLAINED THE SAME WAY EVERY TIME?

Between the cards and his face, as if he was caging a sigh, I could tell there was some frustration.

And then I had a vision of a triangle. It was a prism, transparent like glass, and behind it was a light so white and pure it was blinding. As that light passed through it, though, it fractured into many different colors. Think of Pink Floyd's *Dark Side of the Moon* album: the one light through the triangle becoming many lights of different qualities and colors.

I understood. I'll also be honest: I hate when I understand this way, because it's a message so important, and yet it's conveyed to me in a way that is very hard to translate into speech.

So thank God for Raziel, who could make up for where I lacked.

Balancing act. Compromise of lesser of two evils. Making the best of a bad time. An adversary will challenge you. Friendship after conflict.

Rivalry, disharmony, and transient conflict.

Female intuition, spiritual awareness, acceptance of life's mysteries. Secret knowledge, intelligence, intuition. Consider all factors before a decision.

"The human mind is a powerful thing," he said, "but it is not a perfect thing. It can't understand all that there is at once. People's knowledge is connected across nations, lifetimes, genders, landscapes. There's a reason Azazel revealed gifts of root work to women and gifts of metallurgy to men.

"All the mysteries of this world create a picture, and each of your minds is a piece of its mosaic. Adam was once the only man; he had to shoulder the burden. He was the prism, and all of his offspring—humanity—had their own focus, their ray of colorful light. When you share your talents in harmony, you receive the full power of the mysteries. Nothing can be told the same way twice."

"Oh my God, okay. Heard loud and clear." I shook my head free of the haze that this blanketed my mind with. "That's fantastic. Riffing off of this, though, how does magic tie into the mysteries?"

3. HOW DOES MAGIC TIE INTO THE MYSTERIES?

1. Wonderful opportunities may be missed through pessimistic outlooks.

2. Travel for all the wrong reasons. You can run away from life, not yourself. Detachment from reality, chasing unattainable goals at expense of what's good about life.

3. Injustice, false accusations, prejudice.

Here's where the cards started signifying answers from him I didn't quite expect, and here's another way I know that I was talking to a separate entity: I know what *I* would've said. What I would've said is very simple: magic is our life force that lets us engage with the world and understand its mysteries. Raziel, however, went sliding in an adjacent direction, and as a result, I think this is one of the first interviews that had me genuinely have those *eureka!* moments (the first major one being St. Paul's).

"You already have all the power you will ever need," Raziel said. "There is a reason that you, Sara, felt naturally repulsed at the idea of using magic and meditation to gain power and dominance over the world around you."

I blinked. I had been reading about more left hand path approaches that described the process of becoming a magician as a way to gain more, more, more power and didn't know why it felt odd. Not wrong, per se, but just like the intentions and drive were misplaced. After all, it was only natural that there would be people who felt that gaining power over the physical through the supernatural would be the way to use magic, and people with this idea would create their own resources as a result—but knowing what so many deities, like Hekate and Zorya, had to say about it, and what God thought of it, I couldn't really digest those bits I'd read in the books; they just didn't agree with me.

Raziel continued, "Many magicians have wrongly tried to apply their power to increasing it—as if you could use money to buy more money. Because of this, others have been repulsed throughout time, too—though for reasons they didn't understand. They came to conclusions that made sense to them, but ultimately, they buried their own tools for recognizing their power and its source."

"Ah. So a situation where the baby was thrown out with the bath water."

"Yes. Mystery helps one discover the power already there, in all things."

"In all things, you say?" With my cards in my hands, I shuffled, looking for Raziel's sign to tell me to stop. "I'm interested in that, especially in how creation fits into this picture of magic and mysticism. Some say that it's not a crystal that's 'demonic,' but the way you use it. What do you think?"

4. WHAT DO YOU THINK OF THE IDEA THAT CRYSTALS ARE DEMONIC?

Breaking an addiction, escape from a bad influence, overcoming a vice.

Coveting the success of others while wasting one's own talents. Jealousy, envy.

There can be no winners without losers. Patriarchal authority. Motivated to succeed. Competitiveness. Power, masculine strength.

He cocked his head, considered it. "I think there's some truth to the idea that sin might derive from how you use a piece of creation, yes. But not the way these types realize.

"Oh, no?"

"No. You must understand: the purpose of the mysteries is to remind you that you are all connected. Whether rock or flesh, you all come from the same dust arranged in different, meticulous ways.

"The way sin derives here, is when you use these tools to try and inflate your power over others," he said. "Again, these children you speak of say seeking power is wrong outright, but it's not because power itself is bad. It's because you already have it, and your fellow creation is but a means to help you focus it. They assist and support, but they do not do."

"Oh, damn." My chest filled with discomfort like an upturned bucket in a rain storm. "Am I doing something wrong then, when I ask them to lend their talents and energy to me during spellwork?"

"Not quite," Raziel said, holding a hand out to hush me. "Understand this: they connect with you based on their talents, but they do not surpass you. Nor are they slaves to be abused and directed; they're companions. Power cannot be grown through them, only further discovered within."

A tinier *a-ha!* moment took hold then. Focusing tools. That's what Raziel was saying they were, and that's essentially what we've always said they are, isn't it? Focusing tools. Like Damien Echols says in his book, *Angels and Archangels,* a talented magician should be able to do powerful magic even dropped naked in a jungle.

Creation doesn't make the power of a spell. Its energy helps us make boundaries and focusing borders for our own as we connect with God via that "spark" St. Paul talked about.

Interesting.

"I think I understand," I said, slowly, overturning the idea in my head. "Okay. That's fair. How about angels, then? Where do angels fit into magic?"

5. WHERE DO ANGELS FIT INTO MAGIC?

I was laughing because in the Golden Tarot, the Five of Swords card had a blond man holding a bunch of swords and looking so very tired as other men flailed and cried in the background. It reminded me of Archangel Michael watching over us all.

But moreover, it was the Lovers card that stuck out to me, because it seemed like the man had something a little dark in his gaze. The woman, however, was holding onto a tree, with animals at her side and an angel coming down to touch her head specifically.

"Angels are there to guard and guide you through the traps of the ego," Raziel said. "Powers of the ego cause you to lose sight of the truth of magic; it challenges the egoically fragile in a way that many magicians have not been able to tolerate. Again, there's a

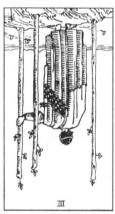

Disappointment, intrigue, and others working against you.

Unfair victory as hollow as defeat. Failure or win against an unmatched opponent demoralizes. Trickery, manipulation, unfair tactics used. Accept it and move on.

Fulfillment through relationships. Love of one creates compassion for others. Material happiness and security.

reason Azazel chose women to learn these secrets—and a reason men resented them for it. But angels are not babysitters. They don't help those who are not ready to receive help. Those who demand help anyway may find themselves hurt."

Cue me blinking at these cards. A lot of talk of ego here also reminded me exactly of *Mary Magdalene Revealed,* which was all about what Mary Magdalene described as the seven powers she had to overcome that were embedded in the ego—seven powers that very well may have been the pre-requisite to the formation of the Seven Deadly Sins.

"Thank you for explaining. I see you're talking quite a bit through the imagery of the cards as well; I appreciate that," I said with a smile. "But okay, so, in this case, then, what do you think of the way people disavow mysticism these days? They act like it's something to be feared and avoided."

6. THOUGHTS ON HOW PEOPLE DISAVOW MYSTICISM ENTIRELY?

Good marriage. Prosperity, stability, happiness. An inheritance. Potential for great joy and love.

Coveting the success of others while wasting one's own talents. Jealousy, envy.

Loss, defeat, and confusion.

Raziel's robes flashed from white to orange with a red-orange sash here, like carnelian.

"You are children of the Sacred Flame," he said, and I interpreted this to mean God, but you might call it the Creator, or Source, or whatever else you think of as the central creative force of our world. "These mysteries, and your power, are your inheritance."

There were so many motifs running through my head as I looked past him, towards the light where God was. There was the triangle, the white light, the concept of Source just laid plain, which I cannot do justice with a description, the orange of Flame itself, like Raziel's robes. It was a lot to parse.

"There is darkness in the minds of those that call themselves righteous," Raziel continued. "They snuffed the light of the Sacred Flame that shows them these mysteries. And that will be their downfall. Mankind needs these mysteries. They need to remember their inheritance, their birthright.

"Whoa." I was still blinking through all the imagery. "I... see. But then, can you speak on why it's important for mankind to learn magic?"

7. WHY SHOULD MANKIND LEARN ANY MAGIC?

1. A shallow person that likes to get what they want regardless of consequences. Spoiled and self indulgent, they should face responsibilities.

2. Dispute, defeat, and possible litigation over petty things. Don't let minor issues become major problems.

3. Disappointments, intrigue, and others working against your best interest.

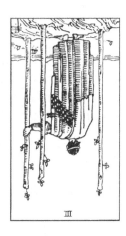

"Mmm." Raziel shook his head; the cards I pulled felt like they were waving me off the idea of magic, but not permanently. "First before magic comes another thing: discipline. You cannot put an empire in the hands of a tyrant, and you cannot put a household in the hands of a child. The mysteries inspire such discipline, and from there, one might responsibly learn to channel their power for the good of themselves and others. Many are too immature to begin recovering their inheritance; the mysteries are like a trust for children."

Let me tell you, I understand now why Jesus was constantly speaking in parables, because here was Raziel's parable of the trust:

"In order to keep a child from spending their inheritance unwisely, the giver of the inheritance will put it in a trust. Then, all transactions must go through the agents that oversee this wealth. It's important that the one receiving this trust has the assets available for them to use, but it's more important that they use it responsibly."

It was all very clear to me, at least. In this parable, God is the giver of the inheritance, the angels the overseers of how it's spent, and us the ones receiving the inheritance.

And another thing that this brought to my mind, which Raziel and I mostly just conveyed to each other through a look, was the "ex witch turned Christian" types, which, unfortunately for them, seemed to be getting ripped up by Angel and Witch alike, given Baba Yaga's distaste for them.

The Page of Cups that Raziel pulled here, though, is exactly that spoiled child that would misspend a trust fund, and so too did it remind me of the people seeking magic for the sake of petty power who, after being confronted with the consequences of their actions, disavowed it all as evil and ran back to what was safe, comfortable, and unchallenging to their ego.

What a waste of an inheritance.

"Alright, alright, I think we have all this under wraps," I said once I finished my note-scribbling. "Do you want to answer a few questions about yourself?"

He shrugged here, like he didn't care to.

"Just one card per question then?" I pleaded with him, unashamed to. "Just a little about yourself?"

One card seemed fine by him from the feelings I was getting, which was a relief. I didn't want to just leave it there, so we went through the last three questions pretty quickly, and they surprised me just as much as anything else.

"How do you see yourself, then?"

8. HOW DO YOU SEE YOURSELF?

"As an adversary."

What? My first thought was how HaShatan (known to us as Satan) is the Adversary, but he then explained:

"Not as a tempter, or one who inspires bad action—rather, I am an adversary *of* bad action. But those who are unrighteous see my work as that of evil."

With a blink, I said, "And how do you want others to see you?"

Rivalry, disharmony, and conflict of a transient nature.

9. HOW DO YOU WANT TO BE SEEN?

Injustice, false accusations, and prejudice.

"I am one who has been ignored and slandered by those without the temperament to see. I am an adversary of these things."

"Oh, I got'cha. Okay. And last, do you have any messages?"

10. ANY LAST MESSAGES FOR ME OR OTHERS?

Carrying a heavy load. Taking on more than you can handle. Too much burden creates a spiritual and emotional low.

"Yes. As important as the mysteries are, they are not worth losing your sanity over. It' a trick of the ego to work oneself to death."

That one felt directed at me, honestly. I spend an awful lot of time buried up to my neck in all things religious, mystical, magical—partly because it's my job, partly because it's part of who I am, and partly because I love it, and God above it all.

But he wasn't being mean about it; he had a half smile as he spoke, a twinkle to those bismuth eyes. He knew my intentions were good, but intentions don't mean much when you run yourself into the ground. When it comes to spiritual things, I've found it's just as important to step away and remind ourselves that this doesn't make us up entirely—that it's okay to spend time on other hobbies, like video games or cooking or reading. It's okay to lean into the Human aspect of ourselves and enjoy it just as much as we do the Divine.

"Alright, I hear you," I said with a nod. "I know. Well, I mean—if you ever want to share any of those mysteries with me, aside from what's already here, I am all ears. But nonetheless, Raziel, thank you so much for your time and attention, and I do hope to see you around in the future."

Then, with a tip of Raziel's head and a few blinks, the image of our space faded away. I sat rubbing my temple, because boy, were those images Raziel showed me something else.

I'll say this: there are concepts in the world that seem universal. The Sacred Flame, the spark within us? We are connected, far more than we realize, as a species. We experience Divinity so differently, and yet we all have the exact same story.

Nonetheless, this is one of those interviews where I really think it best to let it speak for itself. What a wild ride it was, and what a boatload of information came with it. The answers Raziel put forward, I think, put a lot of things in context for me, especially with the parable of the trust fund, and that's why I'm all the more frustrated when people just *refuse* to get it. But we can only be grieved about that for so long before we find ourselves settling into a quiet, knowing peace—one that says, "fine, don't listen to me; go ahead and have a blast thinking you're right."

I used to struggle with that, you know. Constantly having to prove myself right. Having to argue and get the last word. (I still do to an extent; habits are habits.) But with knowledge like this, more and more I find myself realizing that the people who get it, who need this information, will come take it regardless of what others say. I understand that I don't need to have the last word; in fact, I don't need to have a word at all. I can just let people talk themselves blue in the face, all while I sit back and relax, knowing what I know and knowing it with a chilly confidence.

That's what information like this does. It's the first time I've ever felt peace so eerie—real peace, not the numbness of knowledge I'd had with a few of the Goetia. Still, it's a peace worth having, I think.

LEVIATHAN

Naturally, I would make my way back to the infernal divine as we progressed through our new format for this series. And through this new format, the nature of the series was changing rapidly; it was no longer about *investigating* these spirits themselves, finding out more of what they're about and trying, in vain, to patch up inconsistencies in their lore. Rather, it was about exploring our *world* through their eyes, seeing what they have to say about the many things they have dominion over. This month in particular, it was about learning what water is to beings both celestial and infernal— and the first infernal being that comes to mind when I think of water is none other than Leviathan.

One of the most famous demons, Leviathan is a sea serpent that was defeated by God, as per Psalm 74:14; according to this verse, the sea creature was killed and divvied up as food for the ancient Israelites. However, there's more to the story of Leviathan than that, as you might imagine.

For example, did you know that in Canaanite mythology, it's actually Ba'al Hadad that kills Leviathan (in their language Lotan)? Later on, this story became absorbed into the Bible, where God battles Leviathan (Livyatan). In some stories, like in the Book of Enoch, Leviathan is a girl, but in other cases, he's a boy, and in some stories, there was a whole clump of them as a race of creatures, in which God destroyed the females so they couldn't multiply anymore.

As you can see, we have a lot going on with the story of the big sea dragon. Nonetheless, I felt he would have some interesting things to share, and I was happy to have the chance to connect with a different member of the infernal divine. They're such a fascinating bunch, with so many valuable lessons and ideas to share, and I was happy to visit whenever I could. This was no exception—so come take a look at my experience with Leviathan.

Naturally, with Leviathan being associated with water as a sea serpent, I had to crack out the water-related items. Just like with King Paimon, I had offerings that were associated with the element— blackberries, cucumbers, and blueberry liquor—and I also had a tea light I was able to get to float in a small bowl of water (as candles are cool, but are obviously fire—the direct opposite of water). It balanced out in my mind; it made sense. I also had his sigil drawn on paper and five blue stones around the water-candle: lapis lazuli, blue lace agate, and sodalite. Anything that made me think of water.

With my prayers prayed, myself blessed with holy water, and my request to speak with Leviathan spoken to God, I was ready to go soon enough, and I confirmed that Leviathan wanted to use Threads of Fate's Weaver Tarot before fully settling in.

"Hello, Leviathan!" I tapped the cup of liquor. "Welcome! I have here for you some blackberries and cucumber slices, as well as a strong cup of blueberry liquor. Please come chat with me, as I'd love to ask you some things about you and the water!"

Right away, there was the big stormy ocean, stretching on for miles. It was full of little waves, never sitting still, and I was getting snaps of scales, dragon eyes, frills and fins. But eventually, standing there on a rock jutting out from it all, was Leviathan. He appeared as a person, with black clothes and green hair that wasn't staying quite hair-like; I realized after staring at it for a bit that those were actually his way of glamouring his fins. He had deep black eyes and seemed a little androgynous, not quite man but not quite woman, eventually settling on a slightly more masculine way of presenting.

So of course, the first thing I asked about was how he decided how to appear.

"Leviathan, you know—there are some that say they see you as a man, others as a woman, and the stories themselves surely don't give a cut and dry answer. How do you decide how to appear to people, be it in terms of gender, shape, form?"

1. HOW DO YOU DECIDE WHAT FORM TO TAKE ON?

Experiencing hiccups. Put a project aside and come back to it. Progress isn't linear.

Celebration and harmony in life. Riding out ebbs, celebrating good times. Movement.

A need for focus and discipline. It's imperative to stay on the forward path and not get distracted.

Leviathan stood there with his arms crossed, gazing out at the sea, which he would do quite a bit as we went through the interview. He shrugged after I'd asked my question.

"It doesn't matter, he said, showing me images of a great dragon slicing through the water. "It's not important. On the sea floor, you don't think of such things. You move, you hunt, you focus on the goal ahead. I want my children to do the same. There's no need to go picking at irrelevant details—just let them know I'm here, and let them see me as they wish, so long as they work."

"Oh. I understand that," I said, nodding as I recorded his answer. "Makes sense! But you mention work, and I'm curious: what kinds of things do you work on with practitioners?"

2. WHAT DO YOU WORK ON WITH MAGICAL PRACTITIONERS?

"People are so weak when it comes to their perception."

"You think so?"

"Yes. They can't see the forest for the trees. They make judgments off misinterpretations of reality. In the dark, there is no trick of perception. Water becomes black like ink, no light; the mind tries to fill the void with tricks."

For a moment, I was in that water, weightless and feeling it all around me but seeing nothing, not even my hand in front of my face.

"I want my students to separate fact from fiction. To be comfortable with the chaos, the unknown, the dark. To dive in and confront it, accept it. Not to claw after the shimmer and dazzle of a light that blinds them."

"I see. I never thought about the water like that. That's interesting." I

Acknowledgement of success. Be proud of what you've accomplished. Optimistic about challenges. Be careful of your relationship with success and your ego.

Transforming passion to action. Creating containers for success. Doing work most don't like to do. Taking projects seriously.

All things external born out of ego. Detach from your ego and ground yourself to make the best decisions.

cocked my head and pipped, "Learning a lot about perception in this discussion about water!"

He glanced at me. "That's because water is like a mirror. When it's clear, it shows you a strange reflection of reality."

And I understood then why the ocean he put us in was so stormy. No images could come through stormy water and trick people.

"You know, though," I started, catching myself before I dove down a rabbit hole of thoughts on the water, "a lot of these cards you pulled say something about ego, success, and the like, and I wonder: you're frequently associated with envy. What do you think about envy as a concept?"

3. WHAT DO YOU THINK ABOUT THE IDEA OF ENVY?

1. Deep communication with another person. Being honest with a partner. Love is a choice with a life-death-life cycle.

2. Resistance to making changes. We can struggle when we feel powerless. Acknowledge each choice to take back your power.

3. Broken bonds. A relationship fallen out of balance. Communication is more challenging; be open to repairing it. Experiencing hiccups. Put a project aside and come back to it. Progress isn't linear.

Leviathan tapped his temple. "Perception. People perceive that others have something they want. Do they actually want it? Does the other person actually even have it? Who knows? But envy is a stupid thing, blind of reason and rationality. I envy nothing and no one. I wish they wouldn't pin such a silly thing on me. I teach people to break the bonds of envy."

"Agreed, envy does seem like a weird one. Wrath at least is an understandable concept to try ascribing to someone, or pride, but not envy." I stared at my notebook as my brain buffered around the concept, and then I said, "Okay! Beyond that, then, with this ascribing of envy to you, and all these stories, I am curious: how did you become public enemy number one in these stories? What about the water has people making stories like this about you?"

4, WHAT ABOUT YOU HAS EVERYONE MAKING THESE STORIES OF YOU?

Carrying a large burden from yourself or others. It's time to release it. Eliminate this weight from your life.

A clear thinking, ambitious leader. Not centered on luck. Viewing situation with head, not heart, will get a solution quicker.

Pause. May be a time to change course because of challenges, or you may be allowing challenges to break you. Be intentional.

"Men are terrified of what they can't comprehend," Leviathan said with a sigh. "The water claims the lives of so many careless ones, and so many who did everything right. There's no rhyme or reason to the way some come home and others don't. There must've *been* a reason, people said, and that reason must've been me. So they told their tales of glory, made a big fuss about hunts and battles and such. All to believe they could control that which can barely even be contained."

"Ooh." Images of floods, tsunamis, water spilling up onto land started cropping up. "I see that. What do you think of how mankind goes worshipping sea gods, then? All these gods of the ocean to protect them?"

Leviathan smiled as if it was funny.

"Let them have their solace," he mused. "Let them have their perception. It won't save them when the waves rock the boat."

I paused, uneasy. "Yeah, but the gods can stop people from getting killed on the water—don't you think so?"

"Of course they *can*. But will they?"

He asked it with such a cheeky tone, looking at me from the corner of his eye.

"Fair," I said, chewing on the idea. "That is always the tricky bit. But then, what is it about the ocean, and water, that inspires such fear in people?"

5. WHAT ABOUT THE OCEAN SCARES MANKIND SO MUCH?

"There is no way to avoid the sea. Nor do people want to give up its bounty. But the danger still exists, and that's troublesome for people. They spend their lives having already decided, generations ago, that the risk is worth the reward.

"But the bottomless deep is still bottomless, the water still dark. The uncertainty of seeing nothing but water for miles terrifies people. A cloud on the horizon could spell doom. Yet once you're out there, you can only keep going. It represents the unknown, and the unknown is a fearful thing."

I nodded, then started trying to wrap my own mind around my next question. "And that unknown, that chaos and 'uncreation,' as I've heard it so often represents in stories like the ones written about you—can you speak on that?"

Bumps in the road, total life upheaval. Reflect and assess your needs. Be curious of possibilities; don't rely on old ways of thinking.

Rapid movement to emotions. Ready to move forward with actions. Heart-led. A new lover, high emotions, illusion.

You have a few options available and are centering on the one that's best for long term sustainability.

6. HOW IS WATER CONNECTED TO THE ABYSS, OR "UNCREATION"?

A period of solitude. Focus on yourself. Communicate your needs. Relationships have fallen by the wayside.

Imbalance in relationships. Focus on yourself and not others. There may be hidden ego issues in giving so much.

Slow down; examine the situation. You may be moving too quickly. Stick to one thing long enough and be patient.

"I could speak on it forever. Water is life and death: humans come into the world from the dark, in water."

The *a-ha!* moment of remembering how dark it must be in the womb, and the concept of water breaking, had me staring up at him with likely dinner-plate-sized eyes.

"You form there, where it's weightless, empty, yet able to hold you. The 'chaos' of water is simply the lack of things for your mind to latch onto. Water is rest. Water is the blank slate, where rejuvenation occurs. All things start from the dark and unformed."

"Wow. I got'cha. I love that. Thank you for sharing that!" I sat with it a moment longer, then said, "So, that's the last of the topic questions. Now I ask: how do you see yourself?"

7. HOW DO YOU SEE YOURSELF?

Reactive, emotional, imbalanced, moody, and harsh. Emotional disconnect or intensity, or switching between them, creates tension in relationships. Reflect on how you're really feeling.

Pulling King of Cups reversed was a surprise, especially since he seemed a bit detached from the idea of emotion altogether. But as he spoke, it made sense.

"I make an effort not to put my state onto others, but the phrase 'below the surface' exists for a reason. Much damage has been done. Much."

His otherwise mask-like face broke here, and I got the sense he was talking about the others of his group. It seemed there were more than one Leviathan at one point, and it upsets him to be the only one left.

"I see. I can't say I understand, but I can imagine how that would cause a lot of grief. But how do you want others to see you?"

8. HOW DO YOU WANT OTHERS TO SEE YOU?

"I have triumphed," Leviathan said, his voice strong. "I have survived. I am here to stay. I have much to show those who can work past their fear, and I am grateful for the chance to do so."

"Nice. Good!" It uplifted the mood a little to hear him be so stalwart about that. "And now, do you have any messages you'd like to share?"

Enjoying success. Harvest has come. Stability achieved. A long road has been walked; you've worked hard. Don't let it go to your head. No point in abundance if you can't share it.

9. ANY LAST MESSAGES FOR ME OR OTHERS?

"Yes." He stared at me head on and said, "People spread themselves too thin. They think they need to know everything, do everything, see everything. Foolish. I want people, especially my students, to choose a discipline and sit with it. Dedicate time and energy to one thing at a time. You make mistakes when you juggle too many things at once."

And boy, do I ever know about that. We all do it at some point, though— bite off more than we can chew.

"Heard loud and clear," I said, with a slight bow of my head. "Well, that about wraps it up. Leviathan, thank

Those who refuse to pause will get put on pause by the universe. Give yourself permission to rest.

Dissatisfaction with life. Re-establish connections with others and yourself.

Convention in all forms, especially spiritually. Back to tradition; it exists for a reason. Structure and tradition needed.

you so much for your time! It was lovely to get to meet you and hear your perspective. I appreciate you coming to do so. Until next time!"

And then he smiled, and I was drifting away from him as if some tiny speedboat had collected me and ferried me away from him. All the waves, the rocks, the clouds, disappeared, and I was left there in my kitchen, wondering about more than a few things. Namely, all the things I learned that had very little to do with water.

Like the idea that gods *can* stop tragedies, but don't, for whatever reason.

Like the idea that our perception is a bigger enemy than waves and rocks, and that still water makes a mean mirror.

Like the idea that, for all people go fear-mongering about demons and beings like Leviathan, they really do care about humanity—the state of us as a group, and as individuals. They want to see us thrive as much as any angel; they just go about helping us along a totally different way.

It's comforting, you know? To know that the things we were taught to be so scared of really aren't so scary at all, granted we keep our heads and mind our manners. It's interesting, knowing the boundaries we can push, the things we can learn, the places we can go and the things we can see, if we just let go of the fear and take that first shaky step forward into the abyss.

The ocean is a good representation of that abyss. Dark. Cold. Seemingly endless. Full of strange and potentially dangerous finds. But if anything Leviathan said stuck, it's that for all our fear, we just can't keep away from the water. In a more metaphorical sense, it seems we can't stay away from the deep dark of the spiritual world, either. I wonder why. I wonder what about it draws us so close, and why so many earthly forces, like the religious institutions that pad their pockets with tithes while covering up heinous human rights abuses, tell us to ignore it. I wonder why so many well-meaning people, too, preach such fear of it.

I wonder, I say—but I'm pretty sure you and I already have a million and two potential answers to that "why."

Nonetheless, a balanced perspective requires seeing both sides, and if I'm to talk to angels, it's only fair I talk to demons, too. And so far, I haven't met a demon I didn't like. Each one has their own wisdom, talents, and ideas; each one makes you feel just as alive as any other piece of Divinity when you speak to them. Each one wants to help. And so, throughout this series, I'd say I've gone from being pretty spooked about the idea of demons to wholly comfortable with them (even if there are still a couple I'd rather not encounter unless necessary).

Talk about character growth, am I right?

PRINCESS BARI

When I consider doing these interviews, I'll admit: I stick predominantly to Christian or European spirits because I don't, under *any* circumstance, want to stick my behind into a party that is not for me. I don't want to go speaking to deities of cultures I know nothing about, whose customs I don't understand, and I don't want to present a hackneyed, outsider's idea of a deity or spirit as if I'm some authority on them, because what a grave injustice that would be! And not only to the deity, but to the people they preside over and the cultures that wreathe themselves around these gods.

So while there are many deities that interest me—the Chinese Nu Wa, the gods of Japanese Shintoism, the Vedic deities or gods of the Native tribes across North and South America, the Orishas and the Iwa and so on and so forth—I stay to the places I know are open, the religions I know have more modern reconstructionist elements compatible with my framework, and cultures I have some sense of familiarity with. The only exception is one like today.

Thanks to the help of Ji Hae (@neomudang), who is incredibly skilled and educated in the traditions of Korean shamanism, I was able to speak with Princess Bari, a Korean folk goddess of the underworld and a deity credited as the originator of the tradition of Korean shamans (known as mudangs).

Princess Bari has a really interesting story. From what I understand, she was the daughter of a great king that had six daughters before her already. They were expecting Princess Bari to be a son, and so they had a whole feast and lined up for it, but it turned out that Princess Bari was a girl. Her parents had her abandoned as a result (hence her name, likely from Korean 버리, or *beori*, "to be abandoned.")

Some stories of what happen to her after vary (maybe she was adopted by Buddha, maybe by another family looking to raise a child), but when her parents get sick, and none of the other six daughters want to go to the underworld to get the water of life to cure them, her father sends his men out to find out where she is and ask her to take on the task of getting the water.

And she does! But by time she gets back, her parents have already died. Princess Bari interrupts the funeral, reviving her parents with flowers from the underworld and curing them with the water. In some versions, she attains divinity, and in others, she simply lives out the rest of her life.

According to Ji Hae, on top of being the goddess of the underworld and origin of the Korean shamans that followed, given her many magical talents and abilities, she also has folk associations with adoptees (especially Korean adoptees) and even comfort women (which is a whole separate topic of human rights abuses against women in World War II that you are free to look up if you can stomach it). However, there was also a book written (*Princess Bari* by Hwang Sok-yong) using Princess Bari's imagery and story in a modern setting.

I was thrilled to speak to an entity outside of the very European, occultist, and Abrahamic framework I'd worked within throughout my journey thus far, and I very much appreciate Ji Hae's help in making this happen, because it was such a fascinating experience. So without further ado, let me show you a conversation with a well-loved and wonderful Korean deity.

For this interview, I'd done a good deal of preparation. Ji Hae sent me articles about folklore, religious practices, and other recorded details surrounding Buddhism, of which Princess Bari seemed to be at least a little syncretized to, in order to give me some background on a religious system that I honestly didn't know much about. She also shared with me her Spotify playlist of several Buddhist contemplations she brought to life for other observers of the faith. I went through the Contemplation of the Water, as well as did a few full body prostrations, before getting into the zone at the table.

As for offerings, it was critical that if I were to offer a fruit, it be one with no pit (so things like oranges and bananas, which I'd chosen, were fine), and in terms of associations, Ji Hae mentioned that Princess Bari was associated with the rainbow. I unfortunately lost my pieces of bismuth, which would've been perfect for this, so I just surrounded her offering plate with crystals of all different colors. I also lit some iris incense, as she enjoys flowers and good scents, and I lit a single candle to signify the ritual space. Afterwards, Ji Hae and I had a video call, where she performed a ritual to ask Princess Bari's permission for me to speak with her and connect her with me, which was so cool to be able to see. I was fully aware that this was a privilege to go through, from start to finish, and I was so excited to have had a chance like this.

Once the ritual was done, my prayers were done, and everything was lit and set, I was able to feel Princess Bari's presence and confirm that she wanted to use Amrit Brar's Marigold Tarot. After that, I settled in with some music and let myself enter the meditation with full confidence.

"Princess Bari, welcome! Thank you so much for joining me today," I said, my voice ringing out over the infinite space before anything took shape in my mind's eye. "I appreciate and welcome you here with a gift of oranges and banana, and a little iris incense, too. Please enjoy these gifts, and please appear however you'd like me to see you."

It took a little bit to really sink into the image, but once I got there, Princess Bari was there with a pot of tea. She wore a red and blue hanbok covered in silver flower embroidery, and she had a big yellow ribbon holding back some of her slightly wavy black hair. She had a kind smile and deep black eyes, and we soon settled into what looked like a normal house, with a hearth fire embedded in the wooden floor, a couple shelves of simple things, and herbs lining the walls. Directly outside the house was the ocean crashing against the rock the house sat on.

She kept silent and waited patiently as I tried to grasp the full picture, with a soft smile as if she were amused at my clumsy attempts to stitch myself into the space with her.

"Okay, I think I got it now," I said once I could feel the floor beneath me as I sat, and I could clearly see myself within the space. "Again, thank you for coming! But now, I do have some questions for you that I'd love to ask, and the first one is: what is the *water of life* doing in the underworld?"

1. WHY IS THE WATER OF LIFE IN THE UNDERWORLD?

Deception and re-evaluation of whether a relationship or goal is truly fulfilling.

Disinterest and doubt. Introspection, pessimism, and an inability to see the good in life.

We agreed on two cards per question, and she was very clear about which ones she wanted each time. This time, she pulled the Page of Cups Reversed and the Four of Cups Reversed. She also showed me an image of water running between her fingers and spilling onto the floor.

"See how it runs between your fingers? The water. It's so very hard to keep track of. It runs away into the cracks of the floor."

Then she pointed to the wood of the house, where spots of mold and mildew grew in the mists caused by the sea.

"It causes mildew when clinging to living things—mold and damp and rot. It decays. It is of the underworld. But all the same, we die if we have none of it, too. In the land of death, the purest water lives where it has nothing to do with killing. Its purpose is dual, but there in the underworld, it can serve only one purpose: life. This is how water is a nuisance in that land; above, it's a nuisance by its ability to rot things away."

"Oh, wow. I never considered that. Can you say more on it?"

2. THOUGHTS ON THE DUAL NATURE OF THINGS LIKE WATER?

"Of course," she said with such a gentle smile. "Fickle things, all in this world. Everything has a shadow—even the air. The world is full of tricks and illusions, and all wears a double mask. It's important to know when to rebuke the physical world, because sometimes it grows tired and doesn't remember what it must do."

In her cupped hands was a small pool of water.

"Water is a gentle pet. It kills slowly, but it sustains easily."

She must've heard me wonder about tsunamis, because the image popped up, and she addressed it.

"As a wild beast," such as when water takes the form of a tsunami, or a river, or the ocean, "it has a temper, but nothing that doesn't still adhere to this idea. All things that are physical can forget their glory. Only when you leave the physical for good will you truly see."

Overextending oneself or avoiding responsibilities.

Intelligence, trustworthiness, security, generosity, and resourcefulness. Contemplating blessings of the world past material ones. Nurturing, support, responsibility.

This sounded like a familiar idea to me, but I tucked it away, because I was honestly having trouble wrapping my head around it. I think I understood well enough, though the closest thing I could relate it to was the idea in Mary Magdalene's gospel, that we forget who we are and act in ways unbefitting to our divine nature; this is what causes sin (according to Jesus in her gospel).

"I think I get it," I said as I laid my book down. "That's really interesting; thank you Okay! Well, I'd be remiss if I didn't ask you about yourself, too, especially regarding your story. Given the events with your parents, how did you find the compassion to still go to such lengths to help them?"

3. HOW DID YOU FIND THE COMPASSION TO HELP YOUR PARENTS?

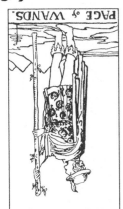

Excess of excitement has resulted in overlooking key details when trying to maintain new projects and relationships.

Unrest and an inability to move on.

The cards were a little confusing at first, the Page of Wands Reversed and the Eight of Swords Reversed. They only made sense together, as I got the sense that the overexcitement & overlooking of key details in the first card had something to do with the "unrest & inability to move on" in the second.

"I'm sorry, Princess Bari—can you explain these cards?"

Then I had an image of her running through a grove of thin trees, sharp and thorny ones that snagged her red coat. It ripped, revealing the white shift of her sleeve underneath.

"They snag you, like a thorny branch on your fine cloak," she said. "Those little details—or even big ones—sometimes they must be left out. Yes, you tore your cloak, but if you stop and despair at that branch, and get angry, and curse at it, all you do is lose time. You delay yourself from approaching that which you were just so dedicated to moving towards. Therefore, it's not that I found the compassion; it's that I let go of what was distracting me from it. I saw a bigger picture than my own experience."

Ah. That made sense. In the materials Ji Hae had given me to read, there was a heavy emphasis on the idea of self-emptying that I thought of as she said that. I don't have the means to explain it well, but it's a piece of Buddhism that is really interesting and helpful for the spirit, in my opinion. Like Pepto Bismol for the soul.

"That does make a lot of sense. Never did I think it had anything to do with releasing versus cultivating something when it comes to compassion, but that does make a big difference in understanding the idea!" Fully in my Divine Reporter groove, I put the thought down for later and kept rolling. "Okay. I guess, then, to follow this idea of your story, with the meaning of your name and the like, I'm curious as to what you would say to those who have been abandoned? Not necessarily with family itself, but in general. People might have ideas like 'what was wrong with me?' or 'why didn't they want me?' and I'd like to know what you would say to them."

4. WHAT WOULD YOU SAY TO THOSE WHO HAVE BEEN ABANDONED?

Here came the clearest message of the night, with Five of Coins and the Eight of Cups reversed. Their meanings were sharp and to the point, and so was she.

"Why dwell on questions like these?" Princess Bari tossed her hand up and huffed. "What answers can you come to that'll satisfy you? You cannot look back and turn over every leaf and stone of the past. What happened, happened."

"That's pretty straightforward, huh?"

1. Financial and material struggles, victim mentalities, rejection. Pained by unfavorable circumstances. Strife is self inflicted.

2. Joy, moving forward. Stagnation is the root cause of a majority of one's challenges.

She nodded, and she was facing away from me, chin up, stoic. "Your only option is to make do with what you have, what you can. One has to be direct with a message like this. It cannot be swallowed beautifully: embrace this discomfort, and the opportunity to liberate yourself from it. Only you can do that."

Sometimes I wondered about the language she used. It was very markedly different from other entities I'd spoken to, with the way she shaped her sentences and the specific words she used, almost like poetry. I mean, *swallowed beautifully* felt like a brand-new phrase in my head, at least. I wondered if it was just an issue with how my mind was translating things, but I didn't let myself get too lost in the idea.

"Understood: I hear you loud and clear. Thank you for sharing! But now, as we are looking to explore the theme of water this month, I was wondering... well, you know... water." I fumbled and bumbled through the idea, tripping on my own mental tongue in my search for the words to convey what I wanted to ask. "It's... watery. Um—"

5. CAN YOU TELL ME SOMETHING ABOUT THE NATURE OF WATER?

Power, prosperity, optimism. Warmth, happiness, comfort, and growth.

Loss, dishonor, and defeat. Defeat even in victory, a hollow triumph.

As I floundered, Princess Bari tapped me and smiled. "You want to know about water? I'll tell you about water."

And then she pulled her cards, and afterwards waved her hand and let the ocean crash up hard on the stone that the house sat on—only for all the spray and roar of it to fall down and dampen the stone. It felt anti-climactic, I guess.

"What water can grant—life, comfort, beauty, purity," all of which came with images of people washing themselves clean, putting on makeup or perfume—"can also be taken away."

Again, there were images of tsunamis, floods, muddy water.

"It fills the container one puts it in," Princess Bari continued. "Fear it, and it will crash against the rock of your mind; it'll erode it away. Try to trap it, and place it in an area where it cannot harm you," there was an image of a clay pot of water on a high shelf in a house, "and it will soon grow stagnant.

"It is not respectful to take something as free and formless as water and demand it choose a shape in some earthen vessel. Water is happiest when it flows free—and people might learn from this."

Again, it was a little difficult for me to wrap my head around this idea, but I understood it was as much a metaphor as it was a statement about water. It had something to do with the human spirit, too. I think.

"I got'cha. Okay. I think I see where you're going with that. Fair enough! Though, speaking of learning lessons, from what I understand, in Buddhism, there are one hundred and eight delusions of the mind. Are there any one of these that you'd like to speak on?"

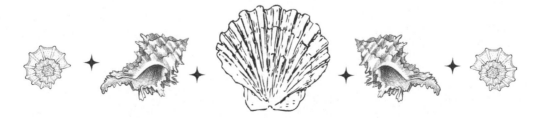

6. ANY THOUGHTS ON THE 108 DELUSIONS IN BUDDHISM?

The number 17 flashed in my mind. I looked it up, and I got translations like deceit and humiliation, and a Japanese word ひまん (*himan*) that only brought up articles about obesity when I tried to get any translation of it. I wasn't really sure what it was or what it was warning against. Thankfully, she explained it.

Behaviors considered self destructive, controlling, dishonest, manipulative.

Hostility, indecision, and disharmony.

"When you think you can poison your body, and that it won't poison your mind, you deceive yourself. This deception breaks you from reality."

My mouth popped open, but no words came out. There was just that *click*, that understanding, as she kept on going.

"To master yourself is to not run from the truth, and to instead acknowledge that what you may find pleasurable is, in fact, the source of your pain," she said. "It is limited to no one idea, be it food or purchasing material items or anything else; any physical pleasure can become a source of the soul's greatest pain. At some point, if you want harmony, you have to show mercy to your soul by denying your body."

I had never heard it described as showing mercy to your soul. What a brilliant way to phrase it. I feel like denying oneself is always described as showing some restraint or proving your mettle by suffering and abstaining from things you like, but the idea that your soul could be pained by hyperfixation and is crying out for a break? That hit me. It also made me again think of Mary Magdalene, and I said so.

"It kind of sounds like one of the seven powers in Mary Magdalene's gospel: the False Peace of the Flesh. What do you think?"

"Mmm, not quite," she said. "That idea there, this false peace, is when you've learned to drown the voice of your soul so that it can't begin to cry. By then, it's difficult to turn back—and then you seek more physical pleasure to fill that void where the voice of your soul once was."

"Wow." I'm not joking when I say I sat there just buffering for a minute. That made a lot of sense. "Okay. Well, then... how can one make sure they stay in harmony with their soul? And not lose the sound of its voice in all that silence, or even get it back from that silence?"

7. HOW CAN ONE STAY IN HARMONY WITH THEIR SOUL?

1. Greed, potentially shallow fulfilment, concerns with the material world.

2. Loss, dishonor, and defeat. Defeat even in victory, a Pessimism, dread, resignation. Hollow triumph.

Again, she seemed to be aiming this message more at whoever, and her face was pinched in a bit of annoyance, her brows furrowed, her eyes wide.

"Why are you settling? When you hold the things you think should give you joy, why are you acting like there's something wrong when you feel nothing?"

Oh, damn.

"When you outsource your joy," she said, "you become sick."

And she showed me images of people with dead eyes as they held things like trophies, like food, like clothing, like trinkets, and she filled me with that feeling of "I should be grateful; I should appreciate this; I should be happy" underscored by deep dissatisfaction—so deep it felt like I was weeping from a deep crack in my chest.

"When you can no longer sit still because the silence is intolerable, sit there longer," Princess Bari whispered. "Don't grab for your nearest distraction to fill the void. Because in the silence, with nothing, if you just wait, you will find yourself again. Listen. The silence holds the voice of your soul deep in it, but you must be patient and let yourself hear it."

Sometimes, there's nothing to say. This was one of the first experiences I had in these interviews where I just stared, not in total bewilderment like I'd done before, but in the very presence of the idea put forward—like I was in a sauna, and all the steam was that idea sitting on me and putting me at ease.

"Thank you for that," I said as I finally found a few spare words. "Well, honestly, that about concludes the questions I had that are specific. Now comes some questions for you that describe you. First, how would you describe yourself?"

8. HOW DO YOU SEE YOURSELF?

KING of PENTACLES

Power, knowledge, success, reliability. Everything one touches turns to gold. Rich in practical knowledge. Keen instincts, cooperative. Sheer abundance and potential.

"It is as it says," she said as she tapped my card, which was sitting on the wooden floor of the house she put us in. "I am rich here, with all I have, even if others only see the ocean and a place to pour my tea. The richness must come from within. It cannot come from outside. I'm one who learned this viscerally."

"Ah, I see. Okay! Now, how would you want others to see you? I know this is going towards a western audience who likely isn't familiar with you, so I'm curious as to how you want them to understand you."

9. HOW DO YOU WANT TO BE SEEN?

"I accomplished what I aimed to," she said, with utmost confidence. "I set my path. I walked it, and I earned my fruits for it. I am sure of myself." Then she added, with such steel in her voice, "Not one piece of my story may ever be used to say I stumbled, or that I was shamed in any way. I achieved my own triumph, and no one can take that from me."

Victory, superiority, confidence, and pride.

I sat there in awe. What a beautiful take. "Incredible. I'm glad to share that! Thank you! And lastly, are there any messages you'd like to share? Maybe topics I didn't ask about that you wanted to mention?"

10. ANY LAST MESSAGES FOR ME OR OTHERS?

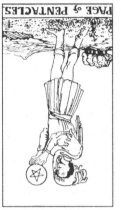

The cards were bleak. Page of Coins reversed, Justice reversed. But as I read the descriptions and felt the overall energy, it didn't seem like Princess Bari was giving a warning. I asked her to explain, and she did.

"I'm not warning anything," she insisted, then drew in a deep breath and sighed. "I'm just describing what I'm seeing. People have no use for each other anymore, unless it's to get something or use them as an outlet for their own vileness. They paint each other in delusion, casting what's inside them onto others. I see a breeding ground for resentment, a wasteland where love should've grown. It's sad. But this is only what I see. It's up to you all to decide to change this."

"Fair enough, yeah. It is a shame, how people act these days; I agree. But that does conclude the list of questions that I had." I bowed my head and beamed at her. "Again, Princess Bari, thank you so much for agreeing to speak to me; it was an incredible experience, and I appreciate you spending the time and energy to tell me these things. With that, I say goodbye."

Bad news, wastefulness, preoccupations with projects at the expense of other priorities in life.

False accusations, disharmony, and general unfairness.

And then I paused my music, mentally unplugged from the space, and let Princess Bari fade away with a smile. Afterwards, I asked Ji Hae what I should do with these offerings. She advised me to eat them and see if they tasted any sweeter.

The banana was already very ripe, so I was expecting it to be sweet. But that and the oranges had a taste that felt a couple degrees off what I expected, as if someone had a very good idea of what they tasted like and tried to replicate it on this plate. It could be described as "sweeter," because the orange for some reason almost reminded me of kiwi, and the banana had a lighter sweetness to it that reminded me of flowers. It was puzzling, and I wasn't sure at all what to make of it, because like many of you, I've eaten bananas and oranges dozens of times. Hundreds, even. I know what they're supposed to taste like, and this just wasn't *quite* it.

But Ji Hae said this was a sign that the offering had been blessed, meaning the interview went well. How exciting a thought! And when I told her about the colors I'd seen, the red, blue, and yellow, she confirmed that this was another good sign—that I'd picked up on the spiritual energies, entities, and guardians around Princess Bari without being primed to do so. All this meant that I'd had, for all intents and purposes, an authentic experience with this goddess.

This made me giddy. I'd pulled it off! I'd made it work! I'd received some *incredible* insights! I mean, really—the idea of restraining ourselves a bit from the many vices of the world as an act of *compassion* towards the soul rather than an ascetic attempt at "punishing the flesh" or however people think about it? I know it's likely an old concept to anyone who follows these traditions, but for someone like myself, who never heard it described that way before, it felt revolutionary—and well timed, given my reading of Mary Magdalene's gospel.

It seems that Divinity points in one direction, no matter which version of it you go to for help and growth. Norse? Celtic? Celestial? Infernal? No matter who you worship or what your beliefs are, it just feels like everything unites under the banner of: *be good to yourself and be good to one another.* Such a simple request, and yet one Humanity has gotten wrong again and again and again.

Still, it certainly gave me a new way to think about the world in relation to myself, and about water, and the way its properties apply both to the simple liquid we drink up everyday and our own selves. Lots of people are "watery," too, you know: people born under the sign of Cancer, Scorpio, or Pisces, people who were born and raised close to the ocean or the lakes or the creeks, they all hold some of those characteristics of water Princess Bari described, I think. And it's important to ask ourselves where we're not respecting ourselves, or leaving ourselves to get stagnant, when going about our day to day lives.

A hard thing to do when you're caught up in the hustle and bustle, but a necessary thing, too. Nonetheless, this was a wonderful experience, and I'm glad to not only have been able to do it with respect to the culture, but to gain such insights to share with you all, too.

MOKOSH

There's a goddess in Slavic folklore that doesn't represent water so much as moisture—that doesn't represent life so much as the bed of dirt and leaves and rot that life grows from. Mokosh, goddess of fertility, women and women's work, childbirth, the harvest, and moisture, is a goddess much beloved, and her worship continues among reconstructionist Slavic pagans and those looking to reconnect with their Slavic ancestry in any way they can. My friend Bolotnitsa (@divchatozlisa) is a devotee of Mokosh, and she helped me verify that Mokosh would be one to speak to about water—and life.

As a part of a religion that's had much of its records lost and erased, and much more of its mythos reconstructed and discussed by later Christian and Muslim scholars, Mokosh's stories are a bit of a jumble. Some say she's consort of Perun, others say she's consort of Veles—some say the great divine battle between Perun and Veles started because Veles kidnapped her from Perun—so on and so forth. She may be the mother of Morana and Jarilo if you ask the eastern Slavs (while according to central Slavs, like the Polish, that would actually be Devana who married Veles and potentially bore Morana, or at least works in tandem with her in spring festivals).

Ask the southern Slavs (like my people, the Slovenians), and the story changes all over again. Mokosh may potentially be consort of Svarog, creating all of humanity with him in various other myths littered around these tribes. Such is what happens when one overarching ethnic group covers literally half of Europe and makes their own specific ideas about the gods in isolation from everyone else.

Either way, Mokosh, as a master of all things living and damp, was a figure of interest for this month's theme of water. As we know, water doesn't just exist in the oceans or the rivers; it exists in the dew of a cool summer morning and the condensation on a cold glass of water, too. I wanted to know more about water from Mokosh's perspective, though I didn't know what to expect when I heard about Mokosh, honestly. Goddesses, the Divine Feminine, all that, you already know: it's not my thing. I was thinking maybe Mokosh would be something like Lada: mild, quiet, gentle.

But boy, was I wrong. Mokosh came through strong and bold, and I'm glad to be able to show you how this conversation went.

As a goddess of the harvest and fertility as much as anything else, for offerings, I had things that represented fertility: nuts, seeds, and so on. A cup of dandelion tea went with it, because if there are two flowers that I know my Slovenian ancestors love to use for tea and food, it's chamomile and dandelion. I also had a bit of my crochet projects around, as being a goddess of women's work—weaving, in particular—it was something to anchor her in my mind and in my space. So was all of the spring-time décor I already had out, as well as the many Ukrainian pysanky I had. I also put out her sigil and a few stones: sunstone, moss agate, and rose quartz, all of which, to me, represented something about the things she has dominion over. Nature, love, wealth and luck—that's all her.

So once I was settled, and I'd done the Lord's Prayer and asked God to set my space up and let Mokosh through, I settled in. She chose M.J. Cullinane's Guardians of the Night tarot, which I thought she might, given it's both for the Slavic gods and full of animals and other nature images, and we agreed on three cards per question, for the most part.

"Hello, Mokosh!" I said as I shuffled the deck. "Welcome! I have here for you some dandelion tea and hazelnuts, pumpkin seeds, and beans. If you'd like to come speak, please do!"

Right away, I got the sense that she'd been there for a while already. Maybe she heard me thinking of talking to her all week and knew I'd be calling on her. Sometimes I do wonder if the gods I plan to talk to know I'm thinking of them beforehand—and this seemed to prove they do.

But immediately, we were in a big grassy field, with a lake off to the side. There were flowers and trees, and there in the middle of it all was Mokosh, a woman with a bright smile and eyes that shined with mirth. Her long brown hair was crowned with a ring of greenery and flowers, and her dress was white and covered with red Ukrainian embroidery around the collar, down the front, and on the sleeves. She was barefoot in the dirt, and she towered over me.

"About time," she said, which startled me. Right away, it felt like I'd encountered someone I already knew well enough to joke with.

"I know, I'm sorry; it took me a second to get everything together! But I've got some questions for you, if you don't mind answering. First things first, you know—we have a saying in English that 'April showers bring May flowers.' What do you think about that? Especially since rain is so cold and icky a lot of the times, and the clouds make things seem a little *blah* when they cover up the sun?"

I. WHAT DO YOU THINK OF "APRIL SHOWERS BRING MAY FLOWERS"?

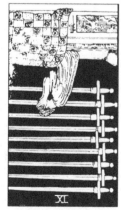

Doubt, shame, suspicion.

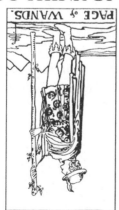

Excitement, over-looking details in projects and relationships.

Breaking bonds, freedom, and detachment.

"I think it's cute! And wise. Because why feel icky? The mists are lovely," and as she spoke, we were no longer in the little grove by the water, but on a grassy hillside where sheep were bleating and where the mists rolled around. "You can't rush this time of year. That's how you end up with dead gardens— because you didn't let the mists seep in deep into the ground and let the rains warm up. See the timing of your expression? April, then May? Yes, you can't rush nature."

"Ah, I got'cha. Yeah, I do like to start my gardens too early, I'll give you that." I'd done it again this year, planting my vegetables just before a sudden rush of cold weather hit. It stunted my tomatoes. I'm still mad about it, and madder that my mother told me to wait another couple weeks to plant. She was right. As usual. "But okay—tell me about these mists, then. What should we learn from them?"

2. WHAT CAN WE LEARN FROM THE MISTS?

Mokosh waved her hand around at the air as we walked through this field. "The mists, the fog—they're thick. They make it hard to breathe. You can't see. But you can't stay standing in the field doing nothing, either. The mists may blind you, but this teaches you to intuitively move.

"Everyone wants the sunny days where all is perfect and pretty, but that's not reality. The mists teach you to move in uncertainty and in less than perfect conditions." Then she tilted her head back in the mists and sat there basking in it, soaking it all up. "They keep your face nice and cool, too."

Indecision, fear of making the wrong move, dealing with responsibility poorly, staying in the dark.

Loneliness, alienation, extreme caution, and isolation.

Loss, theft, un-compromising values, and obses-sion with socially acceptable roles and routines.

Her personality was so big. Huge. It made me smile, and it made me feel cozy warm all throughout my chest. "Understandable, yeah," I said. "I see that. Well, from what I understand about you, Mokosh, you're also a goddess of women and women's work. What is women's work to you?"

3. WHAT IS "WOMEN'S WORK" IN YOUR VIEW?

Here, she chose no cards. But I could see her flexing her hands, as if she were trying to snag the words out of the air. Eventually they came.

"Making things. And unmaking them. That is women's work—to transform things."

I paused, then said, "But men build things, too."

"Yes, but building and destroying aren't the same as making and unmaking, you understand?" She showed me an image of a woman undoing all her weaving, with the string still perfectly usable in her hands to make something else with. "Women make and unmake, or revert things back to what they were."

"Oh, I think I understand!" Interesting. If I understood what she was implying, it was that women could preserve the materials they used to make things with and make anew with the same items. "But what, then, is the most important thing for a woman to make? Or unmake?"

4. WHAT IS THE MOST IMPORTANT THING WOMEN MAKE OR UNMAKE?

Fated romantic or platonic relationships. Common interests, values, goals. Partnership.

Planting seeds for long term goals. Opportunity, possibility. Practical steps lead to success.

Regaining inner strength and alliances.

Mokosh tapped her chin. "Hmm. Women make many things, but what they make most—and have the power to make—is community."

And here, I got the images of women baking, of them dancing in the spring festivals, of them all washing clothes by the river and telling each other all the news about what was going on between families in the village, as they used to do. Connection between households through the women who kept the houses together.

"If you want to talk about 'unmaking,' let them unmake the fences and boundaries between souls. Women are themselves a fountain of things that feed their land and home and family as much as any other food or drink. A poisoned well, a muddy fountain, these kill villages and break them apart. To be a woman is to be a channel, a doorway, for the very cycle of life and death."

"That's a pretty broad idea."

She shrugged. "Because many things fall into this idea. It's no one action women must take or do to be woman, but they need to gatekeep life and death both to keep the community healthy."

That gave me some "if you know, you know" vibes, I won't lie. But I think plenty people of reading this will know, and as I recorded her answer, I was pretty sure I knew, too.

"I get'cha," I said, and then I got back to shuffling. "That's a really cool way to think about it; thank you! But in that vein, then, I imagine you must not be very impressed with the way we clean our homes and live our lives now, huh? What do you think?"

5. THOUGHTS ON HOW PEOPLE LIVE THEIR LIVES IN THE MODERN ERA?

She wrinkled her nose a bit as I pulled the cards.

"How does anyone know what goes on in their own town if they don't talk to each other? Even neighbors become such enigmas to one another. It's too little. You people need other people. You need community. You don't get it doing everything alone.

"Small communities work better than whatever hell you've all sprawled yourselves into, with your big countries and your voting—such

Suppression, or feeling incapable of expression.

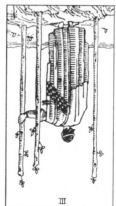

No vision for the future, ignorance of the present.

New beginnings and outlooks, pessimism.

a surprise people have when what they thought was common sense ends up being voted against! Imagine if you all talked to each other again? Made your food together, washed your clothes together by the river? You'd feel much more connected to the world you live in."

The sternness of her voice, the way she planted her hands on her hips and pinched her brows together, it felt like a full-blown Mom Rant. And it was a shockingly relevant take, one I hadn't really thought about. "Oh," I said once she was done speaking. "I really did not expect to be getting political advice here. That's a solid take, though."

"Of course it is." Mokosh waved a hand, held her head high in satisfaction. "Life doesn't happen in solitude and silence; you know this."

"I do. Thank you for the message! I think a lot of people might want or need to hear that." Then I remembered what I was supposed to be investigating with this interview and went back to my list of questions. "But alright, well, back to water itself: I notice it's often associated with emotions, intuition, relationships, stars like Pisces and all that. What about water makes it associated with such things?"

6. WHAT ABOUT WATER MAKES IT THE DOMAIN OF EMOTION?

Envy of a lack of desire to think critically of one's own actions.

Indulgence, sloth, choosing what satisfies immediate needs over long term goals. Avoiding pain and discomfort.

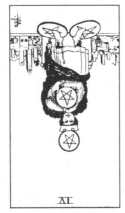

Opposition, feelings of being controlled.

"Water is free," she said as we sat in the grass. "It cuts its own path, goes its own way. Leave it in a cup, and it can make one sick after a while. It encourages movement; you never drink from stagnant waters, only flowing ones."

Mokosh took a deep breath, as if trying to bring all the mist into her lungs, and continued.

"Water represents these things because of how it can express itself so freely in its most natural places. Rivers, oceans, rain and snow. Water never stays still, and neither should we. We should shift and move with each other, and express when we're being left to stagnate. Water teaches us to be anything we want to be."

"I see." I felt small next to her, like a little sister who barely learned how to walk while the big sister was out there being so brave and big and strong. "I love that! Okay, and then to end our personal questions off: where do you like to share your blessings the most?"

7. WHERE DO YOU SHARE YOUR BLESSINGS THE MOST?

Needing to move on. Feelings of alienation and love or relationships long lost.

Keeping up with work, flexibility, inner compassion. Keeping life in balance. Smoothly getting through hard days.

Warm, motherly, generous, supportive. Approach situation with loving energy. Creating space for all to flourish.

"I want to help people heal," she said as she stood up, towering over me with a big smile. "And to be reborn in the sunlight and soft grass! I want to pull people out of the bramble of their minds. I share my gifts with those who need guidance to better fields, where the crops are green and the dew covers the land like honey each morning. There is beauty in the world at its liveliest; I help people find how to flourish with it."

"Beautiful. That's sweet. Now, I'd love to know: how do you see yourself?"

8. HOW DO YOU SEE YOURSELF?

Mokosh shrugged. "I don't fool myself about who I am," she said with her hands on her hips. "I know my talents and when to call on others to help where my talents aren't best suited for a job. Nothing can be done alone, and I don't intend to ever try for the sake of pride. I am strong in my way."

With a nod, I said, "And how do you want others to see you?"

9. HOW DO YOU WANT TO BE SEEN?

Enjoying success. Achievement, pride. Reaping rewards. Confidence, power, abundance.

Her smile took up nearly half her face. "As one who celebrates!" She tossed her hands in the air and twirled, her skirt flaring out. "There's never a reason not to celebrate the fortunes of life—especially fortunes we've earned with hard work. I am one who brings a sense of accomplishment and joy at festivals because we've all earned that moment of satisfaction. If one is to see me at all, may they see me as a sign of joy."

"Aw, that's great! How sweet." It was such a treat to watch her. "Well, before I skip off, Mokosh, is there anything you want to say before we part ways?"

Clarity to see obstacles forming. Seeking the truth behind circumstances. Honesty, integrity, logic, and intuition.

10. ANY LAST MESSAGES FOR ME OR OTHERS?

Facts spoken at expense of feelings, overcoming brain fog.

"Yes." Her smile fell, and the pinched brows, the lips wrenched in a pout, all came back as she said, "It's important to know your stuff, of course—to know the facts and know what you're talking about—but if you tell these truths to people with no regard for how your community feels, does it really help? Whether they don't know what you know or they don't want to hear it because they're upset, the result is the same: no change happens. Be mindful of others."

That was a call out if I ever heard one. A real "if the shoe fits" moment. I can't deny that I've been less than eloquent in my delivery of certain topics many, many times. But it is good advice—some I should take. Some I am taking, in fact, as I go through a chaplaincy program not to learn about Jesus, but to learn about how to properly represent Him, and how to meet people in the world the way He did: with kindness and empathy and grace.

In that moment, though, I clapped my hands and said with a chuckle, "Alright, heard loud and clear. Thank you, Mokosh! I hope you enjoy the spring as everything comes back into bloom, and I'll see you another time!"

Once again, Mokosh gave me a massive, enthusiastic grins. She waved at me and disappeared into the grassy field, and from there, all of it melted away. When I opened my eyes, there was only my living room, the sunlight filtering through the windows, and I sat back against the couch and sighed.

What a goddess. Sometimes, I think we see deities as such ancient beings that we forget that they're still living with us in the modern age. We forget that they know what things like elections and computers are, and that even if they're primordial figures of the dirt and the mist and the seasons, they keep up to speed to help us in the ways we need help. (I mean, did you expect such apt political commentary from a Slavic deity of fertility and weaving? I know I didn't.)

And in a time like today's, her advice is more important than ever. Community doesn't just mean where you live or seeing some familiar faces and striking up small talk. It sure as hell doesn't mean social media communities, where our perception of each other is shaped large in part by over-curated aesthetics, and content made for maximum reach, authenticity be damned. It means going outside and getting to know your neighbor, helping keep your local spaces clean, lending a hand to those in need and working on the lower levels of government to see that your community's needs are met.

I'll tell you: no one realizes just how important their local government is, especially when all the headlines are always so hyperfocused on nonsense happening amongst a group of officials some hundreds of miles away from us. Trust me when I say your state senator or town mayor will have more a vested interest in what you have to say than the top heads running the whole show.

But I digress. Point is, I honestly didn't expect Mokosh to say anything of this nature, and yet she did, and it gave me so much more to think about. I wasn't done thinking about it that day, either, and that's the beauty of direct revelation and speaking to these deities: you might forget you ever had a conversation like this, only to open your notes, read it over, and remember it, getting yourself all fired up all over again in a time where it may be better for you to stop thinking and start taking action.

Seeds. That's what Divinity does: it plants seeds. Once they sprout, though, we're in charge of nurturing them. Nonetheless, when it comes to all things that give life, and all things that remove life, this was certainly a chat for the books, with so many nuggets of wisdom that exhausted me to experience, yet thrilled me to have the privilege to hold nonetheless. And damn, what a privilege it is to be able to do this each week.

NEHALENIA

For my very last interview about water that month, I wanted to take a look at some gods and goddesses I didn't know much about—and that meant looking for help from people much more knowledgeable than I. In this case, I thought: *surely there's a god or goddess in the continental Celtic pantheons that has something to do with water.*

So I reached out to Dīamanios (@dianmanios_craxios on Tiktok) with my question, and he pointed me in the direction of Nehalenia: a goddess of the sea, of seafarers and merchant trade on the waters. It's a bit of a toss-up with which group of gods she truly belongs to—Germanic or Celtic—as many of her shrines are on the coast of the Netherlands, which is where boats would go to and from England and the rest of the Isles. Given that she's often depicted with bread, apples, and a dog, she likely also has something to do with the harvest, spring, and even death; it's said she's a psychopomp, leading souls of the dead to their resting place.

When it comes to understanding what's associated with certain gods or goddesses, and we're drawing a blank on any New Age websites (that we likely should take with a grain of salt or five anyway), it's really important to look at the iconography of the deities: looking at how they were depicted, what symbols or objects they were depicted with, so on and so forth. That's how you discover that Nehalenia is associated with some of the things she is, besides writings: we have pictures of her shrines that show her clearly holding these spring and harvest related items.

Dīamanios cautioned me that, like the sea itself. Nehalenia could be somewhat unpredictable. I certainly didn't walk into the interview as openly and freely as I did Mokosh, but I also made sure I did some solid preparatory work beforehand. Given I live in the Ocean State, it only made sense that I should go down to the beach in the chilly air of March and pick some things up for the table: a bottle of sea water, a few stones, and a few seashells.

I had those sitting for a little bit before I finally found the time to sit down and chat, and when I did, it was quite the experience. Let's take a look.

Along with these ocean items for the table, I also laid out for Nehalenia an apple (of course), a stuffed animal of a dog I'd inherited from my late oma, and a few other blue crystals, namely lapis lazuli, to further represent the water. I had a cup of fresh water for her, as well, to complete the apple offering, and then I was ready to go.

You know the drill already. Lord's Prayer, asking God to let me contact Nehalenia, so on and so forth. By this point, it felt like another day's work—not in the sense that it was drudgery or anything, but in the sense that I was confident in how to do my job without all the tricks and tools I used to. The mugwort, the rosemary to cleanse the space, all that—none of it felt necessary anymore. I would wipe down the table before speaking, yes; I'd never want to invite a deity to a dirty table. But otherwise, I trusted my own abilities to connect, and that was such a far cry from how I'd felt just a short year before. A year really does make a difference when you dive into a practice like this.

But as I settled in, Nehalenia's energy came through, and she chose Amrit Brar's Marigold Tarot to speak through—three cards per question.

"Nehalenia, welcome!" I cleared the space of all the tarot decks I had out and got my notebook open, rambling all the while. "I sure didn't want to bring my cards out to the beach and risk them flying away, so I hope you'll accept that I've brought a bit of the ocean here instead. And for a gift, I have some fresh water and an apple for you, too."

I did not even get to finish my welcome address before I saw her. She had red hair, a flowing, silky-looking bluish-white dress, and a dog at her side, as well as a great golden trident. There was an edge to her features, a light to her blue-gray eyes, that suggested she was not the kind to try whatsoever, and she had us standing on the beach, with huge ships coming towards us through thick mist. The trident seemed to be more a tool she used to direct the ships to the shore, between two great rocks.

"Okay, hello! Thank you for meeting with me." I blinked at the bold image, stunned by it, before I found my bearings and got to shuffling. "So, to start us off: what drew you to watch over seafarers?"

I. WHAT DREW YOU TO WATCHING OVER HUMANITY'S SEAFARERS?

As the ships hit the beach, they let their crew off, and out poured haggard men with sunken, glimmering eyes that ambled along like zombies. They carried nothing and headed for the grass over the sandbanks.

"Look at them. The stink of them," Nehalenia said as she watched them walk. "The moonblink in their eyes. They needed deliverance after so many years on the water. This thing," a gold coin appeared and spun above her hand, "how they crave this. Enough to brave the mists and waves. To put it simply, they called, and I was not the only to answer, but I was the great spirit that descended and claimed these salt-addled men as mine."

Learning, practical goals, reflection, contemplation, connection to reality. Working with one's resources and limits.

Vice, sexuality, bondage, addiction, lack of control, a prison of one's own making.

Deception. Re-evaluation of goals or relationships to see if they're truly fulfilling.

"Okay," I said, confused, "but the Page of Cups suggests some level of regret. Like, re-evaluating whether something is worth having or doing. I'm curious about that; can you tell me about it? About being that great spirit?"

Nehalenia shrugged and said, "I surely don't regret coming to them."

"Okay, I see." One card holds a lot of meanings, and some jump out more than others, so maybe this was more about the deception—of the coin, perhaps. Or maybe it suggested that Nehalenia did re-evaluate, and she found that this was the place she needed to be. After writing it all down, I said, "But that begs the question: how *do* gods decide who they become the patrons of? What makes you choose anything or anyone to watch over?"

2. HOW DO GODS DECIDE WHAT TO BECOME PATRONS OF?

Like the Morrígan, she rarely looked directly at me while speaking, but when she did, it was intense. She stared out at the sea as she answered this question.

"We keep society together," Nehalenia muttered. "You fools go nowhere without some sense of security and promise of safety, however fleeting. We grant your prayers, we eat your sins, we bask in your glory and we bear the scars of your scorn. And you build such empires on our names. It's a thing of terror and beauty.

"So we go where we'll receive what *we're* looking for, in exchange for

Loss, theft, uncompromising values, obsession with socially acceptable roles.

Conformity, wisdom, gaining knowledge, learning while respecting society.

Completion, peace, self awareness, family. Birth, death, and enlightenment.

what you're asking for. For myself, I was born of the mists. Here I shall stay. But it did your empires no good for the unruly sea to swallow up your men constantly, so I began casting lots, making choices—which ones could stay and make it to the isle of the living, and which to the dead." Nehalenia cut a sharp look my way. "We gods have been here longer than your species has existed. We noticed when you appeared and caused a disturbance. We organized you, that you might not be afraid to do your duties and move forward."

"Wow. That's... incredible. Thank you for sharing that."

I felt like there wasn't much I could do except blink at her, dumbstruck. At the same time, I'd taken note of her language—casting lots, eating sins—and couldn't help but think of near Eastern concepts, especially entities like Azazel and the common divinatory custom of lots. I wondered for a second if I wasn't talking to who I wanted, but I knew by the images and the glimmer in her eye that this was more her way of acknowledging all the divine pieces of this world as one system; she was speaking for every god, it seemed. I shook my head and sighed, then jumped back into my questions.

"But then, okay, so you say that you essentially gamble on who stays and goes; is death on the high seas really all up to chance?"

3. IS DYING AT SEA REALLY ALL UP TO CHANCE?

Separation, mistrust, low self-esteem, and disharmony.

Positive change in luck. All things are cyclical, including fortune.

Overextending oneself and re-sources, avoiding responsibilities.

The fact that the Wheel of Fortune sat right there in the middle of her three cards was enough of a confirmation, but she explained further, standing stoic on the sea shore.

"Timidness does you no good when dealing with the sea," she whispered. "No good. Because what will happen will happen, whether you're afraid of it or not. There is no certainty on the seas. You might wait for fair weather, overextending your resources or risking shortage and poverty, only to finally set off and find the storm cloud was just over the horizon.

"Nature does as she wills. I only guide and protect men through it, and I let the sea swallow them where fate demands it. The ocean is a greedy beast. The mists are unforgiving. They must be fed."

"But," I couldn't help but blurt the question, "aren't you a god? I mean, couldn't you just... stop it?"

She looked down on me with a stony face. "It's not about exercising power," Nehalenia said. "It's about maintaining order."

Oh. I—fair enough." The tone of her voice did not leave any room for argument, not a drop. Her answer, however, raised quite a few questions about the meaning of *power*, and *divinity*, that I didn't have time to get into right then, but that I would turn around in my head nonetheless. "I get'cha. Well, then, what do you think of modern seafaring, with the ships we build and the way we navigate now? Pretty hard to have shipwrecks compared to the old days, though they do still happen, I guess."

4. THOUGHTS ON DEVELOPMENTS IN MODERN SEAFARING?

"I think it's precious," she said, her voice dry and a little raspy. Her lips curled into a sharp smile as she continued: "How quickly all your power and bravery wilts when your great ships still capsize. When your hubris has you out in the weather your ancestors would never dare test and you realize your mistake. But men with hardened spirits, you are—after centuries of death on the water, you've determined to conquer it, and you've been mostly successful." She turned to me with that big smile and murmured,

Courage, power, venturing into new experiences. Many paths in life are there to take.

Bad news, pow-erlessness, loneli-ness, self-sabo-tage. Attempted healing.

New beginnings, spontaneity, change, inno-cence. Important mental journeys.

"I admire how far you humans have come in learning to adapt to and embrace the water and its risks. You're aware, yet go on bravely—or stupidly."

I nodded, matching her smile. "Yeah, I can see that. Speaking of our ancestors, though, how do you help people get out on the water without being totally afraid?"

5. HOW DO YOU HELP PEOPLE BRAVE THE OCEAN?

PAGE of CUPS.

Inspiration. New, exciting possibilities blooming. Budding relationships and ventures. Creativity, desire, intuition. Old habits are to be challenged.

Overextending oneself and resources, avoiding responsibilities.

Disloyalty and feeling pressured or lost.

Nehalenia waved a hand, a big grin on her face, a sparkle in her eye.

"How you humans love adventure," she said with a sigh, as if the idea delighted her. "Not everyone was born to be on the seas, but those that were can't be kept away from the thrill of the other side, the voyage, all of it. Those that *had* to be on the water—because of your love of coin, your need to justify life and constantly pay for it somehow—they simply know that if they don't, they'll be letting down quite a few people. Wives, children, their town or even country."

Nehalenia sighed and stared back out at the water. "Shame is quite the motivator; it abates even the deepest fear."

"That makes sense. I guess next I'd like to know what you'd say to—"

"No, no," she said, tapping my notebook. "The underworld. Ask about that."

Huh? I stared at the question I had written, but my hand was already flipping my pencil, already pressing the eraser against the paper. "Are you sure?"

"Yes. I want to talk about that."

With a shrug, I wrote my new question in the freshly blank space: "Okay, then. What does the ocean have to do with the underworld? And the dead?"

6. WHAT DOES THE OCEAN HAVE TO DO WITH THE UNDERWORLD?

1. Bad faith, burnout, and unfinished projects.

2. High energy, impetuousness, and grandstanding. Rashness, overconfidence, and infatuation. Needing to act more recklessly and be more assertive.

3. Financial, material troubles, struggle, victim mentalities, rejection. Unfavorable circumstances. Self-inflicted strife.

XI

KNIGHT of WANDS.

Then we were underwater, and her flowing dress became like the fins of a beta fish, swirling around her body. Her red hair was like a lion's mane around her face. She pulled me down to the ocean floor, where a sunken ship and a few skeletons poked from the sands, swaying with the current.

Then the skeletons got up; they danced, and it was a mirror of the middle card, the Knight of Wands, which had a very bold and happy skeleton on it. These dead things were swirling through the water with permanent bone smiles.

"Look at them, Sara," she said, her grin wolfish as she watched the skeletons. "In life, so sure of their destination and destiny, in death, still alive with adventure. The ocean is their graveyard. The beasts of the sea feast on them and create life anew from them. You might ask: did they create this fate for themselves? And the answer is yes.

"As soon as they boarded their ship, they understood the risks. But their flesh is eaten by the fish, their souls steeped in the water. They had more yet they wanted to do. Not all are ready to take my hand and go to try land just yet—not while their ship and bounty is here."

"Oh, man. That's intense. What an image."

Luckily, we found ourselves back on the beach soon enough, and it finally clicked: none of these people coming off the ships had anything in their hands or any expression in their faces because they were the dead. They were coming to that dry land Nehalenia directed them to after their deaths.

"Uh—okay," I said as I watched the people amble onto their afterlives. "Well, then, final question before we move onto the identifying ones: what would you want to say to seafarers today?"

7. WHAT DO YOU WANT TO SAY TO SEAFARERS TODAY?

Loss, dishonor, and defeat even in the event of victory. Some triumphs can feel ill won or hollow.

I was surprised she only pulled one card, but once again we were in the water, and her eyes were shining with some cold fury, her hair haloed by the sun above the water.

"Seafarers, yes. Do you feel good, seamen? Knowing your prowess, your security on the water, is stripping the ocean bare of its bounty? Remember that balance is a fact and a constant. Tip it too far in your favor, and the loss will be ever more devastating when eventually, inevitably, it tips back the other way."

Short and sweet and very near murderously angry; that's how this answer felt. Her words were like a hand around my neck, their meaning filling my lungs with cold, heavy water.

"Alright, absolutely, I understand what you're saying," I said, nearly spluttering, and I had to remind myself that my actual lungs were perfectly fine and free of seawater before I kept talking. "I appreciate you sharing the sentiment! And now, we get into the final questions: how do you see yourself?"

8 & 9. HOW DO YOU SEE YOURSELF AND WANT TO BE SEEN?

Suffering, betrayal, desolation. Resolution soon to be found. Needing a new starting point.

Power, prosperity, strength, and optimism. Warmth, happiness, comfort, and growth.

Slander, isolation, and being manipulated.

"I have been tossed aside," she whispered. "Branded a fable, a demon, a false god. I have been cast away by those I once protected. And yet I still exist. I am still powerful. I still cast lots in these seas. I always will, for I am a god, no matter how times change."

"And how do you want to be seen?"

"As exactly that: a god."

"Fair, fair," I said, nodding, writing away. Then I looked over all I had and said, "So, Nehalenia, that about wraps it up for me. Is there anything else you want to share before we part ways?"

10. ANY LAST MESSAGES FOR ME OR OTHERS?

To my surprise, she only pulled one card.

"Careful, she said with a sly smile over her shoulder. "Those who cannot set their own sails and stand firm on two feet will be swept away. The ocean is more than water. The ocean is deep, and dark, and all around and within us: learn to keep your head above water or sink, unfulfilled, into the dark."

"Understood. Well, thank you, Nehalenia!" I put my pencil down so I could focus on the image she was giving me with full attention. "This has been a wonderful conversation. I appreciate you taking the time to come speak with me about these things and share your wisdom! Until next time!"

She nodded, then slipped away into the water like a mermaid, disappearing into the dark blue of the infinite sea.

Codependency, miscommunication, and misunderstanding.

And remember when I said that Leviathan was making me think? With his whole "the gods *can* help but don't" shtick? Yeah. I think Nehalenia helped us crack the code on that one. Since these fifty interviews, too, I've spoken to yet more and more gods, as well, and what it looks like, to me, is that there's one concept all the gods in the world are adhering to, and that's Fate.

Yes, even God. I mean, think about it: if He's really omniscient, He already knows what's going to happen, and He knows it has to stay happening for the world's order and balance to stay in tact. And if He isn't omniscient, He still can see from what I call *outside the fishbowl:* He sees all of us, all at once, and knows how all of our actions will affect each other, and what will throw the world out of alignment and what won't. God is God of so many things, but first and foremost, He is a God of *balance.* And so, too, is every other god, if we go by Nehalenia's remarks.

Now, I'm not saying that free will is null and that we have no choice in the matter over anything. What I am saying, though, is that Divinity has a story it wants to tell, and it's sticking to its part of the script while letting us have free reign—from our purview. This, to me, is another part of the reason why divination (or, rather, "fortune telling") was actually *forbidden* in the Bible: not only because God didn't want people trying to basically get a real life Action Replay and learn exactly how to get infinite fortune from the otherworldly spirits that knew the answer, but also because *when we don't know what's supposed to happen, we act in our most authentic ways, thus pushing the World Story forward most authentically, too.*

Gods step in when the story is about to go off kilter. Gods leave things alone when everything is going according to the script they decided on—even if that script kind of sucks for us. I get it. As a writer myself, I know very well how it is when the plot starts derailing and the characters start acting in ways that are natural to their personality, but oh so very bad for the progression of the overall story. It sucks, but it means some tweaking needs to be done.

Which makes life easier to grapple with, and yet harder to live, when you think about it. When you start seeing it for the game, the story that it is, you start to wonder what the point of it all is. I guess if there's anything people would ask after *why can't the gods just fix everything?* it's this: what's the point?

And I guess we'll just have to wait until we're on the other side to see.

AMIDA BUDDHA

A while back, when my friend Ji Hae offered to help me get in touch with Princess Bari, she actually originally had two different deities in mind: Amida Buddha, of Pure Land Buddhism, and Quan Yin, the Chinese goddess of mercy and compassion. So when the poll on Patreon came back with a theme of mercy for the month, I knew we were in a good place to continue what we'd started with such an incredible Korean folk goddess.

Something I didn't know about Buddhism was how many forms it takes. Pure Land Buddhism seems a bit different from other types, and one interesting thing about it is that it's open to anyone who wants to join, anyone who understands and connects to Amida Buddha's teachings. Even if you're at the very end of your life, if you decide to turn it all around and follow Amida Buddha, his mercy is vast, and he'll help you get into his realm.

The term "Pure Land" refers to something like what we might call Heaven: it's a place that, when people follow Amida Buddha and do their best to contemplate the sutras and display them in their hearts, their words, and their actions, can be released from the cycle of reincarnation and achieve bliss in the afterlife. The meditations for such a place are so intense that, honestly, as I went through them, they were a little... headache inducing. So many jewels. So many colors. So much beauty! It's almost too hard to take in when you try to focus on it.

But Amida Buddha, specifically, is a *primordial* Buddha—one who was always there, always trying to help humanity break free from this reincarnation cycle. Buddhas in general are fascinating, several of them being humans who achieved enlightenment and ascended, but it can also be said that each Buddha is simply a reincarnation of the original: one who comes, again and again, to remind people of the mysteries and truths and enlightenment they'd lost. (Sounds a lot like Raziel to me.)

Another cool thing is that Amida Buddha is one that can be contacted by anyone, anytime, anywhere, without any specific rituals or practices necessary to be heard. His realm lies in the West, and his worship remains popular in China, Korea, and Japan. Naturally, I'd never spoken to any kind of Buddha before, and so I was excited to see how this would go—and I hope you are, as well.

After listening to a few more of Ji Hae's recordings of the Contemplations, and doing a few full body prostrations, as well as some more reading of the articles she showed me about Buddha, I felt pretty equipped for this interview. It was fascinating just to read the essays, honestly, because it's such a different understanding of enlightenment and faith than we're used to seeing in the west. I kept all this in mind as I went about setting the table for Amida Buddha.

As an offering, I had a plate of strawberries and some iris incense, as well as jasmine flowers scattered around a white candle. According to Ji Hae, a big part of offerings for deities like Amida Buddha was also acts of charity, in which case I donated to The Trevor Project: an organization aimed to providing counseling and helping prevent suicide in LGBTQ+ youth. I also laid out some clear quartz, rose quartz, and blue lace agate, all items that direct and focus energy, invoke peace, love, and mercy, and help one settle into a calmer state of mind. With all this set up, and my prayers said, and God standing with me, gatekeeping my space as always, I knew I was ready to get started.

Amida Buddha came through in an array of images and colors, but before I got a full grasp of him, I was able to confirm that he wanted to use Threads of Fate's Weaver Tarot, which was all I needed before I let myself get totally lost in these vibrant landscapes.

"Hello, Amida Buddha!" I said as I closed my eyes and let my music play. "Thank you for joining me today and sharing your wisdom with me. For you, I have a bowl of strawberries; please enjoy these as we speak."

Right away, I had an image similar in my mind that was reminiscent of those great golden Buddha statues, with a man in a simple robe & stretched earlobes, as well as a gentle face, eyes half closed as if he was fully relaxed. He sat on a purple cushion in a pagoda, where a field of green grass, a clear blue sky, & a shining sun surrounded the area. He smiled, gentle, and beckoned me forward.

"Alright," I said as I came closer, "thank you again! Now, I suppose the first thing I'm wondering is: what does it mean to be merciful?"

I. WHAT DOES IT MEAN TO BE MERCIFUL?

Light at the end of the tunnel. A new chapter. Confronting fears, coming out more enlightened. Keep balanced.

Struggling, filled with uncertainty. So focused on validation that inner compass is misaligned. Losing sight of intentions.

The unknown and feelings of the unconscious self. Encourage mystery within yourself. Rely on intuition and unseen forces.

When I tell you that the Buddha spoke clearly and easily in my mind, I mean it. He seemed a bit reluctant to speak through cards at first, but when I explained it was for the sake of having something to show others for insight, he obliged. I was thankful for his meeting me halfway, because, as you might guess, the written interview is only half the battle. The other half is always a video counterpart, and I can't transmit images, revelations, and thoughts from my head into a Tiktok video as well as I can through writing. Still, his voice was clear before, during, and after I picked these cards.

"Mercy is hard won," Amida Buddha said, his voice soft and easy on both mind and soul. "It takes time to soften a heart of stone, but the journey starts within. You can't expect to find these secrets of mercy from outside in the world." Then his face fell. "This world knows no love. Love is not a native plant to the soils of war and despair. It must be started, a small seed from within, and planted in fields tilled and filled with hope. To be merciful is to be a tireless laborer from the inside, always working to nourish and cultivate your crop."

"Oh, wow. What a beautiful analogy; thank you." I sat cross-legged on the floor with him, like a child by a mentor listening to ideas and lessons being translated into beautiful stories. "In that regard, though, how can one remember to soften their heart?"

2. HOW CAN ONE SOFTEN THEIR HEART?

As he sat beside me, he waved as if to encompass the whole world.

"There is no one who can survive alone," he said. "But that doesn't mean one should choose just anyone to be their partner and ally in this world. You must surround yourself with those who share your commitment to love and work on removing the splinters of death and war this world tries to dig into you." He gestured to the world outside the pagoda, all sunshine and bird song and sweet green grass. "You must contemplate worlds higher than this one, and seek to embody them. Fill your mind with beautiful thoughts, and you will internalize this

Partnership. Relationships where people are invested and committed. Good things long term.

Confusion. When making decisions, walk slowly through the fog until it clears.

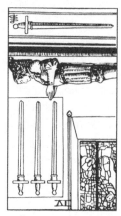

Chronic stress has become a pattern. Addicted to survival mode. Put your mind at rest, reduce stress.

beauty; it will shatter the stone around your heart and remind you of your field of hope."

This, to me, made a lot of sense. There are many Buddhist contemplations that encourage one to imagine the beauty of the Pure Land, from the setting sun to the water to the ground and trees. It makes one feel at peace to do so, even when it's a bit too much to take in for our minds.

"I see, and I appreciate that insight."

Though as I was sitting there, something popped in my head—a wriggling doubt about things I was hearing. I ended up rambling while preparing my next question, explaining all over again my use of the tarot cards to solidify what I was hearing so I could mitigate some doubts, and suddenly he went wide-eyed, waving a hand as if to warn me. It was with the urgency of waving a person away from oncoming traffic. So I erased a less-urgent question from my journal and replaced it with a new one.

"Amida Buddha, is there something you want to say about doubt? And fear?"

3. WHAT WOULD YOU LIKE TO SAY ABOUT DOUBT AND FEAR?

Something underhanded happened. You or someone else are trying to get away with something. Could be necessary, but if it isn't, pause and assess. Reactiveness is no good. Break inherited patterns.

An arrival in many ways, bringing realization of who you really are. Being more focused on yourself than others and empowering yourself. Prioritizing a relationship with yourself.

Creative energy and life cropping up from a creative place. Unseen to the outside world but real to you. Use passion and momentum. A gift, an opportunity. Erase doubts. Be in the flow.

"Voices are blocked for doubt," he said, his eyes still wide. "It creates blockages that stifle truth because of the reliance on the world's reaction. One will couch their words in whispers or swallow them altogether for fear of retaliation. But you cannot. Your soul recognizes Truth even when your and others' eyes do not.

"To doubt is to block the soul's ability to relay it to you and prevent yourself from being in harmony with yourself. It is fear of the outside world that causes doubt, like fear of leaving one's house because of the wolves in the wood." Then he took a deep breath, as if modeling the behavior for me. "Spend more time hearing yourself to mitigate this."

"Ah, yeah. That does make a lot of sense; thank you for your advice! Though, I will say, it makes me think about Jesus." My mind tangled itself in feelings I couldn't put words to. But it all revolved around the idea of Jesus, trying so hard to say what needed to be said, knowing what was coming because He said it. I paused my shuffling and said, "There's a reason to fear."

As I tried to return my focus to my question, Amida Buddha spoke completely outside the cards, in a way that made it feel as if I'd had a seed of pure light warming my chest and taking root there. It was a feeling I can only describe as mercy and empathy, because when Amida Buddha spoke, it hit. It was as if he'd placed a sturdy hand on my shoulder.

"This fear makes you think of your dying Lord."

"Yes."

Amida Buddha nodded. "This is a grief I cannot take from you. Only you can take it from you. But your grief isn't just from a man dying, or even your Lord dying. It's the grief of watching the world's cruel reaction to those that would try to exorcise the cruelty from it. Reasonable grief, yes, but one that must be let go of all the same." He patted my shoulder and added, "Be heartened in your Lord. Be inspired."

"Oh." I was stunned at the message, honestly, but I kept on. "I see what you mean, yeah. But still, we're in this time now, reflecting on how He was put to death for His truth. What do you think about Jesus? Do you know about Him?"

4. DO YOU KNOW ABOUT JESUS? WHAT DO YOU THINK ABOUT HIM?

"Of course I know about Him," Amida Buddha said, smiling. "I think Him a wise, yet rough-and-tumble fellow."

I think this is just how the idea translated in my head, because it seemed out of sorts with the rest of his vocabulary.

Amida Buddha continue: "He's an explosive One, yearning for change the world resists. He is beautifully human in His expression of Divinity. He is Passion seated in Compassion. But this world is cruel. It was never going to forgive one that challenged it. Jesus didn't know right away what was to come, but by time He saw it, it was too late to change course. To be likewise abandoned by His own Lord was a cut on Him so deep it might've never closed, if not for that very same Lord's later intervention.

The devil is in the details. Missing details on plans and what-ifs. Go over everything and get outsider perspective on what's missing.

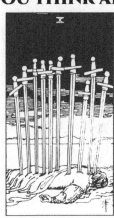

Disaster. A situation has been building. Running from an outcome, but still stuck in it. Face it instead of running from yourself.

Repression of guilt. Trying to justify actions to avoid making amends. Open up about it and forgive yourself to move on.

"It was a transmutation. Like a sponge, your Lord soaked up an eternity's worth of suffering in Himself and transformed it into an eternity's worth of hope. It was a masterful play."

I basked in that answer for a second. It's always so interesting hearing gods and divinities talk about each other. Absolutely fascinating.

"I really am heartened to hear your thoughts," I said. "Thank you for them. But then, what causes all this suffering in the world?"

5. WHAT CAUSES ALL THE SUFFERING IN THE WORLD?

This was the question I'd wanted to ask before getting caught in a ditch about all my doubts, but by time we got here, Amida Buddha only shook his head and refused to pull cards.

"For all our discussion, I think you know," he said. "The world's love of cruelty, and our grief at its every infliction of it."

"Fair." As I wrote, I tried to go as fast as possible, so I could spend as much time in the scene he'd created as possible. "Well, then, might you describe what happens to a soul when it engages in prayer and meditation? I notice this is a large component of Buddhism."

6. WHAT HAPPENS WHEN A SOUL ENGAGES IN PRAYER OR MEDITATION?

PAGE of CUPS.

Creativity, dreaming, raw energy. Youth and impulses of the bizarre. Drawing inspiration from relationships with life. Tossing preconceptions. Living in the unseen gives questions, not answers.

III (THE EMPRESS, reversed)

Stagnancy. Feeling stuck and unable to bring life through. Create a foundation of confidence and self love. Doubting one's ability to hold so much. Ground and focus on self care.

QUEEN of SWORDS.

An evolved, wise person that spent many years healing themselves. Fantastic insights. They're plugged in mentally, but they understand the emotional world. Truth above all and solid boundaries.

With a slow blink, Amida Buddha said, "There is nothing that prayer and meditation on worlds higher than yours cannot do. Through this self discovery, guided by Divinity, you learn to break those patterns of stagnancy. You crush doubt. You powder the stone of your heart.

"Why? Because you are connected to the source of love and beauty, and when you hold the image of such beauty in your mind, you release the memory of pain and death in this cruel world. Prayer and meditation unchain the soul. They set you free."

Ah, yeah, I can see that. I do notice feeling so much lighter after a good bit of meditation, if tired. Okay! And there's one more thing that's really curious to me: in many of the collections of Buddhist stories I read, I notice self immolation is a common theme. But it conflicts with more Near Eastern and Western ideas of the body being a temple, in which this act would be seen as wrong or harmful, uncompassionate to the body. What do you think?"

7. THOUGHTS ON SELF IMMOLATION IN EARLY BUDDHIST TEXTS?

1. Disaster. A situation has been building. Running from an outcome, but still stuck in it. Face it instead of running from yourself.

2. Feeling of being entrapped or stuck with a project that isn't going well. It may be time to move on despite investments. Don't force yourself to keep going for investment.

3. Deep connections. Love coming, a relationship on the mind. Love is a choice and exists in a cycle. Relationships need to die at times to move on. One must be curious about what the future brings.

THE LOVERS.

"I think the body is an interesting animal," he said, "a wonderful beast. Yet it isn't our everything. It can actively deceive us, because like all animals, it fears pain and death. It tries to protect us from these things, but in doing so, it robs our soul of the ability to grow and challenge the darkness.

"The body as a temple? Perhaps. But temples hold no fear. No distortion. No illusion. They are, simply put, what they are. Bodies are more like a good animal, a work horse. Care for them, yes, but don't be afraid to put them to rest when they've had enough of the poison of this world. When in harmony with the soul, the body loses fear of death; it follows its master faithfully to the Pure Land."

"What a fascinating way of looking at this. Thank you for the extra perspective on this, really!" It was hard to sit still, what with all the information I was getting for what felt like nothing—but it wasn't nothing. Just showing up and opening this channel took a good deal of effort. "That certainly gives one more to think about. But that also ends our general questions, so now, I would like to know: how do you see yourself?"

8. HOW DO YOU SEE YOURSELF?

Enduring challenges, but achieving success. Gather your strength; tend to your wounds. Endure the calm day.

"To reach the state I sit in now has not been without great trial. I sit here, overlooking my Land, and I am triumphant. I am at peace, and one day, so too shall all of humanity be."

"And how would you like others to see you?"

9. HOW DO YOU WANT OTHERS TO SEE YOU?

He brought his hands together in his lap and smiled. "I have spent much time contemplating the secrets of this world and the next. But it does no good to lock such secrets away. For all those who wish to see and learn, I am here—and I will always be here. My heart is open to all."

Isolating too much. Reconnect with the world. All good things can deviate to unhealthy places.

"Wonderful! Are there any last messages you want to impress on me, or others, before we part ways?"

10. ANY LAST MESSAGES FOR ME OR OTHERS?

You have a few options available and are centering on the one that will provide the best long term sustainability.

With a slow and graceful nod, Amida Buddha said, "Yes. You know. You all know which choices will lead you away from suffering. But you must *want* to make these choices. You must *want* to be free from agony. While at first it may seem that you do, the world here has a way of tricking you into seeing cruelty as mercy, and hate as compassion. Do not be fooled. Allow your soul to speak and shine in the darkness of this world."

"Wow. That's poignant. What a way to wrap this up!" As I snapped my notebook shut, I spent an undistracted moment with him in the pagoda. "I really appreciate you sharing your wisdom with me, Amida Buddha," I said. "This has been a wonderful meeting! For now, I'll say goodbye, but thank you so much for your time!"

And with that, Amida Buddha broke away from me; the whole world he'd created slipped away, as if it were little more than a dream. I wasn't dreaming, of course; I was sitting there at my kitchen table, fully aware of how much the chair hurt my butt after a good hour in it, but it didn't make the world feel any more real when I opened my eyes. A good clap, that loud sound cracking the connection between worlds, though—that brought me back just fine.

And just as with Princess Bari, my final act of closing out the space was to eat the strawberries. Something about these deities is that when they bless the food, they make it taste so strange. Not completely different, but noticeably a few degrees *off*. In fact, maybe it's the Vitamin C, but both the strawberries I put out for Amida Buddha and the orange I set out for Princess Bari reminded me more of kiwi than their actual respective flavors—kiwi candy. Very sour, very sweet, and almost artificial, as if someone was asked to make a kiwi flavored item after not tasting it for a long time.

So strange. I love it, though.

Nonetheless, in this conversation with Amida Buddha, I found so many fascinating pieces to turn over in my mind for days and weeks afterwards. Even if I'd never spoken to him directly, getting the chance to learn a little bit more about Buddhism and experience the flow of the Contemplations and such was so soothing. It says to me that, no matter your religion, if you can find those texts or traditions or words that can turn your mind away from the material world and towards the heavenly one, you can find a real balm for the soul. You can, as Amida Buddha says, unchain the soul, which is trying so hard to get through to you through the flesh and blood of your body.

I also kept wondering about the "physics" of the spirit world, for lack of a better word. It seems that all entities come circling the same themes again and again: all saying the same general concept with different vocabulary, parables, and priorities of which concept—love, justice, and mercy—to focus on most. Is it just a through-line of human consciousness across time and space? Or is it stitched into the fabric of creation by the gods themselves?

I don't know. All I do know, though, is that after forty-nine interviews, I can feel it in my heart: the gods are connected. All of them. They know each other, know their role in the story of the world, and play it with all they have, for our sake more than anyone else's. It makes one want to look for that "fourth wall" of religion, so to speak: to find out who these gods *really* are behind the masks they wear and the parts they play with us.

Which, funnily enough, would bring us right back to the start of this journey. Funny how things work that way. But as I closed my book and hopped off to bed for the night, I didn't have time to think much about it. I only had time to fall into bed and sleep like a rock, my mind quiet of all its thoughts and questions for at least a little while after such a deep—and illuminating—meditation.

QUAN YIN

Of all the eastern goddesses that might be well known in the west, I think Quan Yin comes out on top. Beloved across the world, in Chinese Buddhism and general mythos, Quan Yin is the god (later turned goddess in the 12th century) of love, mercy, compassion, and beauty. She's cognate with Avalokiteshvara in Buddhism, a name meaning "the Lord that looks on the world with compassion." Quan Yin is the Chinese translation of this name.

Something that interested me while looking deeper into her origins, however, is that this deity can actually switch genders according to Buddhist thought: she'll change to a boy or girl depending on the person about to reach enlightenment. Quan Yin also changes to suit the nature of the one she's speaking to. Whether she's meeting with a monk, a doctor, a girl, a boy, it doesn't matter. This is because, rather than being a full blown Buddha like Amida Buddha, Quan Yin is actually a bodhisattva—a being that stays between the mortal world and the world of the enlightened ones to help humans continue to reach their fullest, truest selves and free themselves from suffering. In western terms, this would make her a bit like a Catholic Saint, or maybe a demigod: one operating between the worlds of the Human and Divine for humanity's benefit and salvation.

As a bodhisattva, Quan Yin is one that, in her lore, had the chance to enter Nirvana and achieve complete enlightenment and bliss, but upon hearing the suffering of the world, chose to stay to help souls escape the cycle of suffering and achieve bliss. The fact that she made the choice to stay and help us, and that she's willing to alter everything about herself—from her appearance to her gender to anything else—to meet us where we are is yet another testament of the Divine as a general concept to me: they don't demand perfection of us. They know they can help us better from where we are than from where they—or where we—want us to be in life.

So naturally, there could be no discussion of mercy without talking to the goddess that helped so many people understand this specific realm of the human experience.

Before I called to her, I asked God to let her through to me, and to bless me that I might be a proper envoy of His. I did five full body prostrations and listened to Ji Hae's recording of the contemplation of the Lotus Throne. Avalokiteshvara is actually mentioned in this, since he does frequently come along with Amida Buddha wherever he goes. On the table as an offering, I had iris incense and apples, as well as a few stones by a lavender candle: amethyst, moss agate, and rose quartz. Beside it all was a carving of a turtle. All these things reminded me of the necessity of patience and peace, which, in my mind, are critical for cultivating a working sense of compassion and mercy.

But before I'd even finished the contemplation, I started getting pulled to a courtyard, with a huge red palace carved of fine wood and paper screen doors, green-leafed trees and flowers and a pond out in the courtyard. In one room, dark and shaded, was a pillow where a woman that looked like an empress sat: she had bright red robes, red makeup on dark, round eyes, ornately decorated black hair, and a gold sash, as well as an almost impish smile.

It puzzled me for a bit, to see her look like that. It wasn't exactly what I expected—nor was the pipe she had smoking away in her hand.

"Hello, hello, Quan Yin!" I just dove in anyway. "Please join me! I have here for you an apple, some iris incense, and a lavender and bergamot candle. I hope this makes a pleasing space for you to answer some questions, if you don't mind."

But she only kept staring at me, smiling. I tried to remember things associated with her, and I was getting a little nervous, because what if this wasn't the right spirit? What if this was someone else?

I stared at her the way a cat stares at an unfamiliar object. "I—I'm sorry, Quan Yin, are you here? Is this you?"

I was getting a yes through my pendulum, but I wasn't sure of what I was looking at. She smiled bigger, a grin of pretty white teeth, her eyes sparkling.

"Well, I know God wouldn't let just anyone in here," I said, more to myself than her. "I just... expected something different."

"Why do you doubt?" She waved me in to sit with her. "Why do you lean so hard on expectations?"

"I mean, well," I was a little unsure even as I sat with her, "I just want to make sure I'm discerning right. I don't want to be like those people I goof on, the ones with absolutely no discernment."

"Ah." Her grin hooked into a knowing half-smile. "That you 'goof on'—that you act so harshly towards, you mean? Like you have in the past couple days? Like you've been feeling a bit badly about?"

Well. slap my ass and call me Humbled.

I had been being a bit rough with the people in my comments the past couple days. Call it burn out, call it bitterness, call it exhaustion, but whatever it was, it was making me unbelievably short with people in my replies, to the point that I even felt bad for the trolls that came onto my page. I looked back to God, who was hovering around as He always did, and He had his arms crossed like He was caging a laugh, a big old grin on His face (or, rather, on the face of the Seraph He uses as a stand-in).

As I'd felt like I'd been hit with a frying pan with the realization, I, too, couldn't help but laugh, and when I looked back, there was a Quan Yin I'd expected more: a woman robed in turquoise and pink, little flower ornaments in her less ornate hair, a bit of ornamental paint on her head and a smile as sweet as honey. She chuckled, too, at my no-doubt dumbfounded expression.

"I suppose, yeah," I said once I'd defrosted from the shock. In between it all, I'd managed to pick up that she wanted Kat Black's Golden Tarot for our discussion, so I pulled it out and cleansed the deck. "But I see where you both were going with that. I am sorry for being a bit rough with people lately; I know I shouldn't. It's just been frustrating, dealing with the same rhetoric and the people that push it over and over."

She shrugged. "Still."

And I knew what she meant. "Yeah. Still. Well!" She blinked as I clapped my hands. "Now that we're all situated here, let's get into it, yeah? I've got some questions for you, and to start, I really would like to know: what's one thing about compassion that people miss?"

I. WHAT DO PEOPLE MISS ABOUT COMPASSION?

Courage in the face of adversity. Taking a stand and overcoming problems. Bravery rewarded.

A strong and opinionated authority figure. Perceptive, strong willed, and intelligent.

A poor investment. Financial doubt or worry.

Success, but tainted with arrogance or impatience about bumps in the road.

When I'd posted this video to Tiktok, someone put forward the idea that I shouldn't be talking to these deities with tarot, because there were other methods of divination native to Quan Yin's region I could've used. Maybe this is true to some extent, but what I want people to understand about divination is that it isn't just a magical tool: it is a language. Unless you can learn to speak a language fluently in a week, how could I have ever picked up an entirely new style of divination with this deity I'd never met and hoped to get clear ideas and messages from her to back up my visions?

And the gods understand this, no matter who they are or where they're from. God knows I don't have an authentic set of Urim and Thummim on hand, nor do I have a Biblical-era prophet I can call up with questions at any time, and that's why He works with me through tarot. Quan Yin understood, too, that I wouldn't have had any concept of any Eastern styles of divination, like pulling yarrow sticks or moon block divination, and so tarot was a fine tool for us to use.

Now, the fun thing about this interview is that, rather than have a set amount of cards for each answer, she preferred to choose a different number for each question. That doesn't always happen, but it's an extra hard divination challenge when it does, honestly—yet sometimes it's also a bit easier. Less is more sometimes when it comes to tarot. But sometimes it means working with the imagery of a card more or leaning harder on the meditation aspect, too.

Nonetheless, she chose four cards for her first answer.

"These people, Sara," she said, with her head resting on her hand as she stared at the floor, "they make shows of their compassion. They turn it into theater, hoping to gain from that should never be done in hopes of a reward. Rarely is compassion a thing that brings rewards of a material nature; the rewards are internal, a lamp light shining in the soul. But people always seek outward approval and fuss when they don't get it."

"That's fair, yeah. I can see that." My pencil's scratching into the paper kept me grounded as I talked. "Well, you know, another thing I notice in your lore is that people ask you for good fortune. As the goddess of mercy, are fortune and compassion related?"

2. ARE FORTUNE AND COMPASSION RELATED AT ALL?

THE WORLD.

One person can make the world better. You've seen and learned much; now put knowledge into action. Others will seek guidance. Share all that fate gave you.

"No," she said before I even found the card. But once I landed on the World, she elaborated. "There is no tie between compassion and fortune in the material and physical sense—only in the spiritual one. Through compassion and wisdom, one might help others through self imposed suffering—like wanting a son over a daughter, missing the joy of having a healthy baby altogether."

"Is that why you stay here? Helping people learn this?"

"This is why I remain Bodhisattva, yes: to help remind the people of this."

"I understand. Thank you for the clarification. But then, speaking of boys and girls, I also see that you, yourself, had a gender swap in your representations." As I shuffled the cards, I said, "It makes me wonder, given some of the ideas that had circulated in Buddhism about enlightenment: does gender actually matter when it comes to attaining it?"

3. DOES GENDER MATTER WHEN IT COMES TO ENLIGHTENMENT?

She shook her head. "Too much focus is put on the body. Too much on the body, and not the ways we've created a world that changes its face depending on the body before it. What kind of world is that? One that breeds suffering based on how one is born?

"It's a lesson you are all still learning. As someone both man and woman once, I see no difference in the quality of enlightenment—only in the paths one chooses to take towards it. As Woman, I see the hole people want me to fill, the gifts and lessons they hope I'll provide. I focus on those now."

"And what are those lessons, if I can ask? What advantages are there to teaching in a female form?"

KNIGHT of SWORDS.

A brash young man, hotheaded but wanting to do what's right. A man of action. Bravery, courage, and heroism.

Grass is always greener elsewhere. Don't take blessings for granted. A tendency to yearn after that which is forbidden or unattainable. Is it worth sacrificing yourself for that which may lose its appeal?

PAGE of CUPS.

An emotional youth. Creativity. Strong emotional ties. An important time in a relationship: a time of deep and significant change. A quiet, gentle, studious youth, or an older person with youthful qualities.

4. WHAT ARE THE ADVANTAGES OF TEACHING IN A FEMALE FORM?

Quan Yin sighed, then looked past me, into the courtyard. "The people sometimes think that because I am a woman, and because I teach the graces of compassion and mercy, that all life's bounties will be given to them for free if they call my name. But a traveler that doesn't mind his purse, or a seafarer that pays no mind to sharp rocks, treats me not with respect, but as a servant—less, a tool, a dispenser of miracle for free. This creates complacency. So I do remind them at times of the nature of things, and that compassion cannot be abused for it to remain compassion." She cut me a pointed look. "The Mother is a forever discerning force. In my womanhood, they know that there is nothing weak about me—and that compassion itself is not weakness."

"Ooh, I see." I swear, answers like these were what made this series even more wonderful; the snap! The directness of it! "That's really interesting, thank you. But now, on the topic of women and compassion, I've heard some compare you to the Virgin Mary. In fairness, every entity even remotely goddess-like or feminine from other religions has been compared to her, but what do you think of this?"

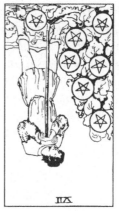

Laziness and desire for wealth without effort.

What you lose on the swing, you gain on the roundabout. Life always sends challenges.

5. THOUGHTS ON YOUR COMPARISON TO THE VIRGIN MARY?

Innocence, faithful acceptance. Remembrance of childhood joys. Unquestioning, unconditional love. Wanting simpler times with less responsibility. Be wary of nostalgia.

Goals can be reached if you set your path and keep to it. Fulfilment of hopes and dreams. Success and critical acclaim of achievements. Joy, health, and happiness.

Obstacles, problems, and resistance.

Quan Yin had a bright laugh, like a tinkling bell.

"Mary is a lovely woman, yes—one that maybe didn't realize her destiny was to be in over her head to such a profound degree. But she navigated it with such grace, didn't she?"

After her laughter died down, she continued.

"I am not her, though. Not at all. But we both face obstacles as women in such stations, don't we? Forever loved, yet forever eyed with suspicion by those who want divinity to have a different face. Such is the fate of all of us, so long as humanity insists on splitting itself so needlessly."

"That's so interesting that you know about her, and have maybe interacted with her, by the way you talk." And after Amida Buddha also spoke about Jesus, I just had to ask: "Can you tell me how divinities learn about each other?

6. WHERE DO THE GODS LEARN ABOUT EACH OTHER?

THE STAR.

Goals can be reached if you set your path and keep to it. Fulfillment of hopes and dreams. Success and critical acclaim of achievements. Joy, health, and happiness.

She shrugged. "The answer is simple: we all have our roles to play. As people move across the world, they carry us all with them. There is no corner of this globe that we can't reach, or haven't seen even in passing. As such, we cross each other's paths continuously, on our quests to help you all relieve your suffering. It's like asking us how we know those we've passed on the street, or heard about from your news channels or some gossip. We talk where we find reason for it, but otherwise we let each other work."

"Oh, wow." The whole concept of spiritual physics that I told you about was, by this point, something I've been thinking of for a long time, and this just added a whole new layer to it. "I think that's amazing. How cool! Okay, okay, to focus again: how can one be mindful of mercy towards their own self? It feels like it's hard to be merciful on ourselves with all we're trying to get done, making us so hard on ourselves."

7. HOW CAN ONE BE MERCIFUL TOWARDS THEMSELVES?

"The answer lies in gratitude," she said, stern. "You all have forgotten gratitude. Forever fixated on where you lack, or haven't achieved, or haven't yet seen or experienced, you take for granted all you have—and you relieve this by wrongly elevating yourselves above those you perceive as having even less than you. There is never a reason to compare yourself to others—not to hurt yourself, and not to falsely prop yourself up against another's lack. There is only a reason for gratitude."

Misguided goals. Poor decisions, or a lack of decision, could lead to destitution and misery. Poor health and misfortune await. Make the most of what you have.

That hit in a way I wasn't expecting. It seems hard, admittedly, to be grateful of where one is when one thinks about where they could be or where everyone else is around them, and I can see how it makes it easier to step on the little guy to cover those wounds. But hearing it laid out like that just made it all click. It also makes sense in why so many people focus on the concept of gratitude in their meditations: because even when all the world feels like it's going to hell in a hand basket, finding something to be grateful for—even just the dragonflies outside or a peaceful moment on the couch, soft and warm and not having to do anything in that particular moment—can go a long way for helping people relax enough to remember themselves.

It's hard to slow down enough to find those moments of pause, is the only thing. Hard to remember to realize where we are and what we do have, rather than always running around in a state of panic, worrying about what we don't have, what we haven't done.

"Thank you for that," I said, letting the message soak in as I sat there by her. "I appreciate that sentiment a lot. That's a great way to put it. But now, I guess we're heading into the end: how do you see yourself?"

8. HOW DO YOU SEE YOURSELF?

Injustice, false accusations, and prejudice.

Shock of all shocks when she pulled Justice Reversed.

"I am not interested in keeping score," she said, plainly, with a little hardness in her voice. "I don't care to settle arguments or preside over petty trials. I am one here for those traveling through the mists of the self. Leave talks of justice to war gods and their hammers."

"Wow! I'll be honest, I didn't expect an answer like that at all." After blinking at her, I asked, "And how do you want others to see you?"

9. HOW DO YOU WANT PEOPLE TO SEE YOU?

Rivalry, disharmony, and transient conflict.

Temperance Reversed was not any less of a surprise.

"I am one that will make people bristle," she insisted. "I will make them fight—those who have lost sight of compassion to the point of seeing it as foreign. I am a challenger, not with swords, but with open arms and seeing eyes." She nodded to herself, her brows pinched with determination. "I want others to see me as a transformative one, a giver of life only if one has understood what it means to live. My gifts are not free to abuse; such is the opposite of showing mercy and compassion."

"Makes sense to me. Alright, then, I guess that's about it. Are there any messages you'd like to get out before we go? Anything to say to me personally, or to others?"

10. ANY LAST MESSAGES FOR ME OR OTHERS?

Grass is always greener elsewhere. Don't take blessings for granted. Wanting the forbidden or unattainable. Is it worth sacrificing yourself for that which may lose its appeal?

Quan Yin had us leaving the manor by then, and she was in a little boat on a massive lake under the light of the full moon. She was ready to leave.

"Every blade of grass is a gift," she said as she looked back to me. "Stop running forward for what you don't even know the value of and look around. Look at where you are right now. Forget all the things that could be, and all the people ahead and behind; find your peace within, and your life will soon come to mirror it. Compassion and mercy spring forth from a place of gratitude and peace with oneself—never forget this."

And then she was off, and I thanked her for her time as she drifted away on the water of the pond. It left me feeling just pure awe, honestly, and I sat there for a second with God once she'd left. There was a sense of peace that was deeper than what I'd expected to get—quieter. A humbling peace, too, because it was—and still is—so hard for me to slow down and break the cycle of being too hard on myself, and by extension on everyone else. It's a killer of mercy and compassion, being too self critical and constantly loading more onto one's plate. It makes people irritable and snappy and harsh, like I'd been (and still sometimes am). But when you're operating in such engrained patterns, it takes a while to undo them.

Nonetheless, I feel like after a solid year of interviewing spirits of all kinds—angels, demons, gods, and Saints—I could at least get a better starting point to begin undoing the nuts and bolts of years and years of ickiness. Not because God didn't, or couldn't, help me with such an idea, of course. But because, in fact, He did. By letting me start this journey at all, He helped me meet so many new people and explore so many new facets of spirituality and religion that have always existed. He stood by my side during all of it, watching as I made mistakes, learned from them, and kept on trucking.

He was my coach, mentor, and guide through the strangest year of my life. And at the end of it all, I couldn't be more thrilled to take a look back and see the incredible amount of growth just one year can do. Quan Yin's message of mercy and compassion—of gratitude and empathy—really cemented that for me here.

AFTERWORD

If you've made it here, congratulations. I know it wasn't easy to get through all of it—especially at the beginning. But that's why we go on journeys like this, isn't it? So we can look back and realize how much we've changed from the start. I believe I've changed a lot since my first foray into speaking with entities that aren't God, honestly—but I'll leave that for you to decide.

However, as I've said throughout this book: the more I learn, the less I know. And yet, funnily enough, the less I know, the more at peace I feel. The real peace, not the eerie one. Why? Because I don't need to fight tooth and nail to defend a worldview that may have some holes in it. I know it has holes in it; I know my worldview isn't perfect. It's okay. All I have to do is stay open, to be willing to listen, and to *never* think I have all the answers—because God knows I certainly never will.

Because here's the problem with religion that so many don't realize: it doesn't matter which you follow. Or what speaks to you. Or what you're "supposed" to do. From the perspective I've gained, all it looks like is people arguing over which equation equals ten: six plus four? Or three plus seven? Or fifteen minus five? They're all correct, and they'll all get you the right answer, but humanity still wants to pick sides and fight for now, I guess.

Still, I don't know how to explain the peace I've found to you. The nonchalance, the utter lack of worry. The only way I can think to try is to tell you about the value of good reading and researching. When I wasn't looking into a deity to interview, after all, I was reading up on God, the Bible, all that, so that I might get answers to questions like these, and even in that research, I found some interesting ideas. The overarching theme of it is: God doesn't really give a damn what I do, so long as I acknowledge Him as my one and only, my supreme God. Besides, knowing that it's God that gave me the greenlight to do all this, and learning what I've learned—that all roads lead to Rome, and that any spiritual path that makes you feel fulfilled is worth walking—I know I'll be fine. (Or, at least, I'll have a hell of an argument to make in the Celestial Court.)

And the connections I've made along the way, the friendships and learning and perspective? That's worth its weight in gold. I can't thank my friends enough along this journey—the ones who pulled me back from the brink when I was doing things all wrong, the ones who reached out with information, rituals, and prayers, the ones who supported me through these wild adventures. It's because of you that a lot of these interviews even happened—and that I was able to become a better spiritual citizen out there in the world of gods and Saints and angels and demons.

I also don't think I'll be done any time soon. Every time I think I will be, or that I'll run out of entities to talk to, I get fifteen more ideas of what to explore. I mean, think of why people travel the world: to learn new things, see how people live their lives in ways totally different from us, *experience* something we're not used to—even if we visit the same place a couple times. The same goes here. I've told friends time and time again: I'm a bit of a spiritual tourist, snapping pictures in the weirdest planes of the Unseen, and I like it that way. I like that I can bump into any of these entities and, rather than get scared or try and run them off, give them a seat at the table to talk. I like that my focus in this journey has changed, from poking at entities' stories to try (in vain) to get one version to exploring the domains and concepts they rule over, hoping to gain more wisdom about the world itself.

One day, this journey will end. But until then, we're going to keep going. Keep talking, keep learning, keep exploring. Keep being a spiritual tourist, walking ahead without knowing where the road takes us, guided only by the One God I call home.

So thanks for walking this far with me, and I hope we can go a little farther together.

REFERENCES

Baring-Gould, Sabine. *Legends of Old Testament Characters.* 1871.

Berlin, Adele, and Marc Zvi Brettler, editors. *Jewish Study Bible: Second Edition.* Oxford University Press, 2014.

Bristow, John T. *What Paul Really Said About Women: An Apostle's Liberating Views on Equality in Marriage, Leadership, and Love.* Harper San Francisco, 2004.

Connolly, S. *The Complete Book of Demonolatry.* Darkwood Publishing Group, 2006.

Copeland, F. S. "Some Aspects of Slovene Folklore." *Folklore*, vol. 60, no. 2, 1949, pp. 277–286, https://doi.org/10.1080/0015587x.1949.9717929.

Echols, Damien. *Angels and Archangels: The Western Path to Enlightenment.* Sounds True, 2020.

Fox, Matthew. *Hildegard of Bingen, a Saint for Our Times: Unleashing Her Power in the 21st Century.* Namaste Publishing, 2012.

Kugel, James L. *The God of Old: Inside the Lost World of the Bible.* Free Press, 2004.

Levine, Amy-Jill, and Marc Zvi Brettler. *The Jewish Annotated New Testament.* Oxford University Press, 2017.

Pamita, Madame. *Baba Yaga's Book of Witchcraft: Slavic Magic from the Witch of the Woods.* Llewellyn Worldwide, Ltd, 2022.

Wangerin, Walther. *The Book of God: The Bible as a Novel.* Lion Book/Lion Hudson PLC, 2011.

Watterson, Meggan. *Mary Magdalene Revealed: The First Apostle, Her Feminist Gospel & the Christianity We Haven't Tried Yet.* Hay House, Inc., 2021.

Wilken, Robert Louis. *The Christians as the Romans Saw Them.* Yale University Press, 2003.

SPECIAL THANKS TO

Mimi (*The Morrígan, Frau Berchta*)
   Tiktok: @feralsouthernhousewife

Dagan (*Persephone, General Hellenic Polytheism Information*)
   Tiktok: @olympianbutch
   Instagram: @olympianbutch

Mika (*General Hellenic Polytheism Information*)
   Tiktok: @hekateanfoodie

Beau (*Anubis, Thoth*)
   Tiktok: @thesacredsycamore

November (*Lada, Veles, Zorya*)
   Tiktok: @olivia.emina

Aziel (*Lucifer, Azazel*)
   Tiktok: @heyaziel
   Instagram: @aziel.2.0

Kyle (*Mother Mary, Isis*)
   Tiktok: @king_kylie1405

Larisa (*Thor*)
   Tiktok: @larisamagick
   Instagram: @larisagorenjak

Beck (*The Morrígan*)
   Tiktok: @thestitchingwitch
   Instagram: @the_stitching_witch

Brittany (*Frau Berchta*)
   Tiktok: @hexmarie

Ji Hae (*Princess Bari, Amida Buddha, Quan Yin*)
   Tiktok: @neomudang

Bolotnitsa (*Mokosh*)
   Tiktok: @divchatozlisa

Dīamanios (*Nehalenia*)
   Tiktok: @dianmanios_craxios

INDEX

ENTITIES BY TYPE

GODS:

Loki, 1
Kresnik, 12
Hades, 19
Brigid, 28
Cernunnos, 34
Freyja, 42
Hekate, 51
Apollo, 60
Persephone, 69

Anubis, 90
Thoth, 90
Veles, 103
Zorya, 103
Lada, 103
Thor, 152
Jesus, 169
The Morrigan, 189
Isis, 218

Morana, 294
Frau Berchta, 302
Odin, 340
Princess Bari, 394
Mokosh, 403
Nehalenia, 410
Amida Buddha, 418
Quan Yin 426

SAINTS & OTHERS

Mother Mary, 123
St. Mary Magdalene, 160
Judas Iscariot, 227
St. Dismas, 264
St. Nicholas, 286
St. Joseph, 318
St. Paul the Apostle, 349
Baba Yaga, 361
St. Cyprian, 369

ANGELS

Michael, 134
Raphael, 142
Gabriel, 198
Azrael, 236
Zadkiel, 279
Uriel, 310
Metatron, 324
Raziel, 378

DEMONS

Lucifer, 79
King Paimon, 207
King Belial, 242
Azazel, 250
Prince Stolas, 272
Prince Vassago, 332
Leviathan, 387

ENTITIES BY ORIGIN

CHRISTIAN / OCCULT

Lucifer, 79
Mother Mary, 123
Michael, 134
Raphael, 142
St. Mary Magdalene, 160
Jesus, 169
Gabriel, 198
Judas Iscariot, 227

King Belial, 242
Azazel, 250
St. Dismas, 264
Prince Stolas, 272
Zadkiel, 279
St. Nicholas, 286
Uriel, 310
St. Joseph, 318

Metatron, 324
Prince Vassago, 332
St. Paul the Apostle, 349
St. Cyprian, 369
Raziel, 378
Leviathan, 387

SLAVIC:
Kresnik, 12
Veles, 103
Lada, 103
Zorya, 103
Morana, 294
Baba Yaga, 361
Mokosh, 403

GERMANIC:
Frau Berchta, 302
Nehalenia, 410

BUDDHIST/EASTERN:
Princess Bari, 394
Amida Buddha, 418
Quan Yin, 426

CELTIC:
Brigid, 28
Cernunnos, 34
The Morrígan, 189

EGYPTIAN:
Anubis, 90
Thoth, 90
Isis, 218

GREEK:
Hades, 19
Hekate, 51
Apollo, 60
Persephone, 69

NORSE:
Loki, 1
Freyja, 42
Thor, 152
Odin, 340

ENTITIES BY THEME

SUN/FIRE:
Kresnik, 12
Brigid, 28
Apollo, 60

DIVINATION:
Uriel, 310
Metatron, 324
Prince Vassago, 332
Odin, 340

WATER:
Leviathan, 387
Princess Bari, 394
Mokosh, 403
Nehalenia, 410

LIFE:
Persephone, 69
Lada, 103
Mokosh, 403

MAGIC:
Hekate, 51
Zorya, 103
Gabriel, 198
Isis, 218
Morana, 294
St. Paul the Apostle, 349
Baba Yaga, 361
St. Cyprian, 369
Raziel, 378

DEATH/WAR:
Hades, 19
Cernunnos, 34
Freyja, 42
Anubis, 90
Thor, 152
The Morrígan, 189
Azrael, 236
Frau Berchta, 302
St. Joseph, 318
Odin, 340
Princess Bari, 394

MERCY:
Zadkiel, 279
Amida Buddha, 418
Quan Yin, 426

DIVINE FEMININNE:
Lada, 103
Mother Mary, 123
St. Mary Magdalene, 160
Princess Bari,
Quan Yin
Mokosh, 4303

KNOWLEDGE:
Thoth, 90
Thor, 152
Jesus, 169
Prince Stolas, 272

CHAOS:
Loki, 1
King Belial, 242

Made in the USA
Middletown, DE
24 September 2023